June 19–23, 2016
Newark, NJ, USA

**Association for
Computing Machinery**

Advancing Computing as a Science & Profession

JCDL'16

Proceedings of the 16th ACM/IEEE-CS
Joint Conference on Digital Libraries

Sponsored by:
ACM SIGIR, ACM SIGWEB, & IEEE TCDL

Supported by:
**Rutgers University, University of Maryland-Baltimore County,
and University of Pittsburgh**

I0131887

**Association for
Computing Machinery**

Advancing Computing as a Science & Profession

The Association for Computing Machinery
2 Penn Plaza, Suite 701
New York, New York 10121-0701

Copyright © 2016 by the Association for Computing Machinery, Inc. (ACM). Permission to make digital or hard copies of portions of this work for personal or classroom use is granted without fee provided that copies are not made or distributed for profit or commercial advantage and that copies bear this notice and the full citation on the first page. Copyright for components of this work owned by others than ACM must be honored. Abstracting with credit is permitted. To copy otherwise, to republish, to post on servers or to redistribute to lists, requires prior specific permission and/or a fee. Request permission to republish from: permissions@acm.org or Fax +1 (212) 869-0481.

For other copying of articles that carry a code at the bottom of the first or last page, copying is permitted provided that the per-copy fee indicated in the code is paid through www.copyright.com.

Notice to Past Authors of ACM-Published Articles
ACM intends to create a complete electronic archive of all articles and/or other material previously published by ACM. If you have written a work that has been previously published by ACM in any journal or conference proceedings prior to 1978, or any SIG Newsletter at any time, and you do NOT want this work to appear in the ACM Digital Library, please inform permissions@acm.org, stating the title of the work, the author(s), and where and when published.

ISBN: 978-1-4503-4229-2 (Digital)

ISBN: 978-1-4503-4601-6 (Print)

Additional copies may be ordered prepaid from:

ACM Order Department
PO Box 30777
New York, NY 10087-0777, USA

Phone: 1-800-342-6626 (USA and Canada)
+1-212-626-0500 (Global)
Fax: +1-212-944-1318
E-mail: acmhelp@acm.org
Hours of Operation: 8:30 am – 4:30 pm ET

Printed in the USA

JCDL 2016 Chairs' Welcome

We are pleased to welcome you to the *2016 ACM/IEEE-CS Joint Conference on Digital Libraries – JCDL 2016*. As more of our interaction with libraries happens digitally, interfaces and tools for access have become increasingly important. An important issue for digital libraries is how to provide users with improved access to materials. We have big data - how can we help scholars use those resources to make new discoveries in their own fields? This year, we focus on new access methods for digital libraries, that develop technologies for analyzing holdings, and that report on innovative uses of digital libraries for discovery and exploration in science, art, and the humanities.

We are delighted to have three outstanding keynote speakers:

- *Future Digital Libraries: Research and Responsibilities,* Maria Zemankova, National Science Foundation (NSF)
- *The State of Practice and Use of Digital Collections: the Digital Public Library of America as a platform for research,* Rachel Frick, Digital Public Library of America (DPLA)
- *The Energy of Delusion: The New York Art Resources Consortium (NYARC) & The Digital,* Stephen Bury, New York Art Resources Consortium (NYARC)

The three represent distinct aspects of the digital library community and will give us several perspectives to compare and discuss. The speakers are leaders who have shaped digital libraries and can speak knowledgeably about where we are and where we are going.

Organizing *JCDL 2016* involved many team members, including the authors who provided the research work and as well as the organizing and program committee. We express our thanks to the authors for their contributions and the committee for their efforts in organizing the event and the program committee for their thorough review and thoughtful feedback. Our special thanks to Rutgers University-Newark for hosting the conference.

We also thank our sponsors, ACM SIGIR and SIGWEB, IEEE TC-DL, Rutgers Institute of Data Science, Learning, and Applications, University of Maryland Baltimore County, University of Pittsburgh – School of Information Sciences.

The program committee has assembled an interesting program with papers and presentations that will provide plenty of opportunity to explore new ideas and follow research trends from leaders of and newcomers to the field of Digital Libraries. Welcome; enjoy the discussions and the society of interesting people from our diverse community.

Nabil R. Adam
Rutgers University

Lillian Cassel
Villanova University

Yelena Yesha
University of Maryland Baltimore County

JCDL 2016 Program Chairs' Welcome

Welcome to the 2016 ACM/IEEE-CS Joint Conference on Digital Libraries. Our conference theme is *Big Libraries, Big Data, Big Innovation*. We invited submissions that proposed new access methods for DLs, developed technologies for analyzing holdings, and reported on innovative uses of DLs for discovery and exploration in science, art, and the humanities.

This year's technical program will feature 27 research papers, to be presented in 7 sessions, with topics ranging from *Wikipedia and Newspaper Analysis* to *Curation and Education* to *Recommendation and Prediction*. We will also host two panel sessions, *Issues of Dealing with Fluid Data in Digital Libraries* and *Preserving Born-Digital News*.

We received a number of high-quality paper submissions with authors from 18 countries around the world. Each paper was read and rated by at least 3 reviewers and a meta-reviewer. All papers were discussed at the Program Committee meeting held in Austin, Texas, where the final slate of accepted papers was determined. We accepted 15 full papers out of the 52 submissions (29% acceptance rate) and 12 short papers out of the 34 submissions (35% acceptance rate).

In addition to papers, we accepted 39 posters and demos in two rounds of submissions; this year with an added round to allow authors who submitted earlier a "second chance" to convert longer submissions into poster form or to present later-breaking work. The 39 posters and demos will be presented on the first night of the conference (Monday) and will be preceded by the popular "Minute Madness" session. During the poster and demo session, attendees will be invited to vote for the *Best Poster/Demo Award*.

At our Tuesday night banquet, we will present the *Vannevar Bush Best Paper Award* and the *Best Student Paper Award*. Here are the nominees for the best paper awards:

- "Low-cost semantic enhancement to Digital Library metadata and indexing: Simple yet effective strategies", Annika Hinze, David Bainbridge, Sally Jo Cunningham, and J. Stephen Downie

- "ArchiveSpark: Efficient Web Archive Access, Extraction and Derivation", Helge Holzmann, Vinay Goel, and Avishek Anand - also nominated for *Best Student Paper*

- "Digital History Meets Wikipedia: Analyzing Historical Persons in Wikipedia", Adam Jatowt, Daisuke Kawai, and Katsumi Tanaka

- "Comparing Published Scientific Journal Articles to Their Pre-print Versions", Martin Klein, Peter Broadwell, Sharon Farb, and Todd Grappone

- "Evaluating the Quality of Educational Answers in Community Question-Answering", Long Le, Chirag Shah, and Erik Choi - also nominated for *Best Student Paper*

We would have not been able to put together this exciting program without the generous help of our Program Committee and other reviewers. We are especially grateful for our meta-reviewers and those who attended the Program Committee meeting. Thank you for your thoughtful reviews.

We hope that you will find the conference program thought-provoking and that you will have the opportunity in Newark to renew old acquaintances, meet new colleagues, and share ideas with researchers and practitioners from around the world.

Richard Furuta   **Michele C. Weigle**

JCDL 2016 Program Co-Chair   *JCDL 2016 Program Co-Chair*

Texas A&M University, USA   *Old Dominion University, USA*

Table of Contents

Keynote Talks

Paper Session 1: Wikipedia and Newspaper Analysis

Paper Session 2: Curation and Education

Paper Session 3: Web Archiving

Paper Session 4: Search

Paper Session 5: Q&A and Gaming

Paper Session 6: Publication Mining

Paper Session 7: Recommendation and Prediction

Posters and Demos

Panels

Tutorials

Workshop Summaries

Author Index

JCDL 2016 Conference Organization

General Chairs: Nabil R. Adam (Rutgers University)
Boots Cassel (Villanova University)
Yelena Yesha (University of Maryland, Baltimore County)

Program Chairs: Richard Furuta (Texas A&M University)
Michele C. Weigle (Old Dominion University)

Treasurer: Basit Shafiq (Rutgers University)

Doctoral Consortium Chairs: George Buchanan (City University London)
Stephen Downie (University of Illinois at Urbana - Champaign)
Uma Murthy (Amazon)

Local Organization Chair: Soon A. Chun (City University of New York)

Publicity Chair: Ingo Frommholz (University of Bedfordshire)

Tutorial Chairs: Hussein Suleman (University of Cape Town)
Glen Newton (Canadian Forest Service, NRCan)

Workshop Chairs: Unmil P. Karadkar (The University of Texas at Austin)
Chirag Shah (Rutgers University)

Panel Chair: Vivek K. Singh (Rutgers University)

Poster and Demo Chairs: Luis Francisco-Revilla (The University of Texas at Austin)
Ian Milligan (University of Waterloo)

Publications Chair: Sampath Jayarathna (Texas A&M University)

Registration Chair: Debopriya Ghosh (Rutgers University)

Student Volunteers Chair: Debopriya Ghosh (Rutgers University)

Meta-Reviewers: Maristella Agosti (University of Padua)
Christoph Becker (University of Toronto)
Sally Jo Cunningham (Waikato University)
Edward Fox (Virginia Polytechnic Institute and State University)
Luis Francisco-Revilla (The University of Texas at Austin)
Ingo Frommholz (University of Bedfordshire)
Dion Goh (Nanyang Technological University)
Marcos Goncalves (Federal University of Minas Gerais)
Xiao Hu (University of Hong Kong)
Sarantos Kapidakis (Ionian University)
Unmil Karadkar (The University of Texas at Austin)
Martin Klein (University of California Los Angeles)
Carl Lagoze (University of Michigan School of Information)
Catherine Marshall (Texas A&M University)
Robert H. Mcdonald (Indiana University/Data to Insight Center)
Michael Nelson (Old Dominion University)
Edie Rasmussen (University of British Columbia)
Frank Shipman (Texas A&M University)
Joan Smith (Old Dominion University)
Hussein Suleman (University of Cape Town)
Herbert Van De Sompel (Los Alamos National Laboratory, Research Library)

Program Committee: Piotr Adamczyk (Metropolitan Museum of Art)
Hamed Alhoori (Texas A&M University)
Robert Allen (Yonsei University)
Ahmed Alsum (Google)
David Bainbridge (University of Waikato)
Sean Bechhofer (University of Manchester)
Nicholas Belkin (Rutgers University)
Maria Bielikova (Slovak University of Technology in Bratislava)
Tobias Blanke (University of Glasgow)
Jose Borbinha (IST / INESC-ID)
Paul Bracke (Purdue University Libraries)
Justin F. Brunelle (Old Dominion University)
George Buchanan (City University London)
Pável Calado (Instituto Superior Técnico, Universidade de Lisboa)
José H. Canós (Universitat Politècnica de València)
Vittore Casarosa (Istituto di Scienza e Tecnologie dell'Informazione)
Jason Casden (NCSU Libraries)
Donatella Castelli (CNR)
Panos Constantopoulos   (Athens University of Economics & Business)
Gregory Crane (Tufts University)
Theodore Dalamagas (IMIS)
Josep Lluis De La Rosa (EASY Innovation Center, UdG & RPI)
Giorgio Maria Di Nunzio (University of Padua)

Program Committee (continued):

Ying Ding (Indiana University)
Boris Dobrov (Recearch Computing Center of Moscow State Univ.)
J. Stephen Downie (University of Illinois)
Fabien Duchateau (Université Claude Bernard Lyon 1 - LIRIS)
Kai Eckert (Stuttgart Media University)
Pierluigi Feliciati (Università degli studi di Macerata)
Nicola Ferro (University of Padua)
Schubert Foo (Nanyang Technological University)
Muriel Foulonneau (Henri Tudor Research Center)
Nuno Freire (The European Library)
Stephane Gancarski (Laboratoire d'Informatique de Paris)
Manolis Gergatsoulis (Ionian University)
C. Lee Giles (Pennsylvania State University)
Elke Greifeneder (Berlin School of Library and Information Science)
Thomas Habing (University of Illinois, Urbana-Champaign)
Martin Halvey (University of Strathclyde)
Myung-Ja Han (University of Illinois at Urbana-Champaign Library)
Carolyn Hank (University of Tennessee)
Bernhard Haslhofer (AIT- Austrian Institute of Technology)
Bradley Hemminger (School Library and Information Science)
Maureen Henninger (University of Technology Sydney)
Annika Hinze (University of Waikato)
Helen Hockx-Yu (Internet Archive)
Jimmy Huang (York University)
Antoine Isaac (Europeana & VU University Amsterdam)
Adam Jatowt (Kyoto University)
Leslie Johnston (NARA)
Jaap Kamps (University of Amsterdam)
Min-Yen Kan (National University of Singapore)
Madian Khabsa (Microsoft Research)
Michael Khoo (The iSchool, Drexel University)
Claus-Peter Klas (GESIS - Leibniz Institute for Social Sciences)
Alberto Laender (Federal University of Minas Gerais)
Ronald Larsen (University of Pittsburgh)
Ray Larson (University of California, Berkeley)
Jonathan Leidig (Grand Valley State University)
Daniel Lemire (Université du Québec)
Chern Li Liew (Victoria University of Wellington)
Ee-Peng Lim (Singapore Management University)
Joan Lippincott (Coalition for Networked Information)
Xiaozhong Liu (Indiana University Bloomington)
Clare Llewellyn (University of Edinburgh)
Fernando Loizides (Cyprus University of Technology)
Clifford Lynch (cni)
Andrew Macfarlane (City University London)

Program Committee (continued):

Linaza Maria Teresa (Visual Communication Technologies VICOMTech)
Byron Marshall (Oregon State University)
P Martin (CDL)
Bruno Martins (IST - Instituto Superior Técnico)
Dana Mckay (Swinburne University of Technology Library)
Ian Milligan (University of Waterloo)
Wolfgang Nejdl (L3S and University of Hannover)
Erich Neuhold (University of Vienna, Austria)
Glen Newton (Natural Resources Canada)
David Nichols (University of Waikato)
Kjetil Nørvåg (Norwegian University of Science and Technology)
Bolanle Ojokoh (Federal University of Technology, Akure)
Christos Papatheodorou (Ionian University, Corfu, Greece)
Dimitris Plexousakis (Institute of Computer Science, FORTH)
Thomas Risse (L3S Research Center)
Seamus Ross (University of Toronto)
J. Alfredo Sánchez (UDLAP)
Heiko Schuldt (University of Basel)
Michalis Sfakakis (Ionian University)
Ali Shiri (University of Alberta)
Lloyd Smith (Missouri State University)
Julie Speer (Virginia Tech Libraries)
Lisa Spiro (Rice University)
Nicolas Spyratos (University of Paris South)
Besiki Stvilia (Florida State University)
Shigeo Sugimoto (University of Tsukuba)
Kazunari Sugiyama (National University of Singapore)
Tamara Sumner (University of Colorado at Boulder)
Sue Yeon Syn (The Catholic University of America)
Atsuhiro Takasu (National Institute of Informatics)
Nicholas Taylor (Stanford University Libraries)
Alex Thurman (Columbia University)
Giannis Tsakonas (University of Patras)
Chrisa Tsinaraki (European Union - Joint Research Center (EU - JRC))
Pertti Vakkari (University of Tampere)
Andre Vellino (University of Ottawa)
Simeon Warner (Cornell University)
Anne L. Washington (George Mason University)
Matthew Weber (Rutgers University)
Michael Witt (Purdue Univeristy)
Mike Wright (UCAR)
Iris Xie (Universty of Wisconsin-Milwaukee)
Maja Žumer (University of Ljubljana)

JCDL 2016 Sponsors & Supporters

Sponsors:

SIGIR
Special Interest Group
on Information Retrieval

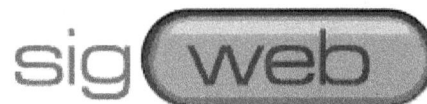

sig web

IEEE
computer
society

Supporters:

RUTGERS
UNIVERSITY | NEWARK

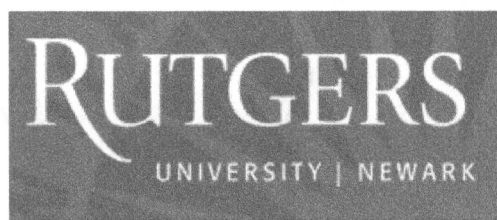

Rutgers University, Newark,
Institute of Data Science, Learning, and
Applications

UMBC
AN HONORS UNIVERSITY IN MARYLAND

University of Pittsburgh

University of Pittsburgh
School of Information Sciences

Future Digital Libraries: Research and Responsibilities

Maria Zemankova
National Science Foundation
mzemanko@nsf.gov

ABSTRACT

In October 1991 the National Science Foundation (NSF) sponsored a workshop to examine the role of the Information Retrieval research community in the emerging environment of Internet, high performance text processing capabilities and ever-increasing volumes of digitized documents. Ed Fox, Michael Lesk and Michael McGill drafted a White Paper, calling for a National Electronic Science, Engineering, and Technology Library. The term "Digital Library" was adopted and for follow-up workshops with the goal to identify research directions, leading to National Science Foundation (NSF)/Defense Advanced Research Projects Agency (DARPA)/National Aeronautics and Space Administration (NASA) Research in Digital Libraries Initiative announced in late 1993. Now, in 2016, 25 years after the first workshop, 15 years after the Joint Conference on Digital Libraries has been established, and many initiatives and developments around the world, what is the state of Digital Libraries? What items should be in digital libraries, who should their custodians, how can the items be organized to support knowledge discovery, how can the contents be safeguarded and preserved? Ebla, Syria (2500 B.C. - 2250 B.C.) constitutes the oldest organized library of tables yet discovered. What will the archeologists discover in year 4400 about the world, politics, economies, technologies, science, climate, species, health, food, culture, art, entertainment and everyday life through the ages?

The talk will examine what we can do to support innovative research and design and implementation of lasting, informative Digital Libraries that will promote global goals of knowledge discovery and international understanding and personal needs to organize and selectively share important facts, creations, and memories.

Keywords

Digital library; preservation; digitized documents; knowledge discovery

BIO

Maria Zemankova joined the National Science Foundation (NSF) as a Program Director in the Information and Intelligent Systems (IIS) Division in 1988. She has been instrumental in developing initiatives on Scientific Databases, Digital Libraries, and Biodiversity and Ecosystem Informatics, and has been active in cross-disciplinary initiatives, including Information Technology Research, Wireless Information Systems, Science of Design, Cyber Trust, Cyber-enabled Discovery and Innovation, Research Infrastructure, EarthCube, Smart & Connected Health, Big Data, and Visual & Experiential Computing. Her research interests include intelligent information systems; information/knowledge organization and evolution, management of uncertainty (fuzzy logic), knowledge discovery environments, data mining, privacy/security, visualization, information retrieval, text mining, social media, multimedia systems, spatio-temporal systems (GIS), scientific databases and data-knowledge life cycle.

Permission to make digital or hard copies of part or all of this work for personal or classroom use is granted without fee provided that copies are not made or distributed for profit or commercial advantage and that copies bear this notice and the full citation on the first page. Copyrights for third-party components of this work must be honored. For all other uses, contact the Owner/Author.
Copyright is held by the owner/author(s).

JCDL '16, June 19-23, 2016, Newark, NJ, USA
ACM 978-1-4503-4229-2/16/06.
http://dx.doi.org/10.1145/2910896.2926740

The State of Practice and Use of Digital Collections: The Digital Public Library of America as a platform for research

Rachel Frick
Digital Public Library of America (DPLA)
rachel@dp.la

ABSTRACT

In 2016, Digital Public Library of America is celebrating the third year of its cultural heritage metadata aggregator service. Since its launch, the DPLA collection has grown to represent over 13 million objects and over 1900 institutions, from small historical societies to large research libraries. With onramps, or hubs, in over 20 states, DPLA is well on its way to complete the coverage map by the end of 2017. As it continues to build this amazing dataset, DPLA is taking the time to examine what lessons are to be learned from this unprecedented resource, as the organization's sustainability is directly tied to how the collection grows, how it measures use, and proving its value to the communities it serves. What does this collection data tell us about the state of bibliographic holdings information, and the knowledge and skills and abilities of those who create records, not just for local use, but for use in other environments and contexts? How well does the metadata perform when it leaves its original context? Working with colleagues at Europeana, DPLA has begun investigating and addressing the problematic issues regarding access and reuse of digital objects in the collective by examining current ways rights are expressed in the metadata, working towards standardization of this information. Ms. Frick will discuss DPLA's rights work, as well as other potential areas of research and DPLA's strategy for future growth.

Keywords
National digital libraries; collection aggregation; open data.

BIO

Rachel Frick is the Director of Business Development for the Digital Public Library of America. In this role, she is responsible for building out DPLA's sustainability plan and forging extensive new relationships in order to strengthen DPLA's visibility and impact. Prior to DPLA, Ms. Frick served as the director of the Digital Library Federation program at the Council on Library and Information Resources, building a large and diverse community of practitioners who advance research, teaching and learning through the application of digital library research, technology and services. She has held senior positions at the Institute of Museum and Library Services and the University of Richmond, among other roles. She is widely known in the library, archive, and museum world for her vision, organizational know-how and commitment to open culture. She graduated with her MSLS from the University of North Carolina at Chapel Hill.

Permission to make digital or hard copies of part or all of this work for personal or classroom use is granted without fee provided that copies are not made or distributed for profit or commercial advantage and that copies bear this notice and the full citation on the first page. Copyrights for third-party components of this work must be honored. For all other uses, contact the Owner/Author.
Copyright is held by the owner/author(s).
JCDL '16, June 19-23, 2016, Newark, NJ, USA
ACM 978-1-4503-4229-2/16/06.
http://dx.doi.org/10.1145/2910896.2926741

The Energy of Delusion: The New York Art Resources Consortium (NYARC) & The Digital

Stephen Bury

New York Art Resources Consortium (NYARC)

bury@frick.org

ABSTRACT

Museum libraries came late to the digitization party - primarily because of perceived copyright issues. Since 2010 the three libraries of the New York Art Resources Consortium (NYARC) have embarked on a series of niche, boutique digitization projects, pushing the boundaries of fair use, but they have also embraced the born-digital, establishing a program to capture art-history-rich websites and to give access to them via an innovative use of a discovery layer which prioritizes web resources in the ranking of results.

Keywords

World Wide Web; digitization; born-digital; art research; discovery layer

1. CONTENTS

The energy of delusion refers to an essay on Tolstoy's plots by the Russian literary theorist, Victor Shklovsky: in searching for the impossible, perfect plot Tolstoy would create and abandon characters and narrative turns, but this frenetic energy would result in such masterpieces as *War and Peace* or *Anna Karenina*.

NYARC consists of the research libraries of three leading art museums in New York City: The Brooklyn Museum, The Frick Collection and The Museum of Modern Art and was formed in 2006 with the goals of improving access to art research resources through technology and of providing leadership in the development of innovative and model information services programs. It created a customized web-based union library catalog, ARCADE. Although NYARC did not take part in the mass digitization project, Google Books, its catalog implements an API linking to Hathi Trust Digital Content, and links to our own niche digitization projects e.g. the collaborative Gilded Age and Vienna Secession (which also have stand-alone websites). We also worked with Tulane University Research as they developed an automatic platform to determine copyright status both in the USA and also in the country of publication, Durationator. We have tried where possible to put our digitized content into as many aggregators as possible – Internet Archive, HATHI Trust (although not a member), the Getty Portal, and shortly DPLA (although the implementation of IIIF is now an alternate strategy).

There were also links in ARCADE to live websites that had been specifically selected under the libraries' collection development policies. This led to a pilot project of web archiving of auction house electronic sales using the Internet Archive's Archive-It

Permission to make digital or hard copies of part or all of this work for personal or classroom use is granted without fee provided that copies are not made or distributed for profit or commercial advantage and that copies bear this notice and the full citation on the first page. Copyrights for third-party components of this work must be honored. For all other uses, contact the Owner/Author.

Copyright is held by the owner/author(s).

JCDL '16, June 19-23, 2016, Newark, NJ, USA

ACM 978-1-4503-4229-2/16/06.

http://dx.doi.org/10.1145/2910896.2926742

service. The Andrew W. Mellon Foundation then funded a yearlong feasibility study, followed by a two-year program to work out workflows for selection, capture, quality assessment, and making available art history-rich websites. Part of the latter involved implementing a discovery layer, PRIMO, which prioritized archived websites in its display: this involved working with ExLibris and an Archive-It API and demonstrates a characteristic of NYARC strategy which is to work closely with tech players when a product or service is just not out there and needs to be developed. We were also fortunate to have a National Digital Stewardship Resident who provided a key document for the workflow for quality assessment of captured websites and for preservation protocols, using the Duracloud-Archive It API. We also had a consultant working on a metadata application profile and data dictionary for the description of websites. Like the quality assessment document, this has been made available to the community, which is another characteristic of NYARC projects.

The Frick Art Reference Library has the main collection of images of artwork in the three NYARC institutions and it began a review, Photoarchive Futures, including scenario planning. The scenario chosen was to move to full digitization but in collaboration with the other major photo archives across the world. We hosted a meeting in NYC and launched PHAROS, and we began to plan a route map involving movement to conversion of all our metadata to CDOC-CRM in conjunction with Research Space, and the implementation of image analysis. We also began the mass digitization of our own photoarchive, beginning with the artists of the American School.

Parallel to this was the creation of a Digital Art History Lab which has the aim to provide workshops to researchers in relevant software and databases to enable mapping, visualization of art history data; to make our digital data open and available; and to promote this new discipline in New York through pop-up digital cafes, open days and lectures. We are working closely with The Tandon School of Engineering, New York University to develop a virtual light box: this will also be part of the PHAROS toolset. Of particular concern is the preservation of digital art history projects. Although our web-archiving project does address this to some degree, there remain other very significant preservation challenges.

Likewise we lack both a sandbox and programming capacity, which constrain what we would like to do. But by working with others (including technical partners, such as the Internet Archive and Ex Libris, as well as individual engineers), and sharing as much as possible we can mitigate this to some degree. At least there are benefits from the energy of delusion, not least in enthusiasm, and experimentalism in trying to make something that does not exist happen.

BIO

Since 2010 Stephen Bury has been the Andrew W. Mellon Chief Librarian of the Frick Art Reference Library and a Director of the New York Art Resources Consortium (NYARC). Previously he was the Head of European and American Collections at the British Library, where he was also in charge of its Web Archiving program, its contribution to Europeana, and the 21st Century Curator Project.

He has a first-class honors degree in Modern History from the University of Oxford and a PhD in Literature and Art History from the University of London. Publications include Artists' Books (1995, 2015), Artists' Multiples (2001), and Breaking the Rules (2007): he was the first advisory editor of the online Benezit's Dictionary of Artists (2010-14).

Querylog-based Assessment of Retrievability Bias in a Large Newspaper Corpus

Myriam C. Traub
Centrum Wiskunde &
Informatica

Thaer Samar
Centrum Wiskunde &
Informatica

Jacco van Ossenbruggen
Centrum Wiskunde &
Informatica

Jiyin He
Centrum Wiskunde &
Informatica

Arjen de Vries
Radboud University

Lynda Hardman
Centrum Wiskunde &
Informatica
Utrecht University

ABSTRACT

Bias in the retrieval of documents can directly influence the information access of a digital library. In the worst case, systematic favoritism for a certain type of document can render other parts of the collection invisible to users. This potential bias can be evaluated by measuring the *retrievability* for all documents in a collection. Previous evaluations have been performed on TREC collections using simulated query sets. The question remains, however, how representative this approach is of more realistic settings. To address this question, we investigate the effectiveness of the retrievability measure using a large digitized newspaper corpus, featuring two characteristics that distinguishes our experiments from previous studies: (1) compared to TREC collections, our collection contains noise originating from OCR processing, historical spelling and use of language; and (2) instead of simulated queries, the collection comes with real user query logs including click data.

First, we assess the retrievability bias imposed on the newspaper collection by different IR models. We assess the retrievability measure and confirm its ability to capture the retrievability bias in our setup. Second, we show how simulated queries differ from real user queries regarding term frequency and prevalence of named entities, and how this affects the retrievability results.

CCS Concepts

•Information systems → Evaluation of retrieval results;

Keywords

Retrievability Bias, User Query Logs, Digital Library, Digital Humanities

Permission to make digital or hard copies of all or part of this work for personal or classroom use is granted without fee provided that copies are not made or distributed for profit or commercial advantage and that copies bear this notice and the full citation on the first page. Copyrights for components of this work owned by others than the author(s) must be honored. Abstracting with credit is permitted. To copy otherwise, or republish, to post on servers or to redistribute to lists, requires prior specific permission and/or a fee. Request permissions from permissions@acm.org.

JCDL '16, June 19 - 23, 2016, Newark, NJ, USA

© 2016 Copyright held by the owner/author(s). Publication rights licensed to ACM.
ISBN 978-1-4503-4229-2/16/06...$15.00

DOI: http://dx.doi.org/10.1145/2910896.2910907

1. INTRODUCTION

For many digital libraries and archives, users are limited to the retrieval system offered by the data custodian. It is important for users that all relevant documents are equally likely to be retrieved, i.e. that retrieved results are not biased by hidden technological artefacts. If, however, the bias in the search technology impacts the findings of research tasks in a way that it renders relevant documents inaccessible or over-represents specific types of documents, this can lead to a skewed perception of the archive's contents. It is therefore important to provide data custodians and users with a measure to quantify the degree to which the retrieval system provides a neutral way of giving access to a document collection.

In the domain of Information Retrieval (IR), Azzopardi et al. introduced a way to measure how retrieval systems influence the accessibility of documents in a collection [1]. The *retrievability score* of a document d, $r(d)$, measures how *accessible* a document is. It is determined by several factors, including the matching function of the retrieval system and the number of documents a user is willing to evaluate. The retrievability score is the result of a cumulative scoring function, defined as:

$$r(d) = \sum_{q \in Q} o_q \cdot f(k_{dq}, c),$$

where c defines the number of documents a user is willing to examine in a ranked list. The coefficient o_q weights the importance of a query. The function $f(k_{dq}, c)$ is a generalized utility/cost function, where k_{dq} is the rank of d in the result list for q. f is defined to return a value of 1 if the document is successfully retrieved below rank c, and 0 otherwise. In summary, $r(d)$ counts for how many queries $q \in Q$ a document d is retrieved at a rank lower than a chosen cutoff c.

Using TREC collections and simulated queries, Azzopardi et al. demonstrated the effectiveness of retrievability as a measure for bias, and how retrievability can be used to compare the bias of different retrieval models [1]. We add to their findings by examining the effectiveness of the retrievability measure, and the query simulation procedure in a more realistic setting and we answer the following research questions:

- *RQ1: Is the access to the digitized newspaper collection influenced by a retrievability bias?*

We use the retrievability measure following a similar experimental setup as described in [1] to the digitized historic newspaper archive of the National Library of the Netherlands. This allows us to investigate the retrievability inequality of documents on a digitized – and therefore error-prone – corpus.

- *RQ2: Can we correlate features of a document (such as document length, time of publishing, and type of document) with its retrievability score?*

We investigate whether documents with specific features are particularly susceptible or resistant towards retrievability bias. This allows to better understand the origin of retrievability bias.

- *RQ3: To what extent are retrievability experiments using simulated queries representative of the search behavior of real users of a digital newspaper archive?*

The availability of user logs allows us to compare retrievability patterns of simulated queries to those generated with real user queries. We investigate how the results differ, for example, what types of documents the queries favor most. Finally, we compare the retrieved document sets with the documents viewed by users to explore how well the results match with users' interests.

Our study investigates the applicability of the retrievability concept to a digitized newspaper collection and the representativeness of simulated query sets of user queries.

2. RELATED WORK

The *Gini coefficient* and the *Lorenz curve* were introduced as means to assess and express potential bias in the accessibility of documents in a collection [1]. Both indicators were originally developed to measure and visualize a degree of inequality in societies [7], such as deprivation and satisfaction [14]. A "perfect tyranny", where one "tyrant" owns the entire fortune, is represented by a Gini coefficient of $G = 1$, whereas for the "perfect communist" scenario $G = 0$. Both have been used in several studies to facilitate the comparison of retrievability inequality of different IR models, subsets of the document collection, parameter sets and cutoff values [1, 2, 12, 11]. We follow these examples and use Lorenz curves and Gini coefficients to assess the retrievability inequality in a digitized newspaper archive, but we also show what other indicators could be used to better understand the *source* of the inequality.

Several additional studies investigated different aspects of retrievability. Most of these studies largely followed the approach introduced in [1], as well as its metrics. Subdomains of IR that are very sensitive to recall are legal and patent retrieval. An IR model that performs poorly on a specific patent collection can therefore have a devastating effect on the result of the search task. A study comparing the retrievability of documents in the MAREC[1] collection through different retrieval models [2] adapted the process used in [1] to generate queries to better simulate the search behavior of patent searchers. They included only bi-term queries as it allowed them to use Boolean operators. Our study shows that even more improvements to the query simulation process are necessary.

To facilitate comparisons across corpora, Bache and Az-

zopardi suggest that the document to query ratio (DQR) should be kept constant [2]. A high DQR, meaning that a relatively small number of queries is applied to a large data set, may lead to an unrealistically high *Gini* coefficient as a large fraction of documents is never retrieved. Low DQR values are very difficult for experiments with large corpora and real queries. None of the studies we found addresses this problem. The main reason for this being that most studies on retrievability make use of TREC document collections [6, 3, 4, 12, 13, 11], or a freely available corpus of patents from the US patent and trademark office [5]. As these data collections are not provided with query logs from real users, the queries for these studies were generated from the terms in the collection, which allows the researchers to create any number of queries to meet a predefined DQR. We show how a high DQR influences the results of a retrievability study with queries based on user logs and suggest compensation strategies.

3. APPROACH

To answer *RQ1*, we explore whether we can identify a retrievability bias with an approach similar to that reported in [1]. We assess the bias by calculating retrievability scores for every document in the collection for three different IR models, two different query sets (real and simulated), and several cutoff values c. For all of these conditions, we calculate the Gini coefficient. Additionally, we visualize the bias in the retrievability results using Lorenz curves.

To verify that the retrievability scores we generated are meaningful, we test in a known-item-search setup, whether documents with a lower $r(d)$ score are actually harder to find than documents with a higher $r(d)$ score. This is achieved by comparing the mean reciprocal ranks (MRR) of target documents of low scoring and high scoring documents for significant differences.

Understanding how specific document features contribute to a potential retrievability bias would allow a data custodian or a user to make a prediction of how likely they would be able to find documents with this feature in a specific retrieval task. We analyze whether features, such as time of publishing, estimated OCR quality or the newspaper title a document originates from, correlates with a higher or lower retrievability of a document (*RQ2*). Furthermore, we investigate the influence of different parameters (specifically stemming, use of Boolean operators and stopwords) on the retrievability of documents.

As queries play an essential role in any retrieval task, we compare how representative simulated queries are for real user queries. We analyze and compare the composition and length of simulated and real queries and how their result sets differ (*RQ3*). To find out which setup best caters to the users' interests, we compare how well the result sets we obtained in our previous experiments overlap with the documents that were actually viewed.

4. EXPERIMENTAL SETUP

We describe the collection of historic newspapers, the query sets and the parameters we used. To obtain comparable results, we followed the experimental setup of [1] as closely as possible, namely to assess the retrievability of documents through a cumulative scoring model. This means that a document score is given for each query for which a docu-

---
[1]www.ir-facility.org/prototypes/marec

ment ranks above a pre-specified cutoff rank (c). We quantified the extent to which the retrievability scores of different retrieval models vary using Lorenz curves and Gini coefficients. To verify the meaningfulness of the retrievability scores, we measure the effectiveness of queries designed to retrieve previously selected documents. An analysis of document features and their correlation with retrievability scores concludes our exploration of the bias in our document collection. The second part of our research investigates the representativeness of retrievability results by comparing the results with view data from the user logs.

4.1 Data Sets

We used three different data sets. The National Library of the Netherlands[2] (KB) provided us with the data of their entire digitized newspaper archive along with server logs from which we could extract the queries users issued via the library's webinterface, Delpher[3]. Additionally, we generated a set of simulated queries from the body text of the documents.

4.1.1 Historic Newspaper Collection

The newspaper data set made available to us ranges from 1618 to 1995[4] and consists of more than 102 million OCRed newspaper items. This comprises articles, advertisements, official notifications, and the captions of illustrations (see Table 1 for details).

As the archive spans almost four centuries, the newspaper pages vary strongly in visual appearance which is known to influence the performance of OCR software [8, 9]. The very high vocabulary size (see Table 1) indicates that the corpus might contain a high number of OCR errors, which can impact retrieval tasks [10]. The OCR quality has not been evaluated, therefore the actual error rates for the documents in this collection are unknown. An estimation of the quality by the OCR engine, however, is included in the metadata in the form of page confidence values.

From the KB data, we extracted and tokenized the body text of the newspaper items, which excludes the headings and meta data. We removed all stopwords and terms with fewer than three characters and kept only numbers with four digits, as these are likely to represent years and can therefore be used as query terms by users. The large majority of items (98%) are written in Dutch. As a stemmer for Dutch text was not available in the Indri[5] search engine, we created a stemmed version during preprocessing. We used the default Snowball stemmer for Dutch[6].

4.1.2 Real Queries

Under conditions of strict confidentiality, the KB made user logs available to us that were collected between March 2015 and July 2015. In order to protect the privacy of the users, the logs had been anonymized by hashing the IP ad-

Newspaper Collection		1618 - 1995
Total Size[7]		102,718,528
Vocabulary Size[8]		353,086,358
Articles	67%	69,237,655
Advertisements	29%	29,591,599
Official Notifications	2%	1,918,375
Captions	2%	1,970,899
User Logs		March - July 2015
Log Size (No. HTTP Requests)		107,684,434
No. Queries		4,169,379
No. Unique Queries		1,051,676
No. Unique IPs		162,536
No. Document Views		3,328,090
No. Unique Documents Viewed		2,732,139

Table 1: Data sets used based on the historic newspaper collection from KB.

Query Set	Composition	Size	DQR
Sim. Queries	single term	2,000,000	
	bi-term	2,000,000	
	total	4,000,000	26
Real Queries	no op., no stopw., st.	957,239	107

Table 2: Sizes and document to query ratios (DQR) of the query sets.

dresses, which enabled us to trace queries that originated from the same address without identifying the user. Delpher provides an advanced search interface, which allows users to apply boolean operators and facets based on metadata to their search queries. We processed the query logs the same way as the document collection by removing operators and stopwords, and stemming. For the latter, we again used the Snowball stemmer[9] (see Table 2 for details).

4.1.3 Simulated Queries

To be able to compare our results with those reported in [1], we created a simulated query set. For this, we counted the unique terms and bigrams in the preprocessed documents and extracted the top 2 million terms as single term queries and the top 2 million bigrams as bi-term queries (see Table 2). The frequencies for the two query sets ranged from more than 180 million to 5 for the single term queries and from more than 10 million to 20 for the bi-term queries. We did not filter for OCR errors, therefore frequently occurring misspellings can still be found in the simulated queries.

4.1.4 Document Query Ratio

Azzopardi et al. use query sets of which the size are comparable to the size of the corpus [1]. In this setting all documents have a fair chance to be retrieved. As we used real user queries in a very large corpus, it was not possible for us to influence the DQR. Consequently, the DQR values in our experiments vary greatly for the different query sets (see Table 2), as opposed to the study reported in [1], where the DQRs were 0.57 (AQUAINT) and 0.43 (.GOV). This issue has not been addressed in previous studies investigating retrievability of large document collections.

---

[2]www.kb.nl

[3]www.delpher.nl

[4]A small number of documents from the 20th century is incorrectly dated to 2011 in the metadata.

[5]http://www.lemurproject.org/indri.php

[6]https://lucene.apache.org/core/4_0_0/analyzers-common/org/apache/lucene/analysis/nl/DutchAnalyzer.html

[7]Number of all articles, advertisements, official notifications and captions

[8]Stopwords removed, length of term at least 2 characters

---

[9]https://pypi.python.org/pypi/PyStemmer/1.3.0

4.2 Setup for Retrievability Analysis

We compute retrievability scores based on three of the retrieval models used in [1]: TFIDF, Language Model using Bayes Smoothing with $\mu = 1,000$ (LM1000), and BM25.

Azzopardi et al. chose to report their results for $c = 100$ [1], therefore we also included these values for comparison. Additionally, we report on a cutoff value of $c = 10$ as it best represents the behavior of our users. The default number of results per page the Delpher interface shows is 10 and an analysis of the user logs showed that only a small fraction of users go beyond this. For the results based on the real queries, we also report on $c = 1000$, as this result set was of comparable size to the $c = 100$ results for the simulated queries.

We did not apply the query weights o_q as the by far largest fraction of real queries were issued only once.

4.3 Setup for Retrievability Validation

We validated the effectiveness of the retrievability scores for the newspaper collection. We examined whether documents with a low retrievability score are harder to retrieve than documents with a high score when a query is *specifically* designed to return the targeted document. We performed one experiment per query set. For simulated queries we follow [1] and use BM25 at $c = 100$ (stemmed, stopwords and operators removed). For the smaller set of real queries, we chose the same parameters but with a cutoff at $c = 1,000$, as the result set is more similar in size to the chosen set for the real queries. We included the documents with $r(d) = 0$, as they represent the group of documents that is supposedly the least accessible one.

For both result sets we generate queries from the target documents which contain OCR misspellings. In the experiment described in Subsection 4.2 the impact of these misspellings was lowered as a side effect of selecting the most frequent terms in the large corpus. Here, we select terms from a single document, which required us to apply filters as very rare misspellings being part of queries led to very high mean reciprocal rank (MRR) values, but are very unlikely to be used as queries by users.

First, we created a dictionary of terms that occurred in more than one document, but in fewer than 25% of all documents and for which the document frequency was *not* equal to collection frequency. This allowed us to exclude extremely rare misspellings that occur in only one document or only once in multiple documents, and very generic terms. The dictionary we created from these terms was used to determine a list of suitable documents. We removed all words from the documents that did not appear in the dictionary or appeared only once in the document. All documents with fewer than four unique words were discarded for the experiment. By applying these filters, we removed 38,026,541 documents from the collection, leaving 64,691,987.

We divided the remaining documents into four bins, the same number of bins as used in [1]. For the division into bins, however, we diverged from the description given in [1] (where documents were ordered by retrievability and then divided into quartiles) because due to a different distribution of $r(d)$ values, the lower scores would have dominated the lower quartiles. Instead of binning on $r(d)$, we used a strategy that is inspired by the distribution of wealth measurements in economics. In our case, wealth is represented as the number of data points per $r(d)$. It is calculated for each $r(d)$ score by

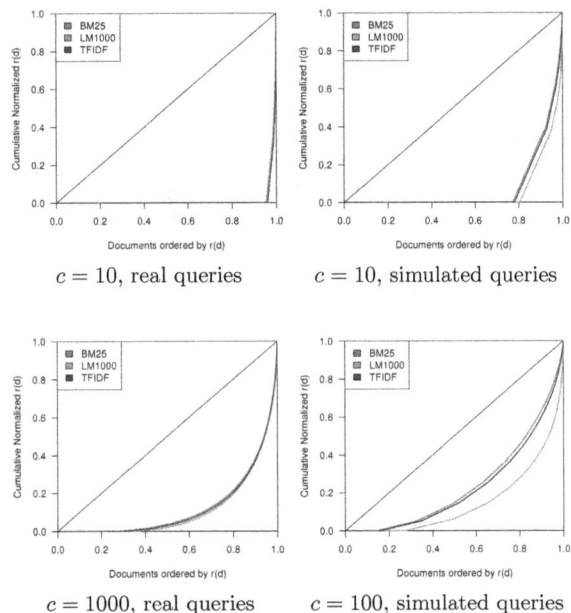

$c = 10$, real queries $\qquad$ $c = 10$, simulated queries

$c = 1000$, real queries $\qquad$ $c = 100$, simulated queries

Figure 1: Lorenz curves visualize the inequality of retrievability scores for the *real queries* (left) and the simulated queries (right) at different cutoff values c.

multiplying the score with its number of documents. Then we successively merged the $r(d)$ bins, until their summed up wealth reached the threshold of 25% of the total wealth. This led to four bins that roughly correspond to quartiles.

From each bin, we picked a random sample of 1,000 documents. We randomly selected 2 to 3 of the most frequent terms of each document to use as a query, as the mean number of terms issued by users was 2.32. The 1,000 queries we created this way were issued against the collection using the same IR model as before, BM25. We determined the rank of the target documents in the result lists and calculated the MRR for each bin as a measure of its retrieval performance.

5. RETRIEVABILITY ASSESSMENT

The high DQR value for our setup suggested that the fraction of documents with $r(d) = 0$ will be relatively high, especially for low cutoff values. Therefore, a large inequality in the retrievability scores was to be expected ($RQ1$). We describe the measured retrievability bias in different result sets and explore how to deal with the non-retrieved documents.

5.1 Assessment of Retrievability Inequality

We first look at the retrievability bias for both query sets at $c = 10$, which is the most realistic representation for the bias users of the archive are confronted with. The *Lorenz* curves depict a high inequality in the retrievability scores (see Fig. 1), with almost identical curves for the TFDIF, BM25 and LM1000 models. This is also reflected in the high *Gini* coefficients ranging from 0.97 to 0.98 for the real and from 0.85 to 0.89 for the simulated queries (see Table 3). The largest part of both curves consists of a flat line, which represents documents that were not retrieved. The setup

	Model	C					
		10		**100**		**1000**	
		G	Z	G	Z	G	Z
Real	TFIDF	0.98	96%	0.91	78%	0.77	30%
	BM25	0.97	95%	0.89	75%	0.76	28%
	LM1000	0.97	95%	0.90	77%	0.78	35%
Sim.	TFIDF	0.86	78%	0.55	16%	-	-
	BM25	0.85	77%	0.52	14%	-	-
	LM1000	0.89	80%	0.71	27%	-	-

Table 3: Gini coefficients (G) and fractions of documents with $r(d) = 0$ (Z) for the complete data set.

	Model	C					
		10		**100**		**1000**	
		G	Z	G	Z	G	Z
Real	TFIDF	0.71	47%	0.74	36%	0.71	13%
	BM25	0.64	40%	0.69	29%	0.70	10%
	LM1000	0.63	39%	0.71	33%	0.73	20%
Sim.	TFIDF	0.52	26%	0.50	5%	-	-
	BM25	0.48	24%	0.46	3%	-	-
	LM1000	0.63	34%	0.67	18%	-	-

Table 4: Gini coefficients (G) and fractions of documents with $r(d) = 0$ (Z) for the $Union_c$ data set.

	Model	C		
		10	**100**	**1000**
		G	G	G
Real	TFIDF	0.46	0.59	0.67
	BM25	0.40	0.56	0.67
	LM1000	0.40	0.56	0.66
Sim.	TFIDF	0.35	0.47	-
	BM25	0.32	0.44	-
	LM1000	0.43	0.60	-

Table 5: Gini coefficients (G) for the *Non Zero* data set from which all documents with $r(d) = 0$ were removed.

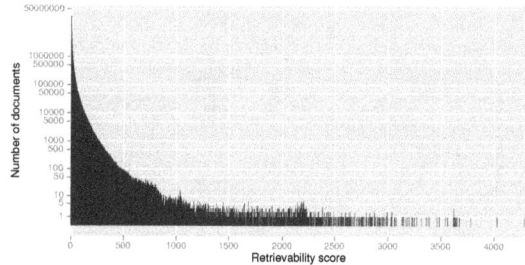

Real queries, $c = 1000$

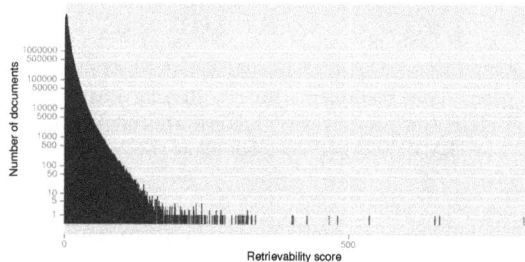

Simulated queries, $c = 100$

Figure 2: Log scale representation of the distribution of retrievability scores $r(d)$ for BM25 based on the complete KB dataset.

with the highest *Gini* coefficient (TFIDF at $c = 10$, real queries) also contains the highest fraction of non-retrieved documents (96%).

By contrast, the *Lorenz* curves for the higher cutoff values depicted in Fig. 1 indicate a more balanced distribution of $r(d)$ values. The curves for all models show a smaller deviation from the equality diagonal and both the *Gini* coefficient, as well as the fractions of documents with $r(d) = 0$, are lower. This suggests that the large number of documents with $r(d) = 0$ has a strong influence on both the shape of the *Lorenz* curve and the *Gini* coefficient. As never-retrieved documents are inevitable in a realistic scenario such as ours, it is important to find a way to address this problem.

To further explore the influence of the $r(d) = 0$ values, we created a $Union_c$ result set, that contains only documents retrieved by at least one of the models. While this removed most of the documents with $r(d) = 0$, a surprisingly large number of zeros still remained in the subset. The number of zero-scoring documents for TFIDF at $c = 10$, for example, was only reduced from 96% to 47%. Even with never-retrieved documents removed, the inequality in the $Union_c$ data set remains quite high for $c = 10$ with *Gini* coefficients ranging from 0.48 (BM25) to 0.63 (LM1000) (see Table 4). The remaining zero-scoring documents are a first indication that, while their Lorenz curves and Gini coefficients are similar, the models actually retrieve very different sets of documents.

We finally removed *all* documents with $r(d) = 0$ to measure the inequality among the retrieved documents. This caused the *Gini* coefficients to drop to values between 0.40 and 0.46 (real queries at $c = 10$). This again shows the large influence of a high fraction of zeros on the overall *Gini* score.

The similarity of the different models' *Lorenz* curves indicates a similar degree of bias in the $r(d)$ scores, but it does not allow insights into the type of bias, i.e. whether it originates from the high DQR, from the users' interest, or from a technological bias towards particular document features.

Fig. 2 shows the frequencies of $r(d)$ values (log scale), with a long tail distribution for both query sets. The maximum $r(d)$ value for the real queries is $r(d) = 4319$, while for the simulated queries this is much smaller (max $r(d) = 807$). This shows one possible cause for the bias towards higher fractions of documents with $r(d) = 0$ within the real queries: they tend to retrieve the same documents more often, leading to a smaller number of unique retrieved documents. This indicates that the query sets themselves may be biased, the real query set towards the users' interest and the simulated query set towards the language use in the document collection.

5.2 Validation of the Retrievability Scores

We validated our results using a known-item-search experiment (see Subsection 4.3) to confirm that documents with low $r(d)$ scores are indeed harder to find.

The results show that the MRR values indeed increase for the bins containing the documents with the higher $r(d)$ values (see Table 6). With one exception the differences in the ranks between the bins proved to be significant in a Kolmogorov-Smirnov test. This suggests that documents in

Query Set		Bin			
		1st	2nd	3rd	4th
Simulated	MRR	0.19	0.28	0.36	0.45
	D	0.20	0.12	0.08	-
Real	MRR	0.17	0.26	0.34	0.38
	D	0.20	0.11	0.05*	-

Table 6: MRR values are higher for items in the quartiles with higher $r(d)$ scores. An * indicates that the Kolmogorov-Smirnov test did not confirm a significant difference (p > 0.05) between the indicated bin and the fourth bin. D is the maximum vertical deviation as computed by the KS test.

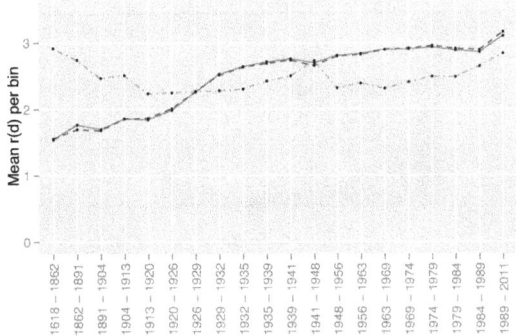

LM1000

BM25

Figure 4: Document length vs. r(d) for c=100, bins of 20,000 documents

Figure 3: The mean $r(d)$ scores (20 equally sized bins, based on $Union_c$ data, real queries for $c = 100$) for BM25 (green) and TFIDF (red) are nearly identical and double in value over time. LM1000 (blue) does not show this upward trend.

the first bin are significantly more difficult to retrieve than documents in the fourth bin.

This pattern is similar to the findings in [1] and confirms that a document's retrievability score is a good indication of how hard it is to retrieve the document by a user.

5.3 Document Features' Influence on Retrievability

To better understand the inequality in our document collection, we explored whether we can identify subsets within the archive that are particularly susceptible or resistant towards retrievability bias ($RQ2$).

• The *time of publishing* of the newspapers in our collection spans a period of nearly 400 years. Newspapers that belong to the early issues are very different from today's newspapers in terms of content as well as visual appearance. This affects the performance of OCR software, which results in high OCR error rates in older newspapers. We are therefore interested if this is reflected in the $r(d)$ values. For the analysis, we ordered the newspaper items in the $Union_c$ set by publishing date, divided them into 20 equally sized bins (1,7M items per bin) and calculated the mean retrievability score for each bin. Note that due to the much lower number of documents in the early periods of the archive, the 20th century occupies by far the most bins. The results for BM25 and TFIDF show a very small upward trend for later documents (see Fig. 3). This trend is, however, not visible for LM1000 and could also not be confirmed in an analysis of the raw data.

• The *document length* in our collection varies from 33

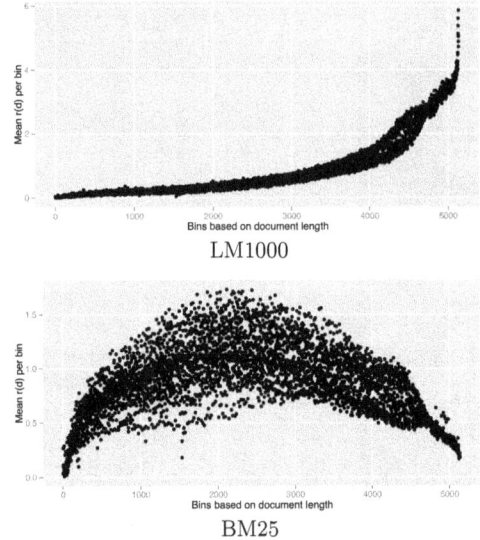

to 381,563 words with a mean length of 362 words. As [1] found that longer documents in their collections were more retrievable than short ones, we were interested in finding out whether the same holds for our collection. We sorted all items in the collection according to their length and divided them into bins of 20,000 documents, leading to 5,135 bins in total. For each bin, we calculated the *mean r(d)*. While the pattern we obtained for LM1000 shows an upwards trend for longer documents and thereby confirms this assumption (see Fig. 4), the results for BM25 and TFIDF[10] indicate that documents of medium length are most retrievable, whereas documents at both extremes are less retrievable. We can see a bias in both patterns, while LM1000 clearly favors longer documents, BM25 and TFIDF overcompensate for long documents, while they seem to fail to compensate for short ones.

• The library's OCR engine assigns *confidence scores* to each page (PC), word (WC) and character (CC) in the corpus. This is intended to give an indication of the quality of the OCR processing. From our contacts with the KB we learned that, during the post-processing, the scores were adapted based on the occurrence of a term in a Dutch word list. A formal evaluation of error rates in the KB data has not yet been performed, therefore we do not know to what extent these PC values are realistic. We divided the collection into bins of 20,000 documents based on their PC value and plotted the mean $r(d)$ score for each bin. The resulting plot shows an upward trend for increasing confidence values (see Fig. 5). Documents with an $r(d)$ score very close to 1.0, however, seem to be less retrievable. A closer look revealed that these documents often contain only very short texts, which makes them harder to find.

• *Newspaper titles* do not only vary with respect to their political orientation, but also concerning the content they provide to their readers. The mean number of articles per newspaper title in the archive is 82,638, with a median of

---

[10]The pattern for TFIDF looks very similar to BM25, therefore we did not include the plot.

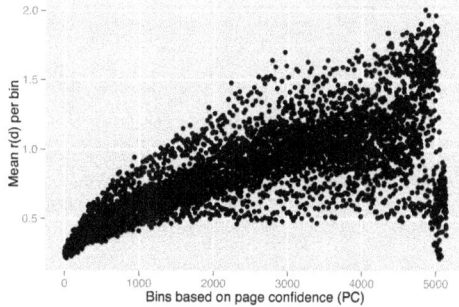

Figure 5: Mean $r(d)$ scores versus page confidence (PC) scores for bins of 20,000 documents

Top 10 Newspaper Titles	Mean r(d)
Rotterdamsch nieuwsblad*	0.05
Algemeen Handelsblad	0.06
De Telegraaf	0.06
Het Vaderland: staat- en letterkundig nieuwsblad	0.07
Leeuwarder courant*	0.07
De Tijd: godsdienstig-staatkundig dagblad	0.08
Het vrije volk: democratisch-socialistisch dagblad	0.10
Limburgsch dagblad*	0.12
Nieuwsblad van het Noorden*	0.14
Leeuwarder courant: hoofdblad van Friesland*	0.15

Table 7: Mean $r(d)$ values for the most prevalent newspaper titles for BM25 at $c = 10$, real queries. An * indicates a regional newpaper title.

127 and a range from one to 16,348,557 documents. We list differences in retrievability scores of the 10 most prevalent newspaper titles in our collection (see Table 7). While the differences seem small, three regional titles have a higher mean $r(d)$ than the seven national titles. Again, this may be caused by a bias in user preferences.

• We computed the mean $r(d)$ scores of the four *types of documents* in the archive for the two query sets. The means resulting from simulated queries show relatively small differences (see Table 8), whereas the mean scores obtained through real queries show a much higher score for official notifications. This again shows the large difference in the document sets retrieved by the two query sets.

From these results we can conclude that the large fraction of never retrieved documents is inevitable in realistic setups and needs to be addressed when assessing retrievability bias. We found evidence for a relation between low OCR confidence values, and short document length and a lower retrievability of documents. When comparing the degree of bias among the three IR models, we found LM1000

	Real	Simulated
Article	0.90	3.89
Advertisement	0.51	3.32
Official notification	4.80	3.22
Caption	0.84	3.06

Table 8: Mean $r(d)$ for different types of articles (BM25, c=100).

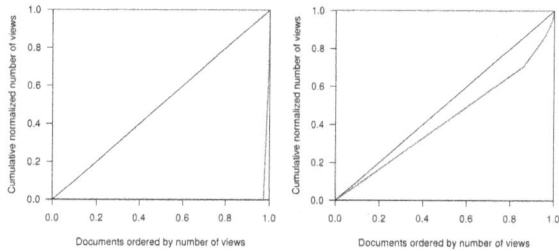

Figure 6: The *Lorenz* curve of viewed documents shows that only a small fraction of the collection was accessed (left) (Gini = 0.98). When non-viewed documents are removed, the inequality largely disappears, because most documents that are viewed, are viewed only once (right) (Gini = 0.16).

to show a greater bias for simulated queries. A comparison of the distributions of retrievability scores indicated a higher variety in $r(d)$ scores for real queries, and a bias towards official notifications for real queries which is not present in the simulated queries.

6. REPRESENTATIVENESS OF THE RETRIEVABILITY EXPERIMENT

We explore to what extent the different types of bias we see in the retrievability experiments are representative for bias in the documents actually viewed on the library's website ($RQ3$). For this purpose we compare the reported results with click data from the user logs, and revisit the use of simulated queries versus real queries.

6.1 Retrieved versus Viewed

The *Lorenz* curve in Fig. 6 (left) shows the inequality in the corpus with respect to the number of views. With only 2.7M out of 102M documents that are viewed, the fraction of documents that is never viewed by users is even larger than the fraction of never retrieved documents in our $c = 10$ experiments. This confirms that a large fraction of not-accessed documents is not only an artifact in our retrievability experiments caused by a relatively small query set: it also reflects the fact that in most large digital libraries, the number of views in any reasonable observation period will be small in comparison to the number of documents in the collection. Since the retrievability and the viewing scores are dominated by the large number of never accessed documents, neither the *Lorenz* curves nor the *Gini* coefficients are very informative measures of bias.

Distribution of r(d) scores and view frequencies.

For documents that are never accessed, it is hard to classify whether this is indeed the result of the small number of user views, the result of bias in user interest, or the result of technical bias in the retrieval system. Focussing only on the accessed documents would ignore the latter type of bias. However, even if we discard the non-accessed documents, the *Lorenz* curve of only the 2.7M viewed documents (see Fig. 6 (right)) is not much more informative. Here we see the opposite: extremely low inequality, which results from the fact that the large majority (86%) of the viewed documents is only viewed once.

13

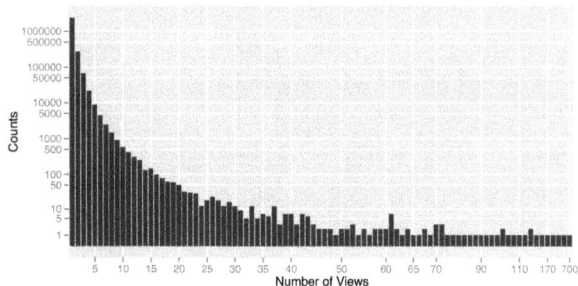

Figure 7: Log scale representation of the frequencies of document views based on the query logs.

Model	C	Real	Simulated
BM25	10	56.19 %	91.19 %
	100	7.94 %	73.51 %
TFIDF	10	53.48 %	91.44 %
	100	8.19 %	75.53 %
LM1000	10	54.74 %	89.24 %
	100	8.75 %	70.62 %

Table 9: The percentages of results from query logs and simulated queries that are *not* found by the other query set show that for small values of c the results vary strongly.

A log scale bar chart of the (non-zero) viewing frequencies (as in Fig. 7) provides more insight than the Lorenz curves. While the viewed documents dataset is smaller, the shape of the view frequency distribution is very similar to that of the retrievability score of the real queries in Fig. 2, and even more similar than the scores of the simulated queries. Again, this suggests that simulated queries do not necessarily represent real user behavior.

Viewed but not retrieved.

To explore if the unique documents retrieved in our experiment using real queries are representative for the 2.7M unique documents actually viewed by the users, we investigated the overlap between the two. Given that most users only look at the first page with 10 results, we looked at the overlap for BM25 at $c = 10$, where we have 4.7M unique documents that are retrieved at least once. Less than 0.6M of these were also viewed, leaving 2.1M documents that were viewed but not retrieved in our top 10.

To find out what the reasons for the small overlap were, we performed a preliminary manual assessment of the top viewed documents that had *not* been retrieved by BM25 at $c = 10$. The most viewed document in this subcollection is a very short article describing an incident, in which a cow accidentally "caught" a rabbit ("Men kan niet weten hoe een koe een haas vangt."[11]). From the user logs, we learned that this was caused by deep linking: the article was accessed in response to a hyperlink in a newsletter, not in response to a direct search action. The second most viewed article[12] was retrieved in response to a direct search action, but by making use of the search interface's time facet which allows users to narrow down the search results to specific time periods.

Other often viewed documents were retrieved in our experiment, but with a ranking slightly above the $c = 10$ cutoff. That this is not just anecdotal but a larger issue is confirmed by the much larger overlap for the higher cutoff values. $c = 100$ retrieved 1.5M viewed documents, and $c = 1000$ retrieved more than 2.4M of the 2.7M viewed documents.

These results can be interpreted in two ways. First, small differences in the ranking scheme can have quite dramatic effects due to the all-or-nothing scoring function. This suggests that a smoother cost function based on the ranking

might be worthwhile. Another potential interpretation is that the experimental setup needs to reflect the real search engine better, and also take the faceted search parameters, pagination, search operators and other more complex search settings into account.

6.2 Real versus Simulated Queries

Since real query logs for large document collections are hard to obtain, most retrievability experiments reported in the literature use simulated queries, typically based on sampling the most popular n-grams. However, our results seem to suggest such queries might not be representative of real user queries.

Qualitative comparison of often retrieved documents.

To get a better intuition of the type of documents retrieved, we manually explored the top 10 articles for both query sets (for BM25 at $c = 10$). The top results for the real queries completely consisted of articles that contained lists of names [13]. This is because the logs from the KB contain a large number of queries with names and locations.

We compared this finding to the top results set retrieved by the simulated queries. Here, the top scoring documents either contain a very repetitive text pattern (e.g. repetitive poems[14]), or the documents themselves are near duplicates of other documents (e.g. chain letters, advertisements with identical text, or other documents that were published multiple times[15]). This finding might indicate another drawback of the way the simulated queries are traditionally sampled: frequently occurring terms are more likely to be included in the query set.

Overlap in retrieved documents.

The variety of $r(d)$ values is much larger on the real queries, indicating that the two query sets might retrieve very different documents (see Fig. 2). We explored the overlap of documents that were retrieved by the real queries and the (larger) set of simulated queries. For all three models, at $c = 10$, more than half of the documents retrieved by the real queries are *not* found in the results from the simulated queries (see Table 9). This again suggests that we should improve the construction of our simulated query set to better represent real queries. Note that the fraction of documents that are retrieved by both approaches is considerably higher for $c = 100$, where less than 9% of the documents in the

---

[11]http://resolver.kb.nl/resolve?urn=ddd:110540686:
mpeg21:a0015

[12]http://resolver.kb.nl/resolve?urn=ddd:000011882:
mpeg21:a0004

[13]see for example http://resolver.kb.nl/resolve?urn=ddd:
010179873:mpeg21:a0001

[14]http://resolver.kb.nl/resolve?urn=ddd:010210514:
mpeg21:a0150

[15]see http://resolver.kb.nl/resolve?urn=ddd:010691557:
mpeg21:a0069

result set of the real queries are not found in the results of the simulated queries.

Differences between query sets.

In addition to the difference between the documents retrieved by both types of queries we also looked at the characteristics of the query sets themselves. The two query sets differ not only in size (as indicated in Table 2). The mean length of the real queries is 2.32 and all queries use a total of 253,637 unique terms. As we followed [1] and only used single and bi-term queries for the simulated query set, its mean query length is much smaller (1.5). The number of unique terms (2,028,617) is, however, much higher. This suggests that even by sampling only the most popular (bi)terms, we would over estimate the vocabulary used by users to formulate their queries.

We manually assessed the number of terms that refer to named entities in the 100 most frequent terms in both query sets. For the simulated queries, we found only 5 mentions of persons or locations, as opposed to 56 named entities in the real queries, confirming again the large differences in this aspect between the two sets.

Table 8 shows a higher retrievability of *official notifications* for the real queries. We compare this finding with the fractions of viewed documents for each type. While these fractions are very low for articles (only 2.61% viewed), advertisements (2.07%) and captions (4.01%), a much higher fraction of the official notifications was viewed (40.10%). This again shows that retrievability measured by real queries are more representative than synthesized queries.

6.3 Representativeness of Parameters used

Apart from queries and document features, retrievability can also be influenced by the parameters used in the retrieval setup, namely the inclusion or exclusion of stopwords and operators, and stemming. While we followed the parameter settings used by [1] so far (PS1), we compare the results obtained with the real queries using two alternative parameter settings (PS2 and PS3):

PS1: operators removed, stopwords removed, stemmed (used by [1])

PS2: operators removed, stopwords kept, unstemmed

PS3: operators, stopwords removed, stemmed[16]

Parameter sets *PS2* and *PS3* resulted in nearly identical *Gini* coefficients to those we reported in Table 3 for *PS1*. This suggests that the removal of stopwords, or the use of stemming and operators, has no influence on the extent of inequality in the document retrieval. The question remains, however, whether and how the underlying retrieved document sets differ and how this relates to the documents the users found sufficiently relevant to view.

Differences in retrieved document sets.

We compared the retrieved document sets from *PS1* and *PS2* for their overlap and found that while the majority of documents retrieved in one setting is also retrieved in

---

[16]As restrictions of the Indri toolkit (http://www.lemurproject.org/) did not allow us to run this set of parameters for BM25 and TFIDF, these results are available only for LM1000.

	PS1	Shared	PS2	C
BM25	1,939,710	2,758,599	1,971,087	
TFIDF	1,667,374	2,485,412	1,689,125	10
LM1000	2,141,563	2,620,988	1,317,420	
BM25	7,436,058	17,923,267	7,232,087	
TFIDF	6,672,656	16,385,354	6,381,519	100
LM1000	7,384,854	16,711,774	4,804,696	

Table 10: Numbers of documents retrieved only by one parameter set (*PS*) and number of documents retrieved by both sets.

	PS1	PS2	PS3	C
BM25	504,022	598,969	-	
TFIDF	435,413	527,461	-	10
LM1000	742,548	706,425	781,908	
BM25	1,422,231	1,511,973	-	
TFIDF	1,323,284	1,423,589	-	100
LM1000	1,788,719	1,741,290	1,840,285	

Table 11: Viewed documents that were retrieved by each model for the different parameter sets (*PS*) for a total of 2,732,139 viewed documents.

the other, still a large fraction is only found in one setting (see Table 10). Note that even though this difference is not reflected in the *Gini* coefficient, *Lorenz* curves or r(d) distribution plots, it is a form of retrieval bias that may have a huge impact on the user's task.

Again, as *c* increases, the fraction of shared documents between the parameter sets increases as well. To judge which of the document sets is the more favorable for our use case, we compare the overlaps of the result sets with documents that were viewed by users (e.g using views as a proxy for relevance judgements).

The combinations of IR model and parameter set vary strongly with respect to their ability to retrieve the viewed documents (see Table 11). BM25 and TFIDF achieved better results with *PS2* than with *PS1*, but both are outperformed by LM1000 in all settings. The best result is achieved by using LM1000 with *PS3* with 29% of the viewed documents retrieved, so that in this case, the retrieval model with the most bias also performs better. This is in contrast to results reported by [1], where better performing models typically also show less bias.

7. CONCLUSIONS AND OUTLOOK

Measuring the variation in the retrievability of documents in a collection complements standard IR evaluations that focus on efficiency and effectivity. No previous study has investigated how well retrievability studies represent the search behavior of real users and how they could be applied to a large collection of digitized documents that contain an unknown number of misspellings due to OCR processing. Our focus was on the exploration of the applicability of retrievability studies to a large digitized document collection and an evaluation of the representativeness of simulated queries for real users' search behavior.

While *Gini* coefficients and *Lorenz* curves allowed us to detect and quantify a retrievability bias in the document collection for three standard IR models, they were not sufficiently expressive to help us understand the source of it. We looked at the differences among the documents retrieved, and showed that large differences are common even for models with similar *Gini* coefficients and *Lorenz* curves.

In addition, we explored several influencing factors: the document to query ratio, document features, characteristics of query sets and the use of different parameter sets.

When comparing the characteristics of simulated queries to those of real users' queries we found substantial differences with respect to composition of the query sets, number of (unique) terms used, and use of named entities. Real users' queries contained a much higher fraction of named entities than we found in the simulated query set.

Finally, we compared how effectively combinations of specific parameter settings could retrieve the documents users viewed. Based on the results from this study, the setup that best covers the users' information needs is the combination of real queries with operators on LM1000. Note that according to the inequality assessment, the least biased model is BM25. This shows, that switch to a model with a lower retrievability bias might hurt the system's performance in terms of retrieving the most relevant documents.

Simulated queries that are representative for the search behavior of real users are a key ingredient for a realistic assessment of retrievability bias. Future work should therefore focus on how the generation of simulated queries can be adapted in a way that they better represent the type of queries real users issue on a specific collection.

Acknowledgments

We would like to thank Marc Bron for pointing us to the retrievability literature, Emma Beauxis-Aussalet for her feedback on the statistical analyses, and the National Library of the Netherlands for their support. This research is funded by the Dutch COMMIT/ program and the WebART project. Part of the analysis work was carried out on the Dutch national e-infrastructure with the support of the SURF Foundation.

8. REFERENCES

[1] L. Azzopardi and V. Vinay. Retrievability: An evaluation measure for higher order information access tasks. In *Proceedings of the 17th ACM Conference on Information and Knowledge Management*, CIKM '08, pages 561–570, New York, NY, USA, 2008. ACM.

[2] R. Bache and L. Azzopardi. Improving access to large patent corpora. In A. Hameurlain, J. Küng, R. Wagner, T. Bach Pedersen, and A. Tjoa, editors, *Transactions on Large-Scale Data- and Knowledge-Centered Systems II*, volume 6380 of *Lecture Notes in Computer Science*, pages 103–121. Springer Berlin Heidelberg, 2010.

[3] S. Bashir. Estimating retrievability ranks of documents using document features. *Neurocomputing*, 123(0):216 – 232, 2014. Contains Special issue articles: Advances in Pattern Recognition Applications and Methods.

[4] S. Bashir and A. Rauber. Improving retrievability and recall by automatic corpus partitioning. In A. Hameurlain, J. Küng, R. Wagner, T. Bach Pedersen, and A. Tjoa, editors, *Transactions on Large-Scale Data- and Knowledge-Centered Systems II*, volume 6380 of *Lecture Notes in Computer Science*, pages 122–140. Springer Berlin Heidelberg, 2010.

[5] S. Bashir and A. Rauber. Improving retrievability of patents in prior-art search. In C. Gurrin, Y. He, G. Kazai, U. Kruschwitz, S. Little, T. Roelleke, S. Rüger, and K. van Rijsbergen, editors, *Advances in Information Retrieval*, volume 5993 of *Lecture Notes in Computer Science*, pages 457–470. Springer Berlin Heidelberg, 2010.

[6] S. Bashir and A. Rauber. Automatic ranking of retrieval models using retrievability measure. *Knowledge and Information Systems*, 41(1):189–221, 2014.

[7] G. Garvy. Inequality of income: Causes and measurement. In *Studies in Income and Wealth, Volume 15*, pages 25–48. NBER, 1952.

[8] R. Holley. How good can it get? Analysing and improving OCR accuracy in large scale historic newspaper digitisation programs. *D-Lib Magazine*, 15(3/4), 2009.

[9] E. Klijn. The current state-of-art in newspaper digitization a market perspective. *D-Lib Magazine*, 14, January 2008.

[10] M. C. Traub, J. van Ossenbruggen, and L. Hardman. Impact analysis of ocr quality on research tasks in digital archives. In S. Kapidakis, C. Mazurek, and M. Werla, editors, *Research and Advanced Technology for Digital Libraries*, volume 9316 of *Lecture Notes in Computer Science*, pages 252–263. Springer International Publishing, 2015.

[11] C. Wilkie and L. Azzopardi. Best and fairest: An empirical analysis of retrieval system bias. In M. de Rijke, T. Kenter, A. de Vries, C. Zhai, F. de Jong, K. Radinsky, and K. Hofmann, editors, *Advances in Information Retrieval*, volume 8416 of *Lecture Notes in Computer Science*, pages 13–25. Springer International Publishing, 2014.

[12] C. Wilkie and L. Azzopardi. Efficiently estimating retrievability bias. In M. de Rijke, T. Kenter, A. de Vries, C. Zhai, F. de Jong, K. Radinsky, and K. Hofmann, editors, *Advances in Information Retrieval*, volume 8416 of *Lecture Notes in Computer Science*, pages 720–726. Springer International Publishing, 2014.

[13] C. Wilkie and L. Azzopardi. Retrievability and retrieval bias: A comparison of inequality measures. In A. Hanbury, G. Kazai, A. Rauber, and N. Fuhr, editors, *Advances in Information Retrieval*, volume 9022 of *Lecture Notes in Computer Science*, pages 209–214. Springer International Publishing, 2015.

[14] S. Yitzhaki. Relative deprivation and the Gini coefficient. *The Quarterly Journal of Economics*, 93(2):pp. 321–324, 1979.

Digital History Meets Wikipedia: Analyzing Historical Persons in Wikipedia

Adam Jatowt, Daisuke Kawai and Katsumi Tanaka

Kyoto University
Yoshida-Honmachi, Sakyo-ku
606-8501 Kyoto, Japan
{adam, tanaka}@dl.kuis.kyoto-u.ac.jp
daisuke@gauge.scphys.kyoto-u.ac.jp

ABSTRACT

Wikipedia is the result of a collaborative effort aiming to represent human knowledge and to make it accessible for everyone. As such it contains lots of contemporary as well as history-related information. This research looks into historical data available in Wikipedia to explore its various time-related characteristics. In particular, we study Wikipedia articles on historical persons. Our analysis sheds new light on the characteristics of information about historical persons in Wikipedia and quantifies user interest in such data. We use signals derived from the hyperlink structure of Wikipedia as well as from article view logs and we overlay them over temporal dimension to understand relations between time, link structure and article popularity. In the latter part of the paper, we also demonstrate different ways for estimating person importance based on the temporal aspects of the link structure.

Categories and Subject Descriptors

H.3.m [**Information Systems**]: Information Storage and Retrieval: Miscellaneous

General Terms

Measurement, Human Factors.

Keywords

Wikipedia, historical analysis, digital history, social networks, temporal link analysis

1. INTRODUCTION

History plays significant roles in our society by giving account of the past, explaining the present and offering lessons for the future. It helps to create meaning, coherence, orientation as well as settles the foundations of nations, our identities and memories, etc. As such, the history is one of the fundamental subjects taught from elementary schools onwards. The field of history science has recently started to benefit from the advances in computer science and information technologies [3,10,24,30,40,47,53], much like social sciences have been fostered by the advent of *computational social science* [35]. *Digital history* (aka. *computational history* or *histoinformatics*) has emerged as a subset of Digital Humanities that utilizes automatic approaches to process, organize, make sense of historical data and to verify or validate historical hypotheses. The growing interest in the application of computational approaches to the history science is also evidenced by dedicated interdisciplinary events (e.g., [28,36]).

Source criticism takes prime position in the history science [5]. The credibility, coverage, origin and other characteristics of sources are usually carefully scrutinized before the start of research. Although typically, primary sources are the main interest of historical analysis, secondary sources are also common subject to investigation. Wikipedia as the largest base of collaboratively created knowledge, is naturally one of them. Despite initial wave of criticism, it has been increasingly used in humanities including the history and memory science (e.g., [7,10,31,36,45,47]). For example, the president of the American Historical Association W. Cronon in the association's publication "Perspectives on History" [7] has recently called historians for embracing Wikipedia in education and research and for actively contributing to make it even better.

The importance of Wikipedia from the viewpoint of history science is due to its powerful educational impact. Wikipedia is hugely popular with nearly 500 million unique visitors each month[1] and constitutes a crucial source of history-related knowledge for majority of users. Typically, users refer to it as a starting point (or springboard) in their search for past-related information. For example, based on controlled user studies conducted in 2014, Wikipedia has been found to be the most frequently visited website for searchers seeking historical knowledge or wishing to corroborate historical facts [29]. Furthermore, Wikipedia and derived from it datasets (e.g., DBpedia[2] [2] or Yago2 [23]) are being commonly used as bases for many knowledge intensive processing tasks (e.g., [13,14,16,25,30,31,32,41,47,48,54]), some of which explicitly focus on historical data (e.g., [16,25,30,31,47]).

Prior studies investigated numerous aspects of Wikipedia including the process of its creation and evolution, the credibility and coverage of its content, controversy, collaboration or lack of it and so on [18,23,33,45]. However, dedicated analysis of history-related content as well as its broad temporal aspects of Wikipedia

Permission to make digital or hard copies of all or part of this work for personal or classroom use is granted without fee provided that copies are not made or distributed for profit or commercial advantage and that copies bear this notice and the full citation on the first page. Copyrights for components of this work owned by others than ACM must be honored. Abstracting with credit is permitted. To copy otherwise, or republish, to post on servers or to redistribute to lists, requires prior specific permission and/or a fee. Request permissions from Permissions@acm.org.

JCDL '16, June 19-23, 2016, Newark, NJ, USA
© 2016 ACM. ISBN 978-1-4503-4229-2/16/06...$15.00
DOI: http://dx.doi.org/10.1145/2910896.2910911

---

[1] Wikipedia is the 7th most visited website globally by Alexa ranking (25/1/2016) http://www.alexa.com/siteinfo/wikipedia.org

[2] http://dbpedia.org

17

articles has not been done so far. In this paper we analyze Wikipedia in order to understand the way in which history is recorded, organized and remembered and through this to better inform future digital history studies. We focus on a particular entity type, persons. Persons are the essence of the history and constitute the large fraction of Wikipedia content. They can be also easily positioned on timeline (provided their birth and death dates are known) unlike other types of entities, e.g., locations, ideas or concepts for which temporal boundaries are harder to be determined. We quantitatively study multiple aspects of historical persons such as the amount of recorded entities per each decade, the link distribution of different cohorts segmented based on their lifetimes and the characteristics of temporal snapshots of social networks. Since the history tends to be defined as an "unending dialogue between the present and the past" [5], we also analyze the connectivity between the present and the past as well as the distribution of viewing frequency of Wikipedia pages on people from different eras.

In particular, a series of questions guide our study:

Q1. *How many historical persons are described in Wikipedia? How much content is available about them?*

Q2. *How are historical persons connected in Wikipedia? What is the effect of time on the link structure and on the overall connectivity within Wikipedia?*

Q3. *How much does user interest in history change with regards to the distance in the past? Is there any correlation between the time when a person lived and its current popularity?*

Q4. *How strongly is the content on the past persons connected to the one on present persons?*

Q5. *How can we estimate historical person's importance using Wikipedia link structure?*

To answer the above questions, we assume a novel analysis style that organizes Wikipedia articles chronologically by the valid time of entities and which associates link-based metrics with time. Note that, unlike this work, prior studies focused mainly on the creation time of Wikipedia content (i.e., on the way in which users collaboratively create content over time or on the recency of information).

To sum up, we exhaustively investigate the characteristics of historical persons described in Wikipedia. We analyze the way in which they are described, the way in which they are inter-connected as well as the extent to which the information on them is accessed by Wikipedia visitors. We then demonstrate the temporal orientation of links to show that link distribution depends not only on semantics but also on time. In addition, we discuss several centrality measures on social historical graph.

The remainder of this paper is structured as follows. In the next section we provide an overview of the related work. Section 3 introduces the dataset and its preprocessing. The next section is the main part of the paper giving the analysis results. Section 5 contains the summary of findings and general discussion. Finally, we conclude the paper and outline the future work in the last section.

2. RELATED WORK
2.1 Wikipedia Analysis and Use
Wikipedia with its vast amount of user-generated content is a goldmine of knowledge both for average readers and for researchers who increasingly use it for many knowledge intensive tasks (e.g., [13,14,16,25,30,31,32,41,47,48,54]). It has been applied to various research areas in computer science ranging from natural language processing, information retrieval, information extraction, ontology construction, etc.

Wikipedia articles have been reported to have, in general, sufficient accuracy [18]. Within the history realm, a recent essay [45] by American historian Rosenzweig have found that mistakes in Wikipedia are as equally common as in reputable sources, and that serious mistakes are typically corrected within hours. Yet, one valid complaint found is the bias of its writers who predominantly are English-speaking males from Western culture. Another shortcoming is that Wikipedia "summarizes and reports the conventional and accepted wisdom on a topic, but does not break new ground." In other words, it lacks original research.

Many works in digital humanities utilize Wikipedia or derived from it knowledge bases. For example, Huet *et al.* [25] studied appearances of historical persons in the past editions of Le Monde based on their attributes derived from the Wikipedia to portray trends in popularity of different professions and the rise of the importance of women in French society. Garcia-Fernandez *et al.* [16] automatically determined publication dates of documents based on a range of linguistic features, one of which is the appearance of historical persons' names in text. The information on the lifespan of detected persons was collected from Wikipedia and used as additional signal for estimating document age. Eom *et al.* [10] studied the hyperlink networks of 24 Wikipedia language editions and automatically extracted the top 100 historical figures for each Wikipedia edition in order to investigate their spatial, temporal, and gender distributions with respect to their cultural origins. Skiena and Ward [47] ranked historical people using PageRank algorithm applied on the hyperlink graph consisting of person pages in Wikipedia. They also used the appearance statistics of person names in Google Books dataset[3]. Takahashi *et al.* [46] estimated influence of historical persons in unsupervised way based on spatio-temporal analysis and the adaptation of PageRank algorithm [44] using Wikipedia link structure. Other examples of using history-related data in Wikipedia can be found in [39] and [50]. Given the popularity of Wikipedia we believe it is important to undertake deeper studies of its history-related content. However, as far as we know, only one work tried to quantify the amount of historical data in Wikipedia. Kittur *et al.* [33] found through sampling that in 2009 about 11% content was strictly devoted to history and the content has grown 143% from 2006 to 2008.

In this work we assume a novel objective. Given the wealth of data on the past in Wikipedia and its frequent usage in education as well as in research, we look closely how the link structure, and the strength of remembering are related to the time periods of historical entities. To the best of our knowledge, this is the first Wikipedia study that considers this kind of temporal analysis of Wikipedia articles.

2.2 Collective Memory Studies
The concept of collective memory (social memory) popularized by Halbwachs [20,22] defines the collective view of society on the past. Collective memory is often contrasted with the concept of *collective amnesia* defined by Jacoby [26] as forceful or unconscious suppressions of memories, especially, those related to disgraceful or inconvenient events. In a similar fashion to personal memory [9], the social memory is known to decrease along time and to be subject to temporal variations following the occurrence of memory triggers such as sudden events or anniversaries [3,31]. Studies of collective memory can help us to understand the

---

[3] https://books.google.com/ngrams/datasets

mechanisms of forgetting and remembering as well as can explain the role of history in our lives. In addition, they have direct implications on the archival selection by memory institutions such as national or dedicated archives [30]. Traditionally, the research on collective memory has been based on small-scale investigations of personal accounts. Relatively few works have been carried out that use computational approaches for quantifying the characteristics of social memory over large text datasets. Cook *et al.* [6] investigated the decay of fame over time on the basis of the collection of news articles that covers 20th century. In [3] we studied memory decay and the way in which past years are remembered using the dataset of English news articles about different countries spanning 90 years. In another work [27] we have also analyzed the way in which users refer to the time in Twitter in order to measure *collective temporal attention* towards the past and the future.

Ferron and Massa [11] and Kanhabua *et al.* [31] proposed to treat Wikipedia as a global memory space. Differently to our work they focused on memory triggers that cause forgotten or poorly remembered events to be brought back into social attention. Anniversaries are natural examples of memory triggers. In another case, current events may also serve as triggers of the memories of similar, past events. Ferron and Massa studied also the way in which memory forms by analyzing the collaboration dynamics of Wikipedia contributors who edit articles on tragic events such as acts of terrorism (e.g., World Trade Center collapse) or natural disasters (e.g., Katrina Hurricane). Our work can be seen as complementary to that of Ferron and Massa [11] and of Kanhabua *et al.* [31].

3. DATA PREPARATION

3.1 Data Collection

We used the English Wikipedia dump provided by Wikimedia foundation[4]. To collect Wikipedia pages about persons we utilized DBpedia ontology datasets (PersonData ontology class) [2]. To capture core article content we used the BeautifulSoup library[5] excluding lists as well as footers under commonly used footer titles: `See also`, `References`, `External links` and `Notes`.

We then collected hyperlinks using Yago2 [23]. Based on the collected links, we could create directed graph, $G(V,E)$, where V is the set of nodes representing persons and E is the set of edges connecting them. An edge e_{ij} from a node v_i to node v_j indicates the presence of a hypertext link in v_i that leads to v_j.

To solve the problem of redirects, nodes redirecting to other pages within Wikipedia were merged with their targets. In addition, self-loops (self-links) were removed by excluding links with identical origin and destination.

3.2 Attribute Assignment

The information on the birth and death of persons has been obtained from Yago2. While many nodes in our dataset have complete attributes, certain fraction lacked either birth or death dates, while some had neither of them. In Fig. 1 we show the rate of persons without the birth date (green line) and the rate of persons without the death date (red line). The former measures the percentage of persons that died at a given decade who lack their birth date, while the latter shows the percentage of persons born at a given decade whose death date is not known. We counted only persons for which at least one of the dates (birth or death) is known (if both are

unknown it is, of course, difficult to assign a person to timeline). The high rate of persons without known death dates in the current and in the last century is not surprising as many are still alive. On the other hand, interestingly, we notice that the rate of persons without the known birth date in the past centuries is higher than the one of persons without the death rate. This may be attributed to the lack of efficient demographics recording (e.g., civil registry) and archiving tools or systems in the past [51]. A death of a person, especially a prominent one, was likely noticed and recorded. Yet, his/her birth related information may not always have been known, unless the person was born to a well-known or noble family. We also notice that the probability of a person article to lack her birth date is higher, the longer time ago the person lived.

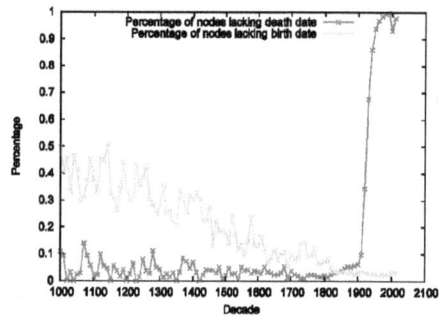

Figure 1 Rate of persons lacking birth or death date per decade.

Note that excluding persons lacking the attribute values would significantly decrease the amount of data at very distant decades, for which, the data is already sparse. We then inferred missing attributes for persons who lack either birth or death dates[6] after first mapping each known date to its decade for minimizing error. Based on the nodes with the complete set of attribute values (i.e., persons with known both the birth and death dates), we first computed: the *mean death date* for people born at a given decade and the *mean birth date* for people who died at a given decade. In result, each birth decade d_b was associated with the most probable death decade computed over the people born at d_b. Similarly, each death decade d_d was associated with the most probable birth decade calculated over the people who died at d_d.

People born in the 20th and 21st centuries who lack their death dates were treated differently. Many of them are still alive so assigning their death decades requires a forecasting procedure to avoid underestimation. We estimated their probable death decades by the least square error method trained on all the persons born after year 200 and before year 1900. The forecasting is reliable when we look at the part of the plot from year 200 until 1900 as shown in Fig. 2. It portrays the average death date for people born at a given birth decade based on the nodes which have complete set of attributes. We can observe a strong linearity for most of the time period except for the two noisy first centuries. After removing the data from the first two and the last two centuries, the fitted linear trend line was: $y = 1.003x + 54.61$ ($R^2 = 0.9173$).

We then assigned the most probable birth and death decades for the nodes that lacked either of the attributes. In the remaining of this paper we will focus on persons born during and after 11th century onwards. The total number of nodes we use in the analysis is 459,991.

---

[4] https://dumps.wikimedia.org/enwiki

[5] https://pypi.python.org/pypi/beautifulsoup4

[6] Nodes that lacked both dates were removed.

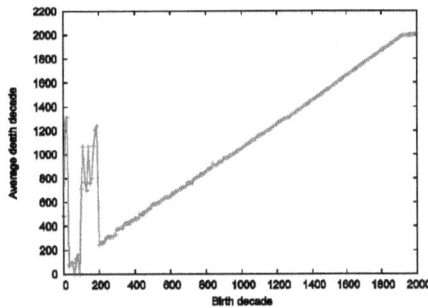

Figure 2 Average death decade for persons at different time.

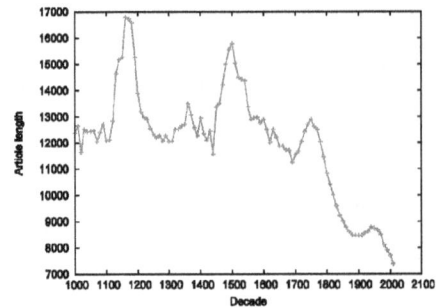

Figure 4 Average article length per decade.

4. ANALYSIS

4.1 Content Analysis

We first look into the average number of persons per decade. Fig. 3 shows on the log scale the counts of persons alive at past decades. A person is associated with a given decade if her or his lifetime overlaps with the decade. We observe a strong increase in the number of persons that have their Wikipedia articles, the closer to the present time. The plot features close to exponential character and could be actually well-approximated by the three straight lines (with corresponding epochs: 1000-1399, 1400-1699, 1700-1990) each having higher slope value than the previous one.

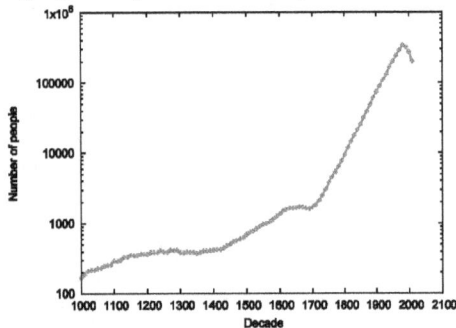

Figure 3 Number of persons per decade in log scale.

The increasing number of people at more recent decades can be of course explained by the demographic trend of rapid population increase over recent times [34]. It also aligns with an intuitive hypothesis that the amount of "remembered" data decreases exponentially with the time elapsed. Previous study on news article collections has demonstrated similar exponential decrease in the strength of remembering of past years [3].

We next examine the effect of time on the amount of content within the Wikipedia articles. According to an intuitive hypothesis, the more time ago a person lived, the less information should be available about her or him, and, hence, the article about the person should be, on average, shorter than ones on more recent people. To the contrary when looking at Fig. 4, which plots the average article length for each decade, it becomes apparent that rather opposite happens.

The mean lengths of articles of people in the 19th and 20th centuries are on average shorter than of persons in the previous centuries. This is likely due to the fact that many less famous persons who lived in the recent past are recorded in Wikipedia. For such persons, Wikipedia contributors may have difficulty to find enough verifiable and informative content, or they may be simply less interested and motivated to contribute.

4.2 Connectivity Analysis

We now look into the connectivity aspects of articles to investigate temporal differences of links. First, we examine the change in the number of links in relation to time. Fig. 5 contrasts the average in- and out-degrees with the time when persons lived. While certain fluctuations can be observed, on average, the mean numbers of incoming (red line) and outgoing (green line) links are decreasing, the more recently a person lived. This suggests that Wikipedia pages about more recent persons are, on average, connected less strongly with other persons than the pages about more distant persons. We also observe that in- and out-degree values tend to correlate over time.

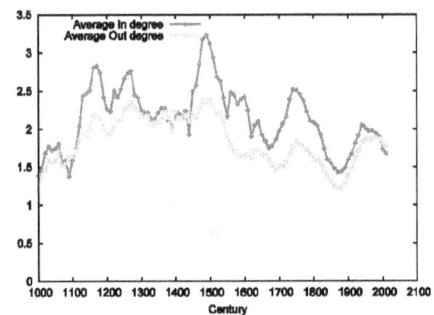

Figure 5 Average in-link and out-link degrees in the past.

To investigate more the decrease in the link rate for the recent persons we show in the upper graph plot of Fig. 6 the ratio of nodes that have at least one incoming link and the ratio of nodes with at least one outgoing link. A person is considered to live in a given century if most of her life span occurred at that century (i.e., the century contains the midpoint of the person's life). We notice that there are relatively more persons without any in- or out-links leading to other persons in more recent centuries. This may be again due to many Wikipedia pages about less known persons in the recent times. Note that, even if a page may have few links to other persons, it still can link to other types of Wikipedia articles that we do not consider in this study (e.g., locations, events or concepts) or to persons who did not live in the second millennium.

We think that, ideally, a person should be well-connected to the social context of its time, that is, to other relevant, contemporary persons. By this visitors could receive contextual information for obtaining more organized and structured view of a person. So weaker connectivity means less chances to understand a target person as well as her context and to discover other related persons. According to the theory of *structuralism* [49], the meaning of concepts resides in the relationships with other concepts. Thus, concepts or entities considered alone may be difficult to be understood and should rather be viewed within their context. Similar idea should apply also to Wikipedia entities. A possible remedy could be adjusting Wikipedia's editing policies and guidelines to put more emphasis on sufficient "grounding" of described persons.

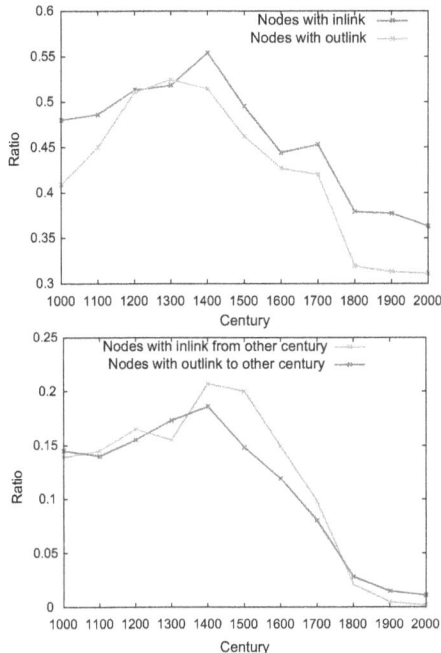

Figure 6 Ratios of persons with at least one in- or out-link from/to any century (top) and from/to centuries different than the one of the target person (bottom).

We next analyze *across-time connectivity* of historical persons. Links between persons from other historical centuries are less likely to indicate physical relationships and actual interaction between the persons. Instead, they tend to be the artefact of historical comparison, family lineage, or point to the start/continuation/end of some processes, etc. In the lower graph of Fig. 6 we show the ratio of nodes that have at least one out-going link to or one in-coming link from someone who lived in another century. We can observe that the persons in the last two centuries have on average less connectivity with the people outside their centuries, than the persons at earlier centuries. This means that Wikipedia pages on persons from the distant past tend to have more *across-century connectivity* than the pages about persons living more recently.

To better portray the inter-century linkage we next plot the aggregate temporal orientation of links in Fig. 7. It displays the rate of links coming from the past persons (blue color), the contemporary persons (green) and the future persons (red) at every decade. Two persons are considered contemporary if their lifetimes have non-empty overlap. Looking at Fig. 7 we notice that on average few links tend to originate from persons living in the past, while most of the links are from the contemporary people. This means that whenever a page has an in-link there is high probability that that link comes from a contemporary person. Note that naturally, the amount of links from the "future persons" decreases the closer to the latest decade.

Figures 6 and 7 do not inform about the distance between linking persons. We then measure the average distance between connected persons and superimpose it over time. The distance is expressed as the number of years that separate the origin and the target of every link. The calculation is done as follows. For each decade d we first collect all persons who lived in that decade. Then, for each person p alive at d we collect all its in-links and compute

the distance between d and the decade from which each such link originates. The latter is represented as the mean decade of the link's origin (mean lifetime point of the person that links to p). Finally, we compute the average distance for all the in-links of all the persons living in d to portray how far the people alive at d are linked from. Fig. 8 shows the results. Interestingly, we notice relatively large distance for people living in the distant past, and, a smaller average distance for more recent persons. This confirms the higher across-time connectivity of past persons.

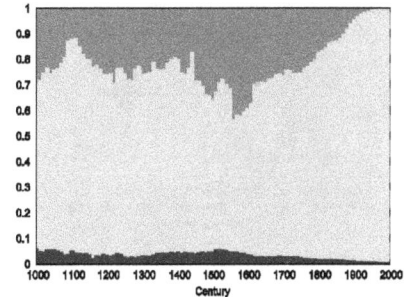

Figure 7 Rate of in-links from past persons (blue), contemporary persons (green) and future persons (red).

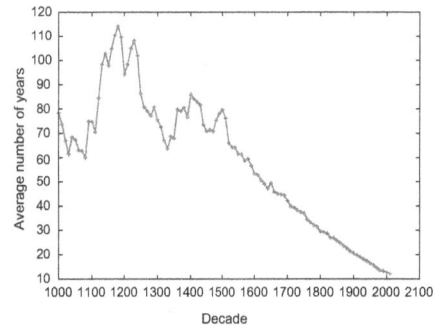

Figure 8 Average distance between link source and link target.

In the next two graphs (Fig. 9) we provide a more detailed view of the relative link distances, separately, for the in- and out-links. For all the people associated with a given century we show the average distribution of their link distances computed as the number of years between the midpoints of connected persons. In particular, the upper graph of Fig. 9 gives the plot for in-links and the lower one for out-links. Note that the midpoints of target persons are always positioned at point 0. The small peaks on the right hand side of the upper graph (the graph showing in-links) are due to links from persons alive at present times. Such peaks are less pronounced at the lower graph of Fig. 9 (the graph showing out-links) suggesting rather weak across-time reciprocity.

The connectivity analysis shown in this section gives rise for forming the hypothesis of a temporal version of social homophily [38] (or "temporal homophily"): *A person tends to be linked more with persons around its time than with persons from distant time.*

This suggests the possibility of automatically dating persons or entities – an important task considering that many entities lack such temporal metadata (as partially shown in the Sec. 3). This is despite the fact that such information is necessary for various processing tasks that harness Wikipedia (e.g., [16,25]). Detecting (or supporting the detection of) an entity's time period could be done by link analysis in a similar way as the one in which approximate page timestamp is gauged by analyzing the timestamps of its neighborhood [43] (i.e., pages linking to the target page).

The above hypothesis has also potential to impact approaches which utilize Wikipedia link structure for entity-to-entity relationship analysis [13,14,32,41,48,54]. The difference between the *activity times* of connected nodes could be taken into consideration when evaluating the relations' strengths or when detecting the topics of such relations.

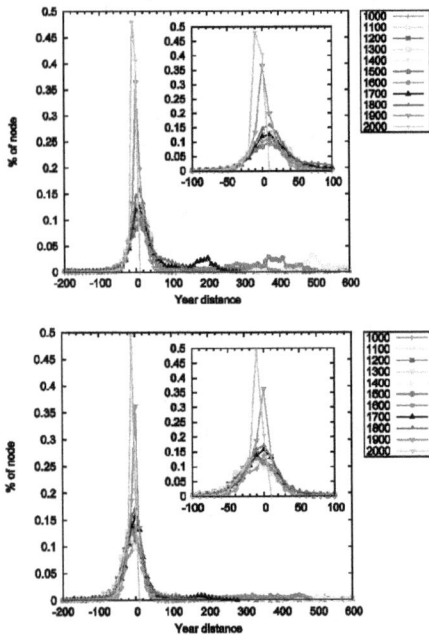

Figure 9 Average in-link (top) and out-link (bottom) distances. The horizontal axis denotes the distance between the linked pages (negative values mean links from/to the past person).

4.3 Historical Social Networks

Studies of social networks are nowadays common due to the popularity of SNSs and the social Web. Analogously, re-creating social networks of the past is also appealing [8]. However, constructing social networks as they existed in the past is inherently difficult and, likely, will never be completely possible given fragmentary data from the past. Instead, as a simple approximation, we can study networks formed by the hyperlink structure between the Wikipedia articles about historical persons.

We define a historical social network in a unit time period t_i as a graph, $G_i(V_i,E_i)$, composed of Wikipedia articles on persons that lived at t_i treated as the set of graph nodes, V_i, and the links between them considered as the edges, E_i. We adopt here the century granularity, hence, t_i represents here a single century. A series of temporal social networks (one for each century) is then created for the entire time period of analysis, $T=(t_1,...,t_i,...,t_n)$. Note that a person is assigned to a given century if the midpoint of his/her life is included in that century. In Fig. 10 we demonstrate the networks for a few selected centuries visualized with the ARF presentation layout [17]. ARF belongs to the class of force-directed graph layouts and is characterized by a circular shape. It is easy to read thanks to the fact that the layout displays as much symmetry as possible and that single nodes are pushed to the outer edges of the circle.

A common way for analyzing social networks is to estimate node importance or prestige by applying centrality measures. We thus first compute node importance using the well-known *PageRank* [44] algorithm in each historical social network, G_i.

Unlike previous works [10,47] in which PageRank is calculated on the entire social graph G, we compute it separately for each social network, G_i. To distinguish between these two approaches, we will call the random walk computation on a historical social network, *Century PageRank*, while the one on the entire graph, *Global PageRank*. Century PageRank score indicates how prominent a person is among people living in her century, while PageRank score measures person's prestige among all the persons in the Wikipedia social graph (or at least in our dataset), irrespectively of time. In Fig. 11 we plot the Pearson Correlation Coefficient between the Century PageRank and Global PageRank scores for each different century. Although the correlation is positive we can see that the rankings based on the two scores are not exactly same, especially, for centuries before the 17th century.

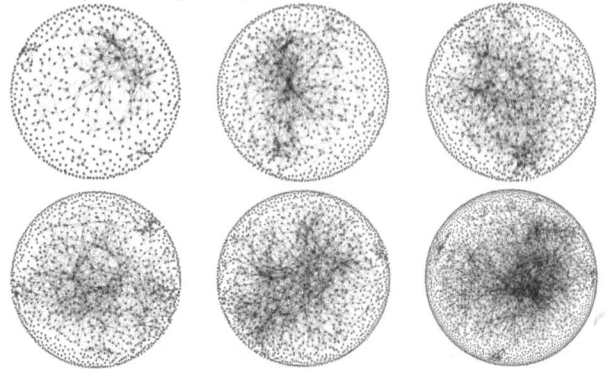

Figure 10 Social networks in the 11th, 12th, 13th, 14th, 15th and 16th centuries (from top left to bottom right).

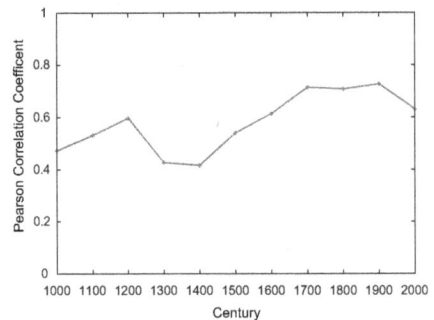

Figure 11 Pearson Correlation Coefficient between Global PageRank and Century PageRank.

The cumulative plot of Century PageRank for people living in different centuries is shown in Fig. 12. As it can be seen, the distributions of the scores are in general quite uniform in each century.

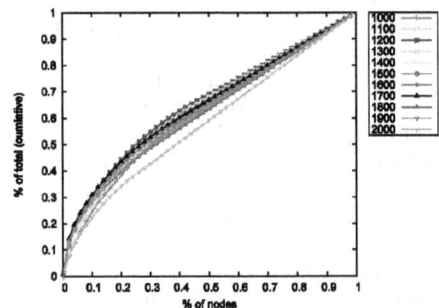

Figure 12 Cumulative plots of Century PageRank distributions in each century. Horizontal axis represents nodes ordered by their Century PageRank scores.

4.4 Remembering Past

We analyze in this section the degree to which past persons are connected with the present and the strength with which they are remembered. We consider the "present-to-past" connectivity as one measure of utility of the history. In fact, the role of history is to teach lessons, and the usefulness of the past accounts relies on how much they can serve the current society [15]. We propose two approaches in this paper: one based on the link analysis and the other based on the view logs. They are described below.

4.4.1 Present-to-Past Connectivity

The first measure quantifies how much a historical person is linked to the present time. In particular, we estimate the connectivity of historical persons with the "present" persons. As present persons we consider people alive during any of the four decades (1970s – 2000s). Note that this period can be arbitrarily chosen. The present-to-past connectivity measure should represent the closeness of nodes denoting historical persons to the nodes corresponding to the present persons. We propose to apply Biased PageRank similar to the concept of TrustRank [19] on graph G where the random walk is biased to the present persons. We call it a *Present-Biased PageRank*.

Fig. 13 shows the average Present-Biased PageRank scores obtained by averaging the scores for people alive at a given decade in the past. The graph can be interpreted as the relation strength between the persons from a given past decade and the present persons. As it can be seen, the rate drastically decreases from the 20th century backwards in time to, more or less, stabilize after 1900s. Notably, people around 15th and 16th centuries seem to be connected bit more to the present. This observation aligns with the relatively higher number of links to such people from "future persons" as shown in Fig. 7.

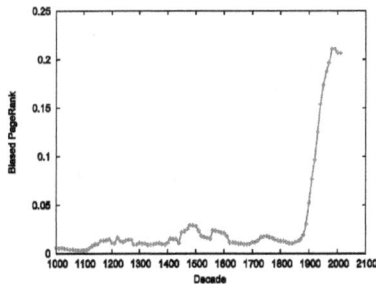

Figure 13 Average values of Present-Biased PageRank per decade.

To understand how Present-Biased PageRank scores distribute in each century we show cumulative plots for each century in Fig. 14. The plots for more distant centuries reveal long tail distributions in which few persons have very high scores while the rest of people have small scores. It suggests a winner-takes-all situation in the past centuries. Only few selected nodes from each century are strongly connected with the present. On the other hand, the last two centuries have close to linear cumulative distribution of scores. When comparing Fig. 14 with Fig. 12 we conclude that the Century PageRank scores for the far away centuries (distant past) are distributed more evenly than ones of Present-Biased PageRank.

We next show in Fig. 15 the Pearson Correlation Coefficient between the scores by Present-Biased PageRank and those by Century PageRank. We can see that prominent people at a given century are not necessarily strongly connected to the present. The correlation for persons living at distant centuries is low indicating

quite weak connectivity of the top prominent persons in those centuries to the people living at the present times.

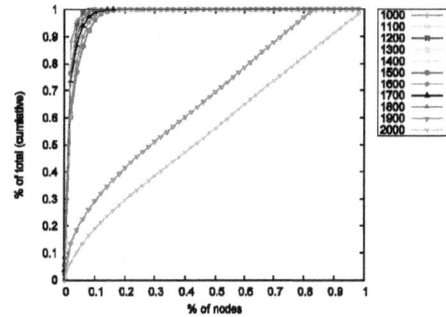

Figure 14 Cumulative plots of Present-Biased PageRank distributions in each century. Horizontal axis represents the percent of nodes ordered by their Biased PageRank scores.

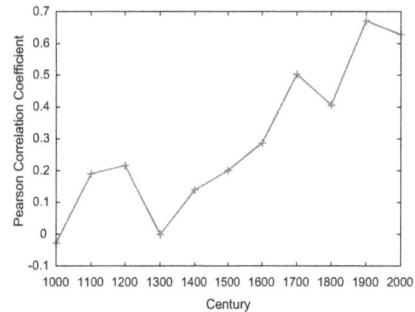

Figure 15 Pearson Correlation Coefficient between Present-Biased PageRank and Century PageRank.

4.4.2 View Frequency

We next analyze the distribution of visitor views in different times. We consider the viewing frequency as a measure of attention and interest in history and the evidence that the past matters. To quantify the popularity of past persons, we make use of the view logs available from the Wikipedia Foundation[7]. We count accesses to every page in our dataset that took place during 5 years long time period from the start of January 2009 to the end of December 2013. The upper plot of Fig. 16 shows in a log scale the average view count of persons alive in a given past decade. We also list the top viewed person for each century in Table 1.

Looking at the average number of views for persons from different centuries we can conclude that the interest to the past persons remains quite strong. We see that although, the average viewership of historical persons differs across centuries, it does not depend on the time segments in a simple way. For example, persons active in 15th and 16th centuries gather the highest attention of visitors. For a comparison we also show the total view count per time at the bottom plot of Fig. 16.

In Fig. 17 we portray changes in the average view rate over the 5 years' long time period (monthly granularity) for which we collected view logs. We can see that the viewership does not remain stable over the viewing time. After examining the peaks, we have found that many can be explained by anniversaries or sudden discoveries related to the past persons. For example, while Shakespeare is an unquestionable "king" of the 16th century (see the last column of Table 1), he has been "dethroned" in February 2013 when Google search engine commemorated the 540th

---

[7] https://dumps.wikimedia.org/other/pagecounts-raw/

anniversary of the birthday of Polish astronomer Copernicus with a related doodle [37]. Similarly, a doodle for the 374ᵗʰ anniversary of the birthday of Danish anatomist, Nicolas Steno's caused a spike in the line for the 17ᵗʰ century on January 2012 [42]. During the same month when Copernicus became the most often viewed person of the 16ᵗʰ century's cohort, Richard III of England "won" the first place within the 15ᵗʰ century cohort (ahead of the usual winner: Leonardo da Vinci) following the remarkable discovery of his remains in Leicester, England [4]. Another example illustrates a very rare case related to past prophecies. The peak on December 2012 within the aggregated view rate of the 16ᵗʰ segment is due to the frequent visits of Nostradamus's (Michel de Nostredame) page, presumably, in association with the alleged Mayan Prophecy.

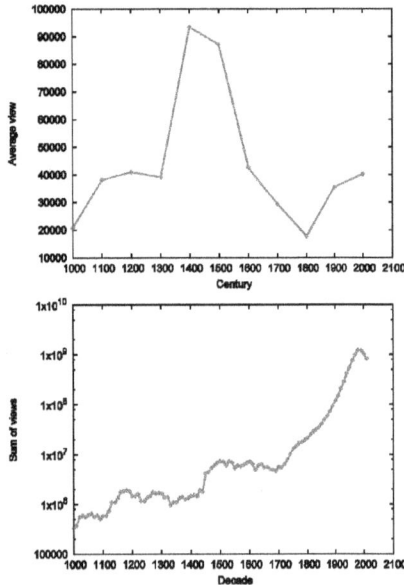

Figure 16 Average views for persons living in a given past century (left) and the total sum of views on log scale (right).

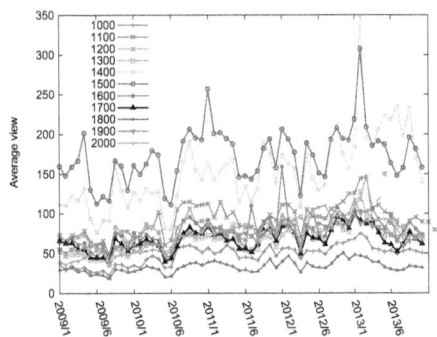

Figure 17 Average views for persons over the viewing time.

Finally, we analyze the cumulative view distribution per century in Fig. 18. In each century the visitors' attention is quite skewed and there are rather few persons whose pages are accessed very frequently, while many pages are visited rarely.

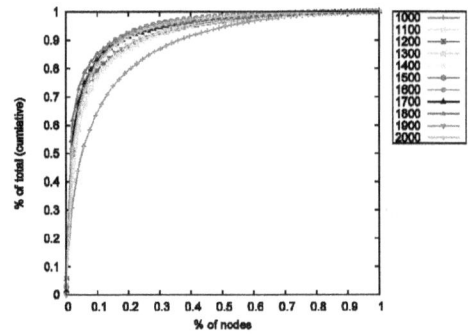

Figure 18 Cumulative plots of visitor views among persons in different centuries.

5. DISCUSSION

In this section we first summarize the main findings of this study and then we provide additional discussion.

· The number of persons recorded in Wikipedia depends on the time when they lived. There appears to be close to exponential growth in the number of person-related articles along with the increase in time.

· The average length of articles about past persons is longer than those about more recent persons.

· The average number of in- and out-links to other persons decreases along with time (from past towards the present).

· Across-time connectivity varies with the time of person's life. Pages on more historical persons tend to be more connected to the people who lived in other centuries.

· For any person, there are more links originating from people who lived in later centuries than from ones who lived in the previous centuries. Temporal orientation of links is then skewed towards the future.

· The link distribution does not solely depend on the semantics, but time plays certain role here, too. In every century there are more links to/from contemporary persons than to/from persons who lived in other times. The distance between the origin and target of the links becomes on average shorter for more recent persons.

· The view log study shows that, in aggregate, there are few views to pages about persons from the distant past. Yet, on average, the articles on the past persons are more frequently accessed than the ones on the current persons.

· The view rate of historical persons is not stable over time. Occasional peaks in the view frequency happen due to anniversaries or other events related to the memory or changes in our knowledge about historical persons.

· Only few persons are strongly "remembered" from the past as quantified by the distributions of Present-Biased PageRank scores and view counts of their pages.

· PageRank on the global social network can be complemented by other time-based centrality measures such as Century PageRank and Present-Biased PageRank. These metrics are correlated, yet, they are not equal.

Table 1 Top ranked persons by *Global PageRank*, *Century PageRank*, *Present-Biased PageRank* and by View Frequency.

Century	*Global PageRank*	*Century PageRank*	*Present-Biased PageRank*	View Frequency
11th	William the Conqueror	William the Conqueror	William the Conqueror	William the Conqueror
12th	Genghis Khan	Saladin	Genghis Khan	Genghis Khan
13th	William Wallace	Thomas Aquinas	Thomas Aquinas	William Wallace
14th	Geoffrey Chaucer	Petrarch	Hafez	Geoffrey Chaucer
15th	Leonardo da Vinci	Joan of Arc	Leonardo da Vinci	Leonardo da Vinci
16th	William Shakespeare	Philip II of Spain	William Shakespeare	William Shakespeare
17th	Isaac Newton	Rembrandt	Rembrandt	Isaac Newton
18th	George Washington	George Washington	George Washington	George Washington
19th	Abraham Lincoln	Abraham Lincoln	Abraham Lincoln	Abraham Lincoln
20th	Michael Jackson	Bill Clinton	Barack Obama	Michael Jackson

Link structure is often used for quantifying relationships on Wikipedia. Thus, properly understanding the role of time and temporal attributes of links ("temporal link signature") can help to improve the results. While there have been studies on the temporal evolution of Wikipedia (e.g., the evolution of Wiki Graph), more investigation should be done on the temporal scope of Wikipedia articles and on time effect on their interconnectivity. In addition, automatic means of time-scoping Wikipedia articles could be proposed using link structure (see Sec. 4.2).

Historical knowledge is especially useful when it strongly relates to the present. Thus computing the importance of historical entities should consider the extent to which the entities are useful for present users. There can be several ways to quantify the past-present relations. We have suggested two such ways in Sec. 4.4.

For improving the usefulness of its articles, Wikimedia Foundation could encourage contributors who edit pages on past entities to try to add more links related to the present time to better explain their roles and importance. At the same time, such entities should not be disconnected from their contemporary context (e.g., social context in the past). An interesting idea would be to propose automatic construction of summaries (e.g., in the form of term clouds) to portray a person's relation to both the current as well as to its contemporary time.

Cultural memory is often categorized into two modes [1]: *passive* (aka. "canon") and *active* (aka. "archive"). The latter represents what is visible to public, while the former comprises what is not "on display". Both the view frequency and the past-to-present connectivity could be regarded as signals useful to distinguish the passive from active memory. This could have implications on archival and preservation decisions [30].

Lastly, additional studies are needed for re-constructing actual social networks in the past. Wikipedia can however provide a foundation for such networks. In addition, link structure based metrics of importance and prestige such as ones listed in this paper and others [8] should be contrasted against the lists of top influential or important persons in the past [12,21] which are manually compiled by professionals.

6. CONCLUSIONS

Studies of the history and the collective memories are important due to the significance of history and its role in our society. At the same time, since Wikipedia constitutes the main source of historical information for online users and for many knowledge processing tasks, the in-depth analysis of its content is needed. The objective of this paper is to help better understand the characteristics of historical data in Wikipedia through applying a novel kind of study. We think that this study and similar ones could support better

design of any systems that utilize historical data in Wikipedia, especially, ones that use information on persons or their social networks. Also, we hope our work can contribute to the collective memory studies.

Several avenues of future work emerge from this research. We first plan to focus on other entities such as events or places. The difficulty here lies in estimating their temporal attributes to position them in time. Second, it is appealing to compare multiple language editions of Wikipedia for the amount and the focus of the historical knowledge they hold. Finally, the comparison of Wikipedia with historical textbooks could shed more light on the coverage and correctness of contained history-related information.

7. ACKNOWLEDGMENTS

This research was supported in part by the Japan Science and Technology Agency (JST) research promotion program Presto/Sakigake: "Analyzing Collective Memory and Developing Methods for Knowledge Extraction from Historical Documents" and by Grant-in-Aid for Scientific Research (No. 15H01718) from MEXT of Japan.

8. REFERENCES

[1] A. Assmann. *Introduction to Cultural Studies*. Schmidt Erich Verlag, 2008 (in German).

[2] S. Auer, C. Bizer, G. Kobilarov, J. Lehmann, R. Cyganiak, and Z. Ives. DBpedia: A Nucleus for a Web of Open Data. In *ISWC'07/ASWC'07*, 722–735. Springer, 2007.

[3] C.-M. Au Yeung, and A. Jatowt. Studying how the Past is Remembered: Towards Computational History through Large Scale Text Mining. In *CIKM 2011*, pp. 1231-1240, 2011.

[4] J. F. Burns. Bones Under Parking Lot Belonged to Richard III, 2/2013, http://www.nytimes.com/2013/02/05/world/europe/richard-the-third-bones.html?_r=1

[5] E.H. Carr. *What is History?* Penguin, London, 1961.

[6] J. Cook, A. Das Sarma, A. Fabrikant, and A. Tomkins. Your Two Weeks of Fame and Your Grandmother's. In *WWW 2012*. ACM, New York, NY, USA, 919-928, 2012.

[7] W. Cronon. Scholarly Authority in a Wikified World. *Perspectives in History*, 2012.

[8] M. Düring. Can Network Analysis Reveal Importance? Degree Centrality and Leaders in the EU Integration Process. *Social Informatics*. Springer International Publishing, 2014. 314-318.

[9] H. Ebbinghaus. *Memory: A Contribution to Experimental Psychology*. 1913.

[10] Y.-H. Eom, P. Aragón, D. Laniado, A. Kaltenbrunner, S. Vigna, D. L. Shepelyansky. Interactions of Cultures and Top People of Wikipedia from Ranking of 24 Language Editions, *PLoS ONE* 10(3), 2014.

[11] M. Ferron and P. Massa. Collective Memory Building in Wikipedia: the Case of North African Uprisings. In *WikiSym '11*. ACM, New York, NY, USA, 114-123, 2011.

[12] R. Friedman. The Life Millennium: *The 100 Most Important Events and People of the Past 1000 Years*, Bulfinch P., 1998.

[13] E. Gabrilovich and S. Markovitch. Computing Semantic Relatedness using Wikipedia-based Explicit Semantic Analysis. In *Proc. IJCAI 2007*, pp. 1606–1611, 2007.

[14] E. Gabrilovich, *et al.* Overcoming the Brittleness Bottleneck Using Wikipedia: Enhancing Text Categorization with Encyclopedic Knowledge. In *AAAI 2006*.

[15] H.-G. Gadamer. *Truth and Method.* London: Sheed and Ward, 1975.

[16] A. Garcia-Fernandez, A.-L. Ligozat, M. Dinarelli and D. Bernhard. When was it Written? Automatically Determining Publication Dates. In *SPIRE 2011*, 2011.

[17] M. Geipel. Self-Organization Applied to Dynamic Network Layout, *International Journal of Modern Physics C* vol. 18, no. 10 (2007), pp. 1537-1549.

[18] J. Giles. Internet Encyclopaedias Go Head to Head, *Nature* 438, 900-901, 2005.

[19] Z. Gyöngyi, H. Garcia-Molina, and J. Pedersen. Combating Web Spam with Trustrank. In *VLDB 2004*, 576-587, 2004.

[20] M. Halbwachs. *La Mémoire Collective.* Les Presses universitaires de France, (in French) 1950.

[21] M.H. Hart. *The 100: A Ranking of the Most Influential Persons in History.* Citadel; Revised edition (June 1, 2000)

[22] C. Hoerl and T. McCormack. *Time and Memory: Issues in Philosophy and Psychology.* No.1. 2001.

[23] J. Hoffart et al. YAGO2: Exploring and Querying World Knowledge in Time, Space, Context, and Many Languages. In *WWW 2011*, 229-232, 2011.

[24] L. Hoffmann. Looking Back at Big Data, *Communications of the ACM*, Vol.56 Issue.4, pp.21-23, 2013.

[25] T. Huet, J. Biega, F. Suchanek Mining History with Le Monde, In *AKBC 2013 workshop at CIKM2013*, 2013.

[26] R. Jacoby. Social Amnesia: *A Critique of Contemporary Psychology.* 1997.

[27] A. Jatowt, E. Antoine, Y. Kawai, T. Akiyama. Mapping Temporal Horizons, Analysis of Collective Future and Past Related Attention in Microblogging, In *WWW 2015*, 484-494, 2015.

[28] A. Jatowt, G. Dias, M. Düring and A. van Den Bosch. The HistoInformatics2014 Workshop, *Socinfo2014 Workshop Proceedings*, Springer LNCS 8852, 2014.

[29] H. Joho, A. Jatowt, and R. Blanco. Temporal Information Searching Behaviour and Tactics, *Information Processing and Management Journal*, Elsevier 51(6), 834-850, 2015.

[30] N. Kanhabua, C. Niederée, and W. Siberski. Towards Concise Preservation by Managed Forgetting: Research Issues and Case Study. In *iPres 2013*.

[31] N. Kanhabua, T. N. Nguyen, C. Niederée. What Triggers Human Remembering of Events? A Large-scale Analysis of Catalysts for Collective Memory in Wikipedia. In *JCDL 2014*, 341-350, 2014.

[32] D. Kinzler. WikiSense — Mining the Wiki. In *Proceedings of Wikimania 2005, The First International Wikimedia Conference.* Wikimedia Foundation, 2005.

[33] N. Kittur, E. H. Chi, and B. Suh. What's in Wikipedia?: Mapping Topics and Conflict using Socially Annotated Category Structure. *In CHI '09*, 1509-1512, 2009.

[34] M. Kremer. Population Growth and Technological Change: One Million B.C. to 1990, *Quarterly Journal of Economics*, Oxford Journals, pp.681-716, 1993.

[35] D. Lazer et al. Computational Social Science, *Science*, 2009, 721-723.

[36] P. Lendvai and K. Zervanou. *Proceedings of the 7th Workshop on Language Technology for Cultural Heritage, Social Sciences, and Humanities (LaTeCH 2013)* at ACL'13, 2013.

[37] T. Malik. Google Doodle Honors 16th Century Astronomer Nicolaus Copernicus, February 19, 2013, http://www.space.com/19868-nicolaus-copernicus-google-doodle.html

[38] M. McPherson, L. Smith-Lovin, and J.M. Cook. Birds of a Feather: Homophily in Social Networks. *Annual Review of Sociology.* 27:415–444, 2001.

[39] O. Medelyan, D. Milne, C. Legg, and Ian H. Witten. Mining Meaning from Wikipedia. *Int. J. Hum.-Comput. Stud.* 67, 9 (2009), 716-754.

[40] J.-B. Michel *et al.* Quantitative Analysis of Culture Using Millions of Digitized Books. *Science*, 331(6014), 176-182, 2011.

[41] D. Milne, O. Medelyan, and I. H. Witten. Mining Domain-specific Thesauri from Wikipedia: A Case Study, In *WI'06*, pp. 442–448, 2006.

[42] Nicolas Steno Google doodle marks his 374th birth anniversary, 2/2012, http://www.theguardian.com/technology/2012/jan/11/nicolas-steno-google-doodle

[43] S. Nunes, C. Ribeiro, and G. David. Using Neighbors to Date Web Documents. In *Proceedings of the WIDM'07 Workshop associated to CIKM'07*, 129-136, 2007.

[44] L. Page, S. Brin, R. Motwani, and T. Winograd. The PageRank Citation Ranking: Bringing Order to the Web. *Technical Report, Stanford University*, 1998.

[45] R. Rosenzweig. Can History be Open Source? Wikipedia and the Future of the Past. *The Journal of Amer. History* 93:1, 2006 117-46

[46] Y. Takahashi, H. Ohshima, M. Yamamoto, H. Iwasaki, S. Oyama, and K. Tanaka. Evaluating Significance of Historical Entities based on Tempo-spatial Impacts Analysis using Wikipedia Link Structure. In *Proceedings of HT '11*. ACM, New York, NY, USA, 83-92, 2011.

[47] S. Skiena and C. B. Ward. *Who's Bigger, Where Historical Figures Really Rank.* Cambridge University Press, 2014.

[48] M. Strube and S. Ponzetto. WikiRelate! Computing Semantic Relatedness using Wikipedia. *In AAAI-06*, 1419–1424, 2006.

[49] J. Sturrock. *Structuralism and since: from Lévi Strauss to Derrida*, Introduction. 1979.

[50] S. Whiting, J.M. Jose and O. Alonso. Wikipedia as a Time Machine. In *TempWeb'14 at WWW2014*, 857-861, 2014.

[51] T. Wood. *An Introduction to Civil Registration.* Federation of Family History Societies (Publications) 1994.

[52] V. Vapnik. *The Nature of Statistical Learning Theory*, Springer-Verlag, 1995.

[53] G. Zaagsma. On Digital History. *BMGN – Low Countries Historical Review*, 128(4):3–29, 2013.

[54] X. Zhang, Y. Asano and M. Yoshikawa. Mining Knowledge on Relationships between Objects from the Web. *IEICE Transactions 97-D(1)*: 77-88 (2014).

Quality Assessment of Wikipedia Articles without Feature Engineering

Quang - Vinh Dang
Université de Lorraine, LORIA, F-54506
Inria, F-54600
CNRS, LORIA, F-54506
quang-vinh.dang@inria.fr

Claudia - Lavinia Ignat
Inria, F-54600
Université de Lorraine, LORIA, F-54506
CNRS, LORIA, F-54506
claudia.ignat@inria.fr

ABSTRACT

As Wikipedia became the largest human knowledge repository, quality measurement of its articles received a lot of attention during the last decade. Most research efforts focused on classification of Wikipedia articles quality by using a different feature set. However, so far, no "golden feature set" was proposed. In this paper, we present a novel approach for classifying Wikipedia articles by analysing their content rather than by considering a feature set. Our approach uses recent techniques in natural language processing and deep learning, and achieved a comparable result with the state-of-the-art.

Keywords

quality assessment, Wikipedia, feature engineering, document representation, deep learning

1. INTRODUCTION

Internet has opened the border of traditional libraries: nowadays everyone can participate and contribute to a common human knowledge repository. Wikipedia is a great example of a knowledge resource receiving contribution from a huge number of authors. At the time of writing, there are more than five millions articles in English Wikipedia, and 38 million articles in all languages[1], and the size of English Wikipedia is over 60 times compared with Britannica[2].

However, due to the huge number of contributors[3] and articles, the quality of Wikipedia articles is not equally distributed [19]. Several research works claimed that the quality of centralized human knowledge resources such as books or Britannica are higher than Wikipedia [7, 11].

---

[1]https://en.wikipedia.org/wiki/Wikipedia:Size_of_ Wikipedia as on 5 - Jan - 2016.

[2]https://en.wikipedia.org/wiki/Wikipedia:Size_ comparisons as on 5 - Jan - 2016.

[3]According to https://en.wikipedia.org/wiki/Wikipedia: Wikipedians, there are more than 100,000 regular Wikipedia editors.

Permission to make digital or hard copies of all or part of this work for personal or classroom use is granted without fee provided that copies are not made or distributed for profit or commercial advantage and that copies bear this notice and the full citation on the first page. Copyrights for components of this work owned by others than ACM must be honored. Abstracting with credit is permitted. To copy otherwise, or republish, to post on servers or to redistribute to lists, requires prior specific permission and/or a fee. Request permissions from permissions@acm.org.

JCDL '16, June 19-23, 2016, Newark, NJ, USA

© 2016 ACM. ISBN 978-1-4503-4229-2/16/06. . . $15.00

DOI: http://dx.doi.org/10.1145/2910896.2910917

In order to improve the quality of Wikipedia, an effective method is needed for quality assessment of its articles. Wikipedia defines quality classes for its articles, including *FA, A, GA, B, C, Start, Stub* where *FA* is the highest quality class and *Stub* the lowest quality class[4].

Assigning the correct quality class for each Wikipedia article is an important task, as authors and reviewers can be notified to pay more attention for improving the low quality articles, and search engines could promote high quality class articles as query result. However, the high velocity of changes on Wikipedia makes impossible a manual quality assessment of articles by human experts. Therefore, it is important to design an automatic approach for quality assessment of Wikipedia articles.

Existing approaches on this topic [3, 6, 10, 12, 17, 19, 21] are all based on defining a feature set that is believed to describe in the best way the quality of a Wikipedia article. Certain approaches claim that longer articles are of a better quality, some others consider that discussions and interactions among authors and reviewers of an article increase the quality of an article and others consider that the quality of an article is determined by contributions of highly respected authors.

There is no standard rule for selecting features, which is considered as one of the most difficult tasks in machine learning. Moreover, feature selection is language dependent. In this paper, we present a new approach that avoids feature engineering and that determines the quality of an article based on its content. We build a deep neural network model where the input is the full content of the Wikipedia articles, and the output is the quality class of the articles. The same approach can be defined for different language data sets.

We start by presenting related works in quality assessment of Wikipedia articles. We then present our classification model including article representation and the deep neural networks technique that we used for the classification. We then describe the evaluation we performed and we compare our results with state-of-the-art techniques. Finally, we present our concluding remarks and we provide some directions for future work.

2. RELATED WORKS

Even though existing research works on automatic quality assessment of Wikipedia articles use a different feature set, they can be classified into two main families: one is analyzing the edit history of an article (for instance, who

---

[4]The description of each quality class is available at https: //en.wikipedia.org/wiki/Template:Grading_scheme.

contributed to the article and the type of their modifications) and the second one is analyzing the article itself (for instance, its length, number of images, presence of an information box).

Belonging to the first family of approaches, [12] measures the quality of Wikipedia articles based on author authority. Using a similar idea, [17] applied authors' *h-index* to measure the quality of articles on Wikipedia. In [18], the authors used both metrics of article's content and authors' authority to measure the quality of Wikipedia articles. However, this research work used a manual evaluation by volunteering students which is not very reliable for verifying the classification. Moreover, the accuracy obtained is not very high. [21] analyzed the edit network around a Wikipedia article to retrieve the information about the quality of that article. [6] presented a model that analysed the collaboration between authors and reviewers on Wikipedia to measure the quality of articles.

On the other hand, as the most simple approach, [3] proposed to use simple word count to evaluate the quality of Wikipedia. Dalip et al [10] analyzed the effect of different feature sets including structure, length, style, review, network and readability in a regression model for measuring the quality of Wikipedia articles and they discussed about a minimal feature set [5]. More recently, [19] used a machine learning model for quality prediction of Wikipedia articles including format-based features such as the number of headings of level 2 of a particular article. Based on the work of [19, 20], Wikimedia Foundation built an online service called ORES to classify the quality class of Wikipedia articles [8], using a set of 24 features for English Wikipedia. This set of features is slightly different for other languages Wikipedia.

Each research work selected and used a different feature set to measure and classify the quality of Wikipedia articles. However, feature selection is mostly based on the heuristic of researchers and so far, there is no "gold - standard" feature set to classify and measure the quality of Wikipedia articles.

In this paper, we claim that the quality of a Wikipedia article should depend on its own content. Certain features can be derived from the article content. Using the full content of Wikipedia articles as the input of training model should avoid missing an important feature that was not manually recognized.

We use the technique *Doc2Vec* [13] to represent Wikipedia articles and a deep neural network to classify their quality. Deep learning is an emerging research field today and, to our knowledge, our work is the first one that applied deep learning for assessing quality of Wikipedia articles. Our approach provides a novel point of view to Wikipedia quality classification.

3. CLASSIFICATION MODEL

In this section, we present how to design and feed the content of Wikipedia articles into a neural network.

3.1 Article representation

Most machine learning algorithms including neural networks require the input to be represented as a fixed-length feature vector. As Wikipedia articles have different lengths, we need an approach that maps Wikipedia articles to fixed-length feature vectors. The most common fixed-length vector representation for documents is the *bag-of-words* [9] where

a document is represented as the bag of its words. However, this approach disregards semantics and even word order.

In this paper, we applied the unsupervised learning algorithm called *Paragraph Vector*, recently known as *Doc2Vec* [13] that learns vector representations for variable-length pieces of texts and overcomes the disadvantages of *bag-of-words* by taking into account the order and semantics of words. In this approach every word and every paragraph are mapped to a unique vector. The paragraph vector is concatenated with several word vectors from the paragraph and trained in order to predict the next word in a text window. While word vectors are shared among paragraphs, paragraph vectors are unique among paragraphs.

We applied the *Doc2Vec* approach where each Wikipedia document corresponds to a paragraph in the above description. While the generated word vectors are not further used, the document vector is given as input for our deep neural network.

3.2 Deep neural networks

Deep learning has been successfully applied for several text classification tasks such as Reuters news or sentiment analysis [14].

Neural networks, or artificial neural networks (ANN), are machine learning models inspired by biological neural networks for the estimation of generally unknown functions that depend on a large number of parameters. Neural networks are typically organized in layers made up of a number of interconnected nodes which contain an activation function. Patterns are presented to the network via the input layer, which communicates to one or more hidden layers. The hidden layers perform the actual processing via a system of weighted connections. The hidden layers then transmit the answer to an output layer. A deep neural network (DNN) [2] is defined as an artificial neural network with multiple hidden layers that allows learning abstraction from data.

In our approach, we used a DNN with four hidden layers to learn and classify the representation vectors of Wikipedia articles computed by *Doc2Vec*.

4. IMPLEMENTATION AND RESULTS

4.1 Implementation

We used the data set contained in around 30,000 English Wikipedia articles which are classified to six quality classes *FA, GA, B, C, Start, Stub* already by Wikipedia reviewers. The data set is provided by Wikimedia Foundations[5]. We separated the data set to training and testing set with the ratio 80/20, similarly to [19] and ORES [8].

We transformed all Wikipedia articles on both training and testing set to *Doc2Vec* vectors by using the library *gensim*[6][7]. The output of the first phase is the collection of vectors for Wikipedia articles in the training and testing set. Therefore, we have a dataset of 30,000 same length vectors. In the second phase, we trained the DNN model on the training set by using *tensorflow*[8], the deep learning library from

---

[5]The data set is available at http://datasets.wikimedia.org/public-datasets/enwiki/.
[6]http://radimrehurek.com/gensim/
[7]Our hypothesis is that the labeled articles in the training set and the unlabeled articles in the testing set are all completed and available.
[8]https://www.tensorflow.org

Google. Our DNN has four hidden layers, with 2000, 1000, 500 and 200 neurons respectively[9]. The number of neurons is selected as a rule of thumb. The final task is to apply the trained DNN model on the testing vector set, and compare the predicting quality labels with correct values assigned by human judgements.

Currently, no standard methodology exists for constructing an optimal neural network with the right number of layers and number of neurons for each layer. An optimal neural network can be built uniquely empirically [15]. However, randomly choosing a structure for a deep neural network is not a good solution as it leads to performances of a random guess, i.e. a low accuracy of 16.7%.

4.2 Results

The predictions obtained by our model are displayed by the confusion matrix in Table 1. The training loss graph in Fig. 1 illustrates the training loss value, i.e. the difference between predicted quality labels and their correct values in the training set, as a function of the number of iterations during the training phase. The graph shows that no local minima is found when the number of training steps reaches a high value (25,000), as the decreasing trend is observed throughout the entire training process.

As the data set we used is balanced, i.e. the number of articles in each class is very close, the *accuracy* metric is suitable to evaluate the classification. Accuracy is defined as a ratio between the number of correct predictions and the total number of articles in the testing data set. The accuracy of our DNN classifier is 55%.

We compare our approach with other popular classification approaches on the same data set. Using the 24 features of ORES as the feature set, k-Nearest Neighbor (k-NN) [1], Classification And Regression Tree (CART) [4] and Random Forest(RF) implemented by ORES, achieved the accuracy of 51%, 48% and 60% respectively. Using the feature set composed of 11 features presented in [19] which is a subset of the 24 features set used in ORES, Random Forest algorithm achieved the accuracy of 58%. The performance of classifiers is summarized in Table 2.

The accuracy of DNN is higher than the one obtained by the k-NN and CART approaches. The lower accuracy of DNN classifier with respect to the RF approach can be explained by the parameter of *Doc2Vec* transformation. Due to our computation power, the size of the vectors was limited to 500, which may lead to the consequence that *Doc2Vec* vectors did not capture all the structure of the Wikipedia articles. Moreover, the low accuracy is also due to our unoptimized DNN, as no standard way exists for constructing a DNN. We can see the improvement from [19] to ORES when more features are added.

To our knowledge, Wikimedia ORES API, which is based on the work of [19, 20] is the only existing approach for classification into all six quality classes. Other works only classified between a subset of classes, such as between *FA* and *Start*[22] with an accuracy of 84%, or between *FA-GA* as a class and the set of *(B, C, Start, Stub)* as another class[16] with an accuracy of 84%, or between *FA-GA* and *C-Start*[21] with an accuracy of 66%. For these binary classification tasks, the DNN approach achieved a very high accuracy compared with previous approaches: 99% to classify

---

[9]The implementation is available at https://github.com/vinhqdang/doc2vec_dnn_wikipedia

	FA	GA	B	C	Start	Stub	Total
FA	778	148	64	17	6	7	1020
GA	160	554	128	88	23	4	957
B	87	187	373	237	143	17	1044
C	28	112	236	376	181	23	956
Start	6	38	119	216	453	133	965
Stub	7	6	20	36	179	701	949
Total	1066	1045	940	970	985	1006	5891

Table 1: Confusion matrix of classifying quality classes. Gray cells are correct predictions. Rows (italic) are actual quality class. Columns are predicted values of the model. For instance, there are 778 articles correctly predicted as FA, and 160 articles which are GA and are predicted as FA.

Classifier	Accuracy
CART [4]	48%
kNN [1]	51%
Doc2Vec & DNN	55%
Warncke et al. [19]	58%
Wikimedia ORES [8]	60%

Table 2: Accuracy scores of different classifiers on English Wikipedia.

between *FA* and *Start*, 86% to classify between *FA-GA* and the other classes and 90% to classify between *FA-GA* and *C-Start*.

We observe that the quality class of a Wikipedia article could be determined by only analyzing its content, so the approach of training the prediction model based on the content and not on feature sets is a promising and interesting approach to be improved in the future. As *Doc2Vec* approach is language independent we expect that our approach can be generally applied to any language Wikipedia.

5. CONCLUSIONS AND FUTURE WORKS

Feature selection is one of the most difficult task in machine learning. Existing research works proposed different feature sets for measuring quality of Wikipedia articles. Each feature set has its own pros and cons, and there is no "golden feature set". As feature selection process is mostly a manual work, we may never know what feature set is the best for assessing quality of Wikipedia articles.

In this paper, we presented an approach to avoid feature selection process. Our approach follows the process of Wikipedia reviewers: first they read the article and then decide what quality class this article should belong to. Using this approach, no feature selection is required to describe a Wikipedia article. We achieved very high accuracy scores for classification into binary quality classes and an accuracy score comparable with the state-of-the-art Wikimedia ORES service for classification between all quality classes.

As a future work we plan to improve performances of our approach by optimizing the deep neural network's structure.

6. ACKNOWLEDGMENTS

Experiments presented in this paper were carried out using the Grid'5000 testbed, supported by a scientific inter-

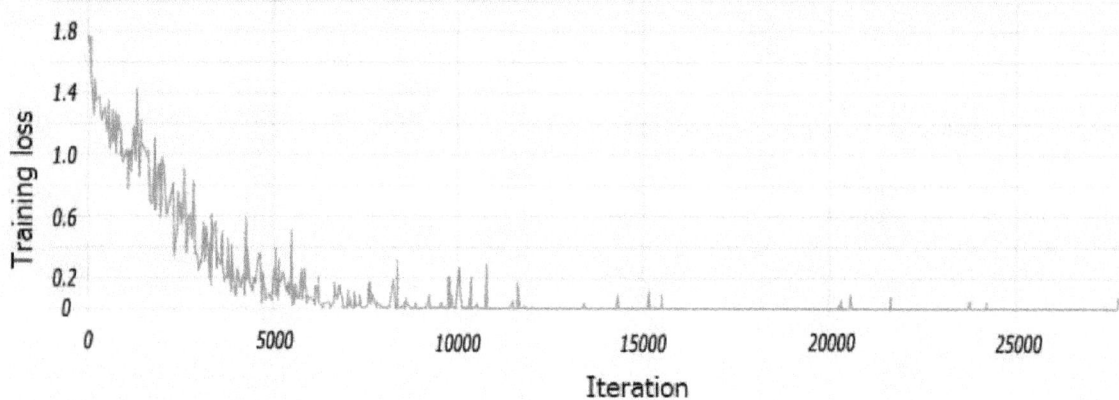

Figure 1: DNN training loss

est group hosted by Inria and including CNRS, RENATER and several Universities as well as other organizations (see https://www.grid5000.fr).

7. REFERENCES

[1] N. S. Altman. An introduction to kernel and nearest-neighbor nonparametric regression. *The American Statistician*, 46(3):175–185, 1992.

[2] Y. Bengio. Learning deep architectures for AI. *Found. Trends Mach. Learn.*, 2(1):1–127, Jan. 2009.

[3] J. E. Blumenstock. Size matters: word count as a measure of quality on Wikipedia. In *Proc. of WWW*, pages 1095–1096, 2008.

[4] L. Breiman, J. Friedman, C. J. Stone, and R. A. Olshen. *Classification and regression trees*. 1984.

[5] D. H. Dalip, H. Lima, M. A. Gonçalves, M. Cristo, and P. Calado. Quality assessment of collaborative content with minimal information. In *Proc. of JCDL*, pages 201–210, 2014.

[6] B. de La Robertie, Y. Pitarch, and O. Teste. Measuring article quality in Wikipedia using the collaboration network. In *Proc. of ASONAM*, pages 464–471, 2015.

[7] P. Dondio, S. Barrett, S. Weber, and J. M. Seigneur. Extracting trust from domain analysis: A case study on the Wikipedia project. In *Proc. of ATC*, pages 362–373, 2006.

[8] A. Halfaker and D. Taraborelli. Artificial intelligence service gives Wikipedians 'x-ray specs' to see through bad edits. https://blog.wikimedia.org/2015/11/30/artificial-intelligence-x-ray-specs, 2015. Accessed: 2016-04-01.

[9] Z. S. Harris. Distributional structure. *Word*, 1954.

[10] D. Hasan Dalip, M. André Gonçalves, M. Cristo, and P. Calado. Automatic quality assessment of content created collaboratively by web communities: a case study of Wikipedia. In *Proc. of JCDL*, pages 295–304, 2009.

[11] L. Holman Rector. Comparison of Wikipedia and other encyclopedias for accuracy, breadth, and depth in historical articles. *Reference services review*, 36(1):7–22, 2008.

[12] M. Hu, E.-P. Lim, A. Sun, H. W. Lauw, and B.-Q. Vuong. Measuring article quality in Wikipedia: models and evaluation. In *Proc. of CIKM*, pages 243–252, 2007.

[13] Q. V. Le and T. Mikolov. Distributed representations of sentences and documents. In *Proc. of ICML*, pages 1188–1196, 2014.

[14] S. Lee and J. Y. Choeh. Predicting the helpfulness of online reviews using multilayer perceptron neural networks. *Expert Systems with Applications*, 41(6):3041–3046, 2014.

[15] N. D. Lewis. *Build Your Own Neural Network Today*. 2015.

[16] E. Lex, M. Voelske, M. Errecalde, E. Ferretti, L. Cagnina, C. Horn, B. Stein, and M. Granitzer. Measuring the quality of web content using factual information. In *Proc. of WICOW*, pages 7–10, 2012.

[17] Y. Suzuki. Quality assessment of Wikipedia articles using h-index. *Journal of Information Processing*, 23(1):22–30, 2015.

[18] Y. Suzuki and M. Yoshikawa. Mutual evaluation of editors and texts for assessing quality of Wikipedia articles. In *Proc. of WikiSym*, pages 18:1–18:10, 2012.

[19] M. Warncke-Wang, V. R. Ayukaev, B. Hecht, and L. G. Terveen. The success and failure of quality improvement projects in peer production communities. In *Proc. of CSCW*, pages 743–756, 2015.

[20] M. Warncke-Wang, D. Cosley, and J. Riedl. Tell me more: An actionable quality model for Wikipedia. In *Proc. of OpenSym*, pages 8:1–8:10, 2013.

[21] G. Wu, M. Harrigan, and P. Cunningham. Classifying Wikipedia articles using network motif counts and ratios. In *Proc. of WikiSym*, pages 12:1–12:10, 2012.

[22] Y. Xu and T. Luo. Measuring article quality in Wikipedia: Lexical clue model. In *Proc. of SWS*, pages 141–146, 2011.

Glyph Miner: A System for Efficiently Extracting Glyphs from Early Prints in the Context of OCR

Benedikt Budig*
Chair for Computer Science I
University of Würzburg
benedikt.budig@uni-
wuerzburg.de

Thomas C. van Dijk
Chair for Computer Science I
University of Würzburg
thomas.van.dijk@uni-
wuerzburg.de

Felix Kirchner
Digitization Center
University Library Würzburg
felix.kirchner@uni-
wuerzburg.de

ABSTRACT

While off-the-shelf OCR systems work well on many modern documents, the heterogeneity of early prints provides a significant challenge. To achieve good recognition quality, existing software must be "trained" specifically to each particular corpus. This is a tedious process that involves significant user effort. In this paper we demonstrate a system that generically replaces a common part of the training pipeline with a more efficient workflow: Given a set of scanned pages of a historical document, our system uses an efficient user interaction to semi-automatically extract large numbers of occurrences of glyphs indicated by the user. In a preliminary case study, we evaluate the effectiveness of our approach by embedding our system into the workflow at the University Library Würzburg.

Keywords

Early Prints; Document Recognition; OCR; Glyph Extraction; Efficient User Interaction

1. INTRODUCTION

Early printed documents are a precious source of information for researchers of various disciplines and a remarkable part of our cultural heritage. Scans of such documents are widely available,[1] but their contents need to be extracted to make the most use of them. Particularly, optical character recognition (OCR) is necessary to make the contained text searchable and available to further analysis. While off-the-shelf OCR systems work well on modern documents, they have trouble with early prints due to lower printing quality, higher visual variance within characters and possibly poor

conservation state.[2] Instead, general purpose OCR software (e.g. Tesseract [13]) has to be trained specifically to the early print to be processed. At best, the trained system can then also be applied to other books printed by the same workshop (*Offizin*). The process of training an OCR system for use on early prints is tedious and requires significant manual effort. Typically, a first step is to catalog all different glyphs that occur in the given corpus. Then, several "representative" occurrences of each of these glyphs are located and cropped from the scans. Finally, the OCR engine can be trained on this set of glyph examples. Each step in this process requires a considerable amount of fine-tuning and domain knowledge – both of the OCR system and of the characteristics of the particular historical document.

In this paper, we describe a new system that replaces part of this pipeline with a more efficient workflow: finding (many) examples of the various glyphs. The main feature of this system is an efficient user interaction to learn the parameters of a template matching algorithm. As output, our software provides the detected glyph occurrences in the PAGE XML format, which can then be used to train (for example) the Tesseract OCR engine.

After reviewing related work (Sect. 2), we describe the features and contributions of our system (Sect. 3). We demonstrate the effectiveness of our approach in a small experiment, comparing our tool to the current workflow at Würzburg University Library, which relies on Aletheia [5] (Sect. 4).

2. RELATED WORK

Since the digitization of early prints has seen increasing attention over the last years, efforts have been made to automatically extract the contents of these documents. Off-the-shelf OCR systems like Tesseract [13] and ABBYY FineReader[3] need to be specifically trained to obtain fair results on early prints. This is a nontrivial task [10]. To make this procedure more convenient for users, several tools simplifying the construction and tuning of training sets have been developed. Clausner et al. [5, 6] introduced the ground-truthing system Aletheia, which provides a convenient user interface for annotating documents. It is focused on the annotation of regions, text lines and glyphs in a given page; for this task, some semi-automated tools are provided. The gathered information can be saved in the PAGE XML for-

---

*Corresponding Author

[1]For example, more than 17 million scanned pages are available through the Early English Books Online (EEBO) project. http://eebo.chadwyck.com/home

Permission to make digital or hard copies of all or part of this work for personal or classroom use is granted without fee provided that copies are not made or distributed for profit or commercial advantage and that copies bear this notice and the full citation on the first page. Copyrights for components of this work owned by others than the author(s) must be honored. Abstracting with credit is permitted. To copy otherwise, or republish, to post on servers or to redistribute to lists, requires prior specific permission and/or a fee. Request permissions from permissions@acm.org.

JCDL '16, June 19 - 23, 2016, Newark, NJ, USA

© 2016 Copyright held by the owner/author(s). Publication rights licensed to ACM.
ISBN 978-1-4503-4229-2/16/06. . . $15.00

DOI: http://dx.doi.org/10.1145/2910896.2910915

[2]This was also identified as a key problem by IMPACT, a European research project focused on digitizing historical printed text. http://www.impact-project.eu/

[3]http://www.abbyy.com/finereader/

mat [11] for further processing. The detected occurrences of glyphs can be used to train the Tesseract text recognition system, but first need to be checked for classification mistakes (and converted to appropriate file formats). Torabi et al. [14] introduced Franken+, a tool that aids this process by reading PAGE XML files, building a database of glyphs and creating synthetic training images for Tesseract.

The Gamera framework by Droettboom et al. [9] uses a different approach: It is a generic toolkit for building custom document recognition applications. It implements various image processing algorithms, including template matching and connected component analysis, which can be used to detect glyphs. Gamera also allows the training of classifiers to distinguish the detected glyphs and can thus be used as an OCR system (potentially using additional plug-ins [7]). The software exposes a variety of algorithms and its user interface is firmly aimed at technical experts who develop recognition processes. Off the shelf, it cannot be considered appropriate for users without a technical background in image processing.

There are various ways to arrange workflows for the digitization of early prints; see Pletschacher et al. [12] for a recent evaluation of options. In the current paper, we evaluate our system in the context of the digitization workflow at Würzburg University Library. First, a table of all occurring glyphs is created (using a spreadsheet software). Next, multiple representative occurrences of each glyph are obtained using Aletheia. Finally, this data is used to train Tesseract OCR through the Franken+ toolkit. This workflow is advocated by Torabi et al. [14] in their eMOP project and follows a sample use case for Aletheia;[4] Clausner et al. [6] describe a similar approach to train Gamera's OCR engine. As noted, our system would replace Aletheia (and the spreadsheet) and produce the table of representatives for each glyph. This would also be useful in a workflow based on Gamera.

Note that the problem of locating many occurrences of a given glyph is not limited to the training of OCR on early prints. In fact, the algorithmic underpinnings of our system were originally developed for locating pictographs and characters on early maps [3].

3. GLYPH MINER: SYSTEM DESIGN

The system presented in this paper simplifies the extraction of multiple occurrences of given glyphs from large corpora of printed text. It is based on an earlier system that we designed for metadata extraction from early maps [3]. In this section, we present our extensions to this system to make it suitable for OCR workflows of early typeset prints. The objective for the new system is to quickly detect a large set of samples for a given glyph, employing efficient user interactions. Note that it was specifically designed towards usability, to enable users without technical knowledge of OCR (e.g. researchers in the humanities) to contribute to the digitization workflow.

We start with two remarks. The system assumes that the images have already been binarized, a step that is commonly included in many digitization pipelines. We further note that depending on the particular use case, it might not be necessary to import all pages of a particular corpus, as long as the desired glyphs occur often enough. This can

[4] http://www.prima.cse.salford.ac.uk/tools/Aletheia/Usecases

Figure 1: Interface for handling a collection of pages from an early print. In the center, all occurrences of the glyph "e" on a particular page are presented.

increase the system's runtime performance without significantly impacting the quality of the results (see Sect. 4).

Mining Glyphs

In the first step, the user indicates a *template* of the glyph he or she is interested in by drawing a rectangle on one of the pages; the corresponding user interface is shown in Fig. 1. Once a template has been provided, the system runs a template matching algorithm on all images of the collection in parallel. This is based on the assumption that occurrences of the same glyph *look* the same, which is reasonable considering that they were printed using the same types. A renewed investigation of template matching in the context of OCR has also recently been advocated by Caluori and Simon [4]. In contrast to glyph segmentation based on connected components of ink (as used, for instance, in Gamera's classification module), this approach is reasonably stable against smudged printing, suboptimal binarization, and glyphs touching each other.

The template matching yields a set of candidate matches together with respective similarity scores, but we do not know which of these matches are in fact semantically correct (that is, depict the desired character). We model this problem as a classification task and apply active learning: The system iteratively presents carefully selected batches of candidate matches to the user, such that his or her time and effort is spent where it is most useful. Typically, the training process can be completed well within a minute and the learned model is applicable to all pages of the corpus. Fig. 2 shows our classification interface, which can be used on desktop PCs as well as on mobile devices. A complete description of this system's algorithmic and machine-learning aspects as well as its user interfaces is available elsewhere [3].

Glyph Library

All candidate matches and their respective classification models are stored in a database. Our system presents the matches to the user in the *Glyph Library* view: see Fig. 3. Here, the user can inspect and filter glyphs aggregated from all images of the chosen collection; by default, only the matches classified as positive are shown. The glyphs are presented in descending order of their similarity scores, allowing the user to easily find particularly clean occurrences of each glyph (as well as particularly distinct edge cases). The selected glyphs can be exported in various formats, including PAGE XML (which can be processed further by Franken+).

Figure 2: The classification interface as shown on a PC and a smartphone. The user's task is to touch all tiles showing the desired glyph (here: "p", three already checked), thereby training the classifier.

Figure 3: The *Glyph Library* view is used to browse and export detected occurrences of glyphs.

Implementation

The implementation of our system is web-based and we have used it in the experiments of Sect. 4. The client side runs in a web browser, providing cross-platform compatibility. The web application communicates through a REST API with a server that is responsible for image handling and maintaining the database of glyph occurrences. Our modular approach and the API design make it possible to quickly change individual components of the system (e.g. integrate a more sophisticated template matching algorithm).

See our demo video of this system at:
`https://youtu.be/T-p_kIdsn6k`

4. EXPERIMENTS AND CASE STUDY

In this section, we present a preliminary case study where we embed our system into the digitization workflow of the Würzburg University Library. Our experiments were run on an incunable printed in Basel in 1497, containing a Latin translation of Sebastian Brant's *Narrenschiff* (GW 5061). The Narrenschiff ("Ship of Fools") is considered an outstanding work in the history of German literature, being the most successful German book until Goethe's *Werther* almost three centuries later. It spectacularly combined the printing techniques emerging at the time, which now poses a considerable challenge to OCR systems. There exist approximately two dozen other prints using the same type inventory, to which OCR training results could be transfered.

All pages of this work were available as high-resolution grayscale scans, which we binarized with a fixed threshold. Unless otherwise noted, we ran the experiments on the first 20 out of 320 pages.

All parameters for the matching algorithm are learned automatically. This is in contrast to Gamera, which for similar tasks depends on a nontrivial set of parameters to be picked by hand (for filtering connected components by size, similarity thresholds, et cetera). Although Aletheia has the official use case of training OCR through Franken+, it is actually a ground-truthing system (including e.g. annotating the page layout), which hampers usability in our context. In contrast to these two systems, our tool outputs directly to Franken+, which is no longer the case for the latest releases of Aletheia.

Experiment: Glyph Miner on early prints

First we consider the precision and recall of Glyph Miner on two example characters. For both, we used our system for 10 iterations in the active learning interface. This takes approximately 90 seconds per character, including indicating the desired character, computation time, and the active learning procedure. We compare the output of our system to the glyphs actually contained in the pages; this ground truth was created manually.

Using a "g" glyph, the system achieved precision 1, recall 0.991, and F1-Score 0.995. There were only two false negatives, one match being wrongly classified and one occurrence not being detected by the template matching at all. With an "a", we achieved precision 0.941, recall 0.969, F1-Score 0.955. Note that for the latter glyph, the system has some difficulty with similar glyphs such as "ä" and marginalia of slightly smaller font size. The false negatives in this case were mostly caused by glyph occurrences undetected by the template matching algorithm. These quality measures are much higher than reported in previous work [3], where the same algorithms were applied to early printed maps with hand-drawn characters. This experiment shows that our system is suitable for finding repeat occurrences of glyphs in early typeset prints.

A particular class of false positives in our system occurs for characters that are visually contained within one another (for example, the character "m" might contain approximate occurrences of "n"). This is a known issue with glyph detection in general [8], but not an important one, since the user can work around it with clever template selection or in postprocessing. We do not specifically address this problem.

Experiment: Glyph Miner vs. Aletheia

Our second experiment was conducted with the help of an OCR engineer at the Würzburg University Library. In this experiment, we assess how our system could be used as an in-place substitute of part of their current workflow.

As the baseline experiment, the OCR engineer worked for 45 minutes using Aletheia following the existing workflow. In this time, he annotated roughly 1⅓ pages. His annotation consisted of 1251 occurrences of 65 different glyphs, with a median number of 7 occurrences per glyph. The seemingly slow progress has two main reasons. First, Aletheia's automatic segmentation of glyphs often fails and needs to be corrected manually. Second, the characters suggested by Aletheia are often wrong and must be checked and corrected.

In the contrasting experiment, the OCR engineer worked on the same pages for another 45 minutes, now using Glyph

Miner. In this time, he processed 26 different glyphs, arriving at 17 426 repeat occurrences, with a median of 498 occurrences per glyph. These repeat occurrences were extracted from the 20 pages of input given to the system. As a byproduct, Glyph Miner has trained a classifier which can be used to extract further occurrences from the remaining 300 pages of the corpus. For the glyph "a", for example, this gives us a total of 21 189 occurrences; for the rarer "ct" ligature we find 648. This extrapolation took 168 seconds per glyph on a single quad-core 3.4 GHz PC, and can be trivially distributed further for additional performance.

In the 45 minutes alloted in the above experiments, Aletheia gets a better coverage of glyphs: 65 versus 26. On the other hand, the Glyph Miner finds a considerably larger number of repeat occurrences: a total of 17 428 versus 1251. The occurrences found with Aletheia are from the first $1^1/_3$ pages; the Glyph Miner covers all of the first 20 pages. Using some additional computational time, the occurrences on the remaining 300 pages can be found fully automatically.

Of the 65 different glyphs covered by Aletheia, only 25 were backed by ten or more occurrences. The limited number of occurrences for the others glyphs may hamper proper training of OCR software. In contrast, the minimum number of occurrences per glyph in Glyph Miner was 29, with many more for most glyphs.

In the current workflow, the OCR engineer goes through a number of pages in full, until sufficiently many occurrences of all common glyphs have been found. Afterward, he or she searches through all other pages (potentially hundreds) to obtain enough examples of the rare glyphs. Our system should provide a particular speed-up for this second stage, because every rare glyph needs to be found only once: The other occurrences will be found by template matching. Evaluating this speed-up in practice would be time-consuming and was beyond the scope of our experiment.

5. CONCLUSION AND OUTLOOK

We have presented a system for efficiently extracting repeat occurrences of given glyphs from scans of early prints. The system can be embedded into a digitization workflow and combines template matching and active learning into an efficient user interaction. We have done a preliminary case study showing that our system has the potential to outperform state-of-the-art approaches in this use case.

The motivating application in this paper is training OCR software. We have shown that we are able to massively increase the number of examples available per glyph. Giving more examples to Franken+ sounds promising, but at present we have not evaluated if this actually leads to an increased OCR performance. Even if not all occurrences are used for training, the large number of glyph examples, sorted by quality, makes it easier for OCR engineers to compose a good training set. Emerging new OCR approaches based on deep learning would certainly profit from the large set of training data. Additionally, we note that a catalog of occurrences of glyphs can in itself be interesting, for example to date or attribute printed works [2]. Such catalogs can also be used to handle particular sets of glyphs in highly specialized digital libraries, for instance handling neumes in medieval chant manuscripts [1].

In future work, we want to further exploit the massive number of detected occurrences. One approach is to use this information to simplify the (manual) search for rare glyphs by fading out everything that has been identified before. Here, a semi-automatic approach to detect unidentified glyphs could also be feasible. Another direction of work is to explore if the high detection accuracy for single glyphs can be expanded into a complete OCR system.

Acknowledgments

We thank H.-G. Schmidt, Head of the Department of Manuscripts and Early Printed Collections and the Digitization Center at Würzburg University Library, and OCR engineer P. Beckenbauer. This research was partially supported by the German Federal Ministry of Education and Research (project KALLIMACHOS, reference ehuman-539-084).

6. REFERENCES

[1] L. W. G. Barton, J. A. Caldwell, and P. G. Jeavons. E-Library of Medieval Chant Manuscript Transcriptions. In *Proc. JCDL'05*, pages 320–329, 2005.

[2] M. Behr. *Buchdruck und Sprachwandel*. De Gruyter, 2014.

[3] B. Budig and T. C. van Dijk. Active Learning for Classifying Template Matches in Historical Maps. In *Proc. DS'14*, pages 33–47, 2015.

[4] U. Caluori and K. Simon. An OCR Concept for Historic Prints. In *Archiving Conf.*, pages 143–147, 2013.

[5] C. Clausner, S. Pletschacher, and A. Antonacopoulos. Aletheia – An Advanced Document Layout and Text Ground-Truthing System for Production Environments. In *ICDAR'11*, pages 48–52, 2011.

[6] C. Clausner, S. Pletschacher, and A. Antonacopoulos. Efficient OCR Training Data Generation with Aletheia. In *Short Paper Booklet of the 11th IAPR Workshop DAS'14*, pages 19–20, 2014.

[7] C. Dalitz and R. Baston. Optical Character Recognition with the Gamera Framework. In *Doc. Image Analysis with the Gamera Framework*, pages 53–65, 2009.

[8] M. P. Deseilligny, H. Le Men, and G. Stamon. Character String Recognition on Maps, a Rotation-invariant Recognition Method. *Pattern Recognition Letters*, 16(12):1297–1310, 1995.

[9] M. Droettboom, I. Fujinaga, K. MacMillan, G. S. Chouhury, T. DiLauro, M. Patton, and T. Anderson. Using the Gamera Framework for the Recognition of Cultural Heritage Materials. In *Proc. JCDL'02*, pages 11–17, 2002.

[10] M. Heliński, M. Kmieciak, and T. Parkoła. Report on the comparison of Tesseract and ABBYY FineReader OCR engines. *Improving Access to Text*, 2012.

[11] S. Pletschacher and A. Antonacopoulos. The PAGE (Page Analysis and Ground-Truth Elements) Format Framework. In *ICPR'10*, pages 257–260, 2010.

[12] S. Pletschacher, C. Clausner, and A. Antonacopoulos. Europeana Newspapers OCR Workflow Evaluation. In *Proc. HIP'15*, pages 39–56, 2015.

[13] R. Smith. An Overview of the Tesseract OCR Engine. In *Proc. ICDAR'07*, pages 629–633, 2007.

[14] K. Torabi, J. Durgan, and B. Tarpley. Early Modern OCR Project (eMOP) at Texas A&M University: Using Aletheia to Train Tesseract. In *Proc. DocEng'13*, pages 23–26, 2013.

Enhancing Scholarly Use of Digital Libraries: A Comparative Survey and Review of Bibliographic Metadata Ontologies

Jacob Jett
Graduate School of Library
and Information Science
University of Illinois at
Urbana-Champaign
jjett2@illinois.edu

Terhi Nurmikko-Fuller
Oxford e-Research Centre
University of Oxford
terhi.nurmikko-
fuller@oerc.ox.ac.uk

Timothy W. Cole
Graduate School of Library
and Information Science
University of Illinois at
Urbana-Champaign
t-cole3@illinois.edu

Kevin R. Page
Oxford e-Research Centre
University of Oxford
kevin.page@oerc.ox.ac.uk

J. Stephen Downie
Graduate School of Library
and Information Science
University of Illinois at
Urbana-Champaign
jdownie@illinois.edu

ABSTRACT

The HathiTrust Research Center (HTRC) is engaged in the development of tools that will give scholars the ability to analyze the HathiTrust digital library's 14 million volume corpus. A cornerstone of the HTRC's digital infrastructure is the workset — a kind of scholar–built research collection intended for use with the HTRC's analytics platform. Because more than 66% of the digital corpus is subject to copyright restrictions, scholarly users remain dependent upon the descriptive accounts provided by traditional metadata records in order to identify and gather together bibliographic resources for analysis. This paper compares the MADSRDF/MODSRDF, Bibframe, schema.org, BIBO, and FaBiO ontologies by assessing their suitability for employment by the HTRC to meet scholars' needs. These include distinguishing among multiple versions of the same work; representing the complex historical and physical relationships among those versions; and identifying and providing access to finer grained bibliographic entities, e.g., poems, chapters, sections, and even smaller segments of content.

CCS Concepts

•**Information systems** → **Ontologies;** *Document filtering;*

Keywords

Digital libraries; bibliographic metadata; ontologies.

Permission to make digital or hard copies of all or part of this work for personal or classroom use is granted without fee provided that copies are not made or distributed for profit or commercial advantage and that copies bear this notice and the full citation on the first page. Copyrights for components of this work owned by others than the author(s) must be honored. Abstracting with credit is permitted. To copy otherwise, or republish, to post on servers or to redistribute to lists, requires prior specific permission and/or a fee. Request permissions from permissions@acm.org.

JCDL '16, June 19 - 23, 2016, Newark, NJ, USA

© 2016 Copyright held by the owner/author(s). Publication rights licensed to ACM.
ISBN 978-1-4503-4229-2/16/06. . . $15.00

DOI: http://dx.doi.org/10.1145/2910896.2910903

1. INTRODUCTION

The heart of the HathiTrust Research Center (HTRC)'s infrastructure revolves around a *non-consumptive research paradigm* in which scholars gather together vast quantities of bibliographic resources and use automated analytics workflows to derive facts about them. The workset is the primary tool that scholars use to interact with the HathiTrust (HT) digital library's corpus. Scholars use metadata records to identify objects of interest and gather them into a workset exactly as they would if they were constructing a personalized research collection. The primary difference is that since much of the HT digital library's corpus remains under copyright (keyword in context access is available for 66% of the HT digital library's corpus of 5 billion digitised pages), users are restricted to metadata alone as a means to gather bibliographic resources into their worksets. Metadata is an important linchpin around which the operational characteristics of the workset revolves.

On the whole, metadata plays a significant role in the context of digital libraries infrastructure. Further complicating the situation is the fact that the HT digital library's records come from multiple sources, and that the corpus contains a certain amount of duplicates and alternatives. Under ideal circumstances deduplication could be carried out through analysis of the metadata records, but, as we noted last year [7], this may be impossible in such cases as where the records themselves purport the uniqueness of each described volume.

Limited access (only 34% of the corpus is freely available without copyright) could act as a barrier to using automated methods for deduplication. The HathTrust Research Center (HTRC)'s non-consumptive research infrastructure — designed specifically with the application of automated analysis methods to very large corpora in mind — would seem the ideal solution. However, as with the texts and metadata records, the OCR text files for each volume's pages also hail from different workflows, and the many idiosyncratic errors (as well as those introduced by the OCR process) serve to reinforce, rather than ameliorate, the problem.

Reconciliation of the metadata records is the most feasible solution remaining to the HTRC and its scholarly users. Bibliographic ontologies form the foundation upon which infrastructure supporting reconciliation of metadata records can be built, and by layering in linked data (i.e., replacing simple strings representing people and places with URIs), disparate assertions about the exact same entities can be brought together. Since scholars cannot directly access more than 5 million volumes in the HT digital library's 14 million volume corpus because of copyright issues, metadata descriptions remain their primary tool for gathering together those objects from the remaining 9 million volumes that are likely to be of interest, and worth obtaining full access to (in order to enable close reading).

The HTRC has objectives beyond that of reconciling the digital library's vast collection of metadata: Interviews and focus groups have indicated that scholars have a great interest in engaging with the HT digital library's corpus at a much finer grained level than that of volumes.[3] They wish to be able to gather small texts like poems and segments of text (e.g. chapters) into worksets as well. Employing some the HTRC's existing experimental outcomes, such as the extracted features dataset[1] the HTRC intends to create a layer of metadata objects that describe finer-grained resources so that scholars can identify them and make use of them in their analyses.

As we previously reported, one of the first barriers that users of the HTRC face when wishing to create a workset is the lack of metadata adequate enough to select resources (be that text, or images, etc.) that are of interest to them. We described three use cases that the HTRC's metadata repository needed to fulfill in order for scholarly users of the HT digital library to aggregate desired resources into worksets intended for analysis:

- Refinement of worksets according to particular facets in order to distinguish particular instances of a work from multiple versions.

- Representation of complex historical and physical relationships among various versions of a work. Our example was of a historical text (*The game and playe of the chesse* by Jacobus de Cessolis), of which a microfilm was produced, and given to another collection. Both the original and the copy were digitized in two independent processes at their respective libraries, and are described by two different metadata records, which do not connect them to each other [7].

- Granularity of the desired resource needs to match the expectations and scope of analysis that the scholar intends to carry out [3].

Metadata is crucial in the formation of worksets. And thus, bibliographic ontologies are fundamentally essential for the improved, informative, predictable, and consistent retrieval of records within the digital library's collection. They enable linking across collections, which is particularly significant in cases where a digital corpora brings together not only disparate collections but the heterogeneous repositories of contributing institutions. The issue of granularity, for example, can be problematic as most metadata records only operate at the level of a physical or digital volume (and not,

for example, differentiating between different pieces within an anthology); others pinpoint to a specific article within a journal, or even to a chapter within a book; many lack the granularity of being able to pinpoint a specific page, or a particular element on a given page, such as an image, or musical notation. Different ontologies are better suited to addressing each of these differing levels of granularity, making understanding of their idiosyncratic nuances, and the way they can fit together, all the more important.

Despite the significant role metadata and ontologies play in the sphere of digital libraries, relatively little work has been done to directly compare bibliographic ontologies to one another. Many of the existing analyses are of very high-level ontologies such as DOLCE and WordNet[6], which are primarily concerned with semantic enrichment of the objects within a corpus itself, rather than providing linked data compliant descriptions of the contents of the corpus. Of the few comparisons that focus on bibliographic ontologies concerned with providing metadata descriptions, most focus on ontologies that support citations and the creation of structured citation data[10][8]. None have created a broad-ranging analysis of bibliographic ontologies' suitability for describing bibliographic resources relative to one another. To address this gap, we carried out a preliminary investigation into bibliographic metadata ontologies [7].

While each of the ontologies reviewed has dozens (and sometimes several hundred) of entity types and properties which were compared, we limited the initial discussion to the 12 comparisons made in Table 1. This paper takes those initial comparisons of MODSRDF/MADSRDF,[2] Bibframe,[3] schema.org,[4] and FRBRoo,[2] and fully develops and extends the analysis. We have also been able to add our analysis of the Bibliographic Ontology (BIBO)[5] back into the mix of comparisons, having excluded it from our initial paper because of the different level of granularity that it operates at — i.e., at that of journal article or conference paper. To further highlight the contrast between this more granular approach we have added the FRBR-aligned Bibliographic Ontology (FaBiO)[6] to our set of comparisons.

In this paper, we discuss each of the selected ontologies in the context of eight core categories of bibliographic metadata. We summarize our findings, and present a number of recommendations for best practice for ontology reuse, and documentation. The paper concludes with a view to future work.

2. METHODOLOGY

The research methodology used is that of conceptual analysis. It has been employed more formally by other scholars in the library and information science (LIS) field to decompose the particulars of notions like "information" [4], in the development of ontologies [12], and for the development of conceptual frameworks for metadata schema [5]. Here we employ it to assess the semantic equivalence and adequacy of entities and properties across several ontologies.

In particular we will be looking at entity types and properties whose instances articulate and assert the core infor-

[1]https://sharc.hathitrust.org/features

[2]http://www.loc.gov/standards/mods/modsrdf/
[3]http://bibframe.org/
[4]http://schema.org/
[5]http://purl.org/ontology/bibo/1.2/
[6]http://purl.org/spar/fabio

Table 1: Excerpts from the original survey [7]

	MODSRDF	Bibframe	Schema.org	FRBRoo
Base Type	Resource	Resource	Creative Work	CRM Entity (E1)
Edition/Version	edition	edition	bookEdition/ version	
Work Entity		Work		Work (F1)
Issuance	Issuance		<rdf:type>	has issuring rule (R11)
Title/Name	Title	Title	Thing:name	Title (E35)
Location	Geographic	Place	Place	Place (E53)
Topicality	subjectTopic or Complex Subject	Topic or subject	CreativeWork:about	Propositional Object (E89) is about (P129) CRM Entity (E1)
Attribution	statementOfResponsibility	Responsibility Statement		Type (E55) "Statement of responsibility"
Manifestation		Manuscript		Manifestation Singleton (F4)
Identifier	hasIdentifier	22 properties		Identifier (E42)
Creation Event				Work Conception (F27)
Temporality	Temporal	Temporal		Event (E5)

mation that past studies on metadata interoperability have used to assess completeness [11]. Whereas Shreeves et al.'s approach examined metadata records conforming to the Dublin Core (DC) metadata standard[7] that had been harvested using the Open Archives Initiative - Protocol for Metadata Harvesting (OAI-PMH),[8] our goal is to compare ontologies across the eight axes of completeness identified in that work.

We have derived general categories for comparison from the eight core DC elements of <title>, <creator>, <subject>, <description>, <date>, <format>, <identifier> and <rights>. Because <subject> is extremely broad, we further divided it into subcategories that are often reflected in traditional research questions and problem spaces: General, Temporal/Event, and Geographic/Geopolitical. Our interest in employing FRBR to identify equivalencies among resources led to the inclusion of two additional factors from this framework - Group Entity Type and Edition/Version. Finally, we added the category of Language, believing it to be a feature of interest to the majority of the HT digital library's scholarly users. The resulting categories are: Title/Colloquial Name, Authorial Agent (e.g., author, contributor, publisher), Topicality, Colloquial Description, Date/Event, Format/Media Type, Identifier/Inventory Control Name, and Rights.

The following review section examines how comparable each of the six ontologies are for each of the 13 listed categories. We also speculate on how any particular ontology's set of entity/property characteristics might meet the needs of the three use cases outlined above.

3. COMPARATIVE REVIEW

3.1 Title/Colloquial Name

All but one of the six ontologies (schema.org) examined in our survey provided at least one property that directly corresponded to our collective notions of "bibliographic title" (Table 2). In two cases, BIBO and FaBiO, this property corresponded directly to an equivalent property (dcterms:title) in the DC metadata schema (a recurring practice observed throughout the comparisons).

In the case of schema.org, the community appears to have made an active decision to generalize the notion of "title" to that of "name." This may seem harmless, but the schema:CreativeWork class introduces another property — schema:headline — which might be more appropriate for one specific kind of creative work. It is defined specifically as "Headline of the article",[9] and is a property of the class of all creative works; the ontology provides more specific subclasses (e.g. schema:Book), which in turn introduce additional properties. The definition for the related property —schema:alternativeHeadline — invokes the LIS notion of "title" by defining an alternative headline as "[a] secondary title of the CreativeWork".[10]

Table 2: Title/Colloquial Name Properties

Ontology	Property/Entity	Property Range
MODS/ MADSRDF	modsrdf:titlePrincipal modsrdf:titleUniform	madsrdf:Title
Bibframe	bf:title	bf:Title
schema.org	schema:name schema:headline	xsd:string
FRBRoo	P102 has title	E35 Title
BIBO	dcterms:title	xsd:string
FaBiO	fabio:hasTitle dcterms:title	xsd:string

Whatever the intended use of the schema:headline property, agencies such as OCLC[11] have chosen to map MARC title field elements[12] to the schema:name property. One might assume that terminology which is clearly described is more likely to be reused — conversely, in the case of schema:name, the lack of documentation may be its most attractive quality: there is nothing in the documentation to imply that it could not be used in every instance of linking any given Thing to the label applied to it.

The two ontologies that are more obviously descended from library cataloging traditions and the MARC metadata schema (MADSRDF/MODSRDF and Bibframe) and

[7] http://dublincore.org/

[8] https://www.openarchives.org/pmh/

[9] https://schema.org/headline

[10] https://schema.org/alternativeHeadline

[11] https://www.oclc.org/en-UK/home.html

[12] http://www.loc.gov/marc/bibliographic/bd20x24x.html

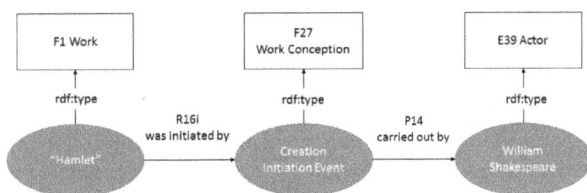

Figure 1: Conception of Hamlet by Shakespeare

the two that are focused more specifically at the level of journal articles (BIBO and FaBiO) each provide additional distinctions regarding titles through either subproperties (e.g., fabio:hasSubtitle) or sibling properties (e.g., bibo:shortTitle). FRBRoo provides a more generalized solution in the form of monolithic hasTitle -Title property-value pairs. Broadly speaking, the Bibframe ontology provides the largest number of options for recording idiosyncrasies with regards to a resource's title. And, since our purpose for the metadata is to aid in the selection of resources for computational analysis, it is likely that such idiosyncratic title details will be of much interest to scholarly users of the HT digital library.

3.2 Authorial Agent

All of the ontologies provide means to at least name a work's author/creator (Table 3). In the case of MODSRDF/MADSRDF,[13] an attempt was made by its editors to generalize the creator role to a more general property ("role").[14] Expressing creative responsibility through the use of an intermediary role vocabulary would have enabled MODSRDF/MADSRDF to reuse the entire relators:role subproperty vocabulary (e.g., relators:author, relators:illustrator, etc.) and thereby provide extremely granular characterizations of the role that each agent plays in the creation of a work.

Bibframe, schema.org, FRBRoo, and BIBO also name multiple roles for various agents (authors, editors, illustrators, and publishers, among others) but they do not interweave with other vocabularies in such a pre-planned way. Of these four, BIBO uses separate properties (bibo:director, bibo:editor, bibo:publisher, etc.) for certain kinds of roles, but represents authors and contributors specifically through aggregate properties (bibo:authorList and bibo:contributorList). This makes for a very verbose description of any work authored by a single person, as they are only linked to the work through the indirection of participating in an rdf:List or rdf:Seq subgraph. This is likely to make the database queries necessary for grouping resources together more difficult to develop and less efficient in the long run.

As with other members of the family of ontologies put forth by the International Committee for Documentation's Conceptual Reference Model (CIDOC CRM), FRBRoo has a very nuanced understanding of authorial agency. In particular, consider the following paired triples illustrated in Figure 1 above. The important (and by far the most subtle)

---

[13]We understand from our conversations with some of the authors of this ontology that its development has largely been abandoned by the Library of Congress in favor of the Bibframe ontology.

[14]Note that the equivalency with the realtors vocabulary may be an indicator that more specific subproperties such as realtors:author are intended for actual usage.

Table 3: Authorial Agency Properties

Ontology	Property/Entity	Property Range
MODS/ MADSRDF	modsrdf:role realtors:role	madsrdf:Name
Bibframe	bf:creator	bf:Authority
schema.org	schema:author	schema:Person schema:Organization
FRBRoo	P14 carried out by	E39 Actor
BIBO	bibo:authorList	rdf:List or rdf:Seq
FaBiO	fabio:hasCreator dcterms:creator	xsd:string

thing to catch is that the way the FRBRoo vocabulary describes it, works are not merely created: they are conceived and the event of that conception is a recordable event. However, this information may not be useful for the purposes of gathering resources for computational analysis (although the graphs produced by FRBRoo's highly structured data would be).[15]

3.3 Topicality

3.3.1 General Topicality

There is a great deal of value in dividing topicality into multiple subcategories, not the least of which is the way in which topic and temporality align with traditional research questions, particularly in the humanities: most will be familiar with examples where the parameters of *what*, *when*, and *where* define a niche or an area of expertise.

Table 4: General Topicality Properties

Ontology	Property/Entity	Property Range
MODS/ MADSRDF	modsrdf:subject	madsrdf:Topic
Bibframe	bf:subject	bf:Authority bf:Work
schema.org	schema:about	schema:Thing
FRBRoo	P129 is about	E55 Type
BIBO	dcterms:subject	xsd:string
FaBiO	fabio:hasSubjectTerm	fabio:SubjectTerm

Each of the analyzed ontologies provides a means of recording a work's "aboutness" or topicality (Table 4). There is an interesting dichotomy in the Bibframe standard between the entities called "Authorities" and those called "Works" — there is also something odd about the FRBRoo standard and its claim that works "are about types".[2]

Bibframe describes a work's topicality as being about another work or something called an "authority." We can see from Table 3 that the entity authority is also used as the range of the bf:creator property. An "authority" is defined as the "[r]epresentation of a key concept or thing."[16]

---

[15]One can imagine that such a deeply interwoven and rich tapestry of structured metadata could be plumbed for a vast wealth of otherwise hidden information regarding relationships among works and agents. This could be especially informative with non-text based works such as games (especially video games), films, television programs, comic books, dance performances, and other kinds of works that require entire armies of agents realize.

[16]http://bibframe.org/vocab-list/#Authority

On the one hand, Bibframe records claim that works are authored by representations of things and are also only about representations of those things or representations of concepts (after all, we would typically claim that the work *Hamlet* was written by Shakespeare, rather than a representation of him). On the other hand, we may argue that the issue is much more complex than the relatively straightforward assertions we would typically like to make about *Hamlet*, especially when it must be realised with the precision of a technical system, i.e., without the implicit ambiguity conveyed in natural language.

We are faced with the issue of a physical, real-world person (e.g., Shakespeare), and an identifier that refers to them.[17] In essence, the server should not respond with a 200 OK status in response to a GET request, as it is not, in fact, returning the physical entity. A URI is then to be understood as a plausible *representation* of Shakespeare. This lack of clarity is indicative of a recurring problem of insufficient and incomplete documentation. Terminology such as "representation" is inevitably nuanced, with multiple possible readings and interpretations.

The use of bf:Authority as the range of bf:subject illustrates a more complex alignment between a work and its subject or topic, but does not do so arbitrarily. Mapping through an authority ensures that even in the case of corpora that combine collections from several diverse collections, a shared vocabulary (and thus understanding) is in use, making resources from all source-collections equally discoverable using the same terminology. This brings us back again to the issue of documentation: to have described bf:Authority with more vigor, or at a minimum as "an authoritative representation of a key concept or thing" would have made the role, purpose, and intended use of the class clearer from the onset.

FRBRoo[18] asserts "F1 Work P129 is about E55 Type". Unlike the Bibframe example, it is possible to interpret the entity type E55 as being intended as a placeholder for instances of particular types, and so in practice, usages of the property P129 have a range of rdfs:Resource or rdfs:Literal (i.e., essentially a work can be about anything). As we show in section 3.3.2, one key problem with this interpretation is that neither E55 nor P129 encompass the key geographical entities E48 Place Name and E53 Place.

3.3.2 Temporal/Event-based Topicality

Differentiating among kinds of temporal topicality is a distinction created by the DC vocabulary and the overly broad scope of its <date> element. Indeed, temporal topicality is one of the more important distinctions, as it allows the development of powerful faceted search algorithms that can distinguish among resources by time period and topic.

Labels related to some notion of Time can be divided into three major categories: firstly, that of *Date*, which is generally represented numerically, and frequently denotes a par-

ticular 24hr period within a calendar year; secondly, there is the *Event*, which most commonly spans days, perhaps months, years or even decades, but it unlikely to refer to a period lasting centuries or millennia; thirdly, there are *Periods*, which often refer to much lengthier sections of time. These differences also carry a spatio-temporal nuance: an event is tied to a place (e.g., a conference), whilst a period as a label can be independent of location (e.g., "the Bronze Age"), and the addition of geography is significant (to extend the example, consider "the Bronze Age" in the Americas in comparison to that in the Middle East, separated by almost three millennia). Of these, only *Period* is considered here as a type of Temporal Topicality - *Date* and *Event* are discussed in section 3.5 below.

Although one might expect genre and other topic-based classifications (particularly those connected to periods, such as works focusing on, for example, "the Renaissance") to rank highly in the needs of (digital) librarians, half of the bibliographic ontologies reviewed here offer no scope for capturing such temporal topicality. Those that do, namely Bibframe, MODSRDF/MADSRDF, and FRBRoo, are inclusive of *Period*, as well as capturing bibliographic *Events* of work biography, but do so with classes that are largely unconnected to Works: F8 Event ≡ E4 Period, for example can only be connected to other instances of E4, to E53 Place, or E19 Physical Object. Similarly, bf:Event and bf:Temporal capture events and "chronological periods,"[19] but are not specified as the range for properties such as bf:temporalCoverageNote.

Only the two ontologies that hail from long traditions of bibliographic cataloging preserve this kind of metadata as distinct kinds of structured data (Table 5).

Table 5: Temporal Topicality Properties

Ontology	Property/Entity	Property Range
MODS/ MADSRDF	modsrdf:subjectTemporal	madsrdf:Temporal
Bibframe	bf:temporalCoverageNote	rdfs:Literal
schema.org	schema:about	schema:Thing
FRBRoo	P129 is about	E55 Type
BIBO	dcterms:subject	xsd:string
FaBiO	fabio:hasSubjectTerm	fabio:SubjectTerm

The absence of this level of topical granularity from the other ontologies may have been expected, but less so for an event-based ontology such as FRBRoo. Adding to this is the existence of CIDOC-CRM entity types[20] that seem wholly appropriate for capturing topicality information at this level of granularity.

3.3.3 Geographic/Geopolitical Topicality

The same issues arise when specifying geographic/geopolitical topicality (Table 6). Schema.org fares as well as both MODSRDF/MADSRDF and Bibframe do, by providing a specific property to separate information about content topicality with regards to geographic or geopolitical location. We hypothesize that this may reflect the primary target au-

---

[17] A known problem in the field of Knowledge Representation, and often addressed using the 303 See Other status code, which has been recommended as a method for responding to instances of real-world objects https://www.w3.org/TR/cooluris/#r303gendocument

[18] It is likely important to realize that CIDOC-CRM's use of the term "type" in this case is limited to kinds of conceptual objects (E28) and encompasses things such as languages (E56), materials (E57), and units of measure (E58). Moreover, it is intended to act as interface for domain specific ontologies [2].

[19] http://bibframe.org/vocab-list/#Temporal

[20] In particular E52 Time-Span seems most appropriate and yet it is not within the range scope of the P129 is about property.

dience for schema.org - online vendors and developers of on-line vending systems. The example they use in their documentation is of a "location in a photograph or painting"[21] which seems pertinent to someone shopping online for paintings, post-cards, or other image-based media.

Table 6: Geographic Topicality Properties

Ontology	Property/Entity	Property Range
MODS/ MADSRDF	modsrdf:subjectGeographic	madsrdf:Geographic
Bibframe	bf:geographicCoverageNote	rdfs:Literal
schema.org	schema:contentLocation	schema:Place
FRBRoo	P129 is about	E55 Type
BIBO	dcterms:subject	xsd:string
FaBiO	fabio:hasSubjectTerm	fabio:SubjectTerm

As for FRBRoo, E48 Place Name and E53 Place might be expected to be in scope of the range of property P129 is about, but the documentation states otherwise. An ontology, which provides such a rich and intricate set of provenance and archival metadata would be expected to be better aligned with one of the cornerstones of search and retrieval faceting.

3.4 Colloquial Descriptions

As expected, each of the six ontologies provides a property that allows for a colloquial description (Table 7). Of particular interest here is that only Bibframe accommodates the linked data approach of allowing any resource to perform this role. Each of the other five ontologies limit the scope of the property to just string data.

Table 7: Colloquial Description Properties

Ontology	Property/Entity	Property Range
MODS/ MADSRDF	modsrdf:abstract	xsd:string
Bibframe	bf:hasDescription	bf:Resource
schema.org	schema:description	xsd:string
FRBRoo	P3 has note	E62 String
BIBO	dcterms:description	xsd:string
FaBiO	fabio:description dcterms:description	xsd:string

Bibframe, like MODSRDF/MADSRDF, has been designed with the idea to incorporate evolving linked data practices:[22] something more than simple text can be used to describe bibliographic entities. Indeed, with the Bibframe approach one can actually describe a bibliographic entity through the use of another bibliographic entity. Although the evolving interest in linked open data for libraries (see for example the Linked Data for Libraries[23] and Linked Open Data for Special Collections[24] projects) has been noted, we still see simple string data types appear as the range for most of these description properties.

FRBRoo stands out as the only other ontology to provide a reference to an entity class. Unlike Bibframe's bf:Resource,

[21]https://schema.org/contentLocation
[22]https://www.w3.org/DesignIssues/LinkedData.html
[23]https://www.ld4l.org/
[24]http://publish.illinois.edu/linkedspcollections/

which is intended to be roughly equivalent in breadth and depth as rdfs:Resource, FRBRoo's E62 entity type aggregates a number of specified mimetypes whose encodings rely on the ASCII character set and calls them all strings. While it's true that a bitmap provides a series of instructions encoded using binary or ASCII, the rendered end products are typically images rather than strings. This appears to be a case where assertions about data encodings are being conflated with assertions about the data (i.e., the content) itself.

3.5 Dates and Events

The ontological representation of temporal entities is complex. There are at least three distinct labels and categories applied to time, already described in section 3.3.2, and summarized as *Date*, *Event*, and *Period*.

Of these, the former two are significant in capturing metadata regarding the biography of a work (dates of publication and modification, for example), whilst the latter is almost exclusively used in the context of *Topicality*. For this reason, only the former two are considered here, whilst the latter has already been discussed in section 3.3.2 above.

Representation of events is one of the areas where the ontologies differ from one another the most. Those originating from bibliographic traditions (namely MODSRDF/MADS-RDF and Bibframe) have vocabulary that captures relatively few events, most of which are concerned with the bibliographic control issues of creation, modification, and copyright. Both ontologies limit their representations to the existence of a handful of properties (as can be seen in Table 8) below.

Table 8: Date/Event Representations

Ontology	No. of Events	Event Types
MODS/ MADSRDF	5	digitization, creation, modification, copyright assertion, validity
Bibframe	6	change, creation, copyright assertion, events (as type of work), provisions (from a vendor), title variations
schema.org	19	business event, children's event, comedy, dance, educations, exhibition, festival, food, literary, music, publication, sale, screening, social, sports, theater, use interaction, visual arts
FRBRoo	30	E5 Event
BIBO	6	conference, hearing, interview, performance, personal communication, workshop
FaBiO	17	update, acceptance, access, copyright assertion, correction, creation, reception, decision, deposit, issuance, modification, preprint dissemination, publication, request, reaction, validity

A rather stark contrast to this is the approach taken by schema.org, FRBRoo, BIBO, and FaBiO, which represent events as first-class entities in and of themselves. BIBO (a descriptive ontology) has very few entity classes, all of which are permutations of public performances such as conferences, hearings, and interviews. The schema.org ontology is similarly focused on representing various kinds of performances, as well as some events, such as *publication event*, *sale event*, and *user interaction* that allow the capture of metadata which records sales and user behavior.

The FRBR-based FaBiO combined traditional metadata interests in bibliographic control with more granular representation of journal article provenance. Among other things, this allows it to capture events particular to the journal article medium such as the dissemination of preprints and the retraction of articles.

FRBRoo provides a granular and rich tapestry of events. While it has much in the way of vocabulary supporting the representation of archival and transaction events (inherited, from CIDOC-CRM), it provides potent means to record granular events within the authorial process. In addition to the aforementioned F27 Work Conception (section 3.2), it provides entities and supporting properties for the creation of expressions (F28 Expression Creation), the carriers through which they are distributed (F32 Carrier Production Event), and even for when particular items are reproduced (F33 Reproduction Event).

3.6 Format/Media Type

As Table 9 demonstrates, MODSRDF/MADSRDF and Bibframe both provide property vocabularies that easily reconcile with the preconceptions of bibliographic traditions. They provide strong distinctions between a work's genre, media type, and physical format. FRBRoo opts for a more generic explanation by acknowledging that the abstract matter of works are only carried through the intervening abstractions of symbolic objects. FaBiO relies on the relatively narrowly scoped dcterms:format property to capture such information.

Table 9: Format/Media Type Properties

Ontology	Property/Entity	Property Range
MODS/ MADSRDF	modsrdf:genre modsrdf:locationCopy-Form modsrdf:mediaType modsrdf:physicalForm	madsrdf:GenreForm xsd:string
Bibframe	bf:format bf:genre bf:mediaCategory	rdfs:Literal bf:Category
schema.org	schema:bookFormat schema:genre	xsd:url xsd:string schema:BookFormat-Type
FRBRoo	P128 carries	E90 Symbolic Object
BIBO	dcterms:format rdf:type	xsd:string bibo:Document
FaBiO	fabio:hasFormat dcterms:format	xsd:string

The schema.org ontology and BIBO (unlike MODSRDF/-MADSRDF, Bibframe, FRBRoo, and FaBio) follow the linked data practice of naming entity types. In the case of BIBO, while it also uses the dcterms:format property to record certain aspects of format, genre, and type, it also provides a rich

vocabulary of named categories for different kinds of documents, including bibo:Article, bibo:Book, bibo:DocumentPart, and bibo:LegalDocument, among others.

Of particular interest for the HTRC's purposes is bibo:DocumentPart, which provides an granular means for identifying sections of text (such as chapters). This particular entity type coincides with the kinds of granularity that meets the needs of humanities scholars [3]. The schema.org ontology provides similar functionality through the use of the property-entity pair schema:bookFormat - schema:BookFormatType and by providing an even broader range of work entity types by including things such as blogs, clips, datasets, music playlists, etc.

3.7 Identifier/Inventory Control Name

Identifiers showcase the similarities between the ontologies (Table 10). Whilst MODSRDF/MADSRDF, BIBO, and FaBiO opt to express identifiers using string literals, FRBRoo, schema.org, and Bibframe offer much more informative options. In FRBRoo's case, it utilizes a class and property from the CIDOC-CRM [2].

Table 10: Identifier Properties

Ontology	Property/Entity	Property Range
MODS/ MADSRDF	mods:identifier	xsd:string
Bibframe	22 subproperties	bf:Identifier
schema.org	dependent on media type	
FRBRoo	P48 has preferred identifier	E42 Identifier
BIBO	bibo:identifier	rdfs:Literal
FaBiO	fabio:hasIdentifier dcterms:identifier	xsd:string

Bibframe provides a greater granularity of represented type, containing a total of 22 distinct subproperties for bf:identifier (each has bf:Identifier as its range). These are largely specific to bibliographic records (such as bf:isbn, bf:isbn10, and bf:isbn13) but include those of universal applicability (such as bf:uri, and bf:urn). For schema.org, the appropriate property is dependent on media type: books possess the property of having an isbn, clips have clip numbers, etc. Objects are considered to be resources in and of themselves, and each is associated with an additional identifier in the form of an URI.

3.8 Rights information

Table 11 showcases how each of the six ontologies represents information about the legal rights that pertain to a work. As the properties named in the table demonstrate, copyrights are a central concern for bibliographic works and, each of the ontologies provides a means to record when such rights were first asserted. The two ontologies that come from bibliographic traditions (MODSRDF/MADSRDF and Bibframe) focus primarily on capturing and representing a particular date on which a copyright is asserted. The other four ontologies (schema.org, BIBO, FaBiO, and FRBRoo) all provide additional properties for recording who holds a particular copyright and what the scope of those rights are. Of particular utility is the broad characterizations that FRBRoo provides through the ability to assert when something

Table 11: Rights Information Properties

Ontology	Property/Entity	Property Range
MODS/MADSRDF	modsrdf:dateOfCopyright	modsrdf:ModsResource
Bibframe	bf:copyrightDate	rdfs:Literal
schema.org	schema:accessibilityControl schema:copyrightHolder schema:copyrightYear	xsd:string schema:Person schema:Organization xsd:integer
FRBRoo	P104 is subject to P105 right held by	E30 Right E39 Actor
BIBO	dcterms:rights	xsd:string
FaBiO	fabio:hasCopyrightDate dcterms:dateCopyrighted fabio:hasCopyrightYear fabio:hasRights dcterms:rights	xsd:string xsd:gYear

"is subject to [a] right" (P104 - E20) and when a "right is held by [an] actor" (P105 - E39). The schema.org ontology provides similar information (albeit more narrowly scoped to copyrights in particular) through its schema:copyrightHolder and schema:copyrightYear properties. It also singles out access control from other kinds of rights that might pertain to a bibliographic resource. BIBO and FaBiO both resort to the much broader dcterms:rights property to capture rights information.

3.9 Edition/Version

Table 12 demonstrates an interesting gap in the FRBRoo ontology. Despite providing a great deal of vocabulary that supports the construction of a highly detailed narrative of all of the changes that a work goes through as it evolves into a finished item, FRBRoo lacks the means to establish relationships among items, manifestations, expressions or works themselves. One might imagine that this is because FRBRoo's developers believe that the FRBR Group 1 entities can be used in this capacity. The notion of "editions" is rather problematic.

Table 12: Edition/Version Properties

Ontology	Property/Entity	Property Range
MODS/MADSRDF	modsrdf:edition	xsd:string
Bibframe	bf:edition	rdfs:Literal
schema.org	schema:bookEdition schema:version	xsd:string xsd:integer
FRBRoo		
BIBO	bibo:edition prism:edition dcterms:isVersionOf	rdfs:Literal xsd:string
FaBiO	fabio:hasEdition prism:edition	xsd:string

In the vernacular of LIS, "edition" can refer to things that are different manifestations of the same expression (e.g., a large print edition and a mass-market paperback edition) and sometimes we use it to mean things that are different expressions of the same work (e.g., Shakespeare's *Hamlet*

translated into German and Shakespeare's *Hamlet* translated into Japanese). Because it is frequently unclear when an edition is an expression of a work and when it is a manifestation of an expression, FRBRoo's inability to name editions and versions means is not always entirely clear or straightforward exactly what kind of FRBR Group 1 entity an assertion is being made about.

The other curious thing that Table 12 demonstrates is the rather wholesale abandonment of the linked data approach by all of the ontologies with regards to representing information that identifies particular versions or editions. It would seem that with regards to editions and versions only plain text strings can be used as descriptors. This seems like an ambiguous position to take with regards to bibliographic resources, and may be due to the confusing part-expression / part-manifestation nature of the things we call editions and versions.

3.10 FRBR Group 1 Entity Type

The two FRBR-oriented ontologies - FRBRoo and FaBiO - provide means of representing each of the Group 1 entities, but such FRBR-esque notions of entities are omitted from the ontologies that evolved from traditional bibliographic practices that predate FRBR. In fact, these ontologies lack much in the way of representation for Group 1 entities in general.

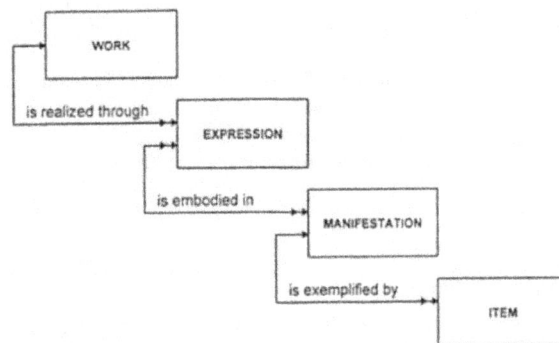

Figure 2: FRBR Group 1 Entities

Table 13 provides insights into FRBR's Group 1 entities. Based on the number of subclasses at the level of FRBR's Work (8 in FRBRoo, 29 in FaBiO, and 38 in schema.org) there seems to be a great deal of specialization taking place. More tantalizing is that while the amount of specialization in FRBRoo contracts at the more concrete entity levels (FRBRoo has 3 subclasses for expression, 1 for manifestation and 0 for items). The specialization of FRBR's Group 1 entities dramatically expands before just as dramatically shrinking in FaBiO (where there are 59 subclasses for expression and 4 each for manifestation and item). What is clear is that many of the communities felt that the Group 1 entities themselves possess sub-classes that frequently map to specific media types (e.g., Book, Blogpost, Video Recording, etc.).

The existence of the subclasses might not be so unforeseeable in and of itself, but the vast majority of sub-classes are for the more abstract Group 1 entities (i.e. Work and Expression) and is not a pattern that repeats for the more

Table 13: Representation of FRBR Group 1 Entities

Ontology	No. of Entities	Levels Represented
MODS/ MADSRDF	0	None
Bibframe	1	Work only
schema.org	39	Work only
FRBRoo	16	All levels
BIBO	0	None
FaBiO	100	All levels

concrete Group 1 entities. This may be indicator that the FRBR Group 1 Entities are not fulfilling the roles that the framework originally set out for them.

3.11 Language

The final category that we examined was that of language. Since the HT digital library's corpus has significant quantities of materials in languages other than English (only about 50% of the 14 million volume corpus is in English) and because computational analytics algorithms are language sensitive, HTRC scholars need reliable means for representing language metadata. As Table 14 shows, each of the six ontologies examined provide such a means. Four of the ontologies even provide methods to represent language metadata in the form of linked data.

Table 14: Language Properties

Ontology	Property/Entity	Property Range
MODS/ MADSRDF	modsrdf:language-OfResource	modsrdf:ModsRe-source
Bibframe	bf:language	bf:Language
schema.org	schema:inLanguage	schema:Language xsd:string
FRBRoo	P72 has language	E56 Language
BIBO	dcterms:language	xsd:string
FaBiO	fabio:hasLanguage dcterms:language	xsd:string

4. CONCLUSIONS

Despite the ongoing deployment of linked data sources, all of the ontologies demonstrated a reliance on string datatypes (i.e., xsd:string) rather than URIs linking to other resources. In particular the reliance on string data for descriptions and versioning information could be a redundant exercise when such information often exists elsewhere (e.g., a book description on Amazon, a play review on a blog post, an annotation of a critical edition, etc.). The semantic web [1], [9] affords vocabulary developers and communities with an easy means of sharing the burden of work needed to provide descriptions of all of their resources. Yet only Bibframe adapts the Linked Data / Semantic Web approach.

We were most surprised by the number of schema.org predicates that have string data as their range. That entities such as names and titles might be strings makes perfect sense, but the inability to link to external resources seems strange for a vocabulary with such a vast community base and that is focused on so ubiquitous of an activity as point-of-sale actions on the Web. One open question is whether

there may be copyright infringement risks involved the application of linked data, especially with regards to activities such as reusing descriptions (in text or through images) from external sources.

Collectively these issues cause problems for the HTRC and its scholarly users as they are limited by the metadata that can be made available and exploited by each of them. Both are limited by the extent of the resources available to them. Despite being more articulate than the HTRC's existing metadata infrastructure, all of the ontologies still possess gaps and idiosyncracies that make their application to the HTRC context a challenge. A highly granular event-based model like FRBRoo might provide scholarly users with a wealth of new information in the form of an overarching archival graph that describes the whole of the HT digital library's corpus, but such a graph is not guaranteed to be useful in and of itself for the selection and gathering of bibliographic resources for analysis. Vocabularies like Bibframe and schema.org may provide means for supporting search and retrieval infrastructure, but they lack some of the depth of more granular vocabularies (BIBO and FaBiO).

4.1 Summary of Findings and Recommendations

The six examined ontologies: MODSRDF/MADSRDF, Bibframe, schema.org, BIBO, and FaBiO share sufficient similarities to be comparable at least, and extensively overlapping at best. The extent of the equivalence between many of the considered classes, and the absence of the explicit assertions of that equivalence, are indicative of a trend in the contemporary practice of ontology development, and showcases a noticeable gap in the review (and reuse) of existing schema, vocabularies, and structures. The motivations for this may be those of prevalent research trends (supporting the creation of new models), insufficient documentation of existing ontologies (causing uncertainty regarding knowledge of the semantics, and preventing users from confidently asserting equivalences between models and their data), an absence of clearly defined and readily accessible best-practice guidelines recommending reuse of exiting ontologies where possible, or a lack of awareness of other initiatives.

Our recommendation for overcoming these problems centers on the identification of suitable classes and properties to incorporate into any underlying ontological structure based on an informed choice after careful consideration of existing alternatives. That is not to say that there are no justifications (particularly in the case of niche domains) for further ontology development — but this ought to be carried out as dictated by requirements as identified through a formal and systematic review.

To ensure appropriate and correct subsequent use, each design and development process ought to spend sufficient time documenting their choices. Ideally, this would include providing clarifying examples (see for example the scope notes at [2]) and using synonyms rather than re-using terminology (i.e., expanding beyond the description of "The name of the item" for the schema:name property).

Where equivalences between ontologies have been declared (see for example Table 11), we are presented with instances of precise ontological structuring (designed to capture very niche entities). However, this alignment is a double-edged sword: the benefit is tangible as an anchoring point to other datasets that have opted to use the generic rather than the (same) domain-specific ontology; the liability, in turn, is that many instances may correctly be captured by the generic, but have attributes and properties which are not true of the specific. Alignment might thus be more safely established by equating the class of the domain-specific ontology as a subclass of the generic. In this way, rather than risking the redundancy of the new class entirely, there is the opportunity to declare the new class as a specialist example of a more generic term. Again, easily accessible, comprehensible, and systematic documentation is key.

The next stage of ontology development may focus on designing overlapping high-level ontologies to bridge relevant and applicable classes from existing ontologies in order to meet the needs of a given dataset. This step makes the reuse of existing structures more likely, and promotes interdisciplinary data sharing via the adoption of common vocabularies and schema, rather than viewing each project as a niche requiring a bespoke and domain-specific structure.

4.2 Future Work

The five descriptive ontologies all provide a wealth of information that will ease the selection and aggregation of bibliographic resources into scholarly worksets (aka scholarly research collections) within the HTRC context. In particular the schema.org ontology is a good fit with the current state of the HTRC's technical infrastructure.

As the infrastructure continues to evolve to accommodate the selection and analysis of more granular bibliographic entities, making additional extensions to the HTRC's rich manifest of metadata will be necessary. In order for scholars to select chapters, sections, poems, and other arbitrary segments of a work, those segments need to be represented using fully featured descriptive metadata. The FaBiO ontology seems particularly well suited to the task, as it simultaneously captures extremely granular portions of text, but also provides vocabulary by which an account of the bibliographic resources as FRBR entities can be built.

This is not to say that narrative ontologies like FRBRoo have no place in the HTRC's infrastructure. Since new scanned images and improved optical character recognition data becomes available on a daily basis, the HT digital library's corpus of data is constantly renewing itself. Not only would FRBRoo provide a narrative of these changes but it would also serve as the nexus around which an event-centric view of the HT digital library's corpus can be built.

Application of existing bibliographic ontologies across multiple axes of the HTRC's infrastructure will allow both the HTRC and its scholarly users to realize a number of benefits regarding the generation of worksets for the creation of analytical data products. The use of ontologies such as FaBiO will enable the HTRC to further leverage existing data products (such as extracted features) as a means to provide metadata describing finer-grained bibliographic entities within the corpus, and open up a world of opportunity for scholars using worksets.

5. ACKNOWLEDGMENTS

We gratefully acknowledge the Andrew W. Mellon Foundation for their generous on-going funding through the Workset Creation for Scholarly Analysis + Data Curation project; the HathiTrust Research Center; and colleagues from the Early English Print in the HathiTrust (ElEPHãT) WCSA Prototyping project.

6. REFERENCES

[1] T. Berners-Lee, J. Hendler, and O. Lassila. The semantic web. *Scientific American*, 284(5):28–37, 2001.

[2] M. Bowman, S. K. Debray, and L. L. Peterson. FRBR object-orientated definition and mapping from FRBRER, FRAD and FRSAD (version 2). *International Working Group on FRBR and CIDOC CRM Harmonisation*, 2013.

[3] K. Fenlon, M. Senseney, H. Green, S. Bhattacharyya, C. Willis, and J. Downie. Scholar-built collections: A study of user requirements for research in large-scale digital libraries. *Proceedings of the American Society for Information Science and Technology*, 51(1):1–10, 2014.

[4] J. Furner. Information studies without information. *Library Trends*, 52:427–447, 2004.

[5] J. Jett, S. Sacchi, J. H. Lee, and R. I. Clarke. A conceptual model for video games and interactive media. *Journal of the Association for Information Science and Technology*, 2015.

[6] J. Lacasta, J. Nogueras-Iso, G. Falquet, J. Teller, and F. J. Zarazaga-Soria. Design and evaluation of a semantic enrichment process for bibliographic databases. *Data & Knowledge Engineering*, 88:94–107, 2013.

[7] T. Nurmikko-Fuller, K. R. Page, P. Willcox, J. Jett, C. Maden, T. Cole, C. Fallaw, M. Senseney, and J. S. Downie. Building complex research collections in digital libraries: A survey of ontology implications. In *Proceedings of the 15th ACM/IEEE-CS Joint Conference on Digital Libraries*, JCDL '15, pages 169–172, New York, NY, USA, 2015. ACM.

[8] S. Peroni and D. Shotton. Fabio and cito: ontologies for describing bibliographic resources and citations. *Web Semantics: Science, Services and Agents on the World Wide Web*, 17:33–43, 2012.

[9] N. Shadbolt, W. Hall, and T. Berners-Lee. The semantic web revisited. *Intelligent Systems, IEEE*, 21(3):96–101, 2006.

[10] D. Shotton. Comparison of bibo and fabio, 2011.

[11] S. L. Shreeves, E. M. Knutson, B. Stvilia, C. L. Palmer, M. B. Twidale, and T. W. Cole. Is 'quality' metadata 'shareable' metadata? the implications of local metadata practices for federated collections. In *In: Proceedings of the Association of College and Research Libraries (ACRL) 12th National Conference. Minneapolis, MN*, pages 223–237, 2005.

[12] K. M. Wickett, S. Sacchi, D. Dubin, and A. H. Renear. Identifying content and levels of representation in scientific data. *Proceedings of the American Society for Information Science and Technology*, 49(1):1–10, 2012.

Data Curation with a Focus on Reuse

Maria Esteva
Texas Advanced Computing
Center
Austin, Texas
maria@tacc.utexas.edu

Sandra Sweat
University of Texas at Austin
Austin, Texas
slsweat7@utexas.edu

Robert McLay
Texas Advanced Computing
Center
Austin, Texas
mclay@tacc.utexas.edu

Weijia Xu
Texas Advanced Computing Center
Austin, Texas
xwj@tacc.utexas.edu

Sivakumar Kulasekaran
Texas Advanced Computing Center
Austin, Texas
siva@tacc.utexas.edu

ABSTRACT

A dataset from the field of High Performance Computing (HPC) was curated with the focus on facilitating its reuse and to appeal to a broader audience beyond HPC specialists. At an early stage in the research project, the curators gathered requirements from prospective users of the dataset, focusing on how and for which research projects they would reuse the data. Users needs informed which curation tasks to conduct, which included: adding more information elements to the dataset to expand its content scope; removing personal information; and, packaging the data in a size, a format, and at a frequency of delivery that are convenient for access and analysis purposes. The curation tasks are embedded in the software that produces the data, and are implemented as an automated workflow that spans various HPC resources, in which the dataset is generated, processed and stored and the Texas ScholarWorks institutional repository, through which the data is published. Within this distributed architecture, the integrated data creation and curation workflow complies with long-term preservation requirements, and is the first one implemented as a collaboration between the supercomputing center where the data is created on ongoing basis, and the University Libraries at UT Austin where it is published. The targeted curation strategy included the design of proof of concept data analyses to evaluate if the curated data met the reuse scenarios proposed by users. The results suggest that the dataset is understandable, and that researchers can use it to answer some of the research questions they posed. Results also pointed to specific elements of the curation strategy that had to be improved and disclosed the difficulties involved in breaking data to new users.

Keywords
Data curation; high performance computing; distributed collections architecture; data publishing and reuse.

Permission to make digital or hard copies of all or part of this work for personal or classroom use is granted without fee provided that copies are not made or distributed for profit or commercial advantage and that copies bear this notice and the full citation on the first page. Copyrights for components of this work owned by others than the author(s) must be honored. Abstracting with credit is permitted. To copy otherwise, or republish, to post on servers or to redistribute to lists, requires prior specific permission and/or a fee. Request permissions from Permissions@acm.org.

JCDL '16, June 19 - 23, 2016, Newark, NJ, USA
Copyright is held by the owner/author(s). Publication rights licensed to ACM.ACM978-1-4503-4229-2/16/06...$15.00
DOI: http://dx.doi.org/10.1145/2910896.2910906

1. INTRODUCTION

Curation of specialized datasets obtained during multi-year research projects involve significant challenges both to the researchers that create them and to the data librarians that prepare them for preservation and publication. In this project, curation is broadly understood as the activities conducted to create data for a specific goal, and those involved in its organization, description, preservation and reuse. Researchers may wait until the research is finalized to organize and document their data, only to find out that these activities require more effort than expected, and that they need to refactor certain data creation processes to meet preservation and publishing requirements. In the case of data generated through research methods and conceptual frameworks that are only familiar to a small niche of researchers, librarians working in institutional repositories (IRs) may not have the domain knowledge to properly document it nor know which are the right venues to promote its reuse. For data that aggregates over time, currently, many IRs do not have the infrastructure to easily upload, store, and provide access to large data.

Evaluation of digital curation strategies is a multi-layered and complex process. Beyond assessing the elements of a curation program (e.g. metadata, data integrity, permanent identification, etc.) against best practices benchmarks, the impact of the strategy in relation to ease of data reuse is often evaluated after the fact, if and when the data is cited in a publication. This approach, which may entail years of waiting, is not necessarily a direct indicator of the success of the curation strategy, nor does it provide opportunities to learn what aspects of the strategy are not working and improve them while solutions can still be implemented.

We present the curation of a growing High Performance Computing (HPC) dataset in which curation tasks were determined based on best practices as well as from requirements gathered from potential users in relation to data reuse. The data is produced by a software called XALT [1], which tracks and collects information about applications used by researchers on open-science HPC systems, or supercomputers.[1] Development of the XALT software is supported by a federal grant, and the resultant data ought to be preserved and made publicly available. The case involved all the curation challenges mentioned above,

---

[1] HPC resources are also known as supercomputers.

which are generalized across data from various domains, as well as specific issues related to this particular data understandability and scope of content.

The research team involved curators from the project's outset. As members of the team, we could evaluate the project at an early stage, in which suggesting changes is expected and implementing them is easier to accomplish. This allowed enough time to learn about HPC concepts and to design curation tasks that were integral to the data creation workflow. A major part of the curation process involved seeking feedback from prospective users, as it became evident to the team that the questions emerging about how to curate the data would be best answered by those that would reuse the data. As a result, the users' responses informed the traditional curation tasks of organizing, documenting, and designing access and preservation strategies, as well as decisions to shape the content of the data. The curation solutions were incorporated in the open source software that generates the data, so they are available to all the software's users.

The feedback obtained from the users also helped to select the outlet for data publication, which led to a successful collaboration between The Texas Advanced Computing Center (TACC) and the Texas ScholarWorks IR [33]. We implemented a distributed collection architecture [14] that spans computational resources and policies from both organizations, within which data is gathered, curated, preserved, and published on a quarterly basis through an automated workflow. This facilitates the work of both parties, and leaves room to make improvements between data installments. Such collaboration can be replicated for future cases of large data that is generated: it can now be stored at a supercomputing center and published through an IR.

Targeted curation also led to the design of an evaluation strategy focused on data reuse. We used data mining and statistics to create proof of concept analyses following basic reuse scenarios suggested by the prospective users. Upon the analyses completion and interpretation, changes were implemented and published in the next data installment in a process of evolving curation. In fact, curation does not stop after data publication. The team continues improving the quality of the data and its documentation, conducting promotion activities to stimulate data reuse, tracking data use, and obtaining feedback until the end of the project's funding.

2. XALT: HPC TRACKING SOFTWARE AND RESULTANT DATASET

HPC resources are maintained by a handful of centers across the country with support from the National Science Foundation (NSF) [34]. Researchers in diverse domains, from Chemistry to Linguistics, and from Aerospace Engineering to Neurobiology log into the supercomputers remotely and at no cost to submit computational jobs. To run their calculations, researchers use community code applications, personal codes, or a combination of the two. Community codes are developed to solve general and specific computing problems, and they have a community of users and developers around them. Such codes are installed and maintained at supercomputer centers based on the needs of the users. HPC resources are shared by many users, and user submitted jobs wait in long or short queues, depending on how busy a supercomputer is at a given time. Because nodes and memory in supercomputers are finite resources, the community code applications installed on the systems must be selected by HPC administrators for continued use and maintenance to ensure optimal performance of the HPC resources. To understand

software usage and performance in HPC resources, NSF funds the development of metrics software, one of which is XALT.

The XALT software is used to support administrative and reporting purposes on selected HPC systems. The software is designed to generate data that can enhance understanding of the HPC users' software needs, identify areas for improving their computational work, and increase the efficiency of limited resources [1]. In its current version, XALT gathers information about parallel jobs run on HPC systems through Message Passing Interface programs (MPI) only, which records jobs that are run in multiple nodes. Another way to do parallel programming is using multiple cores in one node, but, XALT version 0.7.1 does not track the non-MPI executables nor does it account for the serial jobs that are run on supercomputers.

XALT is designed to be a lightweight software because it does not add time to the jobs that are run. Therefore, the resultant data has a precise scope. For example, it shows the number of hours an application runs on an HPC system, which could lead to targeted improvements for efficiency. Open XDMoD, a metrics portal, uses such data along with analysis and charting tools to help HPC administrators identify poorly performing jobs and make decisions about efficient allocation of resources [5, 23]. The data is also used to improve systems security by tracking the shared libraries to detect changes that may point to a hacked library [1]. HPC systems tracking also helps with cost analysis based on compute usage time and number of nodes in relation to overall operational costs.

In this curation project, the data is obtained from the open science HPC system Stampede [31], which is deployed at TACC. XALT is installed at the node level, and at the start of an MPI based parallel computational job it captures job-level information and environmental variables. The resulting information includes among other things, the libraries and executables used, the amount of time the job runs, and the number of nodes and cores used for each job [1]. All collected information goes into a local JSON file; then a script gathers the data and uploads it into a MySQL database located on a Virtual Machine (VM) in Rodeo, a cloud computing system that is also maintained at TACC [30]. The database is the core instrument to organize the data gathered from the computational jobs. The resultant data is dense in content, as it records every execution that is run on Stampede, which averages 1,000 per day [31]. It is also a growing dataset, registering computational activities for Stampede from the point of XALT's development by the end of 2013 until December of 2016, with a possible extension. As it is generated, the resultant data is being documented, preserved, and publicly shared on an ongoing basis.

The XALT software is open source, so all the curation tasks that are integrated to the data generation workflow will be possible in any HPC system where the software is installed. As part of the release is a program called createDB.py, which HPC administrators can use to build the schema into a MySQL database, as well as methods that push the data into the database.

3. RELATED WORK

Concepts and practices of data curation involving overarching library principles of data citation and data sharing [26], are by now widely spread in the academic community. So are the benefits of data curation implemented as a seamless workflow from the point of data creation [14]. However, more often than not, data curation happens at particular stages of a research project's lifecycle and involves different actors. In general, day-to-day data management falls in the lap of the researchers [14], and mostly at the end of the research project. Archivists and data librarians control the selection and storage of information, by methods of "reshaping, reinterpreting, and reinventing" as part of the curation process [27]. Reshaping of data extends to curation when considering issues of anonymization and potential reuse [17].

While data reuse is a major goal in curation projects, it is also elusive, as it is often not clear how to achieve it for particular datasets [6, 13]. Specifically, in the case of computational data, Borgman explains that, "Machine-collected data tend to be consistent and structured, and to scale well, but considerable expertise is required to interpret them" [4]. Others indicate that non-standard file formats used for computational data limit interoperability, human readability, and future use [26]. Indeed, curation practices are needed as an integral part of computational data publishing in order to facilitate interpretation and to exploit reuse [11, 19]. Difficulties with niche data extend to finding an adequate IR for preservation. Currently, there are only a handful of open HPC administration datasets available for public consumption. Examples include the parallel workload archives, published as part of work on parallel job scheduling, and the XDMoD portal, a hardware focused high level overview of computing systems [9, 23], none of which constitute a permanent OAIS compliant repository or publish data with consistent metadata [21].

Evaluation of digital curation strategies often involves benchmarks to assess one or more components of the program, such as: the sustainability of the file formats selected for curation, the stability of the repository, and the completeness of the metadata [10, 18]. As suggested by Faniel and Zimmerman, in this project, we derived curation strategies from data reuse requirements and from research scenarios suggested by prospective users [8]. Such requirements became the benchmarks against which we assessed the results and corrected the curation strategy. The degree of data visibility also affects data reuse. Methods of enhancing visibility include: associating published papers with data, enhancing and using different venues for metadata registry [3, 7, 11], and facilitating encounters between data producers and users [36]. Our approach to increase data visibility uses a combination of the latter strategies and tracks interest in the data for the remainder of the project.

4. CURATION STRATEGIES

As a first step the team, including researchers and curators, conducted a curatorial analysis of the overall project. For the curators this meant that we had to understand both the goals and processes involved in the research, as well as the scope and content of the resultant dataset. The analysis included learning about the functions of the data for purposes of managing HPC resources; and, knowing the workflow steps by which the data is obtained, its contents, the size it would attain by the end of the project, and understanding its reuse prospects. In turn, the researchers learned about the process of curation and agreed to incorporate curation tasks onto the data generation software.

As a result of the analysis we identified outstanding curatorial issues. Users would have difficulties transferring and downloading data, which by the end of the project will reach ~64 GB. Also, we needed to determine a data format to facilitate reuse for analysis purposes. Adequate documentation would be needed so the data would be comprehensible to non-HPC experts. Importantly, data had to be anonymized to preserve the privacy of those running jobs on Stampede, whose identification is

embedded in the data through their supercomputer accounts and the paths to the executables. Finding a permanent repository for the data was another challenge, as there are no computer science specific IRs available, and most open repositories do not normally take large, growing datasets [12, 33]. Given the narrow niche of the HPC administrative field, we considered the limited scope of the data for reuse. Upon concluding the analysis, we identified the need to complete the following curation tasks: a) document the dataset and enhance its understandability, b) expand its reuse scope, c) select a repository for its preservation and publication, d) decide the format, size and frequency of data distribution, e) integrate the processes of data creation and curation and automate the curation workflow, and f) evaluate the curatorial activities.

4.1 User Input on Data Reuse

Throughout the curatorial analysis recurrent questions were which, why, and how would users be interested in reusing this dataset [22]. We decided to seek guidance from prospective data users, for which seven researchers were recruited to answer questions and to provide feedback through the project's development. The selected group comprised of two HPC experts, two data scientists, and three social scientists. We contacted participants due to their expressed interest in the project and through referrals. While we understand that this is not a big pool of interviewees, we considered the very specialized scope of the dataset and the need to reach out to users with knowledge about the project or related interests. For example, expanding the use of HPC data to Social Sciences is a novel concept and it was not easy to find potential users for which this data would fit in their research. In fact, the social scientists we contacted had previously indicated to the XALT team that the data could be used to understand the human factors that influence computing practices. We did not pursue feedback from more HPC administrators because the data was created for HPC administrative use, so we knew that most of their requirements were being addressed. Interestingly, we later found that by pursuing curatorial changes to address social scientists we also helped HPC administrators.

Obtaining curation guidance involved finding out how users wanted to download and manipulate the data for analysis on different platforms (desktop, cloud, supercomputers, etc.) and using different software. It also included discussions about the research questions they expected to answer using the data. We designed a protocol with a few open-ended questions focusing on requirements for data reuse. The interview protocol is published along with the data in the IR [22]. The questions addressed the interviewees computing resources and tools for data analysis, to discover their needs regarding file sizes and format; data transfer modes and broadband; and, to schedule the frequency of data publication. We also asked the interviewees where they expected to find the data. Lastly, we asked them what and how would they use the data for to accomplish their research goals.

Through consensus of responses, JSON was selected as the format for data distribution, pointing to its readability by humans and machines, widespread use, robust documentation, and compatibility with the reported analytic software choices of the users. In terms of file size, most interviewees said they would use laptop or desktop computers to download and analyze the data, and the amounts they needed varied from a few thousand records, to individual months or over a year's worth of data. Other users were interested in analyzing the data in HPC resources, adding that the amount required would depend on the specific research question they wanted to answer. We thus decided to release compressed packages, each containing three individual monthly files of data per quarter, which would support the ample variation in requirements as well as easing download.

When asked where they expected to find the XALT data, interviewees said that they expected to find it via regular web searches and through links in the XALT project's website. HPC users said it would be easy for them to access the data directly from a storage resource that is accessible from other computational resources. Our access strategy, which we describe in section 4.3, incorporates all of these suggestions to accommodate users requests as well as to increase the visibility of the dataset.

Discussing research scenarios with the interviewees, the social scientists suggested that this data could be integrated with other data sources (e.g. online job postings) to identify changes in the software development industry, and to learn if academic development leads or follows industry. They also wanted to understand users' interactions with large computational systems over time and in relation to major events (e.g. weather emergencies), and study usage patterns to determine research cycles based on scientific domains.

HPC administrators wanted more granular information about how much time is spent in a library call and in the computing job to re-evaluate allocated run times. Such metrics could be compared across the network of supercomputing centers to identify optimized codes. HPC administrators also proposed analyzing the data to help long range planning for hiring staff at supercomputing centers and to create user-training tutorials. A software engineer amongst the interviewees said he would want to learn the frequency of use of the community code he developed. In turn, data scientists proposed using the dataset for teaching big data management, database systems, and data analysis using the Hadoop framework. As the curators received and evaluated the users' requirements, we decided to explore if the XALT data could be used to learn the composition of computational workflows. An additional element of the curation strategy was to expand the data visibility once published. Our data visibility strategies are described in Section 6.

4.2 Shaping Content to Address Reuse Scenarios

Understanding what users needed from and expected to do with the dataset was extremely helpful to curate its content. But, the curators in the team also had to become familiar with how users run jobs on HPC resources, what the XALT software does, and what each information element gathered in the data means. A major task was reviewing the information elements that would be part of the public data; and, include new ones to enable its application to the research problems identified in the data reuse scenarios. Studying the information elements included in the XALT data, we observed that some were redundant, others had obscure names that needed to be renamed for clarity, and others were idiosyncratic to the Stampede resource and would be of limited interest to general users. As we were becoming more familiar with the data and the HPC practices, we started preparing a data dictionary to clarify the meaning of the information elements gathered by XALT.

Stampede user names and paths to the users environments had to be anonymized for privacy reasons. It was decided that each user name would be replaced with a unique user identification number to enable analysis based on users. Applications written by users

and considered personal, some of which bear personal names, were also anonymized through the use of hashes.

A new information element, field_of_science, was integrated from the supercomputing center's administrative database. When researchers request time on HPC resources through a supercomputing center's portal, they select a field of science from a list including high level fields of science created by the NSF. We considered that this information would allow learning what fields of sciences use a given resource and what types of jobs are run, and which libraries are used in relation to that field. This information could help answer the research questions posed by social scientists and could also be useful to HPC administrators.

Knowing how users run jobs on computing resources was of importance to make data content decisions. Some users design computational workflows that include executing different community code applications in one job. In other cases, to complete a workflow, users run individual jobs because they need to evaluate results before completing the next step. To understand the composition of workflows, the curators suggested adding job_id information to the data. This element, whose inclusion was not originally planned in the research project, would allow grouping information about applications executed during individual jobs. We also decided to add two other information elements in the public dataset: start_time and run_time, which can be used to calculate a job's end time. Knowing when a job starts and ends would allow identifying if individual jobs are run consecutively by a same user and help infer if those constitute a connected workflow.

Up until the first data installment was published, the team worked on the XALT software side to create clean data: removing duplicate entries, fixing bugs in the job and libraries usage counts, and on files citing null entries.

4.3 Repository Selection and Access Strategy

In selecting an open repository we considered the need for ongoing delivery of data and evaluated which would be the best fit for the data's theme. Searching for Computer Science repositories in the Registry of Research Data Repositories (re3data) and in the Open Access Tracking Project did not yield results [25, 28]. As an alternative, we considered general topics repositories and looked at different DataVerse instances and at the University of Texas DSpace based Texas ScholarWorks. The repositories present varied features: from accommodating up to 1 GB or up to 1 TB of data, they offered different levels of customer service assistance for data upload and metadata entry, and in some cases required the payment of fees [12, 35]. After considering the different options, we saw the advantage of collaborating with Texas ScholarWorks as a publishing outlet [33]. While general repositories serve a large cross-space with little delineation to promote specific topics, it made sense for this data to be amongst other UT academic work.

In coordination with the repository librarian, we implemented an automated workflow from data creation and curation, to long-term storage and publication within a distributed collection architecture that spans multiple resources and policies across two campus organizations. The data is generated, processed, and stored in the HPC resources maintained at TACC, and the Texas ScholarWorks IR is used as a data access point, DOI landing page, and as storage for the data documentation. This solution addresses the limitations in storage space presented by the repository. It also facilitates data movement and analysis across national HPC resources connected through TACC for those users interested in analyzing the data in

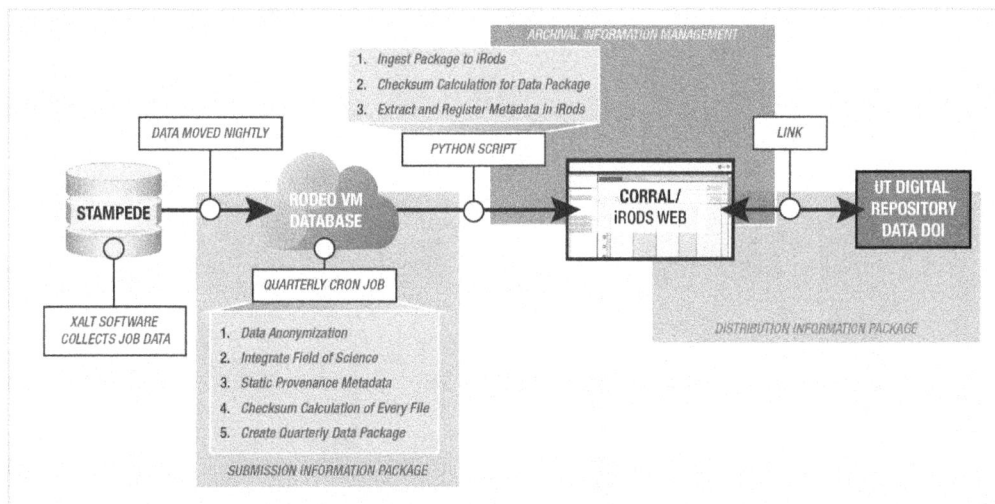

Figure 1. Automated curation workflow from data generation to publication mapped to the OAIS model.

supercomputers. In turn, data segmentation and compression facilitates download to and analysis in the users local computers. In addition, because of the evolving nature of the software development and curatorial work involved in this project, we required flexibility to make workflow adjustments between data installments and to explain those by amending the metadata when needed. The latter was easier to attain working with the local IR.

Importantly, the coordination with Texas ScholarWorks involved a commitment to comply with library standards. In designing the workflow, the stages and processes within the distributed collection architecture were mapped to the OAIS model as well as to best practices for data preservation. This collaboration, which was the first one of this kind between TACC and the UT Libraries, will be generalized to other large datasets that originate on and are stored in supercomputing centers and need to be published to an open repository.

During the interviews, the users mentioned that they expected data access from the software's public repository location and from the research project's page. Taking these suggestions, we cited the data with its DOI in the XALT software GitHub's page and on the XALT project page in TACC's website.[2] Note that the latter sites do not constitute permanent web addresses and may change.

4.4 Automated Curation Workflow within a Distributed Collection Architecture

The XALT data production and curation workflows are integrated and automated across different computational, cloud, storage, and publication platforms. Figure 1 provides an overview of the distributed collection architecture mapped to the OAIS model [15]. Data is gathered by XALT software on the HPC resource Stampede [31] and sent nightly to a database hosted on a virtual machine (VM) located on Rodeo, a cloud computing system also at TACC [30]. Inside the VM, a cron-job that specifies commands to run at the conclusion of every quarter invokes a script to query the database and writes out the three months of data in three individual JSON files. At the same time in the database, each username is converted into a unique string to anonymize the data, and the field of science table for every user is integrated from

TACC's computational accounts database. Provenance metadata, such as creator and publisher, are added to the resultant JSON files which are then hashed for authenticity and time stamped. A readme file recording the three hashes is produced and included in the quarterly package. Up to this point, a script in the XALT software completes the generation of a submission information package (SIP) that complies with authenticity and documentation standards. Therefore, any supercomputing center that uses the XALT software will have this method for producing curated data that they can submit to repositories of their choice.

In the workflow implemented on Stampede, the SIP is moved automatically to an iRODS instance on Corral, TACC's High Performance Storage facility [29]. Using the open source data management broker iRODS allows automating data management tasks through actions that can be initiated from any trigger within the distributed architecture [24]. In this case, when files are scheduled for ingest into the iRODS instance on Corral, a checksum is calculated for each package, and its metadata is extracted and registered on the iRODS metadata catalogue. Using one of the various clients supported by iRODS, curators can view, annotate, change and move or delete files on the storage resource if needed. This access is not available to public users, which can only download the package containing all the files. As an archival information package (AIP), data on Corral/iRODS is redundant and geographically replicated. The resource is monitored 24/7 by systems administrators, while the curators and researchers can focus on managing the AIPs. the Corral/iRODS resource is supported by the University of Texas System to provide reliable and permanent data management and storage services across the UT System [29], assuring that the data will be permanently available. The dissemination information package (DIP) consists of the quarterly data file with embedded dates and provenance information, the metadata dictionary, a catalog of the community codes, and the XML DataCite metadata file (See section 4.5). Thus, regardless of the amount of quarterly packages obtained by a user, the citation information will always be included in the DIP. In this way, the published data preserves representation and integrity information.

For dissemination of the DIP, the project uses the iRODS web interface such that files stored under this collection are automatically available on the open web for the general public to access. A link to the data exists on the Texas ScholarWorks repository, which is the landing page for the data DOI. The

---

[2] GitHub: https://github.com/Fahey-McLay/xalt
TACC: https://www.tacc.utexas.edu/research-development/tacc-projects/xalt

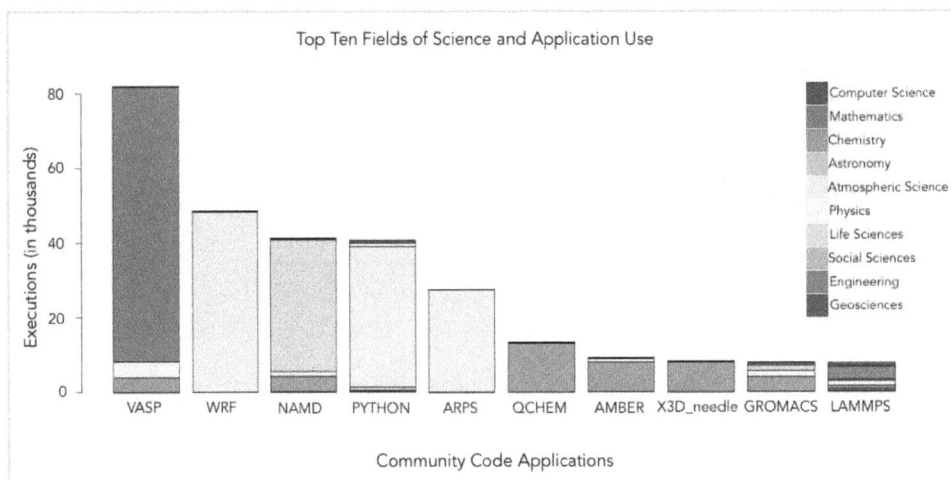

Figure 2. Distribution of users self-selected fields of science over community code applications for one year on Stampede.

landing page contains the project's Dublin Core metadata, another copy of the data dictionary, and a copy of the community code applications catalogue. Due to feedback from the interviewees, most lately we added examples of the proof of concept analysis to illustrate data reuse. Users can search for this dataset within Texas ScholarWorks, access it through its DOI from any available citation, and find it through web searches. Importantly, the distributed collection architecture complies with the functions of a trusted repository.

Creating this workflow involved significant work at the project's outset to identify and implement curation tasks, and improvements are in progress. The goal is to achieve a fully automated workflow to eliminate the need for manual curation. The data first public release was in September of 2015, but the workflow is still undergoing development, and will go into full production before the end of the grant in September 2016.

4.5 Data Understandability and Metadata

Project metadata, including a crosswalk between the DataCite and the Dublin Core schemas was created to publish the data in the Texas ScholarWorks and obtain a DOI [7]. We used the Dublin Core metadata application profile available in the IR to provide an overview of the project, explaining at a high level how the data is obtained and how it can be used [20]. The data dictionary explaining every information element included in the data is key to the dataset's understandability, as the variables recorded can differ in meaning within the field of Computer Science and are largely unknown outside the field [22].

We also created a community applications catalogue of identified community codes used on Stampede. Applications used in HPC systems are often developed by a community of users around scientific problems or domains. As such, they may be sustainable or may have a short duration depending on adoption, and there is no unified catalogue in which they are documented [22]. In the catalogue we point to the community applications projects so data users can learn about the domain that they serve and the types of computational issues they address.

5. CURATION EVALUATION VIA PROOF OF CONCEPT DATA ANALYSES

To evaluate whether our curation decisions were adequate to meet the users' research goals, we designed proof of concept analyses

that use statistical and data mining methods. We based the proof of concepts on basic premises outlined in the research scenarios introduced by the prospective users that we interviewed. Our goal was not to pursue their research questions, but to find out if the information elements selected for publication in the dataset are useful to the kinds of research that the users expressed interest in conducting. We also wanted to find out if the accompanying documentation was adequate to perform analysis on the data and interpret the results. The questions selected for testing are at the tip of more complex research problems, but have the elements to determine if the content of the dataset is adequately curated and identify areas for improvement. To evaluate the analysis results, we obtained feedback from the users that introduced the research scenarios.

Almost a year's worth of data containing 6,987,901 records for the period 2014/07 to 2015/06 was used. Each record in the data file corresponds to one execution of a particular application, so there can be multiple records with the same job_id. All executables that do not correspond to a community code application were filtered out. The final dataset used for the evaluation contains 130 unique executables, 1,868 unique users, 569,811 unique job ids, and 98 unique fields of science. For purposes of showing clear results on this paper, we consolidated the 98 fields of science into ten major fields, and considered only the top ten community codes in the analyses. The proof of concepts were conducted by one of the data scientists interviewed. To conduct the tests, he used Wrangler, the data intensive computing resource at TACC and made use of the data dictionary [32].

The first proof of concept corresponds to the inquiries presented by social scientists and was also useful to HPC administrators. It aimed to answer the following questions: What fields of science are using HPC? What applications do they use? How are those applications shared across different fields of science? The questions relate HPC usage patterns to scientific domains, and allowed evaluation of the integration of the NSF fields of sciences information.

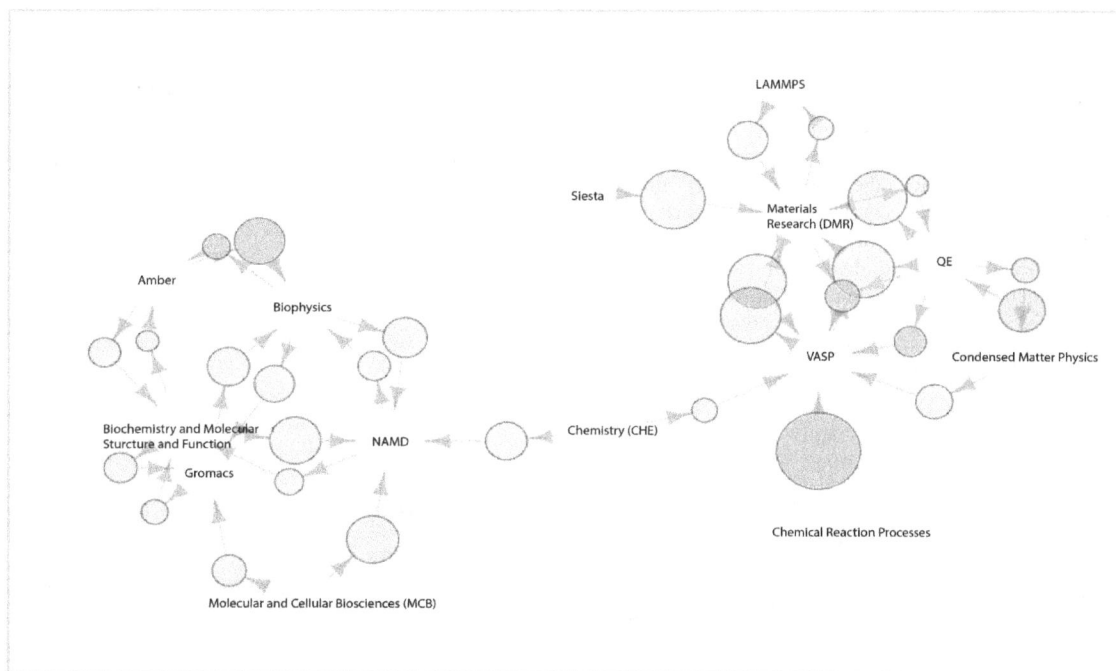

Figure 3. Visualization of association rule mining results showing inferences between fields of science and community code applications.

Figure 2 shows the statistical distribution of self-selected fields of science over the top ten community applications used on Stampede, expressed as number of executions in one year. The HPC experts that provided feedback observed that for the most part the results confirmed their intuition about the users, such as the field of Engineering dominates the usage of Stampede. At the same time, the possibility to mine bigger numbers of users and software exposed more granular information that was new to the administrators. They could now observe that applications that they considered domain specific such as VASP (Vienna Ab initio Simulation Package for Molecular Dynamics in Chemistry), Gromacs (for Biomolecular Dynamics), and LAMMPS (Large-scale Atomic/Molecular Massively Parallel Simulator for soft and hard materials Molecular Dynamics), are actually being shared across various scientific disciplines.

Results interpretation improved our understanding of the possibilities and limitations of the data. Concerning the heavy usage of Python, one of our interviewees said, "I don't know why Atmospheric Science is the top Python user. It's not wrong, necessarily, it just doesn't appear to come from any intuition I have about what gets run by whom on Stampede. We'd have to look into those cases to see if there's a common analysis package used by this community that is written in Python." Another user said, "The large volume of Python jobs might be explained by its use in connection to other executables, or as a tool for pre or post processing if done in parallel. Since Python is just the shell to run other scripts, there is not enough information to indicate what exactly it is used for." These comments helped us understand that the data cannot answer the question of how Python is used in the context of parallel processing using MPI.

Association analysis was used over the same data to understand the relations between scientific fields through the use of community code applications [2]. Association analysis can identify inference rules that can predict the occurrence of one set of variables based on the co-occurrence of another set of variables. The method consists of two steps. The first step identifies objects that commonly occur together as a frequent item set. The second step identifies inference rules among objects

based on their presence in the frequent item set. Figure 3 shows the most relevant patterns found in the data, the fields of science and applications are connected via directional links. One field might be linked to multiple applications and vice versa. The direction of the link indicates the inference from one to the other, and in most cases there are links in both directions between pairs. However, the strength of the inferences can be different for different pairs of objects and directions of inference. The size of the circle in the middle of each link indicates the strength of the inference, the bigger the circle, the stronger the inference. The most revealing pattern shows that users from the field of Chemistry use applications that are also commonly used by Biology and Physics users. The connection is not causal and is established based on executable usage by fields of science. It shows direct connections between field of science and executable, and potential indirect connections among executables. The results indicate that Chemistry users use both VASP (for Quantum Mechanics, Chemistry), and NAMD (Nanoscale Molecular Dynamics for Biophysics), with certain level of significant frequency, and that VASP and NAMD are also significantly used by users from related fields of science. Note that Chemistry users using VASP may or may not be the same users that use NAMD. Such connections are at the tip of understanding the interdisciplinary nature of the computational research conducted on Stampede.

Feedback obtained from one of the evaluators about this scenario referred to the field of science information element. The field of science list used in HPC centers was developed by the NSF and uses a general classification scheme. When users request an allocation on HPC resources they are prompted to select a high level term that relates to their research project. In looking at the results from Figures 2 and 3, the evaluator noted that the list may not always reflect with granularity the domain involved in a research project, and that in cases of multidisciplinary research, users cannot select more than one term. Given that we cannot easily and promptly make changes to the list, we made changes in the data documentation to clarify the field_of_science provenance and scope to our users (See section 5.1).

The second proof of concept involved learning about computational job patterns, useful to understand data provenance and for HPC administration purposes. While XALT software does not have a way of capturing the relation between computational jobs to changes in the data, the assumption for tracking relationships between subsequent computing operations or unique jobs seemed a first step towards a provenance framework in HPC. First we used statistical analysis to identify job patterns. A job is the series of calculations performed on a user's data. A user can submit one job with multiple executables or can submit multiple jobs, each containing a single executable, and each job submitted by a user is identified with a job_id. The results revealed that only 7.2% (41,083 out of 569,811) of jobs use two executables, and there are no known jobs with more than two executables. This shows that the majority of users prefer one execution a time. Jobs using two executables are dominated by the use of ARPS and WRF, both weather forecasting applications, in the same job submission (40994 out of 41083, 99.8%). Another interesting observation is that more than half of the remaining jobs with two executables (54 out of 89) use Python in combination with another executable.

We then used sequential rule pattern mining to identify patterns in the order of the executions for all the jobs run by each user. The sequence of executable paths used by each user was modeled as a list ordered by the starting time of each execution. The results showed that in most cases users run the same executable repeatedly. There are only a few outliers in which different executables are used in a particular order repeatedly. This may suggest a workflow where users use different executables sequentially to achieve a desired analytic result. One example of such pattern is shown as following:

[[VASP*], [QE*], [VASP*]]

The example shows that the executables VASP and QE – Quantum Espresso, are used in alternative sequences by some users. Both executables are popular tools for molecular structure modeling in material sciences, and share similar features and functionalities. The sequential pattern may indicate that users are trying to compare the performance of the tools, or they are attempting to use complementary features from both executables. The results provide interesting observations about how parallel jobs are configured, but more investigation needs to be conducted to corroborate the use of more complex workflows on Stampede. For example, users may wrap a workflow in a personal script and we don't have a way to know the contents of that script, as XALT does not capture this information.

We did not perform HPC specific analysis because this is routinely done by Stampede administrators and we rely on their reports to evaluate the reuse value of the XALT data. At TACC, the data is used to report the top applications and libraries used per month and per year. Also, the data is integrated into TACC-Stats (the center's statistical system) to help understand performance. TACC-Stats measures performance on each node at the start, the end and 10min intervals during a job run and the XALT database is mined to learn what executable is running in the job [23]. Using this data, Stampede administrators discovered which programs were causing delays on the resource's large memory queue and moved those jobs to regular nodes, significantly increasing the efficiency of the tasks [16]. After seeing the proof of concept results, the HPC administrators requested to conduct association analysis to observe connections between libraries, executables and fields of science.

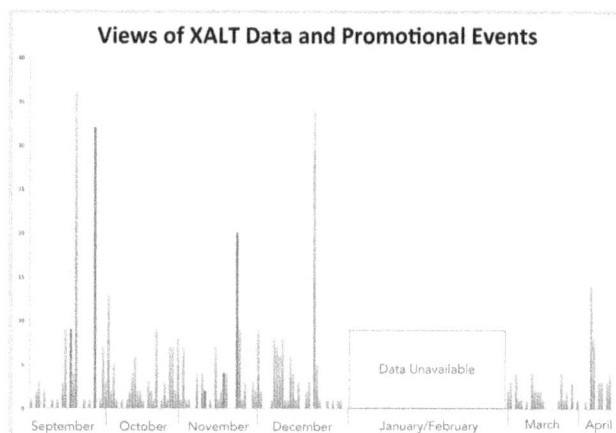

Figure 4. Dataset downloads from Corral/iRODS web-page.

5.1 Lessons Learned

As a result of the analyses we concluded that the curation strategy did expand the scope of the data, but that further explanations in the documentation were in order. To clarify the usage of the field of science information element, we added a description of its provenance in the Texas ScholarsWork landing page metadata and in the data dictionary. Suggestions by evaluators to provide images and descriptions of the proof of concept analyses as part of the data, suggested to us the complexities involved in breaking new uses of a dataset to the public. We incorporated this feedback by including a description and images of the proof of concept analysis in the landing page, obtained a DOI for the software, and furthered examples of data reuse by linking to and citing publications that refer to XALT.[3] In the next data release and in XALT announcements we will highlight the changes made in the documentation to elicit reuse for this niche dataset.

Visualizing the results of the proof of concepts provided a clearer understanding of how much we still need to know about HPC usage that the current version of the XALT data does not capture. We are in the process of writing a proposal to expand XALT to record other non-MPI parallel jobs as well as serial jobs. These changes will render data with more complete information about work and users on HPC resources.

6. TRACKING DATA VISIBILITY

To improve data visibility, we engaged in targeted promotion activities. An initial general promotion featured on the front page of the Texas ScholarWorks occurred with the publication of the data at the beginning of September of 2015. At the end of that month, we sent an email announcing the data public release to those who had expressed interest in the XALT software presentations at HPC events and had subscribed to its mailing list. Social scientists and data analysts were also included in these announcements based on referrals from colleagues that we interviewed. At the same time, we updated the different XALT project pages and included the data citation information.

To evaluate the results of this outreach strategy, we looked at the number of views of the landing page and the number of downloads of the data dictionary from the Texas ScholarWorks reports. Of course, we cannot track data downloads through IR

---

[3] GitHub: https://dx.doi.org/10.5281/zenodo.49772, TACC:https://www.tacc.utexas.edu/research-development/tacc-projects/xalt

metrics because the data is not hosted on the IR. After the beginning of the promotion campaign and for the first twelve days of October, we observed an increase of 12 downloads of the metadata and three data dictionary downloads. In parallel we started tracking data downloads using the aggregated server log information from the Corral/iRODS public web access page. Figure 4 shows the number of downloads from September through December of 2015, where the blue bars are day-to-day downloads and the red bars indicate downloads during a promotional activity.[4] The red bars in September belong to the first data publication and to email outreach activities. The red bars in November correspond to a presentation about the data at the 2015 Supercomputing conference and to Twitter announcements promoting the event and the release of the data. Throughout the promotional activities, the graph consistently shows increase in the number of downloads of XALT data the day of and after an event. The last significant increase in December does not correspond to a known event but to a single user downloading all the data packages. Instead, during the periods which we did not conduct promotional activities, we observed a decrease in data downloads. Overall, the results are consistent with those from the Texas ScholarWorks landing page in relation to data views and documentation downloads. The decrease in views during phases in which there are no promotion activities further demonstrates the value of the conducting outreach for niche datasets.

7. CONCLUSIONS

While data is becoming ubiquitous and IRs are emerging at a rapid pace, it is still not easy for users to find and to identify a dataset's uniqueness and reuse potential. This is exacerbated in the case of computational datasets with a narrow community of users. We curated a growing HPC dataset according to best practices and focused on the needs and suggestions of potential users. The latter led to targeted curation decisions in relation to content, format, and delivery choices to expand the data scope and facilitate its reuse. To overcome the limitations of manual curation we implemented the curation tasks as an automated workflow that spans multiple technical platforms from data generation to publication. Because we integrated the curation functions in the software that generates the data, this strategy can be replicated in other HPC resources. This workflow model can be used to curate large and growing datasets in collaboration between supercomputing centers and IRs or other publication outlets. However, when using a distributed collection architecture, making sure that the system complies with long-term preservation and access standards is key.

Curating data focusing on reuse entails having data creators, curators, and potential users go through the exercise of imagining what data reuse means for a particular dataset from the research project's outset. This strategy derived more focused curation activities and methods for evaluating impact. Data analysis proof of concepts were conducted to understand if the curated data could answer basic questions related to the potential users' research interests. The evaluation showed both the potential and the limitations of the curated dataset. While the data may not be useful to answer all the questions conceived by researchers, the data analysis results provided a flavor of how the data can be used to explore trends in computational research and interdisciplinary collaboration. But, most importantly for assessing the curation

strategy, it indicated how to improve the documentation, tested the precision of the information elements, and directed future improvements to the XALT data. Finally, tracking data views and downloads in conjunction with promotional activities suggests that those are important to increase interest in the data.

The project revealed complex interrelations between understanding a dataset, designing questions and analysis to reuse it, and interpreting its results. We learned that the proof of concept analyses including the response of the users to the results, enhanced our understanding about the possibilities and limitations of the data and how to improve its curation. We also found that changes done to cater the data to a broader public were useful to its regular users. While expanding the data use scope entails an involved process, curatorial time is saved by automating tasks that enable ongoing curation and publication as data is being generated. All of this highlights the importance of implementing curation strategies that can be tested in collaboration with users and throughout the research process.

8. ACKNOWLEDGMENTS

This research was possible through the National Science Foundation Collaborative Research Grant: SI2-SSE: Understanding the Software Needs of High End Computer Users, # 1339708.

9. REFERENCES

[1] Agrawal, K., Fahey, M., McLay, R., and James, D. 2014. User environment tracking and problem detection with XALT. *Proceedings of the First International Workshop on HPC User Support Tools* (Nov. 2014), 32-40.DOI=http://dx.doi.org/10.1109/HUST.2014.6

[2] Agrawal. R. and Srikant, R. 1994. Fast Algorithms for Mining Association Rules in Large Databases. In Proceedings of the 20th International Conference on Very Large Data Bases (VLDB '94), Jorge B. Bocca, Matthias Jarke, and Carlo Zaniolo (Eds.). Morgan Kaufmann Publishers Inc., San Francisco, CA, USA, 487-499.

[3] Arlitsch, K.and O'Brien, P.S. 2012. Invisible institutional repositories: Addressing the low indexing ratios of IRs in Google Scholar. *Library Hi Tech* 30,1 (Mar. 2012), 60-81.

[4] Borgman, C. L. 2012. The conundrum of sharing research data. *Journal of the American Society for Information Science and Technology*. 63, 6 (Jun. 2012), 1059–1078. DOI=http://dx.doi.org/10.1002/asi.22634

[5] Browne, J., DeLeon, R., Patra, A., Barth, W., Hammond, J., Jones, M., and Wang, F. 2014. Comprehensive, open-source resource usage measurement and analysis for HPC systems. *Concurrency and Computation: Practice and Experience* 26, 13 (Sep 2014), 2191-2209. DOI=10.1002/cpe.3245

[6] CODATA-ICSTI Task Group on Data Citation Standards and Practices 2013. Out of Cite, Out of Mind: The Current State of Practice, Policy, and Technology for the Citation of Data. *Data Science Journal* 12,0, (Sep. 2013), CIDCR1-CIDCR75. DOI=http://dx.doi.org/10.2481/dsj.OSOM13-043

[7] DataCite 2015. DataCite Metadata Search. http://search.datacite.org/ui

[8] Faniel, I. and Zimmerman, A. 2011. Beyond the Data Deluge: A Research Agenda for Large-Scale Data Sharing and Reuse. International Journal of Digital Curation, 6, 1 (2011) 58-69. DOI = http://dx.doi.org/10.2218/ijdc.v6j1.172

---

[4] The gap in the graph for the month of January 2016, reflects the logs purges, a common practice in systems administration which we failed to prevent.

[9] Feitelson, D., Tsafrir, D., and Krakov, D. 2014. Experience with using the Parallel Workloads Archive *Journal of Parallel and Distributed Computing*, 74, 10, (Oct. 2013), 2967-2982. DOI=http://dx.doi.org/10.1016/j.jpdc.2014.06.013

[10] Giaretta, D. 2007. The CASPAR Approach to Digital Preservation. *The International Journal of Digital Curation* 3,2 (July 2007), 112-121. DOI=http://dx.doi.org/10.2218/ijdc.v2i1.18

[11] Goodman, A., Pepe, A., Blocker, A. W., Borgman, C. L., Cranmer, K., Crosas, M., … Slavkovic, A. 2014. Ten Simple Rules for the Care and Feeding of Scientific Data. *PLoS Comput Biol. 10*, 4, (Apr. 2014), e1003542. DOI=http://doi.org/10.1371/journal.pcbi.1003542

[12] Harvard Dataverse Project 2015. *Dataset + File Management*. http://guides.dataverse.org/en/4.2.2/user/dataset-management

[13] Hey, T. and Trefethen, A. 2003. *Grid Computing - Making the Global Infrastructure a Reality*. West Sussex: Wiley.

[14] Higgins, S. 2008. The DCC Curation Lifecycle Model. The International Journal of Digital Curation 3,1 (July 2008), 134-140. DOI=http://dx.doi,org/10.2218/ijdc.v3i1.48

[15] International Organizational for Standardization. (2012). ISO 14721: 2012: Space data and information transfer systems – Open archival information systems (OAIS) – Reference model. Genève, Switzerland: International Organization for Standardization.

[16] James,D., McLay, R., Si Liu, R. Evans, T. Barth, W., Lamas-Linares, A., Budiardja, R., and Fahey, M. 2015. Tales from the trenches: can user support tools make a difference?. In Proceedings of the Second International Workshop on HPC User Support Tools(HUST '15). ACM, New York, NY, USA, , Article 2 , 11 pages. DOI=http://dx.doi.org/10.1145/2834996.2834998

[17] Jurczyk, P. and Xiong, L. 2009. Distributed anonymization: Achieving privacy for both data subjects and data providers. In *Data and Applications Security XXIII (Jan. 2009)*, 191-207. Springer Berlin Heidelberg.

[18] Kulasekaran, S., Trelogan, J., Esteva, M., and Johnson, M. 2014. Metadata Integration for an Archaeology Collection Architecture. *International Conference On Dublin Core And Metadata Applications (*Oct. 2013*)*. Austin, TX, USA, 53-63. http://dcpapers.dublincore.org/pubs/article/view/3702

[19] Lubell, J., Rachuri, S., Mani, M., and Subrahmanian, E. 2008. Sustaining Engineering Informatics: Towards Methods and Metrics for Digital Curation. *The International Journal of Digital Curation. 3,2* (Nov. 2008), 59-73. DOI=http://dx.doi.org/ijdc.v3i2.58

[20] Lyon, Colleen; Cofield, Melanie; Borrego, Gilbert; (2015): Reducing Metadata Errors in an IR with Distributed Submission Privileges; University of Texas at Austin. http://dx.doi.org/10.15781/T2KW2

[21] Management Council of the Consultative Committee for Space Data Systems 2012. *Reference Model for an Open Archival Information System (OAIS)* (June 2012). Washington, DC.

[22] McLay, R. and Fahey, M. R. 2015. *Understanding the Software Needs of High End Computer Users with XALT*. Texas Advanced Computing Center. Dataset. DOI=http://dx.doi.org/10.15781/T2PP4P

[23] Palmer, J., Gallo, S., Furlani, T., Jones, M., DeLeon, R., White, J., Simakov, N., Patra, A., Sperhac, J., Yearke, T., Rathsam, R., Innus, M., Cornelius, C., Browne, J., Barth, W., and Evans, R. 2015. Open XDMoD: A Tool for the Comprehensive Management of High-Performance Computing Resources. *Computing in Science and Engineering*, 17, 4, (July 2015)52-62. DOI=http://dx.doi.org/10.1109/MCSE.2015.68

[24] Rajasekar, A., Moore, R., Hou, C. Y., Lee, C. A., Marciano, R., de Torcy, A., Wan, M., Schroeder, W, Sheau-Yen, C, Gilbert, L., Tooby, P. and Zhu, B. 2010. iRODS Primer: integrated rule-oriented data system. *Synthesis Lectures on Information Concepts, Retrieval, and Services, 2*,1 1-143. doi:10.2200/S00233ED1V01Y200912ICR012

[25] Registry of Research Data Repositories 2015. *About re3data*. http://www.re3data.org

[26] Starr, J., Castro, E., Crosas, M., Dumontier, M., Downs, R. R., Duerr, R., … Clark, T. 2015. Achieving human and machine accessibility of cited data in scholarly publications. *PeerJ. Computer Science* 1, 1 (May 2015). DOI=http://doi.org/10.7717/peerj-cs.1

[27] Schwartz, J and Cook, T. 2002. Archives, Records, and Power: The Making of Modern Memory. *Archival Science*, 2, 1-2 (Mar 2002), 1-19.

[28] Tag Team 2015. *Open Access Tracking Project*. http://tagteam.harvard.edu/hubs/oatp/items

[29] Texas Advanced Computing Center 2015a. *Corral User Guide*. http://tacc.utexas.edu/user-guides/corral

[30] Texas Advanced Computing Center 2015b. *Rodeo: General Cloud Computing and Storage*. http://tacc.utexas.edu/systems/rodeo

[31] Texas Advanced Computing Center 2015c. *Stampede User Guide*. https://portal.tacc.utexas.edu/user-guides/stampede

[32] Texas Advanced Computing Center 2015d. *Wrangler User Guide*. https://portal.tacc.utexas.edu/user-guides/wrangler

[33] Texas Scholar Works 2015. Frequently Asked Questions. http://repositories.lib.utexas.edu/pages/faq#getting_started

[34] Towns, J., Cockerill, T., Dahan, M. Foster, I., Gaither, K., Grimshaw, A., Hazlewood, V.,Lathrop, S., Lifka, D., Peterson, G.D., Roskies, R., Scott, J.R., Wilkins-Diehr, N. 2014. XSEDE: Accelerating Scientific Discovery. *Computing in Science and Engineering*, 16, 5 (Sep 2014*)*, 62-74. DOI=http://dx.doi.org10.1109/MCSE.2014.80

[35] UTDR 2015. *The University of Texas Digital Repository: About*. http://repositories.lib.utexas.edu/

[36] White, E., Baldride, E., Brym, Z., Locey, K., McGlinn, D., and Supp, S. 2013. Nine Simple Ways to Make it Easier to (Re)use Your Data. *Ideas in Ecology and Evolution*, 6, 2 (Aug. 2013) 1-10. DOI= http://dx.doi.org/10.4033/iee.2013.6b.6.f

Unraveling K-12 Standard Alignment; Report on a New Attempt

Byron Marshall
Oregon State University
College of Business
byron.marshall@oregonstate.edu

René Reitsma
Oregon State University
College of Business
reitsmar@oregonstate.edu

Carleigh Samson
University of Colorado, Boulder
College of Engr. & Applied Sc.
carleigh.samson@colorado.edu

ABSTRACT

We present the results of an experiment which indicate that automated alignment of electronic learning objects to educational standards may be more feasible than previously implied. We highlight some important deficiencies in existing alignment systems and formulate suggestions for improved future ones. We consider how the changing substance of newer educational standards, a multi-faceted view of standard alignment, and a more nuanced view of the 'alignment' concept may bring the long-sought goal of automated standard alignment closer. We explore how lexical similarity of documents, a World+Method representation of semantics, and network-based analysis can yield promising results. We furthermore investigate the nature of false positives to better understand how validity of match is evaluated so as to better focus future alignment system development.

Keywords

educational standard alignment; semantic analysis; natural language processing; measurement; reliability

1. INTRODUCTION: STANDARD ALIGNMENT REVISITED

Providers of high quality digital learning resources hope that they will be used and reused by educators who are charged with helping students meet externally defined learning objectives called 'educational standards.' To increase dissemination and usability, learning digital libraries and other providers of learning resources want to align their materials to existing, and frequently changing, educational standards. The idea is to help teachers to quickly find relevant; i.e., standards-aligned items, in collections of learning resources as they prepare to teach their classes. Previous work has suggested that developing automatic techniques designed to identify promising alignments is difficult. While some automatic systems have been deployed, the measured accuracy of the resulting alignments has ample room for improvement. Key challenges include the difficulty of establishing a 'correct' set of alignments for training and testing alignment tools [2], quantity and variability in standards and standards sets ([9], [10], [6], [11]), and low agreement among human catalogers when the alignment concept is not decomposed into its various aspects ([2], [9]).

To assess the effectiveness of any automated alignment tool, one must establish what it means to be 'aligned,' and score against a gold standard collection of learning resources, standards, and known-good or vetted alignments. In previous studies, inter-rater reliability between human catalogers for document-standard alignments was shown to be a problem [2]. However, these IRR experiments treated alignment as a one-dimensional, dichotomous concept. Studying the dimensionality of the alignment concept, Marshall et al. [6] and Reitsma et al. [9] propose a multi-faceted interpretation of the alignment concept and explore this refinement as a way to combat low levels of agreement about alignment quality. In particular, teachers must consider both 'World' or 'Content' dimensions (topical or domain -related concepts), as well as 'Method' or 'Inquiry' dimensions (investigative and epistemological principles), when deciding whether or not a learning object is suitable for a given standard ([3], [7], [10]). We observe, however, that whereas previous; i.e., pre-2005 standard frameworks typically represented World and Method elements in separate standards, the current trend in standard setting is to integrate them into single standards ([1], [8]), thereby further complicating both the concept and the practice of standard alignment.

To date, the most comprehensive attempt at automated standard alignment has been reported by Devaul et al. [3]. They apply natural language processing (NLP) methods developed by Yilmazel et al. [14]. Their process of alignment includes the following sequence of NLP steps: sentence detection; part-of-speech tagging; lemmatization; separation of compositional and noncompositional phrases; recognition of special terms (temporal and numeral concepts, named entities, etc.); and categorization of named entities. They do not disclose how the alignment between learning resources and educational standards actually takes place, but they do observe that initial testing against a simpler "no-frills" tf*idf method showed only minor differences. They also find that their method exhibits between 28-51% precision but that precision drops precipitously beyond rank one (83%), and that their method performs better for World standards than for Method ones. Finally, they note that some of the mismatches between their method and the judgments of human catalogers could be the result of errors and/or omissions on the side of the catalogers. They do not, however, further pursue this aspect.

As an alternative or auxiliary to directly aligning between standards and curricular resources on the one hand, and trying to infer relevance from the structural and semantic similarity of standards across standard sets on the other, the feasibility of standard crosswalking – that is, inferring alignment in one set of standards based on alignments in another – has been explored; e.g., [7] and [11]. Results indicate, not surprisingly perhaps, that standard crosswalking can be successful if different standard-issuing agencies base their standard writing on a common source and/or a

Permission to make digital or hard copies of all or part of this work for personal or classroom use is granted without fee provided that copies are not made or distributed for profit or commercial advantage and that copies bear this notice and the full citation on the first page. Copyrights for components of this work owned by others than ACM must be honored. Abstracting with credit is permitted. To copy otherwise, or republish, to post on servers or to redistribute to lists, requires prior specific permission and/or a fee. Request permissions from Permissions@acm.org.
JCDL '16, June 19-23, 2016, Newark, NJ, USA.
© 2016 ACM ISBN 978-1-4503-4229-2/16/0…$15.00.

common approach. Standards written entirely independently by standard-setting agencies, however, exhibit such great variation in wording and abstraction levels that crosswalking them becomes very difficult. The current trend in standard writing to integrate World and Method aspects in single standards further complicates this.

Regardless of these difficulties, teachers as well as content providers would still welcome a reasonably accurate automated standards alignment tool. Teachers, because they typically look for resources which align with standards to which they must teach, and content providers because they want to help teachers and hence, pre-align their content. We offer that perhaps now is the time to try again for several reasons:

- The Devaul et al. work treated alignment as a unidimensional concept but the work by Reitsma et al. [9] indicates that it is not. Separating the alignment concept into multiple dimensions might improve results.

- Devaul et al. consider alignment a dichotomous variable. However, if we would allow for more nuance or different degrees or types of alignment, we might improve results.

- Work so far did not have a good gold standard for testing the results of automated alignment. However, the TeachEngineering.org project ([13]) has recently invested in a relatively extensive set of high quality alignments to NGSS standards ([12]) which might be used as a gold standard, thereby avoiding IRR problems.

- Although standard crosswalking has not been very successful, we might be able to use the information stored in standards involved in existing alignments as just one additional source of information for inferring alignments to other standards. Since one of us developed methods to employ multiple semantic facets within a collection and to leverage structural collection elements ([5]), employing these methods in the alignment process could yield good results.

This work describes our initial efforts revisiting automated standards alignment using a multi-faceted, multidimensional approach employing both World and Method semantics, by leveraging the text of existing aligned standards, and by employing the structural linkages in a collection of educational documents. Initial results are promising and shed some new light on the difficulty of creating a gold standard set in this domain.

2. TESTING PLATFORM

As our experimental data set we used learning resources from TeachEngineering.org, a digital library of 1,400+ K-12 STEM learning resources ([13]), and alignments of TeachEngineering resources to a subset of the Next Generation Science Standards ([8]), comprising 208 standards. All curriculum-NGSS alignment decisions were arrived at manually by no fewer than two independently working K-12 STEM teaching experts. Any discrepancies between alignments were reviewed by a third expert, whose judgement was then reviewed by both the original experts. Only alignments with 100% final agreement were included ([12]). This data set contained 1,902 NGSS alignments covering 1,208 learning resources aligned to 163 different standards.

Rather than testing our methodology on the complete set of TeachEngineering resources and its NGSS alignments, we chose to instead explore a small sample because it provides opportunities for detailed and qualitative feedback on alignment results from NGSS teaching and alignment experts. For our sample we selected all TeachEngineering resources with five or more NGSS alignments, supplemented with all resources residing on the same curricular units as these 'five+' aligned ones. This yielded a sample of 43 resources covering 26 standards and 137 alignments.

3. METHOD

Our intent in constructing our experimental tool was to explore how experts' alignment notions can be usefully employed in guiding automatic alignment computations. The base architecture of our alignment system is similar to previously tested approaches including: sentence detection, part-of-speech tagging, lemmatization, stop wording, and name entity recognition. Document similarity was computed based on tf*idf document similarity calculations over single-word terms and bigrams based on the lemmatized version of the words. However, several potentially useful variations were introduced including:

- We explored expanding and partitioning the lexical content of the resources. To leverage the potential value of existing alignments, we experimented with extending the text of resources with the text of standards included in known-good alignments from other (non NGSS) standard sets.

- We also subdivided resources into subsections: terms from the Learning Objectives sections were cataloged separately from those in the Keywords, Activity Materials, Activity Procedure, Attachments, Background and Prerequisite Knowledge sections.

- Finally, we generated a separate language model for Method terms which have been shown to represent a distinct and important component of the alignment process.

To identify Method terms, we employed two people who we asked to independently extract from the 784 NGSS standards those textual segments which they considered to express Method concepts and terms. Items from these two lists were then extracted if on average both raters tagged them as Method 75% of the time. After stop-wording, this resulted in a Method vocabulary with 326 single-word terms and 151 bigrams. Of these, the bigram design solution was the most commonly occurring bigram Method term, appearing 42 times in the 208 standards in our test set. Other examples with more than 10 occurrences include conduct investigation, interpret datum, provide evidence and apply scientific.

Previous work on the insight of domain experts suggest that structural linkages in a document collection, e.g., activities related to a lesson plan, and structural cues from standards sets, e.g., standards being 'near' each other in a taxonomy of standards, are useful in assigning alignments. To support this notion we implemented a methodology akin to importance flooding to adjust initial alignment scores based on term matching with additional information on linkages between resources and standards. This technique has been shown to be useful in matching educational concept maps ([4]) and was proposed and tested in other multifaceted matching tasks ([5]).

4. RESULTS

Although we have not yet systematically tested the many permutations of our various innovations, we explored a variety of them. Our methods suggested, on average, 33% of the 137 gold standard alignments within the first 10 suggestions, with our best runs exceeding 51% and the worst above 17%. After 20 suggestions our best runs exceeded 83% with a 49% average.

To gain insight into the cases for which our algorithm did not perform well, we submitted a sample set of 86 incorrect automatic alignments to TeachEngineering's master cataloger for review. These were all items that appeared in the top four suggestions from our algorithm but were not part of the gold standard set. The cataloger indicated that eight of the suggested alignments, even though not members of the gold standard set, should in fact be considered acceptable and proper alignments. An additional nine standards were judged as This is a good standard but it is not as good as the one(s) we chose. Another, 22 misalignments were judged, on review by the same cataloger, as Makes some sense but is worse than the one(s) we chose [for this standard]. In other words, the catalogers considered these standards as aligned but did not label them as such and hence, did not include them in the gold standard set. Additional recorded comments suggest that they only needed a handful of alignments for each standard, so if a given standard mapped to a larger number of learning objects, a higher standard of alignment would be needed to 'make the cut.' Adding that up, 45% of the supposedly incorrect alignments were actually not incorrect as much as they were less strong than the best alignments.

4.1 Interesting misalignments and possible ways to avoid them

Or expert judged that 78 of our alignments were not 'correct;' that is, were considered either incorrect or else inferior to the gold standard matches. We asked for both a categorical assessment and for free form comments which we attempt to summarize here.

World && Method ≠ World || Method.

In 11 of the 78 errant cases (14%), the automatically suggested resource was thought to be aligned to the standard either on Method or on World but not on both. This is a significant number reflecting the importance of multi-faceted semantics in this domain.

As suggested earlier, both World and Method alignments are important and newer standards, at least in general, combine some of each. The semantics of matching over two facets might be helpful in that more differentiated standards should provide more robust criteria. Many truly ambiguous alignments may now become more clearly wrong or right. But standards generally have few words. The average number of terms in the 208 standards used in our tests was only 27. After removing stop words there are few meaningful indicators left. We offer the following (random) examples for consideration:

a. Common Core Math, Grade 8: *Know that there are numbers that are not rational, and approximate them by rational numbers.*

b. Common core Math, high school: *Identify zeros of polynomials when suitable factorizations are available, and use the zeros to construct a rough graph of the function defined by the polynomial.*

Clearly, matching the World components of these standards seems quite possible, at least in principle. The terms *number, rational, rational number, factorization, polynomial, etc.* are likely present in resources covering these topics. The Method component, however, is almost entirely implicit. The only explicit components are *approximate* (as verb), *identify* and *use*; terms which are not likely on a stop word list, but which do require a lot of contextualizing before they start making sense. To make matters worse, in b. the Method is conditional, namely it should only be applied *when suitable factorizations are available.*

Semantic ambiguity. Certain combinations of standards and learning resources are quite sensitive to semantic ambiguity. For example, a term such as *solar* means something very different in the phrase *solar system* than in *solar energy* or *solar oven*. An example of this problem is the misalignment of the standard *Analyze and interpret data to determine scale properties of objects in the solar system. Earth's Place in the Universe* with a resource on solar energy. Since educational standards are typically short statements with only a few terms to 'hone in on,' ambiguity can seriously thwart alignment. We propose that one way of ameliorating this problem is by adding carefully chosen keywords to learning resources and/or standards. Devaul et al. ([3]) already noted that adding metadata to their learning resources raised precision.

Everything but the concept. Several misalignments where characterized by having good representation of all the terms in the standard in the resource; often even multiple times, yet the resource being about something different. While tf*idf specifically seeks to assess the degree to which a given resource is 'about' the concept represented by a term, balancing the relative frequency of that term in the resource against the frequency of the term in the collection as a whole, the expert reviewer judged that the main focus of the learning in the resource was not what was called for in the standard. This sentiment was expressed in choosing *Standard is covered but the learning objective of the document is different*. Of course, this could be either because the alignment tool was unable to properly focus on the main idea of the resource or because it was unable to find sufficient matching power in the terms in the standard.

Close but no cigar. Quite a few of the misalignments were caused by our method not picking up the central aspect of a standard, but instead honing in on other relevant but not central aspects. Consider, for instance, the following NGSS standard: *Apply scientific ideas to design, test, and refine a device that converts energy from one form to another. Energy.* The alignment we generated was rejected because "*The activity doesn't focus on the conversion of energy, although forms of energy (or sources) are discussed.*" Clearly, although the *conversion*(!) of energy is what is central here (at least from a World perspective), our computation did not, apparently give sufficient weight to the importance of the *conversion* term.

5. DISCUSSION

We essentially replicated the Devaul et al. [3] architecture using very similar NLP methods in an attempt to align K-12 learning resources with educational standards. We did, however, modify it so that we 1) can separately manipulate different dimensions of alignment, 2) can include different types of metadata, 3) used a different standard set (NGSS), 4) used a gold standard set of vetted alignments and 5) submitted misalignments for careful analysis.

Because our task formulation (find resources for standards given that different standards have different numbers of correct answers) does not correspond to the precision measure used by Devaul *et. al.* both our definition and metric of accuracy (percent of correct matches returned in to 10 or 20) are different from the one used by Devaul *et al.* However, our analysis of misalignments introduces new information which provides important clues for future direction.

- The gold of our gold standard is somewhat tarnished. Although it shines brightly with regards to precision, it is not nearly as good regarding recall. The analysis of initial misalignments uncovered significant numbers of alignments which could very well have been part of the gold standard but were not because the catalogers conducting the alignments that made it into the gold standard decided that they 'had enough' or had better ones, or simply missed them. Reviewing the method by means of which the gold standard set was developed ([12] we suggest that some of its omissions were caused by the developers working from resources to standards (teachers typically work in the opposite direction). Manually trawling a standard set in search of standards that align with a given resource is quite an exhausting activity and we should, in hindsight, not be surprised that some acceptable alignments were missed.

- We must recognize that alignment of education resources with standards is and remains a difficult task, even for subject and teaching experts. The integration of World and Method components in newer standard sets implies having to make difficult decisions when one or the other is missing in a resource. Developing tools to identify the Method elements of standards and learning resources in a way that can be employed in an automatic alignment system seems to be an important direction. While we have not as yet quantified the benefit of including such signals, we have proposed some elements of a way forward: identifying Method terms and employing similarity computations to ensure that multi-faced standards are matched adequately over both dimensions.

Since standards are such short, concise statements, typical bag-of-word methods encounter a 'too little grist for the mill' problem; *i.e.*, there simply is not enough information in those few words and terms to formally and without contextualization reach high precision.

We suggest two approaches to mitigate this challenge: inclusion of information on collection structure; *e.g.*, table of content information, in the alignment computation, and annotation of educational standards with additional terms to help with query expansion. Such query expansion techniques may require further work by subject matter experts to identify how method concepts in particular are actually expressed in learning object texts.

We also note that short-text similarity assessment techniques such as word embeddings may be of use in this effort. It may be that such tools can be trained to recognize and implicitly distinguish between method-focused and world-focused word pairs that occur within short proximities in matching texts.

6. REFERENCES

[1] CCSSI (Common Core State Standards Initiative). 2015. *Read the Standards.* http://www.corestandards.org/read-the-standards/

[2] Devaul, H., Diekema, A.R., Ostwald, J. 2007. Computer-Assisted Assignment of Educational Standards Using Natural Language Processing. *Proc. JCDL'07.*

[3] Devaul, H., Diekema, A.R., Ostwald, J. 2010. Computer-Assisted Assignment of Educational Standards Using Natural Language Processing. *JASIST.* 62. 395-405.

[4] Marshall, B., Chen, H., Madhusudan, T. 2006. Matching Knowledge Elements in Concept Maps Using a Similarity Flooding Algorithm. *Decision Support Systems.* 1290-1306.

[5] Marshall, B., Chen, H., Kaza, S. 2008. Using Importance Flooding to Identify Interesting Networks of Criminal Activity. *JASIST.* 59. 2099-2114.

[6] Marshall, B., Reitsma, R., Zarske, M. 2009. Dimensional Standard Alignment in K-12 Digital Libraries: Assessment of Self-found vs. Recommended Curriculum. *Proc. JCDL'09.*

[7] Marshall, B., Reitsma, R. 2011. World *vs.* Method: Educational Standard Formulation Impacts Document Retrieval. *Proc. JCDL'11*, Ottawa, Canada.

[8] NGSS Lead States 2013. *Next Generation Science Standards: For States, By States.* National Academies Press.

[9] Reitsma, R., Marshall, B., Zarske, M. 2010. Aspects of 'Relevance' in the Alignment of Curriculum with Educational Standards. *Inf. Processing & Management.* 46. 362-376.

[10] Reitsma, R., Diekema, A. 2011. Comparison of Human and Machine-based Educational Standard Assignment Networks. *Intern. Journal on Digital Libraries.* 11. 209-223

[11] Reitsma, R., Marshall, B., Chart, T. 2012. Can Intermediary-based Science Standards Crosswalking Work? Some Evidence from Mining the Standard Alignment Tool (SAT). *JASIST.* 63. 1843-1858.

[12] Samson, C., Reitsma, R., Soltys, M., Sullivan, J. 2015. The Relevance of K-12 Engineering Curricula to NGSS: an Analysis of TeachEngineering-NGSS Alignments. Proc. *ASEE 2015 Annual Conf.* ASEE.

[13] Sullivan, J., Cyr, M., Mooney, M., Reitsma, R., Shaw, N., Zarske, M., Klenk, P. 2005. The TeachEngineering Digital Library: Engineering Comes Alive for K-12 Youth. Proc. *ASEE 2005 Annual Conf.* ASEE.

[14] Yilmazel, O., Balasubramanian, N., Harwell, S.C., Bailey, J., Diekema, A.R., Liddy, E.D. 2007. Text Categorization for Aligning Educational Standards. Proc. HICCS 2007.

Research on the Follow-up Actions of College Students' Mobile Search

Dan Wu
School of Information Management,
Wuhan University
Luojia Hill, Wuhan, China, 430072
woodan@whu.edu.cn

Shaobo Liang
School of Information Management,
Wuhan University
Luojia Hill, Wuhan, China, 430072
johnmillie@foxmail.com

ABSTRACT

This paper focuses on the follow-up actions triggered by college students' mobile searches, which involved 30 participants conducting an uncontrolled experiment in fifteen days. We collected the mobile phone usage data by an app called AWARE, and combined with structured diary and interviews to perform a quantitative and qualitative study. The results showed that, there were three categories of follow-up actions and majority of these actions occurred within one hour after the initial search session. We also found that participants often conducted follow-up actions with different apps, and certain information needs triggered more follow-up actions. We finally discussed the characteristics and the causes of these actions, and stated further studies which include comparing follow-up actions triggered by mobile search and that of Web search, and building a model for the follow-up actions.

CCS Concepts

• Information systems→ Information retrieval→ Information retrieval query processing→ Query log analysis.

Keywords

Follow-up action; Mobile search; Search behavior; User behavior.

1. INTRODUCTION

Mobile search is more popular due to the rapid development of mobile Internet. The iiMedia Research Group studied the Chinese mobile search market in the third quarter of 2015, finding that 16.5% of mobile search users aged 18 to 25, and 26.3% of mobile searchers has college and above educations. College students are the main users of mobile search and extremely active searchers in China, understanding and studying their search activity is therefore of critical importance to search providers.

The study on follow-up actions triggered by mobile search can contribute to understand the relationship between mobile search and other actions, and the research can be applied to help search providers improve the recommendation of search results and enrich the connotation of search behavior.

This work focuses on two research questions:

• *What follow-up actions will be triggered by mobile search and what are the characteristics of these follow-up actions?*

Permission to make digital or hard copies of all or part of this work for personal or classroom use is granted without fee provided that copies are not made or distributed for profit or commercial advantage and that copies bear this notice and the full citation on the first page. Copyrights for components of this work owned by others than ACM must be honored. Abstracting with credit is permitted. To copy otherwise, or republish, to post on servers or to redistribute to lists, requires prior specific permission and/or a fee. Request permissions from Permissions@acm.org.
JCDL '16, June 19–23, 2016, Newark, NJ, USA
© 2016 ACM. ISBN 978-1-4503-4229-2/16/06...$15.00.
DOI: http://dx.doi.org/10.1145/2910896.2910921

• *What are the causes of these follow-up actions?*

We believe that it is important to answer these questions in realistic setting, so we conducted our study using naturalistic observation method. Our study lasted for fifteen days, and combined with structured diary and interview, in order to perform quantitative study and qualitative study.

2. RELATED WORK

Mobile search has been widely studied with the rapid development of mobile Internet. Researchers have carried out some studies based on large scale data analysis. They mainly focused on the diversity of queries [3], different topics searchers were interested in [1] and mixed language using in queries [6], and others.

Differences between mobile search and Web search aroused much attention, such as the category of topics, search time and location distribution by analyzing query length [3], query classification [7], as well as the time and location of searches [11]. Several recent studies focused on how searching cross multiple devices [9], and Sohn, Mori and Setlur believed that sharing user data is the way to achieve continuous search between different devices [10].

Mobile search sessions also played an important role in research. Several different criteria have been used to identify the search session, such as time, IP address, cookie [5]. The search process includes a series of activities, such as submitting the query and selecting the search results [4]. Kotov et al. found that mobile search could across multiple search sessions, from the view of search task [8]. Most of these researches are log-based, whose limitation is that user's motivation and intrinsic factor are not part of the studies.

Some commercial organizations have also studied the conversion of mobile search to actual activities. They studied the follow-up actions of mobile search from the perspective of types of actions, time expended for conversion and so on. Google, IpsosMediaCT and Purchased investigated consumer's search behavior and found that half of the mobile phone users would visit the store they had searched for, which is similar to the results of Teevan's study [12]. Google and Nielsen focused on the conversion of mobile search, finding that 73% of mobile searches will lead to actual activities, such as continuing search, visiting a website, sharing information, visiting the store, shopping, calling, etc. Neustar surveyed the cross-device search behavior and found that the conversion rate of mobile search was the highest, especially when users searched for local information. The method of network questionnaire or interview survey are mainly used, without the support of objective mobile usage data. These researches mainly focused on the connection between mobile search and consumption, while there is a lack of deep academic research on the follow-up actions of mobile search, especially for the specific groups like college students and the analysis of the causes.

3. RESEARCH DESIGN

3.1 Research Method

3.1.1 Data Collection

Concentrate on obtaining study data in the natural setting of the participants, with the aim to learn their real behaviors, we firstly investigated the search frequency, search habits and background information of college students through questionnaire. Then, we chose 30 college students who searched on the mobile at least once per day as the participants, this can ensure the adequacy of dataset. These participants include 9 males and 21 females, coming from seven universities and are majored in fifteen subjects, including linguistics, finance, economics, psychology and so on, and they are denoted as $P_{i\ (i=1,2,\ldots 30)}$.

Participants were asked to install the AWARE, an Android framework, on their mobile phones to collect mobile usage data without any intervention during the experiment. This ensured the integrity and reality of data. We also required the participants to fill in a structured diary every day to describe one mobile search with deepest impression. The structured diary mainly collected the information of mobile search context, like information needs, search motivation, location, etc., and weather the search process was interrupted and the search was successful.

After the experiment, we conducted an interview to investigate the influence factors of participants' mobile search, such as the reasons of changing apps. The structured diary and interview can support qualitative study.

3.1.2 Data Analysis

We used statistical methods to study the log dataset, which were mainly analyzed except for privacy including: (1) *Id*: the unique number of each record; (2) *Timestamp*: the time of keyboard input; (3) *Package_name*: the name of app used; (4) *Current_text*: the content of keyboard input. (5) *Is_password*: whether participants input the password, using binary notation.

In addition, we analyzed the contents of questionnaire, structured diary and the interview, combined with the certain examples to achieve the qualitative analysis for the causes.

3.2 Query and Search Session

In this paper, the *query* is defined as the content that participants input once, and recorded as $Q_{i\ (i=1,2\ldots)}$. The "*Current_text*" in dataset reflected the content of query. A *search session* is defined as a series of queries within 15 minutes submitted by a participant, and denoted as $S_{i\ (i=1,2\ldots)}$, as the most participants continuously used mobile phones for no more than 15 minutes in our dataset. Taking the relevance of the query content into consideration, we divided the 2875 queries requested from 30 participants in 15 days into 1781 search sessions, with 362 search sessions were impressed deeply by the participants in the structured diary.

3.3 Follow-up Action

We found that the participants did not immediately end their mobile searches. On the contrary, they took some actions related to the initial mobile search sessions.

Most of the participants said they would carry out follow-up actions in one day from the interview. So we defined these actions after the initial search session within 24 hours as the *follow-up actions* triggered by mobile search, such as making purchase after searching some food. Due to user privacy protection and limitation of AWARE, we can't identify other actions like calling, navigating the route, visiting certain places, etc.

We identified three categories of follow-up activities in this study. Figure 1 shows the examples of Continuing Searching, Making Purchase and Sharing Information.

P_i	S_i	Q_i	Time	App	Query/ Current_text	Controlled vocabularies	Unique controlled vocabularies in each search session
P_{11}	S_{841}	Q_{1349}	17:16:10	Xiaomi App Store	MIUI	mobile phone, operation system	mobile phone, operation system, mobile software
		Q_{1350}	17:17:35	Android Browser	MIUI root App	mobile phone, operation system, mobile software	
P_{11}	S_{842}	Q_{1351}	17:35:27	Android Browser	MIUI root caution	mobile phone, operation system	mobile phone, operation system

(a) the example of Continuing Searching

P_i	S_i	Q_i	Time	App	Query/ Current_text
P_5	S_{312}	Q_{514}	9:34:10	ele.me	pan pizza
	/	/	9:35:38	ele.me	*"I prefer tomato paste, please help me to put some more, thank you"*

(b) the example of Making Purchase

P_i	S_i	Q_i	Time	App	Query/ Current_text
P_{28}	S_{1686}	Q_{2732}	7:48:31	Android Browser	Lecture on cross culture
		Q_{2733}	7:51:05	Sina Weibo	Lecture on cross culture
	/	/	8:03:04	Sina Weibo	*"#Lecture on cross culture#The lecture will begin on 5pm at 301"*

(c) the example of Sharing Information

Figure 1. The example of follow-up actions.

4. RESULTS ANALYSIS

4.1 Category and Identification of Follow-up Action

4.1.1 Continuing Searching

According to the definition of the search session in section of 3.2, we defined the Continuing Searching as the action that a participant submitted one or more search sessions after initial search session. We identified 179 follow-up actions of Continuing Searching (86.89%). These queries might constitute several subsequent search sessions. Two methods below were used to identification.

4.1.1.1 Co-occurrence of Unique Controlled Vocabularies

We found that the participants would search for relevant information after the initial search session, so we explored the relationship between search sessions to determine the follow-ups of Continuing Searching. Co-occurrence word is an effective way to explore it. We mapped all queries to the controlled vocabularies or its super-verbs by the "Chinese Classified Thesaurus"(CCT), and deleted duplicate controlled vocabulary terms in each search session. If there were more than two same controlled vocabulary terms in the subsequent search session with the initial search session, it was considered to be Continuing Searching. As shown in Figure 1(a), there are two co-occurrence of unique controlled vocabularies between S_{841} and S_{842}. That is, S_{842} is a follow-up action of the Continuing Searching triggered by S_{841}.

4.1.1.2 Recurrence of Query

In the dataset, we also found that the participants submitted the same query after the initial search session within 24 hours, and they used the same app to search in some cases especially. This mobile searching with recurrence of query in the subsequent search session was also considered to be Continuing Searching. In our dataset, 23 follow-ups of Continuing Searching belonged to this type.

4.1.2 Making Purchase

Making Purchase (5.83%) is the action of buying goods after the initial search session, as shown in the Figure 1(b). We confirmed that participants made a purchase after initial search session by payment records from apps, purchase order and leave words on Shopping apps and the content from structured diary and interview. P_5 said in the interview he searched two stocks that he was interested in by entering the stock code (S_{341}, Q_{577} & Q_{578}) through Mobile Baidu and then made a decision to buy the stoc k of ICBC in thirteen minutes. The number of Making Purchase is close to the Google, IpsosMediaCT and Purchased's study on the American users (7%). All Making Purchase during the experiment were mobile shopping, this result reflects that the e-commerce and electronic payment bring convenience for college students. Absolutely, participants might visit the store after the mobile search, but we were not able to record these actions.

We also found that participants made purchase after comparing the different search results. This enables some applications, for example, the shopping apps can provide convenient services for users to comparing the different information to improve efficiency.

4.1.3 Sharing Information

The phenomenon of sharing information on the web, especially misinformation [2], has been studied. Sharing Information in this work is the action of sharing the search results to participant's social network through apps after mobile search, as seen in the Figure 1(c). The proportion of Sharing Information in our study (7.28%) is lower than the Neustar's research (18%). Similar to the Making Purchase, all Sharing Information were online, we couldn't record the actions if the sharing was through word of mouth.

This enlightens us that search engines can support users share the more complex results by some more convenient methods to optimize the search experience.

4.2 Follow-up Actions and Information Needs

In order to understand what category of information searched by the participants will trigger follow-up actions, we used the DMOZ, an Open Directory Project, to classify the needs of each initial search session into twelve first-rate categories and the respective subordinate categories. Results showed that the needs for Reference (26.21%), Shopping (17.48%), Computers (11.65%) and Arts (9.22%) triggered the majority follow-up actions, followed by Society (7.28%), Science (6.8%) and Recreation (5.83%).

The follow-up actions of Making Purchase were mainly triggered by the needs for Food (58.33%). This was largely due to the convenience of takeout food services, as P_5 said "*I preferred searching for takeout food because it was convenient*". While participants' more different information needs could trigger the actions of Sharing Information, such as Society, Science, Reference, Recreation, Computers, News, Health, Arts, etc.

We highlighted the Continuing Searching and discussed the main causes of it. First reason was that participants would continue the same search task to a deeper level after initial session by modifying the queries in the subsequent search sessions. For example, P_7

searched "*Can I return the alternative train ticket?*" (S_{380}). Due to disappointment about results, he continued to submitted "*Can I return the alternative train ticket immediately by 12306?*" (S_{381}). This reflected that their information needs were more clearly.

The second was that participants searched for information related to the initial search session or searched for something inspired by new information needs. For example, P_7 searched the "*feature spot in Suzhou*" and "*Humble Administrator's garden*" (S_{460}, Q_{746} & Q_{747}), after fifty-five minutes he continued searching other feature spots like "*Suzhou's moat*" and "*Songhe Building of Suzhou*"(S_{461}, Q_{748} &Q_{749}). P_{13} had searched for information about Recreation in the initial search session, while searched other information about Reference like Maps later.

The third reason was repeated searching, as described in the section of 4.1.1.2. Participants' search process might be interrupted for some reasons. P_4 said in the interview "*I wanted to know weather the China Post on the bayi road exist (S_{371}), but was interrupted by my friends, so I searched it later (S_{373}).*" Besides, they would use other apps to submit the same query as a result of dissatisfaction with the initial search results.

4.3 Time Interval

We analyzed the time interval between the initial search session and the follow-up actions. The *time interval* is the time difference between the beginning time of follow-up actions and the end time of initial search session. In our dataset, the follow-ups like Making Purchase and Sharing Information were all triggered by one search session, while Continuing Searching (26.26%) were composed of two or more subsequent search sessions. For these Continuing Searching with several sub-sessions, we counted the time interval using the sum of each time interval among sub-sessions, divided by the number for sub-sessions.

The results showed that the average time interval for the Continuing Searching is two hours and forty-six minutes, while the average value for Making Purchase (13 minutes) and Sharing Information (6 minutes) is shorter. The shortest time interval is only 15 seconds, on the contrary, the longest time interval is close to 15 hours. We found that these actions whose time interval were more than 2 hours because of a temporary interruption, or with "*less urgent*" information needs.

We analyzed the follow-up actions whose time interval are more than one hour, finding that these actions mainly triggered by information needs for Recreation. It is often about a plan or arrangement in the future, they didn't need to complete the mobile search immediately.

In general, the vast majority of follow-up actions (48.06%) occurred within one hour and 41.34% follow-ups of Continuing Searching occurred within one hour, which are both less than Google and Nielsen's research. The follow-ups of Making Purchase and Sharing Information were all triggered within one hour, higher than Google and Nielsen's research.

4.4 App Usage of Follow-ups

In this study, we found that participants often used different apps in the 62 follow-up actions. All Sharing Information occurred through different apps, 21.79% Continuing Searching and 66.67% Making Purchase used different apps.

We also found that if the participants used the search engine apps (34.65%) in the initial search sessions, there was more prone for them to use different apps later. They are followed by shopping apps with 18.81% and app store apps at 12.87%.

We use "A → B" to represent using different apps in follow-up actions. The data shown that *"search engine apps → social apps"* and *"shopping apps - search engine apps"* appeared the most. If participants filled *"not entirely successful"* or *"failure"* about the search, and said *"I'm willing to continue searching"* in the structured diary, the probability of using different apps in the follow-up actions is high.

Moreover, participants often compared search results from different apps, especially searching for information of Reference and Shopping category, such as Dictionaries and Beauty Products. P_{12} searched *"Backpack"* through Mogujie, a shopping app, and searched the same goods by Meilishuo to compare their prices. Participants preferred to select the best results from different apps.

5. DISCUSSION AND CONCLUSION

This paper classified the follow-up actions triggered by college students' mobile search, such as Continuing Searching, Making Purchase and Sharing Information, and introduced the definition and identification criteria of these follow-up actions. We studied the characteristics of these follow-up actions and discussed the causes of these follow-up actions.

Interestingly, there is a close connection between the follow-up actions and information needs. The participant's information need could change in the follow-up actions during a search task. These follow-up actions that triggered within one hour mainly were goal-oriented, we can also think so, these actions were purposes of their mobile searches. Besides, participants might use another app or several different apps in the follow-up actions, this mainly because the search results failed to meet participants' information needs, or participants compared different search results, or they did some other activities out of satisfaction with the search results.

Through the analysis of the dataset, structured diary and interview, we think that the feedback for the search results is the main cause for the follow-up actions. If they are satisfied with the search results, they may share some information or make purchase after searching immediately. Otherwise, they will continue searching by using different apps or modifying their queries.

Due to limitation of the AWARE and requirements of privacy protection, only follow-up actions occurred online were recorded and our categories for follow-up actions couldn't cover all follow-up actions from mobile search. Furthermore, the dataset can't be shared publically. We will continue focus on the follow-up actions triggered by mobile search and Web search, and build the model of the follow-up actions.

6. ACKNOWLEDGMENTS

We thank all the volunteers who participated in the experiment. This work was supported in part by Wuhan International Science and Technology Cooperation Fund (No. 2015030809020371) and Wuhan University Youth Fund of Humanities and Social Sciences.

7. REFERENCES

[1] Arter, D., Buchanan, G., Jones, M. and Harper, R. 2007. Incidental information and mobile search. In *Proceedings of the International Conference on Human Computer Interaction with Mobile Devices & Services* (Singapore, September 9-12, 2007). MobileHCI'07, ACM, New York, NY, 413-420.

[2] Chen, X., Sin, S. C. J., Theng, Y. L. and Lee, C. S. 2015. Why do social media users share misinformation?. In *Proceedings of the Joint Conference on Digital Libraries* (Knoxville, Tennessee, USA, June 21-25, 2015). JCDL'15, ACM, New York, NY, 111-114.

[3] Kamvar, M. and Baluja, S. 2007. Deciphering trends in mobile search. *Computer,* 40(8), 58-62.

[4] Daoud, M., Lechani, L. T. and Boughanem, M. 2009. Towards a graph-based user profile modeling for a session-based personalized search. *Knowledge & Information Systems*, 21(3), 365-398.

[5] Eickhoff, C., Teevan, J., White, R. and Dumais, S. 2014. Lessons from the journey: a query log analysis of within-session learning. In *Proceedings of International Conference on Web Search and Data Mining* (New York, NY, USA, February 24-28,2014). WSDM'14, ACM, New York, NY, 223-232.

[6] Fu, H. and Wu, S. 2015. Studying Chinese-English mixed language queries from the user perspectives. In *Proceedings of the Joint Conference on Digital Libraries* (Knoxville, Tennessee, USA, June 21-25, 2015). JCDL'15, ACM, New York, NY, 247-248.

[7] Kamvar, M., Kellar, M., Patel, R. and Xu, Y. 2009. Computers and iPhones and mobile phones, my!: a logs-based comparison of search users on different devices. In *Proceedings of International Conference on World Wide Web* (Madrid, Spain, April 20-24, 2009). WWW'09, 801-810.

[8] Kotov, A., Bennett, P. N., White, R. W., Dumais, S. T. and Teevan, J. 2011. Modeling and analysis of cross-session search tasks. In *Proceedings of SIGIR Conference on Research and Development in Information Retrieval* (Beijing, China, July 24-28, 2011). SIGIR'11, ACM, New York, NY, 5-14.

[9] Montanez, G. D., White, R. W. and Huang, X. 2014. Cross-device search. In *Proceedings of the International Conference on Information and Knowledge Management* (Shanghai, China, November 3-7, 2014). CIKM'14, ACM, New York, NY, 1669-1678.

[10] Sohn, T., Mori, K. and Setlur, V. 2010. Enabling cross-device interaction with web history. In *Proceedings of International Conference on Human Factors in Computing Systems* (Atlanta, Georgia, USA, April 10-15, 2010). CHI '10, ACM, New York, NY, 3883-3888.

[11] Ghose, A., Goldfarb, A., & Han, S. P. (2012). How is the mobile Internet different? Search costs and local activities. *Information Systems Research*, 24(3), 613-631.

[12] Teevan, J., Karlson, A., Amini, S., Brush, A. J. B. and Krumm, J. 2011. Understanding the importance of location, time, and people in mobile local search behavior. In *Proceedings of International Conference on Human Computer Interaction with Mobile Devices & Services* (Stockholm, Sweden, August 30- September 2 ,2011). MobileHCI'11, ACM, New York, NY ,77-80.

Routing Memento Requests Using Binary Classifiers

Nicolas J. Bornand
Los Alamos National Lab
Los Alamos, NM, USA
nbornand@lanl.gov

Lyudmila Balakireva
Los Alamos National Lab
Los Alamos, NM, USA
ludab@lanl.gov

Herbert Van de Sompel
Los Alamos National Lab
Los Alamos, NM, USA
herbertv@lanl.gov

ABSTRACT

The Memento protocol provides a uniform approach to query individual web archives. Soon after its emergence, Memento Aggregator infrastructure was introduced that supports querying across multiple archives simultaneously. An Aggregator generates a response by issuing the respective Memento request against each of the distributed archives it covers. As the number of archives grows, it becomes increasingly challenging to deliver aggregate responses while keeping response times and computational costs under control. Ad-hoc heuristic approaches have been introduced to address this challenge and research has been conducted aimed at optimizing query routing based on archive profiles. In this paper, we explore the use of binary, archive-specific classifiers generated on the basis of the content cached by an Aggregator, to determine whether or not to query an archive for a given URI. Our results turn out to be readily applicable and can help to significantly decrease both the number of requests and the overall response times without compromising on recall. We find, among others, that classifiers can reduce the average number of requests by 77% compared to a brute force approach on all archives, and the overall response time by 42% while maintaining a recall of 0.847.

1. INTRODUCTION

The Memento "Time Travel for the Web" protocol was first introduced in 2009 [17] and its formal specification was concluded in December 2013 with the publication of RFC7089 [16]. The protocol specifies interoperable access to resource versions, named Mementos, and consists of two complimentary components:

- A TimeGate (URI-G) associated with an Original Resource (URI-R) supports datetime negotiation - a variant on content negotiation - to allow access to a Memento (URI-M) for the Original Resource that was the live web version at or around a preferred datetime. That datetime is expressed in a special-purpose HTTP protocol request header.

Publication rights licensed to ACM. ACM acknowledges that this contribution was authored or co-authored by an employee, contractor or affiliate of the United States government. As such, the Government retains a nonexclusive, royalty-free right to publish or reproduce this article, or to allow others to do so, for Government purposes only.

JCDL '16, June 19 - 23, 2016, Newark, NJ, USA

© 2016 Copyright held by the owner/author(s). Publication rights licensed to ACM.

ACM ISBN 978-1-4503-4229-2/16/06. . . $15.00

DOI: http://dx.doi.org/10.1145/2910896.2910899

Table 1: Web archives covered by the LANL Aggregator

Abbreviation	Native - By Proxy	Included
archive.is	native	yes
archiveit	native	yes
ba	native	yes
blarchive	native	yes
es	by proxy	yes
gcwa	by proxy	yes
hr	by proxy	yes
ia	native	yes
is	native	yes
loc	native	yes
nara	by proxy	no
proni	native	yes
pt	by proxy	yes
sg	by proxy	yes
si	by proxy	no
swa	native	yes
uknationalarchives	native	yes
ukparliament	native	yes
webcite	by proxy	yes

- A TimeMap (URI-T) associated with an Original Resource (URI-R) provides an overview of all Mementos for an Original Resource known to the system that provides the TimeMap. For each such Memento, the TimeMap lists the URI-M and the archival datetime.

The Memento protocol can be adopted by web archives and resource versioning systems. At the time of writing, especially the former systems support the protocol either through native or by-proxy implementations. As such, it has become possible to uniformly interact with web archives in order to determine which Mementos a specific archive holds for a given URI-R (TimeMap component) as well as to negotiate access to the Memento for a given URI-R that is held by a specific archive and that is temporally closest to a preferred datetime (TimeGate component). In addition, in order to provide these same functionalities across archives, Memento Aggregator infrastructure has been introduced that provides TimeMaps and TimeGates that cover multiple archives.

The longest running Memento Aggregator infrastructure is operated by the Research Library at the Los Alamos National Laboratory (LANL). As shown in Table 1, it currently covers 19 archives[1], 11 of which are natively Memento compliant, and the 8 others are compliant via proxy implementations. The last column in the Table indicates whether an archive was included in the experiments described in this paper. This Aggregator infrastructure is leveraged to deliver end user web time travel services (e.g. Memento for Chrome[2], the Time Travel web portal[3], Mink[4]) and is also frequently used for research endeavors that require cross-archive lookups. The Aggregator received about 1.5M incoming TimeGate/TimeMap requests in March 2015, nearly 18.5M in October 2015, and over 50M in December 2015.

In essence, the Aggregator infrastructure accepts TimeGate and TimeMap requests and provides responses that reach across all covered archives. Generating a response requires issuing the respective Memento request against each of the distributed archives. Since doing so is predictably resource intensive and time consuming, an Aggregator Cache has been introduced. The cache has URI-R as key and cross-archive TimeMap information (URI-Ms and associated archival datetimes) as value. The URI-Rs that are covered by the cache are a combination of about 500K popular URIs retrieved from Alexa[5] in December 2014 plus URIs that were requested by users over time, for a total of about 1.2M.

On a recurrent basis, and in a background process, the cache is refreshed by re-polling all covered web archives for TimeMaps. TimeGate/TimeMap requests against the Aggregator for any given URI-R are served from the cache if the URI-R exists in the cache and the cache is not considered stale. For responses that can not be delivered from cache (i.e. cache misses), the following approach is currently taken:

1. A TimeGate response is generated by issuing a real-time TimeGate request against each of the Memento compliant archives, excluding by-proxy compliant ones. The exclusion is aimed at reducing response times and required computational resources, and is informed by the intuition that responses from by-proxy implementations will generally be slower than those from native ones. Depending on the application, all TimeGate responses are returned to a client of the Aggregator or only the response with the Memento that has an archival datetime closest to the requested preferred datetime.

2. A TimeMap response is generated by issuing a realtime TimeMap request against all covered archives, both compliant and by-proxy, merging all responses, and returning them to a client of the Aggregator. This approach may yield significant response times but aligns with the Memento protocol that emphasizes completeness of TimeMap responses.

2. PROBLEM STATEMENT

The use of a cache for LANL's Memento Aggregator and the heuristic introduced for handling TimeGate requests for

[1] Full archive names at http://mementoweb.org/depot/

[2] http://bit.ly/memento-for-chrome

[3] http://timetravel.mementoweb.org

[4] http://matkelly.com/mink

[5] http://www.alexa.com/

Table 2: Distribution of the cached URI-R across archives

k	# URI-R stored by k archives	In %
0	270,495	22.17
1	407,998	33.44
2	323,596	26.52
3	120,829	9.90
4	53,212	4.36
5	25,947	2.12
6	11,819	0.97
7-19	6,100	0.50

URI-Rs that are not cached are indicative of a general challenge related to operating Memento Aggregator infrastructure. As the number of web archives increases, delivering aggregate responses becomes more challenging as there is a limit to the number of archives that can be polled when response times and computational costs for the infrastructure are a concern. But, equally important is appropriately handling the load caused by requests on the individual archives. This may not be a serious concern in case of the Internet Archive that has sufficient machine power to handle continuously high traffic from around the globe. But, other archives have more limited resources and sometimes even policies aimed at reducing traffic. For example, in recent Hiberlink[6] research, we experienced a daily cap on the number of requests from a given IP address imposed by the webcite archive. And, soon after the overwhelmingly successful launch of oldweb.today[7] in December 2015, several archives struggled with the load incurred by the service, leading to extreme response times and even a request from an archive not to be polled. For these reasons, Memento Aggregator infrastructures are in need of strategies that inform selective polling of archives instead of brute force polling of all archives. This consideration is supported by Table 2, which shows that 82.23% of URI-Rs covered by the LANL Aggregator have Mementos in 0, 1, or 2 archives only. Clearly, using a brute force strategy, many request are issued that do not return Memento information. But how to know which URI-R to look up in which archive? How to predict whether an archive has Mementos for a given URI-R?

Considering the limitations of prior work in this realm (see Section 3), we set out to explore whether a machine learning approach could be used to inform the decision as to whether a given URI-R should be looked up in a specific archive. Specifically, we conduct experiments in which we use the content of the Aggregator Cache to train one classifier per archive covered by the Aggregator. The training is based on features extracted from the URI-Rs stored in the cache and uses the TimeMap information contained in the cache that indicates whether an archive holds Mementos for that URI-R or not. Once a classifier for an archive has been generated, it can provide a binary response to the question whether the archive should be polled for a given URI-R.

If such an approach were successful in reducing the amount of distributed queries, it would be rather attractive from an operational perspective:

[6] http://hiberlink.org

[7] http://oldweb.today

- Unlike previously explored approaches, it does not require the involvement of third-party data as it is fully based on available cached data.

- As archive holdings, and hence the cached content evolves, classifiers can recurrently be retrained in off-line background processes without affecting overall Aggregator performance. In addition, since we generate the classifiers with fixed features types but dynamically selectable features and number of features per type, they can automatically adapt to a changing web archiving landscape.

- It can be expected that the negligible overhead that would be incurred by realtime querying all classifiers (a fraction of milliseconds) would by far be offset by the benefits of not having to query all archives.

The remainder of the paper is structured as follows: Section 3 provides an overview of prior work in this realm; Section 4 describes how classifiers are generated and details the choice of training features and algorithms; Section 5 provides an evaluation of the classifiers using a large dataset of URI-Rs that are distinct from those in the Aggregator cache; Section 6 summarizes our findings.

3. RELATED WORK

Optimizing Memento query routing has been explored in efforts that rely on archive profiling. In [4], profiles were created based on top-level domain (TLD) that recorded URI-R and URI-M counts per TLD for twelve public web archives. The results show that it is possible to retrieve a complete TimeMap for 84% of URI-R when using only the top 3 archives and in 91% of the cases when using the top 6 archives. This simple approach can reduce the number of queries generated by a Memento aggregator significantly with some loss in coverage. In [3] extensive profiles were created based on URI keys, generated from URI-Rs using various templating approaches. Doing so, they can successfully identify about 78% of URI-R to not be present in an archive by means of a template approach that requires storing only 1% of what would be required to hold all URI-Rs of the archive. Both [3, 4] ideally require obtaining URI-R index files from archives. Profiles could also be generated by sampling archives for URI-Rs, although determining an appropriate sampling approach remains a research challenge in its own right. While these research directions are interesting and promising, generating profiles is resource intensive, requires recurrent updates at unpredictable frequencies as archives evolve, and - in case of the index file approach - relies on the availability of third party data and, hence the willingness of those parties to share it.

Various efforts have used machine learning techniques to predict characteristics of a web page by merely considering its URI. The classification goals are wide ranging and include predicting a web page's topic [6, 7, 13], genre [2], pagerank [13], language [1, 8] or whether it has malicious content [5, 11, 14]. Certain URI feature classes perform better for some goals than others. The lexical features of a URI were successfully used to detect phishing attacks [5, 11, 14]. TLD has been used for language detection [1, 8] but results show that, due to the heterogeneous nature of domains like com and org using TLD only is not sufficient. In [13],

several token segmentation techniques were used to determine web page topic. The resulting classifiers perform well on long URIs but less so on typical web site entry points. An approach that includes the use of tokens has also achieved high accuracy in identifying suspicious URIs [5, 14]. For text classification, n-gram approaches are widely used and have also been applied for URI classification in combination with tokens for topic and genre classification [2, 6, 7] as well as for language detection [1, 8]. These efforts have achieved good results for their respective goals, and we build on their pioneering work. However, we apply their techniques to an entirely different task. As we embark on the research we are unsure whether it will be possible to characterize the respective archives by means of a limited set of features, especially since the holdings of many are highly heterogeneous, covering many languages, topics, and - in the case of on-demand archives - user interest.

4. BUILDING ARCHIVE-SPECIFIC CLASSIFIERS

For the purpose of our experiment, we use a dump of the content of the LANL Aggregator Cache, created on September 8th 2015. It contains 1,219,999 distinct cached URI-Rs for which a total of 239,753,370 URI-Ms are known. Table 3 shows the number of cached URI-Rs for each archive as well as the number of cached URI-Rs for which an archive is the only one to hold Mementos. The Table shows that for 2 of the archives covered by the Aggregator (nara, si), the cache contains no URI-M at all. As a result, these archives are not included in the experiments as no training data is available for them (see Table 1). As can also be seen, for a large majority of URI-R, the Internet Archive (ia) holds Mementos. This observation is aligned both with prior findings and popular knowledge. As any sensible cross-archive lookup strategy would always include the Internet Archive, we decide not to train a classifier for this archive but rather to consistently perform a lookup, the equivalent to having a classifier that returns a positive, irrespective of the requested URI. Overall, the Table clearly illustrates the value of looking beyond the Internet Archive when in need of a comprehensive overview of Memento holdings.

To visualize the performance of the archive-specific classifiers, we use Receiver Operating Characteristic (ROC) curves [15]. Figure 1 illustrates the specific meaning of these curves for the case of routing Memento requests to an archive. In ROC curves, the x-axis represents the False Positive Rate (FPR) and the y-axis the True Positive Rate (TPR). When requesting a prediction from a trained classifier, a specific (TPR,FPR) pair is chosen on the curve that corresponds with the compromise that is most acceptable for a given application. Throughout the paper, we present ROC curves for two archives: the left hand plots are for archiveit that holds Mementos for a significant number of cached URI-R, and the right hand plots are for gcwa that holds Mementos for only a small number. To support a complete understanding, the ROC curves for all archives and all experiments are available[8]. To generate our classifiers, we use Apache Spark MLlib version 1.5.1 (scala)[9] on a MacBook Pro, 2.7 Ghz i7, 16GB 1600Mhz DDR3 and use 10-fold cross-validation to train.

---

[8] http://mementoweb.org/demo/aggregator_learning/
[9] https://spark.apache.org/mllib/

Table 3: Distribution of the cached URI-R in the archives.

archive	#URI-R stored	#URI-R unique
archive.is	319,554	9,971
archiveit	168,286	1,498
ba	110,073	236
blarchive	21,300	659
es	4,170	50
gcwa	1,001	10
hr	1,245	0
ia	920,934	390,604
is	71,015	2,221
loc	150,882	1,012
nara	0	0
proni	3,946	8
pt	32,002	224
sg	3,247	9
si	0	0
swa	895	8
uknationalarchives	24,572	368
ukparliament	14	1
webcite	40,043	108

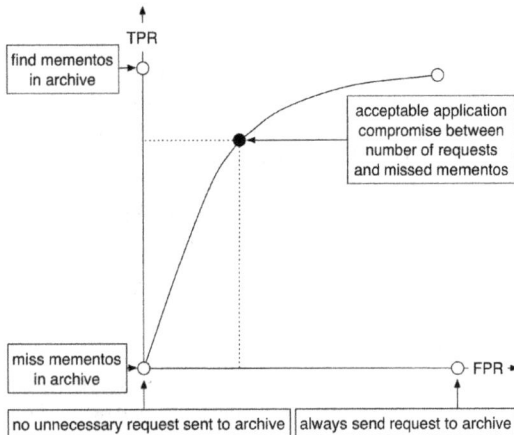

Figure 1: ROC curve for Memento requests to an archive

4.1 Selecting Features

Inspired by the aforementioned literature on using machine learning approaches for URI classification, we decide to use the following *count* features:

- The character lengths of the complete URI-R and of its host, path, and query components.

- The count of special characters (# / . ? - _ % = : $) in the aforementioned URI-R components.

Since the crawling policies of various archives differ, for example regarding depth of crawl, we expect these features to be relevant for our goal. Instead of using a Top Level Domain (TLD) feature as previous work did, we add the Public Suffix List domain[10] - *PSL domains* - feature to our arsenal. It consists of a binary vector with one entry for each considered PSL domain. The extension from TLD to PSL is

[10]List at https://publicsuffix.org/

guided by the observation that most archives cover the same popular TLDs. In addition, we decide to also add *n-gram* (n ranging from 3 to 7) and *token* features extracted from URI-Rs as these have shown to be successful for determining the language of a web page. Since, especially, national archives may be more likely to archive web pages in certain languages, our intuition is that these features should add significant discriminatory power. Full word extraction (tokens) present a challenge in our case as initial tests show that using dictionary lookups is unsuccessful, a result of, for example, the use of trademarks and concatenated words in URI-Rs. Hence, we decide on a simple approach that consists of generating tokens of length 2 to 10 by parsing a URI-R, removing common delimiters, and turning the resulting strings into lower case. Table 4 illustrates these features by means of an example URI-R.

Table 5 shows the features discussed so far, and, for each, the number observed in the set of cached URI-Rs as well as the maximum, if any. Since one of our goals is to incur minimal overhead by querying the archive-specific classifiers in realtime, it is not feasible to exploit all those features for classification. While we need not be concerned about the number of counts features, we do need to limit the number of PSL domains, n-gram, and token features. There are two aspects to the desired reduction:

- Selecting a method to rank features according to their discriminatory ability.

- Selecting the feature types to use, and, for each type, the maximum number of features.

Regarding the selection of ranking methods for features, we explore 4 metrics: the Most Common metric simply ranks features according to their frequency over the whole training set; Difference is the sum of the absolute differences between a feature's frequencies for URI-Rs stored by an archive and the overall frequency of that feature (as used by Most Common); Entropy [12]; and Gini impurity [9]. The latter two are widespread metrics for assessing the usefulness of a split when building decision trees.

To quantify how the choice of a metric impacts the resulting prediction, we select 1,000 features for the n-grams and token categories according to the 4 aforementioned metrics, as well as 1,000 randomly selected features, to be used as a reference point. We then train binary classifiers using the logistic regression algorithm. As the ROC curves of Figure 2 illustrate, we find that the choice of metric does not significantly impact the resulting classifier. We observe the same lack of impact of the choice of metric for classifiers generated for all archives and find that it relates to the significant overlap in choice of features for each metric. For example, we find that when it comes to selecting 1,000 3-gram features for archiveit, the smallest overlap in features is between the Most Common and Entropy metrics, which still share 563 features. Nevertheless, we find small performance differences, leading us to proceed with the Most Common metric for PSL domains, Difference for n-grams, and Entropy for Tokens.

Regarding the selection of types and numbers of features, we evaluate various scenarios for PSL domains, n-grams, and tokens. For each, we choose the respective metric resulting from the above described experiments, and, again, generate classifiers using the logistic regression algorithm to evaluate performance. Regarding PSL domains, we explore the

Table 4: Example of features extracted for http://www.dailymail.co.uk/science-tech/index.html

Type	Features
counts	len(url)=50, len(host)=19, count(., url)=4, count(., path)=1, ...
PSL domains	co.uk
3-grams on host	www, dai, ail, ily, lym, yma, ail
4-grams on path	scien, cien, ince, tech, inde, ndex, html
tokens on whole URI	www, dailymail, co, uk, science, tech, index

Table 5: Observed and maximum features per type

Features	Observed	Maximum
counts	36	36
PSL domains	1,600	7,834
3-grams	40,712	46,656 (36^3)
4-grams	345,988	1,679,616 (36^4)
5-grams	864,992	60,466,176 (36^5)
2-10 tokens	315,798	-
total	1,569,126	-

Table 6: Final features choice

Features Type	Number	Selection Metric
counts	36	Take all
PSL domains	250	Most Common
3-Grams	3,000	Difference
Tokens	2,000	Entropy

use of different numbers of features: 20, 50, 250, 500, and 1,000. Figure 3, top, shows the resulting ROC curves. They illustrate a pattern that occurs for all archives, namely that performance does not increase significantly by using more than 250 PSL domain features, which is the number we select. We next focus on n-grams and tokens and proceed as follows: first, we compare the different types of features (e.g. 3-grams, 4-grams, tokens) to see whether some stand out; next, we determine the number of features per type. We find that 3-grams and 4-grams perform best (Figure 3, second from top) and that a number of features between 2,500 and 5,000 is desirable (Figure 3, third from top for 3-grams, and bottom for tokens). After conducting more detailed assessments in the range 2,500-5,000, we decide to settle on 3,000 3-grams and 2,000 tokens. This is a somewhat arbitrary decision because adding more features further improves the predictions. However, the gains become too small to justify the additional computational cost. Table 6 summarizes the chosen features and respective numbers.

We conclude our exploration of features by assessing the performance of several feature combinations. As Figure 4 shows, we find that performance can substantially be improved by using 3-grams and tokens in addition to the basic (counts and PSL domains) features. Of all the variations we try, it turns out that basic combined with 3-grams and tokens extracted from the whole URI-R perform best.

4.2 Selecting Training Algorithms

So far, we have used logistic regression only as the al-gorithm to train the classifiers. Here, we assess the performance of different algorithms using the features selected above. We are specifically interested in algorithms that result in classifiers that have a low computational load and small memory footprint at runtime. Hence, we exclude algorithms such as Nearest Neighbors that require the availability of the entire training set at runtime. The choice of the Spark framework, selected among others because its ability to deal with extensive datasets, further limits the choice of algorithms to Logistic Regression, Multinomial Bayes, Random Forest, and Support Vector Machine (SVM) with stochastic gradient descent.

Figure 5 shows the ROC curves whereas Table 7 lists, per algorithm, the time required to train the classifier and to obtain 100K predictions. We find that Random Forest yields the worst results both regarding algorithm performance and prediction times; we therefore discard it. We find no clear winner among the remaining 3 algorithms. Their performance and runtime prediction times are very similar; the latter are negligible as anticipated. The learning times differ but are not a significant concern for our application because training can be done in offline processes. We proceed to train 3 classifiers per archive, one using each algorithm. In preparation of evaluating their performance (see Section 5), we need to determine the thresholds under which the classifiers must perform in order to achieve a targeted True Positive Rate (TPR). We initially rely on a subset of the cached entries, distinct from the training set, to determine these thresholds. However, when evaluating the classifiers on third party URI samples, we find that they are overly optimistic in the sense that they recommend too few lookups. We assume this is related to the nature of pockets of cached URI-Rs that share the same baseURL, a result of users looking up batches of URIs for a same domain. Hence, we bring in an external dataset of 100,000 totally unrelated URI-Rs extracted from log files of the Internet Archive covering requests issued on January 27th 2012. We use these URI-Rs to determine the threshold at which to query each archive-specific classifier to achieve a required TPR, and, for each archive, select the algorithm that yields the lowest False Positive Rate (FPR). We find that Logistic Regression performs best for 10 archives (archiveit, ba, blarchive, es, loc, proni, pt, uknationalarchives, ukparliament, webcite) and Multinomial Bayes for 6 (archive.is, gcwa, hr, is, sg, swa). The inclusion of this external data is somewhat of a setback since we had hoped to fully rely on cached data only. Nevertheless, we note that this dataset can be the same for recurrent classifier training as long as associated Memento information would recurrently be updated. Such information can be gathered using TimeGate requests, which are cheaper than TimeMap requests. Also, this information has shown to evolve slowly over time[10], making polling these URI-Rs

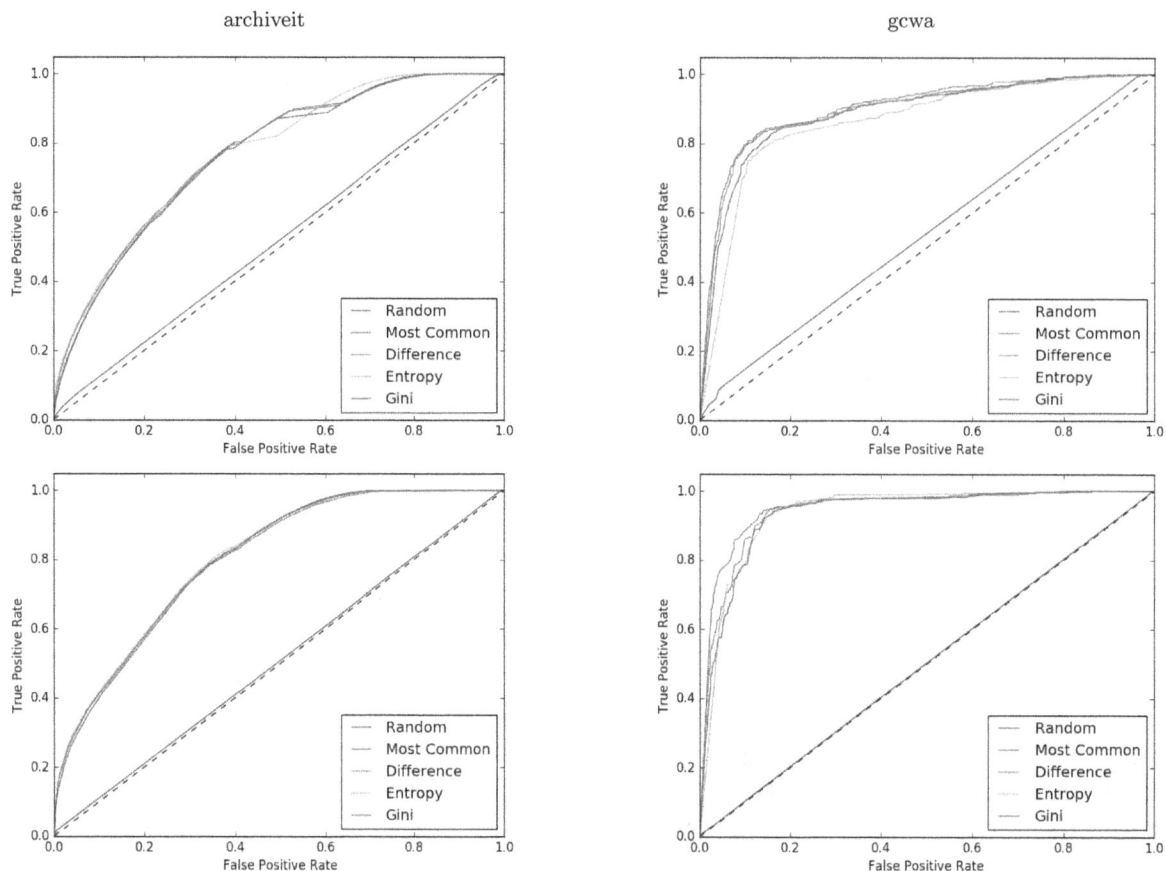

Figure 2: Comparison of feature selection strategies. Plots at the top: 1,000 3-grams. Plots at the bottom: 1,000 tokens.

Algorithm	Learning Time (s)	100K Predictions Time (s)
Logistic Regression	18.47	0.609
Multinomial Bayes	5.14	0.487
Random Forest	76.13	11.45
SVM	261.94	0.48

Table 7: Learning time averages over all archives and 3 runs

for each recurrent classifier training unnecessary, although this finding would need to be reconfirmed.

5. EVALUATION

Having trained the classifiers, we proceed to evaluate their performance using an unrelated datasets consisting of URI-Rs extracted from logs of oldweb.today covering 200,000 randomly selected requests issued in the week of December 14th 2015. We remove URI-Rs that are syntactically invalid, duplicate, already covered by our cache, or blocked by our adult-content filters. The resulting set has 187,449 URI-Rs. Since these originate from requests issued to a service that operates across archives, and are not covered by our cache, they are representative of the URI-Rs for which the Aggregator infrastructure would need to send distributed requests to archives in order to assemble an aggregate response.

To evaluate the performance of the classifier-based approach to sending requests, for each URI-R, we:

- Issue a TimeMap request to determine which archives hold associated Mementos.

- Query each archive-specific classifier to determine whether it advises a lookup in the archive or not. We query the respective classifiers at several FPR levels: 0.9, 0.8, 0.7, 0.6, and 0.5.

- Assess recall, computational cost, and response times using the obtained data.

We use the common definition of recall ($\frac{TP}{TP+FN}$), with TP being True Positive, and FN False Negative. To assess computational cost, we use the sum of the time it takes to poll each archive recommended by the classifiers for a given URI-R as this relates to the load on the Aggregator infrastructure and on the archives. To assess response times experienced by a user of Aggregator services, we take the maximum response time over the archives polled for a given URI-R. In order to avoid issuing hundreds of thousands of requests to archives, we simulate the response time for a given URI-R per archive. To do so, we collect 1,000 response times per archive. Table 8 shows the range of observed response times, listing minimum, average, and maximum. Then, for our computations, we randomly select with replacement - per archive and per URI-R - a response time from the 1,000

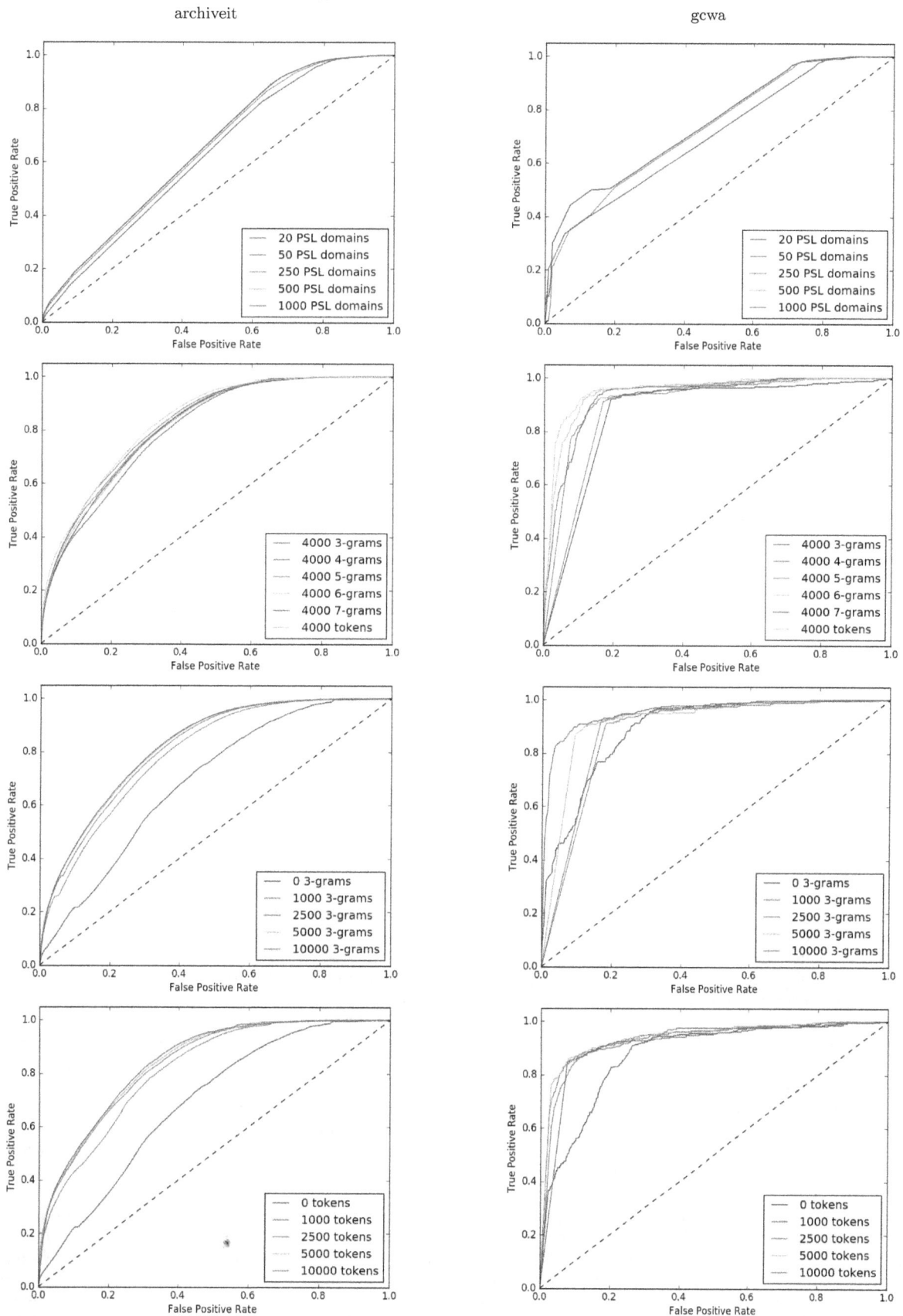

Figure 3: Comparison of number of features. Plots at the top: PSL domains. Plots second from top: n-grams and tokens. Plots third from top: 3-grams. Plots at the bottom: tokens.

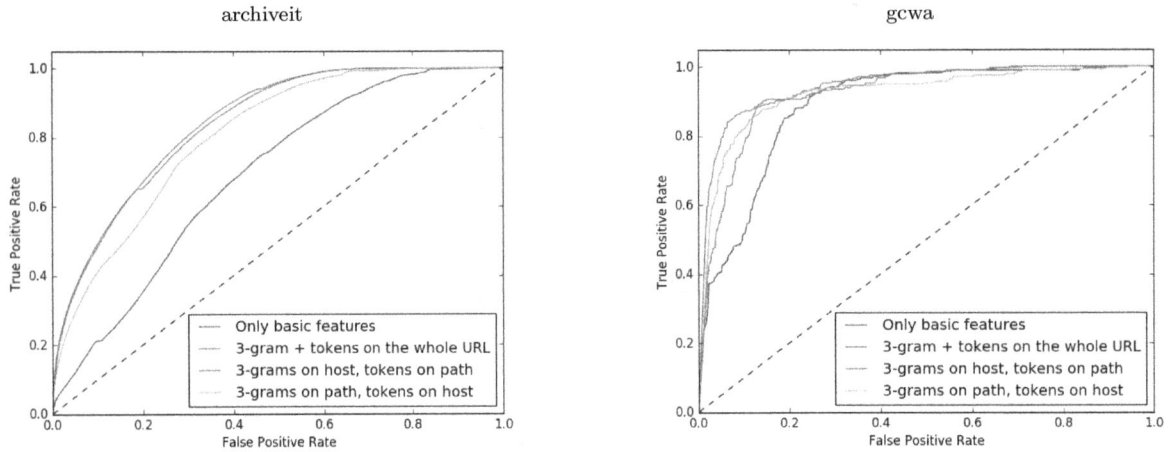

Figure 4: Combining basic (count, PSL domains), 3-grams, and token features

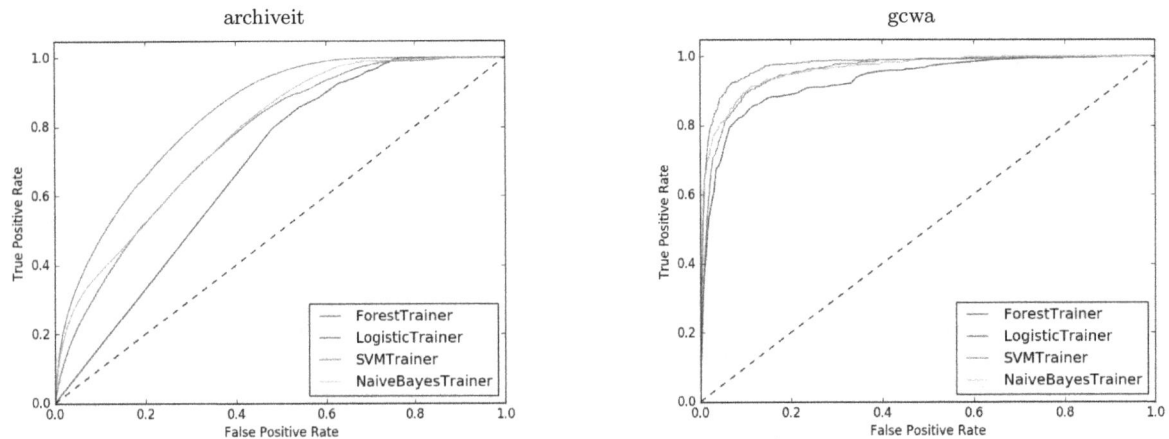

Figure 5: Comparison of training algorithms

observed ones. That selected response time is used for classifiers operated at the different levels of TPR. Table 9 shows the results, based on the 187,449 URI-Rs from oldweb.today, distinguishing between using all archives or only Memento compliant ones. Note that the FPR value of 1.0 corresponds to not using classifiers but rather the brute force approach. The results indicate that the currently used heuristic to query all Memento-compliant archives yields the best recall (disregarding the brute force approach on all archives), yet that computational cost and response time can be reduced by using classifiers without significantly decreasing recall. Viable strategies exist both using all archives or compliant ones only, but the latter consistently perform better regarding recall and response time at equivalent request numbers. The result at TPR 0.6, using Memento compliant archives only, looks extremely attractive: compared to a brute force approach on all archives, classifiers can reduce the average number of requests by 77% (from 17 to 3.985), and the overall response time by 42% (from 3.712 to 2.16 seconds) while maintaining a recall of 0.847. At this TPR level, significant optimizations can be achieved while maintaining acceptable recall, even when compared to brute force on Memento compliant archives only. When operating at FPR level 0.45, we reach an average number of 2.994 requests per URI-R and find that complete TimeMaps are collected for 83.4% of

URI-R. This result fully aligns with [4], which found that it is possible to retrieve a complete TimeMap for 84% of URI-R when using only the top 3 archives. But, in contrast to [4], our approach only marginally relies on third party data, and can actually be brought into production.

We zoom in on the 0.6 TPR level. For that level, Table 10 shows, per archive, the true positives (TP), false negatives (FN), true negatives (TN), and false positives (FP). Note that TP+FN for an archive is equal to the number of URI-R of the sample for which the archive holds Mementos. Also, TP+FP is the number of queries sent to an archive. For sg and ukparliament, only FP is listed as neither archive has Mementos for URI-Rs in the oldweb.today dataset. Since a request is always sent to ia, no FN are listed. Note, for ia, the significant number of URI-R for which it has no Mementos. Table 11 compares the number of requests sent according to various strategies. We see that, when including all archives, the classifiers at TPR level 0.6 recommend sending a total of 916,881 requests: 171,862 TP and 745,019 FP. The high FP count relates to our desire to achieve low FN and hence miss few Mementos; FN stands at 26,304. The total number of requests would have been 3,186,633 for the brute force approach (TPR 1.0) on all archives. In this case, the classifiers achieve a 71% reduction. When only Memento compliant archives are considered a reduction of 67% is achieved.

Table 8: Response time [ms] statistics

Archive	Min	Average	Max
archive.is	35	434	2,770
archiveit	140	342	9,585
ba	226	1,740	60,372
blarchive	338	562	59,087
es	438	464	1,387
gcwa	219	464	2,516
hr	407	428	2,817
ia	71	1,485	24,967
is	402	838	3,215
loc	191	381	3,804
proni	181	234	5,793
pt	57	821	9,328
sg	443	836	9,035
swa	2	3	352
uknationalarchives	190	308	6,320
ukparliament	186	312	32,278
webcite	495	1217	60,050

Table 9: Average (#requests, recall, sum(T), max(T)) per URI-R on oldweb.today sample, with T the response time [s]

TPR	All archives	Memento compliant archives
1.0	(17.00, 1.000, 10.90, 3.712)	(11.00, 0.971, 6.640, 3.084)
0.9	(9.134, 0.955, 6.533, 2.983)	(6.447, 0.929, 4.506, 2.558)
0.8	(7.429, 0.924, 5.562, 2.760)	(5.384, 0.900, 3.995, 2.409)
0.7	(6.213, 0.896, 4.792, 2.534)	(4.619, 0.874, 3.597, 2.283)
0.6	(5.220, 0.867, 4.233, 2.418)	(3.958, 0.847, 3.229, 2.160)
0.5	(4.303, 0.835, 3.614, 2.226)	(3.349, 0.818, 2.867, 2.041)

Figure 6 details the relation between recall and the number of requests sent, again for classifiers operating at 0.6 TPR. The left hand plot considers a situation in which all archives are involved, the right hand one pertains to Memento compliant ones only. In each case, brute force requests are depicted in red and requests based on the advise of classifiers in blue. Each plot covers all URI-Rs of the oldweb.today dataset and the size of the respective dots is proportional to the number of URI-R for a given (recall,requests) combination. The dots at the very right hand side of each plot pertain to URI-R for which no Mementos exist in any archive, and, hence, for which recall is undefined. We see a very significant number of URI-R for which classifiers reach the maximum recall by sending between 1 and 9 requests but also some URI-R for which Mementos are missed even when sending up to 13 requests.

6. CONCLUSIONS

We explored the use of binary classifiers to guide the routing of Memento requests for Memento Aggregators. To train the classifiers, we solely relied on data that is recurrently gathered by the LANL Aggregator as part of its daily operation. We used features that have been shown to perform well for other URI-based classifier tasks and determined a combination of number and types of features that worked well for the novel challenge of routing Memento queries. We

Table 10: Performance on oldweb.today dataset at TPR 0.6

Archive	TP	FN	TN	FP
archive.is	14	62	185,541	2,518
archiveit	7,694	4,927	124,580	50,934
ba	19,888	9,593	95,988	62,666
blarchive	1,665	582	131,985	53,903
es	670	284	135,254	51,927
gcwa	210	113	149,161	38,651
hr	0	3	176,272	11,860
ia	122,787	0	65,348	0
is	5,362	2,381	94,760	85,632
loc	6,625	4,769	111,518	65,223
proni	489	336	140,201	47,109
pt	2,289	909	119,650	65,287
sg	0	0	188,135	0
swa	2,320	1,239	93,093	91,483
uknationalarchives	1,185	531	134,500	51,919
ukparliament	0	0	188,135	0
webcite	664	575	120,989	65,907
Total	171,862	26,304	2,255,110	745,019

Table 11: Number of requests using different strategies

TPR	#Requests all archives	#Requests Memento compliant
1.0	3,186,633	2,061,393
0.6	916,881	676,884

also trained archive-specific classifiers using various training algorithms on the basis of the same data. However, in order to optimally operate the classifiers, we had to bring in a third party set of URI-Rs to compensate for bias in the Aggregator Cache. Our evaluation of this approach, performed on the basis of an unrelated set of URI-Rs from oldweb.today, shows that classifiers can significantly reduce the number of requests sent to archives, and hence reduce the load on both the Aggregator and the archives. It can also reduce overall response times. These reductions can be achieved without significantly compromising recall. Improvements over the reported work are definitely possible. We must ensure that the cache contains URI-Rs with associated Mementos in all archives as the lack of training data led us to exclude two from our experiments. More advanced machine learning techniques can be explored that may yield even better results. But, overall, the results are so compelling that we already devised a workflow based on Spark that can recurrently train archive-specific classifiers on the basis of cached data. The training of classifiers is set up such that it can dynamically adapt with regard to specific features and number of features, as the archives evolve. We plan to bring this capability in production to guide the LANL Aggregator and will also expose a public API to support Memento clients in determining which archives to poll for a given URI-R.

7. ACKNOWLEDGMENTS

This work is supported in part by the International Internet Preservation Consortium (IIPC). Ilya Kreymer provided the oldweb.today dataset. Shawn Jones, Martin Klein, and Harihar Shankar provided comments to a draft paper.

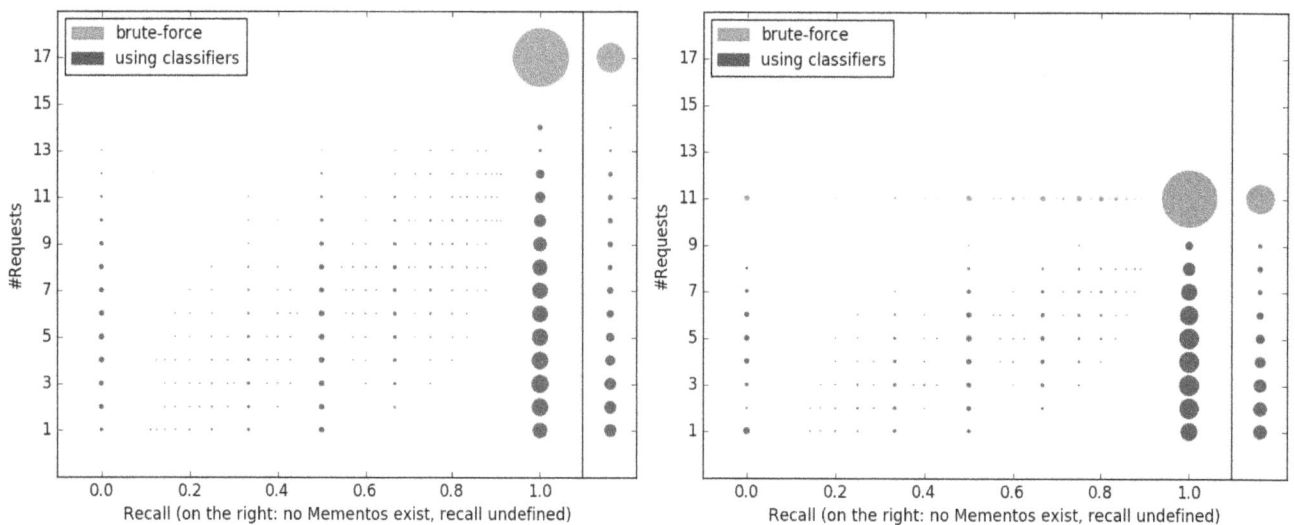

Figure 6: Recall per URI-R versus number of requests sent using all archives (left) and compliant archives (right). Dot size proportional to number of URI-Rs.

8. REFERENCES

[1] A Comprehensive Study of Techniques for URL-based Web Page Language Classification. *ACM Trans. Web*, 7(1), 2013.

[2] M. Abramson and D. W. Aha. What is in a URL? Genre Classification from URLs. Technical Report AAAI Technical Report WS-12-09, Naval Research Laboratory, Washington, DC 20375, 2012.

[3] S. Alam, M. L. Nelson, H. Van de Sompel, L. Balakireva, H. Shankar, and D. Rosenthal. Web Archive Profiling Through CDX Summarization. In S. Kapidakis, C. Mazurek, and M. Werla, editors, *Research and Advanced Technology for Digital Libraries*, volume 9316 of *Lecture Notes in Computer Science*, pages 3–14. Springer International Publishing, 2015.

[4] A. AlSum, M. C. Weigle, M. L. Nelson, and H. Van de Sompel. Profiling Web Archive Coverage for Top-Level Domain and Content Language. *International Journal on Digital Libraries*, 14(3):149–166, 2014.

[5] R. B. Basnet, A. H. Sung, and Q. Liu. Learning to detect phishing URLs. *International Journal of Research in Engineering and Technology*, 3(6):11–24, 2014.

[6] E. Baykan, M. Henzinger, L. Marian, and I. Weber. Purely URL-based Topic Classification. In *Proceedings of the 18th International Conference on World Wide Web*, WWW '09, pages 1109–1110, New York, NY, USA, 2009. ACM.

[7] E. Baykan, M. Henzinger, L. Marian, and I. Weber. A Comprehensive Study of Features and Algorithms for URL-Based Topic Classification. *ACM Trans. Web*, 5(3):15:1–15:29, July 2011.

[8] H. M. Baykan E. and W. I. Web Page Language Identification Based on URLs. In *Proceedings of the VLDBEndowment*, volume 1(1), pages 176–187, 2008.

[9] L. Breiman, J. Friedman, C. J. Stone, and R. A. Olshen. *Classification and Regression Trees*. CRC press, 1984.

[10] J. F. Brunelle and M. L. Nelson. An evaluation of caching policies for memento timemaps. In *JCDL '13: Proceedings of the 13th ACM/IEEE-CS Joint Conference on Digital Libraries*, pages 267–276, 2013.

[11] M. N. C. Whittaker, B. Ryner. Large-scale automatic classification of phishing pages. In *Proc. 17th Annual Network and Distributed System Security Symposium*, 2010.

[12] T. Hastie, R. Tibshirani, J. Friedman, and J. Franklin. *The Elements of Statistical Learning: Data Mining, Inference, and Prediction*. Springer, 2009.

[13] M.-Y. Kan and H. O. N. Thi. Fast Webpage Classification Using URL Features. In *Proceedings of the 14th ACM International Conference on Information and Knowledge Management*, CIKM '05, pages 325–326, New York, NY, USA, 2005. ACM.

[14] J. Ma, L. K. Saul, S. Savage, and G. M. Voelker. Identifying Suspicious URLs: An Application of Large-scale Online Learning. In *Proceedings of the 26th Annual International Conference on Machine Learning*, ICML '09, pages 681–688, New York, NY, USA, 2009. ACM.

[15] T. M. Mitchell. *Machine Learning*. McGraw-Hill Boston, MA:, 1997.

[16] H. Van de Sompel, M. L. Nelson, and R. Sanderson. HTTP Framework for Time-Based Access to Resource States – Memento, December Internet RFC 7089, December 2013.

[17] H. Van de Sompel, M. L. Nelson, R. Sanderson, L. Balakierva, S. Ainsworth, and H. Shankar. Memento: Time Travel for the Web. Technical Report arXiv:0911.1112, 2009.

The Dawn of Today's Popular Domains

A Study of the Archived German Web over 18 Years*

Helge Holzmann, Wolfgang Nejdl, Avishek Anand
L3S Research Center
Appelstr. 9a
30167 Hanover, Germany
{holzmann,nejdl,anand}@L3S.de

ABSTRACT

The Web has been around and maturing for 25 years. The popular websites of today have undergone vast changes during this period, with a few being there almost since the beginning and many new ones becoming popular over the years. This makes it worthwhile to take a look at how these sites have evolved and what they might tell us about the future of the Web. We therefore embarked on a longitudinal study spanning almost the whole period of the Web, based on data collected by the Internet Archive starting in 1996, to retrospectively analyze how the popular Web as of now has evolved over the past 18 years.

For our study we focused on the German Web, specifically on the top 100 most popular websites in 17 categories. This paper presents a selection of the most interesting findings in terms of *volume*, *size* as well as *age* of the Web. While related work in the field of Web Dynamics has mainly focused on change rates and analyzed datasets spanning less than a year, we looked at the evolution of websites over 18 years. We found that around 70% of the pages we investigated are younger than a year, with an observed exponential growth in age as well as in size up to now. If this growth rate continues, the number of pages from the popular domains will almost double in the next two years. In addition, we give insights into our data set, provided by the Internet Archive, which hosts the largest and most complete Web archive as of today.

CCS Concepts

•Information systems → World Wide Web; •Applied computing → Digital libraries and archives;

Keywords

Web Dynamics; Analysis; Statistics; Longitudinal; Retrospective

*This work is partly funded by the European Research Council under ALEXANDRIA (ERC 339233)

Permission to make digital or hard copies of all or part of this work for personal or classroom use is granted without fee provided that copies are not made or distributed for profit or commercial advantage and that copies bear this notice and the full citation on the first page. Copyrights for components of this work owned by others than ACM must be honored. Abstracting with credit is permitted. To copy otherwise, or republish, to post on servers or to redistribute to lists, requires prior specific permission and/or a fee. Request permissions from permissions@acm.org.

JCDL '16, June 19-23, 2016, Newark, NJ, USA

© 2016 ACM. ISBN 978-1-4503-4229-2/16/06. . . $15.00

DOI: http://dx.doi.org/10.1145/2910896.2910901

1. INTRODUCTION

The Web is in a state of continuous change, with websites and pages being continuously added, deleted and modified. As previous studies have reported, the Web has been growing and evolving substantially over its lifetime. Researchers have measured and characterized the nature and degree of change in the past [1, 2, 3, 4, 5]. However, these studies primarily focus on content or structural change rates of rather small collections of websites for time periods from a few weeks to a couple of years. One of the interesting findings of such analyses is that a significant part of the changes on the Web are the creation and deletion of pages [4]. This paper aims to extend those studies with a comprehensive retrospective analysis with a strong topicality, by investigating today's most prominent part of the German Web over an 18 year period from 1996 to 2013. We collected the most popular domains from a diverse set of categories on Amazon's *Alexa* ranking[1] and analyzed on the German Web crawls for this period preserved by the *Internet Archive*[2]. This makes it the longest study of Web evolution so far.

The dataset gives us the unique opportunity to analyze the evolution of what is popular on the Web today and how those websites have evolved from their early days. At the same time it puts us into a role similar to an archaeologist, who studies the past only based on what has remained. What remains of the Web in archives is influenced by crawling policies, which are limited due to the available resources. Furthermore, not only the Web itself but also the crawlers are subject to evolution. Therefore, we will discuss our assumptions and findings on the Internet Archive dataset in a separate section, which by itself is another interesting contribution of the study described in this paper and shows the representativeness of the archive with respect to the most popular websites by comparing the growth to the actual Web in terms of registered domains. In this respect, it is interesting to see that those websites are relatively well covered, even though some years back they might not have been as popular as today. This is a positive observation and an important trait of a Web archive since today's popular websites are likely to be looked up by users of an archive from the past as well.

In the following we will use *domain* synonymously for a *website* including its *sub-domains*, e.g., *google.de* and *news.google.de* belong to one website. In contrast, *webpage* is used interchangeably for *URL* and denotes a single *page* of a website.

---

[1]http://www.alexa.com
[2]http://www.archive.org

The questions we ask in our study are inspired by the popular belief about the structure of the Web, but with a focus on the prominent part that people care about most today in Germany:

- *Are popular websites growing old and if so, how can we characterize it?* We were able to confirm what other researchers found earlier: the majority of pages on the Web are rather young. In addition, however, we found that the small long-living fraction contributes significantly to the age, which is increasing.

- *How has the size of popular websites changed over time?* In terms of the volume of a domain, which we define as the number of URLs, we found the growth has been exponential up to now. This is an interesting finding, which we believe is true for the Web in general. Regarding actual sizes, not just existing pages grow, but also newly created ones are larger every year.

- *Do the popular websites from different categories (like business, universities and technology) have different growth rates?* In almost all the conducted analyses we found distinct differences among the considered categories. We find that 75% of the popular university domains of today have been around since *1999* whereas not even 20% of the popular game websites of today were present back then.

Before we present the results of our analysis (Sec. 4 and 5), we provide a detailed description of the experimental setup and the measurement metrics used in this study (Sec. 3). Since all presented properties and statistics are computed purely on meta data from a crawl index (CDX), the same analysis can be replicated by other researchers with access to such an index. Using the same definitions (Table 2) would allow to compare among datasets, e.g., different national domains. The national top-level domain *.de* constitutes the largest fraction of German-speaking websites, a non-negligible portion of the Web, which we analyze with a focus on the most popular part. The paper ends with an analysis and discussion of this dataset as provided by the *Internet Archive* (Sec. 6).

2. RELATED WORK

Studying and characterizing change and evolution in the Web falls into the broad field of *Web Dynamics*. Change on the Web can be differentiated into content change and structural change in terms of the Web graph as well as the creation and deletion of webpages. This paper investigates the latter together with the growth of Web pages as a result of content change, which is not analyzed in depth though, as we operated purely on metadata.

By contrast, the earliest studies in this field mainly investigated content changes with respect to change rates. Already in 2000, Cho and Garcia-Molina [1] analyzed 720,000 pages over 4 months in a study motivated by the question on *how to build an effective incremental crawler*. They found that 40% of them change within a week based on their checksum. Similar to us, they focused on popular pages, determined by computing PageRank. In a similar study from 2003, Fetterly et al. [2] analyzed 150 million webpages over a period of 11 weeks with more sophisticated features. They found that 67% of the pages never change, 20% are only minor text changes and 10% of the webpages have changes in the non-textual part. Only around 4% of the webpages report

medium to major changes to their text content. The first study in this respect that covers multiple years was done by Koehler [3] in 2002. They analyzed a small sample of 360 pages spanning more than four years from 1996 to 2001 and showed that navigation pages have a better survival rate than content pages. A more fine-grained content analysis was done much later by Adar et al. [5] in 2009, taking hourly and sub-hourly changes into account. They studied page level content changes and tried to capture term-level dynamics on a sample of 55,000 pages with different popularities and different revisitation patterns over 5 weeks. They found that 66% of the visited pages changed during the period under consideration on average every 123 hours.

From a search engine perspective, back in 2004, Ntoulas et al. [4] analyzed the link structure in addition to content of 3-5 million pages over one year. They focused on popular websites once again, according to Google's directory, and observe that 8% of the pages are replaced by newly created ones every week. Out of the remaining about 50% did not change at all during the year under consideration.

With a focus purely on structural change, Baeza-Yates and Poblete [6] investigated the Chilean Web (*.cl*) domain over five years from 2000 to 2004 with questions similar to ours. During this period, their collection grew from 600,000 to 3 million pages. Other studies also focused on national top-level domains, such as *.uk*, which was studied by Bordino et al. [7] in 2008 as well as in a recent study from 2014 by Hale et al. [8]. Bordino et al. [7] analyzed a time-aware Web graph consisting of 100 million pages over one year with monthly granularity. Hale et al. [8] focused on the academic part of the UK under *.ac.uk* from 1996 to 2010 and investigated link patterns. As in our study their collection was also crawled and provided by the Internet Archive. Another recent work by Agata et al. [9] analyzed a collection of 10 million mainly Japanese pages in 2001, which was collected by the Internet Archive as well and is also based on metadata. They report a webpage's average life span of a little more than three years. The most recent study with a national focus was published by Alkwai et al. [10] in 2015. They analyzed around 300,000 Arabic pages in terms of different criteria, such as their coverage on Web archives.

Our work differs from these previous analyses by having a larger temporal coverage as well as new objectives. To this effect, we carry out studies which compare observations across years showcasing evolution of websites in terms of age (s. Sec 4) and growth both in size and volume (s. Sec 5).

3. SETUP AND METHODOLOGY

In our analysis we focused on the aging as well as growth of today's most popular German websites based on a Web archive over 18 years. All information needed for such an analysis are available in the meta data index, called CDX[3], which most Web archives maintain with their collections.

3.1 Dataset Preparations

Our dataset has been provided by the Internet Archive in the context of the ALEXANDRIA project[4] and consists of all their archived text records from the German Web, as defined by the *.de* top-level domain, from 1996 to 2013.

---

[3]http://archive.org/web/researcher/cdx_file_format.php
[4]http://alexandria-project.eu

Table 1: Dataset Details

Category	# Domains	# Sub-Domains	# URLs
Computer	100	561	2138786
Recreation	100	380	981638
Society	100	368	832017
Health	100	274	453282
Kids & Teens	100	234	311705
Culture	100	250	934552
Media	100	512	1981877
Shopping	100	429	6726195
Regional	100	793	3069791
Games	99	304	718348
Sports	100	290	656859
Business	100	546	1534639
Education	100	827	1240196
Science	100	398	579821
Home	100	325	1762361
News	40	117	820163
Universities	100	828	659175
TOTAL	*1444*	*5846*	*20778475*

3.1.1 German Web CDX

The so-called CDX files that we used for our investigation are manifests consisting of all meta information about the crawls in a space-separated format, with one line per capture, i.e. a snapshot of one URL at a given time. The corresponding line in the CDX file looks as follows:

```
<canonicalized_url  timestamp  original_url
mime_type  status_code  checksum  redirect_url
meta_data  compressed_size  offset  filename>
```

Of importance for this work are the URL, the timestamp, the status code, as well as the size. As the CDX files that we used for this analysis only include text files, such as HTML, we could ignore the mime type. Please note that the sizes provided in the CDX files corresponding to the records in the archive, compressed in *GZip* format. Therefore, the analysis on sizes does not present the exact sizes of the websites, but trends over time.

In order to handle the large amount of data, we created an index based on the domains as keys. Each domain points to a list of its URLs, where every URL has attached a sub-list with all its captures in the archive in chronological order, including the data as shown above. This allows quick access to all URLs and captures of any available domain.

3.1.2 Today's Popular Domains

There are three types of Web archives. While the first type attempts to preserve a certain part of the Web completely, for instance a national top-level domain, the second type is more focused, aiming for a certain topic or event. Those broad as well as topical crawls are typically done once or periodically without the attempt to capture all changes in between or to preserve the dynamics of the Web. In contrast to that, the third type of Web archives constitutes continuous crawls over a longer time period, which does not claim to preserve everything, but the most important parts according to a certain crawling strategy. This strategy might even change over time to adjust the crawler for a better coverage of a certain aspect. For instance, a typical strategy is to revisit frequently changing pages more often. Therefore, the temporal coverage of some websites in the archive may be very good, while others are missed completely. This selective crawling introduces a certain bias to the archive, which however is difficult to track retrospectively.

Our collection is of the third type, plus, it includes data donations, which were crawled by third-party organizations. For that reason, it does not cover the entire Web, but constitutes a sample biased by the different crawling strategies. Accordingly, a random sample of the collection would again be biased and it will require further research to analyze what the collection actually consists of to create a more representative sample of the entire German Web.

Therefore, instead of sampling we decided to focus on a well-defined subset, which in addition is inherently substantial for users as well as Web crawlers: the today's popular domains from their early stages in 1996 up to now (2013 to be exact). These websites are of interest for most readers and at the same time have the biggest impact on upcoming research on Web archiving, crawling, IR and related areas, since those disciplines typically focus on rather prominent websites. Also, as we will show later (s. Sec. 6), this subset nicely represents the actual growth of the Web in terms of registered domains.

The selection of domains was taken from *Alexa* by fetching the top websites of different categories, like *Business*, *Society*, *Sports* and others. To match our dataset we only picked those categories listed under German [5]. In addition to the top categories, we also took two sub-categories for news and universities, which we considered especially relevant. As our dataset only consists of domains ending with the German top-level domain *.de* and not all German websites listed on Alexa are under *.de*, we filtered out those websites with another top-level domain. Out of the remaining, we picked the top 100 from every category (or less for smaller categories, like news) to form our dataset. The last time we retrieved the rankings from Alexa was on July, 10th 2014 at 09:26 GMT+1.

3.1.3 Dataset extraction

Based on the selected domains from Alexa, we filtered our CDX dataset by taking only those records with URLs belonging to one of the domains. Additionally, we cleaned the dataset by discarding the following URLs:

- All URLs ending with one of the following extensions: *.jpg, .png, .gif, .css, .js*, because these constitute embeds and not self-contained resources, like websites. Although the dataset only consists of URLs with mime type *text*, it included image types either because the server returned a wrong type or the files were not available and pointed to an error page.
- All URLs that have never returned a successful HTTP status code (starting with 2). Those are most likely broken links, which the crawler followed, but which did not lead to a successful response.
- All URLs that were not crawled anymore in 2013, i.e., the last year of the dataset, even if the last available capture was successful. Keeping them would result in an inconsistent state, because we cannot tell what happened to them after the last time they were crawled.
- All URLs that have been crawled successfully only once, even if this was in 2013. As it exists only a single capture of those pages, they do not contribute to our evolution analysis at this point. Most likely, the Internet Archive crawler has just begun to crawl them.

---

[5]http://alexa.com/topsites/category/Top/World/Deutsch

Table 2: Properties Used in the Statistics

Evolution and *Domain Age* statistics	
$\mathbf{alive}_d(p_i)$	# URLs of d alive in period p_i (were born before t_i and did not die before t_{i+1})
$\mathbf{born}_d(p_i)$	# URLs of d born in period p_i (were born after t_i (included) and did not die before t_{i+1})
$\mathbf{died}_d(p_i)$	# URLs of d died in period p_i (were born before t_i and died before t_{i+1})
$\mathbf{flashed}_d(p_i)$	# URLs of d born and died in period p_i (were born after t_i (included) and died before t_{i+1})
$\mathbf{size}_d(p_i)$	Cumulated sizes of URLs of d at the end of period p_i (all URLs that were alive or were born in period p_i)
$\mathbf{born\_size}_d(p_i)$	Cumulated sizes of URLs of d at the birth of newborn URLs in period p_i
$\mathbf{ages}_d(p_i)$	Ages in months of URLs of d at the end of period p_i (all URLs that were alive or were born in period p_i)

URL Age statistics	
$\mathbf{count}_d(p_i)$	# URLs of d in period p_i / at age i (were born before t_i and reached age i)
$\mathbf{died}_d(p_i)$	# URLs of d that died in period p_i / at age i (were born before t_i and died before t_{i+1})
$\mathbf{size}_d(p_i)$	Cumulated sizes of URLs of d at the end of period p_i (only of URLs that did not die in period p_i)
$\mathbf{died\_size}_d(p_i)$	Cumulated sizes at the death of URLs of d that died in period p_i
$\mathbf{died\_birth\_size}_d(p_i)$	Cumulated sizes at the birth of URLs of d that died in p_i

Ultimately, we ended up with a dataset consisting of 17 categories with today's popular domains from the German Web, as presented in Table 1. The dataset covers in total 1,444 domains with 5,846 sub-domains and more than 20 million URLs (20,778,475 URLs to be exact).

3.2 Statistics and Metrics

Our statistics were gathered in two steps. First, a precomputation step counted different properties of a domain. Afterwards, we aggregated these properties into meaningful metrics. The following subsections describe these two steps in detail and define the terminology used in the analysis results (Sec. 4 and 5).

We use the terms of *birth*, *death* and *life* to describe the lifetime of a URL or domain in our dataset. We consider a URL or domain to be alive from the time it first appeared in the Web archive until it was last seen online.

3.2.1 Precomputations

For each domain, we precomputed three types of statistics: *Evolution*, *Domain Age* and *URL Age* statistics. Each of them describes a collection of properties, such as *size* and *age*, computed in different units, i.e., calendar years, domain years, URL years. For all statistics, one unit i spans a period p_i of one year time from t_i to t_{i+1} (excluded), which may or may not be a calendar year from 1 Jan to 31 Dec, depending on the type of statistics presented.

We decided not to collect more fine-grained statistics, such as monthly or weekly, because a higher resolution would not have had any advantages for our analysis and is not sufficiently supported by the dataset. While studies on change rates would require more steady crawls, this is not required for an evolution study such as the one we present as the overall trends are not affected. Also, we cannot guarantee such fine-grained captures with our dataset (s. Sec. 6).

The following definitions describe the statistics:

- **Evolution statistics:**
  Values are measured per calendar year.
  t_i denotes the beginning of the calendar year i.

- **Domain Age statistics:**
  Values are measured for full years starting from the first date a domain occurs in the dataset (e.g., for a domain that appears first in $t_0 = 04.05.2000\ 10:30:45$, age $i = 0$ spans from to $04.05.2001\ 10:30:44$).
  t_i denotes the beginning of the domain age i.

- **URL Age statistics:**
  Values are measured for full years of the analyzed URLs. As before the statistics are gathered per domain, however, here by combining values of different URLs at the same age.
  t_i denotes the beginning of the URL age i.

Age statistics (*Domain Age* and *URL Age*) do not necessarily reflect the actual age of domains/URLs, but their age as evident from the dataset. These ages probably do not diverge much, but some time might have passed after the creation of a new domain until it is included in the Web archive.

Evolution and *Domain Age* statistics are similar in the sense that both describe the evolution of a domain over time. The *URL Age* statistics on the other hand are relative to the time of a domain's URLs, which reflects different periods of a domain but aggregates URLs at the same age. This enables different kinds of statistics as shown below.

3.2.2 Aggregation

The precomputed statistics were accumulated among the domains in each category as well as among all categories. For the sake of clarity, we present only selected categories in our plots, which best represent the overall observations as well as some outliers. Each metric that we analyze below is defined per period p_i on the set of domains that appeared in this period D_i. For instance, a domain which was born in the year 2000 is not included in D_i for any $i < 2000$ in the *Evolution* statistics. The same applies to *Domain Age* and *URL Age* statistics with i referring to relative years instead of calendar years.

The aggregations with corresponding formulas that we present and discuss in the following of this paper are presented along with the plots. The definitions of the used properties are listed in Table 2. In addition to the given definition of alive URLs, we define the number of URLs alive at a single time point, which is a special case for a period with length 0: while $\mathrm{alive}_d(p_i)$ is defined for a period $p_i = [t_i, t_{i+1})$ and denotes the URLs that were alive the entire interval, $\mathrm{alive}_d(i)$ refers to the very end of this period. It includes the URLs that were alive during the entire period p_i plus the ones that were born in period p_i:

$$\mathrm{alive}_d(i) = \mathrm{alive}_d(p_i) + \mathrm{born}_d(p_i)$$

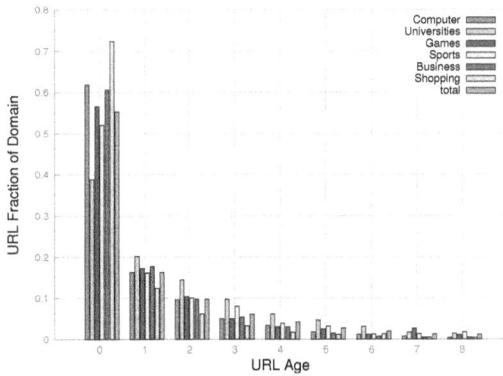

Figure 1: URL Age Distribution

4. THE AGE OF THE WEB

The Web started around 25 years ago and has been maturing ever since. However, is its actual age really increasing or is its content constantly being refreshed, by pages being added and removed? To answer this question we analyzed the age of the Web in terms of how long URLs have been existent. It turns out, while the majority of popular webpages are young, older pages are aging further. We show the distribution of ages among URLs as well as the evolution of the long-living parts of the Web.

4.1 Distribution

It has been shown by other researchers that most URLs on the Web are rather short living [4, 2], i.e., less than a year. However, nothing could be deduced about the URLs which survived after a year. Also, there was no evidence whether the fraction of these short-term URLs increased or decreased over time. To answer these questions, we first investigate the age distribution to determine what fraction of URLs is short or longer living and how this differs among the different categories. In this analysis, we only consider URLs that died during the timespan of our dataset, determined by an unsuccessful status code without another successful status code thereafter. The end time of such a URL is set to the time of the first returned unsuccessful status code. The begin time of the URL is the time it was crawled first.

Figure 1 shows the fraction of URLs per domain that died at age i, averaged over all domains D_i that reached this age. It is defined on the *URL Age* statistics (cp. Sec. 3.2), with p_i referring to the period of a URL's age i:

$$\frac{1}{|D_i|} \sum_{d \in D_i} \frac{\text{died}_d(p_i)}{\text{count}_d(p_i)}$$

The age distribution shows that, indeed, the largest fraction of the URLs of a domain, about 55%, live less than a year. A considerable fraction of URLs die at the age of two to five. These are what we denote as short-living pages. Every page that lives longer than five years is considered long-living and subject to contribute to the aging of the Web. These constitute the long tail in this distribution. We do not show the entire tail in this figure but we considered URLs up to ages of thirteen. It is interesting to observe that the university websites have a significantly higher number of URLs dying after the first year, while less than 40% of webpages die at the age of 0. For each of the subsequent ages they consistently outnumber other categories indicating that

university webpages tend to be rather long-living. In contrast, we have shopping websites, which have the highest number of pages, 73% of all its URLs, that die within their first year.

Now we turn to the second question of how the overall age distribution evolves over time, presented in Figures 2(a) and 2(b). For this, we resort to a different style of analysis by considering the number of URLs at a certain age in the given year, instead of how long they lived in the end. We divided the ages into six age buckets of URLs that lived for less than – a year, 2 years, 3 years, 4 years, 5 years and 6 years or longer, which includes the URLs at age five together with the long-living ones. We observe in Figure 2(a), that over the years the number of URLs for each bucket increases superlinearly. Interestingly, this trend correlates with the domain volume which is presented in the next section.

Further, we investigate the normalized distribution for all years in Figure 2(b). The normalized value of an age bucket α at a given year p_i is defined as follows (on *Evolution* statistics):

$$\frac{\sum_{d \in D_i} |\{a \in \text{ages}_d(p_i) | \alpha \cdot 12 \le a < (\alpha + 1) \cdot 12\}|}{\sum_{d \in D_i} \text{alive}_d(i)}$$

Although the number of URLs overall grows over the years, as suggested by Figure 2(a), the fraction of the URLs at different ages remains more or less stable. As emphasized by the computed fitted line in Figure 2(b), almost 70% of all webpages are younger than a year at any time during the Web's lifetime. The fact that the sizes of all age buckets are equally stable over time suggests that, although the Web is growing, it consists of equal proportions of different aged webpages at any time.

As a result of the retrospective nature of this study, abnormal artifacts that appear in some of the plots are difficult to track. Similar to the peak in year 2007 in Figure 2(a) there are artifacts in the following figures as well. These kinds of abnormalities are most likely due to the different data sources that donated crawls of very diverse volume and size to the Internet Archive. However, as all of them are local phenomena, they do not affect our analysis as the global trend can be clearly recognized in all figures. More details on the dataset are discussed in Section 6.

4.2 Aging

Knowing that the majority of pages on the Web are rather fresh, we now analyze the evolution of the Web's average age. Rather ironically, like humans can grow old but stay younger by eating healthy and doing sports, a similar trend applies to the Web as most of its constituent webpages are frequently replaced. To investigate this, we computed the *average age* of the Web in months at any given year as defined below (on *Evolution* statistics) and plotted in Figure 3:

$$\frac{\sum_{d \in D_i} \sum_{a \in \text{ages}_d(p_i)} a}{\sum_{d \in D_i} |\text{ages}_d(p_i)|}$$

The figure shows that the Web is actually growing older after all. While the average age of the Web was about 10 months during the year 2000, it grew almost 50% by the year 2012. This can possibly be attributed to the stability of age distributions as shown before (s. Figure 3). Specifically, the fraction of long-living webpages, which are constantly aging, contributes to a higher age every year.

(a) Total

(b) Normalized

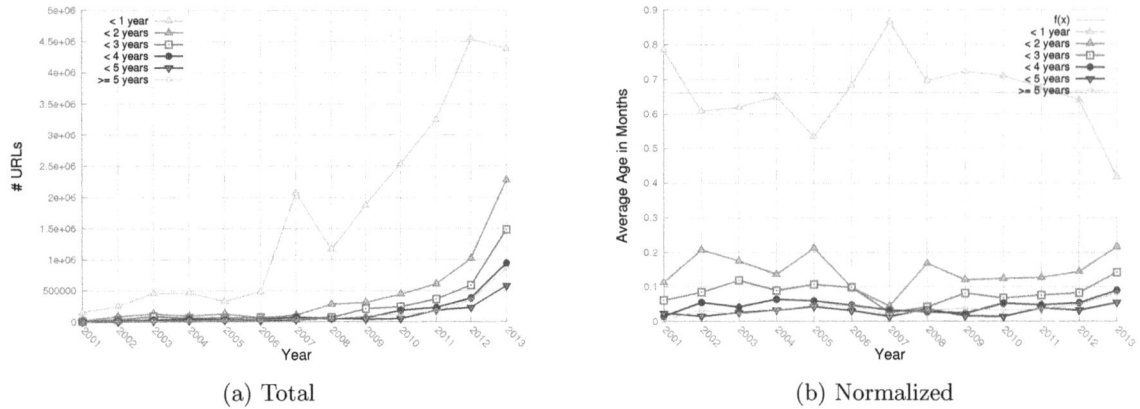

Figure 2: Evolving URL Age Distribution

This aging is almost linear, following the curve $f(x) = a \cdot x + b$, where x is the number of years calculated from 1996. The estimated values for the parameters of this curve are $a = 0.74, b = 4.89$ with an asymptotic error of 8.41% (the corresponding plot is attached in Figure 10(a)). This aging would lead to an average URL age of 23 month in the year 2020, which is double the age of 2005, while the age today or at the end of our dataset (2013) to be exact is 1.5 years. According to this finding, the Web will on average turn three in 2038. However, as our dataset goes back only until 1996, there might be even older pages on the Web. For this reason, our result can be considered as a lower bound.

We further verify our claim that this aging is caused by the long-living pages by analyzing the age of webpages older than five years using the following expression (defined on *Evolution* statistics):

$$\frac{\sum_{d \in D_i} \sum_{a \in \{a \in \text{ages}_d(p_i) | a > 5 \cdot 12\}} a}{\sum_{d \in D_i} |\{a \in \text{ages}_d(p_i) | a > 5 \cdot 12\}|}$$

The corresponding plot in Figure 4(a) visualizes the quite significant growth in age of the long-living URLs. Even though this old part is just a small fraction of the entire Web, its increasing age leads to the slow increase of the Web's actual age that we have shown above. This figure only starts in 2001 as there exist no long-living URLs in our dataset before.

The same observation can be made by analyzing the average age of long-living URLs at a given age of the corresponding domains in Figure 4(b). This is defined by the same formula as used before, but on *Domain Age* statistics with p_i referring to the of age i of a domain (cp. Sec. 3.2). The plot reflects the actual aging of the popular domains in our dataset in contrast to their real age, as shown on the x-axis: when a domain turns 10 years, their URLs are on average only 80 months old, which is about 6.5 years.

Corresponding to what we observed in Section 4.1 all plots in this section acknowledge the characteristics in terms of age for different categories. While websites of universities appear to be the oldest, others such as sports, business and computer websites tend to be much fresher, not to say more up to date.

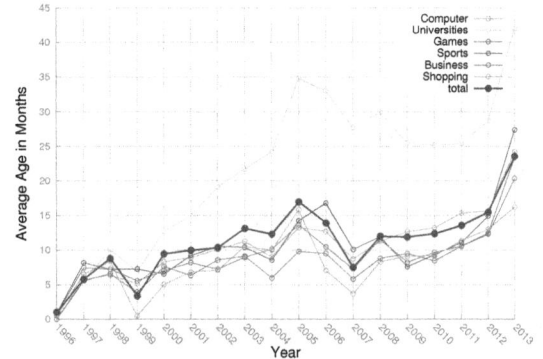

Figure 3: URL Age Evolution

5. THE GROWTH OF THE WEB

We now turn our attention to measuring the *size of the popular Web* and how it has evolved over time. The size of the Web can be interpreted as the number of webpages or as the actual size of its content. We refer to the number of websites and pages as the volume of the Web or a domain, while size refers to the actual file size (including markup as well as the content of a page). In this section we study both interpretations and their evolution over time.

By design, we expect growth as we focus on today's popular domains, which have grown popular over time and therefore, have naturally grown in volume and probably size, too. The question now is how this growth, which made the websites as popular as they are today, can be characterized.

5.1 Volume

Considering that the number of domains in our dataset grows every year as we will see in Section 6, it is not surprising that the number of URLs grows as well. However, if this was the only reason, the growth would be similar to the growth of our dataset, which is not the case. We analyzed this by computing four properties: (a) the number of newborn URLs in a year, (b) the number of URLs that died in a year, (c) the number of URLs that are alive at the end of a year, as well as (d) the growth rate. The growth rate is the difference between the number of born and died URLs. While all other numbers are computed over the period of a

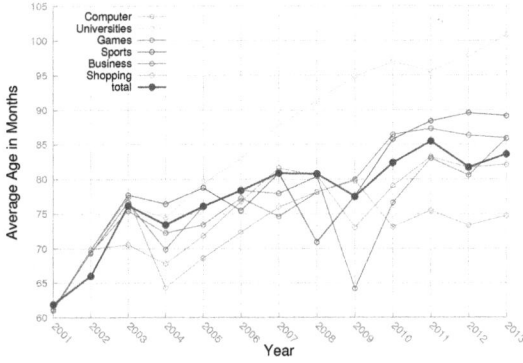

(a) Evolution

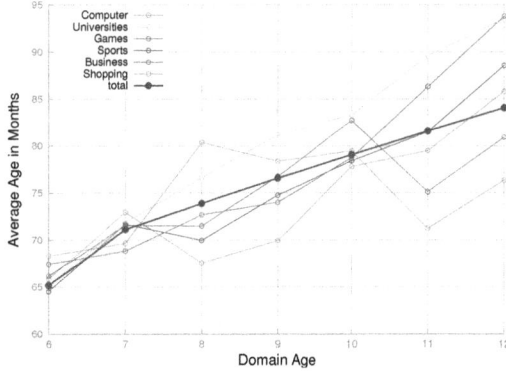

(b) Domain Life

Figure 4: Age of Long-Living URLs (older than five years)

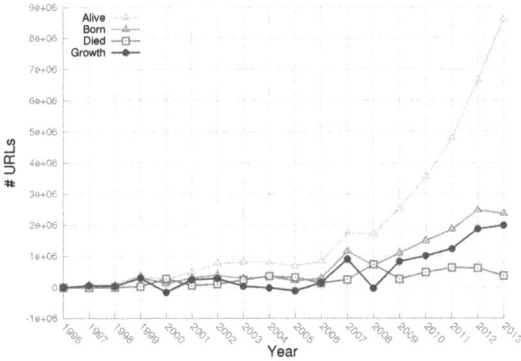

Figure 5: Evolution of the Web's URL Volume

year p_i, the number of URLs alive is considered at the end of the year i, defined as follows (on *Evolution* statistics):

$$\sum_{d \in D_i} \text{alive}_d(i)$$

The results are presented in Figure 5, which shows that the Web is growing a little faster every year. Especially noticeable is the strong growth starting from 2006, which however might be due to the characteristics of the dataset after all. The reason for this growth of the Web is that there are more new URLs born every year, while the number of dying URLs remains almost constant. In order to affirm that this finding is independent from the growing number of domains in our dataset, we investigated the average number of URLs per domain over the years as well. The formula below (defined on *Evolution* statistics) describes this progression, which is shown by the plots in Figure 6(a) per category:

$$\frac{1}{|D_i|} \sum_{d \in D_i} \text{alive}_d(i)$$

Figure 6(b) shows the corresponding average growth rate per domain, as defined below (on *Evolution* statistics), together with birth and death rates. The growth rate describes the difference of born and died URLs of one domain in a given year as fraction of the ones that were alive at the beginning of the year:

$$\frac{1}{|D_i|} \sum_{d \in D_i} \frac{\text{born}_d(p_i) - \text{died}_d(p_i)}{\text{alive}_d(p_i) + \text{died}_d(p_i)}$$

Except for the beginning of this plot, which is most likely due to the transient state at the early years of our dataset, the growth rate is relatively stable at around 30%. Based on this, we can deduce that the number of URLs that are born or die depends on the volume of the Web or their domain. However, among categories the growth varies strongly. While most of them follow the overall trend, university websites barely grow in volume at all, as presented earlier in Figure 6(a). Even in 2013 they still only consist of about 1,000 URLs on average, whereas computer websites comprise almost 8,000 and shopping as well as news websites more than 12,000 URLs.

The average domain volume follows an exponential curve $f(x) = a \cdot b^x + c$, where x is the number of years calculated from 1996. The estimated values for the parameters of this curve are $a = 22.82, b = 1.38, c = 300.18$ with an asymptotic error of 2.07% (the corresponding plot is attached in Figure 10(b)). Assuming the growth continues with the same rate, in the year 2020 the number of URLs of the popular domains would be almost 6.7 times the number of URLs today (2014) and by 2030 it would be 166 times that of today. Already within the next two years the domain volume would be doubled. Even though this prediction might be weakened due to our crawling assumptions for archives (s. Sec 6) or the resource limiting is not exponential with the same degree (which is indeed the case as confirmed by the Internet Archive), the exponential nature is still retained, although not as strong.

Another perspective to look at the growth of websites is from the age of a domain in contrast to absolute years. Instead of plotting total numbers, this time we analyzed the number of URLs at every age of a domain in relation to its initial volume (defined on *Domain Age* statistics):

$$\frac{1}{|D_i|} \sum_{d \in D_i} \frac{\text{alive}_d(i)}{\text{alive}_d(0)}$$

Figure 6(c) gives an impression of this relative volume over the lifetime of a domain for five selected categories. We decided to look only at the first 12 years, as our data is not

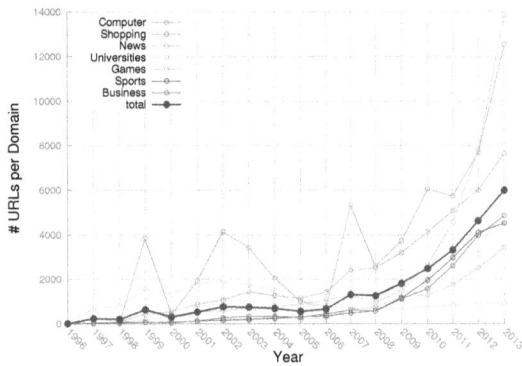

(a) Domain Volume Evolution

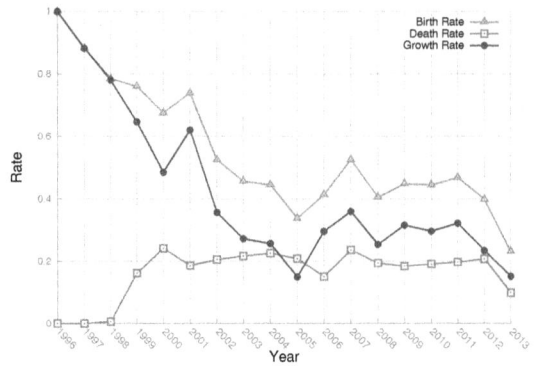

(b) Birth/Death/Growth Rates Evolution

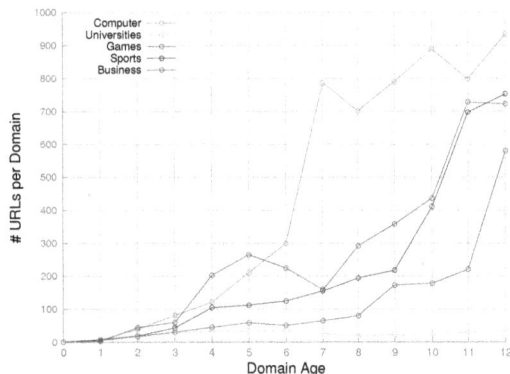

(c) Domain Volume over Domain Life

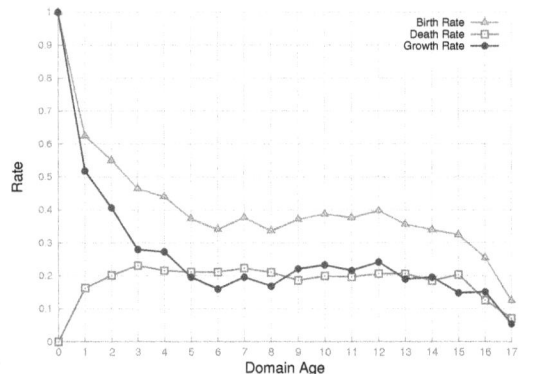

(d) Birth/Death/Growth Rates over Domain Life

Figure 6: Domain Volume

representative enough for older domains. Most noticeable is a quick growth at some point for the websites in most categories. However, the time of this critical take off varies. While computer websites appear to have a strong growth already very early around year six, where they reach 800 times the volume that they started with at birth, and stagnate afterwards, most categories take longer. As observed before, university websites hardly grow in volume at all. Interestingly, the average growth during the lifetime of a domain, as presented in Figure 6(d), looks very similar to the actual growth of the popular German Web over time.

5.2 Size

Apart from the volume also the actual size in bytes has been growing. We found this to be the result of two evolutions: newborn URLs appear to be larger nowadays than they used to be earlier and, in addition, URLs grow in size during their lifetime.

We first analyzed the average size of a URL evolving over time (defined on *Evolution* statistics):

$$\frac{\sum_{d \in D_i} \text{size}_d(p_i)}{\sum_{d \in D_i} \text{alive}_d(i)}$$

Figure 7(a) shows that the size of URLs indeed has increased over the years. This can either mean that websites today consist of more content than they used to in earlier days of the Web, or the markup has grown.

As it turns out, a major growth in size is contributed by

newborn URLs, as defined below (on *Evolution* statistics):

$$\frac{\sum_{d \in D_i} \text{born\_size}_d(p_i)}{\sum_{d \in D_i} \text{born}_d(p_i) + \text{flashed}_d(p_i)}$$

This evolution, presented by Figure 7(b), is similar to the overall growth in size. Its trend follows a linear curve $f(x) = a \cdot x + b$, where x is the number of years calculated from 1996. The estimated values for the parameters of this curve are $a = 866, b = 1320$ with an asymptotic error of 6.9% (the corresponding plot is attached in Figure 10(c)). Based on this, in the year 2038 a new URL will be born on average with double the size as today (2016). As these are compressed sizes (s. Sec. 3.1.1), we cannot state actual numbers though.

Another factor that contributes to the growth of URL sizes is the growth of existing URLs during their lifetime. For this analysis we only took those URLs into account that died at some point within the period of our dataset and computed the average size at birth and at death of all URLs that reached a certain age, as defined by the formulas below (on *URL Age* statistics):

$$\frac{\sum_{d \in D_i, j \geq i} \text{died\_birth\_size}_d(p_j)}{\sum_{d \in D_i, j \geq i} \text{died}_d(p_j)}$$

$$\frac{\sum_{d \in D_i, j \geq i} \text{died\_size}_d(p_j)}{\sum_{d \in D_i, j \geq i} \text{died}_d(p_j)}$$

Figure 8 shows these numbers in a cumulative manner,

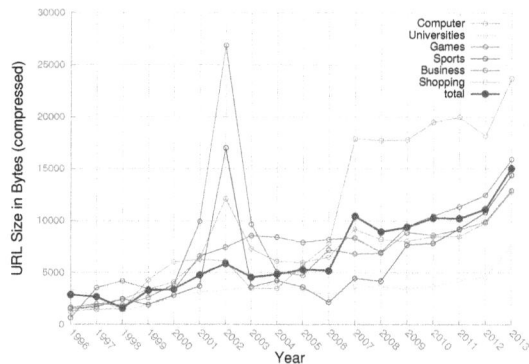

(a) Alive Size

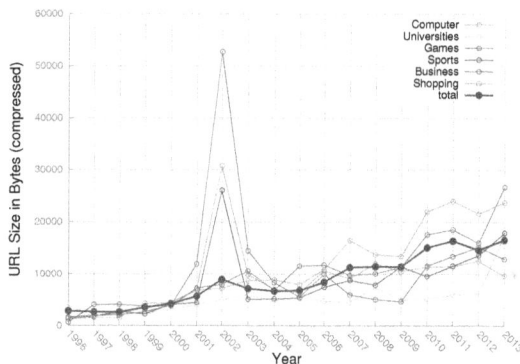

(b) Birth Size

Figure 7: URL Size Evolution

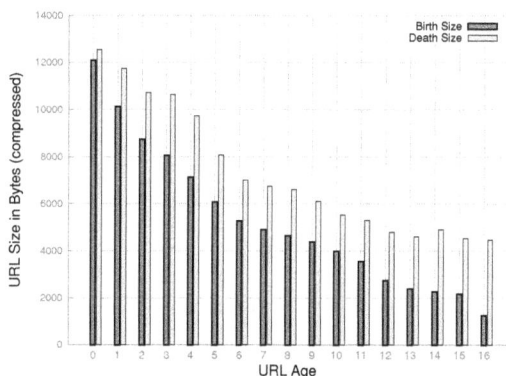

Figure 8: Average URL Birth/Death Size

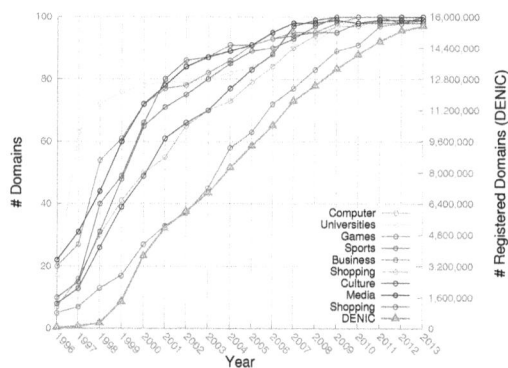

Figure 9: Domain Emergence vs. Registered Domains on DENIC (right y-axis)

averaged over all URLs at a given age. Accordingly, URLs that die earlier tend to be larger than longer living ones. Hence, it appears that less content promises a longer lifetime. Furthermore, the plot shows that URLs grow in size over time, regardless of their age. This growth is almost constant, which indicates that longer living URLs either grow more slowly or that most of the growth takes place in the early years of a URL, as already found by Koehler et. al [3]. In contrast to that observation, short-living URLs with a lifetime of less than a year seem to grow least of all in size.

6. ARCHIVE DATASET DISCUSSION

Our analysis of Web evolution is performed on a dataset comprising German websites under the *.de* top-level domain, which was provided by the Internet Archive. The Internet Archive is the largest and most complete Web archive today. It covers a period of 18 years and constitutes a great source for analysis like ours. Just like in every other archive, not everything can be preserved. What is saved from the Web is influenced by crawl policies and constraints that impact both completeness as well as the change coverage.

We conducted this analysis under the major assumption that, if a domain is crawled, it is crawled completely with respect to the applied crawling policies and limitations, such as certain filters and maximum number of hops from a seed page. Hence, even though this does not cover all URLs of a domain, as long as the crawling strategy does not change

over time, our observed trends are still valid. For Internet Archive crawls performed after 2010 this is actually the case. Thus, at least our results after that time are not affected by changing crawl policies at all. However, due to our focus on popular domains, we expect the assumption to be widely true also before 2010. The Internet Archive received lots of their crawls as donations from different partners. As crawlers, especially from search engines, typically aim for the most prominent part of the Web, we consider our subset consisting of popular domains to be covered with higher priority and hence very comprehensively compared to the rest of the archive.

Moreover, we investigated how well the analyzed popular domains in the Web archive represent the actual Web by comparing to the trend of registered domains on DENIC[6] (the *.de* domain registrar), as shown in Figure 9. The plot gives an overview of presence of domains from the different categories in our dataset at every year under consideration. A domain that is not present can mean two things: 1. it was not online at that time, or 2. it was not considered in the Internet Archive crawls. Although we are not able to distinguish this, the experiment shows a similar trend to the actually existing domains, suggesting that our dataset is fairly representative.

Interesting are also the differences among different categories: whereas about 75% of today's university websites

---

[6]http://www.denic.de/en/background/statistics.html

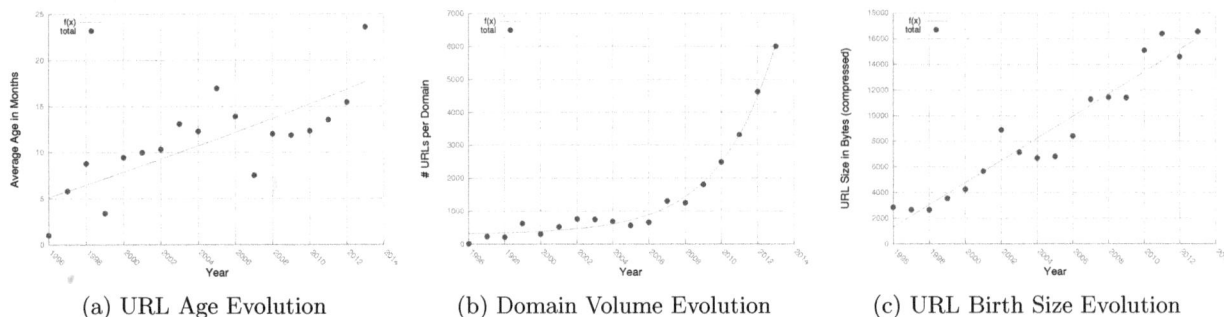

(a) URL Age Evolution   (b) Domain Volume Evolution   (c) URL Birth Size Evolution

Figure 10: Predictions of Evolution Analysis

already existed in 1999 and grew quickly, not even 20% of today's popular game websites were present back then. Most likely, many universities even had a website before 1996, but only got picked up by the crawlers later. By contrast the game websites that are most popular today have been created more recently and grown slowly since. The fact that perhaps not all domains were covered in the very beginning does not affect our analysis, as we investigated volume and size on a per-domain and per-URL basis, respectively.

7. CONCLUSION AND OUTLOOK

In this paper, we have presented an extensive longitudinal study on 18 years of the popular German Web, based on crawls of the Internet Archive. We carried out an in depth analysis on how the popular domains of today were created and how their age, volume and sizes have grown over the last decade. First, we find that most of the popular educational domains like universities have already existed for more than a decade. On the other hand, domains relating to shopping and games have emerged steadily over the period of the last decade. Second, we see that the Web is getting older, not in all its parts, but with many domains having a constant fraction of webpages that are more than five years old and aging further. Finally, we see that popular websites have been growing exponentially after their inception, doubling in volume every two years.

The study has provided us with interesting insights and ramifications on the evolution of the prominent part of the German Web. What we have learned about its growth and size can impact resource allocation strategies for Web archives as well as exhaustive and focused crawling strategies. Especially the identified differences among the studied categories can be of importance when dealing with topical or organizational Web archives from the respective areas. The introduced properties and definitions provide a solid foundation for comparing our findings on growth and aging against different Web archive collections. A possible research question would be: How does the Web of other countries compare to this analysis of the German Web? Furthermore, we lay the foundation for follow-up questions in future research, such as: How do webpages evolve content-wise compared to size and age, and why is the average size of the newborn webpages today larger than the ones in the yesteryear? Is it because of an actual increase in content or is it because of the markup due to constantly increasing web authoring technologies?

References

[1] J. Cho and H. Garcia-Molina. The evolution of the web and implications for an incremental crawler. In *Proceedings of the 26th International Conference on Very Large Data Bases*, VLDB '00.

[2] Dennis Fetterly, Mark Manasse, Marc Najork, and Janet Wiener. A large-scale study of the evolution of web pages. In *Proceedings of the 12th International Conference on World Wide Web*, WWW '03.

[3] Wallace Koehler. Web page change and persistenceâĂŤa four-year longitudinal study. *Journal of the American Society for Information Science and Technology*, 53(2):162–171, January 2002.

[4] Alexandros Ntoulas, Junghoo Cho, and Christopher Olston. What's new on the web?: The evolution of the web from a search engine perspective. In *Proceedings of the 13th International Conference on World Wide Web*, WWW '04.

[5] Eytan Adar, Jaime Teevan, Susan T. Dumais, and Jonathan L. Elsas. The web changes everything: Understanding the dynamics of web content. In *Proceedings of the Second ACM International Conference on Web Search and Data Mining*, WSDM '09.

[6] Ricardo Baeza-Yates and Barbara Poblete. Dynamics of the chilean web structure. *Computer Networks*, 50 (10):1464–1473, 2006.

[7] Ilaria Bordino, Paolo Boldi, Debora Donato, Massimo Santini, and Sebastiano Vigna. Temporal evolution of the uk web. In *Data Mining Workshops, ICDMW'08*, pages 909–918, 2008.

[8] Scott A. Hale, Taha Yasseri, Josh Cowls, Eric T. Meyer, Ralph Schroeder, and Helen Margetts. Mapping the UK webspace: Fifteen years of british universities on the web. In *Proceedings of the 2014 ACM Conference on Web Science*, WebSci '14.

[9] Teru Agata, Yosuke Miyata, Emi Ishita, Atsushi Ikeuchi, and Shuichi Ueda. Life span of web pages: A survey of 10 million pages collected in 2001. *Digital Libraries*, 2014.

[10] Lulwah Alkwai, Michael L Nelson, and Michele C Weigle. How well are arabic websites archived? In *Proceedings of the 15th ACM/IEEE-CS Joint Conference on Digital Libraries*, 2015.

ArchiveSpark:
Efficient Web Archive Access, Extraction and Derivation*

Helge Holzmann
L3S Research Center
Appelstr. 9a
30167 Hanover, Germany
holzmann@L3S.de

Vinay Goel
Internet Archive
300 Funston Avenue
San Francisco, CA 94118
vinay@archive.org

Avishek Anand
L3S Research Center
Appelstr. 9a
30167 Hanover, Germany
anand@L3S.de

ABSTRACT

Web archives are a valuable resource for researchers of various disciplines. However, to use them as a scholarly source, researchers require a tool that provides efficient access to Web archive data for extraction and derivation of smaller datasets. Besides efficient access we identify five other objectives based on practical researcher needs such as ease of use, extensibility and reusability.

Towards these objectives we propose ArchiveSpark, a framework for efficient, distributed Web archive processing that builds a research corpus by working on existing and standardized data formats commonly held by Web archiving institutions. Performance optimizations in ArchiveSpark, facilitated by the use of a widely available metadata index, result in significant speed-ups of data processing. Our benchmarks show that ArchiveSpark is faster than alternative approaches without depending on any additional data stores while improving usability by seamlessly integrating queries and derivations with external tools.

CCS Concepts

•Information systems → Extraction, transformation and loading; •Applied computing → Digital libraries and archives;

Keywords

Web Archives; Big Data; Data Extraction

1. INTRODUCTION

A significant portion of the record of our society exists exclusively on the Web. Web archives aim to capture and preserve this record. Today, a large number of libraries, universities, and cultural heritage organizations have Web archiving programs [1], with a 2011 survey reporting 42 different Web archiving initiatives across 26 countries [2]. With greater availability of Web archives and increasing recognition of their importance, a growing number of historians, social and political scientists, and researchers from other disciplines see them as rich resources for their research [3]. However, as Web archives grow in scope and size, they present unique challenges for creating tools and access methods for researchers.

One of the fundamental tasks in using Web archives for research is *corpora building*. This task involves the selection and filtering of subsets, grouping and aggregation of records of interest and the extraction and derivation of new data (cp. Sec. 2). Consequently, there is a need for a framework that provides this functionality for efficiently constructing corpora out of the original archived collection. However, only providing fast access to the underlying collection is not sufficient. The framework needs to tackle a number of objectives driven by practical requirements (s. Sec. 4.3), like simplicity, expressiveness, extensibility and the ability to produce reusable, well-structured output.

We address these objectives by proposing ArchiveSpark, a framework for distributed Web archive processing based on *Apache Spark* (s. Sec. 5). By developing a tool solely based on standard file formats, we achieve the distinct advantage of institutions being able to easily share and apply the corpus generation specification across different collections. Towards providing efficient access, ArchiveSpark makes use of a metadata index (CDX) that is widely used by other tools in the domain of Web archiving. The CDX provides a lightweight representation comprised of metadata from all records in an archive. We achieve efficiency of access by exploiting the CDX to select records of interest before accessing the original archived content from disk. We also deliver substantial speed-ups by using *lightweight representations* of records to enhance performance of distributed operations, like grouping and aggregation, unlike existing approaches that operate on much larger raw inputs. More specifically, rather than starting with all archived records and stripping them down, we operate on lightweight representation of records from the CDX and iteratively extend it as needed. We consequently observe large improvements in efficiency as we are able to minimize expensive disk operations involved as the researcher modifies and refines her requirements.

We compare and contrast our system with two alternative approaches and perform benchmarks to show differences in speed for select scenarios (s. Sec. 6). The benchmarks show that ArchiveSpark is faster than a similar approach that

*This work is partly funded by the European Research Council under ALEXANDRIA (ERC 339233)

Permission to make digital or hard copies of all or part of this work for personal or classroom use is granted without fee provided that copies are not made or distributed for profit or commercial advantage and that copies bear this notice and the full citation on the first page. Copyrights for components of this work owned by others than ACM must be honored. Abstracting with credit is permitted. To copy otherwise, or republish, to post on servers or to redistribute to lists, requires prior specific permission and/or a fee. Request permissions from permissions@acm.org.

JCDL '16, June 19-23, 2016, Newark, NJ, USA

© 2016 ACM. ISBN 978-1-4503-4229-2/16/06...$15.00

DOI: http://dx.doi.org/10.1145/2910896.2910902

does not make use of the metadata index in the selected scenarios, which we aim at. Also, depending on the task, ArchiveSpark is even faster than a method of filtering based on HBase, a distributed database system, without the space and time overhead of ingesting and storing the archived data into a database.

ArchiveSpark is fully open-source and contributions to extend its functionality are very much appreciated. For this reason, we provide convenient extension points and an architecture that makes it easy to apply third-party tools to create custom derivatives from Web archives as part of an ArchiveSpark job specification. The working source code with the functionality that we provide out-of-the-box is available for open access:
https://github.com/helgeho/ArchiveSpark

2. USE CASE

In order to use Web archives as a scholarly source for scientific research, a required first step in most cases is the extraction of a well-defined corpus to work with [3, 4]. Scientists typically focus on a temporal and/or a topical subset of the archived data within the scope of their research question. In the following example, we consider five steps to be taken by a political scientist who wants to analyze sentiments and reactions on the Web from a previous election cycle.

Step 1: The researcher would need to define and extract a specific Web collection related to her research. In this case, she would only need websites that were archived in the time period of interest. However, this time-based or longitudinal filter alone would result in too many candidate websites as most Web archives are not topically organized. Finding just election related websites from this candidate pool requires domain expertise and/or manual intervention. For that reason, it is useful to have this pool to be as small as possible to begin with.

Step 2: Since the researcher needs to consider only text resources from websites for her sentiment analysis project, she would apply a filter on *MIME types* to only select such resources. However, identifying these resources by their MIME type involves accessing and parsing the HTTP headers of the records in the archive, which is a low-level detail and needs to be abstracted away from the potentially non-technical researcher.

Step 3: Another required filter involves the *HTTP status code* of a particular capture. The fact that a certain URL was captured at some point in time and is part of the archive does not necessarily mean there was a valid Web resource being served at the URL. The URL could have been the result of an invalid link or a dead URL that was valid at a previous time. As our example researcher would only be interested in successful URL fetches, she would need to filter for records with status code 200.

Step 4: At this point, the candidate set is still likely to be very large for manual analysis. The researcher might decide to only focus on websites that contain certain terms or a specific set of entities, e.g., the candidates of the election. While seeming straightforward, this content-based filter involves accessing the content of every candidate record, which in turn involves separating the headers from the response body, encoding the textual response to a string, parsing out raw text from HTML, and finally applying text processing tools, before filtering on the resulting values.

Step 5: Web archives typically contain multiple captures of a website for every time the website was crawled, regardless of whether it has changed or not. Therefore, our researcher might decide to pick only the latest captures of the candidate URLs. In order to apply this filter, all captures of the intermediate corpus need to be grouped by URLs and sorted by their capture times. These types of operations are very expensive when performed on the raw records that include the entire payload. By operating only on metadata records that contain the required fields, they can be made much more efficient. However, this implementation is not something that the researcher should necessarily be concerned with.

Filtering, selection, grouping and extraction steps, like the ones described, can be arbitrarily continued. Depending on the task at hand, it may be necessary to keep track of where a certain value was derived from. As an example, consider the case that the researcher deems entities extracted from the title text to have more value than those extracted from the body text on a page. Keeping track of this lineage is an essential way to document the collection building and derivation process and enable its comprehension and reproduction by other researchers. Therefore, it should be included in the output format to be used by the researcher in her further research process.

ArchiveSpark seeks to tackle the challenges that arise by a research scenario such as the one described above. A researcher or a technical person supporting her on the corpus building process should be able to easily specify her requirements and efficiently extract the required corpus from a Web archive.

3. RELATED WORK

Scientifically published articles on data extraction from Web archives, like ArchiveSpark, have been very limited. To the best of our knowledge, the only comparable system is *Warcbase* by Lin et al. [5], which will be discussed at the end of this section and serves as the baseline in our benchmarking process (s. Sec 6). There are also a number of other approaches in the area of accessing and mining Web archives including tools from industry.

In this discussion on related work we differentiate between specialized Web archive access approaches based on certain properties and more general approaches. The former provide search and lookup operations as the method of access, while the latter provide access to all of the archived data with support for data processing. ArchiveSpark, our tool for general Web archive access, supports arbitrary filtering and data derivation operations on archived data making it much more suitable for the scientific use of Web archives.

3.1 Specialized Web Archive Access

The Internet Archive[1], one of the driving institutions of Web archiving, and most other Web archives, feature the *Wayback Machine*[2] to provide access to their Web collections. The Wayback Machine enables URL based access to the archived captures of a website, based on a server API powered by a metadata index (CDX). Lookups are designed for efficient, random URL based access and accomplished by running binary searches through the sorted index files.

---

[1]http://archive.org
[2]https://github.com/iipc/openwayback

Researchers can query the CDX server for metadata information of a particular URL, host, domain or URL prefix.

In contrast to these structured queries by means of metadata, the *UK Web Archive*[3] is working on an information retrieval system based on the Apache Solr search platform[4]. Their *Shine* project[5] supports faceted searching and more sophisticated trend analysis of Web archive content. Hockx-Yu [3] identifies 15 Web archives that feature similar kinds of full-text search capabilities. While these are largely engineering efforts that exploit existing search systems, there have also been scientific efforts to build indexes specialized on certain properties, such as time [6] or semantic annotations [7]. There are however two major challenges with these approaches that limit their applicability in the area of corpus building from Web archives. First, it is not always feasible to obtain the necessary resources to parse and index all archived Web content and store them in a search index. Second, even if the necessary resources are available, they cannot efficiently support corpus building processes that go beyond these specialized lookups. For these reasons, with ArchiveSpark, we propose a general data processing approach that exploits the CDX for gains in efficiency while not having to rely on an external index.

3.2 General Web Archive Access

Due to the size of Web archives, often in the order of multiple terabytes, a single machine can no longer process or even store those collections. As a result, distributed computing facilities are commonly implemented for processing archived data. In contrast to the previously discussed specialized access approaches, these facilities enable general access to the archives by operating directly on the data records for selection, filtering, aggregation and transformation.

As part of their self-guided workshops, like the *Web Archive Analysis Workshop*[6] and *ARS Workshop* [7], the Internet Archive provides a number of tools for this purpose. These tools enable researchers to batch process data and derive information like hyperlink graphs and mined text using, *Apache Hadoop*, an open-source implementation of the MapReduce programming model for distributed computing of large datasets [8].

AlSum [9] presents with *ArcContent* a tool for archive access based on Hadoop that uses Cassandra [10], a distributed database to store the extracted data. Similar to ArchiveSpark, it involves a data filtering step where records of interest are selected using the metadata fields in the corresponding CDX dataset. However, in contrast to our approach, the extracted records are stored into Cassandra to be queried through APIs powered by a web service. This only works in cases where the research task is clear and well-defined beforehand and does not involve iterative filtering and data transformations.

Most similar to our ArchiveSpark framework is *Warcbase* by Lin et al. [5], an open-source platform for data processing on Web archives. It provides two different methods to access the data and serve as a baseline in our benchmarks (s. Sec. 6). Warcbase was originally developed to be based on

HBase, an open-source implementation of Google's Bigtable [11], a Hadoop-based distributed database system. It features tools to ingest the Web archive records into HBase and allows for temporal browsing of URLs, with efficient, random URL based access similar to the Wayback Machine. The first method requires the storing of data in HBase with researchers leveraging Hadoop based tools to analyze it. However, this has the major drawback of involving an expensive setup phase of duplicating the entire Web archive in HBase. For the second method, Warcbase provides convenience functions to load and process the archive files directly using *Apache Spark*, one of the most popular alternatives to Hadoop. Spark, in contrast to Hadoop/MapReduce makes extensive use of the main memory of nodes, which has shown to lead to impressive speed-ups [12]. On the GitHub repository of Warcbase, the authors recommend the Spark based method in order to avoid the HBase overhead of the first [13]. However, this Spark based method, in contrast to ArchiveSpark which is also based on Spark, does not optimize for efficiency or meet all of the objectives outlined below.

4. OBJECTIVES

ArchiveSpark addresses six objectives, which we identified as being essential for a tool for corpus creation on Web archives, based on practical requirements. These comprise (1) a simple and expressive interface, (2) compliance to and reuse of the standard formats in the domain of Web archives, (3) an efficient selection and filtering process, (4) an easily extensible architecture to support various derivation tools, (5) lineage support to comprehend and reconstruct the process of derivation from the archive, and (6) an output in a standard, readable and reusable format.

4.1 Simple and Expressive Interface

The primary objective, when we designed ArchiveSpark, was a simple interface that lets users access the fields of interest without the need to do any parsing of archived Web records themselves. Users of this interface would be able to easily express any selection and filtering operations and access available information without carrying over complete archived records at each stage of the workflow. Additionally, the idea was to provide a seamless transition from filtering based on just metadata available in the index to that based on the contents of the archive.

Since ArchiveSpark is based on Spark (s. Section 3.2), which is written in Scala, we naturally chose Scala to be the language of choice for ArchiveSpark. Scala enabled us to specify the ArchiveSpark extraction and derivation workflow in a functional manner. This functional approach is less verbose than that of traditional object oriented languages and often simplifies tasks as it allows for a more natural way of expressing thoughts. Our interface is inspired by the existing Spark API and the Scala standard library, to provide the same degree of simplicity and expressiveness.

Even though the interface, in our opinion, is fairly intuitive to use by a computer scientist or a researcher familiar with programming, we do not expect researchers from other disciplines to be able to use it directly in all cases. However, with the aid of a technically savvy person, the researcher should be able to express her thoughts and requirements on the collection building process and get them easily translated into an executable ArchiveSpark workflow.

---

[3]http://www.webarchive.org.uk/
[4]https://github.com/ukwa/webarchive-discovery/wiki
[5]https://github.com/ukwa/shine/wiki
[6]https://webarchive.jira.com/wiki/display/Iresearch/
Web+Archive+Analysis+Workshop
[7]https://github.com/vinaygoel/ars-workshop

4.2 Standard Formats

In the area of Web archiving, there are a couple of file formats for storing archived web resources and derived metadata that have been established and in wide use over the years. As a result, these formats have either become de-facto standards or have been standardized by ISO. Given their common availability in almost every known Web archive, we wanted our system to be based on these file formats. We did not want to introduce any new file format or index structure: while such files or indexes could provide gains in efficiency for access, their generation would necessitate a pre-processing phase consuming expensive compute resources and additional storage. While being based purely on pre-existing file formats, ArchiveSpark maintains its essential objective of efficiency as described in the next sub-section.

The most important format in the world of Web archives is **WARC** (Web ARChive), which is registered as ISO 28500. WARC is a format to store archived web resources. Every record in a WARC file represents the capture of a single web resource at a given instant of time. The WARC record comprises a header section that includes the URL of the resource, the timestamp of capture and other metadata, as well as a payload section that contains the body returned by the web server. In the case of HTTP responses, the payload consists of a HTTP header and body. Before WARC was introduced as a format to store Web archives, archived records were widely stored in the older **ARC** format[8]. Although ARC is not standardized, many Web archives still contain data in this format, and hence ArchiveSpark supports both WARC and ARC file formats.

Another format which is not standardized but is seen as a de-facto standard is **CDX**[9]. This is an index format that contains a number of metadata fields for every web capture including pointers to the (W)ARC file and the file-offset into the file where the capture is stored. A header line specifies the metadata fields contains in the plain text index file. Most commonly generated, however, are CDX files with either 9 or 11 fields, which are utilized by the Wayback Machine to serve records to users browsing the archive. Since the Wayback Machine software is currently the access method of choice for most Web archives, CDX files are generated by and/or readily available to these archives. As an example, CDX files are available for the crawls provided by the Common Crawl initiative[10]. Furthermore, it is possible to generate both WARC and CDX files with the current version of the Unix/GNU download tool *Wget*[11].

In summary, with ArchiveSpark we designed for, first, being compliant to these standard formats, and second, not introducing and depending on any new format. This way we aim to guarantee that any Web archiving institution that has (W)ARC and corresponding CDX files can use ArchiveSpark to extract and mine their Web collections, without requiring any expensive pre-processing steps or prerequisites.

4.3 Efficiency

Efficiency is one of the core objectives of ArchiveSpark. Since Web archives are typically large scale data collections

of terabytes or even petabytes, a scan-based selection over all archive files is a very time consuming process and can potentially run in the order of multiple days. This is in most cases too inefficient to be used for corpus building as part of a scientific research task.

With ArchiveSpark we leverage the available CDX index files (s. Sec. 4.2). As a first step, we apply filters on the metadata fields from the CDX and generate a small candidate pool with the captures of interest that need to be read in from (W)ARC files. This way, we potentially avoid the scenario of reading in all the records in the archive before ending up rejecting a large number of them (s. Sec 5.1). Our approach of CDX-enabled filtering and selective data access results in efficiency gains over the scan-based approach.

Furthermore, when working with the raw archive records, complex operations, like groupings and aggregations, become much more expensive, since the whole records need to be moved around in a distributed setting. This could be optimized by stripping out data that is not required by those operations. However, if needed later, it will need to be recovered from disk, which is often even more expensive.

With ArchiveSpark we turned this around using a selective data access and derivation approach, starting with lightweight records comprising of only metadata and iteratively extending them as needed, resulting in further gains in efficiency.

4.4 Extensibility

In most research applications, instead of working on the raw archived resources, a researcher is interested in extracting or deriving the data of interest for a given research task. Derivations can either be created from the original payload of an archived resource or from previously derived data. An example of such successive derivations on text are Natural Language Processing (NLP) tasks, such as the extraction of named entities from websites. The corresponding derivation tools operate on natural text and thus, first require the HTML parsers to remove markup and extract plain text, followed by the NLP tool, i.e., the named entity extractor, to extract the desired information.

There are a limitless number of other derivations that researchers can be interested in, e.g., audio/video fingerprinting on archived media files, OCR on archived images and many others. With ArchiveSpark we want to ensure any possible derivation from Web captures, regardless of whether they were constructed by us before-hand or not. Therefore, we designed a very flexible architecture with appropriate extension points that allow the application of custom code as well as third-party libraries to build derivatives from the records of a researcher corpus.

4.5 Traceability

An important trait of any scholarly resource is transparency and traceability. In order to make scientific research reproducible it is essential to understand how the research corpus was designed. However, in the case of Web archives, it is difficult to retrospectively reproduce the crawling process. Reasons for this are, among others, an ever-changing Web, a semi-automatic prioritization by Web crawlers, changing crawling strategies as well as multiple, disparate parties being involved in the collection process. As a result, we found it even more important to focus on documenting the data lineage of corpus building from Web archives.

---

[8]http://archive.org/web/researcher/ArcFileFormat.php
[9]http://archive.org/web/researcher/cdx_file_format.php
[10]http://blog.commoncrawl.org/2015/04/announcing-the-common-crawl-index
[11]https://www.gnu.org/software/wget

Also, depending on the needs of the researcher, it may often be sufficient to only deal with derived information and not include the original records. In order to reproduce this derivation process at a later time, a proper documentation of the data lineage is absolutely crucial. ArchiveSpark achieves this objective of traceability by documenting the data lineage of all the derived records. The documentation includes metadata that allows for the identification of all the source records responsible for the derivative as well as the the derivation path outlining the steps undertaken to filter, transform and derive from these records.

4.6 Reusable Output

The extraction and derivations steps performed by ArchiveSpark act as a preprocessing phase in a research pipeline. The data extracted from the Web archive serves as scholarly source for a research tasks, which can either be manual or programmatic. In the case of manual research, researchers would typically create rather small, very selective corpora and read in the results manually. On the other hand, researchers may use tools to analyze the corpora based on different features in a completely automatic or semi-automatic manner.

In either case, the corpus needs to be clean, well-structured and readable. While human readability implies a pretty printed output without too much clutter, machine readability implies data parsing support. The latter can be guaranteed best by producing data in a commonly used format with existing parsers for various programming languages. One such format is JSON, which was originally introduced as an exchange format for JavaScript to be used by Web services. However, because of its simplicity, it has become a widely used format that can be easily parsed by many pre-existing tools.

JSON supports a cascading nested structure with multiple levels of data and is therefore well-suited for supporting the data lineage functionality of ArchiveSpark (s. Sec 4.5). Another advantage is that these nested cascades of data can be easily presented in a fairly human readable form. For these reasons, we decided on JSON as the default output format of choice. Of course, any other output format that meets our outlined objectives can also be implemented and integrated into ArchiveSpark.

It is worth noting that the use of ArchiveSpark is not restricted to such an output. Researchers can also use it to access the archive, apply filters and derivations, and continue using the rich data types provided by ArchiveSpark in a Spark job to perform data analysis at scale, e.g., machine learning or graph analysis.

5. ARCHIVESPARK

ArchiveSpark is a framework that enables efficient data access, extraction and derivation on Web archive data with a simple API that enables flexible and expressive queries. The following sections describe the approach as well as the distinct features of ArchiveSpark, which are designed to meet the previously described objectives.

5.1 Approach

ArchiveSpark makes use of the CDX metadata index (s. Sec 4.2) to selectively access resources from a Web archive. This approach is optimized for efficiency when extracting a defined subset of records as it avoids having to perform a full scan through all records in (W)ARC files. Since corpora used in scientific fields typically comprise of data derived from a small subset of the entire Web archive, ArchiveSpark is well suited for these use cases.

Figure 1 shows how ArchiveSpark works. First, the filtering process is performed using only metadata contained in the CDX files (s. Sec. 4.2). Second, by utilizing the file pointers contained in the CDX records, ArchiveSpark selectively accesses the filtered records from the underlying (W)ARC files. At this stage, we augment the record's metadata with headers and content from the (W)ARC records. Next, users apply what we term *enrichments* to derive new information, such as named entities or hyperlink data, that is added to the records. These enrichments can be applied by executing custom code or external tools. Based on the derived information, further filters and enrichments may be applied iteratively. The resulting corpus can be saved in a custom JSON format that is tailored to support data lineage.

5.2 Interface

The interface of ArchiveSpark is an API (Application Programming Interface) designed to define the specification of a Web archive extraction and derivation workflow. It is based on Apache Spark and greatly inspired by its API. Also ArchiveSpark uses the data structures of Spark and is hence fully compatible with any transformation methods provided by Spark. Like Spark, ArchiveSpark is implemented in Scala, a functional and object-oriented programming language running inside the JVM, Java's runtime environment. As a result, it is compatible with any third-party library running on the JVM as well, for instance all available Java and Scala libraries.

The entry point to ArchiveSpark is a globally available object with the same name. It serves as a starting point by providing methods to load Web archive files into so-called Spark RDDs (Resilient Distributed Datasets). RDDs are partitioned collections of objects spread across a cluster, stored in memory or on disk. Spark programs are written in terms of operations on RDDs.

Currently, we support reading in (W)ARC and CDX files that are stored in Hadoop HDFS (Hadoop Distributed File System). In order to load an ArchiveSpark RDD from HDFS, one simply needs to specify the path to the (W)ARC and corresponding CDX files. The following code is written in Scala, since it is our language of choice for defining an ArchiveSpark workflow specification:

```
val archive = ArchiveSpark.hdfs(
    "/path/to/(W)ARC", "path/to/CDX")
```

The above *archive* variable now references a Spark RDD consisting of specialized ArchiveSpark records. Hence, all methods provided by Spark to manipulate it through a set of parallel transformations, e.g., filter, as well as actions, e.g., count, can be applied. However, at this point these are based on the CDX data and therefore, only allow access to the metadata fields available in the CDX.

The following call applies filters on HTTP status codes and MIME types and only retains those records with a successful response (*HTTP status code 200*) of type *text/html*:

```
val filtered = archive. filter (r =>
    r.status == 200 && r.mime == "text/html")
```

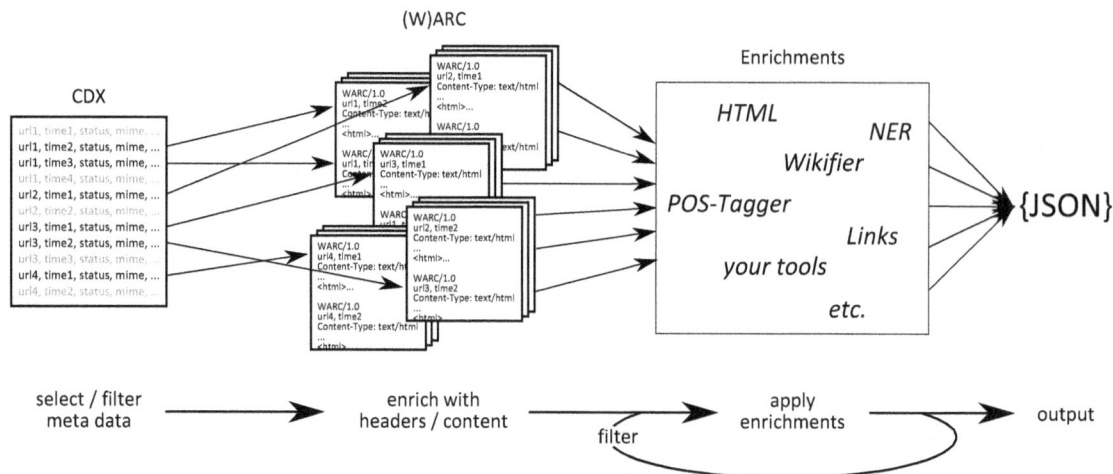

Figure 1: Illustration of the ArchiveSpark selection and enrichment approach.

In the functional paradigm of Scala, every operation returns a new, immutable object instead of modifying the previous one. We have made sure this behavior is provided by ArchiveSpark as well. Hence, *archive* still represents the entire dataset, while *filtered* is a new object representing the filtered one.

As all Spark transformation operations are lazily evaluated, no actual data access will have been performed yet. The original RDD as well as the filtered one are just representations of the corpus to be extracted from the Web archive. The above filter is only evaluated or executed once a Spark *action*, such as a data output, is performed. The advantage of the lazy loading is that, although all CDX records need to be read, only those that have passed through the filters are kept in the dataset consuming much less memory.

To access the actual content of these records in the next step, ArchiveSpark provides a method on archive record RDDs to apply so-called *enrich functions*. The most basic enrich function is *Response*. It opens the (W)ARC records, which are pointed to by the selected CDX records in the dataset, parses the HTTP response and enriches the original records with three fields: 1. (W)ARC header, 2. HTTP header, and 3. Payload:

val response = filtered .enrich(Response)

Enrich functions can depend on each other and be applied consecutively. Each consecutive application derives new information from its parent dependency. While *Response* does not depend on any other enrich function and is usually applied first, *StringContent* depends on *Response*. It transforms the payload of every record in the dataset into a string representation and enriches the record with this string. This works because our filter on the MIME types before made sure that our example dataset only contained text responses and no images or binary files:

val strings = response.enrich(StringContent)

By explicitly enriching the records with both *Response* and *StringContent*, ArchiveSpark marks both these fields to be contained in the output. This way, by specifying what the records should be enriched with, the researcher can control the required features in the final corpus. If the dataset

referenced by the *response* variable had been directly enriched with *StringContent*, only this enrichment would have been part of the output. However, internally, this process would still have first enriched the dataset with *Response* as it is dependent on the payload. And since the payload was already present in the records from an earlier enrichment, the payload would have been used as-is and would not have needed to be re-computed. Note that dependencies specified in enrich functions are defaults but can also be explicitly specified by the user. For the sake of clarity and brevity, we do not show all the currently available methods and options of ArchiveSpark here in this paper.

Based on the enriched information, additional filters can be applied. This process of enriching and filtering can be repeated as needed. For the most efficient execution, it is recommended to apply filters as early as possible i.e. as soon as the data to be filtered on is available. This guarantees that any expensive derivation is performed on as few records as needed. This is especially important for the very first enrichment operation, which involves accessing data from (W)ARC files.

Other than the metadata fields available from the CDX records, the data derived by enrich functions is not typed, as different functions can create fields of various data types. The access to these values is enabled by specifying a path in dot-notation, where each segment specifies a level in the derivation pipeline. ArchiveSpark's *get* method utilizes the ability of Scala to automatically infer data types based on their usage and casts the retrieved value into this type. As an example, the following instruction filters on the content string, i.e., the HTML code in the case of a webpage, and retains only those records that include the term *internet*:

val internet = strings. filter (
     r => r.get("payload.string").contains("internet"))

After the final dataset has been created, it can be written out as JSON using the *saveAsJson* method on archive records RDDs provided by ArchiveSpark. It transforms the records into JSON objects consisting of the metadata and all explicitly enriched data:

internet .saveAsJson("/output/path/results.json.gz")

The *gz* extension is automatically detected by ArchiveSpark and causes it to compress the output using *gzip*. The above six instructions have now created a corpus consisting of all successful text/html responses, i.e., HTML webpages, that contain the term *internet*, formatted as pretty-printed and well-structured JSON in a compressed form. With this workflow approach, we believe we have met our objective of Section 4.1 of a simple and expressive interface.

As an alternative to the JSON output, users are free to transform the archive records that ArchiveSpark uses as its first class citizen into any form they want. We provide all the necessary access methods for this purpose. That way, besides the corpus building use case, ArchiveSpark can be used as a library to access Web archives as part of a larger data analysis application pipeline.

5.3 Extensibility

Currently, we provide the most basic enrich functions to get users started, but we will continue to extend ArchiveSpark with more functions moving forward. As ArchiveSpark is fully open source, any interested parties can also contribute to its development and provide their own tools as enrich functions. To support this, we provide convenient base functions that make it easy for a developer to define custom enrich functions meeting our objective of Section 4.4.

An enrich function consists of the following four properties, which are required in the definition:

1. **Dependency** The enrich function that this function depends on, e.g., *Response*.
2. **Dependency Field** The resulting field of the enrich function that serves as input/source for this function, e.g., *payload*.
3. **Result Fields** The resulting fields of this enrich function, e.g., *string*.
4. **Body** The actual definition of the enrich function, specifying how new data is derived, i.e., the result fields, based on the original record or its dependency. The body can either consist of custom code performing the derivation or call an external tool.

For the sake of simplicity, in addition to the above described *enrich* method we also provide a *mapEnrich* method on archive records RDDs. It allows a user to define enrichments without creating a specialized enrich function. This is especially handy if the enrichment is only used once, a very simple function or a highly custom one that is not worth the overhead of creating a new function. As an example, consider a function to obtain the length of a content string:

```
val enriched = rdd.mapEnrich[String, Int](
        "payload.string",
        "length",
        s => s.length)
```

The syntax of such a *mapEnrich* method is similar to the syntax of Spark's *map* method or the *map* method on standard Scala collections. However, in contrast to *map* functions that transform one value into another, it enriches the original record with the resulting value preserving all the metadata and previously derived information. In the above content length example, *String* specifies the input data type and *Int* the output data type. The first parameter denotes the path from where to load the input and the second pa-

rameter names the result field. Unlike custom enrich functions, *mapEnrich* methods can only create one result field. Instead of specifying the input path with dot separated field names, one can also pass in a dependency enrich function and the dependency field name. The last parameter of the *mapEnrich* method is the body, which derives the required information, the content length in this case, from the value stored in the input path. Applying this method on a dataset creates a new record for each record in the dataset with the result field nested under the input path containing the result value of the body.

5.4 Formats and Lineage Support

Input files required by ArchiveSpark are WARC or ARC files with their corresponding CDX index datasets (s. Sec 4.2). Currently, we support one of the most common CDX formats that is in use by the Internet Archive's Wayback Machine. This format encodes eight metadata fields and three additional fields pointing to the (W)ARC file where the capture is stored along with file-offset and compressed length of the record. However, we can easily support additional CDX metadata as the format evolves in the future.

CDX is a space-separated plain text format with each line representing one record. A single header line at the top of a CDX file denotes the fields: *SURT URL (Sort-friendly URI Reordering Transform), timestamp, original URL, MIME type, HTTP status code, content digest/SHA-1 checksum, redirect URL* (or -), *meta tags* (or -), *(W)ARC record compressed length, (W)ARC record file-offset, (W)ARC filename*.

An example CDX line looks as follows:
```
com,example)/jcdl 20160117113253
http://example.com/jcdl text/html 200 RKMS6XLYED4G8
POFQUIN37WDEWYLD9Z - - 12345 67890 archive.warc.gz
```

For the output format we decided on JSON, a widely used format that meets our objective of Section 4.6. Each output JSON record includes a listing of all the metadata fields from the source CDX identifying the selected resource. If no enrichments are applied, this would be the final output for our example record:

```
{
  "record": {
    "surtUrl": "com,example)/jcdl",
    "timestamp": "2016-01-17T11:32:53.000+01:00",
    "originalUrl": "http://example.com/jcdl",
    "mime": "text/html",
    "status": 200,
    "digest": "RKMS6XLYED4G8POFQUIN37WDEWYLD9Z",
    "redirectUrl": "-",
    "meta": "-"
  }
}
```

Enrichments are added to these JSON objects as additional keys next to *record*. In case the *Response* enrich function is applied, as in our example from Section 5.2, the (W)ARC headers, HTTP headers as well as the raw bytes of the payload will be added in:

```
{
  "record": {...},
  "recordHeader":{
    "subject-uri": "http://www.example.com/",
    "content-type": "text/html",
```

```
    "creation-date": "20160117113253",
    ...
  },
  "httpHeader": {
    "Date":"Sun, 17 Jan 2016 10:32:53 GMT",
    "Connection":"close",
    "Content-Type":"text/html",
    ...
  },
  "payload": "bytes(length: 2345)"
}
```

Any other enrich function that depends on a value produced by *Response*, e.g., payload, will result in the output being added as a nested value. If, for instance, the dataset was enriched with *StringContent*, which calls *Response* implicitly as its dependency, the resulting JSON might look like this:

```
{
  "record": {...},
  "payload": {
    "string": "<html>...</html>"
  }
}
```

In this case, the record and HTTP headers are not included, since the user did not explicitly specify them to be part of the corpus. The payload, however, is required to document the lineage of the string (the string representation of the payload). This meets the traceability objective of Section 4.5 as every derived value can be traced back through the cascades to its origin.

When the user is interested in both the original value as well its derivations, for instance, when *mapEnrich* is called to enrich the dataset records with their string content lengths (s. Sec 5.3), a special underscore key (_) is introduced. The field with this key retains the original value, like in the following example:

```
{
  "record": {...},
  "payload": {
    "string": {
      "_": "<html>...</html>",
      "length": 2345
    }
  }
}
```

Other derivatives based on this string content would be placed next to the underscore, just like *length*. In the same way, if the dataset was explicitly enriched with both *Response* and *StringContent*, the byte representation of the payload along with the header fields would have been placed next to *string*.

Finally, we consider the example of deriving named entities from the titles using the HTML string representation. This example would involve a HTML parser, which depends on StringContent to enrich the dataset with the required title value nested under a HTML field, as well as a named entity extractor tool, which in turn depends on the title to create a set of named entities. The lineage path of this constructed example would look as follows: *payload.string.html.title.entities*.

6. BENCHMARKS

We ran benchmarks to assess the efficiency benefits of exploiting the CDX dataset when accessing Web archives (s. Sec. 5.1). The run times of three different scenarios are compared using ArchiveSpark and two baseline approaches: a scan-based approach using pure Spark, and the Warcbase approach using HBase. For both baselines, we used the tools provided by Warcbase to load and access the datasets (cp. Sec. 3).

6.1 Dataset

One of the services provided by the Internet Archive is Archive-It[12]. It is subscription based and enables partner institutions to run selective focused crawls to create and archive their own thematic and event driven collections. For our experiments, we chose one of these collections, the *Occupy Movement 2011/2012*[13] collection, collected by the Internet Archive itself. Unlike a generic Web crawl collection, this collection features a well-defined scope and is not too large, allowing our benchmarks to be performed in a reasonable amount of time.

The collection contains a total of 17,478,067 (17.4 Million) captures with 10,089,668 (10.08 Million) unique URLs. It contains Web content crawled during the time period Dec 3, 2011 to Oct 9, 2012, with a total storage of 470.9 GB of compressed WARC files. The CDX data, generated by us, adds in 24.4 GB of data size.

6.2 Experimental Setup

The experiments were performed on a Hadoop cluster running the Cloudera distribution[14] (Hadoop 2.6.0-cdh5.4.9). The cluster consisted of 2 master nodes and 24 compute nodes with a total of 256 CPU cores, 2560 GB of RAM and 960 TB of hard disk space.

The three systems we compared in the benchmarks were:

1. ArchiveSpark
2. Spark: Using Warcbase's Spark library
3. HBase: Using Warcbase's ingestion tool

For both ArchiveSpark and pure Spark approach, WARC files from the collection were stored in Hadoop HDFS. The CDX files required by ArchiveSpark were generated using the Internet Archive's CDX Generator, which is available open source on GitHub[15]. Generating the CDX files took 110 minutes, however, this is a one time process and is anyway a necessary step to enable access services like the Wayback Machine. This dataset could have also been downloaded directly from Archive-It. For these reasons, we consider this CDX generation step to be negligible in the benchmarks.

In the HBase (Warcbase) approach, we had to first ingest WARC files into HBase. Warcbase exploits certain properties of HBase to enable access to Web archives. For instance, different captures of a crawled Web resource are stored as timestamped versions of the same record in HBase. URLs are stored in an inverted, sort-friendly format and are used as row keys for fast lookups with the MIME type serving as a column qualifier. These design decisions allow for an efficient selection and filtering process based on these three

---

[12]https://archive-it.org
[13]https://archive-it.org/collections/2950
[14]http://www.cloudera.com
[15]https://github.com/internetarchive

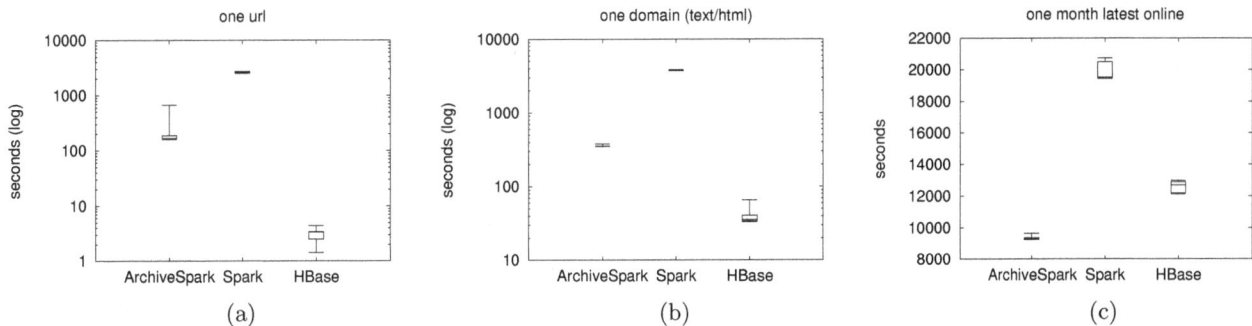

Figure 2: Benchmark times of ArchiveSpark vs. Spark vs. HBase (both by leveraging Warcbase)

properties: URL, timestamp of capture, and the MIME type. When additional fields are required, those need to be parsed from the WARC records, either from headers or the payload, which are stored as values in HBase cells. Due to limitations on the local disk space of our cluster, we had to ingest the data into HBase from the WARC files stored in HDFS. As the current version of Warcbase only supports reading in WARC files from the local file system, we modified this system accordingly. The ingesting process took a little over 24 hours with the resulting database containing a complete copy of the entire collection.

For both the Spark and HBase approaches, we queried the data using Spark and also used it to perform operations on the resulting data. All three systems being compared ran with the same Spark configurations, using 10 executors with 4 GB of memory each. As the cluster was not exclusively available to us, with other jobs running at the same time, the cluster load varied among the benchmarks. To compensate for these variations, we ran every single benchmark a total of five times.

We chose a common task among all benchmarks: select a subset of records from the entire dataset, count the length of the string content of these records and compute the sum of these lengths. This task is well-suited for the benchmarking process since it features the extraction workflow supported by ArchiveSpark. It involves a filtering phase to select the subset of records of interest, an enrichment phase to augment records with content, as well as a derivation phase that enriches the content with its string representation and length. We intentionally did not apply any more sophisticated enrichments that involved third-party libraries as those would only be applied on top of these results and would depend on the performance of these external tools.

6.3 Scenarios and Results

The benchmark consisted of three different scenarios, starting with the most basic filtering operation to only select records of a given URL, and ending with a more sophisticated scenario involving a grouping operation to select the latest online capture of all URL from a specific time period.

6.3.1 Scenario 1

First, we filtered the dataset for all records of one particular URL, i.e., *http://map.15october.net/reports/view/590/*. In case of HBase, this is directly supported and constitutes a simple row query. Therefore, it is understandably very fast

with the query taking between 1.4 and 4.4 seconds. However, when comparing with the other approaches, the preprocessing time required for HBase as well as the additional space requirements need to be kept in mind (s. Sec. 6.2). The times of all three approaches are illustrated in Figure 2a, where the whiskers represent the fastest and slowest runs, while the box covers the ones in the middle, with a centered line representing the median. As shown, ArchiveSpark is about 100 times slower with times between 160.3 and 675.4 seconds, but still around 10 times faster than pure Spark with times between 2522.6 and 2734.0 seconds. This is where ArchiveSpark's incorporation of the CDX index leads to performance benefits as it allows for the selective access of only records of the given URL, while pure Spark performs a scan over the entire dataset and parses every single record in order to find these records.

6.3.2 Scenario 2

In the second scenario, instead of filtering by URL, we selected all webpages, i.e., MIME type *text/html*, belonging to a specific domain, i.e., *15october.net*. The results are shown in Figure 2b. The HBase query performs a targeted row scan again, this time for all keys starting with the specified domain in its inverted, sort-friendly form, i.e., *net.15october*). However, this alone is not sufficient as the scan would also yield rows starting with *net.15octoberx*, which is not the correct domain. Therefore, an additional filtering step is required. Next, the filter by MIME type *text/html* is also directly supported by HBase, since MIME type is available as a column label. With times between 33.4 and 65.6 seconds, the HBase approach is around a magnitude of 10 slower than in the first scenario. ArchiveSpark comes closer to HBase with times between 349.2 and 379.1 seconds, because both values to be filtered are part of the CDX and therefore, the task is similar to the one in the first scenario. The pure Spark approach of a complete scan is around 10 times slower than ArchiveSpark with times between 3737.7 and 3853.2 seconds.

6.3.3 Scenario 3

Finally, we selected the latest successful captures for all URLs crawled in a specific month, i.e., Dec 2011. This is accomplished in two steps: first, all captures from the desired time period (Dec 2011) and with a successful response (status code 200) are selected and next, the latest capture for each candidate URL is chosen. The pure Spark approach takes between 19432.0 and 20744.3 seconds in this scenario. This approach first scans through all records of the dataset, followed by the step of identifying the latest capture of every URL from the set of qualifying records. This may be more efficient when only a few records of a dataset need to be filtered out. However, in scenarios, like this, where users are interested in only a small subset of a large collection, it is very slow. In the HBase approach, although HBase directly supports timestamp based filtering, which is performed on the versions of a URL, filtering on the HTTP status code requires parsing the WARC record to read in the status code. Only then can the latest successful captures be selected as an additional post-processing step. The HBase approach takes between 12117.7 and 12971.5 seconds. For ArchiveSpark, as both properties, timestamp and HTTP status, are contained in the CDX files (cp. Sec. 5.4), the filtering as well as selection of the latest captures is entirely possible using just the CDX. For that reason, ArchiveSpark leads in this benchmark as illustrated in Figure 2c with times between 9639.6 and 9270.8 seconds. This illustrates how the rich potential of ArchiveSpark's selective access approach is unlocked when a large fraction of the dataset can be filtered out based on available metadata.

7. CONCLUSION AND OUTLOOK

Web archives are becoming more and more important as a scholarly source and building a corpus from these archives is typically one of the first steps in any research process. Since researchers working with these Web collections are often from the humanities with no technical background, there is clearly a need to simplify this extraction and derivation process. In the first part of this paper, we presented a number of objectives and discussed why we deem them as essential for any system that supports building research corpora from Web archives. These include simplicity in terms of usage and extensibility, efficiency of access and traceability by documenting data lineage for the purposes of reproduction and reuse.

In the second half of the paper, we presented ArchiveSpark, a framework that effectively tackles these objectives by making use of existing file formats, a functional approach to data processing at scale and utilizing a widely deployed metadata index. By utilizing this index that is a de-facto standard in the area of Web archiving, ArchiveSpark avoids having to perform any pre-processing of the data or having to invest in additional storage space. We also provided benchmarks that show how ArchiveSpark is more efficient than other alternatives when selecting records of interest based on the rich metadata already available in the metadata index. ArchiveSpark, however, is not the best option when a data processing task needs to run across all or a large fraction of the records in a Web archive.

Moving forward, we plan to extend ArchiveSpark to support more data sources, such as streaming data over HTTP, which would allow researchers to efficiently extract corpora from publicly available, remote Web archives without needing a local copy of the complete dataset. Since Python is a popular language among data researchers and scientists, we plan to provide support for PySpark, the Python API for Apache Spark. ArchiveSpark is fully open source, and we hope for many contributions from the broader community, especially in terms of third-party tools to be used as extensions in the ArchiveSpark pipeline.

References

[1] Jefferson Bailey et al. (Internet Archive). Web archiving in the united states: A 2013 survey, 2014. URL http://www.digitalpreservation.gov/ndsa/working_groups/documents/NDSA_USWebArchivingSurvey_2013.pdf. A report of the National Digital Stewardship Alliance. [Accessed: 11/01/2016].

[2] Daniel Gomes, João Miranda, and Miguel Costa. A survey on web archiving initiatives. In *Proceedings of TPDL'11*.

[3] Helen Hockx-Yu. Access and scholarly use of web archives. *Alexandria*, 25(1-2):113–127, 2014.

[4] Niels Brügger. Web history, web archives, and web research infrastructure - between close and distant reading, 2015. URL http://alexandria-project.eu/events/2nd-int-alexandria-workshop-2015. Keynote at the 2nd Int. Alexandria Workshop on Foundations for Temporal Retrieval, Exploration and Analytics in Web Archives on 03/11/2015 [Accessed: 17/01/2016].

[5] Jimmy Lin, Milad Gholami, and Jinfeng Rao. Infrastructure for supporting exploration and discovery in web archives. In *WWW'14 Companion*, 2014.

[6] Avishek Anand, Srikanta Bedathur, Klaus Berberich, and Ralf Schenkel. Temporal index sharding for space-time efficiency in archive search. In *Proceedings of the 34th international ACM SIGIR conference on Research and development in Information Retrieval*, 2011.

[7] Annika Hinze, Craig Taube-Schock, David Bainbridge, Rangi Matamua, and J Stephen Downie. Improving access to large-scale digital libraries throughsemantic-enhanced search and disambiguation. In *Proceedings of the 15th ACM/IEEE-CE on Joint Conference on Digital Libraries*, 2015.

[8] Jeffrey Dean and Sanjay Ghemawat. Mapreduce: a flexible data processing tool. *Communications of the ACM*, 53(1):72–77, 2010.

[9] Ahmed AlSum. *Web archive services framework for tighter integration between the past and present web*. PhD thesis, Old Dominion University, 2014.

[10] Avinash Lakshman and Prashant Malik. Cassandra: a decentralized structured storage system. *ACM SIGOPS Operating Systems Review*, 44(2):35–40, 2010.

[11] Fay Chang, Jeffrey Dean, Sanjay Ghemawat, Wilson C Hsieh, Deborah A Wallach, Mike Burrows, Tushar Chandra, Andrew Fikes, and Robert E Gruber. Bigtable: A distributed storage system for structured data. *ACM Transactions on Computer Systems (TOCS)*, 26(2):4, 2008.

[12] Matei Zaharia, Mosharaf Chowdhury, Michael J Franklin, Scott Shenker, and Ion Stoica. Spark: cluster computing with working sets. In *Proceedings of the 2nd USENIX conference on Hot topics in cloud computing*, volume 10, page 10, 2010.

[13] Jimmy Lin. Warcbase on github. URL https://github.com/lintool/warcbase. [Accessed: 11/01/2016].

Low-cost Semantic Enhancement to Digital Library Metadata and Indexing: Simple Yet Effective Strategies

Annika Hinze
University of Waikato
Hamilton, New Zealand
hinze@waikato.ac.nz

David Bainbridge
University of Waikato
Hamilton, New Zealand
davidb@waikato.ac.nz

Sally Jo Cunningham
University of Waikato
Hamilton, New Zealand
sallyjo@waikato.ac.nz

J. Stephen Downie
Library & Information Science
University of Illinois
jdownie@illinois.edu

ABSTRACT

Most existing digital libraries use traditional lexically-based retrieval techniques. For established systems, completely replacing, or even making significant changes to the document retrieval mechanism (document analysis, indexing strategy, query processing and query interface) would require major technological effort, and would most likely be disruptive. In this paper, we describe ways to use the results of semantic analysis and disambiguation, while retaining an existing keyword-based search and lexicographic index. We engineer this so the output of semantic analysis (performed off-line) is suitable for import directly into existing digital library metadata and index structures, and thus incorporated without the need for architecture modifications.

CCS Concepts

•**Computing methodologies** → **Semantic networks;** *Lexical semantics;* •**Applied computing** → **Digital libraries and archives;** •**Information systems** → *Digital libraries and archives; Search engine indexing;*

Keywords

Semantic analysis; disambiguation; indexing; semantic enrichment

1. INTRODUCTION

Search in large collections—such as the bespoke solutions developed for the HathiTrust Digital Library (HTDL, www.hathitrust.org) and Google Books (books.google.com) or those built through general purpose digital library software, such as the Greenstone toolkit (www.greenstone.org)—is at the core of the services provided by a digital library. Most of these established systems provide access primarily by string-based search over inverted indexes [8] of both document full-texts and metadata, with text-based search that is implemented using lexicographic analysis (such as Solr/Lucene indexes).

Permission to make digital or hard copies of all or part of this work for personal or classroom use is granted without fee provided that copies are not made or distributed for profit or commercial advantage and that copies bear this notice and the full citation on the first page. Copyrights for components of this work owned by others than ACM must be honored. Abstracting with credit is permitted. To copy otherwise, or republish, to post on servers or to redistribute to lists, requires prior specific permission and/or a fee. Request permissions from permissions@acm.org.

JCDL '16, June 19-23, 2016, Newark, NJ, USA

© 2016 ACM. ISBN 978-1-4503-4229-2/16/06...$15.00

DOI: http://dx.doi.org/10.1145/2910896.2910910

Most scholars using these digital libraries, however, are interested not in simple textual keywords but rather in semantic concepts. Having to express their search as keywords is restrictive in its expressiveness, and of limited use for exploring whole collections. Lexicographic search in large collections, such as the HathiTrust's 13,000,000 volumes with 4.6 billion pages, often returns large sets of unrelated documents (due to homographs —same spelling, different meaning—being included), while relevant sources may remain undetected unless the right keyword is found. The problem is exacerbated in documents that have been obtained through Optical Character Recognition (OCR), as recognition errors may lead to misidentification of terms, which are then either mistakenly included or omitted from the search results.

In the Capisco project [3], we introduced a new way of semantic search in large collections that affords the benefits of semantic search while minimizing the problems associated with applying existing semantic analysis at scale. The developed software architecture avoids the need for complete semantic document markup using pre-existing ontologies by developing an automatically generated *Concept-in-Context* (*CiC*) network seeded by *a priori* analysis of Wikipedia texts and identification of semantic metadata. Capisco also provides the means to manually introduce or modify concepts in this *CiC* knowledge base. The disambiguation of large document collections is done automatically using the *CiC* network as a knowledge base for semantic analysis. Capisco's search interface guides the user through a manual disambiguation of query terms into semantic concepts. We showed in [3] that using Capisco reduces the number of *false positives*, includes documents missed when using keyword-based search (increased *true positives*), and can to some extent remedy OCR problems (by excluding out-of-context concepts, which may stem from OCR errors).

To use Capisco in already established digital library systems, however, would require making major changes to the document retrieval mechanism, such as the introduction of semantic document analysis, and changing the indexing strategy, query processing and query interface. Such a major technological change would most likely be disruptive for both the digital library users and the software maintenance team. In this paper, we explore ways of extending the conventional digital library's retrieval capabilities by importing the results of semantic analysis and disambiguation (such as those from Capisco), while retaining an existing keyword-based search and lexicographic index.

The remainder of the paper is structured as follows: Section 2 briefly describes related work on using concepts and semantic relationships mined from Wikipedia. Section 3 outlines the basic components of typical lexical indexing in Digital Libraries (DLs) and indexing in Capisco with specific focus on semantic disambiguation and indexing structures. Section 4 then discusses options to incorporate semantic information into existing DL systems. Section 5 presents results for a number of small test collections, and compares the quality of the results. We then show a worked example of a system using semantic enhancements to index and metadata in Section 6. Section 7 discusses related approaches, lessons-learned from our explorations, and future research directions, while Section 8 concludes the paper.

2. RELATED WORK

Our research is situated in the body of work exploring the application to information retrieval of concepts and semantic relationships mined from Wikipedia. The key insight in this use of Wikipedia is to treat its structure (rather than the contents of its articles) as a semantic resource: the title for each article is a brief phrase describing a single concept, and the links between articles capture the hierarchical and associative relationships between concepts. "Redirects" link alternative expressions of a concept (e.g., synonyms, abbreviations, spelling variations, colloquialisms, scientific terms, *etc.*) to the concept term (the article title) [10].

The mined Wikipedia structures have been exploited to enhance different aspects of a retrieval system architecture and to support user searching: to automatically create a domain-specific thesaurus [10] or a general thesaurus covering all Wikipedia topics [10, 13], to cluster documents based on the semantic relatedness of their associated Wikipedia concepts/articles [4], and to develop search interfaces that support semantic-based query expansion and query refinement [12, 3]. Key to all of these applications is efficient support for automatically cross-referencing document terms with their associated Wikipedia link structure [11, 9].

This earlier work largely developed proof-of-concept systems and included evaluations to establish the potential *effectiveness* of mined concepts and relationships for improving search. In contrast, in this present paper we investigate the *practicality* of including mined concepts and relationships into existing DLs. Our goal here is to explore the opportunities to gain the benefits of semantic enhancements while requiring minimal, if any, changes to a DL's underlying architecture and interface.

3. BACKGROUND: LEXICAL AND SEMANTIC INDEXING

In this section, we introduce an example user's information need and a set of documents that will be used to explore the implications of our different search strategies. We then outline the indexing processes, data structures and search options for both lexical indexing (typical for DLs) and semantic indexing (Capisco), in Sections 3.2 and 3.3, respectively. We assume the existence of a collection of documents, in which each of the documents consists of one page or more and the length of pages is variable. Figure 1 shows a simplified structure of a document (here consisting of three pages) and the catalogue's bibliographic metadata for the document. We focus on text-based indexing; similar processes and structures would be used for other media types. For simplicity, we use *term* to refer to single words, phrases, or n-grams (sequence of n words).

3.1 Example query and documents

Throughout the paper, we use the main example of a user querying for information about the Pacific island nation of Niue over a collection of documents. We selected four example documents to highlight the implications of the various indexing and search strate-

Doc-ID	OCR-ed term	Semantics	Match
$D1_{Niue}^{+}$	"Niue"	*Niue*	yes
$D2_{SI}^{+}$	"Savage Island"	*Niue*	yes
$D3_{SI}^{-}$	"Savage Island"	*primitive place*	no
$D4_{Niue}^{-}$	"Niue"	*Nine*	no

Table 1: Example documents for information need *Niue*

gies, see Table 1.[1] The documents are referred to as D1–D4 with qualifiers indicating whether a document is relevant for our user's information need regarding the Niue island (superscript + or −) and a shorthand notation of the query relevant OCR-ed term in the document (subscript).

$D1_{Niue}^{+}$ The first document is a 1970 book about the *Flora of Niue* [15]. It contains the literal term "Niue" both in its title and on several pages throughout the book. The document is relevant to the user's information need.

$D2_{SI}^{+}$ The second document is an historic collection from 1889 of reports about Niue and other Pacific islands [1]; it is also relevant to the user's information need. As was customary at the time, it refers to the Niue island by the term "Savage Island".

$D3_{SI}^{-}$ The third document is John Redmond's 1910 speech to the Irish Parliament, in which he refers to the Irish Railway system of the time as being as "neglected as if it had been a savage island in some distant ocean" [14]; it is not relevant to the user's information need.

$D4_{Niue}^{-}$ Finally, the fourth document is an historic treatise published 1870 about the church in Wales [5]. It contains an OCR error that interprets the word "Nine" as "Niue". This book is also not relevant to the user's information need.

We now explain how both lexical full-text search and semantic search using Capisco execute this example search and the implications for the respective result sets. This explanation forms the foundation for exploring (in Section 4) how to merge Capisco semantic data into existing digital library metadata and index structures without the need for architecture changes.

3.2 Lexical indexing

Typical full-text indexing (e.g., as provided by Solr[2]) analyzes the contents of each text page (performing lexical transforms such as case folding, stop-word removal and stemming) and creates for each term an index entry with references to the pages on which the term appears (see Figure 1, top). The bibliographic metadata is typically kept in a separate structure, where each metadata field (such as author, title, subject) carries one or several entries, which link to the document (see Figure 1, bottom). Some DL implementations additionally include the metadata in the full-text index.

Common search interfaces for DLs offer 'simple full-text search' and 'advanced full-text search'. Simple search typically offers a single query box for keywords or phrases (see mock-up in Figure 2, left) and executes a search via the full-text and all metadata fields. The advanced search option typically allows a user to specify a Boolean combination of searches in full-text and in each of the metadata fields (see Figure 2, top right). Additionally some

---

[1] These documents and other test collections have been provided by the HathiTrust.

[2] lucene.apache.org/solr/

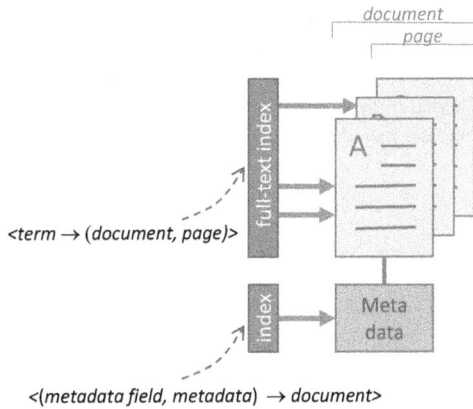

Figure 1: Lexicographic indexing

systems support filtering of results by selected metadata fields (see Figure 2, bottom right). The only metadata fields that can be used for filtering are those that have numerous entries (such as language or format) out of which the user can select the appropriate ones.

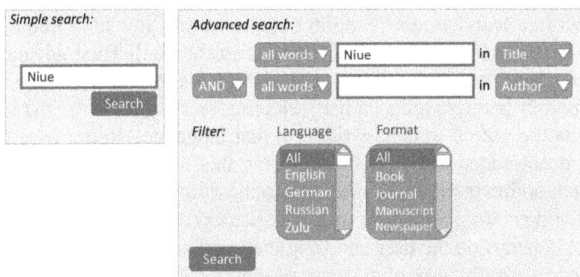

Figure 2: Mock-up of Simple (left) and Advanced (right) Lexical Search interfaces for DL collections

Example 1. (Lexical index & search) *Let us now consider our four example documents $D1$ to $D4_{Niue}^-$ introduced above. Figure 3 shows a simplified full-text index structure (as used in Fig. 1, top) for the terms "Niue" and "Savage Island" appearing in each of the four documents.[3] Even though the two terms have different semantic meanings in the documents, each occurrence will be treated the same in the index.*

Figure 3: Example index structure for full-text (snippet)

Using this index in simple full-text search (see Figure 2, left) will result in documents $D1_{Niue}^+$ and $D4_{Niue}^-$ being included in the result list, and $D2_{SI}^+$ and $D3_{SI}^-$ being omitted. $D4_{Niue}^-$ is a false positive and $D2_{SI}^+$ is a false negative.

Using advanced search (see Figure 2, upper right) on the bibliographic metadata field title, alone or in conjunction to the full-text search, yields the result set $D1_{Niue}^+$ (removing the false positive $D4_{Niue}^-$). This approach, however, excludes other matching documents that do not carry to term "Niue" in their title (such as $D2_{SI}^+$).

---

[3]For simplicity, we abstract from the precise locations in which the terms appear on each page.

Additional filtering of bibliographic metadata by language or format (see Figure 2, lower right) is not useful here as all four documents are books in English.

3.3 Capisco: Semantic indexing

Capisco uses a knowledge base containing information about concepts in context, initially created by mining Wikipedia and potentially further enriched by domain experts (see orange elements in Fig. 7). Each concept is identified by an *id*, and also carries a human-readable *concept label*. Concept labels are derived from Wikipedia article titles. Synonymous terms for a concept are stored with reference to the context in which they appear. The context of a term refers to the main area in which this term is used for this concept (e.g., term "Apple" refers to concept *Apple Record* in the context of *music* and to the concept *Malus domestica* in the context of *horticulture*). Because contexts are also concepts, the knowledge base forms an interlinked Concepts in Context (CiC) network.

Capisco processes each document by first disambiguating each term (i.e., identifying its semantic concept) by reverse look-up of the term in the knowledge base (i.e., querying all synonyms) to identify potentially matching concepts. These concepts are then disambiguated by filtering out those concepts for which no valid context can be found on the document page. This leads to the identification of *significant* topics within a document (i.e., not every noun found in the document matches a concept). For further detail on the disambiguation process, see [3]. The identified concepts for each document are then indexed into a full-concept index, analogous to traditional full-text indexes. For each context, an index entry is created with references to the pages on which the term appears (see Figure 4, middle). The index carries only concept IDs; concept labels and synonyms can be accessed via the knowledge base (see Figure 4, left). Due to Capisco's focus on semantic search, it does not currently employ an index for the metadata; if it did, the index would be identical to the one in lexical indexing.

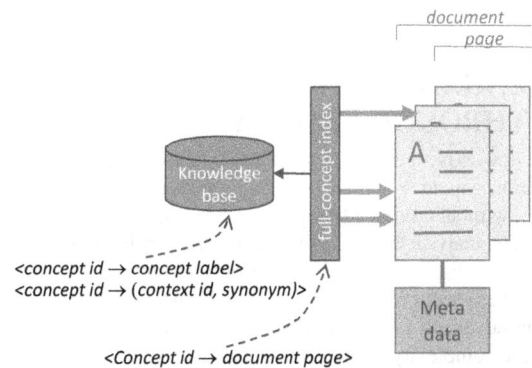

Figure 4: Capisco indexing

Capisco's search interface starts similarly to lexical search by the user inserting search terms (see mock-up in Figure 5, left). One or more keywords can be entered; our example shows the process for the single term "Puck". For each search term, Capisco retrieves all potentially matching concepts and presents these to the user for manual disambiguation (Figure 5, right). Once the user has selected the concept that matches their search interest, the search process is executed via a lookup of the concept IDs in the full-context index. A detailed description of the process with a walk-through with interface screen-shots can be found in [3].

Example 2. (Semantic index & search) *Figure 6 shows the full-concept index structure in Capisco for the terms "Niue" and*

95

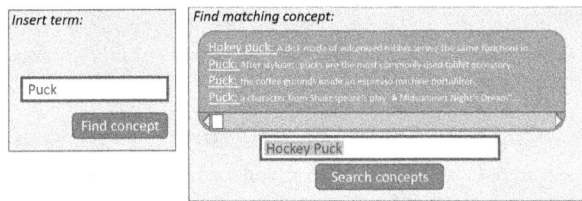

Figure 5: Mock-up of Manual Disambiguation and Search interface

"Savage Island" appearing in our four documents. The terms that are used synonymously for Niue Island (which has the concept ID 14334) are referred to in the knowledge base, while the index itself only contains the concept ID. Note that the use of the phrase "savage island" in document $D3_{SI}^{-}$ is not related to a specific concept, as it was merely a figure of speech, and is therefore not included in the semantic index. Neither is the term "Niue" from document $D4_{Niue}^{-}$ included, as there is no context supporting such a semantic reading.

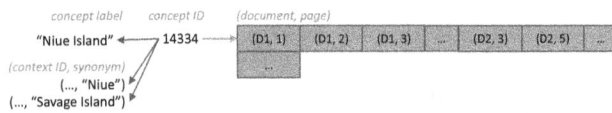

Figure 6: Example index structure for Capsico (snippet)

Searching using Capisco, the user is first guided through the manual disambiguation of the search term "Niue" to the concept Niue Island (id 14334), using an interface like the one shown in Figure 5. Capisco then uses the full-concept index (see Figure 6) to look-up the documents for ID=14334. This will result in documents $D1_{Niue}^{+}$ and $D2_{SI}^{+}$ being included in the result list, and $D3_{SI}^{-}$ and $D4_{Niue}^{-}$ being omitted. In this case, a concept search would return no false negatives or false positives.

4. ENHANCING LEXICAL SEARCH THROUGH SEMANTICS

We now explore strategies that allow us to use the semantic information gained by employing Capisco (see orange elements in Fig. 7), without completely replacing the established lexicographic document analysis, indexing technique, or query interface (see blue elements in Fig. 7). We explore four options open to standard digital libraries (Sections 4.1–4.4), and one further option for DLs supporting advanced metadata structures (Section 4.5). We will explore the complexity of the solution (in terms of changes needed in the DL system's interface and indexing) and implications for query formulation and result quality (by exploring the potential for introducing false negatives and false positives into search results).

4.1 Concept labels added to metadata

Figure 7: Export of semantic concepts into existing DL indexes

The most straight-forward way to incorporate the concepts that have been identified for each document is to create a new metadata field at the document level. Each of the concept labels is then automatically added to this concept field, similar to the treatment of entries in a subject metadata field. Fig. 8 illustrates this approach.

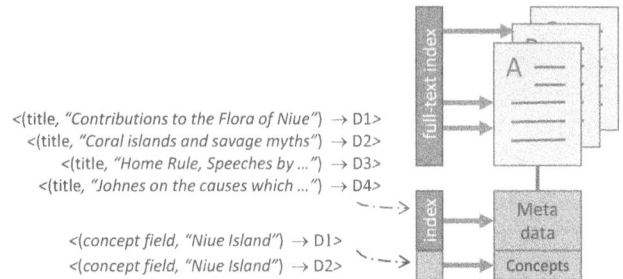

Figure 8: *Approach 1*–Concept labels added to metadata; extended indexing structure (right) and example snippet (left)

Searching for a document using a digital library's advanced catalogue search may then use this metadata field as one of the options either in a search or else as a filter applied at the time of searching. An example of filtering can been seen in the HathiTrust advance query page[4] where the union of all the languages the collection is written in is displayed as a list: selecting an item from the list restricts the search to texts written in that language. In our case of a concept added to the metadata, using this field as a conjunctive search option restricts the result set to those documents for which a matching concept label is found. The success of this strategy, therefore, depends on the user choosing the exact same search keyword as appears in the matching concept label.

Example 3. Approach 1–search *Using this indexing approach with our four documents leads to concept labels being added to the metadata as indicated in Figure 8, left. Results for both simple and advanced search now depend on whether the DL indexer uses a tokenizer: either the metadata is interpreted as the phrase "Niue Island" or interpreted as two words. In the first case, a simple or advanced search for "Niue" will lead to the same results as pure lexical search (see Example 1). In the second case, executing a simple search for "Niue" evaluates the full-text and all metadata fields, leading to a result set containing $D1_{Niue}^{+}$, $D2_{SI}^{+}$ and $D4_{Niue}^{-}$. When comparing to the purely lexical search result (see Example 1), we note that the false positive $D4_{Niue}^{-}$ is retained while the false negative $D2_{SI}^{+}$ from lexical search is remedied. The result of the advanced search for "Niue" in the concept field alone leads to $D1_{Niue}^{+}$ and $D2_{SI}^{+}$, thus removing the false positive $D4_{Niue}^{-}$ and addressing the false negative $D2_{SI}^{+}$ from lexical search. We note that the user here selected a matching keyword "Niue"; any other keyword, such as "Niu" or "Niue-Fekai" (both alternative names for the island) are unsuccessful.*

Using advanced search with filtering (such as shown in Figure 2 bottom right) may have better outcomes. Each concept is represented by one term only and users would select one such concept; thus metadata filtering offers greater transparency to the user (than in metadata search). However, users are still required to scan the complete (alphabetically ordered) list. If the concept labels are listed without further information about their semantic meaning,

---

[4]Such as the advanced search for HathiTrust items at catalog.hathitrust.org/Search/Advanced

misunderstandings are hard to avoid. Providing additional semantic information about a concept would therefore be advised. Overall concept metadata filtering is a simple and easy to achieve option, tempered with the observation that it has some challenges for search interface usability.

If the user filters by the correct concept, the search results will filter out those false positives that would be included in the ordinary lexicographic search through homonyms. However, if they combine the filter with a non-matching full-text search term, the result set is reduced (different to semantic search in Capisco). Best results are therefore achieved if the search keyword matches the concept filter (thus semantically narrowing the search for the term).

Finally, the result list may include large numbers of correctly matching documents which are nevertheless not of particular interest (i.e., no ranking by concept filter). This could be offset through only including the n most important concepts (although this in turn would then limit the filter capability).

Example 4. Approach 1–filter *To use a filter on the concept field, our user first needs to identify a suitable concept label from a list. Fortunately, in this case the concept label "Niue island" is similar to the user's search term "Niue". Filtering by concept field only, leads to the results $D1^+_{Niue}$ and $D2^+_{SI}$ (again removing the false positive $D4^-_{Niue}$, and omitting the negative $D2^+_{SI}$ from lexical search). Using an advanced search, e.g., for "Niue", on the full-text in conjunction with the filter by concept field Niue Island, reduces the result set to $D1^+_{Niue}$ (with false negative $D2^+_{SI}$). Users may habitually try to ask for their search term in several fields, and may therefore not be familiar with these implications.*

4.2 Concepts & synonyms added to metadata

Approach 1, above, is limited by using the concept label only in the metadata. This second approach aims to remedy this by including not only concepts but also all concept synonyms into the same metadata field (see Figure 9 for illustration).

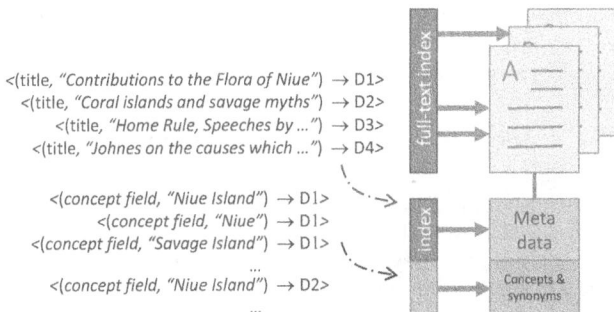

Figure 9: *Approach 2–Concepts and synonyms added to metadata; extended indexing structure (right) and example snippet (left)*

An advanced search using keywords in the concept metadata field will yield much better results than for Approach 1, because the keywords have a much higher probability to be matched by one of the concept synonyms. The best strategy would be to filter by (or search for) a concept and all its synonyms and also include these as keywords in the full-text search.

Example 5. Approach 2–search *Using this indexing approach with our four documents means that the concept label and synonyms will be added as metadata (see Figure 9, left). In this approach, the different indexing options for the metadata fields (phrases vs single words) does not lead to different results. A simple query*

for "Niue" would, different to Example 3, lead to $D1^+_{Niue}$, $D2^+_{SI}$ and $D4^-_{Niue}$, because several synonymous terms for the concept Niue are available.

Advanced search for "Niue" in the concept field *alone would lead to a result set containing $D1^+_{Niue}$ and $D3^-_{SI}$, thus removing the false positive $D4^-_{Niue}$ and omitting the negative $D2^+_{SI}$ from lexical search. Any other keywords, such as "Niu" or "Niue-Fekai" lead the the same result.*

The advanced search strategy using filters would be similar to the one described for Approach 1, with the difference that now the potential list of concepts and their synonyms is much longer. However, a user would be more likely to be able to identify the concept they have in mind (as each concept now has several expressions instead of just one).

The same limitations with regard to the lack of ranking by concept applies as in the Approach 1. Overall, though, the quality of the search results is expected to be better. The number of false positives is potentially reduced (compared to Approach 1) because the user has more opportunity to identify their desired concept (via filter or search). Those search results that would be mistakenly excluded in lexicographic search (false negatives) because a keyword is not matched, could now be included by searching for the keyword in the concept field, which would lead to better results due to the inclusion of synonyms. Here a new set of false positives, however, could now be included as these synonyms are no longer linked to their semantic concept, nor is the semantics of the search keyword clearly identified. The problem of filter results including false positives is increased as more potential matches are now included. Overall this approach offers more options and better user support, but its effectiveness may depend heavily on the collection.

Example 6. Approach 2–filter *When filtering by* concept field *our user now has several options to identify a matching metadata entry (e.g., Niue Island, Niue, Niu, Niue-Fekai). Filtering by concept field only leads to the results $D1^+_{Niue}$ and $D2^+_{SI}$. Using an advanced search, e.g., for "Niue", on the full-text in conjunction with the filter by concept again leads to $D1^+_{Niue}$ only (with false negative $D2^+_{SI}$).*

4.3 Concept labels indexed at page-level

In contrast to the first two approaches, Approach 3 does not merely change metadata but includes the concepts into the index for each page. This means that each page is (virtually) extended by a number of concept keywords, which are in the indexing process being treated as part of the page content. Figure 10 illustrates the approach.

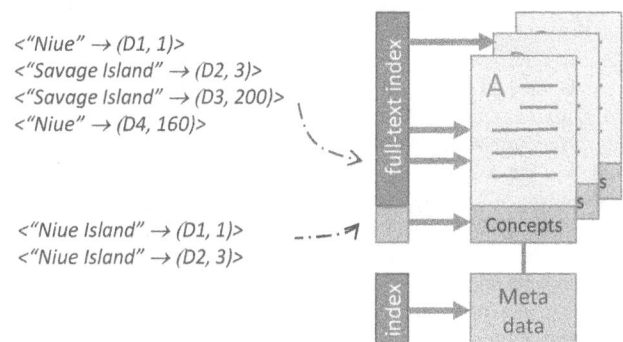

Figure 10: *Approach 3–Concept labels indexed at page-level; extended indexing structure (right) and example snippet (left)*

No change in the user's search interface is required, as the enhancement happens at the indexing level. The chances of semantically matching documents being found for a search are increased, as all concept synonyms in a text are additionally tagged by the concept label. That is, if the document contains a lesser-known term, while the user searches for the more widely used term (which, we assume, matches the concept label) then the document is retrieved. In purely lexical search, the user would have missed this result (false negative). The number of false positives is not directly affected, as there is no filtering (as in Approaches 1 and 2) and potentially more terms can be matched. However, because the context label is included as a term (without semantic meaning), it is now susceptible to being 'misunderstood' during the lexical search (i.e., being a homonym to an unrelated concept), and to introduce new false positives.

Overall, the number of these should be relatively small, as the concept labels are largely very specific, but they can occur. In some documents, the addition of the concept labels may lead to an increased repetition of terms (i.e., if the term used in the document is identical to the concept label). In these cases, naturally there is no change to the number of false negatives (as the document was already included in the result list). However, the increased repetition of the term would lead to a higher ranking of the document within the result list. Documents that use terms other than the one matching the result label, while talking about the same concept, would not be boosted in the same way. Overall, this approach seems to favour documents using established terminology, while also retrieving those using more unusual concept terms.

Example 7. Approach 3 *Using this indexing approach with our four documents leads to concept labels being added into the full-text index (see Figure 10, left). If the concept label is not tokenized, i.e. interpreted as a phrase by the indexer, our user's full-text search for "Niue" leads to the same result as the lexical search, $D1^{+}_{Niue}$ and $D4^{-}_{Niue}$ (see Example 1), because the additionally indexed terms do not match the query. If the user were to search for "Niue Island" instead, the result would be $D1^{+}_{Niue}$ and $D3^{-}_{SI}$. If the concept label is tokenized, the result set for query "Niue" consists of $D1^{+}_{Niue}$, $D2^{+}_{SI}$ and $D4^{-}_{Niue}$. In this case, $D1^{+}_{Niue}$ receives a higher ranking as before as each occurrence of "Niue" now appears twice per page. False positive $D4^{-}_{Niue}$ is still included but ranked very low (single occurrence of "Niue", no re-enforcement through concept labels). $D2^{+}_{SI}$ would be ranked similarly low.*

4.4 Concept label and synonyms indexed

Approach 3 is somewhat limited by the restriction to include the concept label only. Approach 4 aims to overcome this limitation by including not only concept labels but also all concept synonyms into the page such that they are included in the full-text index (see Figure 11).

As before, no change in the user's search interface is required. If the search term matches on the concept synonyms, and assuming correct semantic analysis, all relevant documents should be included in the result set (accompanied by significant reduction in false negatives). At any rate, the results (with regards to false negatives) has the same quality as a semantic search using Capisco. However, because all synonyms are treated as terms only (i.e., without their semantic meaning attached), each of the terms is now open to be misunderstood as belonging to a different concept. Thus the number of false positives is potentially increased (compared to Approach 3). These might be filtered out by a combination with Approaches 2 or 3 (as discussed later in Section 7). Similar to Approach 3, all documents mentioning a concept will receive boosted

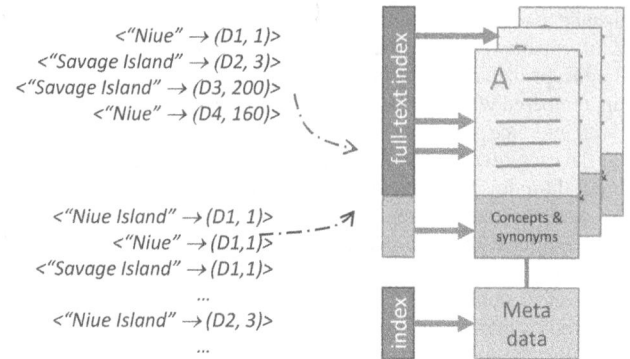

Figure 11: *Approach 4–Concept label and synonyms indexed; extended indexing structure (right) and example snippet (left)*

ranking (through the repetition of the matching concept label or synonyms), but without the skewing of results in favour of texts who use established terminology (i.e., matching the concept label).

Overall, this approach significantly reduces false negatives without users having to change their search habits. However, it may increase the number of false positives. This depends on the document collection; if a wide variety of document subjects is represented, the probability of homonyms occurring is increased. A large collection may very well contain text about both ice hockey ("hockey puck") and Shakespeare ("Puck" in Midsummer Night's Dream). In contrast, specialised collections will likely encounter this problem to a limited extent.

Example 8. Approach 4 *In this approach, concept labels and synonyms are added into the full-text index (see Figure 11, left). In this case tokenization only influences possible rankings, not the selection or exclusion of documents. The search result set for query "Niue" consists of $D1^{+}_{Niue}$, $D2^{+}_{SI}$ and $D4^{-}_{Niue}$. In this case, both $D1^{+}_{Niue}$ and $D2^{+}_{SI}$ receive higher rankings due to repetition of the term through the synonyms. False positive $D4^{-}_{Niue}$ is still included but ranked very low (single occurrence of "Niue", no re-enforcement through concept labels).*

4.5 Concepts & synonyms at page metadata

The final approach that we analyse is only possible for those DL implementations that support page-level metadata fields (such as provided in Greenstone [16]). Following Approaches 1 and 2, concept labels and concept synonyms are added as page-level metadata fields (see Figure 12 for illustration).

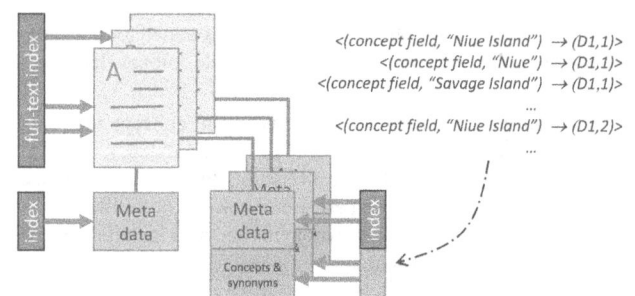

Figure 12: *Approach 5–Concepts & synonyms at page metadata; extended indexing structure (left) and example snippet (right)*

Collection	Coll. size	Tokens	Concepts	Shared	Combined size	(Combined w/synonyms)
A	701 pages	190475	2850 (12%)	783 (2.1%)	205755 (110%)	278699–369879 (149–197%)
B	878 pages	354954	45243 (13%)	13205 (3.7%)	386992 (109%)	515144–675334 (145–190%)
C	1214 pages	518401	29857 (6%)	4642 (0.9%)	543616 (105%)	644476–770551 (124–149%)
D	1649 pages	4379593	75544 (2%)	12580 (0.3%)	4442557 (101%)	4694413–5009233 (107–114%)

Table 2: Test collections and index sizes in #tokens (Solr) and #concepts (Capisco)

This metadata field may then be used in advanced search as a filter to restrict the result set, or in fielded search to increase the result set (reduction of false negatives). As in Approaches 1 and 2, the list of concepts and their synonyms may be quite large. Selecting a concept from a filter list would be easier than having to identify the correct keyword while searching the metadata field. Again, the advanced search using keywords in the concept and/or synonyms metadata fields would be useful for improving result set quality (increase in true positives in comparison to lexical search). As before, a new set of false positives may, however, now be included as these synonyms are no longer linked to their semantic concept, nor is the semantics of the search keyword clearly identified. The lack of ranking information when filtering by document metadata (as in Approaches 1 and 2) is remedied here as the frequency of pages on which a concept is used is known.

Overall the number of false positives and false negatives would be the same as in Approach 1 or 2, depending on the index variation. However, the main advantages of this approach is the support for ranking and the increased ease for a user in identifying why a document has been included in the result set, as each of the matching pages is identified.

Example 9. Approach 5 *Revisiting our four documents, the metadata changes are indicated in Figure 12, right. The search results for this approach contain the same documents as Approaches 1 and 2 (see Examples 3 and 5). However, the result set consists of all the pages on which the matches were found. If both concept label and synonyms are include in the metadata and a tokenizer is used, the result set for simple search for "Niue" is: pages 1,2, 3... in D1, page 3 in $D2_{SI}^{+}$ and page 160 in $D4_{Niue}^{-}$. Advanced search for "Niue" leads to pages 1,2, 3... in $D1_{Niue}^{+}$ and page 3 in $D2_{SI}^{+}$. When filtering by concept field, this leads to only pages 1,2, 3... in $D1_{Niue}^{+}$, page 3 in $D2_{SI}^{+}$. Using an advanced search, e.g., for "Niue", on the full-text in conjunction with the filter by concept selects pages 1, 2, 3... in $D1_{Niue}^{+}$ only.*

4.6 Summary of Approaches

The table in Figure 13 provides an overview of the five approaches that were introduced in Section 4.

Approach	semantically enhances		access via		impact on	
	metadata	text index	search	filter	false positives	false negatives
1	x		x	x	--	o
2	x		x	x	-- / +	--
3		x	x		o/+	-
4		x	x		o/++	--
5	x		x	x	-- / +	--

Figure 13: Overview of approaches (Legend: X = applies, empty field = does not apply; –/- = less, +/++ = more, and o = no change)

Approaches 1, 2 and 5 add information about semantic concepts to the metadata, while Approaches 3 and 4 add information about semantic concepts to the full-text index. Search is then possible via both the simple interface and the advanced interface for filtering and search in metadata-based enhancements. Figure 13 then summarises our rather complex observations about the influence on false positives and false negatives by simple indications on whether more or less of these results can be expected.

5. TEST COLLECTIONS & DOCUMENTS

This section explores the enhanced indexing approaches for their impact on the size of the resulting indexes, and explores the commonality of the tokens indexed by Solr and the concepts identified by Capisco for a set of example documents.

5.1 Lexical vs semantic-enhanced index

We present the results from experiments testing the potential impact of Approaches 3 and 4 on a digital library's full-text index. We created four test collections from Hathitrust documents, and for each, we created a Solr index and a Capisco index. The Capisco index was then serialised and exported as a concept list for each document, and then imported into the Solr index. Table 2 shows for each collection the number of unique tokens that were identified in Solr and the number of unique concepts that were identified in Capisco. We also list the number of concept labels that refer to terms that already exist in the Solr index (column 'Shared'). The combined size of the index is given both in number of tokens and as a percentage. We also estimated the combined index when including not only the concept labels but also the synonyms. The expanded indexes including synonyms were calculated in their size but not built. On average 5 synonyms per concept are included, but manual extension of the knowledge base may lead to a larger number of synonyms.

The combined index (in comparison to the DL's original Solr index) was between 1% to 10% larger. This is an acceptable increase in size that would not create performance problems for most DL systems. Including the synonyms into the index would also at most double the size of the index, which is manageable for DL systems.

Considering the number of concepts identified for each of these collections, however, highlights the user interface issue for filtering by concept metadata: selecting concepts from a list of more than 2000 concepts that occur within the collection is not feasible. Alternative means of presenting the information may need to be found. Here the disambiguation interface that has been developed for Capisco may provide a suitable starting point.

5.2 Lexical vs semantic analysis

Figure 14 plots the number of lexical tokens (blue) against the number of identified concepts (orange) in 30 documents chosen at random from document collections A–D. The percentage of shared concept/tokens is shown as black circles, using the right-hand axis. For documents D8 and D12, the number of tokens is larger than the maximum of the scale shown in the figure. Furthermore, D8 does not seem to contain any semantic concepts. On closer inspection, we find that Document D8 contains only pages with OCR errors (seemingly random symbols, no text). Thus here Capisco can be used to identify potential problems with OCR-ed text. Documents without any concepts should be automatically flagged for the curator to inspect. Other documents, such as D12, contain surprisingly

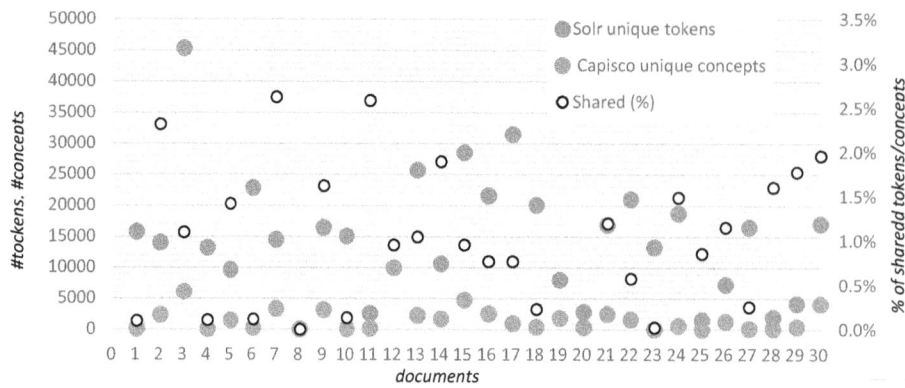

Figure 14: 30 example documents: number of tokens and concepts

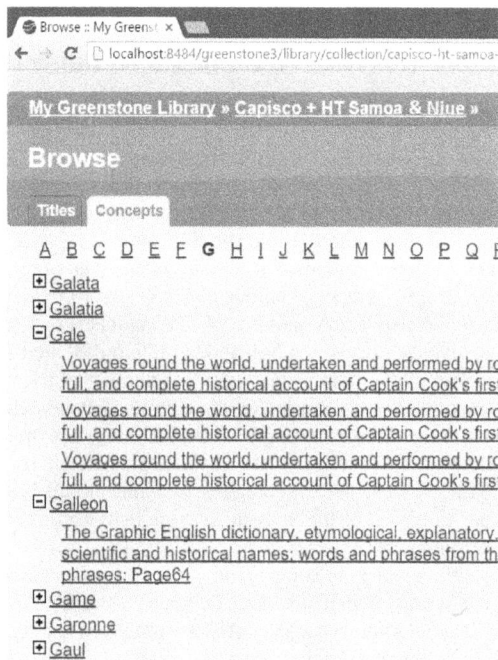

Figure 15: Browsing the assigned concepts: words starting with G

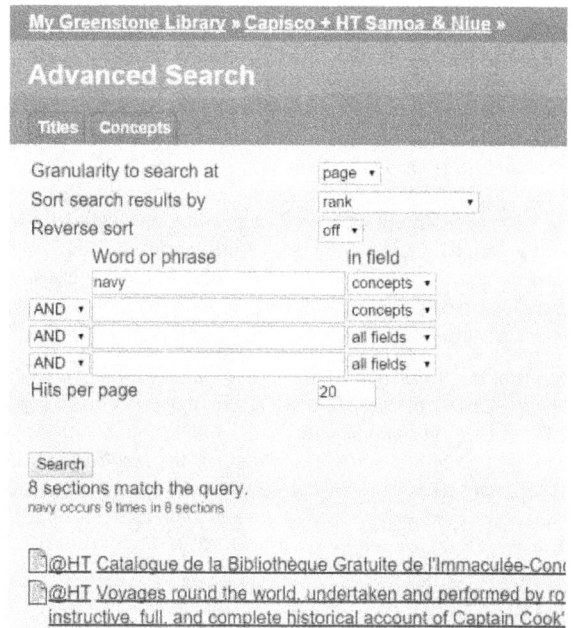

Figure 16: Searching by concept through the advanced search page

few concepts in comparison to the number of tokens. For example, documents D1, D4 and D6 contain 117 concepts vs 15776 tokens, 62 vs 13211, and 210 vs 22804 concepts and tokens, respectively. These documents turned out to be not in English, and the recognised concepts are predominately names of people and locations.[5].

Further research is needed into the significance of particularly low or high commonality between tokens and concepts. These may be indicators of document coherence or writing style (scholarly vs popular writing), or of OCR errors.

6. WORKED EXAMPLE

In this section we present a worked example, based on a Greenstone digital library collection that has incorporated the semantically assigned concepts generated by Capisco when applied to a

collection of texts related to Pacific islands Samoa and Niue (collection C). Greenstone allows for parallel indexes to be built. For the example collection, concepts from Capisco were included as a new metadata field at both document level and page level. With the exception of filtering, this structure is rich enough for the user to formulate queries through the advanced search page that covers all the approaches described and analysed in Section 4. In this worked example we concentrate on Approach 5.

Figure 15 shows how these concept metadata fields have been used to introduce a 'browse by concepts' tab to the digital library. The figure shows the example of concepts starting with 'G': the user has clicked on a couple of these (Gale and Galleon) to expand their contents, to view documents containing these concepts.

For Gale, three pages from the book *Voyages round the world* are shown, and for Galleon a page in *The Graphic English dictionary, etymological, explanatory, and pronouncing:...* has been identified.

Browsing helps give the user a feel for what is in the digital library collection. In Figure 16 we have jumped ahead in the timeline of our user's interaction with the DL. In this figure, they have

---

[5]These collections were created by the HathiTrust using lexical search for research purposes on specific topics regarding the Pacific island nations of Niue and Samoa.

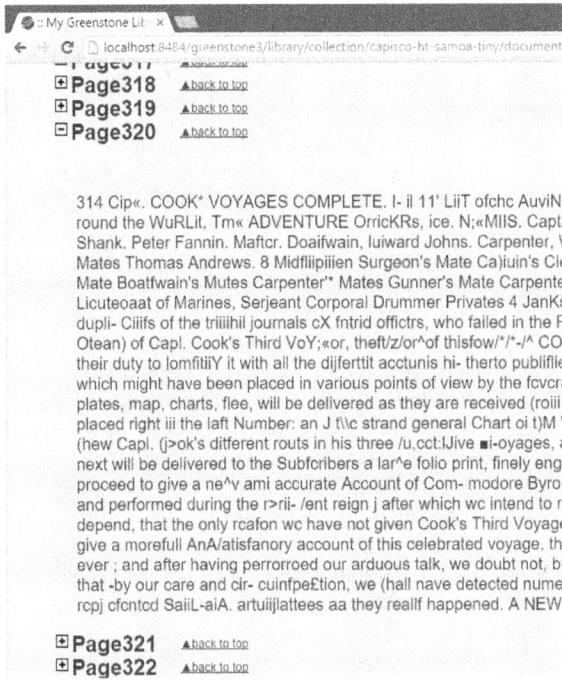

Figure 17: The OCR-ed text of a matching page for concept "navy"

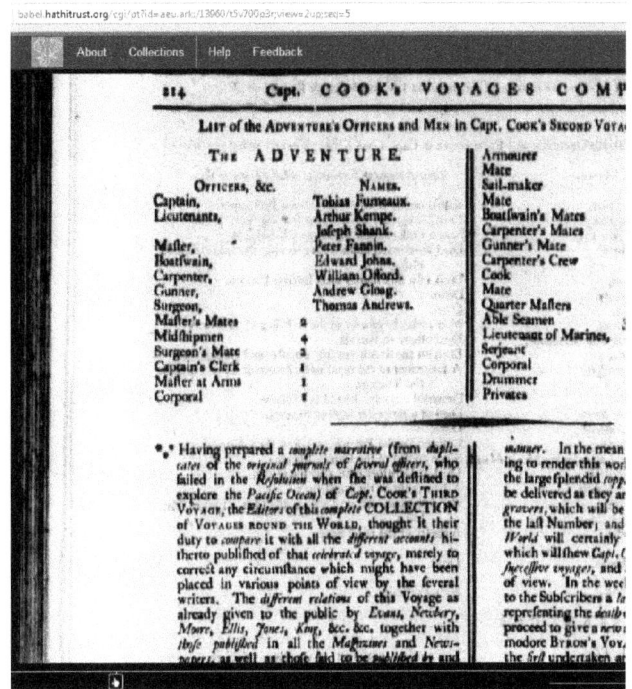

Figure 18: Scanned page corresponding to OCR-ed text in Fig. 17

accessed the advanced search page and configured the interface to search for pages that contain the concept "navy". Shortly we will look at one of the matching documents returned by this query, but first we note the outcome of other searching options available to the user at this point:

- Had the user searched the full-text, then 54 matching pages would have been returned.

- By including the concept labels within the full-text, the number of search results increased to 60.

- Searching by concept label on its own returned 8 pages (the snapshot shown in Figure 16).

From these numbers it can be seen that the concept "navy" has been attributed by Capisco to 2 pages that already have this string literal present, and 6 further pages that do not.

Focusing on the second matching document in the returned result set (the account of Captain Cook's voyages which also appeared in the browsing example), clicking on its link brings up the snapshot shown in Figure 17. In this view, we are shown the OCR-ed text of the document, which is instructive in seeing what text the digital library has actually registered with the page, if not terribly pleasing aesthetically. Using the @HT link on the result page (previous snapshot), the digital library takes the user directly to a scanned version of the document (Figure 18) to view.

Reviewing the information on the page presented, we do indeed see that the page provides details relating to the (British) navy. From the result of the OCR-ed page (the text Capisco has processed), we can see the words and phrases "Marines", "Sail-maker", and "Gunner's Mates" in addition to more generic military terms such as "Captain" and "Lieutenants".

7. DISCUSSION OF APPROACH

Semantic Drift. The accommodation of historical meanings of words, or historical context of words and concepts, can only be achieved if either these are already known to Wikipedia or if these are entered by a scholar who is interested in and aware of the historic meaning of words. Wikipedia does indeed cover some historic concepts, such as the out-of-date usage of "Savage Island" to refer to the Pacific island nation of Niue (as used in our examples). Other aspects may not be covered to the full requirements of a scholar; in these cases the scholars can extend the Concepts-in-Context network as described in [3].

Generalizability of approach. The processes suggested here are directly or with minor adaptations applicable to mainstream digital libraries, such as HathiTrust Digital Library (which was used as our data source) or Greenstone (which was used in our worked example). Any other digital library that uses text-based indexing on full-text and/or indexes on metadata (at page level or document level) would also benefit from the semantic enhancements described here.

Scalability. Test collections have only been explored for Approaches 3 and 4 (see Section 5). Further performance tests are planned for all approaches, including combinations of the approaches. These relatively small test collections are expected to predict the behaviour of *homogeneous* collections adequately. Semantic enhancements of large *heterogeneous* collections are expected to have characteristics similar to those of a combination of smaller homogeneous sub-collections. The performance implications of such combinations will depend on both the homogeneity across the larger collection and the semantic support for each of the sub-collections. These issues will need to be explored further.

Knowledge base seeding. It might appear desirable to use existing ontologies, such as DBpedia, instead of mining Wikipedia. However, these ontologies are too complex for our semantic analysis. They encode rich relationships and hierarchies between concepts. Because of this complexity, they do not cope well with the inherent noise in the documents and would require costly semantic analysis of the sentence structures. The advantage of our CiC network over existing ontologies is its robustness for noise (see [3]). Its simpler semantic analysis is less error-prone and more efficient.

Visualising collection semantics. Enhancing the indexes and metadata of collections with semantic information does not just widen the possibilities for, and quality of, text-based search—it also opens up opportunities to explore the collections. Similar to the existing *ngram* analysis (e.g., [6, 7]), which allows visualisation of changing word use over time, we suggest exploring the semantics over time [2]. While the former allows the linguistic comparison of words, our approach allows the tracking of concepts independent of the actual words used to refer to the concept.

8. CONCLUSION

This paper takes an analytical approach to explore five strategies for low-cost semantic enhancement to DL metadata and indexing. We used a case study of four documents to showcase the differences in result sets for lexical search, semantic search, and each of our five approaches. We also created four test collections for which the performance implications of enriching the full-text index with concept labels was experimentally determined. We additionally estimated the expected growth of the index when using semantic synonyms in addition to concept labels.

We have argued theoretically and shown through examples how using semantic concepts can help identifying OCR errors. Historic documents are particularly susceptible to OCR errors, due to their use of older-style fonts such as *Fractura*, the use of the medial 's' (often misread as f), and general aging and wear of the pages [7]. This aspect has been little explored so far.

Several possible future work directions flow naturally and easily out of having concept information in the full-text index or metadata. Concept information may be useful for relevance feedback on documents. For example, where a user finds a document or page that is of interest to them, they can easily see what semantic concepts were applied. Used this way, the users do not need to "know" the concepts occurring in the digital library or to browse through a list of concept labels. Thus, with no additional effort, query expansion based on semantic concept terms can be supported.

Interface and interaction issues stemming from the joint use of lexical terms and concept labels need to be explored further. For example, since terms in the search may not necessarily match the concept terms, it is not always possible to highlight matching search terms in the document. This is potentially confusing to users.

Further work could also be dedicated to exploring combinations between the approaches introduced in Section 4. For example, a combination of Approaches 2 and 4 promises to offer flexibility and expressiveness to the user.

Even though our work here focused on simply enhancing the lexical search capabilities of traditional digital libraries, the most powerful solution would be a combination between lexical-based search and semantic search as offered in Capisco. Both offer elements that are useful for a scholar; offering merely one of them will always fall short of the full potential.

9. ACKNOWLEDGEMENTS

We thank the recipients of the University of Waikato Summer Research Scholarships, Michael Coleman and Yang Guo, for their work on exploring indexing in Solr and Capisco. The authors thank the Andrew W. Mellon Foundation for their support of this work (grant reference number 41500672). We also thank the staff at the HathiTrust Research Center for their assistance.

10. REFERENCES

[1] H. B. Guppy. *Coral islands and savage myths*. Victoria Institute and Philosophical Society of Great Britain, London, 1889.

[2] A. Hinze, M. Coleman, S. J. Cunningham, and D. Bainbridge. A semantic bookworm: mining literary resources revisited. In *JCDL '16*. ACM, 2016.

[3] A. Hinze, C. Taube-Schock, D. Bainbridge, R. Matamua, and J. S. Downie. Improving access to large-scale digital libraries through semantic-enhanced search and disambiguation. In *JCDL '15*, pages 147–156. ACM, 2015.

[4] A. Huang, D. Milne, E. Frank, and I. H. Witten. Clustering documents using a wikipedia-based concept representation. In *Advances in Knowledge Discovery and Data Mining*, pages 628–636. Springer, 2009.

[5] A. J. Johnes. *Johnes on the causes which have produced dissent from the established church, in the principality of Wales*. Henry Hooper, London, 1870.

[6] P. Leonard. Mining large datasets for the humanities. In *World Library and Information Congress*. International Federation of Library Associations, 2014.

[7] Y. Lin, J.-B. Michel, E. L. Aiden, J. Orwant, W. Brockman, and S. Petrov. Syntactic annotations for the google books ngram corpus. In *Proceedings of the ACL 2012 system demonstrations*, pages 169–174. ACL, 2012.

[8] C. D. Manning, P. Raghavan, H. Schütze, et al. *Introduction to information retrieval*, volume 1. Cambridge university press Cambridge, 2008.

[9] R. Mihalcea and A. Csomai. Wikify!: linking documents to encyclopedic knowledge. In *Proceedings of the sixteenth ACM conference on Conference on information and knowledge management*, pages 233–242. ACM, 2007.

[10] D. Milne, O. Medelyan, and I. H. Witten. Mining domain-specific thesauri from wikipedia: A case study. In *Proc. IEEE/WIC/ACM international conference on web intelligence*, pages 442–448. IEEE, 2006.

[11] D. Milne and I. H. Witten. Learning to link with wikipedia. In *Proc. ACM Conference on Information and knowledge management*, pages 509–518. ACM, 2008.

[12] D. N. Milne, I. H. Witten, and D. M. Nichols. A knowledge-based search engine powered by wikipedia. In *Proc. ACM Conference on information and knowledge management*, pages 445–454. ACM, 2007.

[13] K. Nakayama, T. Hara, and S. Nishio. A thesaurus construction method from large scaleweb dictionaries. In *Advanced Information Networking and Applications, 2007. AINA'07. 21st International Conference on*, pages 932–939. IEEE, 2007.

[14] R. B. O'Brien, editor. *Home Rule, Speeches by John Redmond*. T. F. Unwin, London, 1910.

[15] W. R. Sykes. *Contributions to the Flora of Niue*. Department of Scientific and Industrial Research, Christchurch, 1970.

[16] I. H. Witten, S. J. Boddie, D. Bainbridge, and R. J. McNab. Greenstone: a comprehensive open-source digital library software system. In *Proceedings of the fifth ACM conference on Digital libraries*, pages 113–121. ACM, 2000.

Desiderata for Exploratory Search Interfaces to Web Archives in Support of Scholarly Activities

Andrew Jackson[1], Jimmy Lin[2], Ian Milligan[2], and Nick Ruest[3]

[1] The British Library   [2] University of Waterloo   [3] York University

Andrew.Jackson@bl.uk, {jimmylin,i2milligan}@uwaterloo.ca, ruestn@yorku.ca

ABSTRACT

Web archiving initiatives around the world capture ephemeral web content to preserve our collective digital memory. In this paper, we describe initial experiences in providing an exploratory search interface to web archives for humanities scholars and social scientists. We describe our initial implementation and discuss our findings in terms of desiderata for such a system. It is clear that the standard organization of a search engine results page (SERP), consisting of an ordered list of hits, is inadequate to support the needs of scholars. Shneiderman's mantra for visual information seeking ("overview first, zoom and filter, then details-on-demand") provides a nice organizing principle for interface design, to which we propose an addendum: "Make everything transparent". We elaborate on this by highlighting the importance of the temporal dimension of web pages as well as issues surrounding metadata and veracity.

1. INTRODUCTION

Web archiving refers to the systematic collection and preservation of web content for future generations. Since web pages are ephemeral and disappear with great regularity [13], the only sure way of preserving web content for posterity is to proactively crawl and store portions of the web. Since 1996, the Internet Archive has captured and made publicly accessible hundreds of billions of web pages. Today, many libraries, universities, and other organizations have ongoing web archiving initiatives [7]. Although content capture is by no means a solved problem—in particular, social media and highly-interactive JavaScript-heavy pages present ongoing challenges—scholars now have at their disposal a rich treasure trove of material to study. The focus of our work is how to make these materials accessible to humanities scholars and social scientists.

This paper describes our initial experiences in providing an exploratory search interface to web archives to support scholarly activities. We describe our initial implementation and present our findings in terms of desiderata for such a

Permission to make digital or hard copies of all or part of this work for personal or classroom use is granted without fee provided that copies are not made or distributed for profit or commercial advantage and that copies bear this notice and the full citation on the first page. Copyrights for components of this work owned by others than the author(s) must be honored. Abstracting with credit is permitted. To copy otherwise, or republish, to post on servers or to redistribute to lists, requires prior specific permission and/or a fee. Request permissions from permissions@acm.org.

JCDL '16, June 19 - 23, 2016, Newark, NJ, USA

© 2016 Copyright held by the owner/author(s). Publication rights licensed to ACM.
ISBN 978-1-4503-4229-2/16/06. . . $15.00

DOI: http://dx.doi.org/10.1145/2910896.2910912

system, summarized as follows: It is clear that the standard organization of a search engine results page (SERP), consisting of an ordered list of hits, is inadequate to support the needs of scholars. Shneiderman's mantra for visual information seeking ("overview first, zoom and filter, then details-on-demand" [15]) provides a nice organizing principle for the types of exploratory search interfaces that we desire. Elaborating on this, we discuss the importance of metadata and the issue of veracity—helping scholars understand the quality characteristics of the content, including biases that might be present. To Shneiderman's mantra, we propose an addendum: "Make everything transparent". We argue that a tool in support of scholarship should not have "magic". Every system decision—from the ordering of results to how aggregations are computed—should be available for inspection and manipulation by the scholar.

We view the contribution of this paper as starting a conversation with digital library and information retrieval researchers on the underexplored problem of searching web archives. While our findings are accurately characterized as preliminary, and we are by no means the first to examine the information seeking behavior of scholars (cf. [3]), to our knowledge the focus on web archiving is novel. Our discussion enriches the literature on complex information seeking and system support for such activities.

2. BACKGROUND AND RELATED WORK

Most early work on web archiving has focused on the content acquisition pipeline (collection development, crawling, storage file formats, etc.) as opposed to providing access. In fact, a question the community has perpetually struggled with is "who's using web archives and for what purposes?" The Internet Archive boasts impressive access statistics,[1] but AlNoamany et al. [1] found that most requests are actually by robots. Dougherty and Meyer [5] identified lack of shared practices, accessible tools, and clear legal and ethical guides as obstacles to advancing scholarly use of web archives. According to that article, the Internet Archive has identified three categories of current users, and, surprisingly, scholarly use *is not* one of the categories.

The most popular (and in many cases, the *only*) access method to web archives is temporal browsing, or what is commonly know as "wayback" functionality. Given the URL of a page, a user can view a particular version of a web page, move forward and backward in time to examine different captured versions, and follow links to contemporaneous

---

[1] twitter.com/brewster_kahle/status/364834158285041665

pages. Obviously, browsing is only useful if one knows the exact URL of the desired content. Since this is often not the case, search is an obvious solution [4, 6], but unfortunately, most web archives do not support full-text search. There has been academic work on searching timestamped collections (such as web archives) [12, 10, 2, 8], but these systems have not been deployed in production to our knowledge. Regardless, most previous work has focused on technical issues such as the layout and organization of inverted index structures. In contrast, there has been relatively little work on search interfaces in direct support of users' needs.

3. INTERFACE DESIGN

To begin, a word about methods: this paper represents the distillation of the authors' personal experiences working on web archives over the past several years—the authors include a historian, a librarian, a researcher in information retrieval, and a software engineer working in a major national web archiving effort. Our findings and recommendations are based on these experiences, informal interactions with colleagues at various professional events, and informal feedback from users of our working prototype.

3.1 Task Model

The development of search interfaces must begin with an understanding of who the users are and what they are trying to accomplish. In our case, we wish to support the activities of humanities scholars and social scientists. It is important to recognize that search isn't necessarily the most natural starting point for these users—search presupposes that it is possible to articulate (however poorly) an information need. In our experience, most scholars don't even know "where to start" with a web archive. To a large extent, this is because web archives are relatively novel artifacts that few scholars have had experiences with. Nevertheless, there is usually "something" that occurs before search.[2]

The chess analogy of Hearst et al. [9] for information navigation seems apt for characterizing the task model for humanities scholars and social scientists. In the "opening", they want a high-level overview of what's in a collection and how it was gathered. For the humanist, this is often called "distant reading" (aggregation and large-scale data analysis) to elicit "provocations". For social scientists, exploratory analyses are often intertwined with the process of hypothesis generation. Search is a poor tool for the "opening".

At the other end of the task model is the "end game" in our chess analogy: For a humanist, this might involve the "close reading" of several records (e.g., webpages) to construct a narrative. For a social scientist, this might involve extracting variables of interest from text or metadata and applying a regression to illustrate some hypothesized relationship. Once again, search is not particularly useful for this stage of the game.

Between the "opening" and "end game" lies the "middle game", and this is where we believe search plays a vital role. We readily concede that this three-stage model is a vast oversimplification of reality, eliding many important issues: Scholarly activities extend over many sessions, perhaps lasting months or even years. Scholarship is fundamentally

iterative with false starts, backtracking, and feedback loops, e.g., consideration of pages leads to the reformulation of the hypothesis. Despite these inadequacies, we believe that our model is nevertheless helpful in situating search.

3.2 Current Implementation

We have implemented and deployed a prototype exploratory search interface for web archives, available online at webarchives.ca. The interface was originally developed by the British Library's web archiving team for the Big UK Domain Data for the Arts and Humanities (BUDDAH) project in order to facilitate access to their legal deposit crawl collection. We have adapted the tool to host the Canadian Political Parties and Political Interest Groups collection, gathered by the University of Toronto Library using the Internet Archive's Archive-It platform.[3] The collection contains 14.5 million documents from crawls performed at roughly quarterly intervals between October 2005 and March 2015. Content from around fifty organizations were collected: all of the major Canadian political parties (the Conservative Party, the Liberal Party, the New Democratic Party, the Green Party, and the Bloc Quebecois), as well as minor parties and political organizations such as the Assembly of First Nations, the Canadian Association for Free Expression, Fair Vote Canada, and beyond. The entire collection totals 380 GB in size compressed. The prototype search interface is powered by Apache Solr. The underlying Lucene indexes are generated by Warcbase [11], a platform for managing web archives built on Hadoop and HBase. All components of the system are open source.

In developing this prototype, we faced a classic chicken-and-egg problem: scholars have a difficult time articulating what capabilities they desire in a search interface for web archives, and without some notion of requirements, it is difficult to build a prototype. We attempted to break out of this cycle by implementing, at least in the beginning, an interface similar to what most users today have come to expect from a web search engine: a simple search box and results organized as an ordered list, just like a standard search engine results page (SERP). Note, however, that the results are *not* algorithmically ranked, but simply presented in archival (i.e., temporal) order; we discuss this decision later. A screenshot of the interface is shown in Figure 1 (left) for the query "recession". Running down the left edge of the interface are controls for faceted navigation, which lets users filter content type (HTML, PDF, etc.), year of crawl, site, and a few other facets. Next to each facet we show the number of documents that match the filter criterion. We believe that faceted navigation is sufficiently commonplace today (in sites like Amazon.com) that users will be able to manipulate the controls without requiring instructions or training. In the current results display, different versions of the same document are treated as if they were different documents; we have an experimental feature deployed elsewhere that groups different versions of the same page together. However, as we discuss later, there are issues with both approaches.

As an alternative interface, we developed a "trends visualization" inspired by Google's Ngram Viewer,[4] shown in Figure 1 (right). In this view, we are able to concurrently visualize the prevalence (i.e., frequency) of term matches over time for multiple queries. Here, we show trends for the

---

[2]This is a deliberately vague statement because, as Dougherty and Meyer [5] point out: "researchers have trouble deciding what they want methodologically before they begin".

---

[3]`archive-it.org/collections/227`
[4]`books.google.com/ngrams`

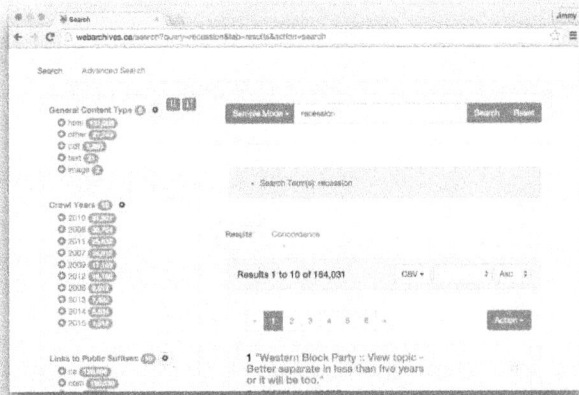

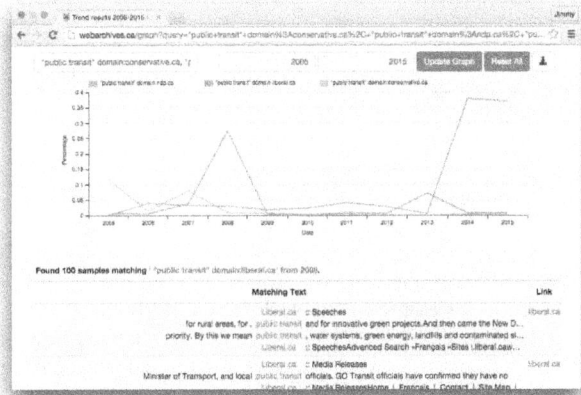

Figure 1: Screenshots of our exploratory search interface: on the left, a standard SERP layout and controls for faceted navigation; on the right, the trends visualization showing the prevalence of the phrase "public transit" on the websites of the Conservative Party, the Liberal Party, and the New Democratic Party.

phrase "public transit" on the websites of the Conservative Party, the Liberal Party, and the New Democratic Party. The user can click on the line graph to obtain sample results, shown as a keyword-in-context concordance. In this example, a scholar might use this interface to explore how each party's views on public transit evolved over time.

4. DISCUSSION

A Standard SERP Isn't Enough. One immediately obvious finding about our existing prototype is the inadequacy of the standard SERP organization. There are two important interacting issues:

First, our choice *not* to rank the results bears some discussion. Although it would be simple enough to provide a ranking model (e.g., BM25), some scholars we interacted with questioned the very idea of relevance ranking. To them, *all* of the matching results are relevant from a scholarly perspective. Often, they are looking for information beyond the documents themselves, i.e., for traces of evidence that allow them to infer information about the authors of those documents or the societal context in which they were created. Because these scholars are treating the tool primarily as a "lens" through which to examine society, all matching documents should be considered. However, without relevance ranking, scholars are frequently presented with overwhelming numbers of results and no way to prioritize their attention. This observation about the needs of scholars deserves further study because it challenges the probability ranking principle [14], one of the central tenants of modern information retrieval research.

Second, regarding the choice between grouping different versions of the same page in the results view or treating them as if they were different documents: both options are problematic. Without grouping, results are frequently populated by duplicates or near duplicates. Grouping versions creates a different issue: pages change over time, and it is often these changes that are of interest (for example, when a particular phrase is removed from a page). An interface that performs grouping can inadvertently hide insights.

The fundamental deficiency with the standard SERP organization is that it offers only a single linear dimension with which to organize search results, whereas scholars desire

a view into a multi-dimensional document space. Faceted browsing helps, but does not solve the problem.

Shneiderman's Mantra. We believe that Shneiderman's mantra for visual information seeking ("overview first, zoom and filter, then details-on-demand" [15]) provides a nice organizing principle for exploratory search interfaces to web archives. The trends visualization in Figure 1 (left) appears to be a useful starting point based on our own experiences and feedback from colleagues—scholars find the trends view preferable to the standard SERP organization. In Shneiderman's mantra, trends provide the "overview first". Interactions with the trends provide "zoom and filter" capabilities. The user is able to click on a particular year and query (e.g., the Liberal party in 2008) and bring up sample results that match the criteria. Finally, "details-on-demand" is supported by the user clicking on a particular sample in the concordance view to bring up the archived page.

Shneiderman's mantra brings to focus what humanities scholars refer to as "distant reading", or understanding text through massive data analysis, and "close reading", which is the careful interpretation of select passages. Exploratory interfaces, especially for humanities scholars, need to support seamless movement between the two modes and to adjust the "distance" of reading: although many trends only become apparent during distant reading, criticism and interpretation requires close reading.

Metadata and Veracity. Although the trends visualization is a good starting point, we have already identified several areas for improvement, the most salient of which is better support for faceted navigation of metadata. Even in the traditional SERP organization, scholars commented positively about the support for faceted browsing. Beyond obvious facets such as content type and source, there are a number of facets that can be straightforwardly derived from page content. For example, we can group sites into categories such as "news" and "social media". This requires only a modest amount of effort, and often these metadata are already available during collection development. We can also break down pages in terms of the number of incoming or outgoing links (appropriately bucketed). Another facet we have been experimenting with is based on named entities. For example, a scholar might be interested in mentions of op-

105

ponents in a particular party's website. The current trends visualization lacks support for faceted browsing, which represents one future direction for development.

Related to metadata is the issue of veracity. Scholars consistently express concerns about the veracity of whatever insights our interface purports to show—for example, is a trend reflective of underlying shifts in content, or merely an artifact of the crawl or decisions made by the system? Many of these concerns stem from unfamiliarity with web archives as objects of study: when a historian approaches a traditional archive to examine the personal papers of an important figure, for example, he or she has a fairly good idea of "what to expect", including potential biases that might be inherent in the collection. Not so with web archives. Part of the solution is to better educate scholars on the technical nuances of web crawling and related technical issues.

We provide a concrete example: mention aggregation, one of the most common and useful tools for distant reading, can be insightful but is fraught with peril. We can learn from our collection, for example, that Liberal Party of Canada leader Michael Ignatieff appeared 160k times on the liberal.ca website in 2008 at the peak of his leadership (approximately 5% of the pages), versus only 22k times or 1.4% of documents in 2012, the year after he resigned. Broadly, we can see the fall from favor of a politician, but to what extent is this finding an artifact of biases in content selection? Crawl volume (in absolute number of documents) can widely vary (for example, due to minor changes in scoping rules), thus distorting frequencies. Even if we take these counts at face value, the aggregates don't tell us the context of the mentions: What fraction of the mentions were from boilerplate (e.g., page footers)? What fraction were mentioned in a policy context? Surely these distinctions would be relevant for a political scientist or a historian. At present, our interface does not provide any mechanism to explore these questions. However, it may be possible to answer many of the types of questions posed above via faceted browsing, provided that we are able to accurately extract the relevant facets.

Make Everything Transparent. Shneiderman's mantra provides a nice organizing principle, to which we propose an addendum: "Make everything transparent". The "magic" of modern search engines in placing relevant results at the top of a ranked list is *not* what scholars want—they are instinctively distrustful of any mechanism they don't understand. If documents are presented in a particular order, scholars will want to know exactly how the ranking was generated. Something simple such as date ordering may be suboptimal, but at least it is understandable. If the system presents an aggregation, it should explain what information is potentially lost. Quite simply, transparency increases veracity.

Note that this recommendation does not preclude the use of machine learning or other automated techniques for ranking, classifying, clustering, etc., simply that the output must be transparent to the scholar. They are not the only group of users with this requirement: lawyers share similar requirements in the context of electronic discovery and health professional in searching the medical literature.

5. ONGOING WORK

Recognizing that search support is directly applicable to only a relatively small portion of scholarly activities (Section 3.1), we are currently exploring tighter integration of our prototype with Warcbase [11], a related project that provides a general platform for analyzing web archives. Using Spark, a framework for large-scale data processing, users can perform arbitrarily complex filtering and aggregations, ranging from gathering page statistics to extracting the hyperlink structure and named entities mentions from page contents. These capabilities complement what scholars can accomplish with search alone.

We fully recognize that what we currently have is a case study focused on a particular collection. While illuminating, there may be idiosyncratic characteristics that prevent us from making generalizations across different web archives. Thus, we hope to engage more scholars to explore different types of collections. We have only begun to scratch the surface in developing tools to support scholarly access to web archives. We hope that this paper begins a conversation with computer scientists and generates community interest in tackling the many challenges in this space.

Acknowledgments. This research was supported by the AHRC under grant number AH/L009854/1, the U.S. National Science Foundation under awards IIS-1218043 and CNS-1405688. Additional support was forthcoming from the Social Sciences and Humanities Research Council of Canada under Insight Grant 435-2015-0011, and the Ontario Ministry of Research and Innovation's Early Researcher Award program. Any opinions, findings, conclusions, or recommendations expressed are those of the authors and do not necessarily reflect the views of the sponsors.

6. REFERENCES

[1] Y. AlNoamany, M. Weigle, and M. Nelson. Access patterns for robots and humans in web archives. *JCDL*, 2013.

[2] K. Berberich, S. Bedathur, T. Neumann, and G. Weikum. A time machine for text search. *SIGIR*, 2007.

[3] G. Buchanan, S. J. Cunningham, A. Blandford, J. Rimmer, and C. Warwick. Information seeking by humanities scholars. *ECDL*, 2005.

[4] M. Costa, D. Gomes, F. Couto, and M. Silva. A survey of web archive search architectures. *WWW Companion*, 2013.

[5] M. Dougherty and E. Meyer. Community, tools, and practices in web archiving: The state of the art in relation to social science and humanities research needs. *JASIST*, 65(11):2195–2209, 2014.

[6] D. Gomes, D. Cruz, J. Miranda, M. Costa, and S. Fontes. Search the past with the Portuguese web archive. *WWW Companion*, 2013.

[7] D. Gomes, J. Miranda, and M. Costa. A survey on web archiving initiatives. *TPDL*, 2011.

[8] J. He, J. Zeng, and T. Suel. Improved index compression techniques for versioned document collections. *CIKM*, 2010.

[9] M. Hearst, P. Smalley, and C. Chandler. Faceted metadata for information architecture and search. *CHI*, 2006.

[10] M. Herscovici, R. Lempel, and S. Yogev. Efficient indexing of versioned document sequences. *ECIR*, 2007.

[11] J. Lin, M. Gholami, and J. Rao. Infrastructure for supporting exploration and discovery in web archives. *WWW Companion*, 2014.

[12] K. Nørvåg. Space-efficient support for temporal text indexing in a document archive context. *ECDL*, 2003.

[13] A. Ntoulas, J. Cho, and C. Olston. What's new on the web? The evolution of the web from a search engine perspective. *WWW*, 2004.

[14] S. Robertson. The probability ranking principle in IR. *Journal of Documentation*, 33(4):294–304, 1977.

[15] B. Shneiderman. The eyes have it: A task by data type taxonomy for information visualizations. *IEEE Symposium on Visual Languages*, 1996.

Content Selection and Curation for Web Archiving: The Gatekeepers vs. the Masses

Ian Milligan[1], Nick Ruest[2], and Jimmy Lin[1]

[1] University of Waterloo   [2] York University

{i2milligan,jimmylin}@uwaterloo.ca, ruestn@yorku.ca

ABSTRACT

Any preservation effort must begin with an assessment of what content to preserve, and web archiving is no different. There have historically been two answers to the question "what should we archive?" The Internet Archive's broad entire-web crawls have been supplemented by narrower domain- or topic-specific collections gathered by numerous libraries. We can characterize this as content selection and curation by "gatekeepers". In contrast, we have witnessed the emergence of another approach driven by "the masses"—we can archive pages that are contained in social media streams such as Twitter. The interesting question, of course, is how these approaches differ. We provide an answer to this question in the context of a case study about the 2015 Canadian federal elections. Based on our analysis, we recommend a hybrid approach that combines an effort driven by social media and more traditional curatorial methods.

1. INTRODUCTION

Any preservation effort must begin with an assessment of what content to preserve: archivists refer to this as appraisal, which is related to what librarians call collection development. This process remains inescapable, even in the digital context. Even if there are no technical barriers (e.g., storage capacity) to simply "keep everything" (and inevitably, there are—in most cases, available budget), such a strategy is not feasible for a variety of other reasons. This is especially true for web archiving, which refers to the systematic collection and preservation of web content.

The web has become an integral part of our daily lives and captures our "collective memory", recording everything from major world events to the rhythm of commerce. Even personal minutiae are valuable in that they offer a snapshot of our society, much in the same way that a diary from the 17th century provides insight into what the world was like then. It would not be an exaggeration to say that the web has become an important part of our cultural heritage worthy of preservation. As web pages are ephemeral and

disappear with great regularity [7], the only sure way of preserving web content for posterity is to proactively crawl and store portions of the web.

Any web archiving effort must begin with the following question: which sites should we crawl and how frequently? Historically, there have been two answers to this question, which has been supplemented by a third more recently. The Internet Archive has been collecting and storing web content since 1996, and to date has amassed hundreds of billions of pages totaling tens of petabytes. The Internet Archive's actual crawl strategy is opaque, but the organization aims to periodically gather a broad snapshot of the web as a whole—this thus serves as the first possible answer to our question: broad across-the-web scrapes. The second answer is supplied by a loosely-organized network of national, academic, and other libraries who adopt a strategy that is similar to the development of special collections. Based on some mandate, librarians scope their crawls—in the case of national libraries the mandate might be preserving pages in their country's domain; in many academic libraries, special web archive collections are created because they capture events of interest. The librarians who undertake such collection development essentially serve as information gatekeepers. Finally, the third, and most recent development, is to drive web archiving efforts based on social media—for example, archive those pages that are linked to from tweets. In contrast to librarians, we might think of this approach as content selection and curation by the masses. The question is how these approaches differ.

The contribution of this paper is an answer to this question in the context of a case study. We compare the contents of three different web archive collections with respect to the 2015 Canadian federal elections: a professionally curated collection by the University of Toronto, a collection formed by gathering pages linked from Twitter, and the general collection in the Internet Archive's Wayback machine. Based on our analysis, we recommend a hybrid approach that combines an effort driven by social media and more traditional curatorial methods. A manually-curated collection provides a robust foundation—site infrastructure, unpopular parties, marginal candidates—to layer the selection of the "masses" upon. On their own, popularly-curated web crawls are insufficient. Yet with contextual data, they can be very powerful.

Permission to make digital or hard copies of all or part of this work for personal or classroom use is granted without fee provided that copies are not made or distributed for profit or commercial advantage and that copies bear this notice and the full citation on the first page. Copyrights for components of this work owned by others than the author(s) must be honored. Abstracting with credit is permitted. To copy otherwise, or republish, to post on servers or to redistribute to lists, requires prior specific permission and/or a fee. Request permissions from permissions@acm.org.

JCDL '16, June 19 - 23, 2016, Newark, NJ, USA

© 2016 Copyright held by the owner/author(s). Publication rights licensed to ACM.
ISBN 978-1-4503-4229-2/16/06...$15.00

DOI: http://dx.doi.org/10.1145/2910896.2910913

2. BACKGROUND AND RELATED WORK

To begin, why is this an important issue to explore? The answer is simple: the content selection and curatorial decisions that we are making today define the source record of tomorrow. Thirty years from now, when historians study contemporary society, we do not want them to have an unnecessarily warped vision of the world today.

We are not the first to note the limitations of manually- or algorithmically-curated web archives. Farag and Fox [3] noted that while manual curation can render "high quality–time consuming" web archives, social media-based curation leads to "low quality–time saving" collections. Using tweets from high-profile events, including the Ebola outbreak and American Thanksgiving, they collected and compared URLs. The emphasis of that work, however, is the construction of an event model, whereas we are focused on providing a historical corpus for researchers; thus, the "low quality" of a citizen-created archive might be an advantage in our case. Similarly, the work of Georgescu et al. [4] in event-model extraction used Wikipedia edits for event detection, concluding that the citizen-generated approach is promising.

A common question, however, is: How comprehensive is archiving coverage? One study has found that between 35% and 90% of the web "has at least one archived copy." [1] This roughly lines up with earlier findings by Payne and Thelwall [8] and Russell and Kane [10]. We add to that literature by comparing three different collections around one event, examining content overlap and potential biases.

Others have explored the power of social media in providing seed lists. In the aftermath of the shooting of Mike Brown in Ferguson, Missouri and the ensuing protests, the Internet Archive's subscription archiving service, Archive-It, announced that they were "accepting URL nominations for web archive collection on Ferguson" to generate their seed list. Ed Summers extracted URLs from the #Ferguson Twitter hashtag and submitted those as seeds [11].

The most significant undertaking in this area was the IIPC-funded Twittervane project, developed by the British Library with the aim of "monitoring and analysing Twitter traffic relevant to a given theme and generate a list of most frequently shared web resources." While they brought the program to a prototype stage, curatorial feedback was lukewarm. The IIPC report found that only 20-30% of the URLs tweeted could be considered valid archival selections. For example, of the top seven URLs found by the Library of Congress test user, only one was relevant to their overall collecting approach [5]. Our project updates this work.

3. A TALE OF THREE COLLECTIONS

Using a study of a recent Canadian election, we compare:

- A collection of 1,988,693 URLs tweeted by users on the #elxn42 Twitter hashtag;
- The holdings of the Internet Archive's Wayback Machine;
- The August and November 2015 crawls of the Canadian Political Parties and Political Interest Groups (CPP) web archive collection.

These represent different collecting paradigms. The first represents the curatorial decisions of the "masses," or of the 318,176 unique users who used the #elxn42 hashtag. The second, the broad yet shallow crawls conducted by the Internet Archive. And finally, the curated collection gathered by the University of Toronto between 2005 and 2015.

3.1 Twitter

For archivists interested in user-generated corpora, Twitter shows promise. It provides insights into the opinions,

Twitter		CPP (Aug./Nov.)	
twitter.com	615421	liberal.ca	55536
cbc.ca	143941	greenparty.ca	45788
youtube.com	66886	policyalternatives.ca	37810
huffingtonpost.ca	66758	socialist.ca	26856
theglobeandmail.com	63401	davidsuzuki.org	25487
thestar.com	53051	canadians.org	24424
ctvnews.ca	49295	ccrweb.ca	19521
globalnews.ca	46488	afn.ca	15879
twimg.com	39989	blocquebecois.org	10899
macleans.ca	35280	egale.ca	7837

Table 1: Top tweeted domains (left) and top CPP domains from the Aug./Nov. 2015 crawls (right).

beliefs, and sentiments of everyday people. This comes in both the form of the 140-character limited tweet content itself, as well as the links shared to tweets, websites, and documents. While Twitter is not a representative sample of broader society—skewing young, college-educated, and affluent (above $50,000 US household income) [2]—it represents a dramatic increase in the amount of information generated, retained, and preserved from ordinary citizens.

A Canadian federal election was called on 3 August 2015, presenting a case study to compare user-tweeted URLs versus the seed list in our more conventional CPP collection (more details below). We carried out harvesting of the #elxn42 hashtag (the 2015 Canadian federal election hashtag) to compare what voters tweeted about with the formal seed list from the CPP collection. In total, we collected 3,918,932 tweets [9]; these tweets and the URLs contained in them form a foundation for the web archive.

To create the social media collection, our team began capturing tweets with the #elxn42 hashtag on 3 August 2015 using twarc [13], a command line tool and Python library for archiving Twitter JSON data, using Twitter's streaming and search APIs. We stopped collecting on 5 November 2015, the day after Justin Trudeau was sworn in as the 42nd Prime Minister of Canada. Using the twarc analysis library, we extracted tweeted URLs. As Twitter uses automatic link shortening, we also unshortened every URL in the dataset so that we would be able to create a canonical list of URLs tweeted for further analysis. We were able to create this using a combination of open-source tools: unshorten.py and unshrtn [12]. A total of 1,988,693 URLs were tweeted (50.9% of all tweets contained a URL), 334,841 of which were unique. By aggregating and sorting the URLs, we could see the domains that were tweeted the most in Table 1 (left). We find that twitter.com is the top tweeted domain largely due to "quoted" tweets, a form of retweeting, commenting upon, and endorsing other content.

3.2 Canadian Political Parties

To compare the Twitter-based web archive with another collection, we used the Canadian Political Parties and Political Interest Groups (CPP) collection. We have been using this for an analysis of Canadian politics between 2005 and 2015, and have provided public access to it through our http://webarchives.ca/ portal. The CPP collection is the product of a quarterly crawl, beginning in 2005, by the University of Toronto Libraries using Archive-It, the Internet Archive's web archiving subscription service. It includes all major Canadian federal parties, many minor ones, as well as a nebulous group of "political interest groups," ranging

	CPP	Twitter	Wayback
CPP	-	0.341%	74.30%
Twitter	0.269%	-	10.06%
Wayback	N/A	N/A	-

Table 2: Intersection analysis. Read as percentage of *row* found in *column*, e.g., 0.341% of URLs from CPP were in the Twitter #elxn42 collection.

from groups advocating for marriage equality, the banning of land mines, environmental issues, and Canada's First Nations. With over fifteen million documents crawled, it is an unparalleled collection of recent Canadian political history.

The collection has a significant downside, in that it has opaque seed list selection criteria. The librarian responsible for scoping this collection in 2005 has retired. Curatorial choices were not documented. While political parties are well covered, the interest groups were largely discovered through keyword searches, some were excluded due to robots.txt exclusions, and the seed list was largely developed by one person.

By aggregating and sorting the URLs, we can see the domains that are most represented in the CPP collection in Table 1 (right).

3.3 Internet Archive

The Internet Archive engages in broad crawling. For example, in the March–December 2011 Wide Web Scrape, they began with the top million URLs based on the Alexa Internet rankings, and crawled from there. These crawls capture many sites, but to a limited depth.

4. INTERSECTION ANALYSIS

To query the Internet Archive's Wayback Machine, we used their Wayback CDX Server API.[1] This takes a URL and determines whether there is an archived, accessible copy in the Wayback Machine. We ran lists of all the unique URLs in the CPP collection and the #elxn42 Twitter collection through the API, which provides a list of all timestamps of available captures. We then checked to see if the Wayback Machine had a copy of the webpage within the August–December period. Results are shown in Table 2.

Of the 1,988,963 URLs that were tweeted (334,841 unique URLs), there was low coverage in the CPP collection (drawing only on the August and November 2015 crawl URLs): of the URLs in CPP, only 0.341% are found in the Twitter collection. We thus have very different collections: the library gatekeepers have captured a very different picture of Canadian politics than the "masses" on Twitter.

To add to this understanding, we subsequently carried out an investigation of what tweeted URLs from #elxn42 would be included in the Internet Archive or the CPP collection. To do so, we took our list of 334,841 unique URLs and submitted them to the Wayback CDX Server API.

Of these URLs, 33,685 were present in the Wayback Machine with a snapshot between August and December 2015. This gives the Wayback Machine a coverage, within our time period, of 10.05%. If we were to remove the time period limit, 68,112 of the URLs (or 20.34%) had at least one snapshot dating back to 1996, but not necessarily within our time period. While both values are below the lower bound of the

[1] https://github.com/internetarchive/wayback/

Included		Excluded	
cbc.ca	3035	twitter.com	173931
youtube.com	2639	linkis.com	11071
thestar.com	1665	youtube.com	6026
theglobeandmail.com	1644	instagram.com	5302
huffingtonpost.ca	1561	globalnews.ca	4709
twitter.com	1550	cbc.ca	4529
ctvnews.ca	1423	facebook.com	4282
nationalpost.com	1262	rabble.ca	3859
globalnews.ca	1062	huffingtonpost.ca	3762
ottawacitizen.com	836	fw.to	3284

Table 3: Top #elxn42 Twitter domains included (left) and excluded (right) in the Wayback (August–December crawls).

35-90% coverage from previous work, this reflects the changing nature of websites—more social media—as well as the early timing of our inquiry.

What #elxn42 URLs were and were not included in the Wayback Machine was fascinating. Table 3 (left) shows the top ten domains that were found in the Wayback Machine. The top ten domains that were *not* present in the Wayback Machine included significant overlap with these same domains, as seen in Table 3 (right). Some of these are social media websites (Facebook, Instagram), and others are Canadian media outlets that are likely not crawled much, such as the left-wing news site rabble.ca, some Canadian Broadcasting Corporation pages, and Global News—in the broad global scope of the Internet Archive, they may receive little attention. However, there was quite a bit of overlap on major traditional print newspapers: The *Toronto Star*, the *Globe and Mail*, and the *National Post*, Canada's three highest-circulation newspapers, also had their websites included in both the #elxn42 corpus and the Wayback Machine. A few omissions were technical. One is a link shortener (fw.to) that is not supported by our link unshortening package. The other, linkis, is a platform that personalizes shared sites (most of these tweets were shared using the linkis client).

Which of the URLs tweeted on the #elxn42 hashtag would have been included—or would be potentially included—in the CPP collection? The actual inclusion coverage is low, amounting to 902 or 0.269%. This does not tell the full story, however. Comparing the domains tweeted with the CPP's fifty seed domains, we found that 59,576, or 17.79%, were part of the fifty domains. While slightly lower than the global Wayback Machine, this is roughly comparable. This suggests that the CPP collection does indeed capture websites of significant public interest.

Finally, we were curious about what URLs found within the CPP collection—drawing on the two most recent crawls in August and November 2015—would be found in the global Wayback. We discovered that 74.3% of CPP URLs were found there with snapshots within the last six months; removing the time limit, we observe 83.94% coverage for CPP URLs in the Wayback dating back to 1996.

While Archive-It and the Wayback Machine are similar, largely due to the former being routinely piped into the latter, they are not identical. The differences were largely driven by changes to crawl scope: the CPP collection included RSS feeds, forms, calendars (often crawler traps), and more discussion forum content. CPP also contained a few hundred YouTube videos that were out of scope in the Wayback. As Archive-It crawl operators have considerable crawl discretion, including the ability to ignore robots.txt, the slight variation is unsurprising.

5. DISCUSSION

The three crawl paradigms discussed in this paper offer relative advantages and disadvantages. The CPP collection provides a broader documentary overview of Canadian politics than the Twitter corpus, as reflected in the low 0.341% coverage. This is due to three reasons beyond the reality of the CPP collection spanning ten years (December 2005 to present) versus the few months of the federal election.

First, several websites that were collected as part of the CPP collection were not tweeted at all. These included unpopular fringe parties who have largely faded from the public eye. While not commanding popular support, they provide useful historical information about the extremes of the political spectrum. Manual curation, done with sensitivity, can ensure the inclusion of more minority viewpoints.

Second, the CPP collection includes entire websites: from calendars, to menus, archived pages, to terms of service, and beyond. Users do not tweet this important content.

Third, the CPP collection has an institutional bias in it. Comparing the top ten domains tweeted in the #elxn42 dataset versus the top ten in the CPP collection (see Table 1) reveals that the only overlap is the Conservative Party of Canada's website. Curation by professionals, performed over a long period of time, tends to focus on stable institutions (understandably). On the other hand, Twitter users tweeted more ephemeral sites and social media: issues of popular discussion and controversy, such as political platforms, controversial press releases, and popular events (which all rank highly in the correlation between the CPP and the Twitter corpus).

We cannot rely on the Internet Archive as a replacement for either professionally-curated collections or Twitter-based crawls. The Internet Archive's main collection is necessarily broad but shallow: websites are only crawled, in some cases, a few times a year, and only to a certain depth. Crawlers may not reach deep into large domains. Without input from Archive-It (which represent the efforts of professional curators), we anticipate that the coverage of the Wayback machine would be even spottier on topics of scholarly interest.

Access is also more easily enabled with smaller, focused collections in a way that providing access to broad crawls has so far been elusive. To use Internet Archive or most national library collections, users must know the exact URL of the resource they are looking for as an entryway; in other cases, such as the British Library, full-text search exists but is severely hamstrung by access and content rendering restrictions [6]. There is room for smaller, more circumscribed collections, as the popular and media success of http://webarchives.ca/ demonstrates: a subject-focused collection can appeal to both scholars and the general public, more importantly.

6. CONCLUSION

A hybrid approach between Twitter-based and traditional curatorial methods is recommended. The Archive-It collections provide a foundation to lay the more specific Twitter-focused collections upon. Curators could be encouraged to collect event-based hashtags alongside traditional methods, perhaps in consultation with researchers. Tweeted URLs have an innate demographic and partisan bias within them, drawing on profiling information about Twitter users, but so do curated collections, which can suffer from a lack of documentation and transparency about how they are collected. For researchers, Twitter-based collections are at least documentable: the parameters of the hashtags chosen, streaming method used, and the rich metadata embedded in the tweet JSON itself can help contextualize further studies. In addition, our work significantly builds upon the earlier IIPC-funded Twittervane project, with more positive research outcomes. While one limitation of this short paper is that we could not explore the quality of the preserved content—instead, focusing more on quantities—future research will explore actual content differences.

We believe that scholarly findings from a Twitter-based web archive would differ substantially from a professionally curated collection. The former is a laser-focused snapshot of collections of immediate interest from potentially millions of users, while the latter is a broader collection of a still relatively narrow band of domains selected by subject-matter experts. They are apples and oranges, but complement each other very well. Most importantly, we need both.

Acknowledgments. This work was supported by the Social Sciences and Humanities Research Council of Canada under Insight grant 435-2015-0011 and the U.S. National Science Foundation under awards IIS-1218043 and CNS-1405688. Any opinions, findings, conclusions, or recommendations expressed are those of the authors and do not necessarily reflect the views of the sponsors.

7. REFERENCES

[1] S. G. Ainsworth, A. AlSum, H. SalahEldeen, M. C. Weigle, and M. L. Nelson. How much of the web is archived? *arXiv:1212.6177*, Dec. 2012.

[2] M. Duggan. The demographics of social media users, Aug. 2015.

[3] M. M. Farag and E. A. Fox. Building and archiving event web collections: A focused crawler approach. *Bulletin of IEEE Technical Committee on Digital Libraries*, 11(2), 2015.

[4] M. Georgescu, N. Kanhabua, D. Krause, W. Nejdl, and S. Siersdorfer. Extracting event-related information from article updates in Wikipedia. *ECIR*, 2013.

[5] H. Hockx-Yu and M. Pitt. Evaluating Twittervane: Project final report, June 2013.

[6] I. Milligan. Web archive legal deposit: A double-edged sword, July 2015.

[7] A. Ntoulas, J. Cho, and C. Olston. What's new on the web? the evolution of the web from a search engine perspective. *WWW*, 2004.

[8] N. Payne and M. Thelwall. A longitudinal study of academic webs: Growth and stabilisation. *Scientometrics*, 71(3):523–539, June 2007.

[9] N. Ruest and R. White. #elxn42 tweets (42nd Canadian Federal Election), Dec. 2015.

[10] E. Russell and J. Kane. The missing link: Assessing the reliability of internet citations in history journals. *Technology and Culture*, 49(2):420–429, 2008.

[11] E. Summers. A Ferguson Twitter archive, Aug. 2014.

[12] E. Summers and D. Krech. unshrtn, Dec. 2015.

[13] E. Summers, H. van Kemenadem, P. Binkley, N. Ruest, recrm, S. Costa, E. Phetteplace, T. G. Badger, M. A. Matienzo, L. Blakk, D. Chudnov, and C. Nelson. twarc: v0.3.3, Aug. 2015.

Towards Better Understanding of Academic Search

Madian Khabsa
Microsoft Research
Redmond, WA
madian.khabsa@microsoft.com

Zhaohui Wu and C. Lee Giles
The Pennsylvania State University
University Park, PA
zzw109@psu.edu, giles@ist.psu.edu

ABSTRACT

Academics have relied heavily on search engines to identify and locate research manuscripts that are related to their research areas. Many of the early information retrieval systems and technologies were developed while catering for librarians to help them sift through books and proceedings, followed by recent online academic search engines such as Google Scholar and Microsoft Academic Search. In spite of their popularity among academics and importance to academia, the usage, query behaviors, and retrieval models for academic search engines have not been well studied.

To this end, we study the distribution of queries that are received by an academic search engine. Furthermore, we delve deeper into academic search queries and classify them into navigational and informational queries. This work introduces a definition for navigational queries in academic search engines under which a query is considered navigational if the user is searching for a specific paper or document. We describe multiple facets of navigational academic queries, and introduce a machine learning approach with a set of features to identify such queries.

1. INTRODUCTION

Academic search engines have become the starting point for many researchers when they draft research manuscripts or work on proposals. Typically, there are two main retrieval systems that are used by academics. The first one is a citation database that is more of a traditional librarian search such as *Web of Science* and *Pubmed*, while the other is more similar to typical web search such as *Google Scholar*, and *Microsoft Academic Search*. Usage statistics tend to reflect user's preference for each type of systems. For example, 30% of Ph.D researchers relied on Google and Google Scholar as their main source for finding information in a survey conducted by the researchers of tomorrow project in 2012[1]. On

[1] http://www.webarchive.org.uk/wayback/archive/20140614040703/http://www.jisc.ac.uk/publications/reports/2012/researchers-of-tomorrow.aspx

Permission to make digital or hard copies of all or part of this work for personal or classroom use is granted without fee provided that copies are not made or distributed for profit or commercial advantage and that copies bear this notice and the full citation on the first page. Copyrights for components of this work owned by others than ACM must be honored. Abstracting with credit is permitted. To copy otherwise, or republish, to post on servers or to redistribute to lists, requires prior specific permission and/or a fee. Request permissions from permissions@acm.org.

JCDL '16, June 19–23, 2016, Newark, NJ, USA.

© 2016 ACM. ISBN 978-1-4503-4229-2/16/06. . . $15.00

DOI: http://dx.doi.org/10.1145/2910896.2910922

the other hand, usage statistics from the University of California, Santa Cruz indicate that Google Scholar was used as a secondary source of information rather than a primary one in 2010 [4].

The need for retrieving relevant information in scientific domains has lead to many contributions in information retrieval [12]. For example, the idea behind indexing documents using keywords have originated from the field of librarianship [12]. Similarly, the intuition behind *PageRank* goes back to citation indexing, and using the number of citation as a proxy for measuring importance.

In this work we focus on academic search systems that use keyword base search. We study user behavior of an academic search engine using query logs of three years. By observing user query patterns, we were then motivated to study the user query intent by classifying academic search queries into navigational and informational queries. Search engine queries have typically been classified into three main categories [2]: 1) Informational: the user is seeking some information available on the web; 2) Navigational: the user is trying to reach a particular website; and 3) Transactional: where the user is trying to perform some type of transaction. Query intent classification is an important part of any search engine because the query type affects how the query is handled. Identifying navigational queries is essential for devising specific ranking functions that rank navigational queries only. Similarly, if a query is known to be navigational, the search engine may choose to present the results page differently by either showing a single result or few results. In this work we introduce the concept of academic navigational query, and define multiple facets through which a query should be considered navigational. To the best of our knowledge, this is the first work that studies academic query classification.

2. RELATED WORK

Although there is a rich literature related to academic search in both information retrieval and data mining community, few work studies the usage of academic search engines and seeks to understand academic search using real world user query data. We briefly review the related research on academic search in the following directions.

Existing academic search engines. Earlier academic search engines that build upon automatic citation indexing and metadata extraction include Citeseer [3], followed by Arnetminer which focuses more on extraction, analysis and mining of academic social network and providing academic rankings [14]. In the industry, two typical instances of

Table 1: Search type percentage. Document and author search

Search Type	Percentage
Document	92.73%
Author	6.9%
Other	0.2%
Total	100%

academic search engines are Google Scholar and Microsoft Academic Search.

Query type identification. Most query type identification has focused on general Web search engines, with different methods applied in different settings. For example, Kang and Kim used the difference of distribution, mutual information, the usage rate as anchor texts, and the POS information for the classification [7]; Jansen et. al. proposed a rule based method based on a set of heuristics [5]; and Lee et. al. studied user-click behavior and anchor-link distribution [9]. The closest work to ours is Kan and Poo [6] where they focused on detecting known item search in online public access catalogs. However, our work introduces the concept of navigational queries and formally categorizes the cases that belong the concept.

Personalized academic search. Some research also investigated the personalized academic search by user modeling based on query log [13].It is worth noting that traditional user models such as collaborative filtering that do not consider document content features may fail since they play a more important role in ranking document than user similarity.

3. ACADEMIC QUERY LOGS

Our work was motivated by examining the usage behavior of academic users of CiteSeerX, which indexes publications in computer science and engineering, physics, and economics. The search engine provides multiple search types, most notably document search and author search. The search sessions received by the search engine between September 2009 and March 2013 are used in this study.

The proportions of search types are presented in Table 1. As seen in the table, the majority (92.73%) of search sessions belong to document search. In addition, there is a reasonable interest in searching for author names with 6.9% of the search requests targeting the authors index. We conjecture two possible reasons for this. In the first scenario users are interested in searching for papers by author name assuming they remember one of the authors of a paper but do not recall the title. The second reason is that individual authors are searching for themselves to track down the number of citations they received, the number of papers they have being indexed by the search engine. Similarly, tenure and promotion committees would use the author search to track down the body of work for a given scholar. An important feature of queries is query length, which might to some extent indicate the user query intent. For example, users issuing longer queries might be more likely searching for more specific information. By examining the queries with type *document search* we found that the average length of a query is 4.76 terms.

4. QUERY TYPE CLASSIFICATION

Most of query intent identification has focused on general search engines with many approaches being applied [7, 5, 9]. However, there has not been any work that identifies navigational queries in academic search, to the best of our knowledge. In fact, we are not aware of any work that categorizes query intent in the academic search. Perhaps because traditional library search was the defacto standard in academic search until recently. The ease of use of current academic search engines such as Google Scholar, combined with their similarity to traditional web search that most people have become familiar with creates an opportunity to study the query intent of the users.

In academic search it is possible to categorize queries into at least two types: *navigational* and *informational*. It is not straightforward how to define transactional queries, if they exist, in the academic setting. Providing a complete taxonomy of query intent in academic search is beyond the scope of this work. Rather, we focus on identifying navigational queries. We define a **navigational query** as a query for which the user is looking for a specific scholarly document, which can be a paper, book, thesis, etc. Correctly identifying navigational queries is important, because rankers are heavily influenced by citations which can lead to highly cited papers being ranked higher than the target paper if the target paper is new or not well cited. Furthermore, papers whose title contains general terms are more likely to be susceptible because there are large number of matches. There are multiple facets for navigational queries in academic search. For example, a user might look for a given document by:

- Document Object Identifier (DOI): *10.1038/nature14106*

- Full title query: *The Google file system*

- A combination of an author and title information: *jeff dean mapreduce*

- Author and year/venue information: *leskovec 2009 news cycle*

- Author names for a well known work: *Cormen Leiserson Rivest Stein*, or *hopcroft motwani ullman*

- A combination of author names along with some paper's distinguishing terms: *dic brin motwani*

In the first scenario when users search by DOI, it is sufficient to check if the query matches a database of DOIs or not. However, other cases are not as trivial. For example, title queries are not easily detectable. First of all, extracting titles from papers is not always accurate. In addition, although a query can be checked against a list of titles, there are many short and ambiguous queries that might match at multiple title positions. On top of that, no search engines contain all academic documents [8], hence identifying a title navigational query that the search engine does not have a result for it may be used as signal to locate this missing document. However, other cases can be more subtle to identify. For example the following queries that were found in the logs of the academic search engine are not as obvious. In the query *leskovec 2009 news cycle* there exists an author name and a year along with subset of a title that would identify

Table 2: Navigational Query Features

Feature	Description
#_tokens	number of tokens in a query
has_year	whether a term in the query matches a regex for identifying year
has_stop_word	whether the query has stop words
has_punctuation	whether the query has punctuation
#_authors	the number of tokens in the query identified as author name
author_ratio	the ratio of query terms identified as author names to the query length
is_title_match	whether the query matches a title in the search engine's index

the work.[2] Similarly, *dic brin motwani* and *lift brin motwani ullman* both refer to the dynamic itemset counting paper by S. Brin and R. Motwani [3]. Finding the correct matching of those queries might need more sophisticated approach than simple rules.

4.1 Approach

The problem is modeled as a binary classification problem. Given a query q, we would like to classify it into one of the following classes {Navigational, Informational}. Each query q is represented as a vector of the features described in Table 2. The features are crafted to capture the multiple facets that represent navigational queries. For example, #_tokens is chosen after noticing that many navigational queries have more terms than informational queries because they contain a title. On the other hand, is_title_match can be a good signal in general, but if the query term is general, a match does not necessarily make the query navigational. Other syntactic features such as has_stop_word, and has_punctuation are aimed at identifying title queries. The intuition is that users rarely use such terms in informational queries, and they are more likely to be part of title.

As shown in the examples, the mention of author names is one facet of navigational queries. However, it is not always the case that a mention of an author means a navigational query. For example, the following query that was found in the logs of the academic search engine is not considered navigational: mccallum nigam because these two authors have coauthored more than one paper together, and this query cannot be interpreted to refer to a single paper. Nevertheless, the presence of an author name is one of the indicators of navigational queries. Therefore, we create a feature to represent the number of query tokens that are identified to be an author name. Identifying whether a token refers to an author name or not was not as trivial as checking against a

---

[2]Meme-tracking and the dynamics of the news cycle (KDD'09).
[3]Dynamic itemset counting and implication rules for market basket data (SIGMOD'97).

dictionary of all possible names. Initially we started by using the author list of DBLP[4] as a names dictionary assuming that it would have low false positive rate since it is manually curated. However, the false positive identification was still high as tokens such as network matched as an author.

Therefore, we adapted a language model approach to identify author names. For every token t we estimate three probabilities: $P(t|author)$, $P(t|title)$, and $P(t|abstract)$ where author, title, and abstract refer to the token appearing in the author, title, or abstract section of the paper, respectively. We estimate each of the probabilities for every token over all the fields in the academic search engine's index. A token t is considered an author iff:

$$P(t|author) > P(t|abstract) \wedge P(t|author) > P(t|title)$$

Gradient Boosted Trees (GBT) are used to train a classifier for identifying navigational queries. The number of stumps and the learning rate parameter are chosen using grid search over the range $[10, 400]$ and $[10^{-4}, 10^{-1}]$, respectively. SMOTE oversampling is used to oversample the navigational queries because the dataset is imbalanced.

4.2 Dataset

To build the dataset, we first randomly sample 1000 queries from the user search logs and then keep only the queries in document search type, which results in 553 in total. However, notice that this small number of samples might not give reasonable coverage of all possible positive samples (navigational queries), we did multiple rounds of sampling and use the aforementioned heuristics to match possible positive candidates. The dataset was then augmented by those positive examples that might not have enough presence in the randomly sampled dataset, such as examples with author names. We also added comparable number of negative examples to counter for that effect. At the end, the dataset contained 579 queries. Each query was manually inspected by two human judges and tagged as either navigational or informational. When the judges had mismatching labels, they conferred and agreed on a mutual tag. In the manually tagged queries, 12.5% were found to be navigational.

4.3 Experiments

The performance of the classifier is shown in Table 3. The numbers are for a 5 fold cross validation, with the training fold being randomly split into 90:10 with the 10% used to validate the grid search parameters. Oversampling using SMOTE was only conducted on the training fold, with the test fold remaining untouched. We compared the performance of the boosted tree classifier with that of an SVM with RBF kernel, and with that of a random forest. All parameters for both baseline classifiers are configured with grid search, similar to the GBT. The highest precision, and overall F score was attained with GBT as can be seen in table 3. The numbers in the table refer to the average precision, recall and F score obtained through the 5 fold cross validation, with the standard deviation reported between parenthesis. The importance of each of the features is shown in Figure 1. The number of tokens within a query is the most important feature, which can be explained by title queries that tend to have higher number of tokens. Similarly, the title match feature which is closely related to the number of tokens in

---

[4]http://www.dblp.org/search/index.php

Table 3: Navigational query classification performance for multiple learning algorithms. Numbers between parenthesis refer to standard deviation in 5 fold cross validation

Method	Precision	Recall	F1
GBT	0.68 (0.03)	0.68 (0.09)	0.677 (0.04)
SVM (RBF)	0.67 (0.05)	0.63 (0.12)	0.64 (0.07)
Random Forest	0.71 (0.06)	0.59 (0.14)	0.62 (0.09)

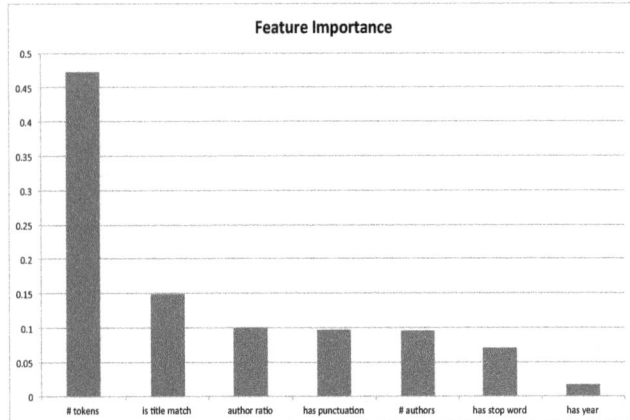

Figure 1: Feature importance of navigational query classification.

the query ranks second in terms of importance, followed by author ratio feature.

It is worth noting that classifying navigational queries is notoriously a hard task in the web domain, and it would be at least as hard within the academic realm. For example, Jansen et al.[5] were only to obtain 74% for overall web query intent classification, which is not limited to navigational. Others were able to obtain 70% precision with high recall for informational queries [1]. Many studies for navigational query classification at web search engines have relied on click through rates [9, 11, 10]. While these methods were effective overall, they remain passive and depend on the presence of queries and clicks in the logs to be able to accurately classify them. This presents a challenge when new queries that have not been seen before arrive, or when users refer to an academic paper using a new combination of keywords.

5. CONCLUSION AND FUTURE WORK

We studied academic search based on user query logs. We then introduced the concept of academic navigational query and studied the problem of academic query type classification on a new dataset with human judgments. We proposed a set of features to learn the classifier. The results showed the effectiveness of the proposed features and demonstrated the challenge of the problem.

One of our ongoing work is on implementing our new academic ranking methods that take advantage of both navigational query classification and the learned academic document rank functions. We could add the navigational query classification result as a new feature for the ranker or train separate rankers for different types of queries.

6. ACKNOWLEDGMENTS

We acknowledge partial funding by the National Science Foundation.

7. REFERENCES

[1] R. Baeza-Yates, L. Calderón-Benavides, and C. González-Caro. The intention behind web queries. In *String processing and information retrieval*, pages 98–109. Springer, 2006.

[2] A. Broder. A taxonomy of web search. In *ACM Sigir forum*, volume 36, pages 3–10. ACM, 2002.

[3] C. L. Giles, K. D. Bollacker, and S. Lawrence. Citeseer: An automatic citation indexing system. In *Proceedings of the third ACM conference on Digital libraries*, pages 89–98. ACM, 1998.

[4] C. Hightower and C. Caldwell. Shifting sands: science researchers on google scholar, web of science, and pubmed, with implications for library collections budgets. *Issues in Science and Technology Librarianship*, (63):4, 2010.

[5] B. J. Jansen, D. L. Booth, and A. Spink. Determining the user intent of web search engine queries. In *Proceedings of the 16th international conference on World Wide Web*, pages 1149–1150. ACM, 2007.

[6] M.-Y. Kan and D. C. Poo. Detecting and supporting known item queries in online public access catalogs. In *Digital Libraries, 2005. JCDL'05. Proceedings of the 5th ACM/IEEE-CS Joint Conference on*, pages 91–99. IEEE, 2005.

[7] I.-H. Kang and G. Kim. Query type classification for web document retrieval. In *Proceedings of the 26th annual international ACM SIGIR*, 2003.

[8] M. Khabsa and C. L. Giles. The number of scholarly documents on the public web. *PLOS one*, 9(5):e93949, 2014.

[9] U. Lee, Z. Liu, and J. Cho. Automatic identification of user goals in web search. In *Proceedings of the 14th international conference on World Wide Web*, pages 391–400. ACM, 2005.

[10] X. Li, Y.-Y. Wang, and A. Acero. Learning query intent from regularized click graphs. In *Proceedings of the 31st annual international ACM SIGIR conference on Research and development in information retrieval*, pages 339–346. ACM, 2008.

[11] Y. Lu, F. Peng, X. Li, and N. Ahmed. Coupling feature selection and machine learning methods for navigational query identification. In *Proceedings of the 15th ACM international conference on Information and knowledge management*, pages 682–689, 2006.

[12] M. Sanderson and W. B. Croft. The history of information retrieval research. *Proceedings of the IEEE*, 100(Special Centennial Issue):1444–1451, 2012.

[13] Y. Sun, H. Li, I. G. Councill, J. Huang, W.-C. Lee, and C. L. Giles. Personalized ranking for digital libraries based on log analysis. In *Proceedings of the 10th ACM Workshop on Web Information and Data Management*, WIDM '08, pages 133–140, 2008.

[14] J. Tang, J. Zhang, L. Yao, J. Li, L. Zhang, and Z. Su. Arnetminer: extraction and mining of academic social networks. In *Proceedings of the 14th ACM SIGKDD international conference on Knowledge discovery and data mining*, 2008.

Investigating Cluster Stability when Analyzing Transaction Logs

Daniel Grech
University of Sheffield
Sheffield
United Kingdom
dgre090@gmail.com

Paul Clough[*]
University of Sheffield
Sheffield
United Kingdom
p.d.clough@sheffield.ac.uk

ABSTRACT

Data-driven approaches have become increasingly popular as a means for analyzing transaction logs from web search engines and digital libraries, for example using cluster analysis to identify common patterns of search and navigation behavior. However, steps must be taken to ensure that results are reliable and repeatable. Although clustering patterns of user interaction behavior has been previously explored, one aspect that has received less attention is *cluster stability* that can be used to aid cluster validation. In this paper we compute stability based on the Jaccard coefficient to investigate the cluster stability when using different subsets of transaction log data from WorldCat.org. Results provide insights into different types of search behaviors and highlight that clusters of varying degrees of stability will result from the clustering process. However, we show that additional investigation beyond the results of cluster stability is required to fully validate the resulting clusters.

1. INTRODUCTION

With the increased availability of user-system interaction data has come reliance on the use of data-driven techniques for mining and analyzing data. One particular area that has received considerable interest in recent years is search or transaction log mining [1]. Valuable insights can be gained from analyzing the traces people leave when they search for and navigate digital information. These transaction logs provide a unique resource to drive the next generation of digital services and applications [2]. The use of unsupervised learning techniques, such as *clustering*, have been widely used for various tasks in transaction log analysis. This includes identifying user interests from query logs, grouping query refinements according to users' information needs, providing query suggestions, identifying changes in user intent and identifying tasks [1, 2].

In this paper we investigate categorizing users' general search and navigational patterns using user-system interaction data derived from WorldCat.org transaction logs, together with cluster analysis. Clustering is often used as a data-driven method to explore and group common patterns of interaction [3, 4, 5]. However, the use of cluster analysis raises many questions, such as what is the optimal set of clusters and how 'good' are the resulting clusters? One approach to validate the results of clustering is to assess *cluster stability* [6]. The stability of clusters could be affected by a variety of factors, including sample size, selected features, algorithm, parameter settings and distance/similarity metric. The idea behind cluster stability is that the optimal clustering of a data set is the clustering that is most stable. Despite the importance of cluster stability, however, there is little empirical work undertaken in the area of transaction log analysis.

We use a simple method based on the Jaccard coefficient and subsets of data to determine cluster stability. Results highlight that clusters of varying stability are produced when using cluster analysis. However, results also show the limitations with relying solely on cluster stability to validate clustering outputs and the need for manual inspection. Our work is similar to [7], but instead of using cluster stability to determine the optimal number of clusters we use it to help with validating the results of clustering. The following research questions are considered: *[RQ1] How stable are the clusters produced from applying cluster analysis to a sample of Worldcat.org transaction logs?* and *[RQ2] How can cluster stability be used to validate the clustering of transaction logs?* The remainder of the paper is structured as follows. Section 2 describes related work; Section 3 describes our experimental setup; Sections 4 and 5 present and discuss results; finally Section 6 concludes the paper and provides avenues for further research.

2. RELATED WORK

2.1 Mining transaction logs

This paper investigates validity when clustering transaction logs into groups that signify distinct patterns of user-system interaction. Examples of past work that have analyzed search patterns of transaction logs using cluster analysis include Chen & Cooper [4] who applied hierarchical agglomerative clustering to detect distinct patterns of user behavior for a library catalog system. They manually derived 47 variables that could be extracted from the transaction

---

[*]This is the primary contact author.

Permission to make digital or hard copies of all or part of this work for personal or classroom use is granted without fee provided that copies are not made or distributed for profit or commercial advantage and that copies bear this notice and the full citation on the first page. Copyrights for components of this work owned by others than ACM must be honored. Abstracting with credit is permitted. To copy otherwise, or republish, to post on servers or to redistribute to lists, requires prior specific permission and/or a fee. Request permissions from permissions@acm.org.

JCDL '16, June 19-23, 2016, Newark, NJ, USA

© 2016 ACM. ISBN 978-1-4503-4229-2/16/06. . . $15.00

DOI: http://dx.doi.org/10.1145/2910896.2910923

logs of an online library catalog. They used cluster analysis to find groups of similar sessions and came up with six clusters of general usage patterns. Wolfram et al. [3] used simila a similar approach to identify distinctive session characteristics from three web search transaction logs. Stenmark [5] used self-organizing maps (SOMs) to identify clusters of user behavior in intranet search logs. Weber & Jaimes [8] base their study of usage patterns on Broder's taxonomy of user intent, but perform automated analyses of users' sessions using features derived from activities within the session and also from external demographic information. Using k-means clustering they show that different user profiles have distinct patterns of search behavior. Jones & Klinker [9] also use supervised learning to automatically segment sessions into higher level *missions* and lower level *goals*. In most cases the stability of clustering is not investigated or reported. Heer et al. [7] is one of the exceptions in which they investigate user-system interaction activity using cluster stability to determine the optimal number of clusters.

2.2 Cluster stability

Clustering methods will generate clusterings for almost any dataset, even if the data is homogeneous by nature. Therefore, performing some form of cluster validation to ensure that the clusters produced are meaningful is an important step in the process [7]. A key concept in the field of cluster validation is the notion of *cluster stability*. The idea behind cluster stability is that the optimal clustering of a dataset is the clustering that is most stable. Hennig [6] captures the intuition behind cluster stability by stating that clusters which are meaningful and valid "shouldn't disappear easily if the data set is changed in a non-essential way". This viewpoint is shared by Von Luxburg [10] who states that a clustering structure on a data set is stable if when it is applied to "several data sets from the same underlying model or of the same data generating process", it outputs fairly similar results. Von Luxburg insists that, in the field of cluster stability, the way that clusters look is not important; all that matters is the clusters can be constructed in a stable manner.

Ben-David et al. [11] describe the possible scenarios that can lead to unstable clusters and state that such clusters are usually the result of one of the following phenomena:

Multiple global optima. If the global optimizer of the clustering objective function is not unique then this will always lead to unstable clusters.

Small sample size. If the sample size is not large enough to ensure that the cluster structure is well-pronounced, then instability will be observed.

Algorithmic instability. If the clustering algorithm can converge to very different solutions by ending up at different local optima then instability will be present. Such instability would not exist if an algorithm which always terminates at the global optimum existed.

Geometric instability. It is possible that the mechanism behind stability based model selection is not consistent with the geometric model of the underlying distribution leading to low score for stability.

All of the definitions emphasize that clusters which are meaningful should be reproducible using different datasets

from the same underlying distribution or under slightly different algorithmic conditions. In this study we identify different 'types' of sessions within a large transaction log using clustering and validate results by quantifying and analyzing the stability of the resulting clusters using the Jaccard Coefficient (see Section 3.3).

3. METHODOLOGY

3.1 Dataset

The dataset used to investigate cluster stability is a search log from WorldCat.org, the world's largest bibliographic data base, with more than 300 million bibliographic records and over 2 billion holdings from more than 70,000 libraries[1]. Log data for two months of WorldCat.org (October 2012 and April 2013) were used (74,711,963 entries in total). Preparation of the logs included filtering out non-human traffic, such as web search engine crawlers, together with segmenting the logs into *sessions* (with sessions consisting of more than 100 queries removed). A simple and efficient time-based method using a 30 minute cut-off period was used to segment sessions, resulting in 25,395,469 user sessions[2]. This paper is not concerned with defining sessions or broader units of interaction, such as tasks or missions [9]; rather, we focus on validating the outputs of cluster analysis on transaction logs where session boundaries have already been defined.

The log data contains many types of user-system interactions, such as the user issuing a query, selecting to view an item from the search results, viewing other pages from the WorldCat interface, navigating links (e.g., related items or further information), logging into a user account, etc. The use of different features from the log are being investigated to characterize patterns of search and navigation; however, in this paper we focus on a small subset of features and the issue of cluster validation. The average duration of a session is 41 secs (σ=81 secs) with 55% of sessions originating from the US. The mean number of actions (queries and viewed items) is 3.07 per session, with a typical session consisting of 2 item views (μ=2.2, σ=2.62). 42% of sessions consist of single query searches with the mean number of queries being 3.3 queries per session (σ=4.1). Sessions with viewed items only are typically referrals from external sites, such as web search engines, and subsequently do not contain query actions that occur within WorldCat.

3.2 Cluster analysis

To cluster sessions from WorldCat.org we first extract the following descriptive features to represent sessions (based on [3]): (i) duration of session; (ii) number of queries used to search for items (issued within WorldCat); (iii) average query length; (iv) number of viewed item pages (excluding clicks on other links within WorldCat, such as viewing help and login pages); and (v) number of different subjects viewed. The final feature represents the diversity in subject of the items (e.g., books or DVDs) that users view. This is based on subject information provided about each bibliographic resource provided by OCLC. In future work we plan to investigate a wider range of features to capture richer

---

[1]http://www.oclc.org/worldcat/catalog.en.html
[2]Various methods can be used to segment transaction logs into sessions, but the 30 minute cut-off heuristic was shown to be adequate for this task (see [12] for further details).

and more complete interaction patterns. Prior to clustering, the scores for the features must be normalized. In this study the feature values were scale normalized using Principal Component Analysis (PCA), which we also used to conduct preliminary exploration of the dataset. Five principal components emerged from the dataset with the first two accounting for 55% of the variability. The clustering algorithm was subsequently applied to the data projected onto the principal components.

Various clustering algorithms have been used in prior work. In our work we use the DBSCAN density-based clustering algorithm [13] as its execution time is almost linear and therefore highly suited to larger datasets, such as transaction logs. Density-based clustering algorithms represent the data in a spatial manner and aim to find regions of high density separated from low density regions. Such an approach has the advantages of being able to identify irregular shaped clusters, requiring only one dataset iteration and does not require the number of clusters to be defined prior to initialization. Two parameters must be set for DBSCAN: ϵ and $MinPts$. In DBSCAN a cluster is defined as a set of densely-connected points (controlled by ϵ) which maximize density-reachability and must contain at least $MinPts$ points. Parameter values of $\epsilon = 0.4$ and $MinPts = 200$ were chosen through empirical investigation.

3.3 Computing stability

We used Hennig's approach for assessing cluster stability that uses the Jaccard coefficient as a measure of similarity between two sets based on set membership [6]. The approach assesses stability by re-sampling the original dataset with the assumption that points drawn from the same underlying distribution should give rise to more or less the same clusterings. The procedure used is as follows:

1. Cluster the entire dataset. This is the 'best' clustering of the dataset as it includes all data points.

2. Re-sample new datasets from the original one and cluster again.

3. For every cluster in the original clustering find the most similar cluster (i.e., that with the highest similarity score) in the new clustering using the Jaccard coefficient and record its value.

4. Compute the cluster stability for every cluster in the original clustering as the mean of the similarity scores over the re-sampled datasets.

In our study cluster stability was calculated by applying the clustering process 100 times on samples (using sampling without replacement) of the original dataset, each containing 10,000 sessions.

4. RESULTS

DBSCAN produced a group of 10 clusters from the log data with around 20% classified as 'noise' – points too far away from any of the produced clusters to be considered for inclusion and discarded from further analyses. Table 1 summarizes the clusters and shows mean values for the original features, as well as stability scores. The clusters can be mapped to attributes through the use of session identifiers. Clusters 1 and 2 account for 54% of the sessions with stability scores of 0.87 and 0.85 respectively.

The most stable clusters are clusters 4 and 5 that account for 19% of sessions. These four clusters have stability scores over 0.80 that suggests they are unlikely to have arisen from the clustering process by chance. Clusters 8, 9 and 10 are the least stable and suggest noise or that they should have been combined with other clusters. The estimated stability is moderately correlated with the size of the cluster ($r = 0.67$, $p < 0.05$) indicating that larger clusters *generally* tend to be more stable than smaller ones.

Cluster 1 is similar to clusters 3, 6, 9 and 10. In fact, these clusters all share the same mean values (0.00) for number of queries and average query length. However, they vary in session duration and the magnitude of items viewed. Sessions that belong to cluster 3 vary from those in cluster 1 by being longer (around 5 minutes in length) and containing more item views which tend to span across two subjects on average. Clusters 6, 9 and 10 are also similar but vary in duration, number of items viewed and number of subjects viewed. These typically reflect sessions in which users are referred to WorldCat.org and therefore have searched in external websites and do not query in WorldCat (i.e., number of queries = 0).

Cluster 2 is the second largest cluster comprising around 25% of the data points not classified as noise. On average, sessions in this cluster have a duration of around 2 mins, contain 1-2 queries (of around 3 words) and involve viewing 1-2 items which generally belong to the same subject.

Clust Num	Size (%)	Duration (secs)	Num of Queries	Query Len	Item Count	Subj Count	Stab score
1	(30%)	123.98	0.00	0.00	2.15	1.00	0.87
2	(24%)	117.31	1.61	3.31	1.51	1.00	0.85
3	(12%)	298.15	0.00	0.00	3.07	2.00	0.76
4	(10%)	468.49	0.00	0.00	0.00	0.00	0.96
5	(9%)	131.18	2.42	2.79	0.00	0.00	0.91
6	(3%)	508.63	0.00	0.00	4.50	3.00	0.66
7	(8%)	211.15	1.83	2.95	2.74	2.00	0.68
8	(2%)	225.28	1.87	2.37	3.64	3.00	0.45
9	(1%)	340.57	0.00	0.00	4.70	4.00	0.44
10	(1%)	296.07	0.00	0.00	7.63	4.00	0.20

Table 1: Cluster summary: size, mean values for original features and stability scores

Clusters 5, 7 and 8 are similar to cluster 2 in the sense they contain sessions involving a couple of queries and viewing of items which tend to belong to different subjects. The average query length is fairly constant across all sessions in these clusters. Sessions in cluster 5 contain the most queries on average (μ=2.42), although do not lead to the user viewing items. On the other hand, sessions in cluster 7 contain less queries on average (μ=1.87), but users in such sessions tend to view on average 3-4 items from 2 or more subjects. Similarly, for users in cluster 8, the average number of queries is 1.87.

The distinguishing factor, however, between sessions in clusters 7 and 8 seem to be that users who are part of the sessions in cluster 8 tend to view a larger number of items which usually span across an average of 3 different subjects. Initial inspection would suggest that cluster 4 seems to be unique in comparison with other clusters. Sessions in this cluster tend to last around 8 minutes but do not contain any queries or the viewing of page items. Reasons for this could include: errors in the sessionization process, interaction behavior not captured by the current feature set or people using Worldcat as a service within external sites.

5. DISCUSSION

With regards to RQ1 cluster stability scores range from 0.20 to 0.96. DBSCAN successfully identifies different types of patterns of user-system interaction that can be interpreted in light of how users interact with WorldCat. However, before drawing inferences from the resulting clusters it is essential to validate the results to reduce the possibility that the clusters were identified by chance and do not actually reflect differences in the underlying data. In relation to DBSCAN unstable clusters represent data points that should either have formed part of another cluster or should have been classified as noise. From results presented in Section 4, the indications are that the most unstable clusters (clusters 8, 9 and 10) should probably have formed part of other more stable clusters. One possible reason for this could be the fact that the ϵ parameter of DBSCAN is a global parameter and cannot be adjusted per-cluster.

With respect to RQ2 cluster stability scores can be used help determine the optimum number of clusters and evaluate the "goodness" of the resulting clusters [7]. Hennig [6] states that large stability values do not necessarily indicate that the underlying clusters are valid. However, he also emphasizes that small stability values are always informative, indicating that the underlying clusters are either meaningless in relation to the true underlying model, or that instabilities exist in the clusters or the clustering methods used. In the case of the results in Table 4 the most stable cluster (cluster 4) is markedly different from other clusters and is likely indicative of users who are using Worldcat via external services, the actions of which are not captured in the current feature set. Since these sessions do not reflect user activity within Worldcat.org one might argue they should be filtered out along with robot traffic. There may also be other reasons for cluster 4, but this does suggest that despite stable clusters typically being meaningful and valid [6] more in-depth analyses must be carried out to better interpret the clusters and gain a complete and accurate picture of user behavior [7, 14]. When utilizing data-driven approaches then applying methods for validating results is important. However, cluster stability alone is not enough to fully validate the results of clustering.

6. CONCLUSIONS

This paper has investigated cluster stability for identifying groups of sessions based on features indicative of user-system interaction. The DBSCAN clustering algorithm is used to form clusters that are then validated using a simple approach for assessing cluster stability based on comparing clusters from samples of the dataset with the original clustering using the Jaccard coefficient. As one might expect the results of the clustering contained a mix of stable and unstable clusters. There is clearly instability when clustering that calls for the need to model varying parameters to arrive at a stable set of clusters. Future work will investigate stability with respect to other criteria, such as varying feature sets, sample sizes, parameter settings and alternative log data. In addition, we plan to investigate alternative methods for computing stability.

7. ACKNOWLEDGEMENTS

Work partially supported by the Google Faculty Award "Developing a taxonomy of search sessions". We also thank OCLC for providing anonymised transaction logs.

8. REFERENCES

[1] Silvestri, F.: Mining query logs: Turning search usage data into knowledge. Found. Trends Inf. Retr. **4** (2010) 1–174

[2] Agosti, M., Crivellari, F., Di Nunzio, G.M.: Web log analysis: A review of a decade of studies about information acquisition, inspection and interpretation of user interaction. Data Min. Knowl. Discov. **24** (2012) 663–696

[3] Wolfram, D., Wang, P., Zhang, J.: Identifying web search session patterns using cluster analysis: A comparison of three search environments. Journal of the American Society for Information Science and Technology **60** (2009) 896–910

[4] Chen, H.M., Cooper, M.D.: Using clustering techniques to detect usage patterns in a web-based information system. Journal of the American Society for Information Science and Technology **52** (2001) 888–904

[5] Stenmark, D.: Identifying clusters of user behavior in intranet search engine log files. Journal of the American Society for Information Science and Technology **59** (2008) 2232–2243

[6] Hennig, C.: Cluster-wise assessment of cluster stability. Computational Statistics and Data Analysis (2007) 258–271

[7] Heer, J., Chi, E.H., Chi, H.: Mining the structure of user activity using cluster stability. In: in Proceedings of the Workshop on Web Analytics, SIAM Conference on Data Mining (Arlington VA, ACM Press (2002)

[8] Weber, I., Jaimes, A.: Who uses web search for what: And how. In: Proceedings of the Fourth ACM International Conference on Web Search and Data Mining. WSDM '11, New York, NY, USA, ACM (2011) 15–24

[9] Jones, R., Klinkner, K.L.: Beyond the session timeout: Automatic hierarchical segmentation of search topics in query logs. In: Proceedings of the 17th ACM Conference on Information and Knowledge Management. CIKM '08, New York, NY, USA, ACM (2008) 699 708

[10] Von Luxburg, U.: Clustering stability: An overview. Now Publishers Inc (2010)

[11] Ben-David, S., Von Luxburg, U.: Relating clustering stability to properties of cluster boundaries. COLT **2008** (2008) 379–390

[12] Wakeling, S., Clough, P.: Determining the Optimal Session Interval for Transaction Log Analysis of an Online Library Catalogue. In: Proceedings of the 38th European Conference on IR Research (ECIR'16). Springer (2016) 703–708

[13] Ester, M., peter Kriegel, H., S, J., Xu, X.: A density-based algorithm for discovering clusters in large spatial databases with noise, AAAI Press (1996) 226–231

[14] Grimes, C., Tang, D., Russell, D.M.: Query Logs Alone are not Enough. In: Proceedings of the WWW 2007 Workshop on Query Logs Analysis: Social and Technological Challenges. (2007)

Experimental Evaluation of Affective Embodied Agents in an Information Literacy Game

Yan Ru Guo, Dion Hoe-Lian Goh, Hurizan Bin Hussain Muhamad,

Boon Kuang Ong, Zichao Lei

Wee Kim Wee School of Communication and Information
Nanyang Technological University
31 Nanyang Link, Singapore
(65) 94527949
{W120030, ashlgoh, muha0193, W130022, leiz0001}@ntu.edu.sg

ABSTRACT

Digital game-based learning (DGBL) has become increasingly popular. With elements such as narratives, rewards, quests, and interactivity, DGBL can actively engage learners, stimulating desired learning outcomes. In an effort to increase its appeal, affective embodied agents (EAs) have been incorporated as learning companions or instructors in DGBL. However, claims about the efficacy of using affective EAs in DGBL have scarcely been subjected to empirical analysis. Therefore, this study aims to investigate the influence of affective EAs on students' learning outcome, motivation, perceived usefulness, and behavioral intention in an information literacy (IL) game. Eighty tertiary students were recruited and randomly assigned in a pre- and post-test between-subjects experiment with two conditions: affective-EA and no-EA. Results showed that participants benefited from interacting with the affective EA in the IL game in terms of attention, confidence, satisfaction, and intention to learn IL knowledge and to recommend. However, there were no significant differences in learning outcome, relevance, or intention to play the game. Contributions and limitations of this study are also discussed at the end.

Keywords

Affective embodied agent, digital game-based learning, educational games, game evaluation, information literacy education.

1. INTRODUCTION

People are generating, discovering, gathering, analyzing, translating, and repurposing an enormous amount of information at great speed. Although the Internet is a valuable information source, it is also a source for misunderstanding, incorrect information, and perpetuation of falsehoods. Information literacy (IL) skills - the ability to seek, locate, evaluate and navigate information effectively - have become important. In particular, university students routinely need to search for and synthesize information from multiple sources, such as digital libraries and academic databases; their IL skills can greatly influence their academic performance [1]. Face-to-face classroom instruction has been the most common method in IL education. However, many students find traditional instruction in

classrooms not engaging enough, and expect to be entertained while being taught [2]. IL education is no exception.

Technology advancements have significantly influenced learning and education. Educators have begun to look for other ways to attract students, including using games. Digital games have found a broad audience, particularly for youth [4]. Digital games can be important teaching tools as they can catch the eye, engage the players, and provoke a deep sense of engagement. Digital games can provide an intrinsically motivating experience and a state of heightened enjoyment that people play them "for its own sake" [3]. Using digital games for educational purposes is often referred to as digital game-based learning (DGBL). It is based on the premise that digital games can serve not only as an engaging way to entertain players, but also as an innovative tool to help build the players' cognitive abilities, encourage problem solving, promote collaboration, and increase self-esteem [5]. Although the concept of DGBL has influenced education in general, such as in mathematics, history, or computer literacy [6-8], it is relatively unknown to IL education. DGBL presents an opportunity for librarians to rethink and reinvent the IL education.

Realizing the important role of affect in learning, researchers began to factor in the learners' affective states when designing educational systems. Some common ways to infuse affect into DGBL include using music, storylines, colors, and narration, but the most effective way is through interface characters, also referred to as "avatars" or "agents" [9]. The term "agent" refers to an autonomous computer program that can "act" on its own [10]. An embodied agent (EA) therefore refers to a life-like agent, i.e., one with a face and body, and communicates with users via speech, facial expressions and body gestures. Designed with the capacity for emotional expression, affective EAs are becoming an increasingly popular technique to incorporate affective elements in computer programs.

Using EAs can make the interactions between humans and computers more natural and enjoyable [11]. In addition, EAs' ability to detect and express affective states is crucial for improving their believability and trustworthiness, eliciting affect in the users, as well as contributing to more entertaining interactions. The use of affective EAs in a pedagogical role such as instructors, mentors, assistants, and companions, can also help students overcome negative affect such as boredom or frustration during learning process. Digital libraries can utilize affective EAs to help users during information search tasks as well. Given the potential of both DGBL and affective EAs, the two concepts have been juxtaposed to achieve synergy.

Despite the increasing sophistication of affective EA design, research has focused more on cognitive, rather than motivational or social aspects of their use in educational systems. Motivation is a

Permission to make digital or hard copies of all or part of this work for personal or classroom use is granted without fee provided that copies are not made or distributed for profit or commercial advantage and that copies bear this notice and the full citation on the first page. Copyrights for components of this work owned by others than ACM must be honored. Abstracting with credit is permitted. To copy otherwise, or republish, to post on servers or to redistribute to lists, requires prior specific permission and/or a fee. Request permissions from Permissions@acm.org.

JCDL '16, June 19-23, 2016, Newark, NJ, USA
© 2016 ACM. ISBN 978-1-4503-4229-2/16/06...$15.00
DOI: http://dx.doi.org/10.1145/2910896.2910897

key ingredient in learning, and social cues play an important role in motivation [7]. It is hence important that both developers and educators realistically assess the potential and limitations of using affective EAs in DGBL so that they can be usefully deployed in learning environments, including in digital libraries. Therefore, this study aims to examine the influence of an affective EA in a digital IL game. Specifically, it investigates its effect on learning outcome, motivation, perceived usefulness and behavioral intention.

The paper is organized as follows. The first section sets the context of this study, and states the research gaps and research objectives. The second section reviews related work in DGBL and affective EAs, and explicates the hypotheses development process. This is followed by a description of the IL game used in this study. The subsequent three sections present the research method, results from data analyses, and detailed discussion. The last section concludes the paper, and points out its contributions, limitations, and future work.

2. RELATED WORK
2.1 Information Literacy Education
Librarians have been at the forefront of IL education to the public and students. This section compares three commonly used methods in IL education: face-to-face library instruction, computer-assisted tutorials, and DGBL.

Face-to-face library instruction has been the most common and widely adopted method in IL education. Face-to-face instruction provides an opportunity for librarians and students to build rapport for future contact. However, most librarians are not able to work with students across an entire semester, and are limited to a single session of an hour or two to teach generic library skills [13]. The amount of material presented in an hour is usually overwhelming. Further, since most university libraries hold such sessions at the beginning of each academic year before students receive their assignments, librarians tend to focus on teaching general knowledge (e.g., how to use Boolean operators), rather than on addressing specific problems related to coursework. matters. This potentially reduces their usefulness. Moreover, students' participation rate is usually low [12]. Studies have shown that many students who are most in need of assistance are precisely those who will not ask for help [13]. A rethink on the timing would be helpful to improve the effectiveness [14].

As much of student learning occurs outside classrooms now, face-to-face instruction can only reach a fraction of students. A more effective method of reaching a large number of students simultaneously may be computer-assisted tutorials [15]. Once online, the tutorials can be accessed and reused anytime, with the advantage of time-savings and cost-effectiveness. Such tutorials can effectively reach out to those students with library anxiety, in case they feel embarrassed to ask for help in face-to-face instruction settings [13].

For example, the Florida Gulf Coast University developed an online IL tutorial to teach freshmen English composition. The tutorial starts with the question *"Does the Skunk Ape exist?"*, and leads students along a typical research process, including topic selection, search strategies formulation, resources location, information evaluation, and writing. In order to evaluate the tutorial, 60 students were invited to write essays after watching the tutorial [15]. Citation and textual analysis were conducted to examine the types and quality of bibliographies in the essays. Students who completed the online tutorials cited a greater number and variety of sources, compared with those who received conventional face-to-face instruction.

Next, Western Michigan University developed *ResearchPath*, an online tutorial with animation, video, audio, and interactivity. The tutorial covers five modules, namely, college-level research, define and refine your topic, using power search, using the Internet, and citing sources. After the implementation, the tutorial was evaluated against the previous version named *SearchPath*. Students completed a quiz, worked on a research project, and participated in focus group interviews [16]. Although there was no significant improvement in learning outcomes, students expressed a strong satisfaction and preference for the new *ResearchPath*.

Computer-assisted tutorials also have drawbacks, such as high dropout rates, absence of personal touch, and the lack of motivation by students to participate when it is not required by the instructors. As [17] noted, "never before has a generation been so defined in the public mind by its relationship to technology" (p.2), it is not surprising that students who are bored in a library instruction session are not likely to recall details about it. DGBL can potentially address this issue. Digital games are able to provide enjoyable experiences so effectively that players often find themselves actively seeking information and solutions [18]. This idea of using DGBL in IL education is explored further in the next section.

2.2 Digital Game-based Learning
Digital game-based learning affords a highly interactive medium with many pedagogical attributes. Elements such as narratives, rules, goals, rewards, and multisensory cues in DGBL can stimulate desired learning outcomes from players. Unlike classroom instruction, DGBL can be adapted to the pace of the learners, present information in multiple visual and auditory modes simultaneously, and capitalize on different learning styles. Players' behaviors in successful gameplay meet most of the IL Standards [19]. Games teach players to "determine the nature and extent of information needed", "access needed information effectively and efficiently", "evaluate information and its sources critically and incorporate selected information into the knowledge base and value system", and "use information effectively to accomplish specific purposes (alone or as a team)".

Some academic libraries in the US have tapped on DGBL to promote their services and IL education to students. For example, Arizona State University created an online IL game called *Quarantined! Axl Wise and the Information Outbreak*. Players can learn IL skills by containing a viral outbreak on campus in the game. To evaluate the game, students were invited to play the game in library instruction sessions. Their responses were mixed: some students found the game too long and complex, while others liked it [20]. In another example, the University of North Carolina created an online board game called *The Information Literacy Game*, to teach IL skills to first-year students. The game allows up to four players to roll a digital die, and move around the board by correctly answering questions in four categories: selecting resources, using databases, citation, and library wild card. Students reported that they enjoyed the game and learned IL skills during the gameplay.

At James Madison University, all undergraduates must pass an IL test during their first year. From the test results, librarians identified that students needed to learn more on citation developed an IL game called *Citation Tic-Tac-Toe*. It is a single-player game that begins by clicking on a blank space on a tic-tac-toe board. A citation for a specific type of resource (e.g., book) pops up on the screen and the player is presented with multiple-choice questions relevant to citation. Students' citation skills improved after playing the game [21]. As can be gleaned from the above examples, most game evaluation relied on anecdotal quotations, rather than rigorous research design.

An exception is *BiblioBouts*, an IL game developed by the University of Michigan. It is one of the few IL games that were extensively documented and evaluated, so it is discussed in more detail here. The game is incorporated into class assignments, allowing students to search for, compile, and evaluate different information sources to produce a higher-quality bibliography. *BiblioBouts* consists of a series of narrowly focused and successive bouts (mini-games): closer bout (finding information), tagging & rating bout (evaluating information), and best bibliography bout (selecting information). Students can check the sources that other players contribute, to discover sources they would not have found otherwise. To evaluate *BiblioBouts*, students were invited to play the game over a two-week period. The extensive evaluation process involved game diary forms, pre-and post-game questionnaires, immediate focus group interviews, follow-up interviews four or more months later, pre- and post-game individual interviews, and game activity logs. While most students reported positive learning experiences during game play, some failed to grasp the educational values in the game. All the above examples failed to take advantage of affective elements in IL education. They focused more on cognitive aspect of IL knowledge acquisition, while the affective and social aspects were largely ignored. Further, their evaluation lacked rigorous experimental comparisons and concrete measures on students' learning performance.

2.3 Affective Embodied Agents

Among the different game elements, avatars are frequently used in digital games. Depending on the stream of research, avatars are also labeled as autonomous agents, animated agents, embodied agents, and virtual agents. This study focuses embodied agents, since the term indicates a low level of artificial intelligence [22]. Researchers have discovered that people blended the signals from the living and the animated, and cannot perceive a difference between mediated images of EAs and real people or objects before them [23]. By providing visual cues, well-designed EAs make it easier to attract people's attention, enriching the learning experience.

To investigate the impact of affective feedback provided by EAs, [24] designed *Crystal Island*, an educational game to teach microbiology and genetics for middle school students. Participants were divided into two groups: affective feedback and neutral feedback. The results suggested that when students experienced boredom, frustration and confusion, it is important to bring about a positive change in such situations, and the impact of providing affective feedback to students are very clear. The authors concluded that any attempt to alleviate frustration can greatly help the students, and consequently, intervention strategies should be used more frequently.

Along the same line of research, [25] designed an online multimedia learning environment that teaches thermodynamics. A hundred and thirty-five college students participated in a 2 (EA vs. no-EA) × 2 (simple feedback vs. elaborate feedback) factorial experiment. Results showed that the mere visual presence of an EA did not have significant impact on learning motivation or performances. However, when combined with elaborate and affective feedback, students' learning motivation and performances increased significantly. Therefore, an EA's ability to foster learning is dependent on its other features, such as affective and elaborate feedback. When designing EAs in DGBL, special attention should be given to their affective features, in order to maximize the positive impact on students' learning.

To examine the influence of EAs on users' learning performance in retaining cultural knowledge, [26] designed two tour guide applications, one with a female EA and one without. Results indicated that participants who used the system with the EA retained the cultural knowledge of variable difficulty more consistently, than those without the EA. More interestingly, the qualitative comments gathered from participants indicated that the use of EAs positively changed their perception of the difficulty of the cultural knowledge, which may lead to enhanced motivation to learn more difficult content.

Nevertheless, empirical findings have not be consistent, and sometimes showed no difference in learning outcomes whether students interacted with the affective EAs or not. One such example is [27], in which an affective EA *Patti* was designed to teach English as a foreign language. Forty-two Brazilian undergraduate students were divided into two groups: EA and no EA. The results showed no significant difference in learning performance between the two groups: using an affective EA failed to improve students' learning performance. Such experimental findings seemed to cast doubt on the effectiveness of affective EAs on improving learning in DGBL.

DGBL presents an opportunity for librarians to rethink and reinvent the IL education. However, as emphasis on Science, Technology, Engineering, and Math initiatives increase, as seen from all above examples, there is very limited literature on its use to teach higher-order thinking skills such as IL skills [28]. Academic IL involves higher-order thinking skills as it teaches important procedural knowledge that synthesizes complex level of thinking and knowledge [29]. Hence, it will be useful to ascertain whether DGBL can be effectively used in IL education, an area that is replete with higher-order thinking skills.

2.4 Hypothesis Development

This section explicates the four major variables in this study: learning outcome, motivation, perceived usefulness and behavioral intention, and presents the hypotheses in this study.

2.4.1 Learning Outcome

Learning outcome is an important aspect of any educational system evaluation because it is the most direct and immediate result from the intervention [6]. Some studies have successfully demonstrated that using affective EAs in DGBL can enhance learners' ability to retain the knowledge and apply it in other contexts, while others have not [30]. For example, [31] designed a 3D affective EA, *Chris*, to help 9th grade students learn algebra. Learning outcome was assessed based on the comparison of pre-test and post-test. Surprisingly, the results indicated that students achieved better learning consistently after working with *Chris*, regardless of their differential evaluations of the EA's affability and their attitudes toward the learning tasks.

2.4.2 Motivation

Motivation may be one of the most important prerequisites in learning, and it is a catalyst to achieving learning goals. Learners feel more engaged when presented with EAs in DGBL. With EAs, learners are more motivated to make sense of what is being presented to them, and more likely to process the information deeply, achieving meaningful learning [32]. To investigate the effectiveness of EAs in promoting learning with different levels of embodiment, [32] conducted a 3 (fully embodied, minimally embodied, vs. voice-only) × 2 (animated vs. static feedback) factorial experiment. Results showed that EAs' effectiveness to facilitate learning was positively associated with the level of embodiment. Higher levels of embodiment led to more effective learning: compared with a minimally embodied agent (i.e., static EAs), students who interacted with the fully embodied agent (i.e., EAs that incorporated locomotion, gesture, and gaze) processed the learning material significantly more deeply.

The ARCS (Attention, Relevance, Confidence and Satisfaction) Model by [33] was selected to examine the motivational support from the EA. The model consists of four components: attention, relevance, confidence and satisfaction. Attention is a critical aspect for learning. To sustain students' attention, instructors should respond to the sensation-seeking needs of the students. The second component is relevance, defined as the extent to which the students perceive the results to be applicable, relevant, usable and helpful. Relevance is commonly used as a criterion to evaluate whether using an educational system can meet their utilitarian needs. The third component is confidence, which refers to the learners' positive expectations towards their performance, and their belief that they have the required knowledge, skill or ability to perform certain tasks. The last is satisfaction, which refers to the extent that users feel good about their accomplishments. The ARCS Model has shown to be widely applicable in interactive online environments. For example, it was used to diagnose motivational problems in instructional programs, and [34] used it to evaluate students' motivation in learning from an IL tutorial where the model showed high reliability. Further, [35] used the model to measure the effect of a digital mathematical game on students' motivation. The model can thus be applied to empirically investigate motivational issues in this study.

The use of affective EAs can minimize the communication gaps in interactions between human and computers, and increase learners' motivation [25]. With affective EAs, learners will feel more engaged, and are more motivated to make sense of what is being presented to them, achieving meaningful learning.

2.4.3 Perceived Usefulness
The third variable is perceived usefulness, defined as the extent to which people believe that using the system will improve their performance. It has consistently been a strong and fundamental driver of behavioral intention, thus it is important to understand the determinants of this variable. Using affective EAs might make people perceive the educational systems to be more relevant and useful to their needs.

2.4.4 Behavioral Intention
Behavioral intention refers to the degree to which people have formulated plans to perform or not perform specified behaviors in the future [36]. In a study to investigate the influence of affective EAs on students' behavioral intention, [34] developed an online IL tutorial and assigned students into one of the three conditions: affective-EA, neutral-EA and no-EA. The results suggested that students who watched the IL tutorial with affective EAs indicated greater intention to use it in the future.

In this study, behavioral intention refers to students' intention to use similar digital IL games, to further improve their IL knowledge, and to recommend the game to others. Behavioral intention has frequently been used as a surrogate for the actual performance.

2.4.5 Hypotheses
Based on the discussion from last section, the following four hypotheses are listed below.

H1: There are significant differences in the means of learning outcome among participants exposed to affective-EA and no-EA conditions in DGBL.

H2: There are significant differences in the means of (a) attention, (b) relevance, (c) confidence, and (d) satisfaction among those participants exposed to affective-EA and no-EA conditions in DGBL.

H3: There are significant differences in the means of perceived usefulness among those participants exposed to affective-EA and no-EA conditions in DGBL.

H4: There are significant differences in the means of intention to (a) play similar IL games, (b) learn more about IL, (c) recommend to others, among those participants exposed to affective-EA and no-EA conditions in DGBL.

3. LIBRARY ESCAPE
The material used for the study, *Library Escape*, is briefly introduced here (see [37] for more details). It is a role-playing game that aims to engage university students in learning IL knowledge. The game starts with a comic strip to introduce the backstory (see Figure 1). The grades of the last semester have just been released, and the protagonist, Tom, only managed a "C" for his IL module. Usually a top student, Tom is disappointed with the poor grade. He consults with the IL module instructor, Prof. Senka, to find out the reason and asks what he could do to improve his grade. Prof. Senka leads Tom to the basement of a deserted library building, and shoves him in, saying that this is the place where he could get some IL education.

Figure 1. Game Backstory

There are six missions in the game. Each mission aims to teach IL-related topics, from foundational concepts such as what is IL and why is IL important, to practical skills such as how to search for information systematically, and how to evaluate information for academic purposes. Players need to locate different objects in each mission to uncover the learning content. In knowledge acquisition, learners need to understand basic concepts before solving actual problems, and missions that introduce of new concepts can only be attempted after students have been exposed to necessary vocabulary and background knowledge. Figure 2 illustrates some conceptual and practical content in the game. Table 1 lists the educational content in each mission, which is explained in more details next.

Mission One is the closed stacks of the library to cast an eerie ambience. It introduces background knowledge about IL. Players need to find the relevant objects to reveal the content. For example, the history of IL development is hidden behind a globe, the definition of IL behind a dictionary, the ARCL IL standards behind a scale, and so on (see Figure 3). Mission Two takes place in the open shelves. An evil ghost sleeps here and wakes up occasionally. Players need to stop moving when the ghost wakes up to avoid being attacked. Mission Two teaches how to select a topic, and library anxiety and its causes. Different types of scientific literature are also included, to help students understand the range of sources they can refer to when working on academic projects. The difficulty level increases as the game progresses, and the learning content becomes more concrete and practical in subsequent missions. Mission Three takes place in the reference section, where the ghost constantly moves and the players need to avoid touching it. It presents scholarly publication cycle, how to use Google Scholar, and the library online public access catalog.

Table 1. Venues of Educational Content in Each Mission

Mission Venues	Quests (objects hidden in)
1. Closed Stacks	1.1. Definition of IL (dictionary) 1.2. Importance of IL (wheel) 1.3. ACRL IL Standards (scale)
2. Open Shelves	2.1. Selecting the Topic to Work On (key) 2.2. Types of Scientific Literature (stool) 2.3. Understanding Library Anxiety and Its Causes (magazine)
3. Reference Section	3.1. Scholarly Publication Cycle (grandfather clock) 3.2. Searching in Google Scholar (painting) 3.3. Using the OPAC (date stamp)
4. Digital Library	4.1. Building Blocks (scooter) 4.2. Pearl Growing (search bar) 4.3. Successive Fractions (torch light)
5. AV Collection	5.1. Evaluating the Articles Retrieved (disk) 5.2. Information Seeking as a form of Information Behavior (umbrella) 5.3. Reflecting on information search process (mirror)
6. Café	6.1. Roles and Responsibilities of an Author (flower) 6.2. Plagiarism (blackboard) 6.3. Citations (menu)

Mission Four brings the players to the virtual digital library with a computer virus inside. Players need to find objects quickly to prevent the virus from infecting the entire digital library. Hands-on information search strategies are introduced here, including building blocks, pearl growing, and successive fractions. The evil ghost becomes furious in Mission Five and spews out fire to burn down the library. Players need to put out the fire timely. Here, some objects can only be activated after others have been found. The players have to find a piano that plays a piece of music first, in order to entertain an owl, behind which hides some information on information search process (see Figure 4). This mission requires players to evaluate the information retrieved, and to reflect on their information seeking process. Reflection is a critical part of the learning process in DGBL, as it affords a cyclic learning process such as sense making, reflecting, reaching conclusion, formulating strategies, and acting. Two ghosts roam around in the café in Mission Six, and the players have to be strategic in their movements. Mission Six concludes the game by listing the roles and responsibilities of an author, plagiarism, and the importance of making citations.

Players have to answer three to five quiz questions at the end of each mission before proceeding to the next. The questions take various forms, such as fill-in-the-blanks, single-choice, multiple-choice, and rank-order questions. In terms of content, there are descriptive, applied and reflective questions (see Figure 5). Players are given two chances to answer each question, and they cannot progress to the next mission without getting the correct answers. They will be led back to the library if both attempts are wrong, after which they can try the questions again.

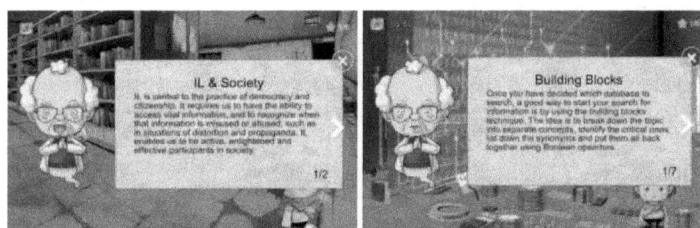

Figure 2. Conceptual and Practical Content

Figure 3. Screenshots in Mission One

Figure 4. Screenshots in Mission Five

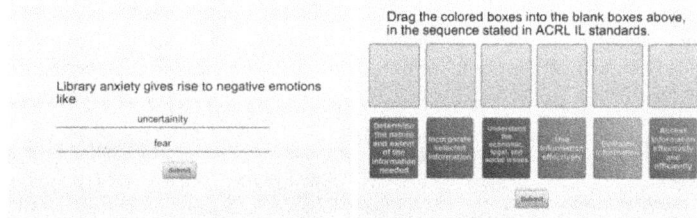

Figure 5. Quiz Questions

The EA in this game takes the form of a ghost librarian. In the affective-EA condition, scripted feedback from the librarian is provided when players successfully find an object, and after they submit answers in the quizzes (see Figure 6). When the player gets the answer correctly, the librarian will display a happy triumphant expression, say "Well done" and explain why the answers are correct. When the player gets the answer wrong in the first time, the librarian will display a patient smile, explain why that answer is wrong, and encourage the players to try the question again. When the players get it wrong the second time, the librarian will gently remind the player why the answer is still incorrect, and redirected them back to the game. Players need to find the objects containing the learning content again, and come back to answer the quiz question. In the no-EA condition, the librarian is absent and all feedback is given in a square box in the center of the screen (see Figure 7). The feedback contains no affective expressions.

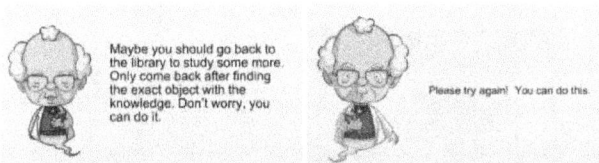

Figure 6. Feedback in Affective-EA Condition

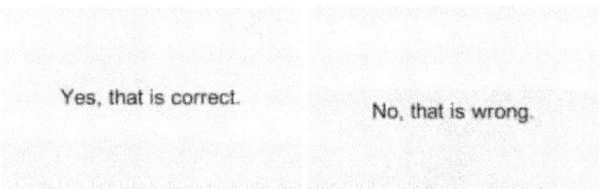

Figure 7. Feedback in No-EA Condition

4. METHODS
4.1 Experimental Design

A pre-test post-test between-subjects design was used to address the research hypotheses. Recruitment was conducted in a major local university in a controlled laboratory setting. Participation in this study was voluntary and confidential. Participants were randomly assigned to one of the two game conditions: affective-EA and no-EA condition.

After the participants arrived at the lab, they were briefed on the study's objective, which was to evaluate a newly developed IL game, and signed the online consent form if they had no objection. The experiment started with a short online pre-test questionnaire to assess participants' prior IL knowledge. Thereafter, they started and played the game on their assigned computers. After the game was completed, they filled in a post-test questionnaire. The entire study lasted approximately two hours. In total, 80 students participated, and they were given S$10 as a token of appreciation.

The pre-test questionnaire assessed participants' prior IL knowledge with ten multiple-choice questions. The post-test questionnaire comprised seven sections. The first section was a single question to assess the EA manipulation. Participants were asked to choose whether the librarian in the game expressed emotions, or was not applicable. The second section assessed the learning outcomes: the amount of IL knowledge that participants retained from the game. The subsequent three sections focused on participants' learning motivations, perceived usefulness and behavioral intention. All items that were used to measure these four variables were formulated based on extant literature, and indicated on a five-point Likert scale, ranging from strongly disagree (1) to strongly agree (5), with a neutral response in the middle. In the penultimate section, participants were asked for their subjective opinions of the game, and how to improve it. The last section collected information on participants' demographic data such as age, gender, nationality and educational background.

Analyses were conducted using SPSS. Analysis of covariance (ANCOVA) was first used to test H1, by controlling for prior IL knowledge differences obtained from the pre-test. The other three hypotheses on motivation, perceived usefulness, and behavioral intention were tested by independent-sample t-tests.

4.2 Operational Definitions

Learning outcome. Participants' IL knowledge was tested in both pre-test and post-test questionnaires, each comprising ten multiple-choice questions. To reduce testing effects, the two sets of questions were different but matched in topic and difficulty. An expert on IL was consulted to improve the questionnaires, and the items were modified based on suggestions given. Example questions include: *"Which of the following is the best criterion to evaluate the credibility of an Internet site?"*, and *"When you are assigned to research a topic that you are unfamiliar with, which of the following sources would you turn to for a brief history and summary about the topic?"*

Motivation. The ARCS scale was adapted with minor changes to suit this study's context [33]. Specifically, the original purpose was to investigate the motivational issues in courses and modules, and used "modules/courses" in the items. So our study used the phrase "IL game" instead. The scale consisted of 36 items, in which 12 items on attention; nine on relevance; nine on confidence, and six on satisfaction.

Perceived usefulness. It was measured using three items [36]. The questions include *"Playing the game would improve my IL skills"* *"Playing the game would make it easier to learn IL knowledge"*, and *"I would find the game useful in my studies"*.

Behavioral intention. It was measured with three sub-constructs and nine items, adopted from an existing survey instrument [38]. The use of "system" was replaced with "IL game" to suit the context of this study. The three sub-constructs are intention to play other IL games, intention to learn more about IL, and intention recommend this game to others.

5. RESULTS

5.1 Sample and Manipulation Check

The demographics of the sample are shown in Table 2, including the breakdown of the two conditions. The sample was balanced in terms of gender, consisting of 39 (48.75%) males and 41 (51.25%) females. Their age ranged between 18 and 29, with an average of 21.76 years and standard deviation of 2.67. With regards to their educational background, slightly more than half (52.5%) were from engineering, 20.0% were from social science, and the rest 27.5% were from the natural sciences and business. The sample can be considered as fairly representative of a technological university that put heavy emphasis on engineering education.

Table 2. Sample Description (N=80)

	Affective-EA (*n*=40)	No-EA (*n*=40)	Total
Gender			
Female	25 (62.5%)	16 (40.0%)	41
Male	15 (37.5%)	24 (60.0%)	39
Age			
20 and below	10 (25.0%)	17 (42.5%)	27
21–25	27 (67.5%)	19 (47.5%)	46
26 and above	3 (7.5%)	4 (10.0%)	7
Education Background			
Engineering	22 (55.0%)	20 (50.0%)	42
Social science	7 (17.5%)	9 (22.5%)	16
Natural science	7 (17.5%)	8 (20.0%)	15
Business	4 (10.0%)	3 (7.5%)	7

Chi-square analysis indicated that the manipulation was successful [$\chi^2(2)$=76.10, p<.000]. Those in the affective-EA condition mostly agreed that the librarian expressed emotions (37 out of 40), while those in the no-EA condition all recognized that there was no librarian in the game (40 out of 40).

5.2 Hypotheses Testing

A one-way ANCOVA was conducted to test H1. The independent variable is the experimental manipulation: affective-EA and no-EA conditions. The dependent variable was the participants' learning outcome in post-test, and the covariate was the prior IL knowledge in the pre-test. First, and manipulation condition and pre-test IL knowledge did not interact [p(.544)>(.05)], so the assumption of homogeneity of regression slopes was met. However, the ANCOVA result was non-significant, $F(1,77)$=0.006, p=.939 (see Table 3). Therefore, H1 was rejected: there were no significant differences in learning outcome across the two conditions (see Figure 8).

Table 3. Learning Outcomes in the Pre-test and Post-tests

	Pretest		Post-test	
Condition	Mean	SD	Mean	SD
Affective-EA	4.78	1.64	4.98	2.02
No-EA	3.98	1.64	4.65	1.94

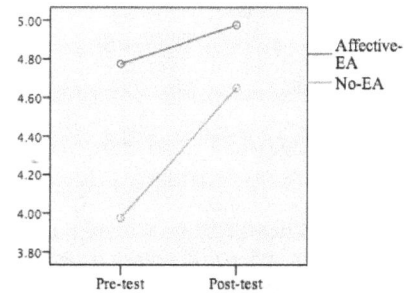

Figure 8. Plots of Learning Outcome in Pre and Post Tests

Table 4. Mean (Standard Deviation) of Dependent Variables

	Affective-EA	No-EA	t
Motivation			
Attention[*]	3.50 (0.47)	3.26 (0.38)	2.50
Relevance	3.52 (0.68)	3.25 (0.68)	1.76
Confidence[*]	3.61 (0.48)	3.36 (0.52)	2.19
Satisfaction[*]	3.60 (0.69)	3.26 (0.81)	2.01
Perceived Usefulness[**]	3.52 (0.65)	3.23 (0.86)	2.87
Behavioral Intention			
Intention To Play Game	3.39 (0.79)	3.08 (1.18)	1.41
Intention To Learn IL[*]	3.69 (0.69)	3.31 (1.00)	2.07
Intention To Recommend[*]	3.77 (0.82)	3.19 (1.19)	2.52

Note: [*], *p*<.05; [**], *p*<.01.

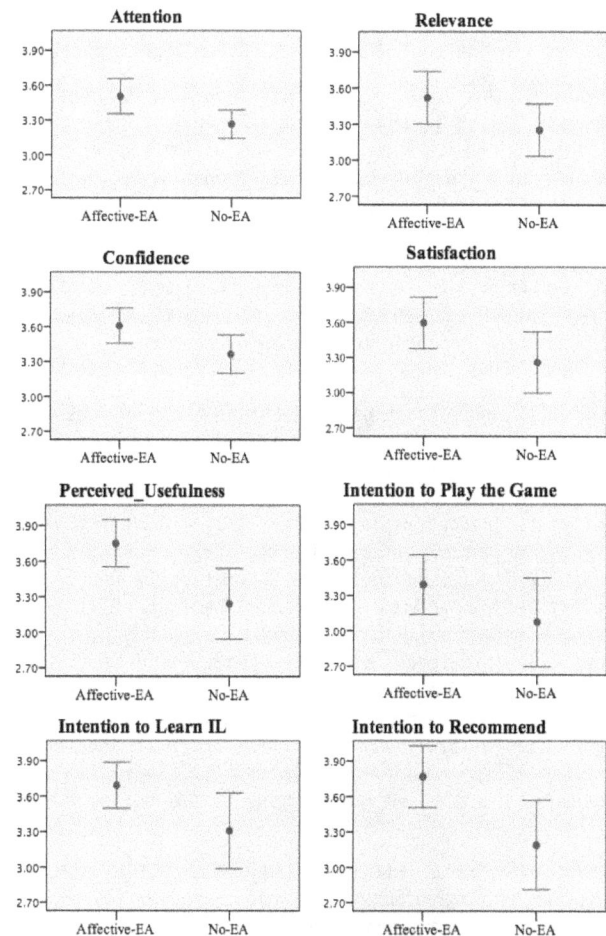

Figure 9. Error Bars for Dependent Variables

Next, independent-sample t-tests were conducted to evaluate the other hypotheses. Table 3 shows the means, standard deviations and t values of dependent variables. Figure 9 shows the error bars of the dependent variables. Results showed statistically significant differences on attention [$t(78)$=2.50, p=.014], confidence [$t(78)$=2.19, p=.03], satisfaction [$t(78)$=2.01, p<.05], perceived usefulness [$t(78)$=2.87, p=.0005], intention to learn IL [$t(78)$=1.41, p=.04], and intention to recommend [$t(78)$=2.07, p=.01]. However, there were no significant differences in terms of relevance [$t(78)$=1.76, p=.08], or intention to play such IL games [$t(78)$=1.41, p=1.62]. Therefore, H2, H3 and H4 were mostly supported.

6. DISCUSSION

Taken together, these results showed that the affective EA had a strong positive impact on participants' learning motivation, perceived usefulness and behavioral intention, compared with no-EA condition. However, there was no difference in learning outcome.

There are a number of salient findings. First, participants who interacted with the affective EA were more attentive, confident, and satisfied than participants from the no-EA condition. They also praised the use of "*avatar and feedback*" in the game as part of qualitative feedback. This confirms previous studies on using affective EAs to motivate students [8, 25, 34], and lends further support to the argument that affective EAs are able to attract and hold students' motivation. They can ease possible negative affect during learning, thus positively influence learners' learning motivation [39]. It is reasonable to infer that the behaviors and feedback from the affective-EA condition contributed to the increased attention, confidence and satisfaction of participants.

Nonetheless, there was no statistically significant difference on relevance. This is possibly because relevance of the game is determined by its educational content (i.e., IL knowledge), which was the same in the two conditions. The similarity of participants' educational levels in the two conditions could be another reason. Typical comments such as "*I realized how important and relevant IL is in daily learning*" showed that both groups found the game and the IL knowledge relevant to their studies. The non-significant impact of affective EA on relevance suggests that players separated the educational content from the gameplay experience. It implies the educational content should be better woven with the gameplay.

Interestingly, even though participants from two conditions rated similarly on the game's relevance, those who interacted with the affective EA perceived the game to be more useful than those who did not. In other words, the use of affective EAs changed participants' perceptions towards the game's usefulness. This suggests that perceived usefulness is not solely influenced by the factual learning content; some other factors brought about by the affective EA were at work. We speculate that using affective EA may have changed people's attitudes and increased their trust in the game, leading to the positive perception. To support this notion, we noticed that participants from the no-EA condition found the "*content*" useful, while participants from the affective-EA condition found "*the comments from the librarian*", in other words, the affective EA, useful. Some commented that "*The praises after I find some objects are very encouraging, he told me I am making good progress.*"

The reason for higher behavioral intention from participants who interacted with the affective EA than those who did not is understandable. Behavioral intention is to a large extent determined by one's attitude and perceived usefulness [40]. In the context of

this study, participants in the affective-EA condition were more motivated and perceived it to be more useful. Thus it is natural that they were more willing to learn more about IL and recommend the game to others in the future. This is confirmed by participants' suggestions from the affective-EA condition such as "*This game could be shared to all, quite enriching.*" On the contrary, in the subjective feedback in no-EA condition, no one mentioned recommending the game to others in the subjective feedback, although they also found the game "*novel and applicable*".

Another point concerns the assumption that affective EAs would improve participants' learning outcome. Knowledge improvement was unsupported in this study, as in many others [6, 34], even though students claimed they gained much useful knowledge in the subjective feedback, such as "*I learnt much about information literacy and it was really fun. The game was tough but nice*". This might be due to the cognitive overload on students' working memory. In other words, with all the activities in the IL game, such as navigating in the environment, finding objects, reading and digesting the knowledge content, answering quiz questions, incorporating the feedback, correcting mistakes, and finishing within one hour, players could have been too distracted to focus on the learning content and their learning efficacy was impeded. Participants from both conditions complained of "*too much information overload. I couldn't remember all the details*". Further, the game lacked audio cues and all information was presented visually. This differs from real world settings, where librarians use both oral and visual means for communication. Some participants expressed the desire that "*I would like to have the content read to me.*" Hence, providing audio cues may help reduce cognitive load, thus improving their learning outcomes.

Additionally, some insights can be obtained the subjective feedback. First and unexpectedly, the design of the game and EA was received favorably, as most participants commented on the design such as "*Librarian as ghost, it is eye catching*", and "*The visual design is very good*". Since only participants from the affective-EA condition interacted with the librarian, its appealing design might have contributed to their positive ratings in the post-test. To some extent, it shows that attractive visual design and enjoyable gameplay experience are prerequisites to engage students in DGBL. They "*liked the idea of teaching information literacy in a game*", which made the learning process more interesting. These positive attitudes can potentially increase their interest in learning IL and interactions with librarians. However, a lesson learnt is to balance the amount of educational content in DGBL, as confirmed from both evaluation results and participants' feedback. Many participants lamented that "*There is too much IL knowledge*" and "*the game is too long*". Educators need to strike a balance between game enjoyment and learning so students will not feel overwhelmed and frustrated. In general, participants' feedback was positive. We believe that the increased learning motivation could reduce students' library anxiety, leading to more interactions with the libraries and librarians in the future.

7. CONCLUSION

Given the rapid rise of online learning environments and DGBL, the findings from this study have important implications. Theoretically, this study reaffirms the positive influence of affective EAs on students learning, and extends it in an IL educational setting. Most prior studies used affective EAs to teach lower-order skills such as facts and concepts, while this study focused on teaching higher-order IL skills. Put differently, it undertook the first step in formally examining the influence of affective EA in an IL digital game. In addition, using EAs with affective expressions and feedback can significantly increase students' motivation, perceived usefulness and behavioral intention. Librarians and educators can tap on this opportunity to tackle the low interest in IL learning from tertiary students. The use of affective EAs is not limited to DGBL, but can be applied to design digital libraries. For example, most digital libraries have implemented recommendation systems, they can incorporate affective EAs to present such recommendations, and embed some affective feedback to users. The positive influence of affective EAs can make digital libraries more user friendly, and ease the information seekers' anxiety, which will potentially lead to better search results.

Some implications on IL game design can also be gleaned from this study. The first is to consider incorporating affective EAs in IL games. Using the image of a librarian as a helpful EA in the game could potentially increase students' trust and positive attitudes towards libraries and librarians. Second, synergizing pedagogical principles with game design heuristics in DGBL design can be challenging, as the two sometimes contradict with each other. For example, although the pedagogical principles advocate fixing learning sequences (from easy to difficult content), game design heuristics encourage player control and exploration. In our study, students responded negatively towards the design decision that they have to answer quizzes correctly before progressing. Hence, designers should carefully weigh the pros and cons for any design decisions. Third, DGBL is promising in enhancing students learning motivation and behavioral usage intention, but potentially limited in improving the learning outcome. Therefore, instead of expecting DGBL to solve all problems faced by students in IL learning, librarians and educators should adjust their expectations, and tap into the safe rich environment provided by DGBL to interact with students, learn about their concerns, design IL syllabus accordingly, and scaffolding the students.

The study is not without limitations. One limitation obtained from participants' subjective feedback is that the game was too long, as they could not proceed to the next level without answering quiz questions correctly. Insisting players to answer all quiz questions correctly may have frustrated them and resulted in low ratings in the post-test questionnaire. This issue will be addressed in the next round of game revision. Additionally, as mentioned in the discussion, there is a lack of audio cues from the EA, which may have resulted in the unsatisfactory learning outcome. Therefore, future research should infuse both visual and audio cues of EAs, to maximize their positive influence. Relatedly, as the EA employed minimal artificial intelligence, the affective expressions and feedback might not be sufficiently lifelike, which might have resulted in negative responses from participants with high expectations. Thus, future work may incorporate more advanced algorithms to deliver more realistic interactions between the EAs and players.

Another fruitful avenue of future research would be to investigate the mechanisms behind findings in this study. For example, the students may have been overloaded with visual information from the IL game, resulting in low learning efficacy. Therefore, eye trackers could be used to examine whether students indeed paid less attention to the learning content. Moreover, in-depth qualitative interviews can be conducted to elicit students' perceptions on the affective EA and the game in more details. Further, while some researchers have argued that simpler games might work better to attract students, the game *Library Escape* used in this study is rather complex. It incorporates many game design elements, such as EAs, backstories, rules, and quests. Therefore, future research can compare this game with simpler ones to ascertain whether the added game elements are useful in motivating students learning.

8. REFERENCES

[1] Loertscher, D. and Woolls, B. 2002. *Information literacy research: a review of the research: a guide for practitioners and researchers*. Hi Willow Research and Publishing, San Jose, CA.

[2] Shurkin, J. 2015. Science and Culture: Cartoons to better communicate science. *Proceedings of the National Academy of Sciences*. 112, 38 (2015), 11741-11742.

[3] Sweetser, P. and Wyeth, P. 2005. GameFlow: a model for evaluating player enjoyment in games. *Computers in Entertainment*. 3, 3 (2005), 3-3.

[4] Olson, C. K. 2010. Children's motivations for video game play in the context of normal development. *Review of General Psychology*. 14, 2 (2010), 180.

[5] Felicia, P. 2009. Digital games in schools: Handbook for teachers. European Schoolnet, Brussels, Belgium.

[6] Atkinson, R. K. 2002. Optimizing learning from examples using animated pedagogical agents. *Journal of Educational Psychology*. 94, 2 (2002), 416-427.

[7] van der Meij, H. 2013. Motivating agents in software tutorials. *Computers in Human Behavior*. 29, 3 (2013), 845-857.

[8] Mayer, R. E. and DaPra, C. S. 2012. An embodiment effect in computer-based learning with animated pedagogical agents. *Journal of Experimental Psychology: Applied*. 18, 3 (2012), 239-252.

[9] Salen, K. and Zimmerman, E. 2005. Game design and meaningful play. *Handbook of computer game studies* (2005), 59-79.

[10] Haake, M., Silvervarg, A. and Sjödén, B. 2010. *Building a Social Conversational Pedagogical Agent-Design Challenges and Methodological Approaches*. IGI Global, Hershey, PA.

[11] Harrison, S., Sengers, P. and Tatar, D. 2011. Making epistemological trouble: Third-paradigm HCI as successor science. *Interacting with Computers*. 23, 5 (2011), 385-392.

[12] Thomas, N. P., Crow, S. R. and Franklin, L. L. 2011. *Information Literacy and Information Skills Instruction: Applying Research to Practice in the 21st Century School Library*. ABC-CLIO, Santa Barbara, CA.

[13] Kuhlthau, C. C. 2004. *Seeking meaning: A process approach to library and information services*. Libraries Unlimited, Santa Barbara, CA.

[14] Van Eck, R. 2011. *Forward*. IGI Global, Hershey, PA.

[15] McClure, R., Cooke, R. and Carlin, A. 2011. The Search for the Skunk Ape: Studying the Impact of an Online Information Literacy Tutorial on Student Writing. *Journal of Information Literacy*. 5, 2 (2011), 26-45.

[16] Sachs, D. E., Langan, K. A., Leatherman, C. C. and Walters, J. L. 2013. Assessing the Effectiveness of Online Information Literacy Tutorials for Millennial Undergraduates. *College & Undergraduate Libraries*. 20, 3-4 (2013), 327-351.

[17] Montgomery, K. C. 2007. *Generation digital: Politics, commerce, and childhood in the age of the Internet.* MIT Press, Cambridge, MA.

[18] Prensky, M. 2005. Engage Me or Enrage Me: What Today's Learners Demand. *Educause Review.* 40, 5 (2005), 60.

[19] VanLeer, L. 2006. Interactive gaming vs. library tutorials for information literacy: A resource guide. *Indiana Libraries.* 25, 4 (2006), 52 – 55.

[20] Gallegos, B., Grondin, K., Allgood, T., Duarte, M. and Rostad, A. 2008. Let the Games Begin! Changing Our Instruction to Reach Millenials! In *Proceedings of the 34th Annual Conference of LEOX* (College Park, Maryland, May 4-6, 2008).

[21] McCabe, J. and Wise, S. 2009. It's all fun and games until someone learns something: Assessing the learning outcomes of two educational games. *Evidence Based Library and Information Practice.* 4, 4 (2009), 6-23.

[22] Nunamaker, J. F., DErrICk, D. C., Elkins, A. C., Burgoon, J. K. and Patton, M. W. 2011. Embodied conversational agent-based kiosk for automated interviewing. *Journal of Management Information Systems.* 28, 1 (2011), 17-48.

[23] Reeves, B. and Nass, C. 1997. *The Media equation: how people treat computers, television, and new media.* Cambridge University Press, Cambridge, UK.

[24] Robison, J., McQuiggan, S. and Lester, J. 2009. Evaluating the consequences of affective feedback in intelligent tutoring systems. In *Proceedings of 3rd International Conference on Affective Computing and Intelligent Interaction and Workshops*, IEEE (Amsterdam, 10-12 Sept. 2009),1-6.

[25] Lin, L., Atkinson, R., Christopherson, R., Joseph, S. and Harrison, C. 2013. Animated agents and learning: Does the type of verbal feedback they provide matter? *Computers & Education.* 67, (Sep. 2013), 239-249.

[26] Doumanis, I. and Smith, S. 2013. An empirical study on the effects of embodied conversational agents on user retention performance and perception in a simulated mobile environment. In *Proceedings of the 9th International Conference on Intelligent Environments–Future Intelligent Educational Environments*, (Athens, 16-17July 2013).

[27] Carlotto, T. and Jaques, P. 2013. Evaluating the Embodied Agent Effect in an English as a Foreign Language Learning Environment. In *Proceedings of XXIV Simpósio Brasileiro de Informática na Educação (SBIE 2013).*

[28] Charsky, D. 2010. From edutainment to serious games: A change in the use of game characteristics. *Games and Culture.* 5, 2 (2010), 177-198.

[29] Anderson, R. E. 2008. *Implications of the information and knowledge society for education.* In *International Handbook of Information Technology in Primary and Secondary Education.* 5-22. Springer, US.

[30] Lee, R. J. E., Nass, C., Brave, S. B., Morishima, Y., Nakajima, H. and Yamada, R. 2007. The Case for Caring Colearners: The Effects of a Computer-Mediated Colearner Agent on Trust and Learning. *Journal of Communication.* 57, 2 (2007), 183-204.

[31] Kim, Y. and Wei, Q. 2011. The impact of learner attributes and learner choice in an agent-based environment. *Computers & Education.* 56, 2 (2011), 505-514.

[32] Lusk, M. M. and Atkinson, R. K. 2007. Animated pedagogical agents: does their degree of embodiment impact learning from static or animated worked examples? *Applied Cognitive Psychology.* 21, 6 (2007), 747-764.

[33] Keller, J. M. 2009. *Motivational design for learning and performance: The ARCS model approach.* Springer Science & Business Media, New York.

[34] Guo, Y. R., Goh, D. H.-L., Luyt, B., Sin, S.-C. J. and Ang, R. P. 2015. The effectiveness and acceptance of an affective information literacy tutorial. *Computers & Education.* 87 (Sep, 2015), 368-384.

[35] Hirumi, A., Sivo, S. and Pounds, K. 2012. Telling stories to enhance teaching and learning: The systematic design, development and testing of two online courses. *International Journal on E-Learning.* 11, 2 (2012), 125-151.

[36] Venkatesh, V. and Bala, H. 2008. Technology acceptance model 3 and a research agenda on interventions. *Decision Sciences.* 39, 2 (2008), 273-315.

[37] Guo, Y. R. and Goh, D. H.-L. 2014. *The Design of an Information Literacy Game.* In *Proceedings of the 16th International Conference on Asia-Pacific Digital Libraries,* (Chiang Mai, Thailand, November 5-7, 2014), 354-364.

[38] McCombs, J. P. 2011. *A path analysis of the behavioral intention of secondary teachers to integrate technology in private schools in Florida.* UNF theses and Dissertations. University of North Florida.

[39] Chen, G.-D., Lee, J.-H., Wang, C.-Y., Chao, P.-Y., Li, L.-Y. and Lee, T.-Y. 2012. An Empathic Avatar in a Computer-Aided Learning Program to Encourage and Persuade Learners. *Journal of Educational Technology & Society.* 15, 2 (2012), 62-72.

[40] Venkatesh, V., Morris, M. G., Davis, G. B. and Davis, F. D. 2003. User acceptance of information technology: Toward a unified view. *MIS Quarterly.* 27, 3 (2003), 425-478.

Evaluating the Quality of Educational Answers in Community Question-Answering

Long T. Le
Department of Computer
Science
Rutgers University
longtle@cs.rutgers.edu

Chirag Shah
School of Communication and
Information
Rutgers University
chirags@rutgers.edu

Erik Choi
Brainly
erik.choi@brainly.com

ABSTRACT

Community Question-Answering (CQA), where questions and answers are generated by peers, has become a popular method of information seeking in online environments. While the content repositories created through CQA sites have been used widely to support general purpose tasks, using them as online digital libraries that support educational needs is an emerging practice. Horizontal CQA services, such as Yahoo! Answers, and vertical CQA services, such as Brainly, are aiming to help students improve their learning process by answering their educational questions. In these services, receiving high quality answer(s) to a question is a critical factor not only for user satisfaction, but also for supporting learning. However, the questions are not necessarily answered by experts, and the askers may not have enough knowledge and skill to evaluate the quality of the answers they receive. This could be problematic when students build their own knowledge base by applying inaccurate information or knowledge acquired from online sources. Using moderators could alleviate this problem. However, a moderator's evaluation of answer quality may be inconsistent because it is based on their subjective assessments. Employing human assessors may also be insufficient due to the large amount of content available on a CQA site. To address these issues, we propose a framework for automatically assessing the quality of answers. This is achieved by integrating different groups of features - personal, community-based, textual, and contextual - to build a classification model and determine what constitutes answer quality. To test this evaluation framework, we collected more than 10 million educational answers posted by more than 3 million users on Brainly's United States and Poland sites. The experiments conducted on these datasets show that the model using Random Forest (RF) achieves more than 83% accuracy in identifying high quality of answers. In addition, the findings indicate that personal and community-based features have more prediction power in assessing answer quality. Our approach also achieves high values on other key metrics such as F1-score and Area under ROC curve. The work reported here can be useful in many other contexts where providing automatic quality assessment in a digital repository of textual information is paramount.

Permission to make digital or hard copies of all or part of this work for personal or classroom use is granted without fee provided that copies are not made or distributed for profit or commercial advantage and that copies bear this notice and the full citation on the first page. Copyrights for components of this work owned by others than the author(s) must be honored. Abstracting with credit is permitted. To copy otherwise, or republish, to post on servers or to redistribute to lists, requires prior specific permission and/or a fee. Request permissions from permissions@acm.org.

JCDL '16, June 19 - 23, 2016, Newark, NJ, USA

© 2016 Copyright held by the owner/author(s). Publication rights licensed to ACM.
ISBN 978-1-4503-4229-2/16/06. . . $15.00

DOI: http://dx.doi.org/10.1145/2910896.2910900

Keywords

Community Question-Answering (CQA); Answer Quality; Features

1. INTRODUCTION

The Internet and the World Wide Web (WWW) have become critical and ubiquitous information tools that have changed the way people share and seek information. Many online resources on the WWW serve as some of the largest digital libraries publicly available. As the number of new resources for communication and information technologies have rapidly increased over the past few decades [18], users have adopted various types of such online information sources in order to seek and share information. These include Wikis, forums, blogs, and community question-answering (CQA). CQAs are one example of a new means of information seeking in which users share information and knowledge in virtual environments.

According to Gazan [12], CQA is "exemplifying the Web 2.0 model of user-generated and user-rated content" (p.2302), creating a critical online repository and an engagement platform where users formulate their information need in natural language and voluntarily interact with each other through the asking and answering of a question. Within CQA, there are other elements, such as commenting and voting, that encourage social interactions for seeking and sharing information. Because of the fast growth of CQA's popularity, a rich body of research has been conducted in order to understand the variety of content and user behaviors in question-answering interactions within the context of CQA. Shah et al. [25] state that previous studies based on user content have focused on content type, quality, and formulation, while studies focusing on user behaviors attempted to understand the motivations for asking and answering a question on CQA.

Many of the initial CQA platforms, such as AnswerBag (the first one in the US), were developed to support general purpose information seeking. They are referred to as horizontal CQA services. Then, other sites were deployed for more specific tasks - vertical CQA. One type of specific task or purpose is online learning. In education, students not only use the Internet to look for new materials but can also exchange ideas and knowledge. The advent of CQA has greatly assisted students in sharing knowledge in virtual environments. As CQA in education is an emerging field, educators hope that they may be able improve learning capability and experience with the help of communication and information technologies.

To further this push for employing CQA services and content for educational purposes, we attempt to examine Brainly,[1] one of the largest CQA services specifically targeted at education. Brainly is

---

[1] http://brainly.com

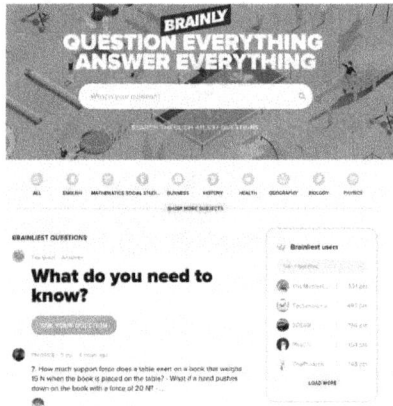

Figure 1: Brainly's homepage in the United States.

a leader in online social learning networks for students and educators with millions of active users. It has approximately 60 million monthly unique visitors as of January 2016 and is available in 35 countries, including the United States, Poland, Russia, Turkey, Brazil, France, and Indonesia. Figure 1 shows the homepage of Brainly in the United States.

CQA is a user-driven community where all contents, including questions and answers, are generated by community members. Thus, content quality is an important aspect in retaining existing users and attracting new members. The quality of information for educational purposes is even more important. For example, students who use the CQA to ask questions about homework problems could be misled by wrong answers. This is an especially problematic issue for struggling students. Thus, quality assessment is a critical aspect. At the moment, traditional CQAs depend on human judgment to evaluate content quality. There are several drawbacks of this mechanism, including subjective (and possibly biased) assessments employed by the assessors, seeming difficulty in recruiting such evaluators, and the time it could take for human assessors to go through the ever-increasing content in CQA sites. The work reported here addresses these concerns by providing a new framework for assessing content quality. Our specific contributions are as follows.

- Empirical study: this is the first large scale study to investigate the quality of answers in an emerging CQA for education.

- Propose a framework to assess the answers automatically. Our framework extracts different aspects of CQA content - such as personal features, community features, textual features, and contextual features - to build high accuracy classifiers. Our work can achieve accuracy higher than 83% in both data sets. Our method also achieves high values on other key metrics such as F1 score and Area under ROC curve.

- Examine the importance of different features and groups of features in assessing the quality of answers. The results show that personal features and community features are more important and have more predictive applications.

The rest of our paper is organized as follows: Section 2 discusses the background and a few related works. The framework is described in Section 3. Section 4 presents the data sets used in our study. We present the results and discussion of our method in Section 5 and Section 6. Finally, the conclusion and future work are presented in Section 7.

2. BACKGROUND AND RELATED WORKS

2.1 Community Question-Answering (CQA)

Community Question-Answering (CQA) services have become popular places for Internet users to look for information. Some popular CQAs, such as Yahoo! Answers or Stack Overflow, attract millions of users. CQA takes advantage of *Wisdom of the Crowd*, the idea that everyone knows something [30]. Users can contribute to the community by asking questions, giving answers, and voting for the posts. Most activities are moderated by humans.

Several works have investigated user interest and motivation for participating in CQA [22], [33]. Adamic et al. [1] studied the impact of CQA. In the work, the authors analyzed questions and clustered them based on the questions' contents. The results showed a diversity of user types in CQA. For example, some users can participate in a large number of topics, while many users are only interested in a narrow topical focus. The work also examined the best answers by using some basic features such as the length and pasts answers given by the corresponding user. Shah et al. [24] compared CQA and virtual reference to identify differences in users' expectations and perceptions. By understanding and identifying these behaviors, challenges, expectations, and perceptions within the context of CQA, we can more accurately highlight potential strategies for more accurately matching question askers with question answerers. Le and Shah [17] developed a framework to detect the top contributors in their early stage by integrating different signals of users. These "rising star" users are crucial to the health of the community due to their high quality and quantity contributions.

2.2 CQA for Online Learning

In recent years, online learning has collapsed time and space [9], which allows users to access information and resources for educational purposes any time and from anywhere. As online learning grows in popularity, a variety of new online information sources have emerged and are utilized in order to satisfy users' educational information needs. For example, social media (e.g., Facebook, Twitter, etc.) has attracted attention for empirical investigations conducted in order to understand the effectiveness of higher education [32]. Khan Academy has become a popular online educational video site that has more than 200 million viewers as well as approximately 45 million unique monthly visitors [21]. Additionally, even though most CQAs are mainly focused on either general topics (e.g., Yahoo! Answers, WikiAnswers, and so on) and/or professional topics (e.g, Stack Overflow, etc.) to seek and share information, new CQAs have emerged to help students participate in question-answering interactions that share educational information for online learning. Some small-scale CQA tools were developed to support small groups of university students [2], [28]. Examples of large educational CQAs include Chegg [2], Piazza [3], and Brainly. Brainly specializes in online learning for students (i.e, middle school, high school) through asking and answering activities in 16 main school subjects (e.g., English, Mathematics, Biology, Physics, etc.) [6].

---

[2]https://www.chegg.com
[3]https://piazza.com/

130

2.3 Quality Assessment in CQA

Since most contents in CQA are generated by users who actively seek and share information with other users, the content quality is a critical factor to the success of the community. Therefore, assessing the quality of posts in CQA is a critical task in order to develop an information seeking environment where users receive reliable and helpful information for their educational information needs. High quality content is the best way to retain existing users and attract new members [19]. However, assessing the quality of posts in CQA is a difficult task due to the diversity of contents and users. The quality of the posts might include quality of the question and quality of the answer. In our work, we focus on the quality of the answer.

Examining the quality of answers can be divided into three types of problems: *(i)* finding the best answer, *(ii)* ranking the answers, and *(iii)* measuring the quality of answers. For example, Shah and Pomerantz [26] looked for the best answers in Yahoo! Answers by using 13 different criteria. Ranking answers is a useful task when a question receives multiples answers. These works focus more on the similarity between an answer and a question [29]. Surynato et al. [31] utilized the expertise of an asker and an answerer to rank the answers. In this work, the authors also recognized that different users are experts in different subjects and used this understanding to rank the answers. Recent work also showed the potential of using graphs to rank users [13], but it is not clear how to rank answers based on users.

The most popular type of problem focuses on regression-related problems, such as predicting how many answers a question will get or how much community interest a post can elicit. Researchers are interested in predicting whether certain questions in CQA will be answered and how many answers a question will receive [34, 11]. This research used features such as asker history, the length of question, and the question category to predict the answerability of the question. Shah et al. [27] studied why some questions remain unanswered in CQA. Particularly, this work explored why fact-based questions often fail to attract an answer. Momeni et al. [20] applied machine learning to judge the quality of comments in online communities, revealing that social context is a useful feature. Yao et al. [36] examined the long-term effect of the posts in Stack Overflow by developing a new scalable regression model. Dalip et al. [10] tried to reduce the number of features in collaborative content, however, the number of reductions was not significant. Furthermore, applying feature selection can solve the issue with many features, such as over-fitting.

Our work is close to measuring the quality of answers. This research uses past question-answering interactions and current question and/or answering activities in order to predict the quality of new answers automatically. The framework incorporates different groups of features including personal features, community features, textual features, and contextual features.

3. EXAMINING THE QUALITY OF AN AN-SWER

In order to reduce the workload by assessing the quality of answers manually, we developed a framework to detect the quality of answers automatically. It is a difficult task due to the complexity of content in the CQA. Here is the formal definition of our problem:

Formal definition:
Given:

- a set of users $U = \{u_1, u_1, ..., u_n\}$
- a set of posts $P = Q \cup A$,

Q is the set of questions $Q = \{q_1, q_2, ..., q_{m1}\}$, and A is the set of answers $A = \{a_1, a_2, ..., a_{m2}\}$

- a set of interactions $I = \{i_1, i_2, ..., i_{m3}\}$ (such as giving thanks, making friends)

Task: For arbitrary answer $a \in A$, predict whether a will be *deleted* or *approved*?

Our framework follows a classification problem. In the first step, we collect the history and information of users in the community, the interactions in the community, and the characteristics of answers. In the second step, we build the classification model based on history. In the last step, we predict the quality of new answers based on our trained models.

3.1 Feature Extraction

In order to classify the quality of answers, we build a list of features for each answer. Table 1 lists the features used in our study. The features are divided into four groups: Personal Features, Community Features, Textual Features, and Contextual Features.

- Personal Features: These features are based on the characteristics of users. Personal features include the activity of an answer's owner, such as the number of answers given by the user, the number of questions asked by the user, the rank that user achieved in the community, and the user's grade level.

- Community Features: These features are based on the response of the community to a user's answers, such as how many thanks they received or how many bans they received. Furthermore, we also consider the social connectivity of users in the community. In Brainly, users can make friends and exchange information. The friendships can be placed on a graph where users are nodes and the edge between two nodes represents the friendship. We extract several features about their connection - such as the number of friends - clustering the coefficient of a user and their ego-net (aka, the friends of friends). The clustering coefficient (CC_i) of a user measures how closely their neighbors form a clique, defined as

$$CC_i = \frac{\# \ of \ triangles \ connected \ i}{\# \ of \ connected \ triples \ centered \ on \ i} \quad (1)$$

Higher values mean that this user and their friends form a stronger connection. We denote $d_i = |N(i)|$ as the number of friends of users i, $|N(i)|$ denotes set of neighbors of i. Average degree of neighborhood is defined as

$$\bar{d}_N(i) = \frac{1}{d_i} \times \sum\nolimits_{j \in N_i} d_j \quad (2)$$

We also use egonet features of a node. A node's egonet is the subgraph created by the node and its neighbors. Egonet features include the size of egonet, the number of outgoing edges of egonet and the number of neighbors of egonet.

These features incorporate four social theories, which are Social Capital, Structural Hole, Balance, and Social Exchange [3]. The capacity of social connection in information dissemination was conducted in [16]. Furthermore, these features are all computed locally, which is scalable and efficient. Computing the community features is an *almost* linear time algorithm, taking *almost* $O(n \log n)$, where n is number of nodes in graph.

- Textual Features: These features are based on answer content, such as the length of answers and the format of answers. We also check whether users use Latex for typing, since many answers provided in mathematics and physics topical areas are easier to read if Latex is used. Furthermore, we measure the readability of the text based on two popular indexes: automated readability index (ARI), and Flesch reading ease score of answer (FRES) [15]. The ARI measures what grade level should understand the text, which is measured by

$$4.71 * \frac{\# \ of \ characters}{\# \ of \ words} + 0.5 * \frac{\# \ of \ words}{\# \ of \ sentences} - 21.43 \tag{3}$$

The FRES index measures the readability of the document. Higher FRES scores indicate the text is easier to understand. FRES index is calculated as

$$206.8 - 1.01 * \frac{\# \ of \ words}{\# \ of \ sentences} - 84.6 * \frac{\# \ of \ syllables}{\# \ of \ words} \tag{4}$$

- Contextual Features: These features contain some contextual features, such as the question's grade level, the device types used to answer the question, the similarity between answer and question, duration to type answer, and the typing speed. The typing speed measures how many words the user types per second. The devices let us know whether the participant used a computer or a mobile device to answer. In order to compute the similarity between the answer and the question, we treat the answer and question as two vectors of words. The cosine similarity between these two vectors returns the similarity between them. Value 0 means that there are no common words between them. We believe that no common words between the answer and the question might indicate unrelated answers.

Building training set: In order to build the training data, we extracted features for each answer as seen in Table 1. These can also be divided into two types of features. *(i): Immediate features:* are the length, device type, typing speed, and similarity between answers and questions. These features are extracted immediately when the answer is posted. *(ii:) History features:* such as the number of thanks and number of answers given, can be built beforehand and be updated whenever these features change. Thus, when a new answer is posted, we can extract all proposed features immediately, which means our method can work in real time. Further details about these settings are described in Section 5. Next, we describe three classifiers used in our study.

3.2 Classification

Since our framework could use almost any classification model, we compared the performance of different models in this study. In particular, we tested the classification algorithms below [4]. Let $X = x_1, x_2, ..., x_n$ be the list of features. The list of classification algorithms are summarized as:

- Logistic regression (log-reg): Log-reg is a generalized linear model with sigmoid function

$$P(Y = 1 | X = \frac{1}{1 + exp(-b)}) \tag{5}$$

Table 1: Lists of features are classified into four groups of features: Personal, Community, Textual, and Contextual. The abbreviations of features are in brackets.

Personal Features
Number of answers given (n_answers)
Number of questions asked (n_questions)
Ranking of users (rank_id)
Grade level of users (u_grade)
Community Features
Number of thanks that user received (thanks_count)
Number of warnings that user received (warns)
Number of spam reports that user received (spam_count)
Number of friends in community (friends_count)
Clustering Coefficient in friendship network (cc)
Average degree of neighborhood (deg_adj)
Average CC of friends (cc_adj)
Size of ego-network of friendship (ego)
Number of outgoing edges in ego-network (ego_out)
Number of neighbors in ego-network (ego_adj)
Textual features
The length of answer (length)
The readability of answer (ari)
The Flesch Reading Ease Score of answer (fres)
The format of answer (well_format)
Using advance math typing: latex (contain_tex)
Contextual features
The grade level of question (q_grade)
The grade difference between answerer & question (diff_grade)
The rank difference between answerer & asker (diff_rank)
The similarity between answer and question (sim)
Device used to type answer (client_type)
Duration to answer (time_to_answer)
Typing speed (typing_speed)

where $b = w_0 + \sum(w_i.x_i)$, w_i are the inferred parameters from regression.

- Decision trees: The Tree-based method is a nonlinear model that partitions features into smaller sets and fits a simple model into each subset. The decision tree includes two-stage processes: tree growing and tree pruning. These steps stop when a certain depth is reached or each partition has a fixed number of nodes.

- Random Forest (RF): RF is an average model approach [14, 5] and we use a bag of 100 decision trees. Given a sample set, the RF method randomly samples data and builds a decision tree. This step also selects a random subset of features for each tree. The final outcome is based on the average of these decisions. The pseudo-code of RF is described in Algorithm 1. There are some advantages of RF. When building each tree in Step 4, RF randomly selects a list of features and a subset of data. Thus, RF can avoid the over-fitting problem of the decision tree. Furthermore, each tree can be built separately, which makes distributively computing the trees extremely easy.

Figure 2 summarizes the architecture of our method. In the framework, textual features and contextual features can be calculated quickly at the moment when a new answer is posted. Personal and community features are extracted from the history database. After querying personal and contextual features, some features related to a user's activities (e.g., number of answers increased over time, etc.) are also updated accordingly.

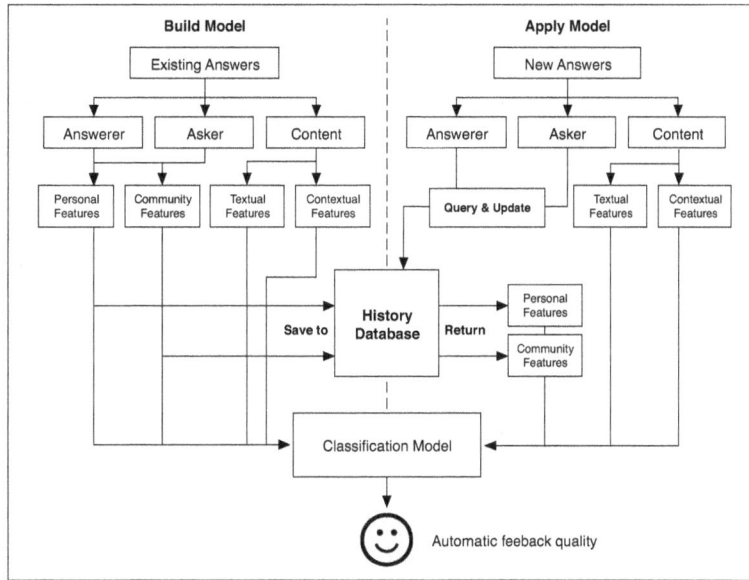

Figure 2: An overview of a framework proposed in the study.

Algorithm 1 Pseudo-code of Random Forest algorithm

Input:

- A set of training input $T = \{(X_i, y_i)\}$, $i = 1, ..., $n.

- Number of trees N_{trees}

- A new feature vector X_{new}

Output: the prediction outcome of X_{new}

1: **for** $i = 1 : N_{trees}$ **do**
2:     Randomly select a subset of training $T_{rand} \subset T$
3:     Build the tree h_i based on T_{rand}
4:     In each internal node of h_i, randomly select a set of features and split the trees based on these selected features
5: **end for**
6: $Pred(X_{new}) = \sum\limits_{i=1}^{N_{trees}} h_i(X_{new})$
7: **return** $Pred(X_{new})$

Next, we will describe the data sets used in our study and some characteristics of users in online learning communities.

4. DATASETS AND CHARACTERIZATION OF THE DATA

Overview: Brainly.com is an online Q&A for students and educators with millions of active users. In our study, we use the data from two markets: the United States (US) and Poland (PL). Table 2 describes some characteristics of these datasets. In our study, we use two types of answers: deleted answers and approved answers. Brainly requires high quality answers. Thus incorrect answers, incomplete answers, or spam posts are deleted by moderators. A moderator is an experienced user who has contributed significantly to the community. The United States is an emerging market for Brainly, which was established in 2013. In contrast, Poland is a well-established market where Brainly has been used since 2009.

The posts in Brainly are divided into three levels (grades): primary, secondary, and high school. There is no detail category for each level.

Table 2: Description about data.

Site	Period	# of Users	# of Posts	# of Answers
US	Nov '13 to Dec '15	800 K	1.5 M	700 K
PL	Mar '09 to Dec '15	2.9 M	19.9 M	10 M

Ranking of users: Brainly uses a gamification-related feature that illustrates how actively users participate in answering questions. In the current Brainly system, there are seven hierarchical ranks, from Beginner to Genius, that users can advance through based on how many points they receive when answering a question, as well as how many of their answers are selected as the best answer by an asker. This mechanism is similar to other CQA sites such as Yahoo! Answers and Stack Overflow, which encourage users to contribute to the site in order to earn a high reputation.

Deleting answers in Brainly: Brainly tries to maintain high quality answers, and moderators are recruited to participate heavily in deleting questions. Only experienced users, such as moderators, are allowed to delete answers. Some reasons for deleting answers are if the answers are incomplete, incorrect, irrelevant, or spam. A significant portion of answers are deleted (30%) to maintain the high quality of the site. But deleting this many answers is time-consuming and labor intensive. Furthermore, manual deleting might not be prompt and unsuitable content can exist on the site until moderators have a chance to review the answers. Thus, developing an automatic mechanism to assess the quality of answers is a critical task.

Friendship in Brainly: Users in this social CQA can make friendships and exchange ideas and solutions. After joining the community, users can request to make friends with other users if their topics of interest are related. The friendship feature in Brainly is a new mechanism that encourages students to exchange ideas and solutions. In traditional CQA such as Yahoo! Answers and Stack Overflow, there is no formalized friendship connection. Figure 3 depicts the distribution of number of friends per user. We see that it follows the power law with long tail. Some users have many connections in the community while others make only a few connections. We expect that users with many connections are more active and more committed to answering questions.

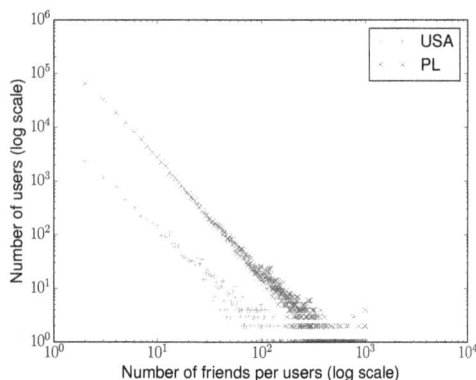

Figure 3: Distribution of number of friends per user in log-log scale. The number of friends follows power law. Some users make a lot of friends in this community.

Activity in Brainly: This is a free community. Anyone can contribute by asking questions, giving answers, giving thanks, and making friends. Due to the nature of the community, the contribution of each user is different and based on their interests and availability. Figure 4 plots the distribution of number of answers given per user. Again, this follows the power law with some very active users. Answering questions is a popular way for users to earn higher scores and increase their ranking in the community. Giving many answers shows that these active users are willing to devote their time to helping others. Answering a high number of questions also helps answerers gain knowledge and trust from the community. Thus, answers from these users could have high quality.

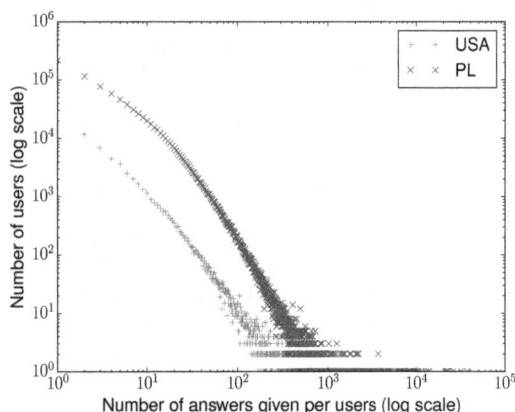

Figure 4: Distribution of number of answers given per user. A small fraction of users answer a lot of questions while many users answer a few number of questions.

Subjects of interest: The questions in Brainly are divided into different subjects/topics, such as Mathematics, Physics, etc. We examine how students participate in these topics between two countries. Figure 5 shows that students in both countries participate more in the topical areas of Mathematics, History, and English. The percentage of posts on mathematics in the United States is significantly higher than in Poland (42% vs. 35%) This might indicate that students in the US need more help with Mathematics.

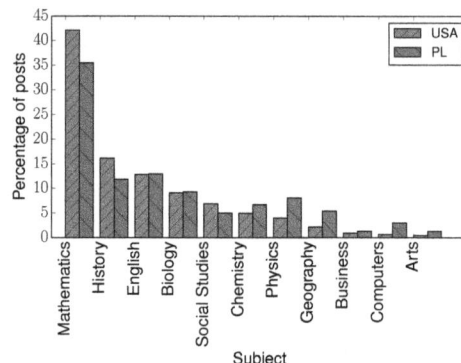

Figure 5: Percentage of posts in different subjects. Both countries are similar and students are most active in discussing Mathematics, History, and English.

The readability of answers: We want to see whether the approved answers are more readable - or clear - than deleted answers. We use ARI to measure the readability of answers. It shows that the ARI of approved answers is 6.9 ± 3.1, the ARI of deleted answers is 5.1 ± 3.2. Similarly, the FRES indexes of deleted and approved answers are 69.9 ± 23.1 and 62.2 ± 22.5 respectively. A higher FRES value means that an answer is easier to read. We see that the standard deviation is large for both indices due to the diversity of content. We conducted a t-test and saw that the difference is significant with $p = 0.05$. The reason for this difference is many answers in primary and secondary levels are deleted. In general, the answers in primary and secondary levels are easy to read.

Quality of experienced and newbie users: We examine the quality of answers from new users and experienced users. We examine the deletion rate of answers based on the ranking of users. Figure 6 plots the rate of answers deleted for differently ranked users. We see that low-ranked users have a very high rate of deletion. Since Brainly is a CQA which supports education, the site expects correct answers. Even incomplete answers are deleted. We see that many intermediate users' (such as rank 3 or rank 4 users') answers are deleted. This demonstrates that Brainly maintains a very high standard to ensure quality answers.

5. EXPERIMENTS AND RESULTS

In this section we will describe our experimental setup, highlight the main results, and provide a discussion around these experiments and findings.

5.1 Experimental setup

We compare the performance of classification using different classification algorithms with different sets of features. In the default setting, we used the Random Forest of 100 decision trees. In the evaluation, we randomly selected 200 K answers in each

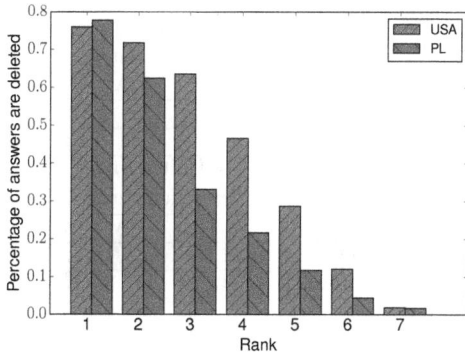

Figure 6: Percentage of answers deleted vs. rank level. Rank 1 is beginner while rank 7 is genius user. Highly ranked users have fewer deleted answers due to their experience. High deletion rate shows the site's answer requirements are very strict.

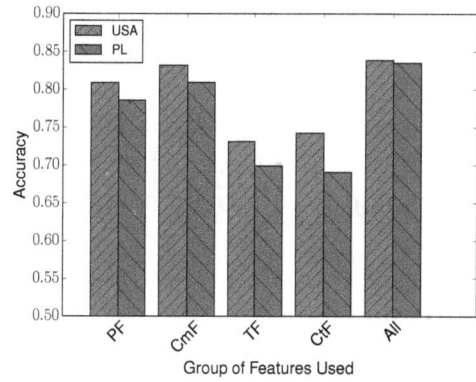

Figure 7: The accuracy of using different groups of features. *PF, CmF, TF, CtF* denotes the results when our frameworks used personal features, community features, textual features, and contextual features respectively. *All* means using all features. *PF, CmF* are more useful in predicting the quality of answers. (Random Forest is the classifier used.)

data set to validate the accuracy of our framework. We used 10-fold cross validation to select parameter classification with 70-30% training, testing set. In order to compare the efficacy, we examined the accuracy, F1-score, confusion matrix, and Area Under Curve.

5.2 Main results

5.2.1 Accuracy

Accuracy is defined as the percentage of answers classified correctly. Figure 7 plots the accuracy of using different groups of features when applying Random Forest. *PF, CmF, TF, CtF* denotes the results when our frameworks used personal features, community features, textual features, and contextual features, respectively. *All* presents the accuracy when using all features in classification. The results show that personal features and community features are more useful in predicting the quality of an answer. The result makes sense because good users normally provide good answers. The textual features have less prediction value due to the complexity of the site's content. We will examine the details of each feature later. Furthermore, our classifier achieves very high accuracy - more than 83% in both markets. These results are very encouraging due to the complexity of answers in the community.

5.2.2 F1-score

We also measure $F1$ score, which considers both precision and recall. Precision is the fraction of instances that are relevant, while recall is the fraction of relevant instances that are retrieved. The value of $F1$ is defined as

$$F1 = 2 * \frac{precision * recall}{precision + recall} \quad (6)$$

Figure 8 shows that using all features achieves the highest $F1$ score, which is more than 84% in both data sets. High $F1$ scores show that our method can achieve both high precision and recall. The results are similar to accuracy, where personal features and community features are the most important features in the model.

5.2.3 Comparing different classifiers

Table 3 compares the accuracy when applying different classification algorithms. We see that Random Forest outperforms logistic

regression and decision trees. The reason is non-linear relation between features and the quality of answers. Furthermore, Random Forest also randomly selects different sets of features to build the trees, which avoids over-fitting in classification. Random Forest is also an efficient algorithm which can work well on large data sets. Our experiment was conducted on a machine with 2.2 GHz quad-core, 16 GB of RAM, implemented in Python code, on a data set is 200 thousand answers. The experiment took 34 seconds to train the model and less than 1 millisecond to predict each answer. Training is one time cost. It implies that our framework can determine the quality of answers in real time. Thus, our suggestion is to use Random Forest as a classifier in a real system.

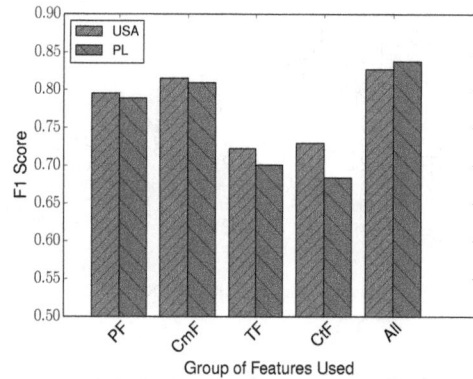

Figure 8: Compare the $F1$ score (higher is better) when using different groups of features. Random Forest is the classifier used. High F1 score shows that our method achieves high value in both precision and recall. Again, personal features and community features are more important in the model.

Table 3: Compare the accuracy of different classifiers. Random Forest (bag of 100 trees) outperforms logistic regression and decision trees.

Classification	USA	PL
Logistic Regression	79.1%	76.8%
Decision Trees	78.2%	77.1%
Random Forest	**83.9%**	**83.5%**

Table 4: Confusion matrix for predicting answer quality.

		Prediction outcome		
		Deleted	Approved	Total
Actual value	Deleted	90.1%	9.9%	100%
	Approved	22.4%	77.6%	100%

a. United States

		Prediction outcome		
		Deleted	Approved	Total
Actual value	Deleted	81.5%	18.5%	100%
	Approved	14.5%	85.5%	100%

b. Poland

5.3 Discussion

5.3.1 Feature importance

In this section, we measure which features are more important. In order to determine this, we use a permutation test to remove the features and measure the accuracy of out-out-bag (OOB) samples. The important features will degenerate the accuracy substantially. Figure 9 reports the importance of different features used in our study. The three most important features are the number of thanks users receive, the amount of spam reported, and the similarity between answers and questions. Some features are believed to have strong correlation with quality but are less important, such as device type or using Latex when typing. For example, participants using mobile devices to submit their answers may make more mistakes, or a participant using Latex markup might indicate a user's high experience with certain topics. Unfortunately, there were only a few answers that were posted from mobile devices or typed in Latex (less than 10%). Thus, these features lost their prediction value.

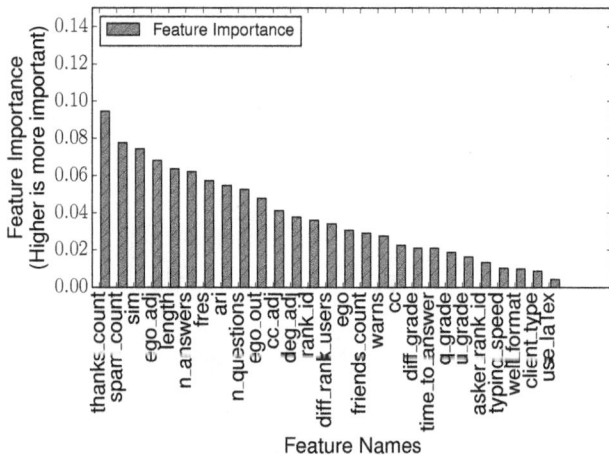

Figure 9: Measure of important features (higher is more important). Most important features are *number of thanks*, *number of spams*, *similarity between question and answer*, and so on. Table 1 lists the notations of used features.

5.3.2 Features selection

One possible concern is whether features selection can improve the performance of our method. The general idea of features selection is to remove features that have no correlation with the outcome, or to remove two similar features. In both cases, such features cause over-fitting in the prediction. In Random Forest, we already randomly select features when building the trees. In particular, Step 4 in Algorithm 1 selects random features to build the trees. Furthermore, the number of features in our study is not large. Thus, features selection is unnecessary and does not help improve accuracy.

5.3.3 High quality answers and low quality answers

We discuss which is more difficult to detect: high quality or low quality answers. Table 4 examines the confusion matrix which describes how answers are mis-classified in the US and PL. We see that detecting deleted questions achieves higher accuracy than detecting approved answers in the US. The reason is that many answers in the US market are answered by newcomers, and this does not satisfy the high quality criteria established by this CQA community. In the PL market, there is no difference due to a well-established community and the fact that the majority of the participants are experienced users.

5.3.4 Receiver operating characteristic (ROC)

We also evaluate the ROC of the approved answers for both data sets. The ROC denotes the ability of the classification to find the correct high quality answers with different thresholds. The curve in Figure 10 plots the True Positive rate against the False Positive rate. We see that the area under ROC is higher than 0.91 in both data sets. In the real deployment, we can set different thresholds to select the approved answers based on various requirements. For example, the administrators of the site might believe that 17% is insufficient and require that the automatic assessments not make mistakes with a rate of more than 0.05. Figure 10 shows that if the False Positive Rate is 0.05, the True Positive Rates of the US and PL are 0.73 and 0.62, respectively. Otherwise, we can detect a majority of the approved answers with a small error rate. The rest of the answers are considered borderline entities, which are hard to differentiate between good or bad. Under these circumstances, we can still take advantage of moderators and askers to evaluate the questions or answers again. In this case, the workload of humans is reduced significantly.

6. DISCUSSION

Asking questions for the purpose of learning is not a new phenomenon within the area of information seeking. It is an innate and purposive human behavior to search information to satisfy a need [8], and information and knowledge received through an asker's questioning behavior may become meaningful in that the information acquired helps solve their problematic situations [35]. In recent years, new information and communication technologies have emerged to develop novel ways for users to interact with information systems and experts in order to seek information. These new resources include digital libraries and virtual references, as well as

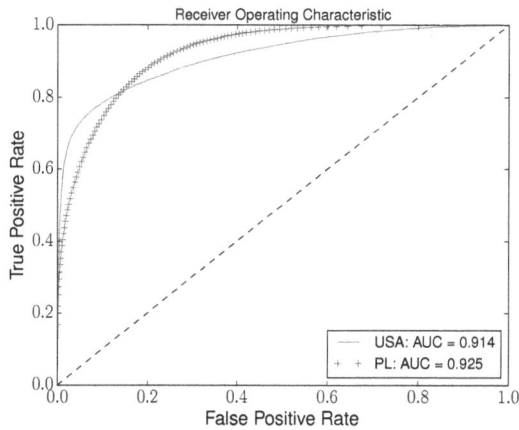

Figure 10: Area Under *ROC* curve for our frameworks are above 0.9 in both data sets.

CQA services where users are both consumers and producers of information.

According to Ross et al. [23], what librarians and experts in brick and mortar as well as virtual reference environments do is a process of negotiating an asker's question, which helps identify an asker's information need and allows him/her to construct a better question and receive high quality answers. However, this process of question negotiation does not occur in the context of CQA, which may cause significant issues for providing high quality answers. Identifying what constitutes the content quality of information generated in CQA (or for that matter, any online repository with user-generated content) can be critical to the applicability and sustainability of such digital resources.

When it comes to CQA in educational contexts, seeking and sharing high quality answers to a question may be more critical since question-answering interactions for educational answers is likely to solicit factual and verifiable information, in contrast to general-purpose CQA services where advice and opinion-seeking questions are predominant [7]. Thus, evaluating and assessing the quality of educational answers in CQA is important for not only improving user satisfaction, but also for supporting students' learning processes.

In this work, therefore, we investigated Brainly, an educational CQA, and attempted to utilize a series of textual and non-textual answer features in order to identify levels of content quality among educational answers. The study first attempted to identify a list of content characteristics that would constitute the quality of answers. In the second step, we applied these features in order to automatically assess the quality of answer. The results showed that Personal Features and Community Features are more robust in determining answer quality. Most of these features are available and feasible to compute in other CQA sites, making our approach applicable to the wider community.

Furthermore, the efficacy and efficiency of our method make it possible to implement within the real system. In our experiment on a standard PC, it takes less than one millisecond to return the prediction. It also only takes less than one minute to train the model with 200,000 answers from Brainly. However, the training step is a one-time cost and can be accomplished using distributed processing. By applying this technique to the real system, we believe that we can reduce the number of deleted answers by giving a warning immediately before a user submits a response to the community. Furthermore, the approach can approve high-quality answers, so that an asker's wait time can be reduced significantly.

Most of the previous work applied logistic regression in order to evaluate the quality of answers. Our work showed that a "wisdom of the crowd" approach, such as Random Forest, can significantly improve the accuracy of assessing the quality of answers due to a non-linear relationship between the features and the quality of answers. For example, the results showed that longer answers are more likely to be approved compared to deleted answers. But very lengthy answers might signal low-quality answers, such as confusing or spam answers. Even though the current study focused on evaluating the quality of answers in terms of educational information on CQA for online learning in particular, the study would also suggest an alternative way of how the quality of answers in the context of general CQA could be investigated by our method - i.e., a "wisdom of the crowd" approach - in order to improve the accuracy of assessing the quality of answers. Moreover, in terms of practical implications of users' interactions for content moderation on CQA, the findings may propose a variety of features or tools (e.g., detecting spams, trolling, plagiarism, etc.) that support content moderators in order to develop a healthy online community in which users may be able to seek and share high quality information and knowledge via question-answering interactions.

There are also limitations to our work. Our work can only detect high- and low-quality answers. It would be helpful if we could provide suggestions to improve the overall quality of these answers. We believe this is challenging work but a highly rewarding task, which might require a significant effort to examine answer meaning. Furthermore, our approach was based heavily on the community's past interactions, which has limited applicability to a newly-formed community.

7. CONCLUSION

In the current study, we focused on the quality of educational answers in CQA. Our work was motivated by a need to improve the efficiency of managing the community in terms of seeking and sharing high-quality answers to a question. Since employing human assessments may not be sufficient due to the large amount of content available, as well as subjective assessments of answer quality, we propose a framework to automatically assess the quality of answers for these communities. In general, our framework integrates different aspects of answers, such as personal features, community features, textual features, and contextual features. This is the first large scale study on CQA for education. Our method achieves high performance in all important metrics such as accuracy, F1 score, and Area under ROC curve. Furthermore, the experiment shows the efficiency of our method, which can work well in a real time system.

We find that personal features and community features are more robust in assessing the quality of answers in an online education community. The textual features and contextual features are less robust due to the diversity of users and content in these communities. Furthermore, all features used in this study can be computed easily, which makes the framework's implementation feasible.

In future work, we plan to study struggling users in the community. We see that many answers were deleted due to low quality. But the reasons these posts were deemed low-quality were not clear. Possibilities include a lack of knowledge on the part of the answerer, an arrogant attitude, or anti-social behavior. Detecting and helping struggle users also increase the quality of the site. We believe that understanding the latent features can help struggling users, improve users' experiences, and make online learning more efficient.

8. ACKNOWLEDGEMENTS

A portion of the work reported here was possible due to funds and data access provided by Brainly. We are also grateful to Michal Labedz and Mateusz Burdzel from Brainly for their help and insights into the topics discussed in this work.

9. REFERENCES

[1] L. A. Adamic, J. Zhang, E. Bakshy, and M. S. Ackerman. Knowledge sharing and yahoo answers: Everyone knows something. In *WWW*, pages 665–674, 2008.

[2] C. Aritajati and N. H. Narayanan. Facilitating students' collaboration and learning in a question and answer system. In *CSCW Companion*, pages 101–106, 2013.

[3] M. Berlingerio, D. Koutra, T. Eliassi-Rad, and C. Faloutsos. Network similarity via multiple social theories. In *ASONAM*, pages 1439–1440, 2013.

[4] C. M. Bishop. *Pattern Recognition and Machine Learning (Information Science and Statistics)*. Springer, 2006.

[5] L. Breiman. Random forests. *Mach. Learn.*, 45(1):5–32, 2001.

[6] E. Choi, M. Borkowski, J. Zakoian, K. Sagan, K. Scholla, C. Ponti, M. Labedz, and M. Bielski. Utilizing content moderators to investigate critical factors for assessing the quality of answers on brainly, social learning Q&A platform for students: a pilot study. In *ASIST*, 2015.

[7] E. Choi, V. Kitzie, and C. Shah. Developing a typology of online Q&A models and recommending the right model for each question type. In *ASIST*, pages 1–4, 2012.

[8] E. Choi and C. Shah. User motivation for asking a question in online Q&A services. *JASIST*, In press.

[9] R. A. Cole. *Issues in Web-based pedagogy: A critical primer*. Greenwood Press, 2000.

[10] D. H. Dalip, H. Lima, M. A. Gonçalves, M. Cristo, and P. Calado. Quality assessment of collaborative content with minimal information. In *JCDL*, pages 201–210, 2014.

[11] G. Dror, Y. Maarek, and I. Szpektor. Will my question be answered? predicting "question answerability" in community question-answering sites. In *ECML/PKDD*, volume 8190, pages 499–514, 2013.

[12] R. Gazan. Social Q&A. *JASIST*, 63:2301–2312, 2011.

[13] S. D. Gollapalli, P. Mitra, and C. L. Giles. Ranking experts using author-document-topic graphs. In *JCDL*, pages 87–96, 2013.

[14] T. Hastie, R. Tibshirani, and J. Friedman. *The Elements of Statistical Learning*. Springer Series in Statistics, 2009.

[15] J. P. Kincaid, R. P. Fishburne, R. L. Rogers, and B. S. Chissom. Derivation of New Readability Formulas (Automated Readability Index, Fog Count and Flesch Reading Ease Formula) for Navy Enlisted Personnel. Technical report, Naval Air Station Memphis, 1975.

[16] L. T. Le, T. Eliassi-Rad, and H. Tong. MET: A fast algorithm for minimizing propagation in large graphs with small eigen-gaps. In *SDM*, pages 694–702, 2015.

[17] L. T. Le and C. Shah. Retrieving rising stars in focused community question-answering. In *ACIIDS*, pages 25–36, 2016.

[18] A. Y. Levy, A. Rajaraman, and J. J. Ordille. Querying heterogeneous information sources using source descriptions. In *VLDB*, pages 251–262, 1996.

[19] Y. Liu, J. Bian, and E. Agichtein. Predicting information seeker satisfaction in community question answering. In *SIGIR*, pages 483–490, 2008.

[20] E. Momeni, K. Tao, B. Haslhofer, and G.-J. Houben. Identification of useful user comments in social media: A case study on flickr commons. In *JCDL*, pages 1–10, 2013.

[21] M. Noer. *One Man, One Computer, 10 Million Students: How Khan Academy Is Reinventing Education*. Forbes, 2013.

[22] J. Preece, B. Nonnecke, and D. Andrews. The top five reasons for lurking: improving community experiences for everyone. *Computers in Human Behavior*, 20(2):201 – 223, 2004.

[23] C. Ross, K. Nilsen, and P. Dewdney. *Conducting the reference interview: A how-to-do-it manual for librarians*. New York: NealSchuman, 2002.

[24] C. Shah and V. Kitzie. Social q&a and virtual reference - comparing apples and oranges with the help of experts and users. *JASIST*, 63:2020–2036, 2012.

[25] C. Shah, S. Oh, and J. S. Oh. Research agenda for social Q&A. *Library & Information Science Research*, 31(4):205–209, 2009.

[26] C. Shah and J. Pomerantz. Evaluating and predicting answer quality in community qa. In *SIGIR*, pages 411–418, 2010.

[27] C. Shah, M. Radford, L. Connaway, E. Choi, and V. Kitzie. How much change do you get from 40$? analyzing and addressing failed questions on social Q&A. In *ASIST*, pages 1–10, 2012.

[28] I. Srba and M. Bielikova. Askalot: Community question answering as a means for knowledge sharing in an educational organization. In *CSCW Companion*, pages 179–182, 2015.

[29] M. Surdeanu, M. Ciaramita, and H. Zaragoza. Learning to rank answers on large online qa collections. In *ACL*, pages 719–727, 2008.

[30] J. Surowiecki. *The Wisdom of Crowds*. Anchor, 2005.

[31] M. A. Suryanto, E. P. Lim, A. Sun, and R. H. L. Chiang. Quality-aware collaborative question answering: Methods and evaluation. In *WSDM*, pages 142–151, 2009.

[32] P. A. Tess. The role of social media in higher education classes (real and virtual) - a literature review. *Computers in Human Behavior*, 29:A60–A68, 2013.

[33] G. Wang, K. Gill, M. Mohanlal, H. Zheng, and B. Y. Zhao. Wisdom in the social crowd: An analysis of quora. In *WWW*, pages 1341–1352, 2013.

[34] L. Yang, S. Bao, Q. Lin, X. Wu, D. Han, Z. Su, and Y. Yu. Analyzing and predicting not-answered questions in community-based question answering services. In *AAAI*, pages 1273–1278, 2011.

[35] S. Yang. Information seeking as problem-solving using a qualitative approach to uncover the novice learners' information-seeking process in a perseus hypertext system. *Library and Information Science Research*, 19(1):71–92, 1997.

[36] Y. Yao, H. Tong, F. Xu, and J. Lu. Predicting long-term impact of cqa posts: A comprehensive viewpoint. In *SIGKDD*, pages 1496–1505, 2014.

Music Information Seeking via Social Q&A: An Analysis of Questions in Music StackExchange Community

Hengyi Fu
School of Information, Florida State University
142 Collegiate Loop, Tallahassee, FL 32306
hf13c@my.fsu.edu

Yun Fan
Répertoire International de Littérature Musicale (RILM),
City University of New York
365 Fifth Avenue, Suite 3108, NY,10016
yfan@rilm.org

ABSTRACT

In this paper we report preliminary findings based on a quantitative analysis of data from a music social Q&A site, *Music StackExchange*, focusing on real-life music information needs, uses, and seeking. Eight major topic categories and a two-level taxonomy for question type/intent and the characteristics of questions in each category are presented. Our findings suggest that Q&A sites are a fruitful resource for identifying users' music information needs, how these needs are expressed, and intended uses for the information. On Music StackExchange, users' questioning behaviors were motivated by the recognition of knowledge gaps, lack of resources, need for others' opinions, or interest in research issues, spanning different topics. This study is explorative in nature and the results could improve the understanding of everyday life music information seeking. The findings can inform music librarians and general-purpose music information systems designers of the needs, requirements, and approaches to enhance music related controlled vocabularies, and improve search engines and online knowledge sharing communities to categorize and provide users with more relevant music information.

Keywords
Music information needs and uses; Music information seeking; Music information behavior; Question type; Social Q&A site.

1. INTRODUCTION
The success of social media has introduced new ways of seeking for information and sharing knowledge via the Internet. An example of such social media is social question and answering (Q&A) sites. Social Q&A sites such as Yahoo! Answers and Stack Overflow allow people to meet their information needs by asking questions and receiving answers from their peers on a broad range of topics. Those questions and answers consist of archives with millions of entries that are of value to the users, as well as the researchers who have interest in studying user information needs, uses, and seeking behaviors. Based on data (e.g. questions, answers, comments, etc.) extracted from social Q&A sites, prior studies have examined users' information needs and the ways in which the needs were expressed in certain knowledge domains, including information technology [1][2], health [3][4], and religion [5].

Permission to make digital or hard copies of all or part of this work for personal or classroom use is granted without fee provided that copies are not made or distributed for profit or commercial advantage and that copies bear this notice and the full citation on the first page. Copyrights for components of this work owned by others than ACM must be honored. Abstracting with credit is permitted. To copy otherwise, or republish, to post on servers or to redistribute to lists, requires prior specific permission and/or a fee. Request permissions from Permissions@acm.org.

JCDL'16, June 19–23, 2016, Newark, NJ, USA.
© 2016 ACM. ISBN 978-1-4503-4229-2/16/06…$15.00.
DOI: http://dx.doi.org/ 10.1145/2910896.2910914

Until now only a small handful of studies have been conducted regarding music information needs, uses, and seeking behaviors by music information retrieval communities[6][7][8].These studies either limited the scope within specific systems which cannot accurately represent the real music needs of users or restricted the scope of music information needs to song related. This study reports preliminary findings based on a quantitative analysis of data from a music social Q&A site, *Music StackExchange*, focusing on the kinds of music information users seek from that site. Eight major topic categories and a two-level taxonomy for question type/intent and the characteristics of questions in each category are presented. This study differs from previous work in a few important respects. First, it examines real-life music information needs and seeking behaviors (not only song related) by analyzing questions and answers from a music social Q&A site. Second, the categories of music information needs and uses identified are more comprehensive and diverse compared to prior studies. This study is explorative in nature and the results could improve the understanding of everyday life music information seeking. The findings can inform music librarians and general-purpose music information systems designers of the needs, requirements, and approaches to enhance music related controlled vocabularies, and improve search engines and online knowledge sharing communities to categorize and provide users with more relevant music information.

2. RELATED WORK
2.1 Music Information Needs, Uses and Seeking
The music information retrieval community examined information needs and seeking behaviors of individuals in "everyday life" in recreational contexts by analyzing music information queries. [6] analyzed 502 music queries posted to Google Answers to learn how users express their music information needs in real-life situations. They identified 10 main categories of the need description types, and the bibliographic metadata category was further divided into 10 subcategories. They also found that users had difficulty coming up with clear descriptions for several of the categories such as date or genre. [8] did a comparative analysis of 107 music queries from the Korean knowledge search portal and 150 music queries from Google Answers to explore what strategies inquirers used when standard access points such as title and creator are not available or unreliable. They found that users experienced difficulty in precisely describing bibliographic metadata, genre, and lyrics, and relied on contextual metadata such as the information about the use of the music sought in other cultural objects or association-based concepts. [7] analyzed 1705 music queries from the Google Answers' music category to develop a taxonomy of expressions of user needs and information features used in queries (e.g. title, date, person's name, etc.).

These studies contributed to identifying the basic types of real-life music information needs but were more focused on the access points that people use when seeking music information.

2.2 Question Types in Social Q&A Sites

Recent studies of social Q&A sites have built on the concept that there are different types of questions in order to better understand user behaviors and community outcomes. [9] proposed two distinct types of questions in social Q&A sites, namely: informational questions which aim to gather information, and conversation questions which stimulate discussion. [10] manually labeled a set of questions posted via Twitter and identified 8 question types, including: recommendations, opinions, factual knowledge, rhetorical, invitations, favors, social connections and others. [11] developed a typology similar to [10] and classified question types within Yahoo! Answers into six types, specifically: factual Information, advice, opinions, chatting, entertainment, and others. [12] utilized a rhetorical framework to develop a typology of question types that fall into six categories, including: Advice, Identification, Approval, Quality, Prescriptive, and Factual. By coding questions drawn from three popular social Q&A sites, they also reported that factual (31%) questions were most frequently asked, followed by identification (28%), advice (11%), and prescriptive (11%) questions. Some researchers also focused on question types regarding a certain domain, including programming [1][2], health [3], and religion [5]. There exist a very limited number of studies regarding music-related question types in social Q&A sites [7][8]. [8] classified 141 Google Answers questions into 11 categories, including: Identify artists/works (32.6%), Seek information (25.5%), Locate works (17%), Acquire lyrics (6.4%), get recommendations (5.0%), Ready references (4.3%), Locate specific version of works (2.8%), Others (2.8%), Seeking scores/tabs (2.1%), Request translation (0.7%), Request research (0.7%). However the questions (queries) in the dataset were mainly related to songs or other music works but didn't cover other music information needs.

3. RESEARCH QUESTIONS

This paper addresses the following questions:

- What are the main discussion topics in Music StackExchange?

- What are the question types (intents) asked in Music StackExchange?

4. STUDY SITE AND DATA COLLECTION

Music StackExchange (http://music.stackexchange.com/) is an online social Q&A site which allows users to post questions about music, provide answers and comments, and evaluate questions and answers among their peers. The site was launched in April 2011, and until now has 13,367 users, 6,225 questions, and 17,359 answers.

This study used the data dump published by Music StackExchange (https://archive.org/details/stackexchange), which has been divided into seven XML documents. For the purpose of this study posts.xml is used, which contains the actual text content of all posts, as well as the view count, favorite count, comment count, score, post type (question, answer, or others), creation date, and ID of the user who created each post. The data dump spans 50 months, from January 2011 to March 2015. After removing other types of posts (e.g. comments to questions or answers) based on

post type id, the final dataset used for this study contains 5,284 questions and 14,821 answers.

5. DATA ANALYSIS

To answer the first two research questions, a random sample of 530 questions (10%) and the associated 1,820 answers was drawn from the dataset. Answers were included in the analysis for two reasons. First, answer posts comprise 74% of the posts in the final dataset, meaning that the majority of text content is located in the answer posts. More importantly, examining all of the question-answer threads could help the researchers understand the interactions between askers and answerers, thus better clarifying the question topics or intents, especially for some recondite music theory or practice questions. Two researchers, who have graduate degrees in musicology, applied open coding approach [13][14] to identify major topic categories by analyzing the titles and body texts of the 530 questions as well as their answers. The researchers independently coded all contents and created a codebook after comparing, discussing, and resolving differences. The researchers then used the codebook to recode all contents and attained an inter-coder reliability of 0.916. The same coding process was conducted in order to identify question types, and the researchers achieved an inter-coder reliability of 0.842. Many questions in the sample contain several interrogative phrases that are distinct in topic or intent. Such compound questions (questions that contain two or more adjacent interrogative sentences, each of which has a separate topic/type, and each of which requires different answers) [12] were coded multiple times in different topic categories or question types.

6. FINDINGS AND DISCUSSION
6.1 Major Discussion Topics

Eight major topic categories were identified, including Instrument/Voice Learning, Music Theory, Sound Recording, Software, Instrument and Equipment, Performance Practice, Music Ability Training, and Creative Process. The number of questions and the question examples (only title) of each category are presented in Table 1:

• **Instrument/Voice Learning**: Questions asking for guidance or solutions to issues for instrument or voice learning.

• **Music Theory**: Questions regarding a specific aspect or aspects of music theory; for example, theories regarding harmony, scale, tempo, mode, counterpoint, key, etc.

• **Sound Recording**: Questions regarding technical or equipment issues that occurred in the sound recording process.

• **Software**: Questions asking for recommendations about software, reviews, or solutions for problems in the use of certain software.

• **Instrument and Equipment**: Questions asking for suggestions or tips for buying an instrument/equipment, or for instrument maintenance, including instrument storage, repair, tuning, and travel.

• **Performance Practice**: Questions regarding performance related issues such as performance preparation and anxiety control.

• **Music Ability Training**: Questions asking for suggestions or tips about how to improve certain music abilities, such as sight-singing or ear training.

• **Creative Process**: Questions about issues concerning creative processes, such as orchestration or improvisation.

Some questions did not fall into a single category. The 530 questions have been coded into 578 items within the eight topic categories: 482 into one category, 48 into two categories. A typical example is a mix of video recording and software questions; users asked for solutions for issues in the use of certain sound recording software, or sought recommendations of software to complete a video recording task. Questions of music theory also tend to overlap with other categories, such as: Instrument/voice Learning, Music Ability Training, or Creative Processes, asking for information about the theoretical background related to issues that occur in learning instruments/voice, training music abilities, and creation.

Table 1. Instance number and question examples in each topic category

Topic Category	Question Examples
Instrument/Voice Learning (242)	• Is it possible for an unamplified acoustic bass guitar to be loud? • How should 3 notes joined with 1 beam line drawn on 5-staff-line?
Music Theory (148)	• What is the theory behind scales? • Can the "music of the spheres" be applied (or projected) to instrumental music?
Sound Recording (20)	• How to record a piano with high quality? • How to sample a certain sound on a song?
Software (28)	• Sight reading by computer: can anyone suggest an usb-to-MIDI interface for Win 7 64-bit? • Is there a way to force Serato Scratch Live to create unique copies of all songs placed in a crate?
Instrument & Equipment (77)	• What Type Of Acoustic Guitar Is This? And Is It Worth Buying? • What is the right way to look after a concert flute after playing it?
Performance Practice (16)	• When should I use a boost pedal in a performance? • How to come over nervousness while stage performance?
Music Ability Training (15)	• Is it possible to learn sight-singing without having learned an instrument? • Tips on identifying intervals by ear?
Creative Process (32)	• Why in the study of counterpoint by johan fux are minor sixths allowed but not augmented fifth? • Writing SATB arrangements so that the bass voice is still audible?

6.2 Question Types

The set of categories about question types that emerged from the analysis, instance number, and question examples are presented in Table 2. The top level of this taxonomy includes five categories, namely: *Seeking Guidance, Seeking Resources, Seeking Opinions, Request Research,* and *Factual Question*. Compared to previous studies about question types in social Q&A sites [3][5], all questions in Music StackExchange focused on seeking information. No conversation, communication, self-expression, or social support questions were identified in this study.

The 530 questions have been coded into 665 items within the five question types: 416 questions into one category, 93 into two categories, and 21 into three categories. Most compound questions are a mix of a factual question and questions from other categories, with that factual question as a starting point. 56 questions are explicitly directed at selected groups, e.g. professional musicians, recording engineers, beginning guitar learners, piano teachers, etc. Overall, 117 questions mentioned supplemental sources (e.g. scores, textbooks, Wikipedia articles, references to other websites, etc.), mostly to provide examples, background, or further illustrations to support their questions.

Table 2. Instance number and question examples in each question type/sub-type

Question Type	Sub-type	Question Examples
Seeking Guidance (289)	Seeking Instruction to complete a specific task (164)	• What is the best way to develop a theoretical approach to practical harmony for guitar? • How long I need to practice piano in general before trying to learn playing blues?
	Seeking Solution for a specific problem (125)	• How can I overcome the fear of performing in front of an audience? • What can I do on the ukulele besides plucking just melody line?
Seeking Resources (50)	Identifying resources (13)	• Is there a piece of music that "inaugurated" Beethoven's middle period, and thus the Romantic era? • Location of ABRSM quote?
	Recommending resources (37)	• Bass-guitar online exercises for not-beginner? • Music software to learn piano on Fantom G8?
Seeking Opinions (93)		• Home recording: Preamp or Dynamic Mic? • Palatino student clarinet compared to a Allora Vienna intermediate one?
Request Research (61)		• What's the difference between sixteenth century counterpoint and eighteenth century counterpoint? • Baroque music composed in the 21st century?
Factual Question (172)		• Is this rhythm called a salsa or samba or something else? • Is it possible to play "Juke - little Walter" on a diatonic harmonica key of C?

The majority of the 530 questions fall into *Seeking Guidance* (289 in total), eliciting a response to fill a knowledge gap in learning, performing, practicing, composing, recording music. The main distinction between the two sub types, *seeking instruction to complete a specific task* and *seeking solutions for a specific problem*, is whether the question is future-focused (asker plans to do something) or past-focused (asker has already made some attempts). Questions from both sub types tend to be highly specific, with an average length of question bodies of 87 and 114 words, respectively. Very few of the desired answers in *Seeking Guidance* are in the form of a statement of fact; the majority of questions did not lend themselves to a simple or straightforward response. Where previous study [3] concluded that a significant proportion of information seeking questions "could easily have been answered by searching the Web with a search engine", most questions here would be very difficult for a novice to answer.

50 questions fall into *Seeking Resources*, looking for practice materials and reference resources, including scores, recordings, books, websites, etc. Two types of resource seeking questions have been found, *Identifying Resources* (13) and *Recommending Resources* (37). The main distinction between those two sub categories is whether the asker already knows which resources s/he wants. An *Identifying Resources* question builds on specific materials the asker has already known or wants to use. In this case the question was posted in order to acquire more details about the resource or simply where s/he could get it. A *Recommending Resources* question is usually associated with a list of materials or a specific learning task; the asker wants others to make recommendations by evaluating and comparing those materials, or to suggest some materials based on the learning task. Requests for suggestions of related materials seem to be a very natural extension or follow-up of a guidance question, thus resulting in overlaps (19) between the *Seeking Guidance* and *Recommending Resources*.

93 questions are identified as *Seeking Opinions*. The distinction between *Seeking Opinions* and *Seeking Guidance* is not always clear-cut. In general the *Seeking Guidance* questions demand more objective, empirical, and explanatory responses, while *Seeking Opinion* questions ask for more subjective, critical, and judgmental reflections. A large number of comparative questions (42) are found in this category, for example which brand of guitar is better or which software is better for home recording.

61 questions are classified as *Request Research*. Questions in this category addressed sophisticated theoretical concepts and usually cannot be answered based only on personal experience or opinion. Some questions (17) expect references to be identified in answers, such as book chapters or academic articles.

7. CONCLUSION AND FUTURE WORK

In summary, this study is an initial effort to contextualize real life, general-purpose music information seeking. The results suggest that Q&A sites are a fruitful resource for identifying users' music information needs, how these needs are expressed, and the intended uses for the information. In Music StackExchange, users' questioning behaviors were motivated by the recognition of knowledge gaps, lack of resources, need for others' opinions, or interest in research issues, spanning different topics. They were particularly interested in finding instructions or solutions to issues that have occurred in a specific learning task. Future research includes applying topic modeling techniques such as Latent Dirichlet allocation [15] to automatically identify music concepts and comparing the results with those identified by expert labeling, as well as validating or expanding current topic categories and the taxonomy of question types by testing them in other music social Q&A sites or music information systems.

8. REFERENCES

[1] Allamanis, M., and Sutton, C. 2013. Why, when, and what: Analyzing stack overflow questions by topic, type, and code In *Proceedings of the 10th Working Conference on Mining Software Repositories*. 53-56.

[2] Treude, C., Barzilay, O., and Storey, M. A. How do programmers ask and answer questions on the web? 2011. In *Proceedings of the 33rd International Conference on Software Engineering*. 804-807.

[3] Bowler, L., J.S. Oh, D., He, E. Mattern, and W. Jeng. 2012. Eating disorder questions in Yahoo! Answers: Information, conversation, or reflection? *In Proceedings of the American Society for Information Science and Technology*, 49, 1, 1-11.

[4] Zhang, Y. 2010. Contextualizing consumer health information searching: an analysis of questions in a social Q&A community. In *Proceedings of the 1st ACM International Health Informatics Symposium*, 210-219.

[5] Cunningham, S. J. and Hinze, A. (2014). Social, religious information behavior: An analysis of Yahoo! Answers queries about belief. *Advances in the Study of Information and Religion*, 4, 1.

[6] Bainbridge, D., Cunningham, S.J., and Downie, J.S. 2003. How people describe their music information needs: A grounded theory analysis of music queries. In *Proceedings of the 4th International Conference on Music Information Retrieval*, 221-222.

[7] Lee, J. H. 2010. Analysis of user needs and information features in natural language queries seeking music information. *J. of the American Society for Information Science and Technology*, 61, 5, 1025-1045.

[8] Lee, J. H., Downie, J. S., and Cunningham, S. J. 2005. Challenges in cross-cultural/multilingual music information seeking. In *Proceedings of 6th International Conference on Music Information Retrieval*, 11-16.

[9] Harper, F. M., Moy, D., and Konstan, J. A. 2009. Facts or friends?: Distinguishing informational and conversational questions in social Q&A sites. In *Proceedings of the SIGCHI Conference on Human Factors in Computing Systems*, 759-768.

[10] Morris, M. R., Teevan, J., and Panovich, K. 2010. What do people ask their social networks, and why?: A survey study of status message Q&A behavior. *In Proceedings of the SIGCHI Conference on Human Factors in Computing Systems*, 1739-1748.

[11] Rodrigues, E. and Milic-Frayling, N. 2009. Socializing or knowledge sharing?: Characterizing social intent in community question answering. In *Proceedings of the 18th ACM Conference on Information and Knowledge Management*, 1127-1136.

[12] Harper, F. M., Weinberg, J., Logie, J. and Konstan, J. A. 2010. Question types in social Q&A sites. *First Monday,*15, 7.

[13] Charmaz, K. 2006. Coding in grounded theory practice. In *Constructing grounded theory: A practical guide through qualitative analysis*, 42-71. Sage Publications, Thousand Oaks, CA.

[14] Strauss, A. and Corbin, J. 1994. Grounded theory methodology: An overview. In *The handbook of qualitative research* pp. 273-285. Sage Publications, Thousand Oaks, CA.

[15] Blei, D. M., Ng, A. Y. and Jordan, M. I. 2003. Latent dirichlet allocation. *Journal of Machine Learning Research*, 3, 993-1022.

PDFFigures 2.0: Mining Figures from Research Papers

Christopher Clark   Santosh Divvala

Allen Institute for Artificial Intelligence
University of Washington
{chrisc, santoshd}@allenai.org

http://pdffigures2.allenai.org

ABSTRACT

Figures and tables are key sources of information in many scholarly documents. However, current academic search engines do not make use of figures and tables when semantically parsing documents or presenting document summaries to users. To facilitate these applications we develop an algorithm that extracts figures, tables, and captions from documents called "PDFFigures 2.0." Our proposed approach analyzes the structure of individual pages by detecting captions, graphical elements, and chunks of body text, and then locates figures and tables by reasoning about the empty regions within that text. To evaluate our work, we introduce a new dataset of computer science papers, along with ground truth labels for the locations of the figures, tables, and captions within them. Our algorithm achieves impressive results (94% precision at 90% recall) on this dataset surpassing previous state of the art. Further, we show how our framework was used to extract figures from a corpus of over one million papers, and how the resulting extractions were integrated into the user interface of a smart academic search engine, Semantic Scholar (www.semanticscholar.org). Finally, we present results of exploratory data analysis completed on the extracted figures as well as an extension of our method for the task of section title extraction. We release our dataset and code on our project webpage for enabling future research (http://pdffigures2.allenai.org).

Keywords

Scalable figure extraction; academic search engine; section title extraction; figure usage analysis

1. INTRODUCTION

Traditional tools for organizing and presenting digital libraries only make use of the text of the documents they index. Focusing exclusively on text, however, comes at a price because in many domains much of the important content is contained within figures and tables. Especially in scholarly domains, authors frequently use figures and tables to compare their work to previous work, to convey the quantitative results of their experiments, or to provide graphics that help readers understand their methods. Therefore parsing figures and tables is a necessary component of any system that seeks to gain a semantic understanding of such documents.

Tables and figures also have the potential to be used as powerful document summarization tools. It is common to get the gist of a paper by glancing through the figures[1], which often contain both the main results as well as visual aids that outline the work being discussed. Being able to extract these figures and present them to a user would be an effective way to let users quickly get an overview of the paper's content. To this end, we introduce PDFFigures 2.0. PDFFigures 2.0 takes as input computer science papers in PDF format and outputs the figures, tables, and captions contained within them.

Our work builds upon the PDFFigures algorithm [5]. The approach used by [5] has high accuracy but was only tested on papers from a narrow range of sources. In this work, we improve upon that method to build a figure extractor that is suitable for use as part of academic search engines for computer science papers. To meet this goal we improve upon the accuracy of PDFFigures [5] and, more importantly, build an extractor that is effective across the entire range of content in a digital library. This requires an approach that is robust to the large number of possible formats and styles papers might use. Particular challenges include handling documents with widely differing spacing conventions, avoiding false positives while maintaining the ability to extract a broad range of possible captions, and extracting a highly varied selection of figures and tables.

Our approach follows the same general structure used in [5] (see Section 3) and employs data-driven heuristics that leverage formatting conventions used consistently in the computer science domain. Following a heuristic approach makes our method transparent and easy to modify [13], which we have found to be important for developing an effective solution to this task.

While our focus is on extracting figures, our method also produces a rich decomposition of the document and analysis of the text. In this paper we demonstrate how this analysis can be leveraged for other extraction tasks, such as identifying section titles. Section titles are important because they reveal the overall structure of the document, and can be a crucial feature for upstream components analyzing

Permission to make digital or hard copies of all or part of this work for personal or classroom use is granted without fee provided that copies are not made or distributed for profit or commercial advantage and that copies bear this notice and the full citation on the first page. Copyrights for components of this work owned by others than ACM must be honored. Abstracting with credit is permitted. To copy otherwise, or republish, to post on servers or to redistribute to lists, requires prior specific permission and/or a fee. Request permissions from permissions@acm.org.

JCDL '16, June 19-23, 2016, Newark, NJ, USA

© 2016 ACM. ISBN 978-1-4503-4229-2/16/06. . . $15.00

DOI: http://dx.doi.org/10.1145/2910896.2910904

---

[1]Throughout this paper we use the term "figures" to refer to both tables and figures along with their associated captions

body text. Section titles can also be used to identify which section figures were introduced in, thereby providing some additional context for interpreting extracted figures. We evaluate our section title extraction method on a dataset of over 50 papers and compare our results against prior work.

In order to evaluate PDFFigures 2.0 against a diverse set of documents, we introduce a new dataset of over 325 computer science papers along with ground truth labels for the locations of figures, tables, and captions within them. We also show how our method was used to extract figures from over one million documents and integrated into the user interface for Semantic Scholar [3], a smart academic search engine for computer science papers. We conclude by using this dataset to study how figure usage has evolved over time, how figure usage relates to future citations, and how figure usage differs between conference venues.

2. RELATED WORK

For a comprehensive survey of previous work in figure extraction as well as relevant open source tools, please see [5]. In this section we review some recent developments in the field as well as exciting applications of figure extraction.

A machine learning based approach to figure extraction was recently proposed in [11]. Their method classifies the graphical elements in a PDF as being part of a figure or not. Elements that were classified as being part of a figure were clustered to locate individual figures in the document. Rather then working primarily with the graphical elements in a document, our approach focuses on identifying body text and then using layout analysis to locate the figures, which allows our approach to not only extract a wide variety of figures but also generalize to extracting tables.

The possibility of being able to semantically parse figures is an exciting area of research, and the figure extraction method of [5] has already demonstrated its ability to facilitate pioneering work in this area. In [12], researchers experimented with an approach to extracting data from line plots. Given a figure, their system uses a classifier to determine whether the figure is a line plot. If the figure is determined to be a line plot, a word recognition system is then used to locate text in the plot and classify that text as being part of an axis, a title, or a legend. Finally, heuristics based on color were used to identify curves in the plot and match them against the plot's legend. Their work used PDFFigures [5] to extract a large corpus of figures from papers published in top computer science conferences. The figures were mined to collect real world examples of line plots. Since PDFFigures can additionally extract the text contained in vector graphic based figures, these figures were also used to provide ground truth labels for the word detection system. Another recent project has similarly found that figures extracted by PDFFigures can be used to generate large amounts of text detection training data for a neural network [4].

Researchers in [14] introduced a novel framework for parsing result figures in research papers. They used PDFFigures [5] to extract figures from computer science papers and subsequently used a classifier to determine the figure type. For line plots composed of vector graphics, heuristics were used to locate key elements of the charts, including the axis, axis labels, numeric scales, and legend. Apprenticeship learning was then used to train a model to identify the lines, and thus the data, contained within the plot. In all these cases PDFFigures provided the critical building block

needed for building tools that are effective on real world figures and papers.

PDFFigures [5] has also been used as a component of PDFMEF, a knowledge extraction framework that extracts a wide variety of entities and semantic information from scholarly documents [15]. In PDFMEF, PDFFigures was used to add figures and tables to the elements PDFMEF is capable of extracting. The authors remarked that PDFFigures is notable for its accuracy and its ability to extract both figures and tables, and concluded by stating "...it[PDFFigures] is arguably one of the best open source figure/table extraction tools."

These projects suggest that the ability to extract figures from arbitrary documents is extremely valuable. With PDFFigures 2.0, we hope to provide a higher quality, more robust tool for researchers wishing to use figures in their work.

The problem of locating section titles within documents has also received attention from researchers, and is addressed in systems such as ParsCit [6], Grobid [8] and SectLabel [9]. All these approaches use machine learning to classify lines of text as being a section title or not. However, we have found that exploiting some natural properties of section titles, such as their use of salient fonts and their location relative to the rest of the document's text, makes heuristic approaches very effective for this task.

3. APPROACH OF PDFFIGURES [5]

Since our work builds upon PDFFigures [5], we review the general strategy employed by [5] in this section. The approach is to focus primarily on identifying the captions and the body text of a document, since these elements are often the easiest to detect in scholarly articles. Once the captions and body text have been identified areas containing figures can be found by locating rectangular regions of the document that are adjacent to captions and do not contain body text. PDFFigures has three phases: Caption Detection, Region Identification, and Figure Assignment.

Caption Detection.

This phase of the algorithm identifies words that mark the beginning of captions within the document. Text is extracted from the document using Poppler [2], and a keyword search is used to identify phrases that are likely to start a caption. False positives are then removed using a consistency assumption: that authors have labelled their figures in a consistent manner as is required by most academic venues.

If the first pass yields multiple phrases referring to the same figure, for example, two phrases of the form "Figure 1", it is assumed that all but one of those phrases is a false positive. If such false positives are detected, an attempt is made to remove them by applying a "filter" that removes all phrases that do not follow a particular formatting convention. Filters are only applied if they do not remove all phrases referring to a particular figure. Filters include (I): Select only phrases that end with a period. (II): Select only phrases that end with a semicolon. (III): Select only phrases that have bold font. (IV): Select only phrases that have italic font. (V): Select only phrases that have a different font size than the words that follow them. Filters are iteratively applied until no false positives are left. If false positives remain but no filter can be applied they fall back on selecting only phrases that start paragraphs, as judged by Poppler's text extraction system.

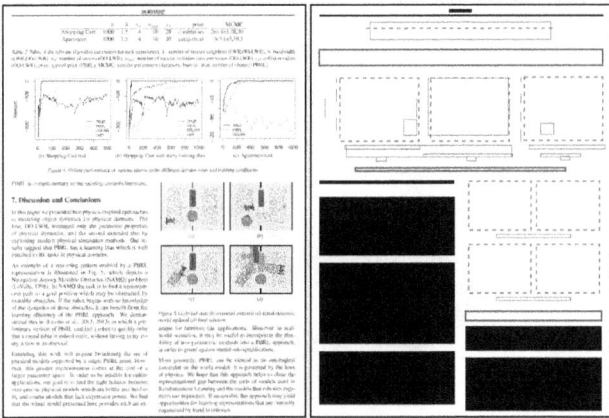

Figure 1: A document page (left panel, from [Scholz et al., ICML 2014]) decomposed into a set of classified regions (right panel). Body text regions are shown as filled boxes, captions and figure text regions as box outlines, and graphical element regions as dashed box outlines.

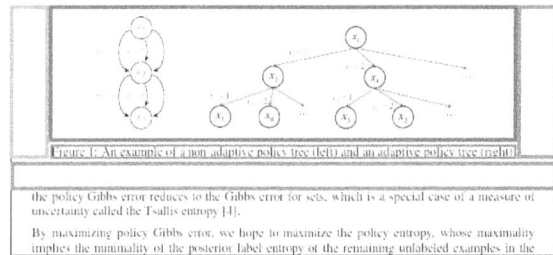

Figure 2: Generating possible figure regions for a caption. For each caption (center blue box), up to four regions are generated as possible figures by maximally expanding boxes that are adjacent to one side of the caption. Page from [Cuong et al., NIPS 2013]

Region Identification.

Region identification decomposes document pages into regions, each one labelled as either caption, graphical element, body text, or figure text. Caption regions are built by starting from the caption phrases found in the prior step, and combining them with subsequent lines of text. The rest of the text in the document is grouped into paragraphs using Poppler's paragraph grouping mechanism. Paragraphs that are either too large or aligned to the left margin of a column are classified as body text, otherwise they are classified as figure text.

Page headers and page numbers are handled as special cases. PDFFigures checks if pages in the document are consistently headed by the same phrase, and if so marks those phrases as body text. Likewise page numbers are detected by checking if all pages end with a number, and if so marking those numbers as body text.

Finally, the graphical elements of the document are located. To do this each page is rendered as a 2D image using a customized PDF renderer that ignores text. The bounding boxes of the connected components in the resulting image are then used as graphical regions of the document. An example of such a decomposition is shown in Figure 1.

Figure Assignment.

The last step is to assign each caption a region of the document containing the figure it refers to. First, up to four "proposal" regions are generated for each caption. Proposal regions are built by generating a rectangular region adjacent to each side of the caption, and then maximally expanding those regions as long as they do not overflow the page margin, overlap with body text, or overlap a caption. This is shown in Figure 2. For two-column papers regions are constrained to not cross the center of the page unless the caption itself spans both columns.

Next, a single proposed figure region is selected for each caption. To do this a scoring function is used to rate each proposed region based on how likely it is to contain a figure. The scoring function gives higher scores to regions that are large and contain graphical elements. To ensure captions are not assigned regions that overlap, they iterate through every possible permutation of how figure regions could be matched to captions. Each permutation is scored based on the sum of the scores of the proposed regions it includes, with regions that overlap given a score of 0. The highest scoring permutation is then selected as the final set of figure regions to return.

An additional complication comes from cases where figures are immediately adjacent, so that they are not separated by any intervening body text or captions. In these cases, proposal regions might get overly expanded and therefore contain multiple figures. To handle these cases, when iterating through permutations, if two proposal regions overlap an attempt is made to split them by detecting a central band of whitespace that separates them. An example of such a figure can be found in Figure 4, second row right column.

4. PROPOSED APPROACH

Our approach builds upon [5] by making crucial updates to its important components. Most of the updates are designed to allow PDFFigures 2.0 to generalize across a wider variety of paper formats. The PDFBox [1] library is used for parsing PDFs.

4.1 Caption Detection

We improve the keyword search of [5] that identifies phrases that might start captions to be effective against more kinds of papers by using a considerably expanded set of keywords. However, naively increasing the number of keywords also increases the number of false positives for each paper. We resolve this problem by adding a number of additional filters to the ones used in [5], such as (I): Select phrases that are all caps. (II): Select phrases that are abbreviated. (III): Select phrases that occupy a single line. (IV): Select phrases that do not use the most commonly used font in the document. (V): Select phrases that are left aligned to the text beneath them. The last filter serves as a general purpose filter for detecting indented paragraphs or bullet points that start by mentioning a figure.

4.2 Region Identification

Our region identification method decomposes each page into caption, body text, figure text and graphical regions as done in [5].

4.2.1 Caption Region Identification

We use a specialized procedure to identify complete captions once the starting line of that caption has been identified. To make our approach robust to the document's choice of line spacing, we compute the median space between lines in the document. Then, for each mention, we construct the caption by adding lines following the mention that are less than the document's median line space away from each other. This works well in many cases, but can fail on documents where captions have been tightly packed against the following text. To add robustness to this problem, we additionally check to make sure new lines have a similar justification to the lines accumulated so far. We also avoid adding lines of text that overlap a graphic region, or lines of text that are of a different font than the previous lines.

4.2.2 Text Classification

Text classification is the process of determining whether blocks of text on each page should be labelled as body text or figure text. Text classification is made difficult by the wide variety of ways text can appear in figures and was a relatively large source of error in PDFFigures [5]. We develop a new set of heuristics to achieve high performance on this task across many kinds of documents. We leverage the insight that the majority of text in a document is body text, and that body text in a document will have a consistent format throughout the document. As a result, text that is formatted in an anomalous way can be assumed to be figure text. We determine the most common font and font size used in the document, the most common line width used, the most common distance between lines and distance between words, and the most common left margins. These statistics are then used in the following heuristics:

1. Graphic Overlap: Text that overlaps a graphic region is classified as figure text.

2. Vertical Text: Text that has a vertical orientation is marked as figure text.

3. Wide-Spaced Text: Text blocks with above median space between its words are marked as figure text. This heuristic is effective for detecting text in tables.

4. Line Width: Text blocks that are several lines long and of the same width as the most commonly used line width in a document are classified as document text.

5. Small Font: Text that is smaller than the most common font size is classified as figure text.

6. Section Titles: Text that is aligned to a margin or centered, starts with a number or is capitalized, and is of a non-standard font or font size, is marked as body text. This heuristic serves to detect section titles, and forms the basis of our section title extraction method (please see Section 7).

7. Margin Alignment: Text that is aligned to a left margin is classified as body text and any remaining text is classified as figure text.

Generalizing to a wide variety of PDFs also requires a more general page header detection method. We have to

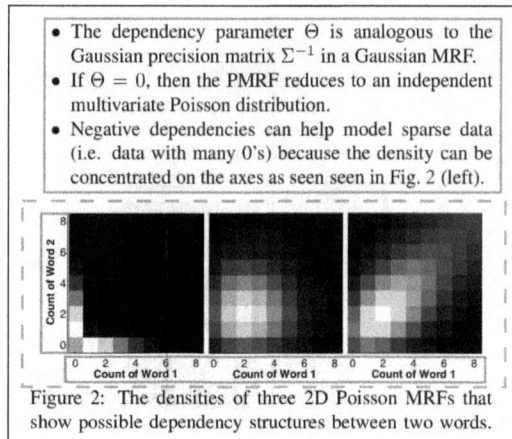

- The dependency parameter Θ is analogous to the Gaussian precision matrix Σ^{-1} in a Gaussian MRF.
- If $\Theta = 0$, then the PMRF reduces to an independent multivariate Poisson distribution.
- Negative dependencies can help model sparse data (i.e. data with many 0's) because the density can be concentrated on the axes as seen seen in Fig. 2 (left).

Figure 2: The densities of three 2D Poisson MRFs that show possible dependency structures between two words.

Figure 3: Using clustering to identify figure regions. In this page from [Inouye et al., ICML 2014] the bullet points were mistakenly misclassified as figure text (box outlines). However clustering elements around the Figure's graphics ensures the bullets are not included in the proposed figure region (dashed line).

handle page headers with inconsistent text, for example page headers that alternate between stating the paper's title and the authors' names, and multiline page headers. PDFFigures 2.0 scans through the first several lines of text on each page. If these lines start above any other text by a sufficiently large margin and appear at the same height on each page they are marked as body text.

4.2.3 Graphical Region Identification

PDFFigures 2.0 locates graphical regions of the document by directly parsing the PDF. Internally PDFs encode graphical elements through the use of various "operators" that draw elements on the page. Operators can be used to draw shapes and curves of different colors or render images embedded in the PDF onto the page. PDFFigures 2.0 scans the PDF and, for each such operator, records the bounding box of the element that operator would draw. To achieve this we make use of functionality introduced in PDFBox 2.0 that provides high level descriptors of the graphical elements being drawn by each operator. The bounding boxes found across the entire page are then clustered by merging nearby bounding boxes, and the resulting merged boxes are used as graphical regions. This approach is much faster than the one used in [5] since it does not require rendering the PDF to a bitmap. This is one of the primary reasons PDFFigures 2.0 is faster than PDFFigures [5] when it comes to locating figures (see Section 6.2).

4.3 Figure Assignment

The final step in our algorithm is to determine the figure regions to return. Possible figure regions are generated for each caption as described in Section 3 (Region Identification). Taking inspiration from [10], where it was found that clustering elements around large graphical regions was an effective way to detect figures, we add a clustering subcomponent to prune the proposed regions. For each proposed figure region, we check to see if a large graphical region is contained within it. If such a region is found, we cluster elements around that graphical region and then remove elements that were not in the cluster. The motivation for this technique is that if a prominent graphical element, like an embedded image or a chart, is part of a figure it is usually the main focus of that figure. Therefore text that is not near that element is unlikely to be part of that figure. This method helps us to be robust to text that was misclassified, for an example see Figure 3.

We make two additional improvements. First, we found that removing proposed figure regions that partially intersect a word in the document was an effective way to remove many incorrect proposals. Second, the region splitting criteria was adjusted to trigger more frequently and prefer splitting regions across the largest band of whitespace rather than the most central band. This allows PDFFigures 2.0 to extract figures that are adjacent to each other in more cases, but also introduces false positives where figures containing whitespace were incorrectly split between nearby captions. We resolve this issue by adjusting our region scoring function to downweight figure regions that were produced using this new splitting procedure.

5. DATASET

We evaluate our approach on two datasets of computer science papers. The first, which we call the "CS-150" dataset, consists of 150 papers from well-known computer science conferences, introduced by [5]. It is composed of 50 papers from NIPS 2008-2013, 50 from ICML 2009-2014, and 50 from AAAI 2009-2014 with 10 papers selected at random from each conference and year. There are 458 labelled figures and 191 labelled tables. This dataset contains papers that are typical of what researchers read, but because it was only drawn from three conferences it does not capture the full range of styles computer science papers have. In order to test our method on a more diverse set of documents, we gather another dataset by randomly sampling papers used by Semantic Scholar [3] that have at least 9 citations and were published after the year 1999. This dataset will be referred to as the "CS-Large" dataset. We used citation and year restrictions to make this data sample more representative of the kinds of documents researchers encounter in search engines. For these sampled papers, we only annotate (and test on) half the pages selected at random, which allowed us to label twice as many papers. We only label up to 9 pages per paper to ensure longer papers do not contribute an overly large portion of the labelled figures and tables. In total, we annotate 346 papers that originate from over 200 different venues. There are 952 labelled figures and 282 labelled tables. Both datasets were annotated by having annotators mark bounding regions for each caption, figure and table using an image annotation tool. These regions were then cropped to the foreground pixels of the page they were marked on, and the cropped regions were used as ground truth labels for evaluation.

6. EXPERIMENTAL RESULTS

6.1 Figure Extraction

We evaluate PDFFigures 2.0 on both datasets and compare its performance to PDFFigures [5], and a figure extraction method developed for the High Energy Physics domain from [10]. Some of the modifications made to caption detec-

Dataset	Extractor	P	R	F1
CS-150	PDFFigures 2.0 (Ours)	0.980	0.961	0.970
	PDFFigures [5]	0.961	0.911	0.935
	PDFPlots [10]	0.624	0.500	0.555
CS-Large	PDFFigures 2.0 (Ours)	0.936	0.897	0.916
	PDFFigures [5]	0.797	0.693	0.741
	PDFPlots [10]	0.678	0.546	0.605

Table 1: Precision (P) and recall (R) on figure extraction.

Dataset	Extractor	P	R	F1
CS-150	PDFFigures 2.0 (Ours)	0.979	0.963	0.971
	PDFFigures [5]	0.962	0.921	0.941
	PDFPlots [10]	0.429	0.363	0.393
CS-Large	PDFFigures 2.0 (Ours)	0.932	0.918	0.925
	PDFFigures [5]	0.804	0.563	0.663
	PDFPlots [10]	0.373	0.317	0.343

Table 2: Precision (P) and recall (R) on table extraction.

tion (see Section 4.1) were ported to PDFFigures, otherwise PDFFigures had a greatly reduced score due to failing to detect certain kinds of captions. Each extractor is expected to return a set of figures for each document. Each returned figure is expected to include a page number, a bounding box for both the figure and its caption, the identifier of that figure (e.g., "Figure 1" or "Table 3"), and optionally the caption text.

We follow the evaluation scheme of [5]. Extracted figures with identifiers that did not exist in the hand built labels, or with incorrect page numbers, are considered incorrect. Otherwise a figure is judged by comparing its bounding box against the ground truth using the overlap score criterion from [7]. A bounding box's score is its area of intersection with the ground truth bounding box divided by its area of union with the ground truth bounding box. We consider a bounding box correct if its overlap score exceeds a threshold of 0.80, otherwise it is marked as incorrect.

Captions are evaluated by comparing the returned bounding boxes with the ground truth using the same overlap criterion, although we also consider captions correct if the text extracted from the ground truth region matches the text returned by the extractor. We use this dual criterion for captions because small differences in the bounding boxes of text extracted from the PDF can sometimes cause correct extractions to be judged as errors by the overlap criterion. Figure regions are usually larger and contain graphical elements, and so are not affected by this problem. We consider an extraction to be correct if both the caption and figure region are correct.

Our approach achieves the highest F1 scores on each dataset for both figures and tables. Relative to [5], PDFFigures 2.0 achieves a 3% absolute gain in F1 on the CS-150 dataset. On the more diverse and challenging CS-Large dataset, we see a much larger gain of over 26.2%. The algorithm by [10], although achieving high results in the domain of high energy physics, did not generalize well to the domain of computer science papers.

Figure 4 shows qualitative results from our method. PDFFigures 2.0 produces very clean extractions in most cases.

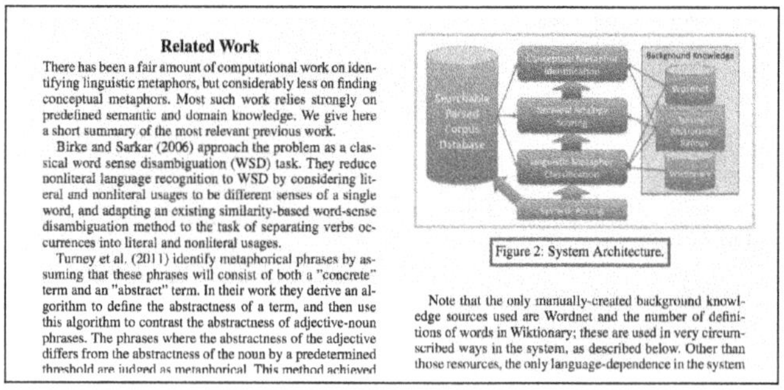

Correct extraction of a figure from [Gandy et al., AAAI 2013]

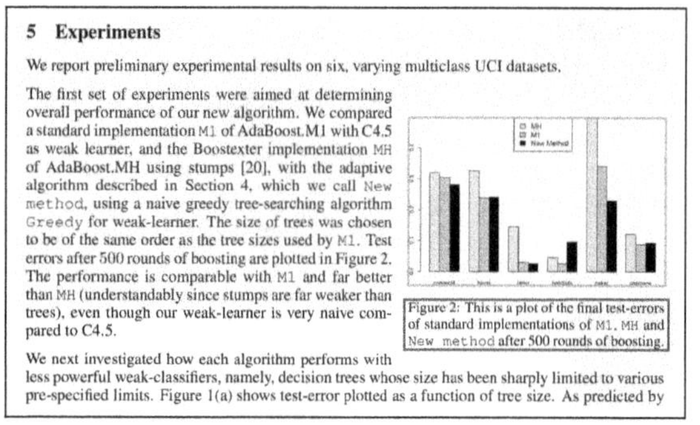

Correct extraction of a figure embedded in text from [Mukherjee et al., NIPS 2010]

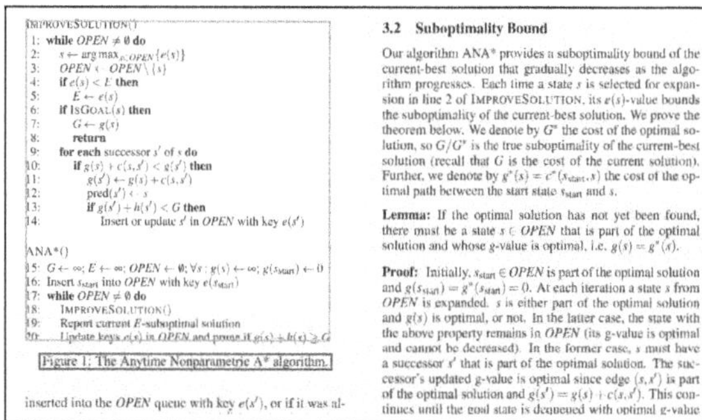

Correct extraction of a figure composed mostly of text [Berg et al., AAAI 2011]

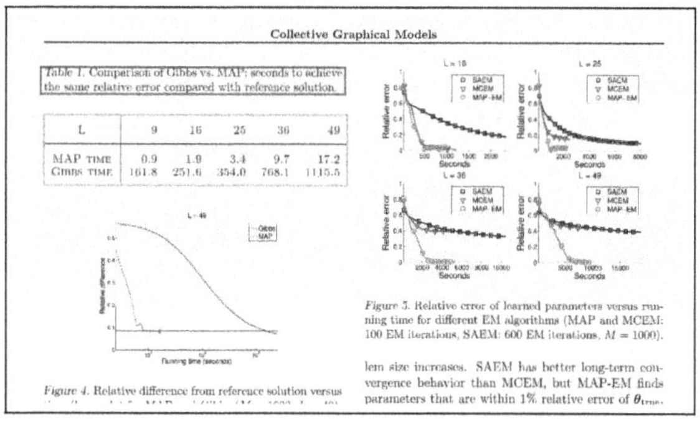

Correct extraction of a table adjacent to a figure [Sheldon et al., ICML 2013]

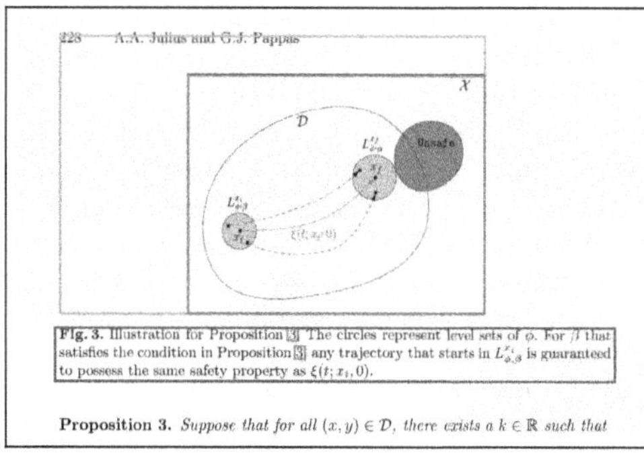

Error caused by mistaking a page header as part of the figure [Julius et al., HSCC 2009]

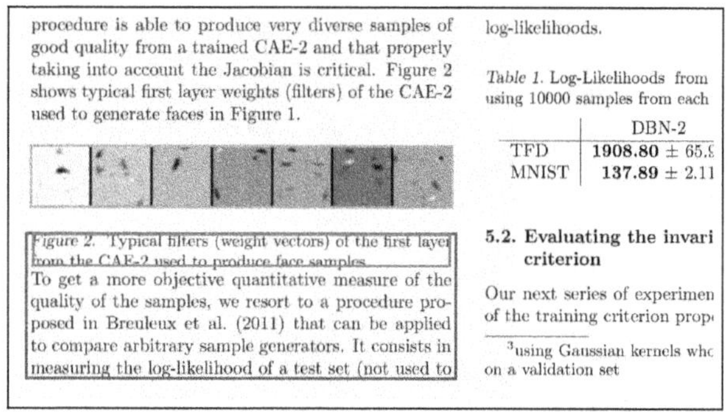

Error caused by including extra text in a caption [Rifai et al., ICML 2012]

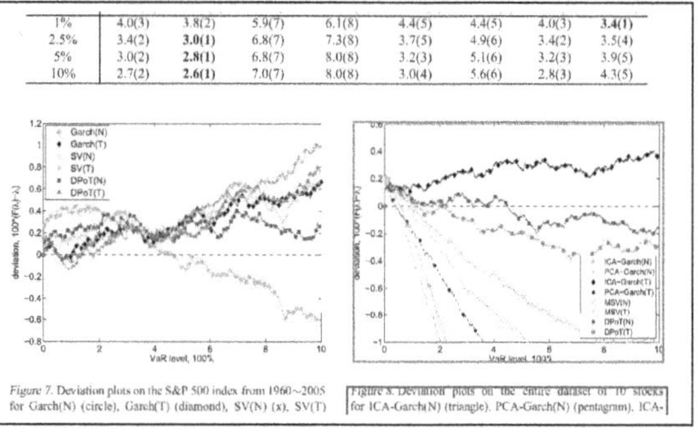

Error caused by inability to separate a 3-way figure layout [Chen et al., ICML 2010]

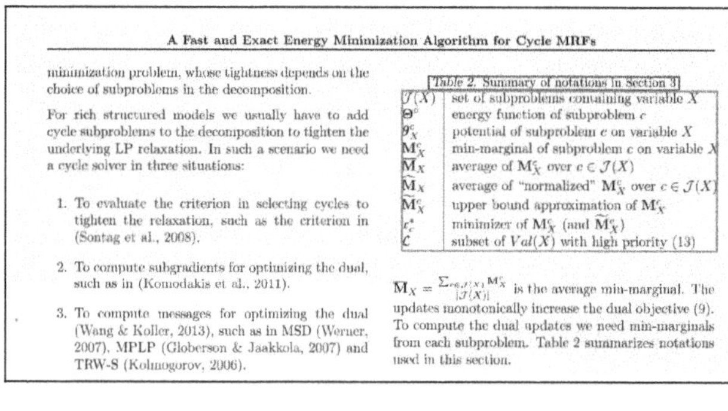

Error caused by mistaking table text as body text [Wang et al., ICML 2013]

Figure 4: **Qualitative results.** Figures that our system extracted are shown in green, captions are shown in blue, and, in the case of errors, correct extractions are marked in red. The top two rows show correct extractions, the third row shows incorrect extractions, and the last row shows figures our system failed to extract.

Dataset	Extractor	Locate	Render
CS-150	PDFFigures 2.0 (Ours)	0.21	2.52
	PDFFigures [5]	0.84	0.93
CS-Large	PDFFigures 2.0 (Ours)	0.27	1.84
	PDFFigures [5]	1.19	1.23

Table 3: Mean number of seconds required to locate, or to both locate and render, the figures in a paper. Our approach is considerably faster at locating figures, but slower when required to render the extracted regions as images.

Dataset	Source of Errors	Count	Percent
CS-150	Text Extraction	10	0.46
	Caption Detection	2	0.09
	Caption Extraction	2	0.09
	Text Classification	2	0.09
	Figure Assignment	2	0.09
	Cropping Error	2	0.09
	Other	2	0.09
CS-Large	Text Extraction	32	0.29
	Caption Detection	6	0.06
	Caption Extraction	15	0.14
	Text Classification	29	0.26
	Figure Assignment	14	0.13
	Cropping Error	12	0.11
	Other	1	0.01

Table 4: Error analysis of our approach. Inaccuracies when extracting text was a major source of error, followed by errors in text classification.

Errors tend to emerge in papers where figures are arranged in complex layouts, or are caused by difficulty correctly classifying blocks of text that do not match the usual flow of body text, such as equations, page headers, or text inside figures.

6.2 Runtime Analytics

We measure our method's runtime performance on both datasets and compare to [5], as shown in Table 3. We measure the time it takes to return the location of the figures in a document, and also the time it takes to both locate the figures and save them as separate image files[2]. PDFFigures 2.0 is considerably faster at locating figure regions. However, rendering the figures using PDFBox [1] proved to be slower then rendering them using Poppler [2], the PDF rendering engine used by [5]. In the future, we might consider using a different library to complete the rendering step in order to remove this performance gap.

6.3 Error Analysis

We perform an error analysis to assess the performance of individual steps of our approach. The analysis is listed in Table 4. We categorize errors (both false positives and false negatives) into one of following six categories. Text extraction errors, referring to errors caused by text not being extracted correctly from the PDF. Caption detection errors, caused by failing to locate captions. Caption extraction errors, where a caption was correctly located but had incorrect

[2]Experiments were run on a single thread on a Macintosh OS X 10.10 with a 2.5GHz Intel core i7 processor.

text. Text classification errors, due to incorrectly classifying body text as figure text or vice versa. Figure assignment errors, caused by generating or selecting incorrect proposal regions during the figure assignment step. Or cropping errors, meaning the returned figure region was approximately correct, but had not been clipped in quite the same manner as the ground truth region. Cropping errors were often due to minor errors in the bounding boxes extracted for text or graphical elements.

Text extraction was a signfiicant source of error, some PDFs that appear correct in PDF viewers yield erroneous text when parsed programmatically. In many cases, other PDF parsing tools beside PDFBox [1], such as Poppler [2], also failed to parse these PDFs, implying these errors stem from how the text was encoded and would be hard to avoid. The next largest source of error was region classification, many errors caused by misclassifying text in page headers, bullet points, equations, or text inside text heavy figures.

7. SECTION TITLE EXTRACTION

While our focus is on extracting figures, the document decomposition produced by our method and our techniques for detecting anomalous text can be valuable when extracting other important elements from documents as well. In this section, we demonstrate how our approach can be extended for extracting section titles. A particular motivation for this task is that section titles can provide additional context when interpreting figures. We have also found open source tools like ParsCit [6] and Grobid [8] to be less effective for this task on our dataset.

7.1 Proposed Approach

Our approach detects lines of text that (I): Are either all caps, or have a font different than the most common font in the document, or are larger than the average font size in the document. (II): Have a uniform font and font size. (III): Have a larger than average amount of space between itself and the line above it. (IV): Have at least one line of text below it. (V): Are centered or left aligned to a column. (VI): Start with a number or are upper case. We remove lines that appear to be part of an equation by removing lines containing many non-alphabetic characters, and we remove lines that appear to be part of a list (ex. "Theorem 1:") by removing lines that end in a number. If any of the remaining lines are consecutively ordered, we have to determine whether they are part of a single, multi-line title or if the following line(s) are a separate section title. Similar to our method of locating captions (Section 4.1), we resolve this problem using the line's justification. If the font and justification of the second line matches the first line the lines are labelled as a multi-line section title, otherwise they are labelled as separate section titles. This phase is run only after the figures and tables have been extracted, since figures and tables often have their own titles which may produce false positives.

7.2 Results

An evaluation of our section title extraction approach was completed on 65 documents, 26 sampled from CS-150 and 39 sampled from CS-Large. For comparison we use the well known PDF parsing program Grobid [8]. We experimented with using all the sections extracted by Grobid, or just the sections that began with a number. We additionally filter

Extractor	Precision	Recall	F1
PDFFigures 2.0 (Ours)	0.946	0.975	0.960
Grobid	0.701	0.818	0.755
Grobid, Numbered Only	0.934	0.670	0.781

Table 5: Precision-recall scores of Grobid and PDF-Figures 2.0 for section title extraction.

out section titles produced by Grobid that were of length one or contained no alphabetic characters. The output of both algorithms was compared against manually extracted section titles. Our results are shown in Table 5. PDFFigures 2.0 shows considerably better performance on this dataset. Many of Grobid's errors are due to extracting bold lines of text that are not section titles, chunking section titles with the line beneath them, or extracting text within a figure or table as a section title. If we only use numbered sections, Grobid's precision becomes much better, although chunking errors still reduce precision while recall drops since many PDFs in our sample do not number their sections. False positives are the primary source of error in our algorithm and are often due to extracting bold lines of text that begin new paragraphs, but were not annotated as section titles.

8. INTEGRATING PDFFIGURES 2.0 INTO A DIGITAL LIBRARY

PDFFigures 2.0 has been featured in a smart online search engine for scholarly computer science documents, Semantic Scholar (www.semanticscholar.org). Semantic Scholar uses state of the art techniques in natural language processing to add semantics to scientific literature search. Integration with a complex, distributed document processing system such as Semantic Scholar requires that our approach is both scalable and easy to integrate into existing codebases. To achieve this goal, PDFFigures 2.0 was implemented in Scala so that it can be easily integrated into JVM based distributed processing environments. We also ensure that PDFFigures 2.0 can be timed out and interrupted if it stalls when parsing a PDF. Using the Apache Spark distributed framework [16], the extractor was run on over one million PDFs. We were able to mine figures from about 96% of these PDFs without errors. In total, 5 million figures and 1.4 million tables were extracted.

The extracted figures are used as part of the user interface of Semantic Scholar. Semantic Scholar features a summary page for each paper, which includes content such as the paper abstract, key phrases, the citations to and from the paper along with highlighted key citations. The extracted figures are shown to the user as thumbnails beneath the abstract. By clicking on an individual figure, users can view it at full scale, or flip through the other figures in the paper. Extracted captions are shown below each figure to provide further context. Figure 5 provides a snapshot of the Semantic Scholar UI. We expect the ability to preview figures in this manner to be especially helpful for mobile users. While it is normally very difficult to view figures on a mobile device, the Semantic Scholar mobile site presents users with a list of the figures in each paper that can be tapped on to be viewed in full screen.

Statistic	Correlation with Citations
Number of Figures	0.0332
Number of Tables	0.0634
Number of Figures and Tables	0.0535
Mean Figure Caption Length	0.0471
Mean Table Caption Length	0.0617
Mean Caption Length	0.0627

Table 6: Spearman rank correlation between figure usage and citations normalized by year and venue. We can observe a slight correspondence between using figures and including longer captions with citations. All values have two sided p-values with $p < 10^{-10}$.

9. EXPLORING FIGURE & TABLE USAGE

As a result of building a database of over 5 million figures (Section 8) we acquired a large collection of rich figure metadata. This metadata gave us an opportunity to investigate figure usage in computer science literature. In this section, we present some of the insights we were able to derive. Note that our analysis is limited to open source documents.

9.1 Figure Usage Over Time

We investigated how the usage of figures has changed over time. A plot of the mean number of figures and tables used in papers during different years can be found in Figure 6. We found both figure and table usage has increased over time, with figure usage undergoing a specially large increase during the years of 1995-2005. The increase in the usage of figures over time provides some empirical evidence that figures have become an increasingly important part of the computer science literature. We also examine how the length of captions has changed over time. The plot in Figure 7 shows that captions tend to be longer in more recent papers, which also suggests authors have devoted more space to presenting and explaining figures in recent years.

9.2 Figures and Citations

We examined how figure usage correlates with the number of citations a paper receives. To control for factors such as time of publication, page count, general topic, and conference prestige, we normalize each paper's citations by conference. That is, we subtract from each paper's citation count the mean number of citations given to papers that were published in the same conference and year. We only make use of a paper if there were 30 other papers from the same conference and year. We then compute the Spearman rank correlation between the number of figures used and citations, and between mean caption length and citations, shown in Table 6. We found that both number of figures and mean caption length has a small correlation with the number of citations a paper receives, and that this trend is stronger for tables than it is for figures. Although these values are small, they are statistically significant and are sufficient to indicate a link between citations and figure usage. One possible explanation is that papers with extensive empirical results, which often leads to higher figure usage, tend to get cited more frequently. Another plausible explanation for this correlation is that leading researchers and authors tend to both use more figures and accrue more future citations.

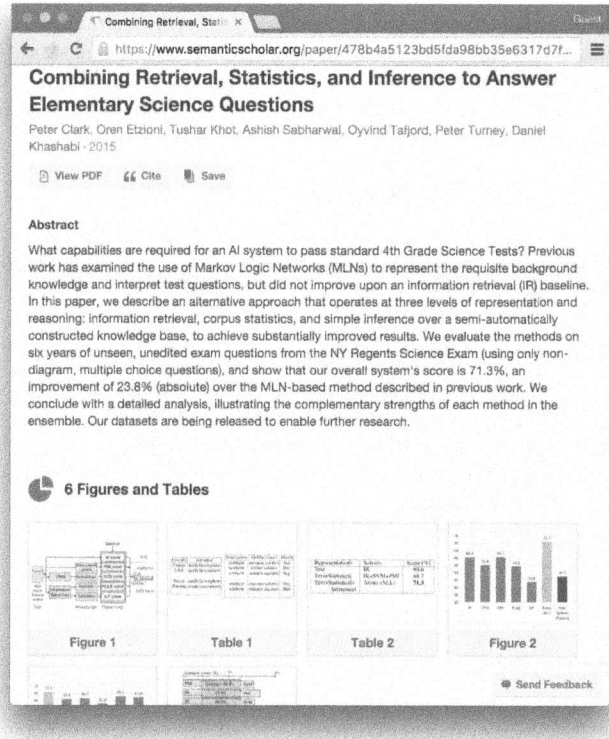

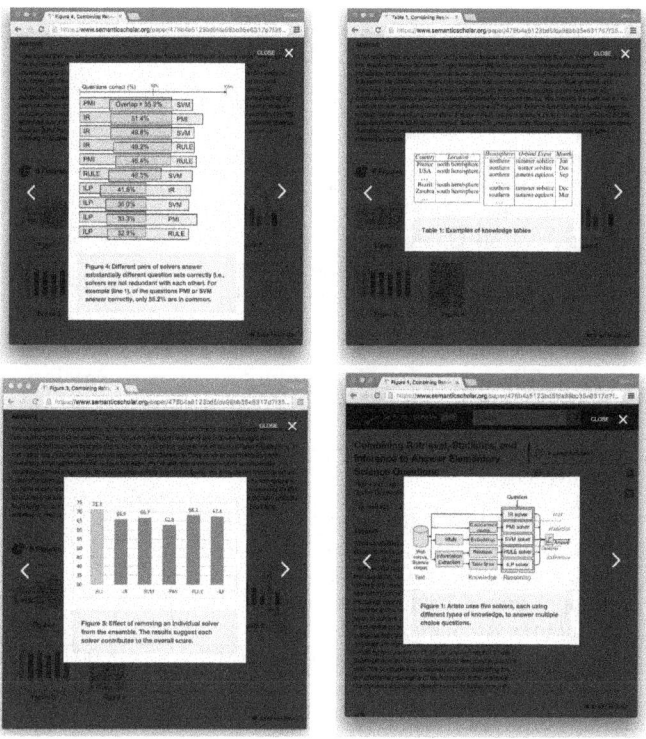

Figure 5: User interface with the extracted figures and tables from Semantic Scholar. Figures are shown as thumbnails below the abstract (left). Users can select a figure to see the full image and its caption (right). This real world example also demonstrates PDFFigures 2.0's ability to extract many different kinds of figures

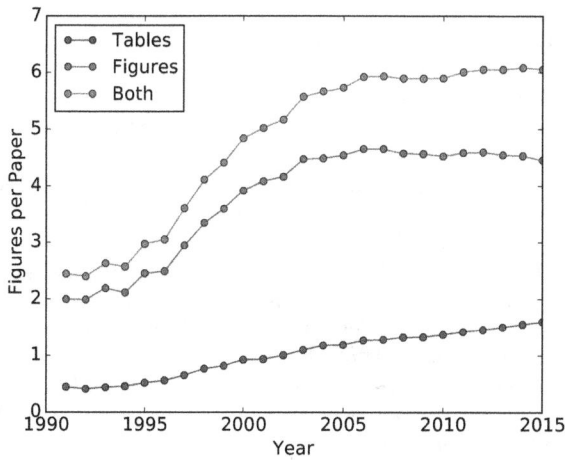

Figure 6: Mean number of tables and figures in papers published in different years. Papers have used more tables and figures in recent years.

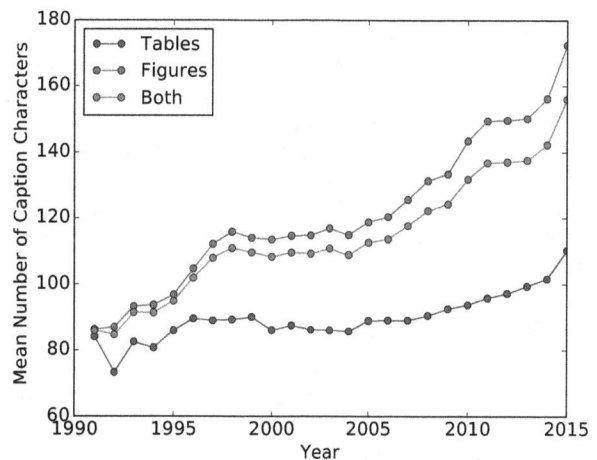

Figure 7: Mean caption length in papers published in different years. Typical caption length has increased over time.

151

Conference	Tables Per Paper
Empirical Methods on Natural Language Processing (EMNLP)	3.86
Conference of Evaluation Information Access Technologies (NTCIR)	3.77
International Joint Conference on Natural Language Processing (IJCNLP)	3.50
Text Analysis Conference (TAC)	3.46
Automatic Speech Recognition and Understanding Workshop (ASRU)	3.44

Table 7: Conferences with the most tables in each paper. This category is dominated by natural language processing conferences.

Conference	Figures Per Paper
International Meshing Roundtable (IMR)	10.23
International Conference on Mobile Systems (MOBISYS)	9.39
Symposium on High-Performance Computer Architecture (HPCA)	8.92
Internet Measurement Conference (IMC)	8.90
European Conference on Computer Systems (EuroSys)	8.06

Table 8: Conferences with the most figures in each paper. Many system conferences can be observed.

9.3 Figures by Conferences

Finally, we investigate how figure and table usage varies between conferences. We compute the mean number of figures and tables used by papers in different conference venues, only including venues for which we had at least 150 documents. The venues with the highest table usage can be found in Table 7, and the venues with the highest figure usage in Table 8. In our dataset, we found that natural language processing conferences dominate the top spots for using tables, an indicator that empirical results and making comparisons has been especially important in that field. The conferences where figures were most frequently used include many system conferences, which tend to both have higher page limits and make frequent use of figures to illustrate circuit or hardware layouts.

10. CONCLUSION

In this paper we considered the challenging problem of developing a scalable figure extraction method that is robust enough to be used across the entire range of content in a digital library. Our contributions include a set of widely applicable text classification heuristics, a clustering mechanism for detecting figure regions, and a novel section title extraction method. Evaluation on manually annotated real world documents and integration with the Semantic Scholar search engine shows the success of our approach. Extracting data from figures and making use of them in user interfaces is an exciting new line of research in digital libraries. We hope that PDFFigures 2.0 will expand upon PDFFigure's success facilitating research in these new fields. While our approach achieves very high accuracy in the computer science literature, future work includes adapting our method to be effective in additional scholarly domains. Combining our heuristic approach with machine learning based approaches is also an interesting avenue for future work.

11. ACKNOWLEDGMENTS

We thank Isaac Cowhey for his help in annotating our dataset. We also thank the Semantic Scholar team for helping with the integration of PDFFigures 2.0.

12. REFERENCES

[1] PDFBox. https://pdfbox.apache.org/.
[2] Poppler. https://poppler.freedesktop.org/.
[3] Semantic Scholar. www.semanticscholar.org.
[4] Text Detection in Screen Images with a Convolutional Neural Network. https://github.com/domoritz/label_generator.
[5] C. Clark and S. Divvala. Looking Beyond Text: Extracting Figures, Tables, and Captions from Computer Science Paper. In *AAAI, Workshop on Scholarly Big Data*, 2015.
[6] I. G. Councill, C. L. Giles, and M.-Y. Kan. ParsCit: An Open-source CRF Reference String Parsing Package. In *LREC*, 2008.
[7] M. Everingham, L. Van Gool, C. K. Williams, J. Winn, and A. Zisserman. The Pascal Visual Object Classes (VOC) Challenge. In *IJCV*, 2010.
[8] P. Lopez. GROBID: Combining Automatic Bibliographic Data Recognition and Term Extraction for Scholarship Publications. In *Research and Advanced Technology for Digital Libraries*, 2009.
[9] M.-T. Luong, T. D. Nguyen, and M.-Y. Kan. Logical Structure Recovery in Scholarly Articles with Rich Document Features. In *IJDLS*, 2011.
[10] P. A. Praczyk and J. Nogueras-Iso. Automatic Extraction of Figures from Scientific Publications in High-Energy Physics. In *Information Technology and Libraries*, 2013.
[11] S. Ray Choudhury, P. Mitra, and C. L. Giles. Automatic Extraction of Figures from Scholarly Documents. In *DocEng*, 2015.
[12] P. M. Sagnik Choudhury, Shuting Wang and L. Giles. Automated Data Extraction from Scholarly Line Graphs. In *GREC*, 2015.
[13] D. Sculley, T. Phillips, D. Ebner, V. Chaudhary, and M. Young. Machine learning: The high-interest credit card of technical debt. In *NIPS Software Engineering for Machine Learning Workshop*, 2014.
[14] N. Siegel. Understanding Charts in Research Papers: A Learning Approach. Technical report, University of Washington, 2015.
[15] J. Wu, J. Killian, H. Yang, K. Williams, S. R. Choudhury, S. Tuarob, C. Caragea, and C. L. Giles. PDFMEF: A Multi-Entity Knowledge Extraction Framework for Scholarly Documents and Semantic Search. In *K-CAP*, 2015.
[16] M. Zaharia, M. Chowdhury, M. J. Franklin, S. Shenker, and I. Stoica. Spark: Cluster Computing with Working Sets. In *USENIX Conference on Hot Topics in Cloud Computing*, 2010.

Comparing Published Scientific Journal Articles to Their Pre-print Versions

Martin Klein
University of California
Los Angeles
orcid.org/0000-0003-0130-2097
martinklein@library.ucla.edu

Peter Broadwell
University of California
Los Angeles
orcid.org/0000-0003-4371-9472
broadwell@library.ucla.edu

Sharon E. Farb
University of California
Los Angeles
orcid.org/0000-0002-7655-1971
farb@library.ucla.edu

Todd Grappone
University of California
Los Angeles
orcid.org/0000-0003-2218-7200
grappone@library.ucla.edu

ABSTRACT

Academic publishers claim that they add value to scholarly communications by coordinating reviews and contributing and enhancing text during publication. These contributions come at a considerable cost: U.S. academic libraries paid $1.7 billion for serial subscriptions in 2008 alone. Library budgets, in contrast, are flat and not able to keep pace with serial price inflation. We have investigated the publishers' value proposition by conducting a comparative study of pre-print papers and their final published counterparts. This comparison had two working assumptions: 1) if the publishers' argument is valid, the text of a pre-print paper should vary measurably from its corresponding final published version, and 2) by applying standard similarity measures, we should be able to detect and quantify such differences. Our analysis revealed that the text contents of the scientific papers generally changed very little from their pre-print to final published versions. These findings contribute empirical indicators to discussions of the added value of commercial publishers and therefore should influence libraries' economic decisions regarding access to scholarly publications.

Keywords

Open Access, Pre-print, Publishing, Similarity

1. INTRODUCTION

Academic publishers of all types claim that they add value to scholarly communications by coordinating reviews and contributing and enhancing text during publication. These contributions come at a considerable cost: U.S. academic libraries paid $1.7 billion for serial subscriptions in 2008 alone and this number continues to rise. Library budgets, in con-

Permission to make digital or hard copies of all or part of this work for personal or classroom use is granted without fee provided that copies are not made or distributed for profit or commercial advantage and that copies bear this notice and the full citation on the first page. Copyrights for components of this work owned by others than the author(s) must be honored. Abstracting with credit is permitted. To copy otherwise, or republish, to post on servers or to redistribute to lists, requires prior specific permission and/or a fee. Request permissions from permissions@acm.org.

JCDL '16, June 19 - 23, 2016, Newark, NJ, USA

© 2016 Copyright held by the owner/author(s). Publication rights licensed to ACM.
ISBN 978-1-4503-4229-2/16/06...$15.00

DOI: http://dx.doi.org/10.1145/2910896.2910909

trast, are flat and not able to keep pace with serial price inflation. Several institutions have therefore discontinued or significantly scaled back their subscription agreements with commercial publishers such as Elsevier and Wiley-Blackwell. At the University of California, Los Angeles (UCLA), we have investigated the publishers' value proposition by conducting a comparative study of pre-print papers and their final published counterparts. We have two working assumptions:

1. If the publishers' argument is valid, the text of a pre-print paper should vary measurably from its corresponding final published version.

2. By applying standard similarity measures, we should be able to detect and quantify such differences.

In this paper we present our preliminary results based on pre-print publications from arXiv.org and their final published counterparts obtained through subscriptions held by the UCLA Library. After matching papers via their digital object identifiers (DOIs), we applied comparative analytics and evaluated the textual similarities of components of the papers such as the title, abstract, and body. Our analysis revealed that the text contents of the papers in our test data set generally changed very little from their pre-print to final published versions; these results suggest that the vast majority of final published papers are largely indistinguishable from their pre-print versions. This work contributes empirical indicators to discussions of the value that academic publishers add to scholarly communication and therefore can influence libraries' economic decisions regarding access to scholarly publications.

2. GLOBAL TRENDS IN SCIENTIFIC AND SCHOLARLY PUBLISHING

There are several global trends that are relevant and situate the focus of this research. The first is the steady rise in both cost and scope of the global science, technology and medicine (STM) publishing market. According to Michael Mabe and Mark Ware in their STM Report 2015 [13], the global STM market in 2013 was $25.2 billion annually, with 40% of this from journals ($10 billion) and 68% − 75% coming directly out of library budgets. Other relevant trends are the growing global research corpus [3], the steady rise in research funding [12], and the corresponding recent increase in open access publishing [1]. One longstanding yet infrequently mentioned factor is the critical contribution of faculty and researchers to the creation and establishment of journal content that is then licensed back to libraries to serve students, faculty and researchers. For example, a 2015 Elsevier study (reported in [12]) conducted for the University of California (UC) system showed that UC research publications accounted for 8.3% of all research publications in the United States between 2009 and 2013 *and the UC libraries purchased all of that research back from Elsevier.*

2.1 The Price of Knowledge

While there are many facets to the costs of knowledge, the pricing of published scholarly literature is one primary component. Prices set by publishers are meant to maximize profit and therefore are determined not by actual costs, but by what the market will bear. According to the National Association of State Budget Officers, 24 states in the U.S. had budgets in 2013 with lower general fund expenditures in $FY13$ than just prior to the global recession in 2008 [8]. Nearly half of the states therefore had not returned to pre-recession levels of revenue and spending.

2.2 Rise in Open Access Publications

Over the last several years there has been a significant increase in open access publishing and publications in STM. Some of this increase can be traced to recent U.S. federal guidelines and other funder policies that require open access publication. Examples include such policies at the National Institutes of Health, the Wellcome Trust, and the Howard Hughes Medical Center. Bo-Christer Björk et al. [2] found that in 2009, approximately 25% of science papers were open access. By 2015, another study by Hammid R. Jamali and Maijid Nabavi [5] found that 61.1% of journal articles were freely available online via open access.

2.3 Pre-print versus Final Published Versions and the Role of Publishers

In this study, we compared paper pre-prints from arXiv.org to the corresponding final published versions of the papers. For comparison, the annual budget for arXiv.org is set at $826,000$ for $2013-2017$. While it is not possible to determine the precise corresponding costs for commercial publishing, the National Center for Education Statistics 2013 found that the market for English language STM journals was approximately $10 billion dollars annually. It therefore seems safe to say that the costs for commercial publishing are orders of magnitude larger than the costs for an organization such as arXiv.org.

Michael Mabe [7] describes the publishers' various roles as including, but not limited to entrepreneurship, copyediting, tagging, marketing, distribution, and e-hosting. The focus of the study presented here is on the publishers' contributions to the content of the materials they publish (specifically copyediting and other enhancements to the text) and how and to what extent, if at all, the content changes from the pre-print to the final published version of a publication.

3. DATA GATHERING

Comparing pre-prints to final published versions of a significant corpus of scholarly articles required obtaining the contents of both versions of each article in a format that could be analyzed as full text and parsed into component sections (title, abstract, body) for more detailed comparisons. The most accessible source of such materials proved to be `arXiv.org`, an open-access digital repository owned and operated by Cornell University and supported by a consortium of institutions. At the time of writing, arXiv.org hosts over 1.1 million academic pre-prints, most written in fields of physics and mathematics and uploaded by their authors to the site within the past 20 years. The scope of arXiv.org also enabled us to identify and obtain a sufficiently large comparison corpus of corresponding final published versions in scholarly journals to which our institution has access via subscription.

3.1 arXiv.org Corpus

Gathering pre-print texts from arXiv.org proceeded via established public interfaces for machine access to the site data, respecting their discouragement of indiscriminate automated downloads.[1]

We first downloaded metadata records for all articles available from arXiv.org through February of 2015 via the site's Open Archives Initiatives Protocol for Metadata Harvesting (OAI-PMH) interface.[2] We received $1,015,440$ records in all, which provided standard Dublin Core metadata for each article, including its title and authors, as well as other useful data for subsequent analysis, such as the paper's disciplinary category within arXiv.org and the upload dates of its versions (if the authors submitted more than one version). The metadata also contained the text of the abstract for most articles. Because the abstracts as well as the article titles often contained text formatting markup, however, we preferred to use instances of these texts that we derived from other sources, such as the PDF version of the paper, for comparison purposes (see below).

arXiv.org's OAI-PMH metadata record for each article contains a field for a DOI, which we used as the key to match pre-print versions of articles to their final published versions. arXiv.org does not require DOIs for submitted papers, but authors may provide them voluntarily. $452,017$ article records in our initial metadata set (44.5%) contained a DOI. Working under the assumption that the DOIs are correct and sufficient to identify the final published version of each article, we then queried the publisher-supported Cross-Ref citation linking service service[3] to determine whether the full text of the corresponding published article would be available for download via UCLA's institutional journal subscriptions.

To begin accumulating full articles for text comparison, we downloaded PDFs of every pre-print article from arXiv.org with a DOI that could be matched to a full-text published version accessible through subscriptions held by the UCLA Library. Our initial query indicated that up to $12,666$ final published versions would be accessible in this manner. The main reason why this number is fairly low is that, at the time of writing, the above mentioned CrossRef API is still in its early stages and only few publishers have agreed to making their articles available for text and data mining via the API. However, while this represented a very small pro-

---

[1]https://arxiv.org/help/robots
[2]http://export.arxiv.org/oai2?verb=Identify
[3]https://github.com/CrossRef/rest-api-doc/blob/master/rest_api.md

portion of all papers with DOI-associated pre-prints stored in arXiv.org, the resulting collection nevertheless proved sufficient for a detailed comparative analysis.

The downloads of pre-prints took place via arXiv.org's bulk data access service, which facilitates the transfer of large numbers of articles as PDFs or as text markup source files and images, packaged into .tar archives, from an Amazon S3 account. Bandwidth fees are paid by the requesting party.[4] This approach only yields the most recent uploaded version of each pre-print article, however, so for analyses involving earlier uploaded versions of pre-print articles, we relied upon targeted downloads of earlier article versions via arXiv.org's public web interface.

3.2 Corpus of Matched Articles

Obtaining the final published versions of articles involved querying the CrossRef API to find a full-text download URL for a given DOI. Most of the downloaded files (96%) arrived in one of a few standard XML markup formats; the rest were in PDF format. Due to missing or incomplete target files, 464 of the downloads failed entirely, leaving us with 12,202 published versions for comparison. The markup of the XML files contained, in addition to the full text, metadata entries from the publisher. Examination of this data revealed that the vast majority (99%) of articles were published between 2003 and 2015. This time range intuitively makes sense as DOIs did not find widespread adoption with commercial publishers until the early 2000s. The data also shows that most of the obtained published versions (96%) were published by Elsevier.

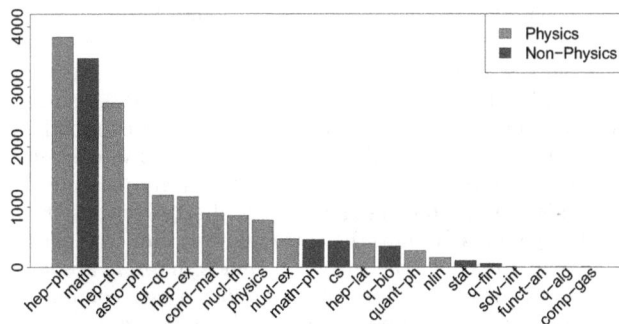

Figure 1: arXiv.org categories of matched articles

The disciplines of articles in arXiv.org are dominated by physics, mathematics, statistics, and computer science. It is therefore not surprising to find a very similar distribution of categories in our corpus of matched articles as shown in Figure 1.

3.3 Data Preparation

For this study, we compared the texts of the titles, abstracts, and body sections of the pre-print and final published version of each paper in our data set. Being able to generate these sections for most downloaded papers therefore was a precondition of this analysis.

All of the pre-print versions and a small minority of final published papers were downloaded in PDF format. To identify and extract the sections of these papers, we used the

GROBID[5] library, which employs trained conditional random field machine learning algorithms to segment structured scholarly texts, including article PDFs, into XML-encoded text.

The markup tags of the final published papers downloaded in XML format usually identified quite plainly their primary sections. A small proportion of such papers, however, did not contain a demarcated body section in the XML and instead only provided the full text of the papers. Although it is possible to segment these texts further via automatic scholarly information extraction tools such as ParsCit,[6] which use trained conditional random field models to detect sections probabilistically, for the present study we elected simply to omit the body sections of this small number of papers from the comparison analysis.

As noted above, the GROBID software used to segment the PDF papers was probabilistic in its approach, and although it was generally quite effective, it was not able to isolate all sections (title, abstract, body) for approximately $10-20\%$ of the papers in our data set. This situation, combined with the aforementioned irregularities in the XML of a similar proportion of final published papers, meant that the number of corresponding texts for comparison varied considerably by section. Thus, for our primary comparison of the latest pre-print version uploaded to arXiv.org to its final published version, we were able to compare directly 10,900 titles and abstract sections, and 9,399 body sections.

The large variations in formatting of the references sections (also called the "tail") as extracted from the raw downloaded XML and the parsed PDFs, however, precluded a systematic comparison of that section. We leave such an analysis for future work. A further consequence of our text-only analysis was that the contents of images were ignored entirely, although figure captions and the text contents of tables usually could be compared effectively.

4. ANALYTICAL METHODS

We applied several text comparison algorithms to the corresponding sections of the pre-print and final published versions of papers in our test data set. These algorithms, described in detail below, were selected to quantify different notions of "similarity" between texts. When possible, we normalized the output values of each algorithm to lie between 1 and 0, with 1 indicating that the texts were effectively identical, and 0 indicating complete dissimilarity. Different algorithms necessarily measured any apparent degree of dissimilarity in different ways, so the outputs of the algorithms cannot be compared directly, but it is nonetheless valid to interpret the aggregation of these results as a general indication of the overall degree of similarity between two texts along several different axes of comparison.

4.1 Editorial Changes

The well-known Levenshtein edit distance metric [6] calculates the number of character insertions, deletions, and substitutions necessary to convert one text into another. It thus provides a useful quantification of the amount of editorial intervention — performed either by the authors or the journal editors — that occurs between the pre-print and final published version of a paper. Our work used the edit ratio calcu-

---

[4]https://arxiv.org/help/bulk_data_s3

[5]https://github.com/kermitt2/grobid
[6]http://aye.comp.nus.edu.sg/parsCit/

lation as provided in the Levenshtein Python C Implementation Module,[7] which subtracts the edit distance between the two documents from their combined length in characters and divides this amount by their aggregate length, thereby producing a value between 1 (completely similar) and 0 (completely dissimilar).

4.2 Length Similarity

The degree to which the final published version of a paper is shorter or longer than the pre-print constitutes a much less involved but nonetheless revealing comparison metric. To calculate this value, we divided the absolute difference in length between both papers by the length of the longer paper and subtracted this value from 1. Therefore, two papers of the same length will receive a similarity score of 1; this similarity score is 0.5 if one paper is twice as long as the other, and so on. It is also possible to incorporate the polarity of this change by adding the length ratio to 0 if the final version is longer, and subtracting it from 0 if the pre-print is longer.

4.3 String Similarity

Two other fairly straightforward, low-level metrics of string similarity that we applied to the paper comparisons were the Jaccard and Sørensen indices, which consider only the sets of unique characters that appear in each text. The Sørensen similarity [11] was calculated by doubling the number of unique characters shared between both texts (the intersection) and dividing this by the combined sizes of both texts' unique character sets.

The Jaccard similarity calculation [4] is the size of the intersection (see above) divided by the total number of unique characters appearing in either the pre-print or final published version (the union).

Implementations of both algorithms were provided by the standard Python string distance package.[8]

4.4 Semantic Similarity

Comparing overall lengths, shared character sets, and even edit distances between texts does not necessarily indicate the degree to which the meaning of the texts — that is, their semantic content — actually has changed from one version to another. To estimate this admittedly more subjective notion of similarity, we calculated the pairwise cosine similarity between the pre-print and final published texts. Cosine similarity can be described intuitively as a measurement of how often significant words occur in similar quantities in both texts, normalized by the lengths of both documents [9]. The actual procedure used for this study involved removing common English "stopwords" from each document, then applying the Porter stemming algorithm [10] to remove suffixes and thereby merge closely related words, before finally applying the pairwise cosine similarity algorithm implemented in the Python scikit-learn machine learning package[9] to the resulting term frequency lists. Because this implementation calculates only the similarity between two documents considered in isolation, instead of within the context of a larger corpus, it uses raw term counts, rather than term-frequency/inverse document frequency (TF-IDF) weights.

---

[7]https://pypi.python.org/pypi/python-Levenshtein/0.11.2
[8]https://pypi.python.org/pypi/Distance/
[9]http://scikit-learn.org/stable/

5. EXPERIMENT RESULTS

We calculated the similarity metrics described above for each pair of corresponding pre-print and final published papers in our data set, comparing titles, abstracts, and body sections when available. From the results of these calculations, we generated visualizations of the similarity distributions for each metric. Subsequent examinations and analyses of these distributions provided novel insights into the question of how and to what degree the text contents of scientific papers may change from their pre-print instantiations to the final published version. Because each section of a publication differs in its purpose and characteristics (e.g., length, standard formatting) and each metric addresses the notion of similarity from a different perspective, we present the results of our comparisons per section (title, abstract, and body), subdivided by comparison metric.

5.1 Title Analysis

First, we analyzed the papers' titles. A title is usually much shorter (fewer characters) than a paper's abstract and its body. That means that even small changes to the title would have a large impact on the similarity scores based on length ratio and Levenshtein distance. Titles also often contain salient keywords describing the overall topic of the paper. If those keywords were changed, removed or new ones added, the cosine similarity value would drop.

Figure 2 shows the comparison of results of all five text similarity measures applied to titles. Since all measures are normalized, they return values between 0 and 1. Values closer to 0 represent a high degree of dissimilarity and values close to 1 indicate a very high level of similarity of the analyzed text. The horizontal x-axis in Figure 2 shows results aggregated into ten bins. The bin with the largest values between 0.9 and 1.0 is located on the far left of the axis followed by the bin with values between 0.9 and 0.8 and so on. The bin with values between 0 and 0.1 can be found on the right end of the x-axis. Each bin contains five columns, each of which represents one applied similarity measure. A column's height indicates the number of articles whose title similarity scores fall into the corresponding bin. The height of a column refers to the left y-axis and is shown in absolute numbers. The red diamond-shaped point in each column indicates the relative proportion of articles in the entire corpus that is represented by the corresponding column. The value of a diamond refers to the right y-axis where the percentage is shown.

Figure 2 shows a dominance of the top bin. The vast majority of titles have a very high score in all applied similarity measures. Most noticeably, almost 10,000 titles (around 90% of all titles) are of very similar length, with a ratio value between 0.9 and 1. The remaining 10% fall into the next bin with values between 0.8 and 0.9. A very similar observation can be made for the Levenshtein distance and the Sørensen value. About 70% of those values fall into the top bin and the majority of the remaining values (around 20%) land between 0.8 and 0.9. The cosine similarity is also dominated by values in the top bin (around 70%) but the remaining values are more distributed across the second, third, fourth, and fifth bin. Just about half of all Jaccard values can be seen in the top bin and most of the remainder is split between the second (25%) and the third bin (20%). In many cases, this metric is registering low-level but systematic differences in character use between the pre-print and final published ver-

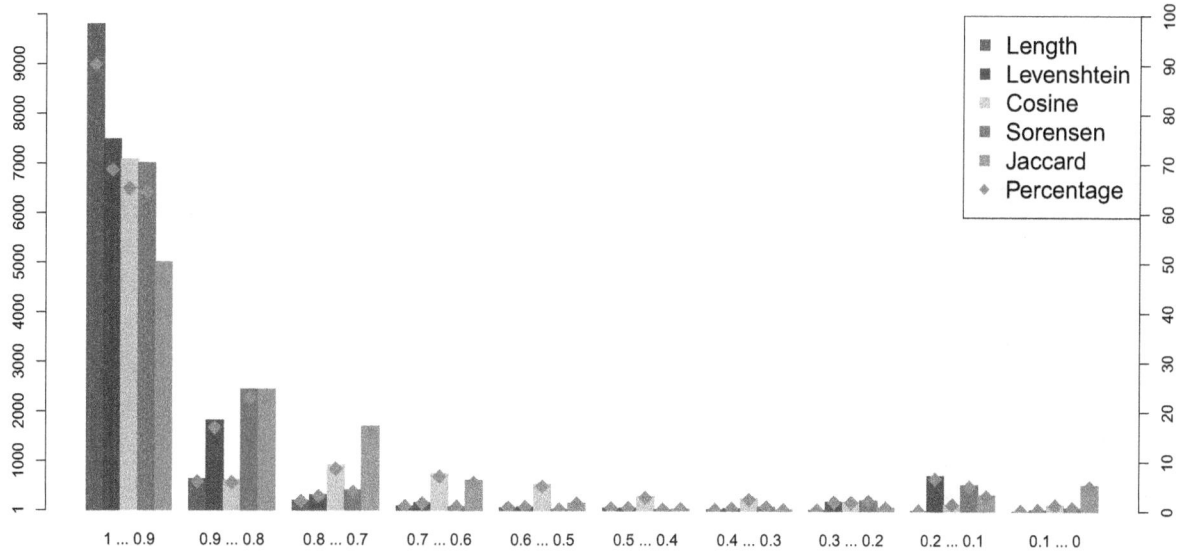

Figure 2: Comparison results for titles

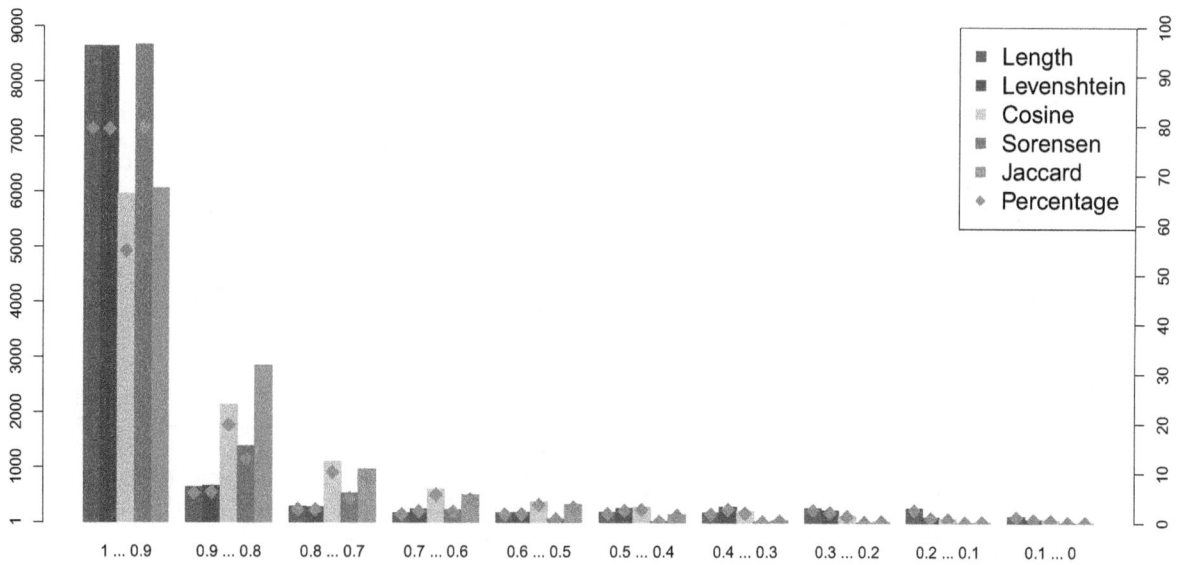

Figure 3: Comparison results for abstracts

sions as filtered through the download methods described above: for example, a pre-print may consistently use em-dashes (–), whereas the published version uses only hyphens (-). This sensitivity of the Jaccard similarity score to subtle changes in the unique character sets in each text is apparent for other sections as well.

The results of this comparison, in particular the fact that the majority of values fall between 0.9 and 1, provide very strong indicators that titles of scholarly articles do not change noticeably between the pre-print and the final published version. Even though Figure 2 shows a small percentage of titles exhibiting a rather low level of similarity, with Levenshtein and Sørensen values between 0.1 and 0.2, the overall similarity of titles is very high.

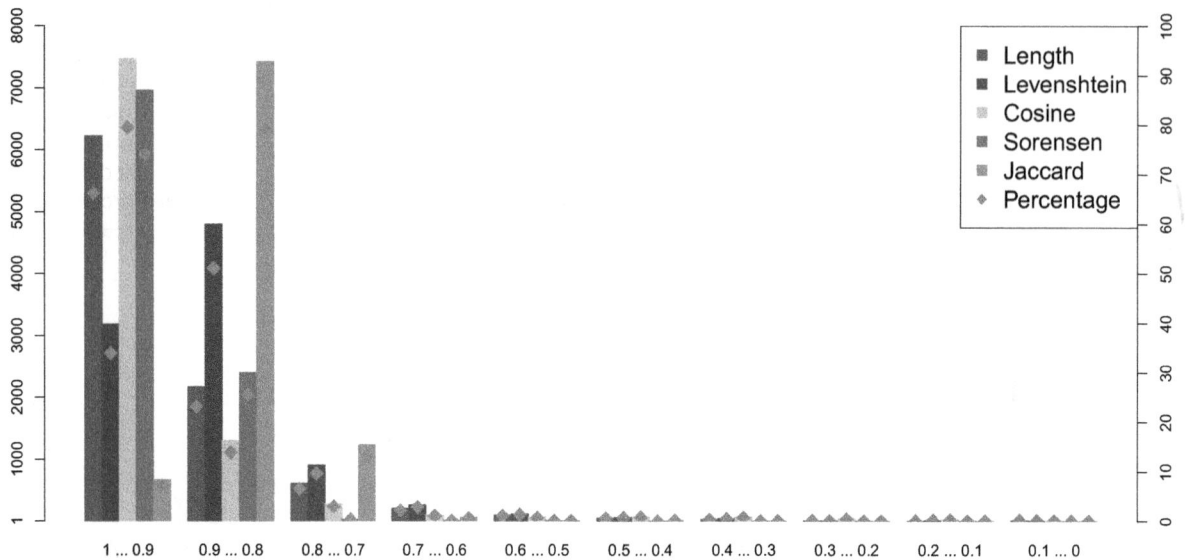

Figure 4: Comparison results for body sections

5.2 Abstract Analysis

The next section we compared was the papers' abstracts. An abstract can be seen as a very short version of the paper. It often gives a brief summary of the problem statement, the methods applied, and the achievements of the paper. As such, an abstract usually is longer than the paper's title (in number of characters) and provides more context. Intuitively, it seems probable that we would find more editorial changes in longer sections of the pre-print version of an article compared to its final published version. However, a potentially increased number of editorial changes alone does not necessarily prove dissimilarity between longer texts. We expect similarity measures based on semantic features such as cosine similarity to be more reliable here.

Figure 3 shows the comparative results for all abstracts. The formatting of the graph is the same as previously described for Figure 2. To our surprise, the figure is dominated by the high frequency of values between 0.9 and 1 across all similarity measures. More than 8,500 abstracts (about 80%) have such scores for their length ratio, Levenshtein distance, and Sørensen index. 6% of the remaining length ratio and Levenshtein distance values as well as 13% of the remaining Sørensen index values fall between 0.8 and 0.9. The remaining pairs are distributed across all other bins. The cosine similarity and Jaccard index values are slightly more distributed. About 5,000 abstracts (55%) fall into the top bin, 20% and 26% into the second, and 10% and 9% into the third bin, respectively.

Not unlike our observations for titles, the algorithms applied to abstracts predominantly return values that indicate a very high degree of similarity. Figure 3 shows that more than 90% of abstracts score 0.6 or higher, regardless of the text similarity measure applied. It is also worth pointing out that there is no noticeable increased frequency of val-

ues between 0.1 and 0.2 as previously seen when comparing titles (Figure 2).

5.3 Body Analysis

The next section we extracted from our corpora of scholarly articles and subjected to the text similarity measures is the body of the text. This excludes the title, the author(s), the abstract, and the reference section. This section is, in terms of number of characters, the longest of our three analyzed sections. We therefore consider scores resulting from algorithms based on editorial changes to be less informative for this comparison. In particular, a finding such as "The body of article A_2 contains 10% fewer characters than the body of article A_1" would not provide any reliable indicators of the similarity between the two articles A_1 and A_2. Algorithms based on semantic features, such as the cosine similarity, on the other hand, provide stronger indicators of the similarity of the compared long texts. More specifically, cosine values are expected to be rather low for very dissimilar bodies of articles.

The results of this third comparison can be seen in Figure 4. The height of the bar representing the cosine similarity is remarkable. Almost 7,500 body sections of our compared scholarly articles, which is equivalent to 80% of the entire corpus, have a cosine score that falls in the top bin with values between 0.9 and 1. 14% have a cosine value that falls into the second and 3% fall into the third bin. Values of the Sørensen index show a very similar pattern with 74% in the top bin and 25% in the second. In contrast, only 7% of articles' bodies have Jaccard index values falling into the top bin. The vast majority of these scores, 79%, are between 0.8 and 0.9 and another 13% are between 0.7 and 0.8. It is surprising to see that even the algorithms based on editorial changes provide scores mostly in the top bins. Of the length ratio scores, 66% fall in the top bin and 23% in the second bin. The Levenshtein distance shows the opposite proportions: 34% are in the top and 51% belong to the second bin.

The dominance of bars on the left hand side of Figure 4 provides yet more evidence that pre-print articles of our corpus and their final published version do not exhibit many features that could distinguish them from each other, neither on the editorial nor on the semantic level. 95% of all analyzed body sections have a similarity score of 0.7 or higher in any of the applied similarity measures.

5.4 Publication Dates

The above results provide strong indicators that there is hardly any noticeable difference between the pre-print version of a paper and its final published version. However, the results do not show which version came first. In other words, consider the two possible scenarios:

1. Papers, after having gone through a rigorous peer review process, are published by a commercial publisher first and then, as a later step, uploaded to arXiv.org. In this case the results of our text comparisons described above would not be surprising, as the pre-print versions would merely be a mirror of the final published ones. There would be no apparent reason to deny publishers all credit for peer review, copyediting, and the resulting publication quality of the articles.

2. Papers are uploaded to arXiv.org first and later published by a commercial publisher. If this scenario is dominant, our comparison results would suggest that any changes in the text due to publisher-initiated copyediting are hardly noticeable.

Figure 6 shows the order of appearance in arXiv.org versus commercial venues for all articles in our corpus, comparing the publication date of each article's final published version to the date of its latest upload to arXiv.org. Red bars indicate the amount of articles (absolute values on the y-axis) that were first upload to arXiv.org, and blue bars stand for articles published by a commercial publisher before they appeared in arXiv.org. Each pair of bars is binned into a time range, shown on the x-axis, that indicates approximately how many days passed between the article's appearance in the indicated first venue and its appearance in the second venue. Figure 6 show clear evidence that the vast majority of our articles (90%) were published in arXiv.org first. Therefore our argument for the second scenario holds. We can only speculate about the causes of certain time windows' prominence within the distribution, but it may be related to turn-around times of publishers between submission and eventual publication.

6. VERSIONS OF ARTICLES FROM THE ARXIV.ORG CORPUS

About 35% of all 1.1 million papers in arXiv.org have more than one version. A new version is created when, for example, an author makes a change to the article and re-submits it to arXiv.org. The evidence of Figure 6 shows that the majority of the latest versions in arXiv.org were still uploaded prior to the publication of its final published version in a commercial venue. However, we were motivated to eliminate all doubt and hence decided to repeat our comparisons

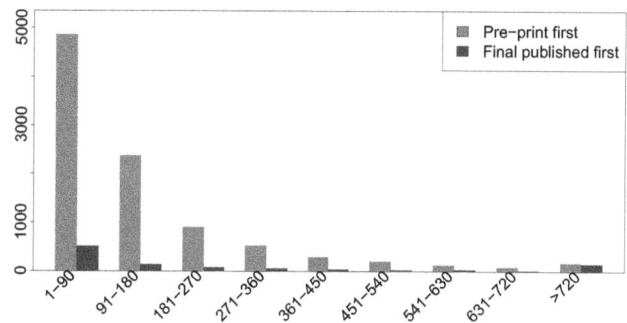

Figure 6: Numbers of articles first appearing in the specified venue, given the date of the last pre-print upload and the commercial publication date, binned by the number of days between them

of the text contents of paper titles, abstracts, and body sections using the earliest versions of the articles from arXiv.org only. The underlying assumption is that those versions were uploaded to arXiv.org even earlier (if the authors uploaded more than one version) and hence are even less likely to exhibit changes due to copyediting by a commercial publisher. It follows, then, that if the comparisons of these earlier pre-print texts to their published versions show substantially greater divergences, then it is possible that more of these changes are the result of publisher-initiated copyediting.

Our corpus of pre-print and final published papers matched by their DOIs and available via UCLA's journal subscriptions exhibits a higher ratio of papers with more than one version in arXiv.org than is found in the full set of articles available from arXiv.org. 58% of the papers we compared had more than one version, 39% had exactly two, and 13% had exactly three versions; whereas only 35% of all articles uploaded to arXiv.org have more than one version. We applied our five similarity measures (see Section 4) to quantify the similarity between the first version of all articles and their final published versions. Rather than repeating the histograms of Figures 2, 3, and 4, we show the divergences from these histograms only. Figure 5 displays a positive/negative barplot that represents the differences between our first comparison and this one.

Figure 5a depicts the deltas of the title comparisons. The top bin contains only negative bars, meaning that our second comparison, using the earliest uploaded versions only, returned fewer similarity scores in that bin. The number of title comparisons in the top bin for the length ratio, for example, dropped by almost 1,000 and the number in the top bin for the Levenshtein ratio dropped by 800. While these numbers may at first seem dramatic, the bigger picture shows that the decrease is not that significant. We merely see a 10% drop in the top bin for length ratio and Levenshtein, a 9% drop for the Sørensen and Jaccard index, and a drop of less than 6% for the cosine similarity. The second bin shows positive bars for the length ratio and cosine similarity, which means that our comparison using the first uploaded version to arXiv.org returned more values for those measures in this bin relative to our comparison using the latest uploaded version. The absolute counts for the following bins decrease relative to our initial comparison, and it is difficult to interpret the corresponding shifts in their proportional values when they are plotted visually (as red

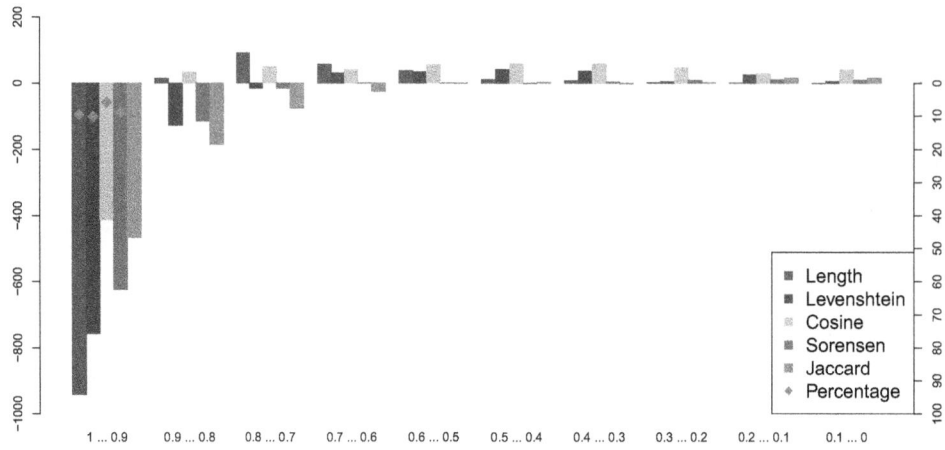

(a) Title deltas

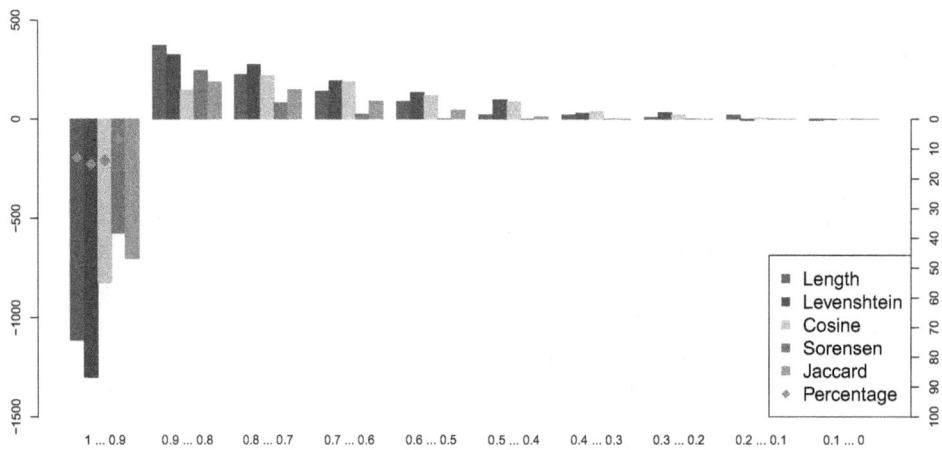

(b) Abstract deltas

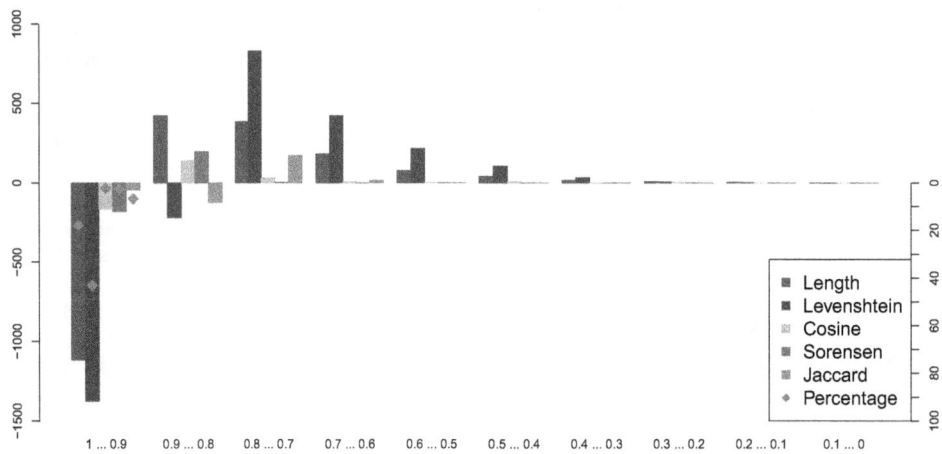

(c) Body deltas

Figure 5: Deltas of paper section comparison bins for the five similarity metrics in the legend, showing the differences in the bin values relative to those in Figures 2, 3, and 4

Table 1: Deltas of the proportions of paper titles in the entire corpus that belong to the specified bins for each comparison metric, giving the differences between the proportional values (red diamonds) in Figure 2 and those generated when each article's first uploaded version in arXiv.org is considered (shown in Figure 5a)

Measure	Bin 1	Bin 2	Bin 3	Bin 4	Bin 5	Bin 6	Bin 7	Bin 8	Bin 9	Bin 10
len	-9.61	2.37	45.73	61.29	61.29	20.00	32.00	9.52	10.00	-50.00
lev	-10.12	-7.04	-4.81	19.50	43.04	72.41	68.52	2.60	3.48	23.08
cos	-5.84	5.36	5.43	5.47	10.15	20.27	22.75	24.87	21.01	33.33
sor	-8.91	-4.70	-3.64	1.25	0.00	-3.45	4.71	4.17	2.04	14.93
jac	-9.34	-7.62	-4.47	-4.08	-0.66	7.50	-8.00	2.82	4.88	3.02

Table 2: Proportional deltas for abstracts (shown in Figure 5b)

Measure	Bin 1	Bin 2	Bin 3	Bin 4	Bin 5	Bin 6	Bin 7	Bin 8	Bin 9	Bin 10
len	-12.87	58.95	79.36	83.23	51.46	12.09	12.36	3.08	7.25	-5.13
lev	-15.08	49.39	100.73	81.43	74.30	38.34	10.49	14.68	-6.25	-3.64
cos	-13.86	6.85	19.91	31.66	30.69	31.54	18.84	15.67	13.04	-2.17
sor	-6.63	17.89	15.55	10.53	-1.56	-5.26	0	0	0	0
jac	-11.60	6.55	15.45	17.84	13.62	8.22	-5.13	0	0	0

diamonds). We instead detail these relative changes between our two sets of comparisons in Table 1.

The numbers for the abstract comparison are fairly similar. Figure 5b shows a drop for all measures in the top bin and corresponding gains in the following bins. However, the relative numbers again are not dramatic. Table 2 lists all relative differences.

The results for the body comparison are interesting. As shown in Figure 5c, we observe a 18% drop in length ratio and even a 43% drop in Levenshtein scores for the top bin. However, cosine scores drop by only 2% in the top bin. Given that in our first body comparison (see Section 5.3) 80% of cosine scores belonged in the top bin, the drop in this second body comparison is almost negligible. The detailed list of relative differences can be found in Table 3.

These results confirm our initial assessment that very little difference can be found between pre-print articles and their final published versions. Even more so, these findings strengthen our argument as they show that the difference between the earliest possible pre-print version and the final published one seems insignificant, given the similarity measures we applied to our corpus.

6.1 Publication Dates of Versions

The scenarios discussed in Section 5.4 with respect to the question of whether an article was uploaded to arXiv.org before it appeared in a commercial venue are valid for this comparison as well. Figure 7 mirrors the concept of Figure 6 and shows the number of earliest pre-print versions uploaded to arXiv.org first in red and the final published versions appearing first represented by the blue bars. As expected, the amount of pre-print versions published first increased and now stands at 95% as shown in Figure 7 (compared to 90% shown in Figure 6). Our argument for the second scenario described above is therefore strongly supported when considering the earliest uploaded versions of pre-prints.

7. DISCUSSION AND FUTURE WORK

The results outlined in this paper are from a preliminary study on the similarity of pre-print articles to their final published counterparts. There are many areas where this

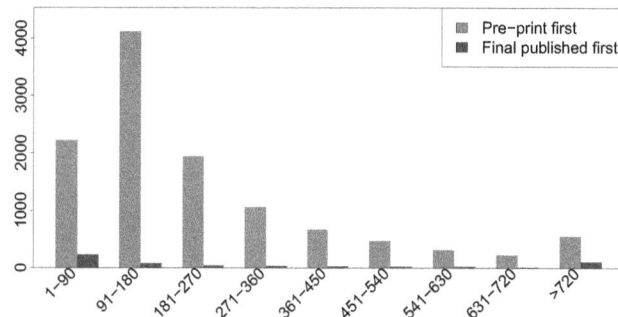

Figure 7: Numbers of articles first appearing in the specified venue, given the date of the first pre-print upload and the commercial publication date, binned by the number of days between them

study could be improved and enhanced. One limitation to this work is the focus on arXiv.org as the sole corpus of pre-print articles. As a result, all of the articles are from a relatively limited slice of the STM domain — specifically, physics, mathematics, statistics, and computer science, as shown in Figure 1. Expanding this line of experiments to other domains such as the biological sciences, humanities, social sciences, and economics might return different results, as the review and editorial practices in other disciplines can vary considerably. As part of our future work, we are planning to conduct this experiment again with articles from the RePEc.org corpus (economics) and from bioRxiv.org (biology), for example.

The matching of a pre-print version of an article to its final published version was done by means of the article's DOI. While this is an obvious choice for a paper identifier, by only relying on DOIs we very likely missed out on other matching articles. For future experiments, we will include the paper's title and author(s) in the matching process. Note also that we could only match articles that we have access to via the UCLA Library's serial subscriptions. It might be worth expanding the matching process to a collaborat-

Table 3: Proportional deltas for body sections (shown in Figure 5c)

Measure	Bin 1	Bin 2	Bin 3	Bin 4	Bin 5	Bin 6	Bin 7	Bin 8	Bin 9	Bin 10
len	-17.93	19.43	62.58	90.05	79.38	85.11	60.00	88.89	133.33	0
lev	-43.14	-4.61	91.59	158.65	183.76	177.97	74.42	83.33	14.29	0
cos	-2.25	10.62	10.79	7.37	-1.64	10.00	-3.03	11.11	-4.76	0
sor	-2.63	8.14	3.85	0	0	0	0	0	0	0
jac	-6.90	-1.70	13.87	25.00	0	0	0	0	0	0

ing organization with ideally complementary subscriptions to maximize access to full text articles.

One typical article section we have not analyzed as part of this research is the references section. Given publishers' claims of adding value to this section of a scholarly article, we are motivated to see whether we can detect any significant changes between pre-prints and final published versions there. Similarly, we have not thoroughly investigated changes in the author sections. We anticipate author movement, such as authors being added, being removed, and having their rank in the list of authors changed — although changes in author order due to publishers' name alphabetization policies must be considered as well. Initial experiments in this domain have proven difficult to interpret, as author names are provided in varying formats and normalization is not trivial.

Another angle of future work is to investigate the correlation between pre-prints and final published versions' degree of similarity and measured usage statistics such as download numbers and the articles' impact factor values. When arguing that the differences between pre-print articles and their final published versions are insignificant, factoring in usage statistics and "authority values" can further inform decisions about spending on serial subscriptions.

8. CONCLUSIONS

This study is motivated by academic publishers' claims of the value they add to scholarly articles by copyediting and making further enhancements to the text. We present results from our preliminary study to investigate the textual similarity of scholarly pre-prints and their final published counterparts. We apply five different similarity measures to individual extracted sections from the articles' full text contents and analyze their results. We have shown that, within the boundaries of our corpus, there are no significant differences in aggregate between pre-prints and their corresponding final published versions. In addition, the vast majority of pre-prints (90% - 95%) are published by the open access pre-print service first and later by a commercial publisher. Given the fact of flat or even shrinking library, college, and university budgets, our findings provide empirical indicators that should inform discussions about commercial publishers' value proposition in scholarly communication and have the potential to influence higher education and academic and research libraries' economic decisions regarding access to scholarly publications.

9. REFERENCES

[1] B.-C. Björk. Have the "mega-journals" reached the limits to growth? *PeerJ*, 3:e981, 2015.

[2] B.-C. Björk, P. Welling, M. Laakso, P. Majlender, T. Hedlund, and G. Guðnason. Open access to the scientific journal literature: Situation 2009. *PLoS ONE*, 5(6):e11273, 2009.

[3] L. Bornmann and R. Mutz. Growth rates of modern science: A bibliometric analysis based on the number of publications and cited references. *Journal of the Association for Information Science and Technology*, 2015.

[4] P. Jaccard. *Etude comparative de la distribution florale dans une portion des Alpes et du Jura*. Impr. Corbaz, 1901.

[5] H. R. Jamali and M. Nabavi. Open access and sources of full-text articles in Google Scholar in different subject fields. *Scientometrics*, 105(3):1635–1651, 2015.

[6] V. I. Levenshtein. Binary Codes Capable of Correcting Deletions, Insertions and Reversals. *Soviet Physics Doklady*, 10(8):707–710, 1966.

[7] M. Mabe. (Electronic) Journal Publishing. *The E-Resource Management Handbook*, 2006.

[8] Office of Management and Budget (U.S.). *Fiscal Year 2014 Analytical Perspectives: Budget of the U.S. Government*. Office of Management and Budget, 2013.

[9] T. Pang-Ning, M. Steinbach, and V. Kumar. *Introduction to Data Mining*. Pearson Addison Wesley, 2006.

[10] M. F. Porter. An Algorithm for Suffix Stripping. *Electronic Library and Information Systems*, 14(3):130–137, 1980.

[11] T. Sørensen. A Method of Establishing Groups of Equal Amplitude in Plant Sociology Based on Similarity of Species and its Application to Analyses of the Vegetation on Danish Commons. *Biol. Skr.*, 5:1–34, 1948.

[12] University of California. Accountability Report 2015. http://accountability.universityofcalifornia.edu/2015/chapters/chapter-9.html.

[13] M. Ware and M. Wabe. *The STM Report - An Overview of Scientific and Scholarly Journal Publishing*. International Association of Scientific, Technical and Medical Publishers, 2015.

Extracting Academic Genealogy Trees from the Networked Digital Library of Theses and Dissertations*

Wellington Dores   Fabrício Benevenuto   Alberto H. F. Laender

Department of Computer Science
Universidade Federal de Minas Gerais
Belo Horizonte, MG, Brazil
{wellingtond, fabricio, laender}@dcc.ufmg.br

ABSTRACT

Along the history, many researchers provided remarkable contributions to science, not only advancing knowledge but also in terms of mentoring new scientists. Currently, identifying and studying the formation of researchers over the years is a challenging task as current repositories of theses and dissertations are cataloged in a decentralized way through many local digital libraries. In this paper, we give a first step towards building a large repository that records the academic genealogy of researchers across fields and countries. We crawled data from the Networked Digital Library of Theses and Dissertations (NDLTD) and develop a framework to extract academic genealogy trees from this data and provide a series of analyses that describe the main properties of the academic genealogy trees. Our effort identified interesting findings related to the structure of academic formation, which highlight the importance of cataloging academic genealogy trees. We hope our initial framework will be the basis of a much larger crowdsourcing system.

CCS Concepts

•**Information systems** → *Digital libraries and archives;*

Keywords

Academic Genealogy Trees; NDLTD; ETD

1. INTRODUCTION

Along the humanity history, science has evolved in different directions and rhythms, allowing humans to approach the main challenges of each era. For example, some disciplines like Computer Science or Neuroscience are considered to be in their infancy in comparison with others such as Physics and Biology. In this context, many researchers have played a vital role on the different research areas and are of extreme importance to this dynamics of science, not only for their findings, usually accounted by means of their publications, but also in the formation of new researchers.

The formation of researchers over the years is usually represented as an academic genealogy tree [6, 7, 12], which is a representation very similar to the well-known genealogy tree. It simply consists of a direct graph, where nodes represent researchers and relations indicate that a researcher was the advisor of another. Tracking this sort of relationship over time is important for many reasons. For example, it would allow us to identify the important researchers within areas and the role they have played on the creation and evolution of scientific communities, and even of novel fields. It would also provide a better understanding about where research areas came from, the birth and death of research communities, the identification of one's academic lineage, and the role of interdisciplinary formation on the evolution of specific research fields. Ultimately, it would allow us to better comprehend the evolution of science and consequently, of our society.

Despite its clear importance, little attention has been given to preserving the academic genealogy. The identification of researchers' ancestors is indeed a challenging task as current repositories of theses and dissertations are usually cataloged in a decentralized way through many local digital libraries [5]. As a consequence, existing efforts on this context have focused on specific fields, such as Mathematics [12] and Neuroscience [7], or on the use of well maintained repositories but restricted to a specific country [19]. Although these efforts are valuable for providing answers to important research questions, they do not provide the big picture about the academic genealogy nor allow us to comprehend many aspects behind the formation of scientists across fields and countries.

In this paper, we give a first step towards building a large network that records the academic genealogy of researchers across fields and countries. We believe that this is the first large-scale effort to generate a general academic genealogy tree involving as much distinct research fields as possible. Our preliminary effort here consists of constructing and analyzing academic genealogy trees from a large existing collection of electronic theses and dissertations, the Networked Digital Library of Theses and Dissertations – NDLTD[1] [8]. To do that, we crawled the entire NDLTD as it records theses and dissertations from many institutions around the world and from different disciplines. Then, we developed a basic

*This research is funded by projects InWeb (MCT/CNPq grant 573871/2008- 6) and MASWeb (FAPEMIG/PRONEX grant APQ-01400-14), and by the authors' individual grants from CAPES, CNPq and FAPEMIG.

Permission to make digital or hard copies of all or part of this work for personal or classroom use is granted without fee provided that copies are not made or distributed for profit or commercial advantage and that copies bear this notice and the full citation on the first page. Copyrights for components of this work owned by others than the author(s) must be honored. Abstracting with credit is permitted. To copy otherwise, or republish, to post on servers or to redistribute to lists, requires prior specific permission and/or a fee. Request permissions from permissions@acm.org.

JCDL '16, June 19 - 23, 2016, Newark, NJ, USA

© 2016 Copyright held by the owner/author(s). Publication rights licensed to ACM.
ISBN 978-1-4503-4229-2/16/06. . . $15.00

DOI: http://dx.doi.org/10.1145/2910896.2910916

---

[1]http://www.ndltd.org/

framework to extract information from the NDLTD, identify and disambiguate authors, and identify their advisor relationships. Finally, we carried out a series of analyses that describe the main properties of the genealogy trees we were able to construct. We hope our initial framework can evolve into a much larger crowdsourcing system that stores a comprehensive collection of academic genealogy trees.

The rest of the paper is organized as follows. Next, we briefly survey existing efforts in this field. Then, we describe our methodology and the data gathered from the NDLTD, and present our characterization study of academic genealogy trees and discuss our preliminary findings. Finally, we conclude the paper and provide directions for future work.

2. RELATED WORK

Since Newman's seminal work on scientific collaboration networks [16], there has been a tremendous effort aiming to understand the structure of such communities [13, 15], characterize their patterns of collaboration [9, 17], and analyze their evolution throughout the years [1, 2]. Likewise, there has also been some recent effort to document, analyze and classify the advisor-advisee academic relationship networks. For instance, Chang [6] presents a career retrospect of prominent American physicists and describes their academic genealogy trees. Jackson [12] seeks to maintain the genealogy tree of all mathematicians around the world[2], whereas David and Hyden [7] have maintained the genealogy tree of researchers in the neuroscience field[3]. In common, these projects collect data about all researchers that work in those fields in order to establish their academic relationships. Other relevant efforts are the PhDTree[4] and the Academic Family Tree[5], which try to document the academic family trees of researchers worldwide and share their information trough a Wiki. Both projects rely on a crowdsourcing system to keep their data up-to-dated.

Other works aim to analyze, understand, and model the structures and properties of such specific academic networks. For instance, Tuesta et al. [19] have analyzed the advisor-advisee relationship in the Brazilian exact and earth science field. Their intention was to explore the correlation between time and productivity throughout the advising relationship. Malmgreen et al. [14] have investigated the role of mentorship in protégé performance by studying mentorship fecundity using data from the Mathematics Genealogy Project. On the other hand, Rossi and Mena-Chalco [18] have introduced some topological metrics to characterize the individuals in academic genealogy trees, whereas Griffiths [10] has shown that a class of genealogy trees is related to unlabelled graph-theoretical trees, which allows to solve some counting problems associated to such trees.

Differently from the above studies, our paper gives the first, yet preliminary, step towards building a large repository that records the academic genealogy of researchers across fields and countries. Thus, to the best of our knowledge, our effort is complementary to the existing ones.

3. THE NDLTD GENEALOGY TREES

To construct the academic genealogy trees from NDLTD data, we first gathered data from all researchers with records

on this digital library. The NDLTD is formed by collections of Eletronic Thesis or Dissertation (ETD) records from hundreds of academic institutions around the world. Its repository is mainly maintained by harvesting individual ETD records from other sources by using the Open Archives Metadata Harvesting Protocol (OAI-PMH)[6], which are then encoded in XML. Calado et al. [5], for instance, describe one of such efforts, in which ETD records were created by automatically extracting data from thousands of webpages.

3.1 Dataset

After collecting all ETD records stored in the NDLTD, the respective XML documents were parsed and transformed into a CSV file keeping only the ETD fields showed in Table 1. In total, 4,588,474 ETD records were collected. Despite the Dublin Core initiative[7] to standardize the set of adopted metadata, many collections do not follow the proposed specification causing the lost of important information. For instance, there were cases in which some metadata did not follow the required format, or were simply not present in the ETD records. Additionally 279,811 records returned the status deleted.

Table 1: Metadata gathered from NDLTD.

Field	Records with values
Title	4,166,668
Creator	4,116,325
Subject	2,222,814
Description	3,588,628
Publisher	2,451,501
Contributor	1,737,371
Date	3,986,625
Type	2,973,366
Format	1,683,547
Identifier	4,162,019
Language	3,550,054
Coverage	125,804
Rights	877,778
Thesis.degree	1,532

3.2 Data Extraction

Finished the data collection, the second step was to extract specific data from the EDT records. However, to find a general solution to clean such data is not a simple task. Thus, we adopted an intermediate solution between an automatic process and a totally manual intervention. For this, we first removed all fields whose content included text in non-occidental characters. Then, we applied some data cleaning procedures to eliminate inconsistent content (e.g., general abbreviations such as "s.n." and "s.l.", emails and general comments such as "Text Here", among others). In this process, the fields Creator and Contributor were the most important ones because they would be used to link the theses' authors with their respective advisors. This task, however, presented a major challenge to our purposes due to the limited number of records (1,737,371, which is about 38% of the total) containing the field Contributor. Finished the cleaning process, only 638,812 records were considered to construct the genealogy trees, resulting a forest with 95,169 components.

---

[2]http://genealogy.math.ndsu.nodak.edu/

[3]http://neurotree.org/

[4]http://phdtree.org/

[5]http://academictree.org/

[6]Proposed by the Open Archives Initiative (OAI)

[7]http://dublincore.org/

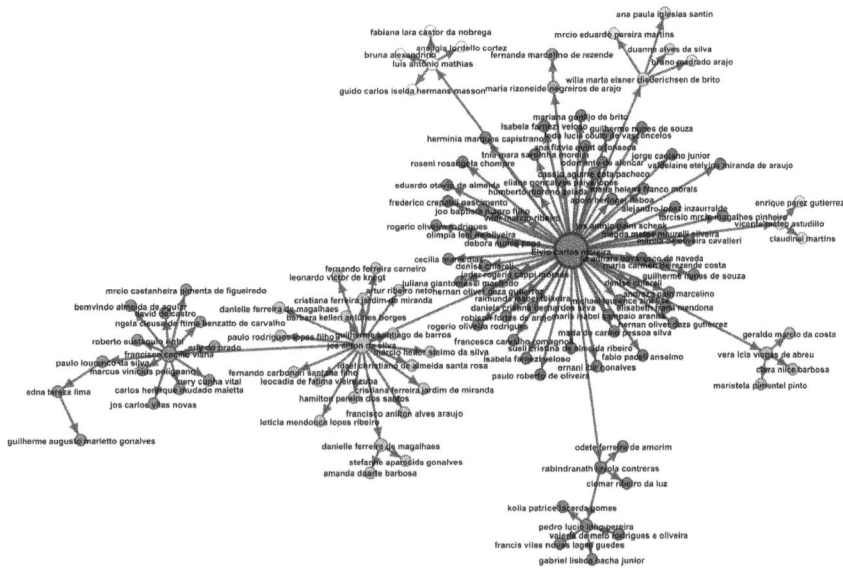

Figure 1: Excerpt of the genealogy tree constructed from NDLTD data.

3.3 Name Disambiguation

The main task in the construction of the genealogy trees is to link the researcher's name found in the *Contributor* field of each EDT record with the name of some researcher in the *Creator* field of another record, since the field *Contributor* is primarily used to store the advisor's name. To achieve such a goal, we adopted a simple solution based on the BK-tree data structure [4]. A BK-tree is a metric tree specifically designed to discrete metric spaces. Thus, it provides a simple and effective solution to search for the most similar names in our dataset, since our major difficulty here is the lack of information to help correctly matching two names. The BK-tree allows one to search for strings that are similar to the query by using a Jaro string comparator. In our case, we used a similarity threshold of 95%.

3.4 Characterizing the Genealogy Trees

The legacy of a researcher can be measured not only in terms of her publications and scientific discoveries, but also in terms of the formation of other researchers. Next, we analyze a small example of an academic genealogy tree as an attempt to visualize this second part of a researcher's legacy, which is the research families and communities that emerge around a particular researcher. Figure 1 shows an excerpt of the genealogy tree of researchers from the Graduate Program in Animal Science of the Universidade Federal de Minas Gerais (UFMG) in Brazil. The colors in the figure represent the graph modularity, which can be understood as a "family" core of researchers. The tree includes a main subtree (the red one), which includes the graduate (PhD and MSc) students that have been advised by Prof. Élvio Carlos Moreira, a senior faculty member in that program. His tree spans seven other trees which, in turn, span three additional subtrees. Thus, by analyzing such a kind of tree we hope

to be able to better understand the role of these families on coauthorship and community formation. More important, this example elucidates that the system we aim at developing can be helpful for those interested in understanding the impact that individual researchers have in a community in terms of scientific formation.

We now investigate some metrics that describe the structure of the trees we have been able to construct. The *width* is the number of advisees a researcher has advised (the researcher's out-degree), whereas the *depth* represents her lineage size. Together, these two metrics provide an overview of the legacy of a researcher in terms of academic formation. In our example in Figure 1, Prof. Moreira's tree has width 60, which is the number of all his advisees, and depth 5, which is the size of his largest lineage. In our dataset, an average researcher has an advising rate of 0.30 researchers. In contrast, the advisor with the highest advising rate formed 169 students. In fact, the 100 most prolific researchers advised 5,948 students, which corresponds to 7% of all nodes in the trees we analyzed. Figure 2 shows the distribution of these two metrics in our dataset.

These results also suggest that academic genealogy trees are much wider than deeper. In fact, if we consider the width and the depth of a tree as its largest width and depth, respectively, we noted that trees are on average 2.48 wider than deeper. The Pearson correlation coefficient between the width and the depth of a tree is 0.60, which suggests that the largest trees are also the deepest ones. In order to better understand this correlation between width and depth, we have considered a variation of the well known *h-index*, adapted to the context of academic genealogy trees.

The h-index [3, 11] is a metric originally proposed to measure a researcher's scientific output. Its calculation is quite simple as it is based on the researcher's set of most cited

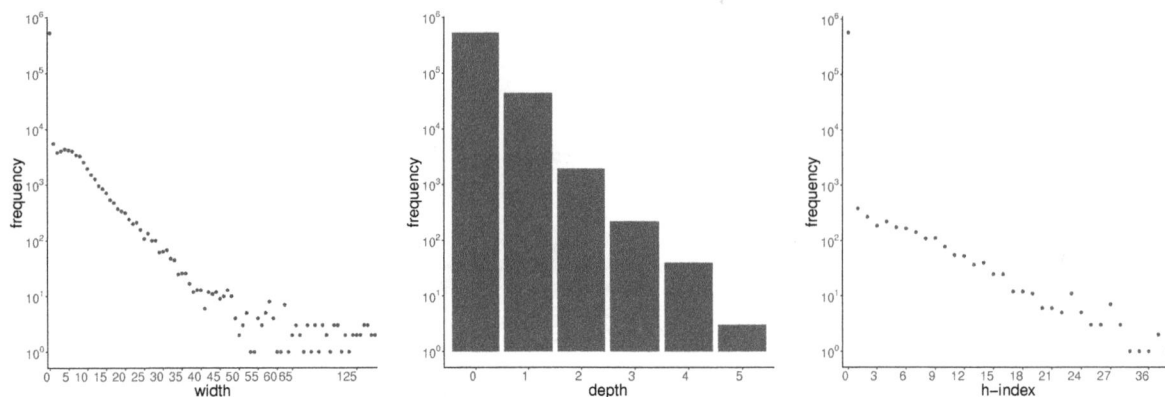

Figure 2: Width, depth, and h-index distributions of genealogy trees.

publications and the number of citations they have received. More specifically, a researcher has an h-index h if she has at least h publications that have received at least h citations. In our context, the metric is computed slightly different as proposed by Rossi and Mena-Chalco [18]. A researcher has an genealogy h-index h if she has at least h advisees and, at least one of them, has advised at least h advisees as well. Thus, if a researcher has at least 10 advisees and one of them has advised at least 10 other advisees, her genealogy h-index is 10. We can note from Figure 2 that most researchers have a low h-index, but some of them reach really high values. For example, the largest h-index in our dataset is 76.

4. CONCLUSIONS AND FUTURE WORK

In this work, we used data crawled from the Networked Digital Library of Theses and Dissertations (NDLTD) to construct academic genealogy trees. Although still preliminary, our effort identified a number of interesting findings related to the structure of academic formation, which highlight the importance of cataloging academic genealogy trees. Our effort showed that NDLTD is a valuable collection for this purpose and that it also allowed us to identify many challenges that we need to tackle towards developing a large repository that records the academic genealogy of researchers across fields and countries. First, we were able to identify researcher names and advisor relationships of a relatively small amount of records. This is because the content on these entries is free text and present many challenges for being properly processed. Proposing an algorithm able to unveil more nodes for our trees is in our research agenda. Second, we aim at identifying the research disciplines of the researchers based on specific EDT fields and also incorporate data from other sources in addition to NDLTD. Finally, we plan to develop our system in a way that researchers and other interested people can help us to curate our genealogy trees, which may also pose other challenges.

5. REFERENCES

[1] B. L. Alves, F. Benevenuto, and A. H. F. Laender. The Role of Research Leaders on the Evolution of Scientific Communities. In *Proc. of WWW (Companion Volume)*, pages 649–656, Rio de Janeiro, Brazil, 2013.

[2] A.-L. Barabâsi, H. Jeong, Z. Néda, E. Ravasz, A. Schubert, and T. Vicsek. Evolution of the social network of scientific collaborations. *Physica A: Statistical Mechanics and its Applications*, 311(3):590–614, 2002.

[3] F. Benevenuto, A. H. F. Laender, and B. L. Alves. The h-index paradox: your coauthors have a higher h-index than you do. *Scientometrics*, 106(1):469–474, 2016.

[4] W. A. Burchard and R. M. Keller. Some approaches to best-match file searching. *CACM*, 16(4):230–236, 1973.

[5] P. Calado, M. A. Gonçalves, E. A. Fox, B. A. Ribeiro-Neto, A. H. F. Laender, A. S. da Silva, D. de Castro Reis, P. A. Roberto, M. V. Vieira, and J. P. Lage. The Web-DL Environment for Building Digital Libraries from the Web. In *Proc. of JCDL*, pages 346–357, Houston, USA, 2003.

[6] S. Chang. Academic genealogy of american physicists. *AAPPS Bulletin*, 13(6):6–41, 2003.

[7] S. V. David and B. Y. Hayden. Neurotree: A collaborative, graphical database of the academic genealogy of neuroscience. *PLoS ONE*, 7(10):e46608, 2012.

[8] E. A. Fox, M. A. Gonçalves, G. McMillan, J. L. Eaton, A. Atkins, and N. A. Kipp. The networked digital library of theses and dissertations: Changes in the university community. *J. Comp. in H. Educ.*, 13(2):102–124, 2002.

[9] W. Glänzel. National characteristics in international scientific co-authorship relations. *Scientometrics*, 51(1):69–115, 2001.

[10] R. C. Griffiths. Counting genealogical trees. *J. of Math. Biol.*, 25(4):423–431, 1987.

[11] J. E. Hirsch. An index to quantify an individual's scientific research output. *PNAS*, 102(46):16569–16572, 2005.

[12] A. Jackson. A labor of love: the mathematics genealogy project. *Notices of the AMS*, 54(8):1002–1003, 2007.

[13] X. Liu, J. Bollen, M. L. Nelson, and H. Van de Sompel. Coauthorship networks in the digital library research community. *IPM*, 41(6):1462–1480, 2005.

[14] R. D. Malmgren, J. M. Ottino, and L. A. N. Amaral. The role of mentorship in protégé performance. *Nature*, 465(7298):622–626, 2010.

[15] G. V. Menezes, N. Ziviani, A. H. F. Laender, and V. A. F. Almeida. A Geographical Analysis of Knowledge Production in Computer Science. In *Proc. of WWW*, pages 1041–1050, Madrid, Spain, 2009.

[16] M. E. Newman. The structure of scientific collaboration networks. *PNAS*, 98(2):404–409, 2001.

[17] M. E. Newman. Coauthorship networks and patterns of scientific collaboration. *PNAS*, 101(s. 1):5200–5205, 2004.

[18] L. Rossi and J. P. Mena-Chalco. Caracterização de árvores de genealogia acadêmica por meio de métricas em grafos. *Anais do XXXIV CSBC*, pages 21–32, 2014.

[19] E. Tuesta, K. Delgado, R. Mugnaini, L. Digiampietri, J. Mena-Chalco, and J. Pérez-Alcázar. Analysis of an Advisor-Advisee Relationship: An Exploratory Study of the Area of Exact and Earth Sciences in Brazil. *PloS One*, 10(5):e0129065–e0129065, 2014.

Predicting Medical Subject Headings Based on Abstract Similarity and Citations to MEDLINE Records

Adam K. Kehoe
Graduate School of Library and Information Science
University of Illinois at Urbana-Champaign
Champaign, IL, USA
kehoe2@illinois.edu

Vetle I. Torvik
Graduate School of Library and Information Science
University of Illinois at Urbana-Champaign
Champaign, IL, USA
vtorvik@illinois.edu

ABSTRACT

We describe a classifier-enhanced nearest neighbor approach to assigning Medical Subject Headings (MeSH®) to unlabeled documents using a combination of abstract similarities and direct citations to labeled MEDLINE records. The approach frames the classification problem by decomposing it into sets of siblings in the MeSH hierarchy (e.g., training a classifier for predicting "Heterocyclic Compounds, 2-Ring" vs. other "Heterocyclic Compounds"). Preliminary experiments using a small but diverse set of MeSH terms shows the highest performance when using both abstracts and citations compared to each alone, and coupled with a non-naive classifier: 90+% precision and recall with 10-fold cross-validation. NLM's Medical Text Indexer (MTI) tool achieves similar overall performance but varies more across the terms tested. For example, MTI performs better on "Heterocyclic Compounds, 2-Ring", while our approach performs better on Alzheimer Disease and Neuroimaging. Our approach can be applied broadly to documents with abstracts that are similar to (or cite) MEDLINE abstracts, which would help linking and searching across bibliographic databases beyond MEDLINE.

Keywords

Controlled vocabularies; Medical subject headings; Machine Learning; Curation of bibliographic databases

1. INTRODUCTION

The Medical Subject Headings (MeSH) controlled vocabulary is a powerful tool for organizing the biomedical literature. However, accurate automatic annotation of new documents is difficult. It has been previously shown that simple nearest neighbors approaches outperform other strategies.[9] The nearest neighbor approach bases its annotation on the labels from similar abstracts identified in MEDLINE, bypassing some of the myriad of challenges in natural language processing and concept identifiability in the input

Permission to make digital or hard copies of all or part of this work for personal or classroom use is granted without fee provided that copies are not made or distributed for profit or commercial advantage and that copies bear this notice and the full citation on the first page. Copyrights for components of this work owned by others than the author(s) must be honored. Abstracting with credit is permitted. To copy otherwise, or republish, to post on servers or to redistribute to lists, requires prior specific permission and/or a fee. Request permissions from permissions@acm.org.

JDCL '16 June 19–23, 2016, Newark, NJ, USA

© 2016 Copyright held by the owner/author(s). Publication rights licensed to ACM.
ISBN 978-1-4503-4229-2/16/06. . . $15.00

DOI: http://dx.doi.org/10.1145/2910896.2910920

text. Here, we propose a more sophisticated nearest neighbors approach that uses both abstract similarity and direct citations to identify the nearest neighbors, and then uses trained machine learning classifiers to transform the labels of the nearest neighbors into predicted MeSH terms.

We hypothesize that combining abstract similarity with citations to identify nearest neighbors will improve the annotation performance because some abstracts use non-standard vocabulary or lack key ideas described in the full-text of a document. Furthermore, all MeSH are not equally represented in MEDLINE so optimizing a classifier for each term should further improve performance.

In order to test this hypothesis, we designed a series of experiments that assessed the performance of the proposed approach under a variety of settings: a) using MeSH terms from different parts of the MeSH hierarchy, b) using several different kinds of classifiers (one rule, logistic regression and random forest), c) including only the abstract similarity predictors, only the direct citation predictors and with both combined. Additionally, we compared its performance with the NLM's Medical Text Indexer (MTI) using only the abstract text as input.

The proposed approach can be applied to a variety of different bibliographic databases, as long as the documents have an abstract similarity or citations to MEDLINE. Our particular efforts are directed toward biomedical patents and grants, which often have both.

2. BACKGROUND

The Medical Subject Headings (MeSH) controlled vocabulary is created and maintained by the National Library of Medicine to annotate MEDLINE records. The 2015 version of MeSH contains approximately 27,000 descriptors with over 87,000 entry terms. MeSH terms are organized at the top-level into 16 categories. Each category is further subdivided and arrayed hierarchically from most general to the most specific, though it is important to note that some MeSH terms have multiple parents. Most papers have approximately a dozen MeSH terms applied to them.[11]

The NLM Indexing Initiative has developed the Medical Text Indexer (MTI) system to assist indexers by providing MeSH recommendations for papers to be included in MEDLINE.[5] The MTI system takes inputs of an identifier, title and abstract but is also capable of processing arbitrary biomedical text.[5] Recommendations are computed using two methods: MetaMap indexing and a K-nearest neighbors (KNN) algorithm that identifies similar citations.[4]

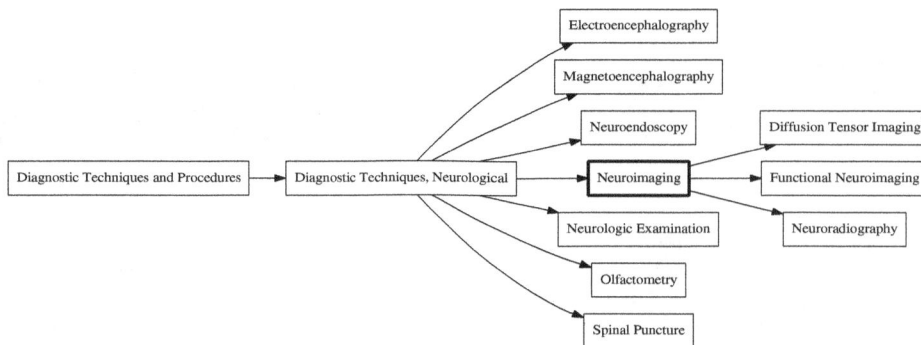

Figure 1: Ancestors, children, and siblings of Neuroimaging in the MeSH hierarchy.

MetaMap processes the title and abstract to identify UMLS Metathesaurus concepts that are then mapped to MeSH. Precision and recall performance for the MTI system is typically around .60.[4]

The high cost of manually classifying records inspires an ongoing interest in automating the process. As a result, numerous research groups have developed MeSH prediction systems and recommenders. Most MeSH prediction efforts rely on one of three techniques.[2] The first is to compute the k-nearest neighbor documents, and utilize the MeSH terms of those documents as recommended terms. [2, 9, 6, 3] The second uses machine learning techniques to identify patterns between the document and MeSH terms[11, 10, 7]. The third uses domain-specific tools like MetaMap to directly process the document and apply terms to a document. The MTI system is the most prominent example of this approach[4].

In distinction to previous work on this topic, our approach implements classifiers at each branch of the MeSH hierarchy rather than attempting to predict the entire MeSH vocabulary in one pass. Figure 1 shows a portion of the MeSH hierarchy around the descriptor "Neuroimaging". In our approach, the classification problem is restricted to the level of MeSH siblings. In the "Neuroimaging" example, we train a classifier for each sibling term of Neuroimaging. We make use of both abstract similarity and citations and leverage the large set of MEDLINE records that already have labels to build these classifiers. If the probability of a child term is sufficiently high, its children terms are subsequently processed. The combination of the parent and child's probability can be used to obtain a final adjusted probability. Here, we report on some preliminary but promising results on classifiers trained in three locations in the MeSH hierarchy: Heterocyclic Compounds, Neurological Diagnostic Techniques, and Dementia.

3. DATA AND METHODS

We selected one million of the most recently added papers in MEDLINE 2015 for which we had two or more references (extracted from PubMedCentral) and contained at least one assigned MeSH. From this set, we identified all the papers with the following MeSH terms (or one of its descendants i.e., operating in an "exploded" mode): "Neurological Diagnostic Techniques" (number of papers = 8,179), "Heterocyclic Compounds" (n = 26,687), or "Dementia" (n = 3,833). For each of these three sets of papers, we formulated a 0/1 classification problem where the label corresponds to a particular

child term. In other words, the goal is to train a classifier so as to optimally distinguish a particular term from its siblings and parent. As such, the classification problem is harder than distinguishing arbitrarily chosen MeSH terms. Table 1 shows the parent terms and their corresponding child terms chosen for the class label. These were selected because they are of particular interest in a separate project and they represent well-established concepts with thousands of papers each and are situated at different levels of the MeSH hierarchy from three broad categories: Techniques, Chemicals and Drugs, and Diseases. Note that a paper can, and often does, have multiple siblings terms so it is reasonable to build separate 0/1-classifiers for each sibling and utilize these classifiers independently of each other. However, if all siblings (or none) are predicted as labels, then perhaps the parent term is the more appropriate label. This hypothesis we leave for a future study.

For each paper in the datasets, we identify the most closely related MEDLINE papers. First, the top 15 or so are selected using a variant of the BM25 score (implemented using Sphinx coupled with MySQL). We have made a publicly available tool called AbSim for retrieving these scores.[8]. Second, the entire set of papers that the paper cites are selected. For each MeSH term at hand, we count the number of different papers with that term, and these numbers make up the set of predictor variables. For example, a paper to be labeled 0/1 for Alzheimer Disease might cite 20 papers of which 4 contain the term Alzheimer Disease, 2 with Lewy Body Disease, 1 with Huntington Disease, and 0 for all other siblings, and might have 16 papers with similar abstracts of which 6 contain Alzheimer Disease, 2 with Lewy Body Disease, 0 for all other siblings. The datasets exhibit strong correlations between the counts found by abstract similarity and the counts based on citations. However, as we shall see, the two sets of predictors both contribute to improved classification performance, indicating that they are complementary. Figure 2 shows a plot of these correlations.

We tested three 0/1-classifiers for each sibling term in each dataset: a one-rule classifier as a baseline, followed by logistic regression, and a random forest which is the least restrictive of the three because it can capture highly nonlinear patterns. All performance estimates were calculated using ten-fold cross validation for all the classifiers except MTI which was assessed on the entire set because it was not privileged to training data. Each abstract was processed through the MTI batch tool using its default parameters,

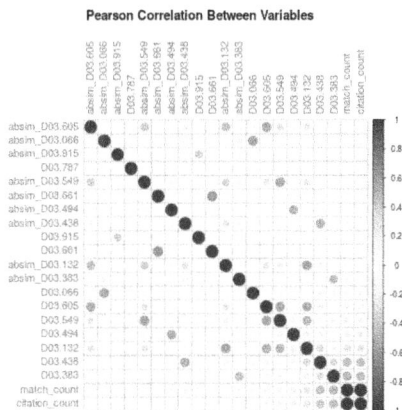

Figure 2: Correlations between the abstract similarity predictors vs. citation predictors for Heterocyclic Compounds dataset.

and assigned the target label if it contained the target term or a descendant.

In order to evaluate the importance of the abstract similarity vs. direct citation independent variables, we trained three variants of each model. Every model was run with both abstract similarity and direct citations included, with only the abstract similarity features and with only direct citation counts.

4. RESULTS

Table 2 details model performance on a particular MeSH term from each of the three datasets.

Overall random forests capture a slight performance gain over logistic regression, probably because it is less restrictive and the data is likely to contain some non-linearities. Furthermore, performance is strongest using both abstract similarity and direct citation counts in all models. Abstract similarity alone performed better than just citation counts, except for Alzheimer disease. Although performance is high for all three terms, there are notable differences. The "Heterocyclic Compound 2-Ring" term had the lowest performance. This likely reflects the differing levels of granularity and semantic similarity between sibling terms. In the case of heterocyclic compounds, many of the sibling terms are similar in that they describe variants of a chemical structure. The sibling terms in the dementia category demonstrate an opposite extreme where the terms are largely semantically distinct. These differences influence the difficulty of the classification problem and are reflected in the varying performance profiles shown.

Random forests also have a useful property for assessing variable importance. In the case of the heterocyclic compound 2-ring classifier, the most predictive variables were highly related to the class. Figure 2 shows that abstract similarity for D03.438 (Heterocyclic Compound 2-Ring) and D03.383 (Heterocyclic Compound 1-ring) were the most useful, followed by the same counts from direct citations.

The strong performance across the Chemicals and Drugs, Techniques and Equipment, and Diseases categories provisionally suggests that the classification technique may be effective throughout the MeSH hierarchy. The heterocyclic compound test case is particularly difficult due to the strong

Table 1: Three MeSH parent terms represent three different classification problems. The child terms chosen for the class label are italicized and bolded.

Diagnostic Techniques, Neurological
Electroencephalography
Magnetoencephalography
Neuroendoscopy
Neuroimaging (5,164/8,179)
Neurologic Examination
Olfactometry
Spinal Puncture

Heterocyclic Compounds
Acids, Heterocyclic
Alkaloids
Heterocyclic Compounds with 4 or More Rings
Heterocyclic Compounds, 3-Ring
Heterocyclic Compounds, 2-Ring (8,136/26,687)
Heterocyclic Compounds, 1-Ring
Heterocyclic Compounds, Bridged-Ring
Heterocyclic Oxides
Phytochemicals

Dementia
AIDS Dementia Complex
Alzheimer Disease (1,275/3,833)
Aphasia, Primary Progressive
Creutzfeldt-Jakob Syndrome
Dementia, Vascular
Diffuse Neurofibrillary Tangles with Calcification
Frontotemporal Lobar Degeneration
Huntington Disease
Kluver-Bucy Syndrome
Lewy Body Disease

similarity between candidate terms. Despite this similarity, the predictors showed strong coherence and the final classification accuracy was high.

MTI performs better on "Heterocyclic Compounds, 2-Ring", while our approach performs better on Alzheimer Disease and Neuroimaging. However, MTI's performance measures vary more than our approach suggesting that it is less robust.

5. DISCUSSION

These preliminary experiments demonstrate that classifiers trained on both abstract similarity and direct citations perform well across a diverse selection of MeSH terms. Differentiating between highly related MeSH siblings given very limited information is inherently difficult. We found that the classification difficulty between MeSH siblings varies in our test cases. Further work is required to test how this variance impacts prediction of the MeSH vocabulary as a whole. One benefit of the proposed approach is that it generates probabilities for each MeSH term, and it does so independent of each other. We plan to study whether these probabilities can be further adjusted by taking advantage of the probabilities of other terms related by ancestry or by imposing constraints that can be gleaned from typical MeSH assignments in MEDLINE.

We plan to study whether the approach is effective beyond the scholarly literature. Biomedical USPTO patents are amenable to the proposed classification strategy in that most they are readily available, and have abstracts and direct citations to MEDLINE, particularly in recent years.

Table 2: Comparison of MeSH prediction performance

Heterocyclic Compounds 2-Ring

Model	Precision	Recall	F-Score	AUROC
1Rule-Both	.83	.84	.83	.79
1Rule-Absim	.83	.84	.83	.79
1Rule-Cit	.75	.77	.74	.66
Logistic-Both	.88	.89	.88	.93
Logistic-Absim	.88	.88	.88	.93
Logistic-Cit	.81	.81	.80	.86
RandomForest-Both	.90	.90	.90	.95
RandomForest-Absim	.88	.88	.87	.93
RandomForest-Cit	.81	.81	.81	.86
MTI	**.99**	**.99**	**.99**	NA

Neuroimaging

Model	Precision	Recall	F-Score	AUROC
1Rule-Both	.86	.84	.84	.85
1Rule-Absim	.86	.84	.84	.85
1Rule-Cit	.81	.81	.81	.79
Logistic-Both	.91	.90	.90	.96
Logistic-Absim	.90	.90	.90	.95
Logistic-Cit	.85	.84	.83	.91
RandomForest-Both	**.91**	**.91**	**.91**	**.97**
RandomForest-Absim	.89	.89	.89	.96
RandomForest-Cit	.85	.86	.85	.92
MTI	.85	.81	.83	NA

Alzheimer Disease

Model	Precision	Recall	F-Score	AUROC
1Rule-Both	.91	.91	.91	.89
1Rule-Absim	.88	.87	.87	.87
1Rule-Cit	.91	.91	.91	.89
Logistic-Both	**.98**	**.98**	**.98**	**.99**
Logistic-Absim	.91	.91	.90	.97
Logistic-Cit	.96	.96	.96	.99
RandomForest-Both	.97	.97	.97	.99
RandomForest-Absim	.90	.90	.90	.97
RandomForest-Cit	.95	.95	.95	.99
MTI	.93	.95	.94	NA

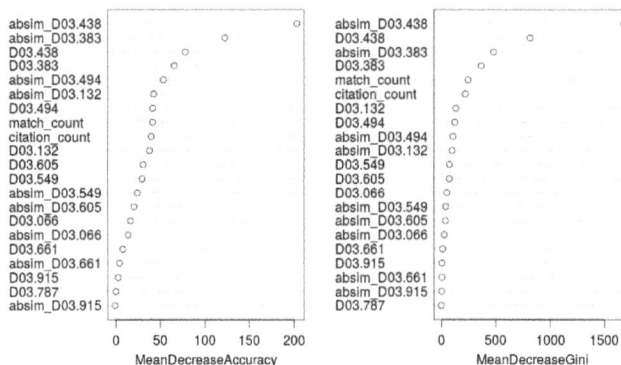

Figure 3: Relative importance of variables in the "Heterocyclic Compound, 2-Ring" prediction problem.

Though many patent citation strings are noisy, robust data on citations from patents to the biomedical literature are available through the citation matcher called Patci.[1] We also anticipate exploring potential applications in literature based discovery and information retrieval enabled by applying shared controlled vocabulary across biomedical bibliographic databases.

6. ACKNOWLEDGMENTS

We thank Abbott Nutrition for partially funding this research.

7. REFERENCES

[1] S. Agarwal, M. Lincoln, H. Cai, and V. I. Torvik. Patci: A probabilistic citation matcher. http://abel.lis.illinois.edu/cgi-bin/patci/search.pl. Accessed: 2016-01-26.

[2] M. Huang, A. Névéol, and Z. Lu. Recommending mesh terms for annotating biomedical articles. *Journal of the American Medical Informatics Association*, 18(5):660–667, 2011.

[3] W. Kim, A. R. Aronson, and W. J. Wilbur. Automatic mesh term assignment and quality assessment. In *Proceedings of the AMIA Symposium*, page 319. American Medical Informatics Association, 2001.

[4] J. G. Mork, D. Demner-Fushman, S. Schmidt, and A. R. Aronson. Recent enhancements to the nlm medical text indexer. In *Working Notes for CLEF 2014 Conference, Sheffield, UK*, pages 1328–1336, 2014.

[5] J. G. Mork, A. Jimeno-Yepes, and A. R. Aronson. The nlm medical text indexer system for indexing biomedical literature. In *BioASQ@ CLEF*, 2013.

[6] P. Ruch. Automatic assignment of biomedical categories: toward a generic approach. *Bioinformatics*, 22(6):658–664, 2006.

[7] S. Sohn, W. Kim, D. C. Comeau, and W. J. Wilbur. Optimal training sets for bayesian prediction of mesh® assignment. *Journal of the American Medical Informatics Association*, 15(4):546–553, 2008.

[8] V. I. Torvik. Absim: A tool for calculating bm25 similarity among pairs of abstracts in pubmed. http://abel.lis.illinois.edu/cgi-bin/absim/search.py. Accessed: 2016-01-26.

[9] D. Trieschnigg, P. Pezik, V. Lee, F. De Jong, W. Kraaij, and D. Rebholz-Schuhmann. Mesh up: effective mesh text classification for improved document retrieval. *Bioinformatics*, 25(11):1412–1418, 2009.

[10] M. Wahle, D. Widdows, J. R. Herskovic, E. V. Bernstam, and T. Cohen. Deterministic binary vectors for efficient automated indexing of medline/pubmed abstracts. In *AMIA annual symposium proceedings*, volume 2012, page 940. American Medical Informatics Association, 2012.

[11] W. J. Wilbur and W. Kim. Stochastic gradient descent and the prediction of mesh for pubmed records. In *AMIA Annual Symposium Proceedings*, volume 2014, page 1198. American Medical Informatics Association, 2014.

Profiling vs. Time vs. Content: What does Matter for Top-k Publication Recommendation based on Twitter Profiles?

Chifumi Nishioka
Kiel University, Germany
ZBW – Leibniz Information Centre for
Economics, Germany
chni@informatik.uni-kiel.de

Ansgar Scherp
ZBW – Leibniz Information Centre for
Economics, Germany
Kiel University, Germany
a.scherp@zbw.eu

ABSTRACT

So far it is unclear how different factors of a scientific publication recommender system based on users' tweets have an influence on the recommendation performance. We examine three different factors, namely profiling method, temporal decay, and richness of content. Regarding profiling, we compare CF-IDF that replaces terms in TF-IDF by semantic concepts, HCF-IDF as novel hierarchical variant of CF-IDF, and topic modeling. As temporal decay functions, we apply sliding window and exponential decay. In terms of the richness of content, we compare recommendations using both full-texts and titles of publications and using only titles. Overall, the three factors make twelve recommendation strategies. We have conducted an online experiment with 123 participants and compared the strategies in a within-group design. The best recommendations are achieved by the strategy combining CF-IDF, sliding window, and with full-texts. However, the strategies using the novel HCF-IDF profiling method achieve similar results with just using the titles of the publications. Therefore, HCF-IDF can make recommendations when only short and sparse data is available.

1. INTRODUCTION

The social media platform Twitter is popular among scientists to share and discuss their professional thoughts and interests [14]. Thus, they are a natural resource for building up a user's professional profile and using it for recommending scientific publications. Recommending scientific publications based on a user's social media items has several advantages: First, users receive recommendations based on their current and ongoing professional interests. In contrast, systems like Google Scholar and Sugiyama et al. [26] recommend scientific publications based on a user's publication record. It can take up to two years (for conferences) or longer (for journals) until a paper is taken into consideration by the recommender system. Second, content-based profiling from a user's social media items mitigates the well-

Permission to make digital or hard copies of all or part of this work for personal or classroom use is granted without fee provided that copies are not made or distributed for profit or commercial advantage and that copies bear this notice and the full citation on the first page. Copyrights for components of this work owned by others than the author(s) must be honored. Abstracting with credit is permitted. To copy otherwise, or republish, to post on servers or to redistribute to lists, requires prior specific permission and/or a fee. Request permissions from permissions@acm.org.

JCDL '16, June 19 - 23, 2016, Newark, NJ, USA

© 2016 Copyright held by the owner/author(s). Publication rights licensed to ACM.
ISBN 978-1-4503-4229-2/16/06...$15.00

DOI: http://dx.doi.org/10.1145/2910896.2910898

known cold-start problem observed in collaborative filtering systems [11]. The cold-start problem refers to the initial situation where a recommender system yet does not know anything about a user's interests. Collaborative filtering systems need to analyze a large amount of user activities in order to provide reasonable recommendations. In contrast, content-based recommender systems like our work make recommendations based on similarity scores between a user profile and candidate items. Therefore, they can generate recommendations based on a single user profile already.

There is various research on user profiling from social media items [5, 21, 24, 29] and recommending scientific publications [15, 26, 28]. However, it is unclear how different profiling methods affect the recommendation performance. In addition, the age of social media items as well as scientific publications has an influence on profiling [24, 21]. But again, it has not been compared. Finally, we investigate whether it is possible to make reasonable recommendations when using only the publications' titles, i.e., when only short and sparse information about the candidate items is available. We have conducted an online experiment to evaluate these three factors of top-k recommendations of scientific publications based on a user's social media profile. In detail, the factors are:

(i) Profiling Method: The first factor is the *Profiling Method*, where we use Concept Frequency Inverse Document Frequency (CF-IDF) [7] as baseline. CF-IDF is a modification of TF-IDF where term frequencies are replaced by frequencies of semantic concepts. In an experiment with 19 participants, Goossen et al. have shown that CF-IDF outperforms TF-IDF for news article recommendations [7]. Recently, we have extended the statistical strength of CF-IDF with the semantics provided by a hierarchical knowledge base [19]. The resulting Hierarchical CF-IDF (HCF-IDF) model is capable of revealing semantic concepts that are not explicitly mentioned in texts but still are highly relevant. This is achieved by applying a spreading activation over a hierarchical knowledge base, which is typically provided as domain-specific taxonomy. Please note that we also considered using BM25 and TF-IDF as profiling method. However, our earlier work showed that HCF-IDF performs better for user profiling from social media items [19]. As third method, we apply Latent Dirichlet Allocation (LDA) [2, 1], a state-of-the-art topic modeling method. LDA is a generative machine learning approach and thus does not require any prior information such as a knowledge base.

(ii) Decay Function: As the second factor, we investigate two temporal *Decay Functions*. They are based on the idea that the importance of information declines gradually as time passes. We compare sliding window [24] and exponential decay [21, 26]. Both decay functions have been used in the past for user profiling [24, 21, 26]. But so far no comparative study was carried out.

(iii) Document Content: The third factor defines the richness of *Document Content* used for profiling candidate items (i.e., scientific publications). We compare the use of full-texts and titles of scientific publications for profiling versus profiling only based on titles.

We compared twelve recommendation strategies making use of different combinations of the three factors described above. For the experiment, we have recruited $n = 123$ participants who are posting about their professional interests on Twitter. For each strategy, the participants have received recommendations of five publications from a large corpus of $|D| = 279,381$ scientific publications in the broader field of economics. We used rankscore [4] to measure the recommendation performance. We also computed Mean Average Precision (MAP), Precision, Mean Reciprocal Rank (MRR), and normalized Discounted Cumulative Gain (nDCG), which show similar results and documented in the TR [20].

The results are very interesting: The strategy that employs the profiling method CF-IDF and the decay function Sliding window with both titles and full-texts achieves the overall best recommendation performance. Although the strategy using CF-IDF shows the highest performance, it has a drawback that it requires full-texts of scientific publications. Thus, it is remarkable that the strategies with HCF-IDF can achieve comparable results using only titles. We observe no significant difference between the best performing strategy and strategies with HCF-IDF. Thus, we conclude that the use of the spreading activation function over the hierarchical knowledge base enables HCF-IDF to compensate for the sparseness when only titles are available due to e.g., legal reasons to hinder the use of full-texts. Please note, there is no lack in domain-specific hierarchical knowledge bases such as the one used in the experiment for economics. In fact, these knowledge bases are freely available for many domains[1]. Furthermore, they are manually crafted by domain experts and thus are of high quality.

In addition, we have applied a correlation analysis between the recommendation performance and the number of tweets a participant has published, the number of concepts extracted from these tweets, the number of concepts extracted per tweet, and the percentage of tweets containing at least one concept respectively. Our results show no significant correlations in any strategies. Thus, the methods are robust against the amount of tweets.

Subsequently, we review related work in Section 2. Section 3 introduces the problem definition. In Section 4, we describe the three experimental factors used in o4ur recommender system. We present the experiment setup and procedure in Section 5. The results are presented in Section 6 and discussed in Section 7 before we conclude the paper.

2. RELATED WORK

Recommender systems are categorized into content-based recommender and collaborative filtering [11]. Collaborative filtering requires analyzing a large amount of user activities in order to predict items to other users [29]. In contrast, we

focus on content-based recommender, which suggest items based on similarity scores between a user profile and candidate items. A content-based recommender can make recommendations based on data from a single user already. Thus it does not suffer from the cold start problem. Recommender systems for scientific publications mostly employed user profiles based on publications [26, 27] or clicks [15]. Instead, we create user profiles based on social media items.

Many works have extracted user interests from social media platforms [5, 21, 24, 29]. Chen et al. [5] studied a recommender system incorporating Twitter, which recommended URLs based on a user's tweets and follower-followee relationships. In order to find out the best recommendation strategy, they evaluated twelve strategies from three factors: content sources, topic interest models for users, and social popularity. Referring to the factor content sources, Chen et al. showed that profiling based on one's own tweets performed better than based on tweets by one's followees. Hence, we build up user profiles from social media items produced by the users themselves.

In the past years, profiling methods based on semantic concepts (i.e., ontology-based profiling) extraction have been developed [7, 16]. They extract semantic concepts from texts, using a structured knowledge base, e.g., DBpedia. Goossen et al. [7] proposed CF-IDF, as an extention of TF-IDF. CF-IDF counts frequencies of a concept instead of a term. Their news arcticle recommendation experiment with 19 participants demonstrated that CF-IDF outperforms TF-IDF. Lu et al. [16] proposed a recommender system for tweets based on what a user tweeted. They constructed user profiles represented as a set of weighted Wikipedia concepts that correspond to Wikipedia articles. The experiment demonstrated that concept-based approaches outperform TF-IDF. Other works employed a hierarchical structure of a knowledge base for profiling [12, 18, 16] and demonstrated their effectiveness. These approaches can reveal user interests that are not explicitly mentioned in the texts, using a structure of a knowledge base and spreading activation. In particular, Middleton et al. [18] constructed user profiles based on a hierarchical knowledge base using spreading activation for a recommender system of scientific publications. Their user experiment compared a profiling method using the structure of a hierarchical knowledge base and a method not using the structure. The result demonstrated superiority of using the hierarchical knowledge base. Topic modeling such as LDA [2] is one of the most popular profiling methods. It is used in the context of social media [10] but particularly suited for document profiling.

Time-aware user profiles are constructed based on the assumption that the degree of user interests declines as time passes. The decline of user interests is modeled by a decay function. In the past, the decay functions sliding window [24] and exponential decay [21, 26] have been employed for user profiling. However, they have not been compared so far like we do in this work.

3. PROBLEM DEFINITION

We address the problem of taking the social media stream as input in order to recommend items such as scientific publications the user might be interested in. The problem can be decomposed into three parts: (1) First, we need to extract the professional interests that a user exposes through his social media stream and represent the interests in a user

---

[1]http://www.w3.org/2001/sw/wiki/SKOS/Datasets

Table 1: Symbol Notation

u	a user
i	a social media item
I_u	the set of u's social media items
c	a concept
C	the set of concepts
d	a candidate item (scientific publication)
D	the set of candidate items
t_i, t_d	the time stamp of i and d, respectively
P_u	u's user profile
P_d	d's document profile
Φ	a profiling function
w'	a weighting function (not considering temporal decay)
f	a decay function
w	a weighting function that extends w' with temporal decay
σ	a similarity function

Table 2: Three factors and their choices for the experiment spanning in total $3 \times 2 \times 2 = 12$ strategies

Factor	Possible Design Choices		
Profiling Method	CF-IDF	HCF-IDF	LDA
Decay Function	Sliding window		Exponential decay
Document Content	All (title + full-text)		Title

profile. (2) Likewise, we profile candidate items (i.e., scientific publications) and represent them in a way that they are comparable with the user profile. (3) We need a ranking function to compute the top-k items based on similarity scores between the user profile and each candidate item. In the following, we formalize the three steps required to create a recommender system based on a user's professional interests extracted from the social media stream. Symbols used in this paper are summarized in Table 1.

(1) User profiling from social media items. We consider I_u as set of social media items i produced by user u. A social media item $i \in I_u$ has a certain time stamp t_i. Subsequently, P_u, the user profile of the user u, is created over a set of concepts C by assigning a specific weight for each concept $c \in C$. Generally speaking, a concept c is a key subject in a dedicated field, coming from a given domain-specific knowledge base C. For instance, "financial crisis" is a concept in the field of economics. We construct P_u by employing different user profiling functions Φ and we compare them. Formally, user profiles are defined as:

$$P_u = \Phi(I_u, C) := \{(c, w(c, I_u)) \mid \forall c \in C\} \qquad (1)$$

Here, w is an arbitrary weighting function that returns a weight of a concept c in a user's social media stream I_u. Thus, it determines how important a concept c is for the user u. Profiling functions Φ and weighting functions w are described in Sections 4.1 and 4.2. Specifically, we describe weighting functions w' that do not consider temporal decay in Section 4.1 and provide weighting functions w which extend w' with temporal decay in Section 4.2.

(2) Profiling candidate items. We have a set of candidate items D. A candidate item $d \in D$ has a time stamp t_d, indicating its published year. To determine the similarity scores between a user profile P_u and each candidate item $d \in D$, we need to construct profiles of candidate items in a way that they are comparable with the user profile. Formally, we represent a candidate item d as a profile $P_d = \Phi(d, C) := \{(c, w(c, d)) \mid \forall c \in C\}$. Since our candidate items are scientific publications, we refer to this process document profiling.

(3) Ranking candidate items. We rank candidate items based on similarity scores between the user profile P_u and a document profile P_d. A similarity function σ takes as input a user profile P_u and document profile P_d. It is defined as $\sigma(P_u, P_d) \rightarrow [0, 1]$. The similarity function is applied to all candidate items $d \in D$. Finally, the top-k most relevant

items (i.e., documents whose similarity scores with P_u are ranked in the top-k) are recommended to the user u. The similarity functions σ are described in Section 4.3.

4. EXPERIMENTAL FACTORS

According to the three factors (i)-(iii) stated in the introduction, we form the design space of our experiment. We illustrate the design space in Table 2, where each cell is a possible design choice we can make in one of the three factors. Subsequently, we detail the factor *Profiling Method* in Section 4.1 and the factor *Decay Function* in Section 4.2. Further, we describe similarity functions σ in Section 4.3. The factor *Document Content* investigates whether full-texts of scientific publications enhance the recommendation performance compared to using only titles.

4.1 Profiling Method

We investigate three methods for user profiling and document profiling. For each method, we define a weighting function w' that gives a certain weight to each concept c. The final weighting function w taking temporal decay into account is described in Section 4.2.

CF-IDF: Compared to the traditional TF-IDF, CF-IDF (Concept Frequency Inverse Document Frequency) counts frequencies of a semantic concept instead of term frequencies [7]. Semantic concepts or short concepts are stored in an external knowledge base. Each concept has a unique resource identifier (URI) and one or more labels describing the concept [2]. The concept's labels are treated as synonyms. As an example, the concept "clothing industry" has the URI http://zbw.eu/stw/version/latest/descriptor/13128-2 and is defined in the thesaurus STW, a domain-specific knowledge base for economics (described in Section 5.3). The concept has not only the label "clothing industry" but also the synonymous labels "garment industry" and "apparel industry". We count the label frequency, i.e., the number of times the label appears, in the social media items and candidate items. Subsequently, we calculate the concept frequency, i.e., the number of times the concept appears, by summing up the frequencies of the labels referring to the concept. For instance, if the labels "clothing industry" and "garment industry" appear twice and once in a text, the total frequency of the concept referring to "clothing industry" is three.

For the social media items I_u of the user u, CF-IDF is computed along with Equation 2.

$$w'_{cf\text{-}idf}(c, i) = cf(c, i) \cdot \log \frac{|I_u| + |I_r|}{|\{i \in I_u \cup I_r : c \in i\}|}, \qquad (2)$$

where $cf(c, i) = \frac{\text{the number of times concept } c \text{ appears in } i}{\text{the number of times all concepts appear in } i}$. The denominator $|\{i \in I_u \cup I_r : c \in i\}|$ counts the number of social media items that contain a concept c. I_r is a set of random social media items.

---

[2]https://www.w3.org/DesignIssues/LinkedData.html

We employ a set of random social media items I_r, because it allows to better distinguish the relevant concepts in the user's social media items I_u, as Chen et al. [5] and Lu et al. [16] did for TF-IDF. For instance, assuming there are two social media items from a user u and both include the concept "currency competition". Although "currency competition" should have a high weight in the user profile, in this case IDF and a final CF-IDF score would be 0 because "currency competition" is common in a user u's social media items. The random social media items are sampled from public microblog postings. In our case, they are obtained from the public Twitter stream using the Twitter API.

We have conducted a simple pre-experiment to empirically determine the optimal amount of random tweets to be used in the profiling method in the context of our experiment of recommending economics publications. Given this pre-experiment, we set the size of random social media items to five times of $|I_u|$. In more detail, we applied different sizes of I_r, starting from 0 to 1000 random tweets. For 26 Twitter accounts, we computed the IDF scores for user profile over $I_u \cup I_r$ and compared it using cosine similarity with the user profile computed only over I_u. The Twitter accounts were taken from a list of famous economists[3] that are frequently tweeting. We ensured that the set of random tweets I_r is disjoint do the user's tweets, i.e., $I_r \cap I_u = \emptyset$. Particularly, we looked into the changes of the cosine similarity while adding more random tweets. We observed the changes in the IDF scores became stable after about a factor of five w.r.t. to $|I_u|$. The changes indicate the influence of the IDF scores to user profile. Using this technique is effective as the IDF score ensures that too generic concepts do not get too high weights in the user profiling. Those generic concepts are at the upper levels of the hierarchy of the domain-specific knowledge base. In our case those concepts are like "product" and "economics". Please note that the factor may depend on the domain of economics considered in this paper and that a different factor may be chosen for other domains.

Regarding document profiling, CF-IDF is computed as defined in Equation 3. The computation is basically identical with the one for user profiling shown in Equation 2. The difference is that CF is computed over single documents and IDF is computed over the document collection.

$$w'_{cf\text{-}idf}(c,d) = cf(c,d) \cdot log \frac{|D|}{|\{d \in D \ : c \in d\}|} \quad (3)$$

HCF-IDF: The novel profiling method HCF-IDF (Hierarchical CF-IDF) [19] extends CF-IDF by using a hierarchical knowledge base, where the concepts are hierarchically organized in a taxonomy. HCF-IDF can reveal concepts that are indirectly mentioned in texts by applying a spreading activation over the hierarchical knowledge base. Figure 1 shows an example where a user's profile includes the concept "social recommendation". Due to the hierarchical structure of the knowledge base, also the concepts "web searching" and "world wide web" are activated and obtain non-zero weights even if they are not mentioned. Different from the profiling methods using spreading activation [12, 18], HCF-IDF avoids to provide too high weights to generic concepts like "economy", as it employs IDF. Specifically, HCF-IDF combines the statistical strength of CF-IDF with semantics

[3]http://www.huffingtonpost.com/2012/11/13/economists-twitter_n_2122781.html

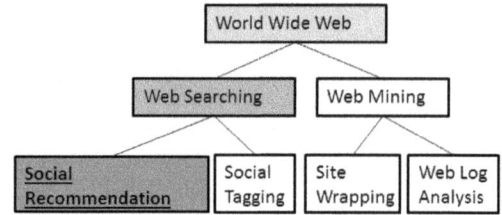

Figure 1: An example of HCF-IDF

provided by the hierarchical knowledge base. We compute HCF-IDF along with Equation 4.

$$w'_{hcf\text{-}idf}(c,i) = BL(c,i) \cdot log \frac{|I_u| + |I_r|}{|\{i \in I_u \cup I_r : c \in i\}|} \quad (4)$$

$BL(c,i)$ denotes the spreading activation function BellLog from Kapanipathi et al. [12]. It returns a weight of a concept c in a social media item i and is defined below:

$$BL(c,i) = cf(c,i) + FL(i) \cdot \sum_{c_j \in C_l(c)} BL(c_j,i), \quad (5)$$

where $FL(c) = \frac{1}{log_{10}(nodes(h(c)+1))}$. $h(c)$ returns the level where a concept c is located in the knowledge base and $nodes$ provides the number of concepts at a given level in a knowledge base. For example, in Figure 1 h("web searching") returns 2 and $nodes(h($"web searching"$) + 1)$ returns 4. $C_l(c)$ returns the set of concepts located in one level lower than the concept c. In Figure 1 the function C_l("world wide web") returns "web searching" and "web mining".

For scientific publications, weights are computed as defined in Equation 6. The computation is basically identical with the one for user profiling as shown in Equation 4. The difference is that BL is applied over single documents and IDF is computed over the document collection.

$$w'_{hcf\text{-}idf}(c,d) = BL(c,d) \cdot log \frac{|D|}{|d \in D : c \in d|} \quad (6)$$

LDA: As third profiling method, we use LDA [2, 1], an unsupervised topic modeling method. LDA identifies latent topics in a document collection, where each document is represented as a probability distribution over topics, while each topic is again represented as a probability distribution over a number of words. Please note that for user profiling, we treat the set of social media items I_u published by a user u as one *single* social media document in this profiling method. It is known that topic models that treat a user's microblog postings as one combined social media document outperform topic models computed over single postings of a user for recommendation tasks [10]. We first create a topic model for the entire document collection D (using the parameters and tools described in detail in Section 5.3). Subsequently, we run LDA with the given topic model for the document collection D and infer a probability distribution over topics for the user's social media document I_u.

Again, we use the same notation of concepts c as introduced above: Each topic generated by LDA is treated as a concept $c \in C$. The weight of a concept c is defined by $w'_{lda}(c,I_u) = p(c \mid I_u)$ for user profiles and $w'_{lda}(c,d) = p(c \mid d)$ for document profiles, where $p(c \mid d)$ and $p(c \mid I_u)$ denote the probability of the concept (i.e., topic) c in the social items I_u and document d, respectively.

4.2 Decay Function

We compare two decay functions f, namely sliding window and exponential decay. In the past, both functions have been used in recommender systems [24, 21, 26]. However, so far they have not been empirically compared. The profiling functions w' described in the previous section are combined with a decay function f in order to obtain a final weight w. The final weights are computed by Equation 7 for the set of social media items and Equation 8 for the candidate items.

$$w(c, I_u) = \sum_{c \in i : i \in I_u} f(t_i) \cdot w'(c, i) \qquad (7)$$

$$w(c, d) = f(t_d) \cdot w'(c, d) \qquad (8)$$

Please note that when employing LDA, the decay functions can only be applied on the candidate items, because we treat the user's social media items as one single document.

Sliding Window: There are two kinds of sliding window functions, whose window size is defined by (a) the number of items [13] and (b) the period of time [25]. The approach (a) is employed to identify relatively short-term features (e.g., user interests from web browsing histories) [13], while the approach (b) is used to identify long-term features [25]. We aim at extracting a user's professional interests, which are rather long-term. Thus, we take the approach (b) and use only social media items and documents that are younger than a given threshold point in time $thresh$. The sliding window function can be represented as Equation 9.

$$f_{sw}(t) = \begin{cases} 1 & for\ t \geq thresh \\ 0 & for\ t < thresh \end{cases} \qquad (9)$$

For user profiles, we set the threshold based on the work by Orlandi et al. [21]. They found out that the half life time is $thresh_{social} = 250\ days$. For document profiles, Sangam et al. [22] observed that the half-life time of the scientific publications in the field of social science is $9.04\ years$. In our experiment, we use a dataset of scientific publications in economics (see Section 5.3), which has a large overlap with social science. Thus, we set $thresh_{doc} = 9.04\ years$ [22] and remove scientific publications published more than $9.04\ years$ ago from the candidate items.

Exponential Decay: The exponential decay function is defined as shown in Equation 10.

$$f_{exp}(t) = e^{-(t_{current}-t)/\tau}, \qquad (10)$$

where $t_{current}$ denotes the current time and τ is a positive number presenting mean-life [21]. For user profiles, we set $\tau = 360\ days$ based on Orlandi [21]. Since Sangam et al. [22] found out that the mean-life of scientific publications in social sciences is $13.05\ years$, we set $\tau = 13.05\ years$ for document profiles.

4.3 Similarity Functions

We calculate the similarity scores between a user profile P_u and each document profile P_d. We cast a user profile P_u and document profiles P_d to a user profile vector $\vec{p}_u$ and document profile vectors $\vec{p}_d$, respectively. Each element in the vectors corresponds to a weight of a concept c.

Temporal Cosine Similarity: We employ the temporal cosine similarity function described in Equation 11 for the profiling methods CF-IDF and HCF-IDF.

$$\sigma_{tcossim}(P_u, P_d) = f(t_d) \cdot \frac{\vec{p}_u \cdot \vec{p}_d}{||\vec{p}_u|| \cdot ||\vec{p}_d||}, \qquad (11)$$

It extends the cosine similarity by the function $f(t_d)$, which results in higher similarity score to newer documents. $f(t_d)$ is a decay function from Equation 9 or Equation 10. t_d is time stamp of a scientific publication d. i.e., the year at which d was published.

Dot Product: For LDA, we employ the dot product computed as $\sigma_{dp}(p_u, p_d) = \vec{p}_u \cdot \vec{p}_d$. Since LDA represents documents as probability distribution, it is more reasonable to use Kullback-Leibler divergence (KL divergence). However, the dot product outperforms cosine similarity and Kullback-Leibler divergence (KL divergence) when representing documents using LDA [9].

5. EVALUATION

We conducted an online experiment with $n = 123$ participants in order to identify the best strategy for a recommender system along the factors described in Section 4. As social media platform, we choose Twitter as it is widely used in scientific communities [14]. We design our experiment following the experiment setup and procedure of Chen et al. [5]: Each participant obtains top-5 recommendations for each of the twelve strategies formed from the three factors. The recommendation performance of each strategy is measured by the rankscore [4]. Below, we describe the details of our experiment procedure and participants. Subsequently, we explain the dataset and the knowledge base used in the experiment. Finally, we introduce our evaluation metric.

5.1 Procedure

The participants are invited to a web application implementing the twelve recommendation strategies. First, participants input their public Twitter handles and e-mail address. Then, the participants' tweets are retrieved from the Twitter API. Subsequently, user profiles are created from the tweets using each of the three profiling methods and two decay functions. Based on the user profiles, personalized top-k recommendations of scientific publications are generated for each of the twelve strategies. We set the number of recommendations per strategy $k = 5$ along with Chen et al. [5]. After computing the recommendations, the participants receive an e-mail invitation to assess the recommendations. The participant go through all of the twelve strategies like as Chen et al. [5]. Thus, we apply a repeated measures design. Each participant obtains $12 \cdot 5 = 60$ recommendations in total throughout the experiment.

Prior to starting the experiment, participants are informed about the task of the experiment, i.e., rating the recommended publications based on relevance to their research interests, and confirmed consent. On each of the subsequent pages, the participants see a list of five recommendations produced by one of the twelve strategies. An example screenshot of the evaluation page is shown in Figure 2.

For each recommended scientific publication, the participants see its bibliographic information, i.e., authors, title, and year of publication. In addition, participants can look into the original PDF files by clicking on a link attached to

Figure 2: Screenshot of our experiment web page showing a randomized list of top-5 recommendations for the first of twelve strategies (which again are randomly ordered). For each recommendation the participants could assess the bibliographic record as well as click on the full-text document. The participants rated each recommended publication as "interesting" or "not interesting"' based on their research interests.

the bibliographic record. In order to avoid bias, the participants go through the twelve strategies in random order. For each strategy, the participants receive one list of five recommendations. The five recommendations in the lists are again shown in random order to the participants to avoid the well-known ranking bias. Typically, participants assume that top-ranked recommendations are essentially more relevant [3, 5]. Thus, again prior to starting the experiment we have explicitly informed the participants that we have randomized the order of the items in the top-5 lists. However, the actual ranks of the recommendations as well as their positions where the recommended items appeared on the participants' screen are stored in the database for later analyses. Participants evaluate each recommendation as "interesting" or "not interesting" by clicking on radio buttons next to the publication records like Chen et al. [5]. Please note, the participants had to evaluate all recommended items.

At the end of the experiment, we collect the demographic information of each participant, including gender, age, highest academic degree, major, years of profession, and current employment status (academia/industry). Finally participants could state free comments regarding the experiment.

5.2 Participants

We recruited $n = 123$ participants through mailing lists, tweets, and word-of-mouth on the Internet. Initially 160 participants registered their Twitter handles and email address for our experiment. Among them, 134 participants started the experiment after receiving the e-mail invitation. From these 134 participants, only eleven dropped in the course of assessing the recommendations in the twelve strategies. Thus, finally we obtain evaluations for all strategies from $n = 123$ participants. From these, 27 participants are female. The average age of the participants is 32.83 years (SD: 7.34). Regarding the highest academic degree, we have acquired 21 with a Bachelor, 58 have a Master, 32 a PhD, and 12 are lecturers/professors. While 83 participants work in academia, 40 work in industry. Tweets of the participants were retrieved via Twitter API. We only collected tweets in English as the scientific publications are also in English. The participants published on average 1096.82 En-

glish tweets (SD: 1048.46). The maximum and minimum numbers of tweets are 3192 and 2, respectively. Twitter users who have not produced any tweets in the last 250 *days* could not register and participate in the experiment, since we use a 250 *days* threshold for the decay function Sliding window (see Section 4.2). Five Twitter users could not participate in the experiment for this reason.

The participants spent on average 517.54 seconds to complete the assessment of the $5 \times 12 = 60$ recommendations (SD: 376.72). This does not include the time spent to register for the experiment, read the instructions, and filling out the final questionnaire. As incentive, each participant received the information about his most similar economist among 26 famous economists[4] and the top-5 dominant semantic concepts in their tweets after the experiment. In addition, the participants could opt-in to a raffle for one of two Amazon vouchers worth of 50 €.

5.3 Dataset Preparation

We use a large-scale dataset of scientific publications in the field of economics as candidate items and a high-quality taxonomy as a knowledge base for profiling methods.

Dataset of Scientific Publications. We collaborate with the providers of EconBiz[5], a portal for scientific publications in economics managed by ZBW, the German National Library of Economics. From this portal, we obtained 1 million URLs of open access publications and extracted full-texts and metadata (i.e., authors, title, year of publication) of 413,098 scientific publications. Finally, we determined the document language[6] and got 279,381 scientific publications in English, which were used in this experiment.

Knowledge Base in Economics. The ZBW also maintains and further develops the hierarchical knowledge base STW[7], a thesaurus specialized for the field of economics. The STW is freely available and is of high quality due to its manual maintenance by domain experts. The knowledge

---

[4]http://www.huffingtonpost.com/2012/11/13/economists-twitter_n_2122781.html
[5]http://www.econbiz.de/
[6]https://code.google.com/p/language-detection/
[7]http://zbw.eu/stw/version/8.12/about.en.html

base is poly-hierarchically organized with six levels. It contains $6,335$ semantic concepts and $11,679$ labels. The hierarchically organized concepts are connected with each other via $14,875$ edges. In order to extract as many labels as possible, we enhanced the original STW with DBpedia redirects[8]. From DBpedia redirects we can retrieve the synonymous labels for a concept. STW contains $2,692$ concepts that have both a DBpedia mapping and one or more DBpedia redirects. As an example, for the concept "Telecommunications industry" in the thesaurus, we obtain the DBpedia redirects "Telecommunications operator" and "Telephone companies" and use them as synonymous labels referring to the concept "Telecommunications industry". Finally, our extended STW contains $6,335$ concepts and $37,733$ labels. This extended STW is used for the profiling methods CF-IDF and HCF-IDF. For CF-IDF, we ignore the edges between concepts.

Processing of the tweets and publications. For the profiling methods CF-IDF and HCF-IDF, we extract semantic concepts from the participants' tweets and the scientific publications by matching the texts with the labels from the extended STW (i.e., a gazetteer-based approach). Before processing, we lemmatize both the tweets and the scientific publications using Stanford Core NLP[9] and remove stop words. Regarding the tweets, some of them contain hashtags indicating topics (e.g., #election) and user mentions (e.g., @UNICEF). We remove only the symbols # and @ from the tweets as Feng et al. [6] observed that the combination of the tweets' textual content with the hashtags and user mentions made the highest performance for tag recommendation.

This process extracts only the users' professional interests from tweets and helps to avoid noise (i.e., topics not relevant to professional interests in economics). A participant has published on average 1096.82 tweets (SD: 1048.46). On average $1,214.93$ concepts (SD: 1181.43) are contained in a participant's tweets and 1.07 concepts (SD: 0.31) are contained per tweet. Regarding CF-IDF and HCF-IDF, we calculate the ratio of the number of tweets containing at least one concept and the total number of tweets the user has published. This indicates the percentage of tweets that have contributed to creating the user profile. On average, 62.24% of the tweets (SD: 13.55) that a participant has published contain at least one concept in economics. These tweets are assumed to be relevant to the professional interests.

LDA. For constructing profiles by LDA, we use JGibbLDA[10]. We first run LDA to generate the topic model based on the given document set D. Following Blei et al. [1], we lemmatize the scientific publications using Stanford NLP Core. Subsequently, we remove stop words and words that appear in fewer than 25 scientific publications. We optimized the number of topics K regarding the maximum mean log likelihood of words given topics as suggested by Griffiths et al. [8]. We experimented with $K = 20, 50, 100, 200, 500, 1000,$ and 5000 and obtained the highest log likelihood for $K = 100$. All topic models were computed over 500 iterations. Regarding the further parameters for LDA, we set $\alpha = 0.5$ and $\beta = 0.1$ as suggested by Griffiths et al. [8]. To infer a topic distribution over a user's tweets, we run LDA again using the topic model for the document set D with 200

iterations. Prior to this, we prepare the tweets of a user u in a single social media document as described in Section 4.1.

5.4 Evaluation Metric

In order to assess the recommendation performance, we compute the rankscore [4] as used by Bostandjiev et al. [3] and introduced by Jannach et al [11]. Rankscore posits that each successive item in a list is less likely to be viewed by users with an exponential decay, as defined in Equation 12.

$$rankscore' = \sum_{d \in hits} \frac{1}{2^{\frac{rank_d - 1}{\theta - 1}}} \quad (12)$$

θ denotes a viewing halflife parameter controlling the speed of the exponential decay. As suggested by Breese et al. [4], we set $\theta = 5$. $hits$ refers to the set of documents d evaluated as "interesting" and $rank_d$ denotes the rank of a recommended item d in a list. Please note $rank_d$ denotes the actual rank stored in the database different from the position where a item d appears in the list (cf. Section 5.1). The normalized rankscore is computed by $rankscore = rankscore'$ $/rankscore_{max}$, where the maximum rankscore $rankscore_{max} = \sum_{j=1}^{k} \frac{1}{2^{\frac{j-1}{\theta - 1}}}$. Here, k is the number of the recommended items. We set $k = 5$. We also computed Mean Average Precision (MAP), Precision@5, Mean Reciprocal Rank (MRR), and normalized Discounted Cumulative Gain (nDCG). Overall, the results are similar to the rankscore and thus omitted for reasons of brevity. The interested reader may refer to the details in the appendix [20].

6. RESULTS

In this section, we document the results of the experiment[11] and conduct the statistical analyses. We set a significance level of $\alpha = 5\%$ for all statistical tests (please do not confuse with α for LDA in Section 5.3).

6.1 Quantitative Analyses

We first report the best performing strategy among the twelve strategies. Subsequently, we analyze the influence by the experimental factors followed by investigating the correlations between the recommendation performance and the numbers of tweets written by a user. Finally, we analyze the performance related to the number of times the participants clicked on the full-text of a publication.

Best performing strategy. Table 3 documents the average rankscores of the twelve strategies sorted in decreasing order. Overall, the best performing strategy is the strategy CF-IDF $\times$ Sliding window $\times$ All. We apply a one-way repeated-measure ANOVA in order to identify if there are significant differences between the strategies. For using ANOVA, we first need to verify whether the variances of the rankscores of the twelve strategies are equal. This is done by using Mauchly's test, which reveals a violation of sphericity in the strategies ($\chi^2(65) = 435.90$, $p = .00$). It may lead to positively biased F-statistics and increases the risk of false positives. To reduce this risk, we apply a Greenhouse-Geisser correction of $\epsilon = .61$ and run the one-way repeated-measure ANOVA. It reveals a significant difference in the rankscores of the strategies ($F(6.60, 805.33) = 21.98$, $p = .00$). To assess the pair-wise significant differences between

[8] http://oldwiki.dbpedia.org/Downloads39#redirects
[9] http://nlp.stanford.edu/software/corenlp.shtml
[10] http://jgibblda.sourceforge.net/

[11] The anonymized experimental data is available from: http://dx.doi.org/10.7802/1224

the twelve strategies, a post-hoc analysis is conducted. We have applied Shaffer's modified sequentially rejective Bonferroni procedure (Shaffer's MSRB procedure) [23] that takes into account the number of different experiment conditions, i. e., the number of recommendation strategies. The result of the post-hoc analysis is presented in Table 4. The vertical and horizontal dimensions of the Table 4 show the eleven-by-eleven comparison of the twelve strategies. As one can see, we observe various significant differences between the strategies ($p < .05$, marked in bold font). For example, while we observe a significant difference between the strategies CF-IDF $\times$ Sliding window $\times$ Title and HCF-IDF $\times$ Sliding window $\times$ All ($t(122) = 4.77$, $p = .00$), there is no significant difference between the strategies CF-IDF $\times$ Exponential decay $\times$ Title and LDA $\times$ Sliding window $\times$ Title ($t(122) = 2.43$, n.s., $p = .41$).

Table 3: Rankscores of the strategies in decreasing order. M and SD denote mean and standard deviation, respectively.

	Strategy			Rankscore
	Profiling Method	Decay Function	Content	M (SD)
1.	CF-IDF	Sliding window	All	.59 (.33)
2.	HCF-IDF	Sliding window	All	.56 (.34)
3.	HCF-IDF	Sliding window	Title	.55 (.33)
4.	HCF-IDF	Exponential decay	Title	.52 (.30)
5.	CF-IDF	Exponential decay	All	.51 (.32)
6.	HCF-IDF	Exponential decay	All	.49 (.30)
7.	CF-IDF	Exponential decay	Title	.41 (.29)
8.	CF-IDF	Sliding window	Title	.39 (.27)
9.	LDA	Exponential decay	Title	.35 (.31)
10.	LDA	Sliding window	Title	.33 (.31)
11.	LDA	Exponential decay	All	.32 (.30)
12.	LDA	Sliding window	All	.27 (.33)

Difference in experiment factors. Subsequently, we analyze the results with respect to each experimental factor. To this end, we first apply Mendoza's test [17] to check for violations of sphericity against the factors. Mendoza's test is an extension of Mauchly's test to adopt to multi-way repeated-measure ANOVA. It shows significances with the global ($\chi^2(65) = 435.90$, $p = .00$) and the factors *Profiling Method* ($\chi^2(2) = 12.21$, $p = .00$), *Profiling Method $\times$ Decay Function* ($\chi^2(2) = 20.02$, $p = .00$), and *Profiling Method $\times$ Document Content* ($\chi^2(2) = 8.61$, $p = .01$). Subsequently, we run a three-way repeated-measure ANOVA with a Greenhouse-Geisser correction of $\epsilon = .60$ for the global and $\epsilon = .91$ for the factors *Profiling Method*, $\epsilon = .87$ for *Profiling Method $\times$ Decay Function*, and $\epsilon = .93$ for *Profiling Method $\times$ Document Content*. Table 5 shows the results of the ANOVA with F-ratio, effect size η^2, and p-value. The effect size is small when $\eta^2 > .02$, medium when $\eta^2 > .13$, and large when $\eta^2 > .26$. The analyses reveal significant differences in all three factors and their contributions except the factor *Decay Function*. For all factors with significant differences, we apply again a post-hoc analysis using Shaffer's MSRB procedure with respect to each factor. In terms of the factor *Profiling Method*, the post-hoc analysis reveals significant differences between all pairs of HCF-IDF, CF-IDF, and LDA (details of the post-hoc analysis are omitted for the reasons of brevity and documented in our TR [20]). Although the strategy CF-IDF $\times$ Sliding window $\times$ All performs best as shown in Table 3, the best *Profiling Method* is

HCF-IDF as it performs under all other factors better than CF-IDF and LDA. Regarding the factor *Document Content*, "All" outperforms "Title" ($F(1, 122) = 5.18$, $p = .02$). Regarding the factor *Profiling Method $\times$ Decay Function*, the result suggests that the strategies with the Exponential decay function perform better than those with the Sliding window function when LDA is employed. In addition, there are significant differences among the three profiling methods when a decay function is fixed. In both decay functions, HCF-IDF performs best, followed by CF-IDF, and LDA. Referring to the factor *Profiling Method $\times$ Document Content*, the result indicates that All is a better choice than Title, when CF-IDF is employed. In profiling methods HCF-IDF and LDA, the factor *Document Content* makes no significant difference. It indicates that HCF-IDF does perform well when only titles of candidate items are available. In addition there are significant differences among the profiling methods when a choice of *Document Content* is fixed. In those cases, HCF-IDF always outperforms others. In terms of the factor *Decay Function $\times$ Document Content*, All is a better choice than Title, when Sliding window is used.

Correlation of recommendation performance with the number of tweets, the number of concepts, the number of concepts per tweet, and the percentage of tweets containing at least one concept. We computed Pearson's r and Kendall's τ between the users' mean rankscores and each of the number of tweets, concepts, concepts per tweet and the percentage of tweets containing at least one concept. A correlation may show a dependency that could influence the recommendation performance. The results show no significant correlation: As stated in Section 5.3, a participant has published on average 1096.82 tweets (SD: 1048.46). There is no significant correlation with the rankscores ($r(121) = .04$, n.s., $p = .62$ and $\tau = .00$, n.s., $p = .98$). Referring to the number of concepts, on average $1,214.93$ concepts (SD: 1181.43) are contained in a participant's Twitter stream. The correlation coefficients are non-significant ($r(121) = .05$, n.s., $p = .60$ and $\tau = -.01$, n.s., $p = .94$). Regarding the number of concepts per tweet, a participant's tweet contains on average 1.07 concepts (SD: 0.31) with again no significant correlation to the rankscores ($r(121) = -.05$, n.s., $p = .59$ and $\tau = -.02$, n.s., $p = .71$). Regarding the tweets that contribute in computing the user profiles for the methods with CF-IDF and HCF-IDF, we calculate the percentage of the number of tweets containing at least one concept and the number of tweets for each user. On average, 62.24% of the tweets (SD: 13.55) that a participant has published contain at least one concept, with no significant correlation ($r(121) = -.04$, n.s., $p = .67$ and $\tau = -.03$, n.s., $p = .73$)

6.2 Questionnaire Feedback

At the end of the experiment, the participants were asked to rate: "How easy it was to make the decisions whether a recommended publication is interesting". Using a 5-point Likert scale, where values between 1 and 5 refer to very difficult to very easy, the result is fairly high with an average of 3.68 (SD: 0.88). Regarding question "Whether the participants noticed a difference among the twelve strategies", the result is similarly high with an average of 3.46 (SD: 1.20). In the free text feedback, one participant denoted that the recommender system failed to pick up his primary field de-

Table 4: Post-hoc analysis with pairwise p-values over the twelve strategies using Shaffer's MSRB procedure. The p-values are marked in bold font if $p < .05$, which indicates a significant difference between the two strategies. Strategies are sorted by rankscores as shown in Table 3.

				All	Title	Title	All	All	Title	Title	Title	Title	All	All
				Sliding window	Sliding window	Exponential decay	Exponential decay	Exponential decay	Exponential decay	Sliding window	Exponential decay	Sliding window	Exponential decay	Sliding window
				HCF-IDF	HCF-IDF	HCF-IDF	CF-IDF	HCF-IDF	CF-IDF	CF-IDF	LDA	LDA	LDA	LDA
				2.	3.	4.	5.	6.	7.	8.	9.	10.	11.	12.
1.	CF-IDF	Sliding window	All	.99	.97	.72	.22	.12	**.00**	**.00**	**.00**	**.00**	**.00**	**.00**
2.	HCF-IDF	Sliding window	All		.99	.99	.99	.99	**.00**	**.00**	**.00**	**.00**	**.00**	**.00**
3.	HCF-IDF	Sliding window	Title			.99	.99	.99	**.00**	**.00**	**.00**	**.00**	**.00**	**.00**
4.	HCF-IDF	Exponential decay	Title				.99	.99	**.01**	**.00**	**.00**	**.00**	**.00**	**.00**
5.	CF-IDF	Exponential decay	All					.99	**.04**	**.00**	**.00**	**.00**	**.00**	**.00**
6.	HCF-IDF	Exponential decay	All						.12	**.02**	**.00**	**.00**	**.00**	**.00**
7.	CF-IDF	Exponential decay	Title							.99	.99	.41	.28	**.01**
8.	CF-IDF	Sliding window	Title								.99	.84	.61	**.03**
9.	LDA	Exponential decay	Title									.99	.99	.72
10.	LDA	Sliding window	Title										.99	.99
11.	LDA	Exponential decay	All											.88

Table 5: Three-way repeated-measure ANOVA with Greenhouse-Geisser correction with F-ratio, effect size η^2, and p-value.

Factor	F	η^2	p
Profiling Method	58.40	.48	**.00**
Decay Function	1.17	.01	.28
Document Content	5.18	.04	**.02**
Profiling Method × Decay Function	4.63	.04	**.01**
Profiling Method × Document Content	17.09	.14	**.00**
Decay Function × Document Content	4.69	.04	**.03**
Profiling Method × Decay Function × Document Content	3.35	.03	**.04**

spite having tweeted about that field. Apart from this, we received many positive comments (e.g., interesting, useful).

7. DISCUSSION

The strategies with HCF-IDF perform almost equally well compared to the best performing strategy CF-IDF × Sliding window × All. There is no significant difference between them as described in Table 4. The strong advantage of HCF-IDF is that it reaches its performance already when using only the titles of the scientific publications. The reason is that spreading activation over the hierarchical knowledge base used in HCF-IDF successfully reveals concepts that are not explicitly mentioned in the texts. CF-IDF works well when full-texts are available. Referring to LDA, the recommendation performance of the strategies with LDA is overall low, even if full-texts are available. A possible reason is that LDA cannot construct accurate user profiles because of the shortness and sparseness of social media items. Without accurate user profiles it is impossible to make good recommendations, even if full-texts are available. In fact, a slight correlation between the rankscores of LDA and the number of tweets is observed [20]. It indicates that participants with more tweets receive better recommendations.

Please note as documented in [20], rankscores are almost exact same values with Precision@5 and nDCG. Although rankscores are slightly different with MAP and MRR, the order of performance of strategies are almost identical. Thus, the arguments described in this paper do not be influenced by differences among those evaluation metrics.

Our dataset covers scientific publications in the broader field of economics. Thus, although the dataset is obtained from a portal of economics literature, it contains scientific publications from various fields including, e.g., social sciences, political sciences, and information sciences. In the experiment, 31 of 123 participants do not have a major in economics. We have conducted an ANOVA test to identify whether the recommendation performance is significantly different for participants from economics and those not in economics. The result shows that majors make no significant difference ($F(1, 121) = 0.01$, n.s., $p = .94$). Thus, we assume that our approach may be transferred to other domains. Furthermore, there are a lot of domain-specific hierarchical knowledge bases in other domains freely available such as Medical Subject Headings (MeSH) for medicine and ACM Computing Classification System (ACM CCS) for computer science. An overview of freely available hierarchical knowledge bases is maintained by the W3C as cited in the introduction. The knowledge bases are of similar structure to the STW used in this paper. They are of high quality as they are manually crafted by domain experts. Therefore, HCF-IDF can be easily applied to other fields. Our approach could be integrated with other social media platforms (e.g., Facebook, LinkedIn), where users generate short and sparse texts. In addition, HCF-IDF is robust against the number of tweets a user published, because there is no correlation between the number of tweets and the rankscores of the strategies with HCF-IDF.

Our results may potentially be influenced by the amount of time that each participant spent for evaluating the $5 \times 12 = 60$ recommended publications by the twelve strategies in the experiment. However, they spent on average 517.54 seconds (SD: 376.72) to complete the evaluation of the 60 recommendations. In addition, we randomized the order of the strategies presented to the participants to counterbalance any influence on the order of the strategies. Thus, we think that our results are not influenced by it. Another potential threat to the validity of our results could be the procedure how we recruited the participants. We believe that the risk is low since we collected enough participants regarding each demographic factor (as shown in Section 5.2). Regarding the demographic factors, we found significant differences only for the participants' highest academic degree and participants' gender (details are documented in the TR [20]). However, they do not affect the order of the recommendation performance of the different strategies.

8. CONCLUSIONS

This paper contributes to content-based recommender systems for scientific publications based on user profiles extracted from social media platforms. We have constructed twelve different recommendation strategies along three factors, namely profiling method, decay function, and document content. The online experiment revealed that titles of scientific publications are sufficient to achieve competitive recommendation results when employing the profiling method HCF-IDF. Thus, the spreading activation over the hierarchical knowledge base enables HCF-IDF to extract a sufficient number of concepts from titles to compute competitive recommendations. This is an important result as full-texts are not always available, e.g., due to legal reasons.

Acknowledgement. This research was co-financed by the EU H2020 project MOVING (http://www.moving-project.eu/) under contract no 693092. We like to thank the anonymous participants of our study to support this research.

9. REFERENCES

[1] D. M. Blei and J. D. Lafferty. Dynamic topic models. In *ICML*. ACM, 2006.

[2] D. M. Blei, A. Y. Ng, and M. I. Jordan. Latent dirichlet allocation. *JMLR*, 3, 2003.

[3] S. Bostandjiev, J. O'Donovan, and T. Höllerer. Taste-Weights: a visual interactive hybrid recommender system. In *RecSys*. ACM, 2012.

[4] J. S. Breese, D. Heckerman, and C. Kadie. Empirical analysis of predictive algorithms for collaborative filtering. In *UAI*. Morgan Kaufmann, 1998.

[5] J. Chen, R. Nairn, L. Nelson, M. Bernstein, and E. Chi. Short and tweet: experiments on recommending content from information streams. In *CHI*. ACM, 2010.

[6] W. Feng and J. Wang. We can learn your# hashtags: Connecting tweets to explicit topics. In *ICDE*. IEEE, 2014.

[7] F. Goossen, W. IJntema, F. Frasincar, F. Hogenboom, and U. Kaymak. News personalization using the CF-IDF semantic recommender. In *WIMS*. ACM, 2011.

[8] T. L. Griffiths and M. Steyvers. Finding scientific topics. *NAS*, 101, 2004.

[9] T. J. Hazen. Direct and latent modeling techniques for computing spoken document similarity. In *the Spoken Language Technology*. IEEE, 2010.

[10] L. Hong and B. D. Davison. Empirical study of topic modeling in Twitter. In *SOMA*. ACM, 2010.

[11] D. Jannach, M. Zanker, A. Felfernig, and G. Friedrich. *Recommender systems: an introduction.* Cambridge University Press, 2010.

[12] P. Kapanipathi, P. Jain, C. Venkataramani, and A. Sheth. User interests identification on Twitter using a hierarchical knowledge base. In *ESWC*. Springer, 2014.

[13] M. K. Khribi, M. Jemni, and O. Nasraoui. Automatic recommendations for e-learning personalization based on web usage mining techniques and information retrieval. In *ICALT*. IEEE, 2008.

[14] J. Letierce, A. Passant, J. G. Breslin, and S. Decker. Understanding how twitter is used to spread scientific messages. In *WebSci*. Web Science Trust, 2010.

[15] Y. Li, M. Yang, and Z. M. Zhang. Scientific articles recommendation. In *CIKM*. ACM, 2013.

[16] C. Lu, W. Lam, and Y. Zhang. Twitter user modeling and tweets recommendation based on Wikipedia concept graph. In *AAAI Workshops*, 2012.

[17] J. L. Mendoza. A significance test for multisample sphericity. *Psychometrika*, 45(4), 1980.

[18] S. E. Middleton, D. C. De Roure, and N. R. Shadbolt. Capturing knowledge of user preferences: ontologies in recommender systems. In *K-CAP*. ACM, 2001.

[19] C. Nishioka, G. Große-Bölting, and A. Scherp. Influence of time on user profiling and recommending researchers in social media. In *i-KNOW*. ACM, 2015.

[20] C. Nishioka and A. Scherp. Profiling vs. time vs. content: What does matter for top-k publication recommendation based on twitter profiles? - an extended technical report. http://arxiv.org/abs/1603.07016.

[21] F. Orlandi, J. Breslin, and A. Passant. Aggregated, interoperable and multi-domain user profiles for the social web. In *I-SEMANTICS*. ACM, 2012.

[22] S. L. Sangam and S. S. Mogali. Obsolescence of literature in the field of social sciences. *PEARL*, 7(3), 2013.

[23] J. P. Shaffer. Modified sequentially rejective multiple test procedures. *J. of the ASA*, 81(395), 1986.

[24] W. Shen, J. Wang, P. Luo, and M. Wang. Linking named entities in tweets with knowledge base via user interest modeling. In *KDD*. ACM, 2013.

[25] S. J. Soltysiak and I. B. Crabtree. Automatic learning of user profiles - towards the personalisation of agent services. *BT Tech. J.*, 16(3), 1998.

[26] K. Sugiyama and M.-Y. Kan. Scholarly paper recommendation via user's recent research interests. In *JCDL*. ACM, 2010.

[27] K. Sugiyama and M.-Y. Kan. Exploiting potential citation papers in scholarly paper recommendation. In *JCDL*, pages 153–162. ACM, 2013.

[28] C. Wang and D. M. Blei. Collaborative topic modeling for recommending scientific articles. In *KDD*. ACM, 2011.

[29] Z. Zhao, Z. Cheng, L. Hong, and E. H. Chi. Improving user topic interest profiles by behavior factorization. In *WWW*. IW3C2, 2015.

Early Prediction of Scholar Popularity

Masoumeh Nezhadbiglari, Marcos André Gonçalves, Jussara M. Almeida

Department of Computer Science, Universidade Federal de Minas Gerais, Brazil
{masoumeh,mgoncalv,jussara}@dcc.ufmg.br

ABSTRACT

Prediction of scholar popularity has become an important research topic for a number of reasons. In this paper, we tackle the problem of predicting the popularity *trend* of scholars by concentrating on making predictions both as *earlier* and *accurate* as possible. In order to perform the prediction task, we first extract the popularity trends of scholars from a training set. To that end, we apply a time series clustering algorithm called K-Spectral Clustering (K-SC) to identify the popularity trends as cluster centroids. We then predict trends for scholars in a test set by solving a classification problem. Specifically, we first compute a set of measures for individual scholars based on the distance between earlier points in her particular popularity curve and the identified centroids. We then combine those distance measures with a set of academic features (e.g., number of publications, number of venues, etc) collected during the same monitoring period, and use them as input to a classification method. One aspect that distinguishes our method from other approaches is that the monitoring period, during which we gather information on each scholar popularity and academic features, is determined on a per scholar basis, as part of our approach. Using total citation count as measure of scientific popularity, we evaluate our solution on the popularity time series of more than 500,000 Computer Science scholars, gathered from Microsoft Azure Marketplace[1]. The experimental results show that the our prediction method outperforms other alternative prediction methods. We also show how to apply our method jointly with regression models to improve the prediction of scholar popularity values (e.g., number of citations) at a given future time.

CCS Concepts

•**Information systems** → *Data management systems;*

Keywords

Popularity prediction, Scholar popularity, Early Trends, Academic Scholar Features

---

[1] https://datamarket.azure.com/dataset/mrc/microsoftacademic

Permission to make digital or hard copies of all or part of this work for personal or classroom use is granted without fee provided that copies are not made or distributed for profit or commercial advantage and that copies bear this notice and the full citation on the first page. Copyrights for components of this work owned by others than ACM must be honored. Abstracting with credit is permitted. To copy otherwise, or republish, to post on servers or to redistribute to lists, requires prior specific permission and/or a fee. Request permissions from permissions@acm.org.

JCDL '16, June 19–23, 2016, Newark, NJ, USA.

© 2016 ACM. ISBN 978-1-4503-4229-2/16/06. . . $15.00

DOI: http://dx.doi.org/10.1145/2910896.2910905

1. INTRODUCTION

We have witnessed a steep increase in the volume of scholarly publications, such as scientific articles, conference papers, books and other types of scientific communications in basically all research fields. Such phenomenon is followed by an increasing competition among scientists, as the amount of financial and human resources to produce high quality research is limited. Accordingly, funding agencies and academic departments have relied on some measures of academic success in order to try to better distribute such resources among scholars. One of such measures, which aims at assessing the impact of a scholar's research is " popularity", usually quantified by metrics such as overall number of citations [16, 13, 32] or the well-known h-index [10].

In this context, a natural question that arises in many contexts is "How *popular* will a scholar be in the near future or in the long run? " Answering such question is valuable for several goals. From an organization's perspective, knowing the scientific potential of a scholar can be very helpful in decisions for hiring faculty members or for guiding funding agencies in their decision processes. Moreover, academic search engines such as Google Scholar and Microsoft Academic or scientific recommender systems (e.g.,[23]) can benefit from such information as a feature for improving their rankings. More importantly, answers for such question, and mainly the factors that influence such answers, can help an individual scholar to better manage her scientific career.

Traditionally, the *total number of citations* has been widely used as a measure of *popularity* for both publications and scientific researchers [27, 13, 32, 16]. Indeed, it has already been argued that citation counts are better indicators of the scientific contribution of researchers than impact factors such as the h-index [13]. Accordingly, we focus on this metric in this paper.

Some prior studies on scholar popularity focus on studying the impact of academic features on popularity [27, 13, 16]. Others aim at developing popularity prediction methods [5, 10]. Among the latter, most attempt to predict the popularity of individual publications. Some studies, for instance, predict the future citation counts of articles based on learning models [33, 6, 34]. Despite such efforts, we are aware of only two previous studies on predicting the popularity of scholars. In [1], the authors use regression models to predict the h-index of scholars at a future time. In [20], the author aims at predicting the scholars' scientific impact in terms of future number of citations and found that the current number of citations is the best reliable predictor for such a prediction.

Complementing prior work, we here are interested in predicting the *trend* that the popularity of a scholar will follow in the future (or her popularity curve), as opposed to predicting popularity values at specific future times. Prediction of popularity trends is valuable as it may bring insights into the evolution of the research impact of a scholar. It may also contribute to improving the effectiveness of models to predict future popularity values, as demonstrated in [26, 35]. Moreover, producing prediction models of scientific impact can also induce interesting services for a digital library, such as a career profile prediction service and expert recommendation.

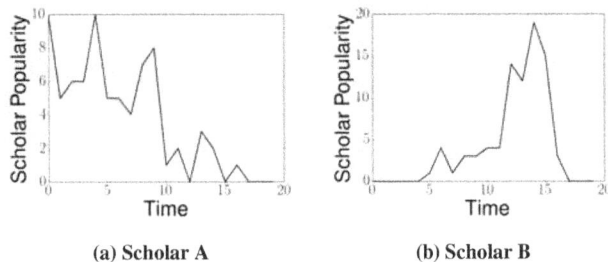

(a) Scholar A   **(b) Scholar B**

Figure 1 :Popularity Evolution of two scholars during 20 years

Another significant contribution of our study is that we aim at solving a tradeoff that is inherent to any prediction task. On one hand, we want to make the prediction as early as possible. The sooner we make a prediction, the earlier corrective measures (if any) can be applied[2]. On the other hand, we want to make predictions as accurate as possible. These two goals are often conflicting as one needs to monitor the scholar features for longer periods to guarantee more accurate predictions. Unlike prior work, we here solve this tradeoff on a per scholar basis (i.e., the monitoring period is different for different scholars), recognizing that different scholars may present quite different popularity evolution curves.

This is better illustrated in Figure 1, which shows the popularity curves of two scholars. Scholar A receives most of her citations at the beginning of her academic career, whereas scholar B becomes more popular later in her profession. Thus, if we monitor both scholars during the same period (e.g., 8 years) to make the prediction, a large portion of the popularity of scholar A would have already passed. Perhaps more accurate and useful predictions could have been made much earlier in scholar A's lifespan. In contrast, predictions before the first 5 years most certainly would not capture the correct trend of scholar B. Thus, the aforementioned tradeoff must be solved separately for each scholar, which implies that determining the duration of the monitoring period for each scholar is part of solving the prediction task.

We tackle the problem of predicting popularity trends of individual scholars by applying a novel two-step learning approach called TrendLearner which was originally proposed for user generated content (UGC) on the Web [12]. In this approach the popularity trends of UGC are predicted based on a tradeoff between prediction effectiveness and remaining interest in the content after prediction. In here, we adapt TrendLearner to our context of predicting scholar popularity trends by solving the tradeoff between prediction effectiveness and remaining citations (or remaining popularity) after prediction. Our adaptation of TrendLearner to the scholar domain has two main steps:

1. In the first step, the popularity trends of scholars are identified by applying a time series clustering algorithm, named K-Spectral Clustering (K-SC) [35]. K-SC extracts popularity

trends from a training set based on the centroids of clusters, being agnostic to the volume and length of the time interval.

2. In the second step, a classifier is first built to predict the popularity trend (i.e., class) of each scholar based on distances between her popularity time series and the trends previously extracted by K-SC. This classifier produces as output the probability of the scholar belonging to a particular trend/class. Finally, we build upon this classifier by combining those probabilities with a set of academic features associated with the scholars (e.g., number of publications, number of venues) to an ensemble learner, named Extremely Randomized Trees classifier [14].

We here refer to this adaptation of TrendLearner to the scholar domain as ScholarTrendLearner. We evaluate ScholarTrendLearner prediction results with respect to both Micro and Macro F1 scores, which are often used for measuring classification performance, as well as remaining popularity, defined as the fraction of all citations remaining after prediction. Our prediction results show that the combination of estimated class probabilities with scholar academic features significantly improves prediction effectiveness compared with using either probabilities or scholar features separately. We also show that ScholarTrendLearner can be applied jointly with two regression-based prediction models (ML and MRBF models) to improve the prediction of citation counts at a given future date.

The rest of this paper is organized as follows. Section 2 discusses related work and we present our prediction model in Section 3. The dataset and experimental setup used in our experiments are described in Section 4. Our experimental results on predicting popularity trends as well as improving regression-based popularity prediction models are presented in Sections 5 and 6, respectively. Finally, Section 7 concludes the paper and offers some directions for future work.

2. RELATED WORK

Some previous studies aimed at measuring the influence of scientific research based on different metrics. These metrics can be classified into two categories: publication level and author level metrics. A number of previous efforts focused on estimating the influence of scientific publications. As an example, Yan et al. implemented a system that takes a series of features of a specific publication as input and predicts its number of citations after a given time period [33].

Regarding the influence of individual scholars, Ding and Cronin [8] proposed the use of weighted citation counts as a measure of the prestige of a scholar, whereas unweighted citation counts should be used as an estimate of the scholar popularity. J. E. Hirsch [17] proposed $h-index$, a measure that combines both productivity and citation impact of a scholar by capturing the number of publications and the number of citations per publication. More recently, some approaches have been introduced that improve some limitations of $h-index$. For example, unlike $h-index$, $g-index$ [11] depends on the full citation count of very highly cited papers and it can be defined as the number of highly cited articles, such that each of them has an average of g citations. Two years later Schreiber introduced $h_m-index$ [28], a modification of $h-index$ that takes multiple co-authorships into account by counting each paper only fractionally according to (the inverse of) the number of authors. In a different perspective, Gonçalves et al. [16] quantified the impact of various academic features (e.g., number of publications, quality of publication venues, properties of the co-authorship network, etc) on scholar popularity by applying regression analysis. The au-

---

[2]We acknowledge that there are also some important boundary events in a scholar career's in which such predictions are useful such as job applications, midterm review before going up for tenure and tenure decision. In any case, our method can be easily adapted to predict in specific points in time.

thors also uncovered five profiles (or trends) of scholar popularity evolution.

Chakraborty et al. [6] tackled the problem of predicting citation counts of a given article by proposing a two-stage prediction model. The first step of the model fits the pattern of early popularity measures of the article into one of six given patterns. Next, a regression model predicts future citation count of the article based on the subpopulation of scholars (in a training set) who follow the same fitted pattern. Aiming at *predicting* the future popularity of a scholar, Mazloumian [20] examined the predictive capability of citation counts and found that they are reliable predictors of future success (e.g., future citation counts and approval of research grants) for scientists. Acuna et al. proposed a model to predict the future h-index of a scholar based on linear regression with elastic net regularization [1]. The authors evaluated their model on a set of 3,085 neuroscientists. On a different direction, Penner et al. provided evidence that, for the purpose of predicting a scientist's future h-index, linear regression models suffer a variety of flaws and their performance strongly depends upon career age [25].

Van Djik [31] focused on a slightly different problem: predicting whether a scholar will become a principal investigator (PI). They found that it depends on the number of publications, the impact factor (IF) of the journals in which those papers are published, and the number of papers that receive more citations than average for the journal in which they were published (citations/IF). However, both the scholar's gender and the rank of their university are also of importance, suggesting that non-publication features play a statistically significant role in this process. Hirsch [18] on the other hand focused on an comparison of the predictive power of different metrics, namely, h-index, total citation count, citations per paper, and total paper count. He found that h-index *appears* to be more suitable to predict future achievement than the other metrics but explicitly stated that further studies are required to confirm this.

Compared to these studies, we here focus on a somewhat different problem: predicting the popularity trend (or curve, evolution pattern) of a scholar as early and accurate as possible. Yet, we show that our popularity trend prediction model can be applied to improve regression-based models that predict the future popularity value of a scholar. This is achieved by developing specialized regression models for each trend (as proposed in [26]).

Ours is the first study we are aware of that aims at predicting popularity trends of scholars. However, similar efforts in other domains, notably popularity of user generated content (UGC), can be cited. For instance, Nikolov [24] proposed a method that predicts whether a tweet will become a trending topic by applying a binary classification model (trending versus non-trending), learned from a set of objects from each class. In [2], the authors designed a prediction model in two steps. First they classify UGC objects (e.g., videos) based on their popularity trends and then predict the popularity of that object in the future. Unlike those studies, our method considers the tradeoff between remaining citations after prediction and prediction effectiveness, adapting a model called TrendLearner, previously proposed to the context of UGC popularity trend predictions [12], to the particular context of scholar popularity trends. Like TrendLearner, our approach determines the duration of the period during which each scholar should be monitored before prediction on a per scholar basis, while other studies such as [2, 6, 29, 26, 19] considered fixed monitoring periods for all objects/scholars. Prediction of popularity trends has also been studied in social networks and search engines. For instance Vakali et al. [30] designed a cloud-based application named Cloud4Trend to cluster streams of web data and detect the trend of user generated content on Twitter and blogging systems. Golbandi et al. [15]

explored a search trend detection algorithm [9] to devise a method for predicting query counts in order to detect search trends.

In sum, to the best of our knowledge, ours is the first study that tackles the prediction of scholar popularity trends as early and accurately as possible recognizing that different scholars may exhibit quite different popularity trends (as identified by [16]). Our solution determines the best monitoring period for each scholar so as to achieve a good tradeoff between prediction effectiveness and remaining citation (or popularity) after prediction.

3. PREDICTION MODEL

In this section we describe our scholar popularity trend prediction model, which was adapted from a method that was originally proposed for predicting the popularity of UGC. As mentioned before, we tackle the tradeoff between prediction effectiveness and the capability of making such prediction as soon as possible, a problem to which we refer to as *early prediction of scholar popularity*.

Our model can be summarized into two parts. Firstly the goal is to extract the scholar popularity trends using a training set (Section 3.1). Next, we predict the popularity trend (or class) of each scholar in a test set by training a classification method using various scholar features as input (Section 3.2).

3.1 Extracting Popularity Trends

We identify scholar popularity trends by clustering the popularity time series of scholars in a given training set. To that end, we exploit a clustering algorithm called K-Spectral Clustering (K-SC), as done in [16]. The K-SC algorithm effectively finds temporal patterns based on a time series similarity measure. Similarly to the K-Means algorithm [36], which minimizes the sum of the squared Euclidean distances between the members of the same cluster, K-SC computes cluster centroids by introducing a new distance metric that is invariant to scaling and translation of the time series [35]. That is, given two vectors p_x and p_y that represent the popularity time series of two scholars, the distance $dist(p_x, p_y)$ between both vectors is defined as following:

$$dist(p_x, p_y) = \min_{\alpha, q} \frac{||p_x - \alpha p_{y(q)}||}{||p_x||} \qquad (1)$$

where $p_{y(q)}$ is the shifted time series p_y by q time units. Note that $dist(p_x, p_y)$ is symmetric in p_x and p_y. For a fixed value of q the optimal distance can be computed by setting its gradient in terms of α equal to zero. Therefore the exact solution for α is $\alpha^* = \frac{p_x^T p_{y(q)}}{||p_{y(q)}||^2}$ which minimizes $dist(p_x, p_y)$. However there is no simple manner to find the optimal q. Thus, as in [16, 12], we search for the optimal value of q considering all integers in the range $(-n, n)$, where n is the length of the input vectors p_x and p_y. Note that K-SC requires all time series have the same size n. Thus, we represent each scholar by a vector with n elements where each element represents the scholar popularity (i.e., number of citations) in one year. We discuss how we set the value of n in Section 4.1. The detailed description of K-SC algorithm can be found in [35].

Though there exists other clustering methods, such as K-Means and Affinity Propagation [22], we chose to use K-SC as it has some desirable properties for our application. Firstly, we need a time series clustering method compatible with our focus on trends (i.e., popularity evolution patterns), as opposed to specific popularity and time values. Secondly, the euclidean distance used in the aforementioned methods has major drawbacks for this goal, as pointed out by previous studies [3, 35]. For instance, it fails to account for the shifted behavior of time series. K-SC, on the other hand, employs $dist(p_x, p_y)$, which is invariant to time shifts and popularity scale. Thus, it is an algorithm capable of finding the optimal alignment between different time series. Thirdly, it has been shown that K-SC can be very effective on the task of extracting trends from social media [35] and should be easily adaptable to our goals

Given a number of clusters k and the set of time series to be clustered, K-SC starts by randomly setting the initial centroids. Next, each time series p_y is assigned to the closest centroid based on $dist(p_x, p_y)$. Each new centroid C_{K_i} should be updated such that:

$$C_{K_i}^* = \arg\min_C \sum_{p_x \in K_i} dist(p_x, C)^2$$

The algorithm updates the centroids until it converges, i.e., until all time series remain within the same cluster. Each cluster's centroid represents the popularity trend that the time series in the cluster follow. So we refer to each cluster as a class K_i, which is represented by centroid C_{K_i}. We discuss how we define the given number of clusters k in Section 4.2. The next step of our method consists of predicting the cluster (or class) to which each scholar in a test set belongs. Such prediction is performed given the identified cluster centroids (classes) as well as early measures of the scholar popularity (i.e., early points in the scholar popularity curve) and possibly the values of a set of academic features computed over the same monitoring period. We discuss this step of our method in the following section.

3.2 Predicting Popularity Trends

Given the k centroids (classes) obtained in the previous step using a training set, we now aim at predicting the popularity trend, i.e., determining the class, of each scholar in a given test set as early and as accurate as possible. Hence, we perform our prediction task by building a classifier which monitors the popularity time series (and possibly other academic features) of each scholar x during a monitoring period t_x. As soon as the classifier is "confident enough" that it can determine the class of x, the algorithm stops and returns the detected class. This is performed for each scholar in the test set independently. We experiment with four classification strategies. The first strategy exploits solely the distances between the popularity curve of each vector p_x (up to the monitoring period t_x) and the centroid of all classes (section 3.2.1). We also explore two other classification strategies that employ a state-of-the-art learning method – extremely randomized trees (ERTree) [14] – to build a classification algorithm. In one strategy, we use the same computed probabilities as input to the ERTree. In the other, we experiment with a set of academic features, whose values are computed over the same monitoring period t_x, as input to ERTree (Section 3.2.2). Finally we combine the two former approaches in a fourth algorithm by using both probabilities and academic features as input to ERTRee. We show that this algorithm, which we call ScholarTrendLearner, improves the quality of prediction task considering the tradeoff between prediction effectiveness and citations after prediction (section 3.2.3).

3.2.1 Prediction Based on Class Probabilities

We build a classifier that computes the probability of belonging to class K_i based on the distances between the initial points in the popularity curve of x (captured in vector p_x) and each curve C_{K_i} (denoting the centroid of class K_i). Regarding the shifting invariants in computing the distances, we consider all possible alignments between p_x and C_{K_i}. That is, given a monitoring period t_x, we take a starting time window t_s and vary it from 1 to $|C_{K_i}| - t_x$, where $|C_{K_i}|$ is the number of time windows in C_{K_i}. Thus, given

centroid C_{K_i}, the monitoring period t_x and a starting window t_s, this probability is obtained as follows:

$$P(p_x \in K_i | C_{K_i}; t_x, t_s) \propto e(-dist(p_x[1:t_x], C_{K_i}[t_s:t_s+t_x-1])) \quad (2)$$

As already discussed, different popularity time series may need different monitoring periods. Thus, given Equation 2, the classifier computes the probability of each scholar belonging to each class at the end of each time window, starting with t_x equal to 1, and returns the class K_i with the highest probability. For each scholar x, the algorithm stops this procedure once the computed probability exceeds a class-specific threshold $\theta^{[i]}$ or the monitoring period t_x exceeds a maximum limit γ_{max}. Threshold $\theta^{[i]}$ captures the minimum confidence required to state that a scholar belongs to class K_i. We also consider that a minimum monitoring $\gamma^{[i]}$ period is provided for each class K_i, given that different classes, exhibiting different popularity dynamics, may require quite different monitoring periods. This procedure is shown in Algorithm 1.

Algorithm 1 computes probabilities and monitoring periods for all scholars in a given test set D_{test}. The algorithm takes as input the time series of all scholars in D_{test}, vector C_K with all class centroids, vector θ with the minimum confidence thresholds for each class, vector γ with the minimum thresholds for monitoring period for each class, and γ_{max}, the maximum threshold for the monitoring period. The output is a vector t with the number of monitored time windows for each scholar and a matrix M with the probabilities of each scholar belonging to each class.

The algorithm begins by initializing matrix M and vector t with 0 in all elements. Starting with a monitoring period t_x equal to the minimum possible for all classes, the algorithm monitors each time series in D_{test}, and computes the probability of it belonging to each class using function *ComputeProb*. This works as follows: for a given t_x, the function computes the probability by trying all possible alignments between the initial elements of p_x (up to t_x) and the corresponding cluster centroid. This is done by applying Equation 2 using all possible values of t_s. The algorithm then takes the largest of all computed probabilities along with the associated class. The algorithm stops searching for the class of a scholar x when both the computed probability and the monitoring period t_x exceed class-specific thresholds $\theta^{[i]}$ and $\gamma^{[i]}$, respectively. At this point, it saves the identified class in matrix M and the current t_x in vector t. The algorithm repeats this procedure for all scholars in D_{test}, returning matrix M and vector t. Note that matrix M may contain only zeros for some scholars, indicating cases for which the algorithm was not able to predict a class with minimum confidence, within the maximum monitoring period allowed (γ_{max}). This classification strategy exploits only the probabilities of a scholar belonging to each class. We refer to it as *ProbClassifier*.

3.2.2 Prediction Using ERTrees

Inspired by [7], we propose to use the probabilities obtained by Algorithm 1 as input features to a feature-learning method. Specifically, we use the estimated probabilities as input to an Extremely Randomized Trees (ERTree) classifier, a tree-based ensemble method [14]. We refer to this prediction method as *ProbERTrees*. We chose ERTree as classification algorithm because of its good effectiveness and computational efficiency on large scale datasets. The method builds regression trees according to the classical top-down procedure but randomly choosing the most appropriate features to grow up the trees. A majority voting of the individual regression trees at classification time leads to the final prediction. We refer to the original paper [14] for more information on ERTree.

As a variation of the aforementioned strategy, we also exploited the ERTree classifier using as input a set of academic features as-

Algorithm 1 Producing Matrix M and vector t

Require: $D_{test}, C_k, \theta, \gamma$ and γ_{max}

Initial $t[i] = 0$; $M[i][j] = 0$; $i \leftarrow |D_{test}|$ $t_x \leftarrow min(\gamma)$

while $(t_x \leq \gamma_{max})$ and $(i > 0)$ **do**

    for all $p_x \in D_{test}$ **do**

        for all $C_{K_i} \in C_k$ **do**

          $P^{[i]} \leftarrow ComputeProb(p_x, C_{k_i}, \theta^{[i]}, t_x)$

        end for

        $prob \leftarrow max(P)$; $k \leftarrow argmax(P)$ $\triangleright$ Identify class k with largest probability

        if $(prob > \theta^{[k]})$ and $(t_x \geq \gamma^{[k]})$ **then**

          $t^{[x]} \leftarrow t_x$; $M^{[x]} \leftarrow p$

          $i \leftarrow i - 1$; $D_{test} \leftarrow D_{test} - \{p_x\}$ $\triangleright$ Classification of x is done, remove it from D_{test}

        end if

    end for

    $t_x \leftarrow t_x + 1$

end while

return t, M

function $ComputeProb(p_x, C_{k_i}, \theta^{[i]}, t_x)$

    $t_s \leftarrow 1$; $p \leftarrow 0$

    while $(t_s \leq |C_{k_i}| - t_x)$ and $(p < \theta^{[i]})$ **do**

        $p' \leftarrow e\,(-dist(p_x[1:t_x], C_{K_i}[t_s:t_s+t_x-1]))$ $\triangleright$ Check all possible alignments between the first t_x windows of p_x (monitoring period) and C_{K_i} by varying t_s. Stops once probability exceeds minimum threshold

        $p \leftarrow max(p, p')$ $\triangleright$ Take the largest probability (best alignment)

        $t_s \leftarrow t_s + 1$

    end while

    return p

end function

---

sociated with each scholar. These features are presented in Table 1. Note that the feature values used as input are computed over the same monitoring period t_x. We call this approach *FeatERTrees*.

Table 1 : List of Considered Academic Features

Feature Notation	Description
# citations	total number of citations
# publications	total number of publications
# coauthors	total number of coauthors
# venues	total number of distinct venues
h − index	h-index of the scholar
short impact factor	average yearly number of citations in the whole period
long impact factor	average yearly number of citations in the last two years

3.2.3 ScholarTrendLearner

Finally, we propose to "merge" the two former approaches by combining the probability features with "domain-specific" features. In other words, we use as input features to the ERTree classifier both the set of probabilities taken from matrix M and the scholar's associated feature values (Table 1). We refer to this approach as ScholarTrendLearner.

4. EVALUATION METHODOLOGY

In this section, we present the dataset we used to evaluate our prediction models (Section 4.1) as well as the experimental setup adopted in these experiments (Section 4.2).

4.1 Dataset

We evaluate our prediction models using an experimental research dataset developed by Microsoft Academic named as Microsoft Azure Marketplace (MAM)[3]. MAM indexes 19,856,190 scholars covering a total of over 39 million publications by those scholars. The dataset also contains other types of information such as publication venues for journals and conferences as well as keywords and references for each publication. In order to exclude very inactive scholars, we restricted our dataset to authors having at least 10 publications. After applying this filtering, we obtained data about roughly 1,500,000 scholars. Using this data, we produced the yearly time series of the number of citations for each such scholar, considering the period between 1995 and 2014 (20 years). We note that MAM records are very sparse before and after this period. Thus, we set the parameter n, the length of the popularity time series, of the K-SC algorithm (see Section 3.1) equal to 20 elements[4]. Then we eliminated time series containing more than 80% elements equal to 0 indicating that the corresponding scholars were not very popular throughout their academic careers. After this filtering, we were left with 500,000 scholars, over which we evaluate our prediction models. For each scholar we also extracted the time series associated with the other features shown in Table 1, namely: total number of publications, distinct venues and coauthors as well as the value of h-index, short impact factor (the average number of citations of articles published in the last two years), and long impact factor (average number of citations received by papers published so far).

4.2 Experimental Setup

Since our popularity prediction problem is formulated as a clustering task combined with a classifier algorithm, we here discuss how we defined the input parameters of the K-Spectral clustering algorithm, Algorithm 1 and the Extremely Randomized Trees classifier. Similarly other clustering algorithms, K-SC requires the number of clusters k as input. To set such parameter, we relied on the β_{CV} clustering quality metric [21]. The β_{CV} is defined as the ratio of the coefficient of variation (CV)[5] of the intra-cluster distances to the CV of the inter-cluster distances. The intra-cluster distance is the distance between a cluster member and its centroid, and the inter-cluster distance is the distance between different cluster centroids. The general purpose of clustering is to group elements so as to obtain high similarity among members of the same cluster, and low similarity across members of different clusters. Thus, the idea behind β_{CV} is to minimize the variance of the intra-cluster distances while maximizing the variance of the inter-cluster distances. The value of β_{CV} should be computed for increasing values of k. We select the lowest value of k after which the value of β_{CV} becomes stable, implying that intra and inter-cluster distances are stable as well. This indicates that the clustering process converged. After applying the β_{CV} heuristic in our data, we identified 5 different clusters, as further discussed in Section 5.

---

[3]The dataset is of public use and can be downloaded from https://datamarket.azure.com/dataset/mrc/microsoftacademic.

[4]Note that scholars with fewer years of activity or no citations in some of those years have elements equal to 0 in their corresponding popularity vector.

[5]The ratio of the standard deviation to the mean.

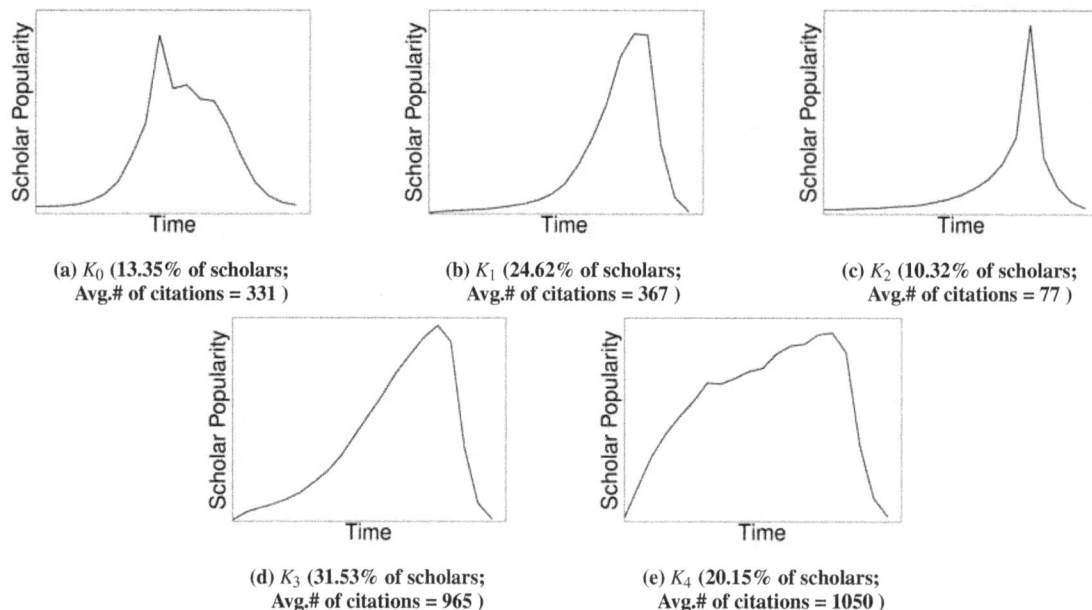

(a) K_0 (**13.35% of scholars;**
Avg.# of citations = 331)

(b) K_1 (**24.62% of scholars;**
Avg.# of citations = 367)

(c) K_2 (**10.32% of scholars;**
Avg.# of citations = 77)

(d) K_3 (**31.53% of scholars;**
Avg.# of citations = 965)

(e) K_4 (**20.15% of scholars;**
Avg.# of citations = 1050)

Figure 2 :Scholar Popularity Trends Extracted by K-SC.

Regarding the parameters of Algorithm 1, namely vectors θ and γ, we adopt the same parametrization approach as in [12]. Notably, we apply an One-Vs-All classification (OVA) algorithm [4] for all classes separately. OVA is implemented for all scholars in the training set that are classified previously by considering different values for $\gamma^{[i]}$ from 1 up to γ_{max}. We select the smallest value of $\gamma^{[i]}$ (the minimum monitoring period for class K_i) for which the classification performance exceeds a given target (e.g. classification above random chance, meaning Micro-F1 above 0.5). Using the selected value for $\gamma^{[i]}$, the minimum confidence $\theta^{[i]}$ is the average probability computed for all scholars in class K_i. Regarding parameter γ_{max}, we set its value equal to the total number of points in the popularity time series (i.e., 20), as done in [12]. Table 2 shows the best parameter values obtained following the aforementioned procedure for each of the 5 identified classes. These parameter values were used by all four classification approaches described in Section 3. We note that in order to be able to compare those approaches under fair conditions, all of them monitor each scholar x until t_x, the monitoring time produced as output of ScholarTrendLearner.

Table 2 :Best values for vector parameters θ and γ (average results across all training sets)

Cluster/class	θ	γ
K_0	0.279	13
K_1	0.228	13
K_2	0.226	13
K_3	0.229	14
K_4	0.226	14

Finally, the Extremely Randomized Trees classifier has three parameters K, M and n_{min}. Parameter K determines the strength of the feature selection process, and was set to the square root of the total number of features, as often suggested. The averaging strength parameter M denotes the number of trees in the ensemble, set to 20, a default value suggested by the majority of the works on ERTrees. We then apply cross-validation within the training set to choose the

smoothing strength parameter n_{min}, the minimum number of samples required for splitting a node, considering values equal to 1, 2, 4, 8, 16, 32. For more information concerning the parameterization of Extremely Randomized Trees we refer to [14].

5. PREDICTION RESULTS

In this section we present our experimental results regarding the extraction and prediction of scholar popularity trends. The results are assessed by means of a 5-fold cross validation[6] such that the original dataset is randomly partitioned into 5 equally sized folds. One of the folds is used as test set (D_{test}) whereas the remaining 4 folds are used as training set for learning the model (with one of the training folds used as validation set for parameter setting). The cross-validation process is then repeated 5 times with each of the 5 folds used exactly once as the test data. The results from the 5 test folds are then averaged to produce a single prediction result.

As discussed in section 4.2, the β_{CV} metric was used to determine the number of clusters of the K-SC algorithm. We found that the β_{CV} value stabilized around $k = 5$, which was used as input parameter for the K-SC algorithm. Figure 2 shows the centroids (i.e., popularity trends) of the 5 clusters for scholars in the training set[7]. The figure also presents, for each cluster, the percentage of scholars belonging to it as well as the average number of citations of them. Absolute values in both axes are omitted to emphasize the scale and time shifting (x-axis) invariants of the algorithm. We note that both the number of clusters and the cluster centroids are very similar to those obtained in [16]. This strong similarity provides validation to our findings, since that study was performed on a different dataset.

Classes K_1, K_3 and K_4 correspond to scholars who managed to become increasingly popular over time, acquiring more and more citations over time. Particularly, the popularity of scholars identified in cluster K_4 is roughly stable over a longer period of time. Moreover, those scholars tend to be the most popular ones, on average. Scholars in clusters K_1 and K_3 exhibit a sharper increase (par-

---

[6]A standard technique for estimating the performance of predictive models.

[7]The same clusters were found in all 5 training sets.

ticularly those in K_1) towards their popularity peak, having also a smaller total number of citations, on average, compared to scholars in K_4. Although there are similarities between these two patterns, the main difference regards the popularity growth rates. In contrast, scholars in clusters K_0 and K_2 are the least popular ones. They tend to loose popularity later in their academic life, possibly after a peak. The main differences between scholars in K_0 and K_2 are the rates of popularity growth and decay before and after the peak, which are much sharper for scholars in K_2. As mentioned, these popularity profiles are similar to those identified in [16]. However, unlike in that work, we here take a step further and try to predict the popularity trend of each scholar and use such trend predictions to improve the prediction of popularity values.

Recall that we here investigate four trend prediction strategies: ScholarTrendLearner, ProbClassifier, ProbERTree and FeatERTree. As discussed in Section 3, ProbClassifier is trained with probabilities and assigns the class (i.e., popularity trend) with largest probability (based on the distance to the closest cluster centroid) in matrix M to a scholar. ProbERTrees predicts a class for scholars by training an extremely randomized trees learner using only probabilities as input features. FeatERTrees predicts the class of a scholar by training an extremely randomized trees learner using only the scholar features. ScholarTrendLeaner, in turn, uses both sets of features as input to the learner. As mentioned, all methods use the monitoring period optimized by ScholarTrendLearner (presented in Table 2), to ensure a fair comparison[8]. All results are averages over all test sets, along with 95% confidence intervals.

Before discussing our popularity trend prediction results, we note that, as shown in Table 2, classes K_3 and K_4 require more monitoring time windows (i.e., larger value of $\gamma^{[i]}$), as these classes experience some fluctuations that may be confused as peaks. Thus, it is harder to determine whether the scholar belongs to one of those classes. On the other hand, classes K_0, K_1 and K_2 exhibit sharper peaks, requiring somewhat shorter monitoring periods, making it easier to classify scholars in these classes.

Table 3 show the results of the four prediction approaches in terms of prediction effectiveness. Since our prediction problem is a classification task, we assess prediction effectiveness using the Micro and Macro F1 scores. These measures are computed based on precision and recall measures. Precision for a class K_i, $p(i)$, is the number of correctly classified scholars out of those assigned to K_i by the classifier, while the recall of class K_i, $r(i)$, is the number of correctly classified objects out of those that should have been classified to that class. The F1 measure of class K_i, $F1(i)$ is computed as:

$$F1(i) = \frac{2p(i) \times r(i)}{p(i) + r(i)}$$

Macro F1 is the average F1 across all classes, whereas Micro F1 is computed based on global precision and recall, calculated for all classes.

Table 3 : Evaluation of Scholar Popularity Trend Prediction Methods (averages and 95% confidence intervals)

	Macro F1 Score	Micro F1 Score
ProbClassifier	0.743± 0.006	0.785± 0.003
ProbERTree	0.731±0.005	0.803±0.004
FeatERTree	0.352±0.005	0.459±0.005
ScholarTrendLearner	0.754± 0.007	0.814± 0.003

[8]All features are computed considering this optimized time window.

As shown in Table 3, ScholarTrendLearner improves the results over the other three alternative classification methods. Combining probabilities and scholar features brings explicit advantages over using either set of probabilities or scholar features separately. As shown in Table 3, the average improvements of ScholarTrendLearner over the other prediction approaches in Micro and Macro $F1$ reach up to 36% and 39%, respectively. In order to illustrate the results obtained with ScholarTrendLearner, Figure 3 shows the true popularity curve and the *predicted* trend of three example scholars. Note that the predictions, which match the correct classes, capture reasonably well the popularity dynamics of all three scholars.

As a note regarding prediction effectiveness, recall that, as discussed in Section 3.22, ScholarTrendLearner may not be able to properly identify the class of a scholar within the maximum monitoring period allowed (γ_{max}). In such cases, the algorithm produces no prediction result. However, we found that this happened for only a small fraction of scholars in our dataset (10%), which exhibit quite different popularity curves which could not be matched (with enough confidence) to any identified cluster.

Recall that ScholarTrendLearner was derived from TrendLearner [12], a model proposed to predict popularity trends of UGC. When comparing our results to those of the original method, we find much higher Micro and especially Macro $F1$ values. Moreover, unlike observed in [12], the use of only scholar features as input to ERTree (FeatERTree) proved to be a much worse approach, compared to the others. A third difference is that the improvements of ScholarTrendLearner over using only probabilities or scholar features, though statistically significant, are somewhat less impressive than the corresponding gains of the original TrendLearner on UGC. Such differences reflect the idiosyncrasies of each particular domain, and indicate that the adaptation of the original technique to a very different domain (the scientific one) does produce new important insights, being a significant contribution of our work.

We now turn our attention to how early the prediction of ScholarTrendLearner is made, as one of our goals is to make the predictions as early as possible. Recall that we assess this measure based on remaining popularity (citation) after the prediction. Figure 4 presents the complementary cumulative distribution of the fraction of remaining citations (RC) after prediction, produced for all scholars in the five test sets. In this graph, the x-axis represents the fraction of total citation counts after prediction while the y-axis represents the fraction of scholars with remaining citations higher than the corresponding value in the x-axis. We note that for around 48% of the scholars, the prediction could only be made after all the citations had been received (remaining citations equal to 0). This reflects the diversity of popularity profiles across the scholars and indicates that the prediction task we are tackling is quite hard. However, for 21% of the scholars, ScholarTrendLearner was able to make predictions before more than 50% of their citations were still to be received. For 40% of the scholars, this fraction is still quite significant (30%). Thus, there is a significant diversity in the required monitoring periods produced by ScholarTrendLearner. We also observe that for more than 45% of scholars, ScholarTrendLearner could make predictions before half of the maximum monitoring time windows (i.e., before 10 years). Other scholars required longer monitoring periods. In sum, the diversity of the results shown in Figure 4, considering both remaining citations and required monitoring period confirms the necessity of personalizing the monitoring period on a per-scholar basis, which our ScholarTrendLearner approach addresses.

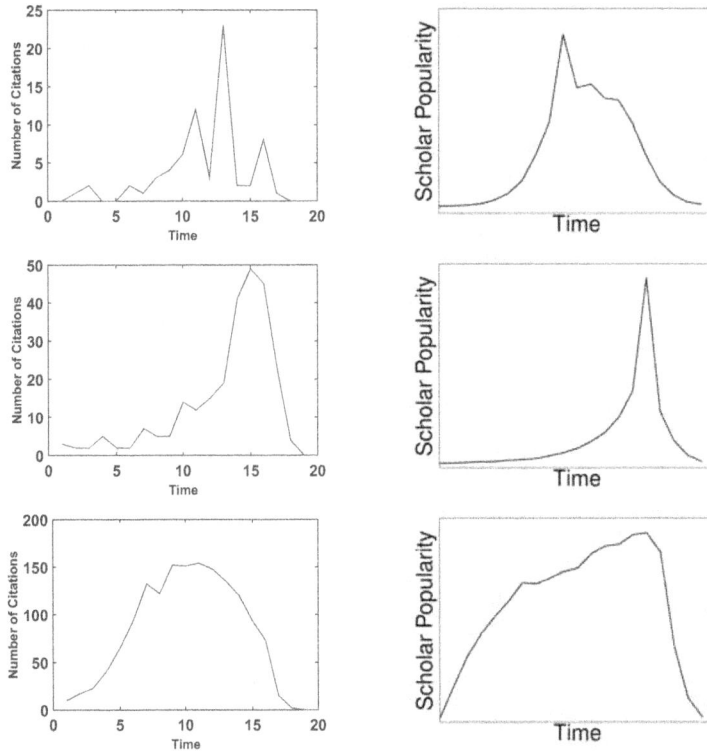

Figure 3 : True popularity curve (left) and predicted (right) for three example scholars

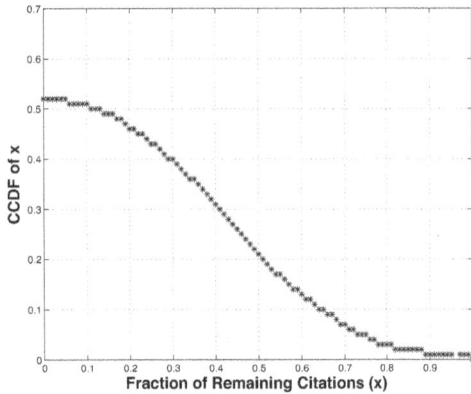

Figure 4 : Remaining citations after prediction

6. APPLYING RESULTS TO REGRESSION-BASED PREDICTIVE MODELS

Finally, we show how to apply the predicted trends to estimate the popularity of a scholar at a given future time. For this, we exploit ideas first proposed in [26], which builds specialized regression popularity prediction models for Web objects (in the case, YouTube videos) with similar popularity patterns. In that work, the authors demonstrated that the specialized models can, at classification time, reduce the prediction errors.

We combine our trend predictions with the state-of-the-art ML and MRBF regression-based models proposed in [26] to predict the future popularity of scholars. The original ML model is a multivariate linear regression model that receives the popularity (number of citations, in our case) acquired by an object (scholar) at multiple given points in time, up to a given reference date t_r and predicts the popularity of the object at a target date t_t ($t_r < t_t$). The MRBF model is an extension of the ML model that includes additional features that capture the similarity between the popularity curves of the object and of known examples from a training set, based on Radial Basis Functions (RBFs). The used performance criterion by these two models is the mean Relative Squared Error (mRSE).

We also exploit such error measure to assess the prediction effectiveness of the ML and MRBF models applied to the context of scholar popularity, considering two approaches, also proposed in [26]: a general and a specialized model. In the former, the parameters of the regression model are configured using the whole set of objects in the training set, while in the latter, the parameters are trained using only specific information of each cluster previously identified by the first step of our ScholarTrendLeaner method. We consider the monitoring time window t_x previously set by our model (see Table 2) as the reference date t_r and set $t_t = t_r + \delta$ as target date for δ equals to 1 and 4, that is, one and four years in the future, respectively.

Table 4 shows the average mRSE along with 95% confidence intervals produced by the two approaches: general and specialized. We notice that for both $\delta = 1$ and $\delta = 4$ the two MRBF models are much better than the ML results, which is consistent with [26]. We also note that for both values of δ, the specialized models generate better results than the general ones, mainly for the "specialized MRBF" vs. "general MRBF" case, though statistical superiority cannot be guaranteed due to the high variance in the results. Finally, notice that, as expected, the effectiveness for predicting farther in the future is smaller than for just one year later. Yet, the overall errors can be considered very small, meaning that our predictions are quite accurate, particularly for the "specialized MBRF" model.

Table 4 Prediction Errors mRSE for ML and MRBF models (Averages and confidence intervals; $\delta = 1, 4$)

Regression Model	$\delta=1$	$\delta=4$
General ML	0.043±0.000	0.282±0.005
Specialized ML	0.040±0.006	0.268±0.047
General MRBF	0.019±0.003	0.062±0.018
Specialized MRBF	0.018±0.004	0.047±0.009

7. CONCLUSIONS AND FUTURE WORK

In this paper, we introduced ScholarTrendLearner, a supervised prediction model that estimates the popularity trends of scholars using a combination of distance-based and associated academic features. Our main contribution is a method that aims at making predictions as early as possible while keeping prediction effectiveness as high as possible. Our method determines the monitoring time window on a per scholar basis, considering the diversity on the popularity of scholars throughout their careers.

Our experimental results show that high Macro and Micro F1 values can be obtained (above 0.75 and 0.81, respectively), with statistically significant gains over the alternative approaches Moreover, our solution is able to reliably predict the popularity of more than 20% of the scholars in our dataset before 50% of the total number of citations obtained by them in their entire career is acquired. Thus our method can provide an effective solution to the tradeoff between prediction effectiveness and remaining popularity after prediction. Furthermore, we concluded that combining our predicted popularity trends with two recently proposed regression based prediction models (ML and MRBF) can lead to highly accurate popularity predictions.

As possible directions for future work, we note that different academic features may affect differently the prediction effectiveness. Thus, we intend to investigate the effectiveness of ScholarTrendLearner using different subsets of features as well as possibly new academic features. Moreover, our present study is focused only in one knowledge area: Compute Science. Scholars from different areas may exhibit different popularity evolution patterns and idiosyncrasies. Therefore, a natural follow-up study is to apply our proposed methods to other knowledge areas, including a thorough comparison of the trends discovered for each of them. Another aspect we plan to investigate is the impact of data quality issues (missing information, name ambiguity, etc) on our prediction results. Finally, we also want to study the impact in our methods of changing the target popularity metric to h-index as there is evidence (though not strong yet) that it may have better predictive power than other metrics [18].

8. ACKNOWLEDGEMENTS

This work was partially funded by the InWeb (grant MCT/CNPq 573871/2008- 6) and MASWeb (grant FAPEMIG/PRONEX APQ-01400-14) projects, and by the authors' individual grants from CNPq, CAPES, and FAPEMIG.

9. REFERENCES

[1] D. E. Acuna, S. Allesina, and K. P. Kording. Future impact: Predicting scientific success. *Nature*, 489(7415):201–202, 2012.

[2] M. Ahmed, S. Spagna, F. Huici, and S. Niccolini. A peek into the future: Predicting the evolution of popularity in user generated content. In *Proceedings of the Sixth ACM International Conference on Web Search and Data Mining*, pages 607–616. ACM, 2013.

[3] G. E. Batista, E. J. Keogh, O. M. Tataw, and V. M. de Souza. Cid: An efficient complexity-invariant distance for time series. *Data Mining and Knowledge Discovery*, 28(3):634–669, 2014.

[4] C. M. Bishop. *Pattern Recognition and Machine Learning*. springer, 2006.

[5] C. Castillo, D. Donato, and A. Gionis. Estimating number of citations using author reputation. In *String Processing and Information Retrieval*, pages 107–117. Springer, 2007.

[6] T. Chakraborty, S. Kumar, P. Goyal, N. Ganguly, and A. Mukherjee. Towards a stratified learning approach to predict future citation counts. In *Proceedings of the 14th ACM/IEEE-CS Joint Conference on Digital Libraries*, pages 351–360. IEEE Press, 2014.

[7] A. Coates and A. Y. Ng. Learning feature representations with k-means. In *Neural Networks: Tricks of the Trade*, pages 561–580. Springer, 2012.

[8] Y. Ding and B. Cronin. Popular and/or prestigious? measures of scholarly esteem. *Information Processing & Management*, 47(1):80–96, 2011.

[9] A. Dong, Y. Chang, Z. Zheng, G. Mishne, J. Bai, R. Zhang, K. Buchner, C. Liao, and F. Diaz. Towards recency ranking in web search. In *Proceedings of the Third ACM International Conference on Web Search and Data Mining*, pages 11–20, 2010.

[10] Y. Dong, R. A. Johnson, and N. V. Chawla. Will this paper increase your h-index?: Scientific impact prediction. In *Proceedings of the Eighth ACM International Conference on Web Search and Data Mining*, pages 149–158. ACM, 2015.

[11] L. Egghe. Theory and practise of the g-index. *Scientometrics*, 69(1):131–152, 2006.

[12] F. Figueiredo, J. M. Almeida, M. A. Gonçalves, and F. Benevenuto. Trendlearner: Early prediction of popularity trends of user generated content. *Information Sciences*, 349-350:172–187, 2016.

[13] T. F. Frandsen and J. Nicolaisen. Effects of academic experience and prestige on researchers' citing behavior. *Journal of the American Society for Information Science and Technology*, 63(1):64–71, 2012.

[14] P. Geurts, D. Ernst, and L. Wehenkel. Extremely randomized trees. *Machine Learning*, 63(1):3–42, 2006.

[15] N. G. Golbandi, L. K. Katzir, Y. K. Koren, and R. L. Lempel. Expediting search trend detection via prediction of query counts. In *Proceedings of the Sixth ACM International Conference on Web Search and Data Mining*, pages 295–304, 2013.

[16] G. D. Gonçalves, F. Figueiredo, J. M. Almeida, and M. A. Gonçalves. Characterizing popularity: A case study in the computer science research community. In *Proceedings of the 14th ACM/IEEE-CS Joint Conference on Digital Libraries*, pages 57–66. IEEE Press, 2014.

[17] J. E. Hirsch. An index to quantify an individual's scientific research output. *Proceedings of the National Academy of Sciences of the United States of America*, 102(46):16569–16572, 2005.

[18] J. E. Hirsch. Does the h index have predictive power? *Proceedings of the National Academy of Sciences of the United States of America (PNAS)*, 104(49):19193–19198, 2007.

[19] Y. Matsubara, Y. Sakurai, B. A. Prakash, L. Li, and C. Faloutsos. Rise and fall patterns of information diffusion:

model and implications. In *Proceedings of the 18th ACM SIGKDD International Conference on Knowledge Discovery and Data Mining*, pages 6–14, 2012.

[20] A. Mazloumian. Predicting scholars' scientific impact. *PLOS One*, 7(11):e49246, 2012.

[21] D. A. Menascé and V. Almeida. *Capacity Planning for Web Services: metrics, models, and methods*. Prentice Hall PTR, 2001.

[22] M. Mohri, A. Rostamizadeh, and A. Talwalkar. *Foundations of machine learning*. MIT press, 2012.

[23] C. Nascimento, A. H. Laender, A. S. da Silva, and M. A. Gonçalves. A source independent framework for research paper recommendation. In *Proceedings of the 11th Annual International ACM/IEEE Joint Conference on Digital Libraries*, pages 297–306. ACM, 2011.

[24] S. Nikolov. *Trend or no trend: a novel nonparametric method for classifying time series*. PhD thesis, Twitter Inc, 2012.

[25] O. Penner, R. K. Pan, A. M. Petersen, K. Kaski, and S. Fortunato. On the predictability of future impact in science. *Scientific Report*, 3, 2013.

[26] H. Pinto, J. M. Almeida, and M. A. Gonçalves. Using early view patterns to predict the popularity of youtube videos. In *Proceedings of the Sixth ACM International Conference on Web Search and Data Mining*, pages 365–374. ACM, 2013.

[27] P. Riikonen and M. Vihinen. National research contributions: A case study on finnish biomedical research. *Scientometrics*, 77(2):207–222, 2008.

[28] M. Schreiber. To share the fame in a fair way, hm modifies h for multi-authored manuscripts. *New Journal of Physics*, 10(4):040201, 2008.

[29] G. Szabo and B. A. Huberman. Predicting the popularity of online content. *Communications of the ACM*, 53(8):80–88, 2010.

[30] A. Vakali, M. Giatsoglou, and S. Antaris. Social networking trends and dynamics detection via a cloud-based framework design. In *Proceedings of the 21st International Conference Companion on World Wide Web*, pages 1213–1f220, 2012.

[31] D. van Dijk, O. Manor, and L. B. Carey. Publication metrics and success on the academic job market. *Current Biology*, 24(11):516–517, 2014.

[32] E. Yan and Y. Ding. Applying centrality measures to impact analysis: A coauthorship network analysis. *Journal of the American Society for Information Science and Technology*, 60(10):2107–2118, 2009.

[33] R. Yan, C. Huang, J. Tang, Y. Zhang, and X. Li. To better stand on the shoulder of giants. In *Proceedings of the 12th ACM/IEEE-CS Joint Conference on Digital Libraries*, pages 51–60. ACM, 2012.

[34] R. Yan, J. Tang, X. Liu, D. Shan, and X. Li. Citation count prediction: Learning to estimate future citations for literature. In *Proceedings of the 20th ACM International Conference on Information and Knowledge Management*, pages 1247–1252. ACM, 2011.

[35] J. Yang and J. Leskovec. Patterns of temporal variation in online media. In *Proceedings of the Fourth ACM International Conference on Web Search and Data Mining*, pages 177–186. ACM, 2011.

[36] M. J. Zaki and W. Meira Jr. *Data mining and analysis: fundamental concepts and algorithms*. Cambridge University Press, 2014.

Evaluating Link-based Recommendations for Wikipedia

Malte Schwarzer
TU Berlin
ms@mieo.de

Moritz Schubotz
TU Berlin
schubotz@tu-berlin.de

Norman Meuschke
University of Konstanz
norman.meuschke@uni-konstanz.de

Corinna Breitinger
University of Konstanz
isg@uni-konstanz.de

Volker Markl
TU Berlin
volker.markl@tu-berlin.de

Bela Gipp
University of Konstanz
bela.gipp@uni-konstanz.de

ABSTRACT

Literature recommender systems support users in filtering the vast and increasing number of documents in digital libraries and on the Web. For academic literature, research has proven the ability of citation-based document similarity measures, such as Co-Citation (CoCit), or Co-Citation Proximity Analysis (CPA) to improve recommendation quality.

In this paper, we report on the first large-scale investigation of the performance of the CPA approach in generating literature recommendations for Wikipedia, which is fundamentally different from the academic literature domain. We analyze links instead of citations to generate article recommendations. We evaluate CPA, CoCit, and the Apache Lucene MoreLikeThis (MLT) function, which represents a traditional text-based similarity measure. We use two datasets of 779,716 and 2.57 million Wikipedia articles, the Big Data processing framework Apache Flink, and a ten-node computing cluster. To enable our large-scale evaluation, we derive two quasi-gold standards from the links in Wikipedia's "See also" sections and a comprehensive Wikipedia clickstream dataset.

Our results show that the citation-based measures CPA and CoCit have complementary strengths compared to the text-based MLT measure. While MLT performs well in identifying narrowly similar articles that share similar words and structure, the citation-based measures are better able to identify topically related information, such as information on the city of a certain university or other technical universities in the region. The CPA approach, which consistently outperformed CoCit, is better suited for identifying a broader spectrum of related articles, as well as popular articles that typically exhibit a higher quality. Additional benefits of the CPA approach are its lower runtime requirements and its language-independence that allows for a cross-language retrieval of articles. We present a manual analysis of exemplary articles to demonstrate and discuss our findings.

The raw data and source code of our study, together with a manual on how to use them, are openly available at: https://github.com/wikimedia/citolytics

Permission to make digital or hard copies of all or part of this work for personal or classroom use is granted without fee provided that copies are not made or distributed for profit or commercial advantage and that copies bear this notice and the full citation on the first page. Copyrights for components of this work owned by others than the author(s) must be honored. Abstracting with credit is permitted. To copy otherwise, or republish, to post on servers or to redistribute to lists, requires prior specific permission and/or a fee. Request permissions from Permissions@acm.org.

JCDL '16, June 19 - 23, 2016, Newark, NJ, USA
Copyright is held by the owner/author(s). Publication rights licensed to ACM.
ACM 978-1-4503-4229-2/16/06...$15.00
DOI: http://dx.doi.org/10.1145/2910896.2910908

Categories and Subject Descriptors

H.3.7 [**Information Storage and Retrieval**]: Information Search and Retrieval – *information filtering, relevance feedback*

General Terms

Information Systems, Recommender Systems, Wikipedia

Keywords

Co-Citation, Co-Citation Proximity Analysis, digital libraries, large-scale evaluations, citation analysis, document similarity measures, link-based, literature recommendations, big data

INTRODUCTION

Literature recommender systems (LRS) are a crucial filtering and discovery tool to manage the vast and continuously increasing volume of documents available in digital libraries and on the Web. Most LRS (approximately 55%) employ content-based document features and corresponding similarity measures to provide recommendations [1].

Especially in academia, LRS are a central fixture among research support tools. Keeping track of the latest research in one's field by identifying the most relevant papers is essential for research progress. The exponentially increasing number of published articles (approximately 1.9 million in 2015[1]) and the increased speed of article availability, e.g. due to Open Access and preprint publishing options, makes thorough literature research even more important, but at the same time more tedious and time consuming for researchers. In academic LRS, citation-based features and document similarity measures have proven valuable [24, 36].

Wikipedia is a large and rapidly growing digital library. As of April 2016, all language-specific versions of the Wikipedia combined contain approximately 39 million articles, of which five million are in English[2]. The English Wikipedia grew by approximately 1,000 articles per day in 2015. All Wikimedia projects received on average 18 billion page views (crawlers excluded) per month in 2015[3]. Despite Wikipedia's size, popularity and rapid growth, little research has addressed the issue of improving information search in Wikipedia through automated generation of article recommendations. Wikipedia relies entirely on manually created and curated links to related articles.

In this paper, we investigate the performance of citation-based similarity measures in recommending related articles in Wikipedia. Our study focusses on comparing the well-established

---

[1] We estimate the number of articles using a regression model that Bornmann et al. [4] derived from Web of Science data.

[2] http://en.wikipedia.org/wiki/Wikipedia:Size_of_Wikipedia

[3] http://reportcard.wmflabs.org

citation-based similarity measure Co-Citation (CoCit) to its proximity-weighted enhancement Co-Citation Proximity Analysis (CPA). We use Wikipedia links instead of citations to compute the two measures. By including the MoreLikeThis (MLT) function of the Apache Lucene framework, we evaluate a traditional text-based similarity measure employing a term vector space model. MLT was also used in comparable studies [25, 33].

1. BACKGROUND

1.1 Citation-based Similarity Measures

The link-based concepts Co-Citation [31] and Co-Citation Proximity Analysis [11, 12] originate from the field of Library Science. Academic *citations* can be regarded as the offline equivalent of *links* in Wikipedia or on the Web in general. The Co-Citation measure independently proposed by Small and Marshakova-Shaikevic [23, 31] reflects the frequency with which two documents are cited together in other documents. The more frequently two documents are co-cited, the more strongly related they are according to the CoCit measure. Figure 1 illustrates the CoCit concept, where Doc A and Doc B have a co-citation strength of two, since they are co-cited by Doc C and Doc D.

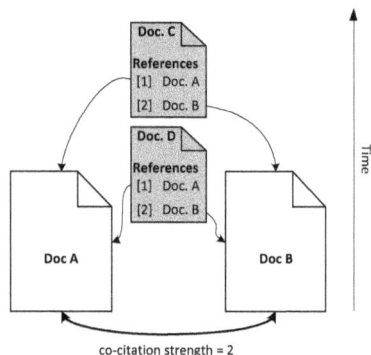

Figure 1: CoCit relationship between documents. Source [8]

The CoCit measure is representative of an era, in which the large majority of academic full texts was not readily available in digital form. Therefore, CoCit exclusively considers entries in the bibliography of academic documents, since this information was accessible using traditional citation indexes [7]. CoCit assigns equal weight to each pair of co-cited documents regardless of *where* in the citing document the citations occur.

Coinciding with the increase in digital availability of academic full texts, Gipp and Beel [12] proposed that taking into account the proximity of co-citations can enhance the effectiveness of the CoCit measure. When the citation markers of co-cited documents appear in close proximity within the citing document, the co-cited documents are more likely to be related. Gipp and Beel coined the concept Co-Citation Proximity Analysis (CPA).

Figure 2 illustrates the CPA approach. The documents B and C are considered more strongly related than A and B, because B is co-cited with C in the same sentence, whereas the citation of document A occurs in a different section of the document. To quantify the degree of relatedness of co-cited documents, CPA assigns a numeric value, the Co-Citation Proximity Index (CPI), to each pair of documents co-cited in one or more citing documents. The CPI reflects the smallest distance between the citation markers of two co-cited documents within a citing document. Gipp and Beel distinguished five levels of co-citation proximity, each of which is assigned a static CPI: same sentence (CPI=1), same paragraph (CPI=1/2), same chapter (CPI=1/4), same journal issue or book (CPI=1/8), same journal, but different

issue (CPI=1/16). The CPA score is formed by summing up the proximity weighted co-citations over all co-citing documents.

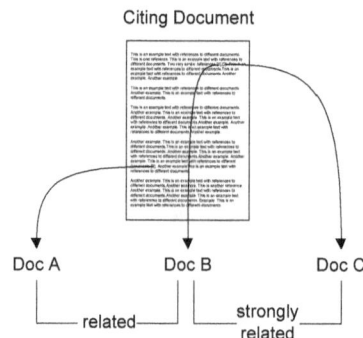

Figure 2: Document similarity assessment according to Co-Citation Proximity Analysis. Source [8]

1.2 Text-based Similarity Measures

To compare the results of the link-based similarity measure, we use the text-based MoreLikeThis (MLT) function of Apache Lucene. MLT uses a Vector Space Model (VSM) of terms as introduced by Salton, Wong and Yang [30] in combination with Term Frequency-Inverse Document Frequency (TF-IDF) weighting proposed by Jones [19]. Several studies and its widespread use among websites have proven MLT's suitability for determining website similarity [5, 20, 29].

2. RELATED WORK

Several publications investigate the placements of citations within the full-texts of documents as additional information for co-citation analysis. Tran et al. [33] and Eto [6] showed the increase in effectiveness of employing sentence-level, over paper-level, citation proximity on the task of retrieving related articles. Liu and Chen [22] analyzed the distribution of co-citations at four levels of proximity: article, section, paragraph and sentence level. They found that sentence-level co-citations can increase the accuracy and efficiency of co-citation analysis.

Gipp et al. investigated the analysis of citation patterns in academic documents to identify disguised forms of academic plagiarism such as paraphrases or translations. They proposed several detection algorithms, which aside from citation proximity also consider the order of citations, citation counts, and other properties to identify suspicious citation patterns [13]. They demonstrated the effectiveness and efficiency of their approach "Citation-based Plagiarism Detection" by analyzing known plagiarism cases [10] and by discovering previously unknown cases in a large full text collection [9].

Recommending citations for academic papers is a well-researched problem. Early approaches used collaborative filtering [24] or (co-)citation information [32]; hence, they required author profile information or partial bibliographies. More recent works focus on citation context analysis to identify suitable citations for specific parts of a paper. For instance, He et al. [14] trained a probabilistic topic model for the citation context, i.e. text range, surrounding user-specified placeholders for citations to identify and rank documents most relevant to the topic of the citation context. Huang et al. [17] extended this approach by proposing a translation model to map the topic of citation contexts to the topics of potential sources while accounting for differences in the vocabulary of the citation contexts and the sources. Most recently, Huang et al. [16] used a probabilistic neural network to model the relationship between citation contexts and potential sources.

For finding related pages in the English Wikipedia, Ollivier and Senellart [25] proposed the Green Measure, which uses Markov chains, and compared the measure to other methods. They found that Green Measure has both the best average results and the best robustness compared to Co-Citation, Cosine similarity with TF-IDF weighting and PageRank [26] of links. Aside from this work, we are unware of research addressing the recommendation of related pages in Wikipedia.

So far, the performance of the CPA approach has been evaluated for academic citations, but not for a large-scale hyperlinked environment, such as the English Wikipedia corpus. Additionally, no large-scale evaluation using "See also" links and clickstreams as quasi-gold standards has yet been performed on Wikipedia.

3. EXPERIMENTAL SETUP

3.1 Test Collection

Our test collection is a dump of the English version of Wikipedia. The dump was created in September 2014, consists of 4.6 million Wikipedia articles in XML Wiki markup, and has a size of 99 GB. To get an overview of the test collection's composition and to enable a comparison with other collections, we collected information on article length and the number of in-links. Figure 3 shows the distribution of words and in-links among articles. The word frequencies are grouped into bins of 20 words.

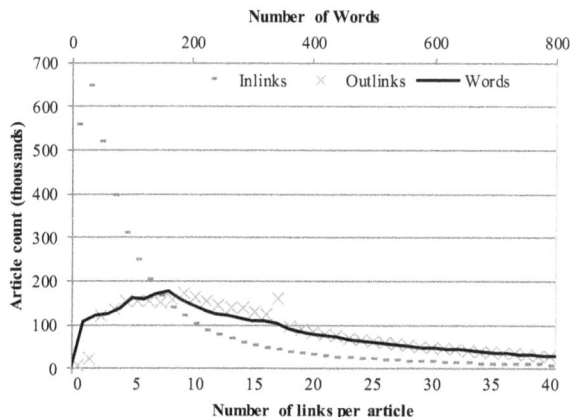

Figure 3: Distribution of word frequency (solid), in-links (dashes), and out-links (crosses) of articles.

On average, articles contained 740.54 words. The longest article contained 75,178 words. There is a consistently strong correlation between the number of out-links and the number of words for all article lengths. The distribution of in-links is heavily skewed. About 1.7 million of the 4.6 million articles have less than three in-links. On average, an article had 20.5 in-links. The most linked to article was "United States", which received 392,494 in-links. As reported by Belomi and Bonato [3], Wikipedia articles with a high number of in-links are mainly about geopolitical topics, famous people, abstract nouns, or common words.

3.2 Information Need

Our goal was a large-scale evaluation of the performance of similarity measures in recommending related Wikipedia articles. Instead of selecting a number of topics and defining topic-specific information needs, we wanted to obtain an understanding of how well the methods perform for the entire Wikipedia with its vast range of topics. Therefore, we defined a generalized information need for our study as follows:

"Recommend related Wikipedia articles that may be of interest to a reader of the source article".

3.3 Quasi-Gold Standards

Given the large scope of our study, we required human relevance judgments that suit our information need, are available for large parts of the collection and a broad range of topics, and are obtainable in an automated fashion. We derived two quasi-gold standards satisfying these requirements from analyzing (a) "See also" links and (b) clickstream data. In contrast to a traditional user study, which is typically limited to a few hundred articles at most, these datasets allowed an evaluation for 779,716 articles using "See also" links and 2.57 million articles using the clickstream data set.

Nonetheless, this evaluation approach lacks completeness. "See also" links and clickstream data are only approximations of complete relevance judgments. Therefore, we refer to them as quasi-gold standards, not gold standards. A quasi-gold standard is an approximation of a 'perfect' reference model. Both quasi-gold standards are being applied for the first time, and have yet to be evaluated by the research community.

3.3.1 "See Also" Links

A unique characteristic of Wikipedia articles is not only that they contain links to additional information in the form of internal references or external links, but also that they contain so-called "See also" sections. The purpose of these sections is to provide links to topically related Wikipedia articles [35], which results in these links acting as recommendation sets for relevant literature. Correspondingly, "See also" links are equivalent to a quasi-gold standard that allows a performance evaluation of a recommendation system.

Therefore, we classified articles as relevant if the retrieved article is listed in the "See also" section and as irrelevant otherwise. However, it is in this second assumption that we see a problem: We expect the "See also" links to be an incomplete quasi-gold standard created by a few Wikipedia editors. We assume that the main objective of Wikipedia editors lies in creating textual content, rather than providing useful literature recommendations, which means that if a retrieved document is not included in the "See also" links, it can still be topically related, i.e. relevant. Therefore, we can only decide if a result is relevant, but not if it is irrelevant. A true binary classification is not possible.

Hence, we expect a precise true positive classification for articles that exist as "See also" links. However, many results could be classified as false negatives, even if a result is truly relevant because the recommendation is missing in the "See also" links.

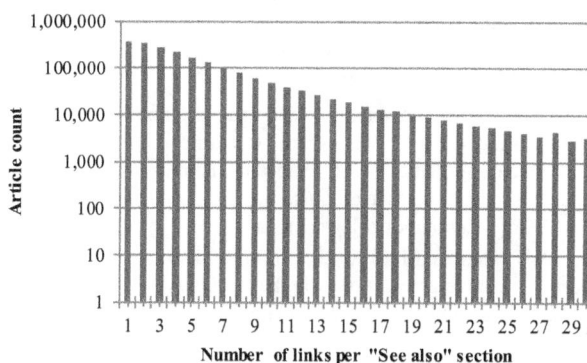

Figure 4: Number of links per "See also" section.
Avg.: 2.6 links. Total: 2,028,146 links.

We extracted the "See also" section and its links using an automated process. Figure 4 shows the distribution of the number of "See also" links in the Wikipedia dataset. The test collection contained 779,716 Wikipedia articles with "See also" sections (17% of the corpus), where each section on average contained 2.6 links. This low number of links per section additionally contributed to the incompleteness of relevance judgments, since the number of relevant recommendations that could be made from the Wikipedia corpus is likely greater than the number of available "See also" links.

3.3.2 Clickstreams

The recent publication of Wikipedia clickstreams by WikiResearch [28, 37] allowed us to use a second quasi-gold standard. The dataset contains clickstreams for 2,572,063 articles (56% of the corpus) in the form of aggregated HTTP referrer information during the month of February 2015. The HTTP referrer indicates the page from which a user clicked to the article in question. Using this data, we can determine the number of clicks on out-links for articles. For out-links, which occur multiple times in an article, only the total number of clicks is provided. WikiResearch cleaned the dataset from computer-generated clicks (bot activity). However, researchers of the Wikipedia foundation have observed that the filtering of bots should be improved [34]. We assume that the dataset contains some noise from bot activity, but we cannot quantify or reduce the noise level, since only aggregated clickstream data was available to us. In the future, WikiResearch plans to release more datasets, which would increase the value of clickstreams as a quasi-gold standard.

We consider the number of clicks on a link as a cardinal relevance classification regarding the linked article. The more often a link is clicked, the more relevant we assume the article to be. Whether this assumption holds true for *all* articles, and whether it is the major force driving clicks, has not been proven. Other factors can also affect the number of clicks, such as the descriptiveness value of the link, or the link's position within the article. A recently published study showed that the Click-Through-Rate decreases in proportion to the link's position from the top [27].

The two quasi-gold standards differ in their conceptual properties: While the "See also" quasi-gold standard is created by the Wikipedia editors; clicks are relevance judgments by all readers. Moreover, clicks can only occur on links that exist in the article content. Such in-content links are also included for navigational purposes, while "See also" links are exclusively literature recommendations. The Wikipedia manual states to only add links in "See also" sections that do not exist in other parts of the article.

3.4 Performance Measures

Each quasi gold standard is evaluated separately to ensure that all Wikipedia articles contribute equally to the results, independent of an article's number of "See also" links or its popularity.

In the "See also" evaluation, we use the rank-based Mean Average Precision (MAP) score (equation 1) to quantify recommendation quality. MAP represents the mean of the average precision scores for a set of queries Q (In our case: Wikipedia articles). $R_{q,j}$ denotes a relevant result for query q retrieved at rank j. We calculate MAP for the 10 top-ranked results, i.e. k=10. All articles are weighted equally in the final MAP score regardless of the article's number of "See also" links.

$$\text{MAP}(Q) = \frac{1}{|Q|} \sum_{q \in Q} \frac{1}{|R_q|} \sum_{j=1}^{|R_q|} \text{Precision}(R_{q,j}) \qquad (1)$$

We also performed test runs that calculated the performance measure Mean Reciprocal Rank (MRR) in addition to MAP during the "See also" evaluation. MRR represents the rank position of the first relevant result averaged over all queries. Evaluating the approaches according to MAP or MRR yielded no significant differences in the performance relation of the approaches. Therefore, we chose to only report MAP results in this paper, since we consider MAP as more representative of the performance of an approach with regard to all results. The code to calculate MRR is included in the GitHub repository for this paper.

In the clickstream evaluation, we measure recommendation performance using the Click-Through-Rate measure (CTR) (equation 2) for the top-k-results with k set to 1, 5, and 10 respectively. CTR represents the ratio of clicks $C_{s,d}$ on a link from article s to article d and the number of all outgoing clicks for article s [18]. Popular Wikipedia articles can generate more clicks than niche articles. Nevertheless, we followed the approach of equally valuating each article independent of its popularity.

$$\text{CTR}(s,d) = \frac{C_{s,d}}{\sum_{j=1}^{|C_s|} C_{s,j}} \qquad (2)$$

3.5 Implementation

For the sake of transparency and to improve reproducibility in recommender system research [2], we have published the data and source code used in our study together with a manual on GitHub: https://github.com/wikimedia/citolytics

3.5.1 More Like This

To generate the MoreLikeThis result set, we used a Java application and an Elasticsearch cluster. The application consists of four sub-tasks: extracting all articles from the Wikipedia XML dump, adding them to the Elasticsearch index, performing MoreLikeThis queries and storing all results as CSV.

3.5.2 CPA

We implemented the CPA algorithm as an Apache Flink job [21] in Java. In contrast to MLT, CPA does not require an indexing process. Instead, the CPA results are directly generated from the Wikipedia XML dump. This requires extraction of the full link graph and performing CPI computation. These operations are expressed in the MapReduce programming model. For completeness, we also resolve redirections for Wikipedia links that do not point directly to their destination.

The static classification of CPI values originally proposed by Gipp and Beel [12] (see Section 1.1) does not fit our test collection. Wikipedia articles are not organized in journals, nor do they follow the structure of scientific documents. Thus, we introduce a new dynamic model of CPI that can be adjusted depending on the requirements of the test collection.

We considered the proposal of Tran et al. [33] to generalize the citation proximity level. Analogous to the Term-Document Matrix, used in text-based approaches like VSM, we define the Link-Position Matrix $v_{i,j}$ of dimension $m \times m$ that stores the link position for all m documents. Specifically, the column for document j, $v_{*,j}$ holds the positions for links to other documents in words counted from the beginning of the document. Without loss of generality, we assume that a document links only once to another document. This complies with the conventions for authoring Wikipedia articles, which state that only the first mention of a concept should be linked.

Thus, for our use case, we redefined CPI as:

$$\mathrm{CPI}(a,b) \equiv \sum_{j=1}^{m} \Delta_j(a,b)^{-\alpha}, \tag{3}$$

$$\text{with } \Delta_j(a,b)^{-\alpha} = \begin{cases} \left| v_{a,j} - v_{b,j} \right|^{-\alpha} & v_{a,j} > 0 \wedge v_{b,j} > 0 \\ 0 & \text{otherwise} \end{cases}.$$

This definition states that for a document pair (a,b), the CPI is the sum of the proximity of their co-citations Δ_j, where the proximity is the link-distance damped by an exponential tuning parameter α, which determines the influence of the distance. The value of α needs to be computed depending on the document type, i.e. the model needs to be optimized. Note that negative values for α are counter-intuitive, because a negative value of α would result in a weighting that prefers co-citations with a greater distance. Furthermore, the case of $\alpha = 0$ implies:

$$\mathrm{CPI}(a,b) = \sum_{j=1}^{m} \begin{cases} 1 & v_{a,j} > 0 \wedge v_{b,j} > 0 \\ 0 & \text{otherwise} \end{cases}. \tag{4}$$

In this specific case, CPI is independent from link distance and equivalent to CoCit, since only the number of co-citations is counted, i.e. proximity has no effect.

3.5.3 "See Also" Evaluation
We collected the data for the "See also" quasi-gold standard from the Wikipedia dump by looking up sections titled "See also" and extracting the sections' links. We merged the resulting dataset with the MLT and CPA results using the article name. Lastly, we ensured that a "See also" link existed for each retrieved article.

3.5.4 Clickstream Evaluation
The data required for the clickstream evaluation was obtained from Wikiresearch as a CSV file. Therefore, no pre-processing was required. We assigned the clickstream data to CPA and MLT results, i.e. we assigned each article recommendation the respective number of clicks on the link and its CTR. In the final evaluation process, we merged all result sets with the corresponding quasi-gold standards.

3.5.5 Computing Infrastructure and Runtime
The experiment was performed on a cluster of 10 IBM Power 730 (8231-E2B) servers. Each machine had two 3.7 GHz POWER7 processors with 6 cores (12 cores in total), 2 x 73.4 GB 15K RPM SAS SFF Disk Drive, 4 x 600 GB 10K RPM SAS SFF Disk Drive and 64 GB of RAM.

Table 1: Approximated runtimes for each task.

Task	Runtime
MoreLikeThis (Elasticsearch)	
Indexing	7h 30min
Retrieval	53h 45min
CPA (Apache Flink)	
Computing Results	7h 45min
Evaluation (Apache Flink)	
"See also"-links	45min
Clickstream	50min

We used Apache Flink v0.8 (2015-01-19) and Hadoop v2.4.1 (2014-06-21). The text-based similarity measure was evaluated using Elasticsearch v1.4.2 (2014-12-16). All versions were the latest stable releases at the time of the experiment. We used the software's default settings, i.e. neither Apache Flink nor

Elasticsearch had been optimized for runtime performance. Although we did not focus on runtime performance and none of the tested document similarity measures had been optimized, the difference in runtime between CPA and MLT, as listed in Table 1 shows that MLT involves a more extensive computation than CPA. This is conceptually obvious, since the data volume for the recommendations based on words vs. links differs significantly. Also, MLT requires additional cleaning techniques such as stop word removal and TF-IDF weighting.

4. RESULTS
4.1 Optimizing the CPI Model
Since we use a dynamic CPI model instead of the static CPI values used in the original approach by Gipp and Beel (Section 1.1), we need to adjust CPA for Wikipedia articles before benchmarking the approach. We need to find a value for the constant α that achieves the best MAP score for the "See also" evaluation and the best CTR score for the clickstream evaluation. Since our goal is to optimize α specifically for the Wikipedia collection, we use the full collection instead of splitting up the collection into a training and test dataset. The later procedure would be appropriate if we were searching for an α value that performs best for different collections.

To find the value for α that performs best for our collection, we applied CPA with α values from -1 to 5 in 0.01 increments. Then, we evaluated the retrieved top-k results with k=10 of each batch by calculating the MAP and CTR scores (Figure 5). CPA performed best in terms of MAP with α set to 0.81 and in terms of CTR with α set to 0.90 (see marks in Figure 5). Thus we used these optimized α values in the corresponding CPI models during the "See also" and clickstream evaluation.

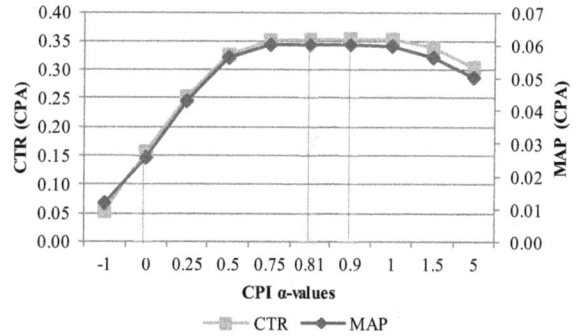

Figure 5: CTR and MAP scores for CPA with various CPI α-values. MAP$_{max}$ at $\alpha = 0.81$, CTR$_{max}$ at $\alpha = 0.9$

Moreover, the graph in Figure 5 proves the consistently lower performance of CoCit compared to CPA. CoCit is a special case of CPA with α set to zero (left mark in the graph). Only for negative α values, CoCit performs better than CPA. Using negative α values would cause CPA to assign higher scores to more distant co-citations, thereby effectively reversing the concept of the CPA measure and reducing CPA's performance. The graph therefore proves the benefit of assigning higher scores to co-citations at closer proximity.

4.2 Evaluation for Quasi Gold Standards
In the following, we present the evaluation results for the two quasi-gold standards presented in Section 3.3. To be included in the "See also" evaluation, a Wikipedia article must contain a "See also" section, which was true for 779,716 articles. To be included in the clickstream evaluation, clickstream data had to be available for the article in question, which was true for 2,572,063 articles.

To enable optimal comparability of the evaluated similarity measures, the following sections report results for a "unified dataset", i.e. those articles, for which all three evaluated measures retrieved the same number of related articles. For example, CoCit and CPA cannot generate recommendations for articles without in-links, hence we excluded such articles from the unified dataset. This procedure reduced the dataset for the "See also" evaluation from 779,716 articles to 659,642 articles (-120,074) and the dataset for the clickstream evaluation from 2,572,063 articles to 2,535,987 articles (-36,076). To ensure that unifying the datasets did not skew the evaluation, we calculated all performance scores for CoCit, CPA and MLT also based on the sets of all related articles that the measures could identify. The maximum difference in any score was 1.3% (average number of clicks for CPA) and for most scores less than 1% compared to the results of the unified dataset. The GitHub repository for this paper includes the results for the unified dataset and the results for set of all related articles.

4.2.1 "See Also" Links

Figure 6 shows that MLT performed better than CPA in terms of MAP and the average number of retrieved relevant documents, while CoCit performed worst. The MAP score of CPA is less than half of MLT's score; CoCit's score is less than a quarter of MLT's score. The average number of relevant documents of MLT and CPA tripled from k=1 to k=5 and nearly quadrupled from k=1 to k=10. We expected significant performance differences between CoCit and CPA, since the CPI optimization already showed that CoCit is an under-performing variation of CPA. On the other hand, we see an advantage of text-based MLT over the citation-based similarity measures, when judging recommendation relevance using "See also" links.

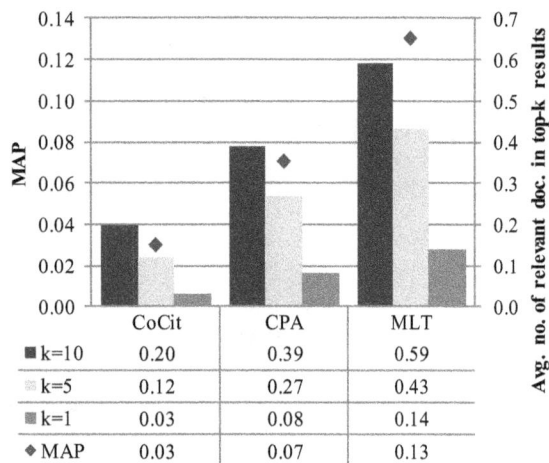

	CoCit	CPA	MLT
■ k=10	0.20	0.39	0.59
k=5	0.12	0.27	0.43
■ k=1	0.03	0.08	0.14
◆ MAP	0.03	0.07	0.13

Figure 6: Results of "See also" link-based evaluation.

4.2.2 Clickstreams

Figure 7 shows the CTR ranking of the clickstream evaluation. CPA accounted for more clicks than MLT for any value of k. MLT achieved the highest CTR, however, the ratio of the CTR scores of MLT and CPA (1.13) was significantly lower than the ratio of the MAP scores of the two approaches (1.92). CoCit again performed worst with regard to both scores.

The improved performance of CPA in this evaluation compared to the "See also" evaluation indicates that CPA performs better than MLT for popular articles, while MLT is more effective for niche articles. In the following, we present possible interpretations for this observation, which, however, need further investigation.

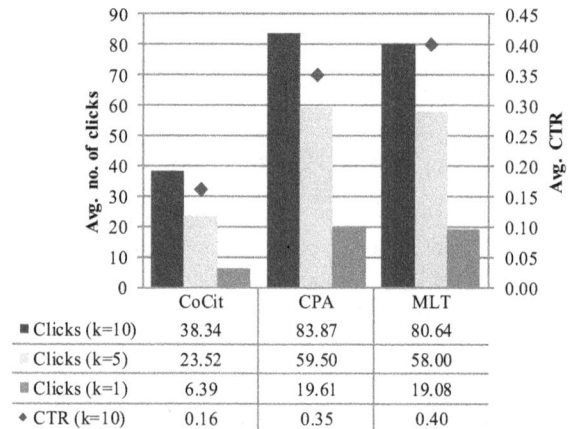

	CoCit	CPA	MLT
■ Clicks (k=10)	38.34	83.87	80.64
Clicks (k=5)	23.52	59.50	58.00
■ Clicks (k=1)	6.39	19.61	19.08
◆ CTR (k=10)	0.16	0.35	0.40

Figure 7: Results of clickstream evaluation.
MLT yields best CTR, while CPA generates the most clicks.

Popular articles typically attract many visitors and thus have a larger impact on the total click count than niche articles. However, CTR values every article equally, thus CTR does not reflect the comparably better performance of CPA for popular articles as strongly as the average number of clicks.

Popular articles also tend to have more co-authors. Therefore, the collaboratively generated 'link set' contained within popular articles might be of higher relevance, thus generating higher numbers of clicks and CTRs. To be able to support this hypothesis, we would need to evaluate the performance with regard to indicators of article quality [15].

Additionally, popular articles likely receive more in-links, which affects CPA's performance. We further investigate this property in Section 4.3.2. Another cause for CPA performing better for popular articles might be that bots, i.e. computer generated clicks, have a proportionally larger impact on niche articles. Consequently, the quality of the quasi-gold standard for these articles might be lower than for articles of average popularity. As we explain in Section 3.3.2, we cannot quantify this effect, since the data we used had been aggregated, thus preventing us from filtering bots on our own.

4.3 Article Properties

In this subsection, we provide details on the evaluation of CPA and MLT depending on article properties, such as the number of words and in-links. We omit CoCit in this evaluation, since the previous "See also" and clickstream evaluations already showed its inferior performance compared to CPA.

Figure 8 and Figure 9 show the performance in terms of MAP and CTR with respect to words and in-links. The graphs do not cover the full corpora: For the sake of visibility we do not plot results for articles with more than 3,000 words (9.07% of the articles in the in "See also" dataset, 5.90% of the articles in the clickstream dataset) or 400 in-links (2.66% of the articles in the "See also" dataset, 1.22% of the articles in the clickstream dataset).

4.3.1 Words

The performance plot with respect to article length, see Figure 8, reveals some interesting results. First, we see that MLT consistently performs better than CPA, when using MAP, but when using CTR, the performance ranking varies depending on the number of words. For articles with less than around 1,400 words MLT is superior, otherwise CPA performs slightly better.

Second, MLT's and CPA's MAP and CTR graphs show similar tendencies, but with one exception: MLT's MAP and CTR scores for very short articles (30-50 words) are exceptionally high, but drop sharply for slightly longer articles (60-150 words). For articles with more than approximately 150 words, MLT's MAP and CTR scores increase steadily and peak at article lengths of approximately 250 words. For articles longer than 250 words, MLT's MAP and CTR scores steadily decline. CPA's MAP and CTR scores, on the other hand, increase with article length up to lengths of approximately 400 words. Beyond this point, the CPA's MAP and CTR score remain relatively stable.

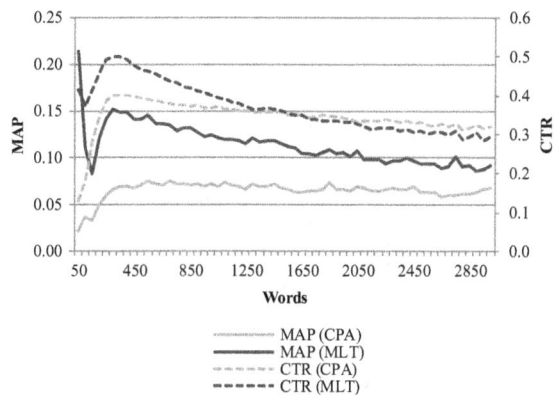

Figure 8: Performance evaluation in relation to number of words per article.

MLT's performance is more strongly affected by article length than CPA's. Short articles simply offer less data for both a text-based and link-based similarity assessment. If an article contains few words, it is difficult to determine topic-defining keywords and find other articles with matching topics. Short articles also typically have fewer in-links, e.g., because they are stubs. Therefore, both MLT and CPA require an article length of approximately 250 or more words to perform well. MLT's MAP peak for articles with around 50 words is an outlier phenomenon. Such very short articles normally contain only a single sentence on one topic, a list, a table, or specific vocabulary. Therefore, such articles often allow an accurate text-based similarity assessment.

While CPA reaches a relatively stable performance in terms of MAP and CTR, MLT's MAP and CTR score decline steadily for articles with 450 words or more. Long articles often cover several subtopics, which decrease the performance of VSM-based text similarity approaches like MLT. The vocabulary of subtopics can vary, thus making it difficult to determine a set of words that represents the breadth of topics present in the article. CPA's performance is hardly affected by article length, given a critical mass of in-links has been reached. This result is intuitive given that CPA's performance exclusively depends on in-links.

4.3.2 In-Links
Figure 9 shows the plot of MAP and CTR scores depending on the number of in-links. Both MLT and CPA performed best for approximately 20 in-links. For more in-links, the performance declines steadily as the number of in-links increases. This plot also shows a change in the CTR performance ranking of CPA and MLT. For less than 50 in-links MLT performs better; for more than 50 in-links CPA performs better. On the contrary, the ranking according to MAP does not change.

In-links as a data source are essential for link-based similarity measures, but do not directly affect text-based similarity measures. Seeing MLT perform better than CPA in terms of CTR

for articles with less than 20 in-links is therefore intuitive. It is also intuitive that CPA's CTR scores increase as the number of in-links increases in the range of 0 to 20 in-links.

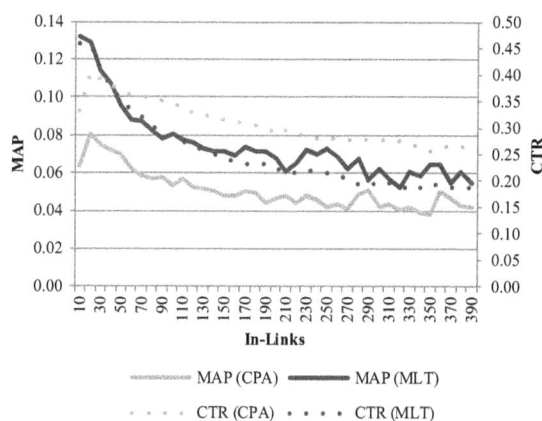

Figure 9: Performance evaluation considering number of in-links per article.

The reason that CPA's CTR scores peak at 20 in-links and decline thereafter and MLT's CTR scores decline steadily as the number of in-links increase may not be as intuitive. We attribute this behavior to the nature of articles that receive many in-links. Such articles typically cover broad topics, e.g. countries, as Belomi and Bonato [3] also reported before. We explain in Section 4.3.1 that text-based similarity measures like MLT perform comparably worse for such articles than for articles with narrowly similar topics. Figure 9 demonstrates that also link-based measures like CPA perform worse for broad-topic articles, because such articles receive in-links from many and topically diverse articles. This diversity of received in-links reduces the likelihood that the article in questions is frequently co-cited in closer proximity with other articles, hence reducing the performance of CPA.

4.4 Manual Sample Examination
To test the validity of "See also" links and clickstreams as gold standards, we manually evaluated a small and random subset of corpus articles. From these articles, we present and discuss the three exemplary articles shown in Tables 2 - 4. We chose the articles for their diversity and comprehensibility. Tables 2 - 4 show the recommendations of CoCit, CPA and MLT with the corresponding rank, similarity score for each measure in parentheses, and click counts. Recommendations that are part of the "See also" links are underlined.

4.4.1 Technical University of Berlin
The article about the Technical University of Berlin (TUB) includes information about the university's history, campus, organization, and a list of notable alumni and professors.

Both link-based measures retrieved two documents, which were included in the "See also" links and received clicks (HU-Berlin and FU-Berlin, underlined in Table 2). The MLT results have a clear focus on "University" as the topic, since all recommended articles are about universities, but from other cities and countries.

In this case, it can be said that the best results were produced by the CPA algorithm, followed by CoCit and MLT. While the CPA results can all be considered relevant, the MLT approach in particular produced a list of irrelevant institutions. For example, the University of Economics Varna in Bulgaria, or the Technological University Hpa-An in Myanmar.

Table 2: Results for "Technical University of Berlin"

	CoCit result	Clicks	CPA result	Clicks	MLT result	Clicks
1	Germany (660)	0	Germany (20.0)	0	Technical University of Sofia (0.86)	0
2	Berlin (487)	20	Berlin (17.6)	20	University of Economics Varna (0.74)	0
3	Humboldt University of Berlin (245)	42	Humboldt University of Berlin (10.0)	42	Vilnius College of Technologies and Design (0.64)	0
4	Ludwig Maximilian Uni. of Munich (229)	0	RWTH Aachen University (8.4)	0	Braunschweig University of Technology (0.63)	0
5	World War II (178)	0	Technische Universität München (5.9)	0	Technical University of Gabrovo (0.60)	0
6	United States (174)	0	Charlottenburg (5.6)	0	Chemnitz University of Technology (0.59)	0
7	RWTH Aachen University (172)	0	Mathematics (5.3)	0	Technische Universität Ilmenau (0.56)	0
8	Free University of Berlin (170)	0	Free University of Berlin (4.9)	0	Technical University of Dortmund (0.51)	0
9	Heidelberg University (142)	0	Habilitation (4.3)	0	Dresden University of Technology (0.50)	0
10	Mathematics (139)	0	Ludwig Maximilian Uni. of Munich (3.8)	0	Technological University Hpa-An (0.49)	0

"See also" links: Hertie School of Governance, Berlin University of the Arts, Free University of Berlin, Humboldt University of Berlin, Berlin School of Economics and Law, Beuth University of Applied Sciences Berlin

Total clicks: 596

Table 3: Results for "Elvis Presley"

	CoCit result	Clicks	CPA result	Clicks	MLT result	Clicks
1	AllMusic (5977)	0	The Beatles (115.5)	247	Sun Studio (1.16)	0
2	The Beatles (5030)	247	Frank Sinatra (61.9)	139	From Elvis in Memphis (1.14)	516
3	Billboard magazine (4425)	0	Johnny Cash (53.2)	140	List of songs recorded by Elvis Presley on the Sun label (1.10)	240
4	United States (3146)	52	Jerry Lee Lewis (50.7)	73	Peter Guralnick (0.99)	0
5	Frank Sinatra (2756)	139	RCA Records (45.1)	175	Colonel Tom Parker (0.96)	1175
6	The Rolling Stones (2374)	0	Rock and roll (42.9)	306	The Blue Moon Boys (0.94)	100
7	Billboard Hot 100 (2203)	12	Heartbreak Hotel (38.0)	720	Elvis Presley's Army career (0.89)	619
8	Johnny Cash (2157)	140	Jailhouse Rock song (36.4)	260	Jailhouse Rock film (0.87)	1132
9	Cliff Richard (1996)	0	Roy Orbison (34.8)	96	I Want You, I Need You, I Love You (0.86)	83
10	Bob Dylan (1930)	77	United States (30.4)	52	Elvis Presley albums discography (0.83)	6084

"See also" links: Honorific nicknames in popular music, Elvis Presley Enterprises, List of best-selling music artists, Personal relationships of Elvis Presley, List of artists by number of UK Albums Chart number ones, List of artists by total number of UK number one singles

Total clicks: 92,379

Table 4: Results for "Newspaper"

	CoCit result	Clicks	CPA result	Clicks	MLT result	Clicks
1	United States (4130)	0	Broadsheet (428.0)	59	The Daily Courier Arizona (0.90)	0
2	Broadsheet (2569)	59	Magazine (331.5)	119	Online newspaper (0.88)	142
3	English language (1732)	0	Tabloid newspaper format (246.7)	35	History of British newspapers (0.86)	168
4	Tabloid newspaper format (1690)	35	United States (225.4)	0	List of newspapers in the United States by circulation (0.86)	0
5	Race and ethnicity in the United States Census (1257)	0	Publishing (102.2)	0	Newspaper circulation (0.84)	23
6	The New York Times (1041)	118	English language (96.2)	0	Midland Daily News (0.78)	0
7	New York City (890)	0	Journalist (86.2)	32	The Huntsville Times (0.77)	0
8	World War II (831)	0	Book (80.3)	11	Decline of newspapers (0.75)	0
9	Magazine (822)	119	Comic strip (80.0)	37	The Leaf-Chronicle (0.74)	0
10	United Kingdom (805)	0	Radio (78.9)	0	The Ann Arbor News (0.74)	0

"See also" links: List of newspaper comic strips, Lists of newspapers

Total clicks: 4,516

The universities considered relevant by the CPA approach are all well-known Universities in the region with a strong technical focus, similar to the technical university of Berlin.

The poor performance of MLT in this case can be explained by the weakness of text-based approaches where a strong emphasis lies on similar words in the documents. Text describing a university is usually similar, given that generic characteristics such as the number of students, etc. is described, which automatically leads to a "high" similarity. Possibly, Wikipedia authors reused text when writing the article about the university in Burma. Citation-based approaches are not affected by text reuse.

4.4.2 Elvis Presley

The biographical Wikipedia article about the American singer and actor Elvis Presley is relatively long. The article contains 24,298 words, received 5,834 in-links and provided 92,379 out-clicks.

None of the articles recommended by any approach were part of the "See also" links, but most recommendations are related to the topic. The topics recommended by CoCit and CPA are broader than the results of MLT. Furthermore, CoCit's recommendations

for the articles "AllMusic", an online music database, and "Billboard magazine" are notable: Even though both articles are music-related, they lack a direct connection to Elvis Presley. These recommendations were caused by links that did not belong to the actual article text, e.g. infoboxes or the article footer.

4.4.3 Newspaper

The "Newspaper" article contains general information on newspapers as periodical publications, their historical development, their categories, formats, and other newspaper related topics. The article consists of 6,313 words and is linked by 7,611 other articles. The "See also" section includes two links to newspaper related lists: "List of newspaper comic strips" and "Lists of newspapers".

MLT, CPA, and CoCit all failed to retrieve any of the "See also" links, which is not surprising, since the only two "See also" links linked to another list. Despite all articles retrieved by MLT being newspaper related, they were also overly narrow and irrelevant for the broad and internationally-oriented 'Newspaper' article. MLT recommended articles on actual newspaper publications, e.g. "The

Daily Courier Arizona", or "Midland Daily News"; However, these publications are so provincial, that they will be irrelevant to most readers. CPA, on the other hand, retrieved a broader spectrum of related topics, for example newspaper formats ("Tabloid", "Magazine", "Broadsheet") or other media ("Book", "Comic strip", "Radio"). Two of CPA's results ("United States" and "English language") were not topically relevant. CoCit retrieved many irrelevant articles from the geopolitical category ("United States", "New York City", etc.).

4.4.4 Summary Manual Evaluation

The results presented for these three examples were typical of other articles examined. MLT tended to retrieve topically more narrow articles compared to the citation-based approaches. CPA usually produced more relevant recommendations than CoCit. We observed that the recommendations were of a different nature for each approach. While CPA's recommendations were consistently plausible, MLT had the tendency to recommend obscure articles. For example, MLT recommended a University in Myanmar (Technological University Hpa-An) for the article 'Technical University Berlin' or an internationally virtually unknown newspaper ('The Daily Courier Arizona') at rank 1.

The result of the manual evaluation showed that CPA recommends topically broader articles, but with consistent relevance compared to the often niche results of MLT. However, because this evaluation approach is highly subjective and dependent on a user's specific information need, we invite the reader to examine the examples in the Tables 2 - 4 as well as additional results available in the repository to make a judgement.

5. DISCUSSION

In the "See also" evaluation, the text-based MLT measure retrieved more related articles and achieved higher MAP than both link-based measures. CPA followed at second rank and clearly outperformed the third-ranked CoCit in this evaluation. Links outside of the article text, e.g., in information boxes or article footers, were a source of irrelevant CoCit and CPA results, since such links are commonly less related to the article's topic.

For example, in the article on Elvis Presley, CoCit identified the link to the "AllMusic" category at the top rank. Devaluating or ignoring these links in future studies should improve the performance of the link-based similarity measures. Such a procedure would correspond to the stop word removal in MLT. For the CPA approach, adjusting the CPI weighting scheme could reduce the effect of such Wikipedia-specific unrelated results. For instance, the quantification of citation proximity should be adjusted for article length or the number of in-links an article receives. Such a normalization can devalue links to general articles that are frequently co-cited but often have no topical relevance, e.g. geopolitical articles such as "United States".

Not surprisingly, articles that CPA retrieved as relevant consistently achieved the highest number of clicks in the clickstream evaluation. MLT followed at second rank and CoCit at third rank in this regard. Yet, MLT achieved slightly higher CTR scores than CPA in this evaluation, with CoCit again following at rank three.

These results indicate that traditional text-based methods are a well-performing "general purpose" approach for recommending related Wikipedia articles regardless of specific article properties. CPA is better suited to retrieve popular articles. Due to Wikipedia's collaborative approach to article curation, popular articles are also typically longer and of higher quality.

Manually examining samples also indicated that CPA and MLT have different strengths that are not adequately reflected by the "See also" quasi-gold standard. The link-based approaches, especially CPA, tended to retrieve articles from a broader range of related topics than MLT. For instance, for the query "Newspaper" MLT mostly recommended actual newspapers, e.g. "The Daily Courier Arizona". CPA on the other hand retrieved more generally related topics, e.g., newspaper formats such as "Tabloid" or "Broadsheet". In our perception, CPA and MLT performed similarly well in identifying related articles, yet the type of relatedness differed.

Two advantages of the link-based measures over the text-based measure are their significantly lower runtime requirement (see Table 1) and their language-independence. Citation or link analysis can be performed for texts in any language and can also be employed for retrieving texts across languages. Text-based measures like MLT are language-dependent.

Summarizing our findings, we conclude that the advantageousness of the link-based over the text-based approach depends on the information need of the user. If a user is interested in articles that address a specific topic, in a single language and from a relatively narrow perspective, text-based recommendations likely suit the user's needs better than link-based recommendations.

If the user desires a broader overview of a topic, and also wants to retrieve articles in different languages, or if the user values factors, such as article popularity and quality, then link-based recommendations fulfill these requirements better than text-based recommendations. Ultimately, a combined approach that includes link-based, text-based and potentially other document similarity measures is likely to achieve the best recommendation quality.

6. CONCLUSION

This paper introduced the first implementation of Citation Proximity Analysis (CPA) for a hyperlink environment use case. We adapted the CPA's Citation Proximity Index (CPI) from the academic literature domain, i.e. citation analysis, to the analysis of links. Subsequently, we performed a large-scale evaluation of the performance of the adapted CPA approach, Co-Citation (CoCit), and Apache Lucene's MoreLikeThis (MLT) function for recommending related documents in two datasets of 779,716 and 2.57 million Wikipedia articles. We used the Big Data processing framework Apache Flink and a ten-node computing cluster to compute article similarities for each approach.

To perform this large-scale evaluation, we introduced two novel quasi-gold standards: the links in Wikipedia's "See also" sections and a comprehensive clickstream dataset as estimators of the relevance for Wikipedia articles.

We found that the link-based and text-based approach to recommending articles in Wikipedia have complementary strengths. The text-based MLT method performs well in identifying closely related articles. The CPA approach, which consistently outperformed CoCit, is better suited for identifying a broader spectrum of related articles as well as popular articles that typically exhibit a higher quality. Additional benefits of the CPA approach are its lower runtime requirements and its language-independence, which allows cross-language retrieval of articles.

Our findings suggest that an approach that combines link-based, text-based, and potentially other recommendation algorithms, shows the most promise for recommending related articles in Wikipedia. We will investigate this hypothesis in future research.

To ensure reproducibility, we have made the data and source code of our study available at: https://github.com/wikimedia/citolytics.

7. REFERENCES

[1] Beel, J. et al. 2015. Research-paper recommender systems: a literature survey. Int. Journal on Digital Libraries. (2015).

[2] Beel, J. et al. 2016. Towards reproducibility in recommender-systems research. User Modeling and User-Adapted Interaction (UMAI). 26, (2016).

[3] Bellomi, F. and Bonato, R. 2005. Network Analysis for Wikipedia. Proc. of Wikimania. (2005).

[4] Bornmann, L. and Mutz, R. 2015. Growth rates of modern science: A bibliometric analysis based on the number of publications and cited references. Journal of the Association for Information Science and Technology. 66, 11 (2015).

[5] Cohen, D. et al. 2007. Lucene and Juru at Trec 2007 : 1-Million Queries Track. TREC 2007 (2007).

[6] Eto, M. 2013. Evaluations of context-based co-citation searching. Scientometrics. 94, 2 (2013).

[7] Garfield, E. 1964. Science Citation Index - a New Dimension in Indexing. Science. 144, 3619 (1964).

[8] Gipp, B. 2014. Citation-based Plagiarism Detection – Detecting Disguised and Cross-language Plagiarism using Citation Pattern Analysis. Springer Vieweg Research.

[9] Gipp, B. et al. 2014. Citation-based Plagiarism Detection: Practicability on a Large-scale Scientific Corpus. Journal of the American Society for Information Science and Technology. 65, 2 (2014).

[10] Gipp, B. et al. 2011. Comparative Evaluation of Text- and Citation-based Plagiarism Detection Approaches using GuttenPlag. Proc. of 11th ACM/IEEE-CS Joint Conf. on Digital Libraries (JCDL'11) (2011).

[11] Gipp, B. et al. 2009. Scienstein: A research paper recommender system. Proc. of the Int. Conf. on Emerging Trends in Computing (ICETiC'09). (2009).

[12] Gipp, B. and Beel, J. 2009. Citation Proximity Analysis (CPA)-A new approach for identifying related work based on Co-Citation Analysis. Proc. of the 12th Int. Conf. on Scientometrics and Informetrics (ISSI'09). 2, (2009).

[13] Gipp, B. and Meuschke, N. 2011. Citation Pattern Matching Algorithms for Citation-based Plagiarism Detection: Greedy Citation Tiling, Citation Chunking and Longest Common Citation Sequence. Proc. of the 11th ACM Symp. on Document Engineering (2011).

[14] He, Q. et al. 2010. Context-aware citation recommendation. Proc. of the 19th Int. Conf. on World Wide Web. (2010).

[15] Hu, M. et al. 2007. Measuring Article Quality in Wikipedia. Proc. of the 16th ACM Conf. on Information and Knowledge Management - CIKM '07 (2007).

[16] Huang, W. et al. 2015. A Neural Probabilistic Model for Context Based Citation Recommendation. Proc. of the 29th AAAI Conf. on Artificial Intelligence. (2015).

[17] Huang, W. et al. 2012. Recommending Citations : Translating Papers into References. Proc. of the 21st ACM Int. Conf. on Information and Knowledge Management. (2012).

[18] Joachims, T. et al. 2005. Accurately interpreting clickthrough data as implicit feedback. Proc. of the 28th Annu. Int. ACM SIGIR Conf. on Research and Development in Information Retrieval. (2005).

[19] Jones, K.S. 1973. Index term weighting. Information Storage and Retrieval.

[20] Konchady, M. 2008. Building Search Applications: Lucene, Lingpipe, and Gate.

[21] Leich, M. et al. 2013. Applying Stratosphere for Big Data Analytics. BTW (2013).

[22] Liu, S. and Chen, C. 2011. The effects of co-citation proximity on co-citation analysis. Proc. of ISSI. (2011).

[23] Marshakova, I. 1973. System of document connections based on references. Scientific and Technical Information Serial of VINITI. 6, (1973).

[24] McNee, S.M. et al. 2002. On the Recommending of Citations for Research Papers. Proc. of the 2002 ACM Conf. on Computer Supported Cooperative Work (2002).

[25] Ollivier, Y. and Senellart, P. 2007. Finding Related Pages Using Green Measures : An Illustration with Wikipedia. Proc. of AAAI. (2007).

[26] Page, L. et al. 1998. The PageRank Citation Ranking. World Wide Web Internet And Web Information Systems. 54, (1998).

[27] Paranjape, A. et al. 2015. Improving Website Hyperlink Structure Using Server Logs. arXiv preprint arXiv:1512.07258. (2015).

[28] Research: Wikipedia clickstream: 2015. http://meta.wikimedia.org/wiki/Research:Wikipedia_clickstream. Accessed: 2015-05-27.

[29] Rubens, N. 2006. The Application of Fuzzy Logic to the Construction of the Ranking Function of Information Retrieval Systems. arXiv preprint cs/0610039. 10, (2006).

[30] Salton, G. et al. 1975. A Vector Space Model for Automatic Indexing. Communications of the ACM. 18, (1975).

[31] Small, H. 1973. A New Measure of the Relationship Two Documents. Journal of the American Society for Information Science. 24, (1973).

[32] Strohman, T. et al. 2007. Recommending Citations for Academic Papers. Proc. of the 30th Annu. Int. ACM SIGIR Conf. on Research and Development in Information Retrieval. (2007).

[33] Tran, N. et al. 2009. Enriching PubMed Related Article Search with Sentence Level. AMIA Annu. Symp. Proc. 2009, (2009).

[34] Wikipedia Clickstream: Getting Started: http://ewulczyn.github.io/Wikipedia_Clickstream_Getting_Started/. Accessed: 2015-05-25.

[35] Wikipedia:Manual of Style/Layout: 2014. https://en.wikipedia.org/wiki/Wikipedia:Manual_of_Style/Layout#See_also_section. Accessed: 2015-04-15.

[36] Woodruff, A. et al. 2000. Enhancing a Digital Book with a Reading Recommender. Proc. of the SIGCHI Conf. on Human Factors in Computing Systems (2000).

[37] Wulczyn, E. and Taraborelli, D. 2015. Wikipedia Clickstream. figshare. (2015).

Context Matters: Towards Extracting a Citation's Context Using Linguistic Features

Daniel Duma
University of Edinburgh
danielduma@gmail.com

Charles Sutton
University of Edinburgh
csutton@inf.ed.ac.uk

Ewan Klein
University of Edinburgh
ewan@inf.ed.ac.uk

Keywords

Citation context; context extraction; window of words; citation recommendation; information retrieval

1. INTRODUCTION

Keyword-based search engines are becoming increasingly sophisticated, and yet navigating the ever-increasing collection of academic knowledge remains an arduous task. Keeping abreast of relevant scientific literature is often a fragmented process that breaks the workflow of academic writing.

Wouldn't it be helpful if your text editor automatically suggested papers that are contextually relevant? Our vision of future access to digital libraries is entirely integrated into the writing process and works to augment the writer's knowledge and capabilities. We concern ourselves with the task of *context-based citation recommendation*: we desire to recommend contextually relevant citations. One example of this is getting relevant suggestions of related work at the early draft stage as the author is typing.

Citation contexts are a very important source of information for scientific discovery. The text that surrounds a citation to another paper inside an academic paper has been variously used to generate summaries of academic papers [8], to inform metrics of a paper's impact [10], as "anchor text" in information retrieval scenarios [9], and within these, especially for context-based citation recommendation [4, 3, 2, 5]

Context extraction is a key sub-task in context-based citation recommendation, yet it has received painfully little attention in the literature to date. Previous approaches to context extraction fall into two big groups: *symmetric window* approaches and *sentence selection* approaches. Symmetric approaches use for example a window of words, where the context is considered to be n tokens before the citation token and n tokens after it, or a window of sentences, where the citing sentence is included, plus n sentences before and/or after it.

Permission to make digital or hard copies of part or all of this work for personal or classroom use is granted without fee provided that copies are not made or distributed for profit or commercial advantage and that copies bear this notice and the full citation on the first page. Copyrights for third-party components of this work must be honored. For all other uses, contact the owner/author(s).

JCDL '16 June 19-23, 2016, Newark, NJ, USA

© 2016 Copyright held by the owner/author(s).

ACM ISBN 978-1-4503-4229-2/16/06.

DOI: http://dx.doi.org/10.1145/2910896.2925431

The task of citation recommendation seems to have exclusively used symmetric windows so far. We propose that these methods are excessively simplistic and can be significantly improved upon. In this paper, we show that sentence selection methods are indeed superior to symmetric windows for the task of citation recommendation.

2. RELATED WORK

For the task of context-based citation recommendation, He et al. [4] used a symmetric window of words (50 before, 50 after) as did Liu et al. [7] (300 before, 300 after). He et al. [3] used passages (splitting the article into half-overlapping fixed-size windows of words). Huang et al. [5] used a window of sentences: citing sentence + 1 before + 1 after. Similarly, [9] used symmetric windows of words and sentences to build external document representations.

It is clear that always using a fixed window size and not dealing with coreference is guaranteed to introduce false positives and false negatives in extracted keywords, which leads to noise.

Instead of dealing with this noise exclusively by using weighting schemes based on topic modelling and word embeddings (e.g. [5]), we propose that those approaches will also benefit from a better selection of the context.

Sentence selection approaches have been applied primarily to summarization and sentiment analysis. Kaplan et al.[6] manually annotated a small corpus (50 citations) with relevant sentences to each citation and trained a coreference resolver on it in order to generate summaries of those papers. Similarly to this and also for summarization, Qazvinian et al. [8] manually annotated a corpus of 203 citations with relevant sentences to each citation within a 4-sentence window (2 up, 2 down) and trained a classifier which decided which sentences to include. More recently, Athar [1] built a larger annotated corpus and trained a classifier for sentiment analysis.

3. METHODOLOGY

3.1 Evaluation

We aim to recommend contextually relevant citations. To evaluate this, we exploit the human judgements that are already implicit in available resources, and so we avoid purpose-specific annotation. That is, we make it our task to to recover the original citations in papers that have already been published and we judge our system's accuracy at this task.

As others before, we frame this task as information retrieval, and we treat an existing citation's context as the query and the corpus of papers as our document collection. For all experiments, we use the ACL Anthology Corpus (AAC) enriched with AAN metadata. We select and separate a subset of documents in our collection as our *test set*. For each document in our test set (see 3.2 below), we:

1. select all references in the test document that can be resolved to documents inside our document collection (*collection-internal references*) and remove all other references we cannot match and the citations to them
2. substitute each citation token to a collection-internal reference with a *citation placeholder*
3. generate a *query* from the *context* of this placeholder
4. perform the query, aiming to rank the original cited reference as high in the results as possible

3.2 A corpus of annotated contexts

We employ the sentiment- and relevance-annotated corpus of Athar et al.[1] for our test set. In this corpus, 20 papers were selected from the ACL Anthology, and approximately 1700 citation contexts to these papers were manually annotated by a single annotator. Within a window of 2 sentences before the citing sentences and 2 after (2 up, 2 down), each sentence receives two annotations: *a)* whether it is relevant to the citation and *b)* its sentiment. The sentiment can be one of: *p* - positive, *n* - negative and *o* - objective.

4. EXPERIMENTS AND RESULTS

We have compared the following methods for extracting a citation's context:

- **window**: a window of n tokens, the same number before and after the citation token
- **sentence**: a window of sentences
  - **1only**: only the citing sentence.
  - **[n]up_[m]down**: n sentences before (up) and m after the citing sentence (down). This window always includes the citing sentence.
  - **paragraph**: the full paragraph where the citation appears.
- **annotated_sentence**: sentences that were human-annotated as relevant to the citation.

The results are previewed in Table 1. They indicate that forming the context out of sentences that were manually annotated to be relevant to the citation leads to generating superior queries than using any other symmetric method. The minimal pair here is *sentence_2up_2down* and *annotated_sentence_pno*, showing that selecting which sentences to include within a 5-sentence window leads to higher scores. Interestingly, selecting sentences based on their annotated sentiment polarity produces worse results, leading us to conclude that sentiment classification, at least as present in this corpus, is not a useful feature.

5. REFERENCES

[1] A. Athar and S. Teufel. Context-enhanced citation sentiment detection. In *Proceedings of the 2012 Conference of the North American Chapter of the Association for Computational Linguistics: Human Language Technologies*, pages 597–601. Association for Computational Linguistics, 2012.

[2] D. Duma and E. Klein. Citation resolution: A method for evaluating context-based citation recommendation systems. In *Proceedings of the 52nd Annual Meeting of the Association for Computational Linguistics*, 2014.

Table 1: **Experiment results. Manually selecting sentences within a 5-sentence context is superior to symmetric methods, irrespective of sentiment annotation.**

Context extraction method	Avg. MRR score
annotated_sentence_pno	**0.1575**
annotated_sentence_po	0.1533
annotated_sentence_no	0.1505
window500_500	0.147
sentence_0up_1down	0.1403
window50_50	0.1382
sentence_1up_1down	0.1378
sentence_2up_2down	0.136
window100_100	0.134
window30_30	0.134
sentence_paragraph	0.1313
sentence_1only	0.1309
sentence_1up	0.1287
annotated_sentence_p	0.0182
annotated_sentence_n	0.0134

[3] J. He, J.-Y. Nie, Y. Lu, and W. X. Zhao. Position-aligned translation model for citation recommendation. In *String Processing and Information Retrieval*, pages 251–263. Springer, 2012.

[4] Q. He, J. Pei, D. Kifer, P. Mitra, and L. Giles. Context-aware citation recommendation. In *Proceedings of the 19th international conference on World wide web*, pages 421–430. ACM, 2010.

[5] W. Huang, Z. Wu, C. Liang, P. Mitra, and C. L. Giles. A neural probabilistic model for context based citation recommendation. In *In Proceedings of the Twenty-Ninth AAAI Conference on Artificial Intelligence*, 2015.

[6] D. Kaplan, R. Iida, and T. Tokunaga. Automatic extraction of citation contexts for research paper summarization: A coreference-chain based approach. In *Proceedings of the 2009 Workshop on Text and Citation Analysis for Scholarly Digital Libraries*, pages 88–95. Association for Computational Linguistics, 2009.

[7] X. Liu, Y. Yu, C. Guo, Y. Sun, and L. Gao. Full-text based context-rich heterogeneous network mining approach for citation recommendation. In *Proceedings of the 14th ACM/IEEE-CS Joint Conference on Digital Libraries*, pages 361–370. IEEE Press, 2014.

[8] V. Qazvinian and D. R. Radev. Identifying non-explicit citing sentences for citation-based summarization. In *Proceedings of the 48th annual meeting of the association for computational linguistics*, pages 555–564. Association for Computational Linguistics, 2010.

[9] A. Ritchie. Citation context analysis for information retrieval. Technical report, University of Cambridge Computer Laboratory, 2009.

[10] S. Teufel, A. Siddharthan, and D. Tidhar. Automatic classification of citation function. In *Proceedings of the 2006 Conference on Empirical Methods in Natural Language Processing*, pages 103–110. Association for Computational Linguistics, 2006.

Knowledge Curation Discussions and Activity Dynamics in a Short Lived Social Q&A Community

Hengyi Fu
School of Information
Florida State University
hf13c@my.fsu.edu

Besiki Stvilia
School of Information
Florida State University
bstvilia@fsu.edu

ABSTRACT
Studying the dynamics and lifecycles of online knowledge curation communities is essential to identify and assemble community type specific repertoires of strategies, rules, and actions of community design, governance, content creation and curation. This paper examines the lifecycle of a short lived social Q&A community on Stack Exchange by performing the content analysis of the logs of member discussions and content curation actions.

Keywords
Online communities; knowledge curation; social Q&A; community lifecycle.

1. INTRODUCTION
Knowledge and data curation online communities have become essential parts of the Web's knowledge and information infrastructure providing free knowledge resources to both human and software agents (e.g., search engines). Although there is a significant body of literature on the design and management of online communities and data curation, there have been only a few studies of the dynamics and lifecycles of online knowledge curation communities in general, and social Q&A communities in particular. This poster presents part of a larger study which examines the work organization and dynamics pertaining to knowledge curation in Stack Exchange social Q&A communities. In particular the poster presents analysis of the work organization and dynamics of a short-lived social Q&A community which lasted only 30 weeks, from its inception to its closing. The study's findings can inform the design and management of similar knowledge creation and curation communities, as well as the definition and provision of infrastructure components, including policy and software tools to support their work and development at different stages of their lifecycles.

Online Social Q&A sites are powerful tools for users to seek knowledge by posing questions and getting answers from peer communities. Prior research on social Q&A communities falls into two main categories. The first category focused on analyzing the content of posts from social Q&A communities to identify and understand information needs and motivations for asking questions [1], evaluate and predict the quality of the questions and answers [2], and identify the experts in social Q&A communities [3]. The second category considered Q&A communities as sociotechnical systems focused on understanding the social organization of Q&A systems, such as what factors enable the social Q&A communities to thrive, how people interact with each other in these sites, and how the community design (reputation and badge system, user groups, governance mechanisms, etc.) could facilitate user contributions and community growth (e.g., [4, 5]). This paper reports on early results of an exploratory study which extends that later literature by focusing on the dynamics and lifecycle aspects of a social Q&A community.

2. RESEARCH QUESTIONS
The study investigated the following research questions:

1. What are some of the actions used in community building, maintenance, and knowledge curation activities in social Q&A communities?
2. What are some of the strategies used in those activities?
3. What are the temporal distributions of those actions and related discussions throughout the community's lifecycle?

3. METHOD AND DATA
To address the above questions, the authors performed content analysis of the logs of member actions and discussions from one of the closed Q&A sites at Stack Exchange called *Economics* (http://area51.stackexchange.com/proposals/1618/economics).
The site successfully passed the definition, commitment, and private beta phases defined by Stack Exchange management (http://area51.stackexchange.com/faq), but failed to be launched and was closed by Stack Exchange after staying in the public beta phase for 206 days. The log data from the Economics site spans 8 months, from October 2011 when the site entered private beta, to May 2012 when the site was closed. It contains data from both the main site (topic specific question-answering threads) and the meta-site (site management discussion threads). The authors used the data dump of the Economics site published by Stack Exchange and performed content analysis with open coding of 166 entries from the meta site (51 entries posted as questions, 115 posted as answers and comments). Next, the authors iteratively clustered codes into 13 categories and recoded the data within those categories. Finally, the authors generated descriptive time series statistics for 30 weeks for both the 13 meta discussion categories (417 instances) and 38 action type codes (3,284 instances) defined and assigned by Stack Exchange software to 1,007 question-answering threads in the main site. The action frequencies of each user on the Economics main site and the meta site were also calculated.

4. FINDINGS AND DISCUSSION
4.1 Community Building Actions
The analysis of the time series data of action type codes showed that members did a fair amount of quality assurance work by actively revising submitted questions and answers during the first 11 weeks of the site's existence (Fig. 1). In week 12, however, the frequency of that activity experienced a sharp

Permission to make digital or hard copies of part or all of this work for personal or classroom use is granted without fee provided that copies are not made or distributed for profit or commercial advantage and that copies bear this notice and the full citation on the first page. Copyrights for third-party components of this work must be honored. For all other uses, contact the Owner/Author.
Copyright is held by the owner/author(s).

JCDL '16, June 19-23, 2016, Newark, NJ, USA
ACM 978-1-4503-4229-2/16/06.
DOI: http://dx.doi.org/10.1145/2910896.2925432

decline, relative to the number of questions asked and answered in the same time period. Another decline in the question and answer revision activity occurred in week 21, right before a trolling attack was discovered and a decision was made by Stack Exchange to close the site. A total of 303 unique users have been identified in the main site, while the unique user number in the meta site was 49. The numbers of user action/contributions in both the main and meta sites followed power law distributions: a small group of community members did a large amount of work and site managing discussions.

Figure 1. Temporal distribution of community building actions in the main site (only the top 10 categories included)

4.2 Community Building Strategies

The most frequently occurring discussion categories on the meta site were discussions about the site's scope definition, community governance, and work organization. The community struggled with the following: defining an optimal scope definition for the site; developing strategies to recruit new members and to increase member participation; to generate content; to promote the site; to intervene effectively to ensure the quality of questions and answers; to educate and enculturate new members and users; and to fight off malicious agents (e.g., trolls). The time series data of meta discussions showed ongoing discussions both in the private beta and the public beta phases on whether to restrict the scope of the site to high level, graduate questions (to recruit and retain experts) or allow lay, normative, and homework type questions as well (to increase the traffic to the site; see Fig. 2). Identifying an optimal scope for a community's site at a particular phase of the community's lifecycle is essential to successfully jumpstart and/or grow the community. In the private beta phase the founders of the *Economics* site chose a narrow scope for the site limiting it to advanced, graduate level questions, while more general, basic level questions could be allowed once the site entered public beta. They were concerned that a broader or ambiguous scope would encourage low quality and/or simple questions and discourage experts from joining the community during the community's early building stage.

This strategy was also partially influenced by Stack Exchange's policy which required a site in its private beta phase to have a certain number of highly rated questions as well as a certain number of members who had achieved high reputation levels at Stack Exchange.

The literature shows that while proving access to a large collection of high quality content can help to jumpstart an online peer curation community, setting its scope to a narrowly defined topic or population may hamper its growth. Some of the existing or potential members may not buy into it and/or may not see their place within that narrow scope. Knowledge curation work is a complex set of activities. In addition to experts, who can provide high quality content, online peer knowledge curation

communities need members who are willing to perform routine but important quality assurance activities (e.g., copyediting, content migration, resolving conflicts, and, fighting spammers and trolls) [1,7]. Experts might not be interested in performing those types of work.

Figure 2. Temporal distribution of member discussion categories in the meta site

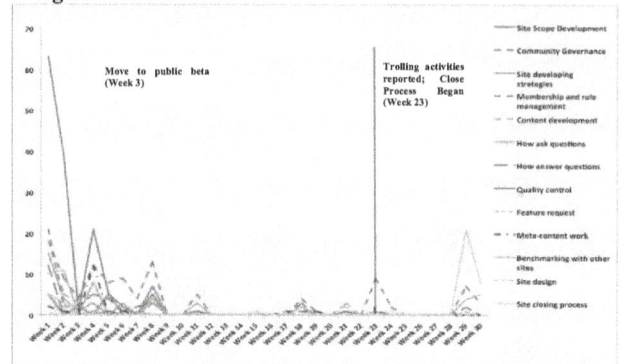

5. CONCLUSION AND FUTURE WORK

The preliminary findings of the study point to the importance of setting an appropriate scope and continuous quality assurance (e.g., evaluating, deleting, revising questions and answers, fighting trolls) for a Q&A community to succeed. The findings point to difficulties in striking a balance between making the content of a Q&A site interesting and challenging enough to lure in and retain experts and in making the site's scope general enough to accrue a critical mass of participants and traffic. Immediate future work will include expanding this study to a successful Q&A community and comparing and contrasting its repertoires of activity strategies, patterns and dynamics to the findings from the examination of the Economics social Q&A community.

6. REFERENCES

[1] Cunningham, S. J., and Hinze, A. 2014. Social, religious information behavior: An analysis of Yahoo! Answers queries about belief. *Advances in the Study of Information and Religion*, 4, 1, 3.

[2] Harper, F. M., Raban, D., Rafaeli, S., and Konstan, J. A. 2008. Predictors of answer quality in online Q&A sites. In *Proceedings of the SIGCHI Conference on Human Factors in Computing Systems*, 865-874.

[3] Pal, A., Harper, F. M., and Konstan, J. A. 2012. Exploring question selection bias to identify experts and potential experts in community question answering. *ACM Transactions on Information Systems*, 30, 2, 10.

[4] Mamykina, L., Manoim, B., Mittal, M., Hripcsak, G., and Hartmann, B. 2011. Design lessons from the fastest q&a site in the west. In *Proceedings of the SIGCHI conference on Human factors in computing systems*.

[5] Tausczik, Y. R., Kittur, A., and Kraut, R. E. 2014. Collaborative problem solving: a study of mathoverflow. In *Proceedings of the 17th ACM conference on Computer supported cooperative work & social computing*, 355-367.

[6] Resnick, P., Konstan, J., Chen, Y., and Kraut, R. E. 2012. Starting new online communities. In *Building Successful Online Communities: Evidence-based Social Design*, 231-280.

[7] Stvilia, B., and Les Gasser. 2008. An activity theoretic model for information quality change. *First Monday*, 13, 4.

Avoiding the Drunkard's Search: Investigating Collection Strategies for Building a Twitter Dataset

Clare Llewellyn
University of Edinburgh
2F2 Buccleuch Place
Edinburgh, UK
s1053147@sms.ed.ac.uk

Laura Cram
University of Edinburgh
2F2 Buccleuch Place
Edinburgh, UK
Laura.Cram@ed.ac.uk

Adrian Favero
University of Edinburgh
2F2 Buccleuch Place
Edinburgh, UK
A.Favero@ed.ac.uk

ABSTRACT

We investigate methods for collecting data to form an archive on the debate within Twitter surrounding the UK's inclusion in the EU. We use three strategies, gathering data using hashtags, extracting data from the random stream and collecting from users known to be discussing the debate. We explore the various bias in the resulting datasets.

Keywords

Data Analytics; Social Media Analysis; Data Selection

1. INTRODUCTION

We are gathering data from Twitter to create an archive on the debate surrounding the UK's inclusion in the European Union (EU). We are tracking opinion leading up to a referendum on the UK's membership. Twitter is being used to find out what people are saying and to investigate how this changes over time. Twitter can be used to track trends in response to emerging events and this analysis allows us to gain a more nuanced understanding of those who are motivated to comment on UK-EU-related topics.

Twitter studies are often criticised because they employ a 'drunkard's search' method, where researchers only look at what is easy to find, like a drunk person looking for keys under a street light because that is the only place where they can see.

An easy way to generate a topic specific Twitter dataset is by querying the Twitter API using hashtags. This method provides data that has been annotated by authors using a keyword or phrase that generally suggests a topic label or a context. The generation of a dataset using this method, however, biases the content in favour of the hashtags chosen. Badly chosen hashtags will mean not all data is covered, hashtags may change over time as debate evolves [4] and data maybe missed if it is not marked with a hashtag.

To address this problem this paper contrasts three methods for collecting data from Twitter: 1) using hashtags cho-

sen by an expert panel as search queries; 2) collecting the random sample without specified search terms and extracting appropriate data [2]; 3) collecting from specific users that are known to be contributing to the debate [3].

2. BACKGROUND

Twitter provides access to a small sample of data through two API methods, a streaming method and a search method. Both give access to 'a small sampling' [1] of the data as it is produced (streaming) or that previously published (search), as results from a query or a random sample. It is possible to share datasets by providing the user id, tweet id and software for gathering data directly from Twitter.

UK citizens will vote on whether to remain within the EU in a referendum that is to take place on the June 23, 2016. The debate over whether the UK should remain as part of the EU is between those who favour remaining as a member (pro-remain) and those who wish the UK to leave the EU (pro-leave). We are monitoring how shifts in opinion relate to the wider public debate and the extent to which Twitter can be used to measure public opinion in relation to the EU.

Data has been gathered as part of an on-going process since Aug 6, 2015 using three strategies:

The Hashtags Set data is collected from the streaming API using UK-EU specific hashtags, chosen by a panel of experts, as query terms. This includes referendum specific terms such as #brexit, #euref, those reflecting topics which will likely be debated such as #migrants and #refugees and more general relevant terms such as #EU and #Europe.

The Stream Set data is extracted from the streaming API using a method based on [2]. This involves collecting the data from the streaming API without any search terms, thereby receiving a random selection. Data is then extracted from this selection using a set of commonly used relevant terms. This gives a topic specific set from the random set. This topic specific set is analysed and the top 100 unigram, bigram and trigram terms are identified. Two annotators then assign each of these terms as relevant or not to UK-EU discussion and the relevant terms are used to search the wider random set to expand the topic specific set. This approach aims to reduce the bias introduced through human defined search terms.

The Official Set data is collected from a group of users that are known to be discussing the referendum, the official campaign groups, StrongerIn, LeaveEUOfficial, Grassroots_Out and Vote_Leave. The data is collected daily via the search API.

Permission to make digital or hard copies of part or all of this work for personal or classroom use is granted without fee provided that copies are not made or distributed for profit or commercial advantage and that copies bear this notice and the full citation on the first page. Copyrights for third-party components of this work must be honored. For all other uses, contact the owner/author(s).

JCDL '16 June 19-23, 2016, Newark, NJ, USA

© 2016 Copyright held by the owner/author(s).

ACM ISBN 978-1-4503-4229-2/16/06...$15.00

DOI: http://dx.doi.org/10.1145/2910896.2925433

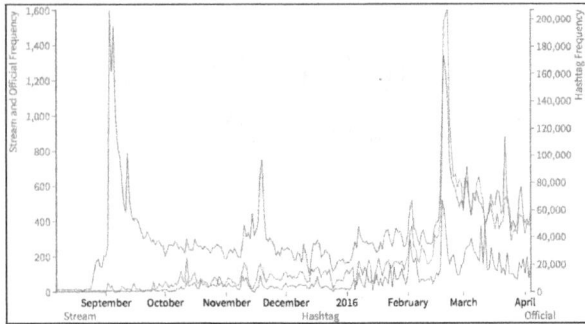

Figure 1: The Frequency of tweets over time.

3. ANALYSIS

We present results based on a comparison of the three data collection methods. We analyse the overall frequency of tweets, the frequency over time in response to specific events, an evaluation of relevance to topic, and an evaluation of how hashtags are used in each set.

During an eight-month collection period the hashtag set contained over ten million tweets, the stream set over forty two thousand and the official set over sixteen thousand. Showing that the hashtag approach collects the largest set by a considerable amount. The frequency of tweets over time graph (Fig.1) shows various similar peaks in the data indicating that all collection strategies are picking up an increase on specific dates. There is a peak in data collected on October 12 2015 when the StrongerIn campaign was launched, and on October 9 2015 after a speech on the EU by David Cameron. There is a large amount of data collected by hashtags on September 3 2015 that is not in the other sets, this was found to be related to refugees and migrants.

Relevance is evaluated independently by three annotators in two tasks. 100 tweets were randomly selected from each dataset. Firstly the annotators were asked to determine if each tweet was directly relevant to the debate on the UK-EU referendum. In the second task the annotators were asked to determine if each tweet was referendum relevant or about a topic that would likely influence voter opinion.

We can see that data in the official and the stream set is more relevant to both the referendum and topics relating to the referendum than the hashtag set (Tab. 1). The hashtag has a low relevance score for 'directly relevant to the referendum debate' but this rises significantly when the topics that will influence the debate are considered. The results indicate that although the hashtag set contains non-relevant information it also covers the topics likely to influence voters not identified in the other sets.

We investigated if hashtags are used differently in the collections through the use of three specific hashtags, one pro-remain (#strongerin) one pro-leave (#leaveeu) and one neutral (#brexit). For each of the sets we gathered 50 random tweets that contained each of the hashtags. Two annotators were asked to mark if each tweet was pro-remain, pro-leave or neutral. We can see (Tab. 3) that all three of the hashtags, thought to represent pro-leave, pro-remain and neutral points of view, are used in tweets that have a pro-leave sentiment. Although #strongerin is used to present a pro-remain opinion in the official set by the pro-remain campaign group.

Table 1: Relevance of data to the EU

	Task 1				Task 2			
	A1	A2	A3	Average	A1	A2	A3	Average
Hashtag	18	8	24	16.67	49	38	68	51.67
Official	91	72	85	82.67	94	80	95	89.67
Stream	95	58	83	78.67	96	79	92	89

Table 2: Opinion (Leave/Remain/Neutral)

		leaveeu %			strongerin %			brexit %		
		L	R	N	L	R	N	L	R	N
Hashtag	A1	94	0	6	42	46	12	76	10	16
	A2	84	0	16	52	42	6	58	6	34
Official	A1	94	0	6	0	100	0	96	0	4
	A2	80	0	20	2	96	2	88	0	12
Stream	A1	100	0	0	60	32	8	78	14	8
	A2	88	0	12	62	34	6	48	4	46

4. CONCLUSIONS

Both the stream and hashtags sets are heavily influenced by the terms used for data collection. The terms differ when automatically extracted (the stream set) or chosen by experts (the hashtag set). The automatic method is most similar to the official set in terms of relevance and frequency of tweets over time. These sets are both very specific to the topic and small in comparison to the hashtag set. The expert method includes a variety of terms that the experts expect will become discussion topics over the longer-term referendum debate. This approach therefore, has a low direct relevance but it gathers information on wider associated topics likely to influence voter choices that may be missed by the other two methods. We cannot extrapolate from this set that these topics will influence the debate, only that they are being discussed. The top hashtag lists for each set and the use of #brexit, #strongerin and #leaveeu suggest that either all of the data selection strategies to collect the data are biased towards the pro-leave opinion or that the data from Twitter contains a strong pro-leave opinion. It is also likely that the term brexit is not as neutral as we thought. Future work includes, gathering relevant data using a supervised machine learning approach, using frequent hashtags in the official/stream sets to update the query terms in the hashtag set and comparing the content of tweets that contain hashtags and those that do not.

5. REFERENCES

[1] Twitter developer pages. https://support.twitter.com/articles/160385. Accessed: 2016-01-22.
[2] C. Llewellyn, C. Grover, B. Alex, J. Oberlander, and R. Tobin. Extracting a topic specific dataset from a twitter archive. In *Research and Advanced Technology for Digital Libraries*, pages 364–367. Springer, 2015.
[3] D. O'Callaghan, N. Prucha, D. Greene, M. Conway, J. Carthy, and P. Cunningham. Online social media in the syria conflict: Encompassing the extremes and the in-betweens. In *ASONAM, 2014 IEEE/ACM*, pages 409–416. IEEE, 2014.
[4] Z. Tufekci. Big questions for social media big data: Representativeness, validity and other methodological pitfalls. *arXiv preprint arXiv:1403.7400*, 2014.

BIBSURF - Discover Bibliographic Entities by Searching for Units of Interest, Ranking and Filtering

Trond Aalberg
NTNU
Trondheim, Norway
trondaal@ntnu.no

Tanja Merčun
University of Ljubljana
Ljubljana, Slovenia
tanja.mercun@gmail.com

Maja Žumer
University of Ljubljana
Ljubljana, Slovenia
maja.zumer@ff.uni-lj.si

ABSTRACT

BIBSURF is a system demonstrating search, ranking and filtering of bibliographic RDF data that is organized in form of entities representing intellectual endeavor at different levels of abstraction: item, manifestation, expression, work.

Keywords

Models; RDF; LRM; keyword search; ranking; filtering

1. INTRODUCTION

Memory institutions such as libraries and museums have embraced the Semantic Web as the main enabler for reuse and exploration of cultural heritage data. Significant effort has been invested in the development of reference models and metadata schemas, and large amounts of data are already made available as result of the Linked Open Data movement. Within the library community main focus has been on FRBR and other reference models published by the The International Federation of Library Associations and Institutions (IFLA), which are being merged into a common Library Reference Model (LRM) [6]. The core of this model is the depiction of intellectual endeavor and products at different levels of abstraction: *item, manifestation, expression, work*, as well the *agents* related to these entities. Various vocabularies have been published for implementing and coding such data in RDF, with the RDA vocabulary[1] currently appearing as the most relevant as it builds directly on the IFLA models and the RDA international cataloguing rules.

However, usage of this model in real world applications tailored to the needs of real users has been less systematically explored, although some protoypes and studies can be found [4, 2, 7]. Model and vocabulary development as well as the creation of data sets is often driven by domain expert and needs to be complemented by best practice knowledge from application development and studying users. *BIBSURF* is

---

[1]http://rdaregistry.info/

Permission to make digital or hard copies of part or all of this work for personal or classroom use is granted without fee provided that copies are not made or distributed for profit or commercial advantage and that copies bear this notice and the full citation on the first page. Copyrights for third-party components of this work must be honored. For all other uses, contact the owner/author(s).

JCDL '16 June 19-23, 2016, Newark, NJ, USA

© 2016 Copyright held by the owner/author(s).

ACM ISBN 978-1-4503-4229-2/16/06.

DOI: http://dx.doi.org/10.1145/2910896.2925434

developed to experiment with search, ranking and "after-search" filtering of library data that is shaped according to the Library Reference Model and coded and stored as RDF. A main difference from traditional library search systems is that we now are interacting with databases containing entities of different types and the system has to make decisions on what type of entities the user has a preference for, what constitutes a meaningful unit in the results listing, what related entities to include in the unit and how to present other relationships. Experience from development and use of the system will also be important to determine how specific bibliographic patterns need be represented. The main contributions of the demonstration are:

- Demonstrate indexing and search on top of LRM data represented and stored in RDF.

- Highlight major design and implementation issues related to indexing and ranking.

- Exemplify solutions for listing and presenting results.

- Contribute with best practice examples for implementing the LRM model.

2. SYSTEM DESCRIPTION

The core of our search system is a database for storing data in RDF, with support for text indexing and keyword search. The current dataset covers a variety of bibliographic patterns and is originally extracted from library catalogues, but enhanced and transformed into rich LRM-data coded in RDF utilizing the RDA vocabulary.

The web-based user interface is inspired by library search interfaces with a single field for entering keywords. Rather than the traditional listing of single publications, BIBSURF organizes the found bibliographic entities in units that correspond to the abstraction level of interest to the end user, as well as improves the search experience by presenting an efficient and comprehensive listing that further can be explored using filtering and hide-show features.

2.1 Indexing and ranking

Keyword search in RDF data is a needed complement to structured queries, particularly when it comes to information needs of users of bibliographic data. A main question when implementing text-indexing and search for RDF is what unit to extract terms from, and what unit to return when querying the index. Different approaches have been explored in research e.g. [3] and most current triplestores have some kind of support for text indexing such as the native repository in the Sesame framework[2] which supports indexing RDF subjects by including the text from associated literal properties [5]. In our context this means that it is possible to index each work, expression etc. as separate units. A more flexible approach is supported in the GraphDB triplestore[3], which extends the subject-based indexing with the possibility to predefine property chains. Essentially this means that it is possible to index larger units of RDF data, sometimes called fragments or RDF molecules [1]. Other alternatives include storing the RDF data in XML databases that support text indexing. Our solution uses property chaining and precomputes RDF fragments which are stored and indexed using the eXist open source database[4]. An important side effect of precomputing fragments is that it removes the severe performance penalties for constructing fragments from the query result runtime.

2.2 Units of interest to users

The decisions on what units to index and return for queries need to be aligned with the expectations of the end users of the system: what we have named as *UIU* - Unit of Interest to User. In BIBSURF, we index works, expressions and manifestations based on the assumption that from any given node of these types we can follow property chains to collect the bag of terms that are relevant for each entity. An example for indexing works is shown in Figure 1 and a query explaining the logic behind this chaining could be "Orient Christie Suchet Movie". In this case it is natural to assume that the top ranked item should be the movie adaptation of Agatha Christie's "Murder on the Orient Express" where David Suchet plays the famous detective. To create the bag of terms related to this unit, one needs to traverse the graph to find the related entities that naturally describe the index centroid, as shown using arrows. The indexing of the original novel would follow other paths and will reach Suchet through the expression where he is the narrator, but this unit will not include the term Movie and will thus be ranked lower.

2.3 Display and interaction

Various forms of grouping items when displaying the results in bibliographic search are increasingly being used. Because of the nature of existing library records such groupings are hard to do consistently and systematically and most implementations are only loosely based on LRM. As our data is elaborated with a rich set of relationships, we have the possibility to experiment with groupings and listings beyond what is found in available library search interfaces. In our display we utilize tabbed boxes for showing e.g. works with tabs for each category of expressions. Other techniques included are hide and show features to display subtrees such as content listings for manifestations.

The use of "after search" filtering is a technique that naturally complements the grouped display lists. Checkboxes for the various facets of the search results, such as the person names related to entities in the result, enable users to easily explore subsets of the results.

To support comparative studies of user preferences we have developed three alternative displays: respectively work-

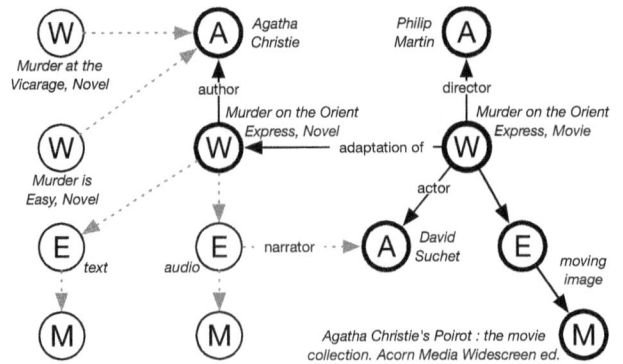

Figure 1: Indexing works.

centric, expression-centric as well as a manifestation-centric. In addition, we have a feature for looking up each UIU both as RDF-fragment and as a SVG-based graph.

2.4 Conclusion

BIBSURF is a search application developed to support the exploration and implementation of search systems for RDF-based bibliographic data. The system is currently used in research to extract best practice knowledge for implementing the Library Reference Model and represents an efficient approach for searching such data. Future work includes generalizing the system to support other reference models and adding support for large scale user studies by implementing logging of search sessions.

3. REFERENCES

[1] Li Ding, Tim Finin, Yun Peng, Paulo Pinheiro da Silva, and Deborah L. McGuinness. Tracking RDF Graph Provenance using RDF Molecules. Technical Report TR-05-06, UMBC, 2005.

[2] Zorana Ercegovac. Multiple-Version Resources in Digital Libraries: Towards User-Centered Displays. *JASIST*, 57(8):1023–1032, 2006.

[3] Wangchao Le, Feifei Li, Anastasios Kementsietsidis, and Songyun Duan. Scalable Keyword Search on Large RDF Data. *IEEE Transactions on knowledge and data engineering*, 26(11), November 2014.

[4] Tanja Merčun, Trond Aalberg, and Maja Žumer. FrbrVis: An Information Visualization Approach to Presenting FRBR Work Families. In *TPDL 2012*, volume 7489 of *LNCS*. Springer, September 2012.

[5] Enrico Minack, Leo Sauermann, Gunnar Grimnes, Christiaan Fluit, and Jeen Broekstra. The Sesame LuceneSail: RDF Queries with Full-text Search. NEPOMUK Technical Report, 2008.

[6] Pat Riva and Maja Žumer. Introducing the FRBR Library Reference Model. In *IFLA WLIC 2015*, Cape Town, South Africa, August 2015.

[7] Krzysztof Sielski, Justyna Walkowska, and Marcin Werla. Methodology for Dynamic Extraction of Highly Relevant Information Describing Particular Object from Semantic Web Knowledge Base. In *TPDL 2012*, volume 7489 of *LNCS*. Springer, September 2012.

---

[2]http://rdf4j.org

[3]http://ontotext.com/products/graphdb/

[4]http://exist-db.org/exist/apps/homepage/index.html

Mining Advisor-Advisee Relationships in Scholarly Big Data: A Deep Learning Approach

Wei Wang, Jiaying Liu, Shuo Yu, Chenxin Zhang, Zhenzhen Xu, Feng Xia
School of Software, Dalian University of Technology
Dalian 116620, China
xzz@dlut.edu.cn

ABSTRACT

Mining advisor-advisee relationships can benefit many interesting applications such as advisor recommendation and protege performance analysis. Based on the hypothesis that, advisor-advisee relationships among researchers are hidden in scholarly big data, we propose in this work a deep learning based advisor-advisee relationship identification method which considers the personal properties and network characteristics with a stacked autoencoder model. To the best of our knowledge, this is the first time that a deep learning model is utilized to represent coauthor network features for relationships identification. Moreover, experiments demonstrate that the proposed method has better performance compared with other state-of-the-art methods.

Keywords

Deep learning; Relationship mining; Stacked autoencoders

1. INTRODUCTION

The benefit of mentorship for advisee is obvious. On the one hand, the extent to which advisee mimic their advisors' career choices and academic preferences, and learn their mentorship skills is unclear [1]. On the other hand, the lack of dataset for advisor-advisee relationships makes it not easy to handle these issues. There are several projects that aim to collect mentorships relationships, such as Mathematics Genealogy Project [1], The Academic Family Tree [2], and Academic Genealogy Wiki [3]. However, these methods heavily rely on volunteers' efforts, which results in limited records.

Fortunately, advisor-advisee relationships are usually hidden in the coauthor network [2], which enables us to automatically uncover these relationships. In this paper, we propose a deep learning based advisor-advisee relationships

---

[1] http://genealogy.math.ndsu.nodak.edu/index.php
[2] http://academictree.org/
[3] http://phdtree.org/

Permission to make digital or hard copies of part or all of this work for personal or classroom use is granted without fee provided that copies are not made or distributed for profit or commercial advantage and that copies bear this notice and the full citation on the first page. Copyrights for third-party components of this work must be honored. For all other uses, contact the owner/author(s).

JCDL '16 June 19-23, 2016, Newark, NJ, USA

© 2016 Copyright held by the owner/author(s).

ACM ISBN 978-1-4503-4229-2/16/06.

DOI: http://dx.doi.org/10.1145/2910896.2925435

mining methods with a computer science bibliographic network extracted from DBLP and Academic Genealogy Wiki project. A stacked autoencoder model is used to learn both scholars' personal properties and network characteristics. Experimental results demonstrate that our proposed method has superior performance compared with four classical machine learning methods.

2. PROPOSED SCHEME

We employ the Stacked Autoencoder (SAE) as the foundation of our methods, which is a famous deep learning model. The SAE model allows users to easily inject the personal features and network characteristics as input without the manual effort of feature selection.In this section, the SAE model details and its settings are introduced.

2.1 Autoencoder

An autoencoder is an artificial network with one input layer, one hidden layer, and one output layer, which can find a lower-dimensional representation of input features. Given input vector $x \in [0,1]^N$, it aims at seeking a lower-dimensional representation $y \in [0,1]^M$ with $M < N$. The mapping function f between x and y is called encoding function and can be the logistic sigmoid function

$$f(x) = f(Wx + b) = \frac{1}{1 + exp(Wx + b)} = y \qquad (1)$$

where, W is a weighted matrix, b is an encoding bias vector. Then the autoencoder finds a second mapping function $f'(y) = f(W'x + b') = z$, such that the output z is equal to the input x.

2.2 Stacked Autoencoders

A SAE model is a series of autoencoder. Considering SAE with k layers, the first layer will be the autoencoder, with the training set as the input. After gaining the kth hidden layer, the input of the $(k + 1)$th layer is the output of kth hidden layer. Thus, multiple autoencoders can be stacked together. Meanwhile, to use the SAE model to identify the advisor-advisee relationships, we put a logistic regression layer after the last output layer for relationship classification.

2.3 SAE Training Method

The SAE model is trained with a greedy layerwise unsupervised learning algorithm. The key point is to first pretrain the deep network layer by layer in a unsupervised way. Then, fine-tuning with BP is used to tune the model's parameters in a top-down direction to gain better results. To

Table 1: Description of input features

Feature	Description
AA_i	academic age of i when first collaborating with j
AA_j	academic age of j when first collaborating with i
N_i	No. of i's publication before collaborating with j
N_j	No. of j's publication before collaborating with i
AD	academic age difference value between i and j
N_{ij}	collaborating times between i and j
CD	collaborating duration between i and j
FTA	number of times i and j being first two authors
$Cohesion$	similarity between i and j (first 8 years)

Table 2: Performance comparison for SAE, LR, KNN, and SVM

Method	Accuracy	Precision	Recall	F1-Score
LR	0.89	0.90	0.86	0.88
KNN	0.87	0.91	0.83	0.87
SVM	0.91	0.85	**0.94**	0.81
DT	0.83	0.84	0.82	0.83
SAE	**0.91**	**0.92**	0.91	**0.91**

be specific, the procedure can be described as follows: 1) Train the first layer by minimizing the difference between input vector x and reconstructed vector z; 2) Train the second layer by taking the first layer's output as the input; 3) Iterate the second step for the desired hidden layers; 4) Use the output of the last layer as the input for the identification layer, and the weights of each layer as the initialized parameters for BP supervised training; 5) Optimize the parameters of all layers with BP method in a supervised way.

2.4 Settings of SAE Model

To apply the SAE model to mining advisor-advisee relationships, we need to determine the number of input features, the number of hidden layers, and the number of hidden units in each hidden layer. For the input features, we both consider the advisor and advisee personal properties, and the ego network properties. Specifically, given a advisee i and his/her collaborator j, the input features can be seen from Table 1. These features are collected from the first 8 years of i's academic career. One's first academic age is the time point of publishing first paper. The Cohesion between i and j after collaborating $t(t \leq 8)$ years can be calculated as:

$$Cohesion_{ij}^t = \frac{T_{ij}}{2}\left(\frac{1}{T_i} + \frac{1}{T_j}\right) \quad (2)$$

where, T_{ij} is the number of co-publications between i and j in t years, T_i is the number of i' publications, and T_j is the number of j' publications. We calculate the cohesion values every year between two collaborators. Thus, we have 16 input features in total. Meanwhile, we normalize all the input features into $[0, 1]$.

In this work, we choose the hidden layer size from 1 to 6, and the number of hidden layer units from 1 to 15. After performing grid finding task, we acquired the best setting for our methods. The best settings consist of two hidden layers, and the number of hidden layer units in each layers is 8.

3. EXPERIMENTS

3.1 Data Description

The proposed deep learning model was applied to the data collected from the Academic Genealogy Wiki project. The mentorship dataset is collected from 16 famous universities such as Carnegie Mellon and Stanford in the field of computer science. The dataset contains 3423 advisees and corresponding 343 advisors. We then gain collaborators of each advisee and their properties from DBLP. Thus we can get

the ego network of each advisee. Obviously, one of the collaborators in each scholar's ego network is his/her advisor. We randomly select 80% nodes as the training set and the rest as the testing set.

3.2 Results

To evaluate the effectiveness of our model, we use four performance indexes, which are the Accuracy, Precision, Recall, and F1-Score. We compared our method with four supervised learning methods. They are Logistic Regression (LR), K Nearest Neighbor (KNN), Support Vector Machine (SVM), and Decision Tree (DT).

Table 2 summarizes the performance comparison of above methods on DBLP data set. From the experimental results, we can see that SAE model outperforms other machine learning methods. The stacked autoencoder as our deep learning architecture result in a accuracy of 0.91. Meanwhile, other machine learning methods can also reach the accuracy more than 0.83. Similarly, our proposed methods has the highest precision and F1-Score. The higher accuracy, precision, and F1-Score underlines the idea that deep learning algorithms can outperform classical machine learning algorithms. Meanwhile, the results also indicate that the deep learning approach can be successfully applied into social network analysis.

4. CONCLUSION

In this work, we propose a deep learning approach with a SAE model for mining advisor-advisee relationships. We consider both the scholar's personal properties and network characteristics as input features. Experimental results show that our method can achieve better performance compared with several classical machine learning methods. In the future work, we will apply our proposed model to the whole DBLP digital library to obtain a large-scale mentorship data set, which will enable us to study the interesting application such as mentor recommendation.

5. REFERENCES

[1] R. D. Malmgren, J. M. Ottino, and L. A. N. Amaral. The Role of Mentorship in Protégé Performance. *Nature*, 465(7298):622–626, 2010.

[2] C. Wang, J. Han, Y. Jia, J. Tang, D. Zhang, Y. Yu, and J. Guo. Mining Advisor-Advisee Relationships From Research Publication networks. In *Proceedings of the 16th KDD*, pages 203–212. ACM, 2010.

Who are the Rising Stars in Academia?

Jun Zhang, Zhaolong Ning, Xiaomei Bai, Wei Wang, Shuo Yu, Feng Xia
School of Software, Dalian University of Technology
Dalian 116620, China
zhaolongning@dlut.edu.cn

ABSTRACT

This paper proposes a novel method named ScholarRank to evaluate the scientific impact of rising stars. Our proposed ScholarRank integrates the merits of both statistical indicators and influence calculation algorithms in heterogeneous academic networks. The ScholarRank method considers three factors, which are the citation counts of authors, the mutual influence among coauthors and the mutual reinforce process among different entities in heterogeneous academic networks. Through experiments on real datasets, we demonstrate that our ScholarRank can efficiently select more top ranking rising stars than other methods.

Keywords

Rising star; Heterogeneous networks; HITS; PageRank

1. INTRODUCTION

The success of academic career not only depends on researcher's personal capacity, but also closely relates to the supports from both governments and institutions. This drives the emergence of more and more research achievements on evaluating the scientific impact of scholars, because it can provide basis for foundation application etc. However, on the contrary, little efforts have been devoted to quantifying the future potential of academic new talents. Therefore, we propose a novel method based on heterogeneous academic networks to find potential academic new talents, which are known as rising stars.

In our paper, rising stars refer to scholars who are not outstanding among peers or with low research profiles at the beginning stage of their scientific career, but tend to become influential researchers in the future. Currently, the existing approaches for the evaluation of rising stars generally ignore a vital fact [1], which is the mutual reinforce process among the components of academic networks. Most of previous studies only consider the mutual influence among coauthors and use homogeneous networks for evaluation. However, as a matter of fact, the real academic networks consist of

various kinds of entities and links. Therefore, it is essential to evaluate the impacts of rising stars under heterogeneous networks. In addition, the reputations of scholars are mainly represented by their publications, while on the contrary, the qualities of publications are also affected by the capacities of its authors. As a consequence, when evaluating the impacts of rising stars, the mutual reinforce process among scholars, articles and corresponding venues should also be considered.

In this work, inspired by the facts mentioned above, we propose a novel method called ScholarRank to evaluate the scientific impact of rising stars. In order to measure the mutual influence among coauthors, we first compute the value of our proposed indicator as introduced in [2]. Then we use our hybrid algorithms to depict the mutual reinforce process among different entities in academic networks. Finally, we apply our proposed ScholarRank on real datasets to evaluate the impacts of rising stars, the architecture of ScholarRank is shown in Figure. 1.

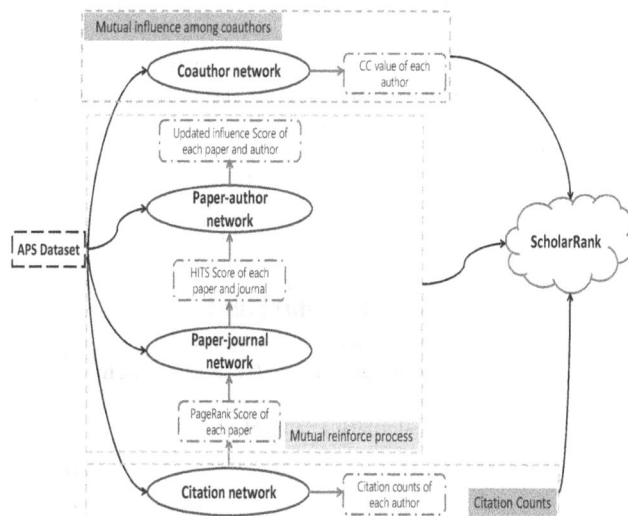

Figure 1: Architecture of ScholarRank.

2. SCHOLARRANK METHOD

2.1 The mutual influence among coauthors

In order to measure the mutual influence among coauthors, we use the indicator named the caliber of collaboration (CC) to capture the researchers' capacity of collaborating with scholars from diverse backgrounds as we proposed

Permission to make digital or hard copies of all or part of this work for personal or classroom use is granted without fee provided that copies are not made or distributed for profit or commercial advantage and that copies bear this notice and the full citation on the first page. Copyrights for components of this work owned by others than ACM must be honored. Abstracting with credit is permitted. To copy otherwise, or republish, to post on servers or to redistribute to lists, requires prior specific permission and/or a fee. Request permissions from permissions@acm.org.

JCDL '16, June 19–23, 2016, Newark, NJ, USA.

© 2016 ACM. ISBN 978-1-4503-4229-2/16/06. . . $15.00

DOI: http://dx.doi.org/10.1145/2910896.2925436

in [2], because scholars can benefit a lot by cooperating with diverse scholars. The specific method is illustrated as follows.

$$entropy(a_i^t) = -\sum_{\vartheta=1}^{r} w_\vartheta^t \log_2\left(w_\vartheta^t\right) \qquad (1)$$

$$CC(a_i) = \sum_{t=1}^{u} entropy(a_i^t) \qquad (2)$$

where a_i represents an author, r is the total number of the words in all the institutions' information of a_i's cooperators in year t, and w_ϑ^t is the possibility of word ϑ in all the institutions' information of a_i's cooperators in year t. The value of $CC(a_i)$ is the sum of $entropy(a_i^t)$ according to specific time intervals, where u refers to the time intervals as we set.

2.2 Mutual reinforce process in heterogeneous academic networks

In this paper, our hybrid algorithms on measuring the importance of nodes are applied in order to measure the mutual reinforce process in heterogeneous academic networks, which compose of three sub-networks, i.e. citation network, paper-journal network and paper-author network. We first compute the importance of papers under citation network according to PageRank algorithm.

Then we consider the mutual reinforce process between papers and corresponding journals to measure the influence of journals. The HITS algorithm is applied to calculate the influence of journals in paper-journal network. In the initial step, if the node is a paper, the values of it are set equal to the PageRank score we get under citation network, else we set the initial value equal to 1.

After the calculations in paper-journal network, we can get the new impact scores of papers and journals. We then measure the influence of authors also according to HITS algorithm in paper-author network. In the initial step, if the node is a paper, the values of it are set equal to the influence score we get in paper-journal network, else we set the initial values as 1. Then we can get the final influence score of authors by considering the mutual reinforce process between papers, journals and authors in heterogeneous academic networks.

2.3 Calculation of ScholarRank

In our proposed ScholarRank, it contains three main parts, which are citation counts, value of CC and our hybrid algorithms in heterogeneous academic networks. The following equation is used to calculate the final score of authors:

$$ScholarRank(a_i) = \frac{1-\alpha-\beta-\delta}{n} + \alpha\frac{CC(a_i)}{T_{CC}} + \beta\frac{Cita(a_i)}{T_{Cita}}$$
$$+ \delta\frac{auth(a_i)}{T_{hyb}} \sum_{j=1}^{\varpi} con(a_i^j)PR(j)auth(V_j)$$
$$(3)$$

where α, β and δ are parameters, ϖ is the number of total papers written by author a_i and n is the number of authors in the network. $Cita(a_i)$ is the total citation counts of author a_i and T_{Cita} is the total citation counts of all the authors. T_{CC} is the total CC values of all the authors. $con(a_i^j)$ means a_i's contribution in paper j and we set it as $1/\theta$ for simplicity, where θ is the order of a_i in paper j. $PR(j)$ is paper j's PagaRank score in citation network, $auth(V_j)$

is the corresponding venue's impact score in paper-journal network and $auth(a_i)$ is the influence score of author a_i in paper-author network. T_{hyb} is the total values of the hybrid results by all the authors.

3. EXPERIMENTS AND RESULTS

We use datasets from American Physical Society and select authors beginning their scientific careers at the year of 1993. We compare ScholarRank with the following methods to evaluate its effectiveness. **CocaRank** is proposed in [2] and **StarRank** is introduced in [3], we choose these two methods for comparison.

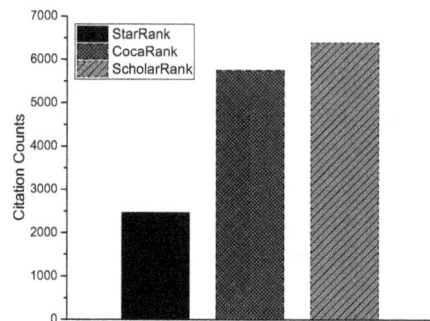

Figure 2: Comparison of average citation counts.

The time intervals we select for evaluation is the initial 5 years of researchers' scientific careers. We assume that the higher citation counts a scholar gets, the more influential he is. In order to validate the performance of our proposed ScholarRank method, we compute the top 10 rising stars' average citation counts in 2013 by our ScholarRank and the above comparison methods. As shown in Fig. 2, the ScholarRank achieves the highest average citation counts among all the comparison methods, and it indicates that our proposed ScholarRank can efficiently select top ranking researchers than other methods.

4. CONCLUSIONS

In this paper, we propose the ScholarRank method to evaluate the impact of rising stars, and the experiments on real datasets indicate that our method can find more top ranked rising stars than other methods. In future work, we will test the performance of ScholarRank on more datasets and consider more factors which correlate with the influence of scholars, such as the social relations of scholars, and the download times of papers.

5. REFERENCES

[1] X. Li, C. S. Foo, K. L. Tew, and S. K. Ng. Searching for rising stars in bibliography networks. In *Database Systems for Advanced Applications*, pages 288–292. Springer, 2009.

[2] J. Zhang, F. Xia, W. Wang, X. M. Bai, S. Yu, B. T. Megersa, and Z. Peng. Cocarank: A collaboration caliber-based method for finding academic rising stars. In *WWW'16 Companion*, pages 395–400, 2016.

[3] A. Daud, R. Abbasi, and F. Muhammad. Finding rising stars in social networks. In *Database Systems for Advanced Applications*, pages 13–24. Springer, 2013.

Can you learn it? Probably!
Developing Learning Analytics Tools in R

Giorgio Maria Di Nunzio
Department of Information Engineering
University of Padua
Via Gradenigo 6/a, 35131 Padua, Italy
giorgiomaria.dinunzio@unipd.it

ABSTRACT

Automatic text categorization is an effective way to organize large text datasets in Digital Libraries (DL). However, most of the available machine learning tools are complex and go beyond the scope of what a digital library curator need or is able to do in order to classify the objects of a DL. Drawing inspiration from the field of Learning Analytics and Interactive Machine Learning, we design and implement visual interactive classifiers that are intuitive to train and easy to use. In this poster, we present an interactive Web application in R that allows users to use text classifier in an innovative way. The source code of the application is available at the following link:
https://github.com/gmdn/educational-data-mining

Keywords

Automated Text Classification, Naïve Bayes, Interactive Machine Learning, Learning Analytics, R programming

1. INTRODUCTION

Automatic text classifiers provides an effective way to categorize large datasets of documents of a Digital Library and to facilitate, for example, the browsing of digital objects by topic, the creation of controlled vocabularies [3], the implementation of content-based recommendation services [8], and many other services that support the fruition of the content of a Digital Library. However, the algorithms that implement these classifiers often require specific optimization processes in order to obtain an accuracy comparable to the one given by professional catalogers [10]. In this context, Interactive Machine Learning (IML) studies interactive approaches that allow non-expert users to solve classification problems with minimum effort by means of intuitive visualization tools [1]. In fact, by means of visualisation techniques, we can help researchers to examine the large information streams at the right level of abstraction through appropriate visual representations [7]. One example is the

Permission to make digital or hard copies of part or all of this work for personal or classroom use is granted without fee provided that copies are not made or distributed for profit or commercial advantage and that copies bear this notice and the full citation on the first page. Copyrights for third-party components of this work must be honored. For all other uses, contact the owner/author(s).

JCDL '16 June 19-23, 2016, Newark, NJ, USA

© 2016 Copyright held by the owner/author(s).

ACM ISBN 978-1-4503-4229-2/16/06.

DOI: http://dx.doi.org/10.1145/2910896.2925437

Interactive and Classification approach [2] that has been designed to enable lay people to train interactively classifiers using large datasets. There is also a recent field of research named Learning Analytics (LA) that focuses, among other things, on the analysis about users and their learning contexts, for purposes of understanding and optimizing learning and the environments in which it occurs. [1]

In this work, we present a Web application developed in R that draws inspiration from the principles of IML and LA with the goal to build an interactive tool that addresses the following problems: (i) teach probabilistic classifiers in an innovative way; (ii) use simple geometrical primitives that allow lay people to understand intuitively how probabilistic classifiers work; (iii) distribute open source code of the application. We use the two-dimensional representation of probabilities proposed by [6, 5] which allows us to provide an adequate data visualization approach to understand, step by step, how to present complex concepts like parameter optimization and cost sensitive learning in an easy and intuitive way. At each step, we suggest exercises that can be monitored to track the learning curve of the user and we apply this geometrical interpretation to a real case scenario of text classification to show how this intuitive visualization can be used to organize large textual collections quickly and effectively.

2. TEACHING NAÏVE BAYES CLASSIFIERS

The two-dimensional representation of probabilities [6], based on the idea of Likelihood Spaces [9], is a very intuitive way of presenting the problem of classification on a two-dimensional space. Given two classes c_1 and c_2, in its simplest form, a Bayeisan classifier puts an object o into category c_1 if the following statement is true:

$$\underbrace{P(o|c_2)}_{y} < m \underbrace{P(o|c_1)}_{x} + q \qquad (1)$$

where $P(o|c_1)$ and $P(o|c_2)$ are the likelihoods of the object o given the two categories, while m and q are two parameters that depend on the misclassification costs that can be assigned by the user to compensate for either the unbalanced classes situation or different class costs. If we interpret the two likelihoods as two coordinates x and y of a two dimensional space, the problem of classification becomes 'visible' and can be presented on a two-dimensional plot. The decision of the classification is represented by the 'line' $y = mx + q$ that splits the plane into two parts and all

---

[1] https://tekri.athabascau.ca/

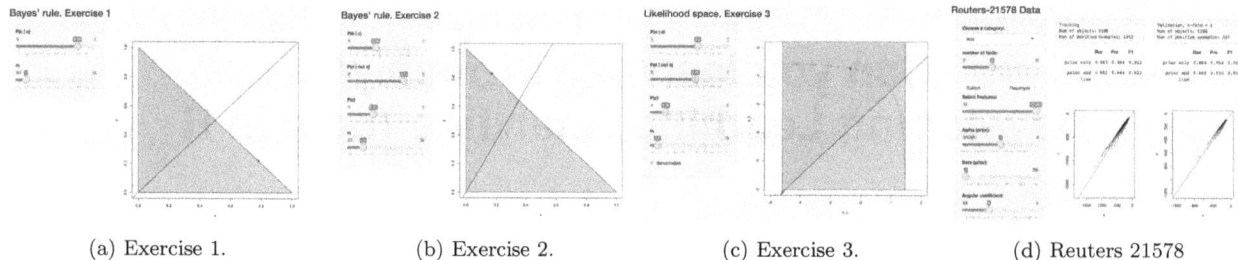

(a) Exercise 1. (b) Exercise 2. (c) Exercise 3. (d) Reuters 21578

Figure 1: Examples of exercises in increasing order of difficulty.

the points that fall 'below' this line are classified as objects that belong to class c_1.

When a Naïve Bayes (NB) approach is chosen, the two likelihoods are factorized into the product of the class conditional probabilities $P(f|c)$ for each feature f of the object o:

$$\underbrace{\prod_{i=1}^{M} P(f_i|c_2)}_{y} < \underbrace{m \prod_{i=1}^{M} P(f_i|c_1) + q}_{x} \qquad (2)$$

where M is the number of features chosen to describe the objects. For computational reasons, we compute the logarithm of the likelihood to transform products into sums and avoid arithmetical anomalies:

$$\log \left(\underbrace{\sum_{i=1}^{M} P(f_i|c_2)}_{y} \right) < \log \left(\underbrace{m \prod_{i=1}^{M} P(f|c_1) + q}_{x} \right) \qquad (3)$$

By introducing the logarithm, we have transformed a linear decision function into a logarithmic curve

$$\log(y) < \log(mx + q) \qquad (4)$$

that, given $m > 0$, for positive values of q is convex, while for $q < 0$ is concave.

2.1 Implementation

We have implemented the NB classifier with the Shiny package in R [4], and the source code of the application is freely available for download[2]. This interactive Web application can be used to show how the theoretical concepts of a NB classifier work on a two-dimensional space both on a toy-problem and on a real case scenario of text classification of Reuters newswires [3]. The idea is to present to the user the classification problem in increasing order of difficulty: the user interacts with the application and has to set the correct values of the parameters according to a set of questions (that are not shown here for space reasons) before he/she can advance to the next level of difficulty. The interface will also show new features and parameters as the difficulty increases (i.e., from likelihoods to class conditional probabilities, from linear to logarithmic curves). At the end of this process, the user is ready to interact with a real dataset of textual documents. In Figure 1, we show examples of

the Web application in increasing order of difficulty, from left to right, where the last picture shows a real machine-learning scenario that uses a standard benchmark for text classification: the Reuters-21578 dataset.

3. CONCLUSIONS

In this work, we have discussed the problem of the complexity of some ML tools that are used to classify, recommend, and index documents in Digital Libraries. We have shown how interactive visual environments allow even lay people to optimize complex ML problems with minimum effort. We have presented a Web application developed in R that draws inspiration from the principles of IML and LA with the aim to build a probabilistic classifier that can be used for real text classification tasks and that can be optimized very efficiently by any user.

4. REFERENCES

[1] S. Amershi, M. Cakmak, W. B. Knox, and T. Kulesza. Power to the People: The Role of Humans in Interactive Machine Learning. *AI Magazine*, 35(4):105–120, 2014.

[2] S. Amershi, M. Chickering, S. M. Drucker, B. Lee, P. Simard, and J. Suh. ModelTracker: Redesigning Performance Analysis Tools for Machine Learning. In *Proceedings of the 33rd Annual ACM Conference on Human Factors in Computing Systems*, CHI '15, pages 337–346, New York, NY, USA, 2015. ACM.

[3] H. Avancini, A. Rauber, F. Sebastiani, and T. U. Wien. Organizing digital libraries by automated text categorization. In *Proceedings of ICDL 2004, TERI, 2004, 919*, page 931, 2002.

[4] W. Chang. *Shiny: Web Application Framework for R*, 2015. R package version 0.11.

[5] G. Di Nunzio. Using Scatterplots to Understand and Improve Probabilistic Models for Text Categorization and Retrieval. *Int. J. Approx. Reasoning*, 50(7):945–956, 2009.

[6] G. Di Nunzio. A New Decision to Take for Cost-Sensitive Naïve Bayes Classifiers. *Information Processing and Management*, 50(5):653–674, 2014.

[7] G. Di Nunzio. Visual Classification. In C. C. Aggarwal, editor, *Data Classification: Algorithms and Applications*, pages 607–632. CRC Press, 2014.

[8] R. J. Mooney and L. Roy. Content-based book recommending using learning for text categorization. In *Proceedings of the Fifth ACM Conference on Digital Libraries*, DL '00, pages 195–204, New York, NY, USA, 2000. ACM.

[9] R. Singh and B. Raj. Classification in Likelihood Spaces. *Technometrics*, 46(3):318–329, 2004.

[10] T. Wang and B. C. Desai. An Approach for Text Categorization in Digital Library. In *Database Engineering and Applications Symposium, 2007. IDEAS 2007. 11th International*, pages 21–27, Sept 2007.

---

[2]https://github.com/gmdn/educational-data-mining
[3]http://www.daviddlewis.com/resources/testcollections/reuters21578/

Characterizing Users Tagging Behavior in Academic Blogs

Lei Li
Department of Information Management
Nanjing University of Science & Technology
No.200 Xiaolingwei Nanjing 210094, China
lileiwelldone@gmail.com

Chengzhi Zhang
Department of Information Management
Nanjing University of Science & Technology
No.200 Xiaolingwei Nanjing 210094, China
zhangcz@njust.edu.cn

ABSTRACT

Along with popular of academic social media, academic blogs are one of the user generated academic information that can be annotated using social tags for user's information retrieval and organization. In order to improve the existing social tagging system to satisfy the users' needs, users' tagging behavior need to be understood. However, there is no researches on characterizing user tagging behaviors of academic resources. In this paper, using the tag of academic blog as the research object, the author analyze user's tagging behaviors based on the characteristics of tags (tags-based features) and those related to blog contents (content-based features). These characteristics can be used to the academic tagging system to promote organization and propagation of academic knowledge.

Keywords

Tagging behavior; academic blogs; narrow folksonomy; academic social media

1. INTRODUCTION

Academic social media are changing the ways that the scholars obtain academic information. The academic blog is one of the user generated academic information resources that can be annotated by the social tags in some social tagging systems. Social tagging systems provide users with a platform to organize and search resources through tags. Previous studies showed that the design of social tagging systems will be guided and the user demands will be satisfied if user's tagging behaviors can be clearly defined [1]. Thomas proposed two types of folksonomy: "broad folksonomy" and "narrow folksonomy". The former means that a tag can be labeled by different users, while the latter means that a tag can only be labeled by the resource provider or specific users [2]. There are a plenty of researches about broad folksonomy, such as tagging distribution, tags reuse, tags growth and types of tag [3, 4], and the application of tags on broad folksonomy context, such as automatic generation of tags, improvement of retrieval effects with tags [6]. Existing researches on tagging behaviors rarely concentrate on user's tagging behaviors in narrow folksonomy domain, particularly in academic context.

Specialized in user's tagging behaviors in narrow domain and academic context, this paper studies the tagging behaviors for academic blog posts whose tags can be annotated only by the

Permission to make digital or hard copies of all or part of this work for personal or classroom use is granted without fee provided that copies are not made or distributed for profit or commercial advantage and that copies bear this notice and the full citation on the first page. To copy otherwise, or republish, to post on servers or to redistribute to lists, requires prior specific permission and/or a fee. Request permissions from Permissions@acm.org.

JCDL '16, June 19-23, 2016, Newark, NJ, USA.
© 2016 ACM. ISBN 978-1-4503-4229-2/16/06…$15.00.
DOI: http://dx.doi.org/10.1145/2910896.2925438

publisher. Tagging behaviors are studied specific to characteristics of tags (tags-based features) and those related to blog post contents (content-based features). These features studied in this paper are chose from the metrics that previous works studied in broad folksonomy and can be drawn to the narrow tagging special domain on academic blog context. We illustrate these features by analyzing the tagging data of the academic blogs, in order to study the narrow tagging behavior of academic resources and support to efficiently promote academic knowledge organization and sharing on the academic tagging system.

2. METHOD

In this paper, blog post tags from blog.sciencenet.cn [1] were selected as the research object, and we crawled the webpages of each blog post to get the blog post profile in a tuple format <post author, post name, post content, post tags, post category, post time>. The data acquisition period lasted from March 6, 2007 to August 25, 2013. Then, 705 blog posts (concerned with 403 blog users) and 2000 corresponding tags were selected randomly, and the attribute value of each tag was calculated. Tag attributes consist of tags-based features and content-based features. Tags-based features values are determined by the tags without considering the blog content. All these attributes are described as follows.

Part of speech of tags: we used the part of speech annotating tool[2] to automatically label the part of speech of tags.

Tag length: to count the word length of each tag, the character number of tags is used as the word length.

Whether it is a subject headings: to judge whether the tag is in the list of Chinese subject headings[3].

Whether it is a named entity: name of people, name of place, name of organization and time word can be identified when using the part of speech annotating tool. To guarantee the result accuracy, then we manually checked the correctness of the named entity tags identified by the tool.

Content-based features' values can be determined and calculated combined with contents of blog posts. All these attributes are described as follows.

Entropy: information entropy is used to measure the probability occurrence of information. The entropy of tag is computed using the following equation:

$$H(x) = -\sum_{i=1}^{12} P(x_i) \log(P(x_i))$$

---

1 http://blog.sciencenet.cn, is a blog of science and technology.
2 https://pypi.python.org/pypi/jieba/
3 http://www.91marc.cn/cct/

Where, i is the number of categories of blog posts in the blog.sciencenet.cn, which have a total of 12 categories; we define x_i as each category. $P(x_i)$ is defined as the following equation:

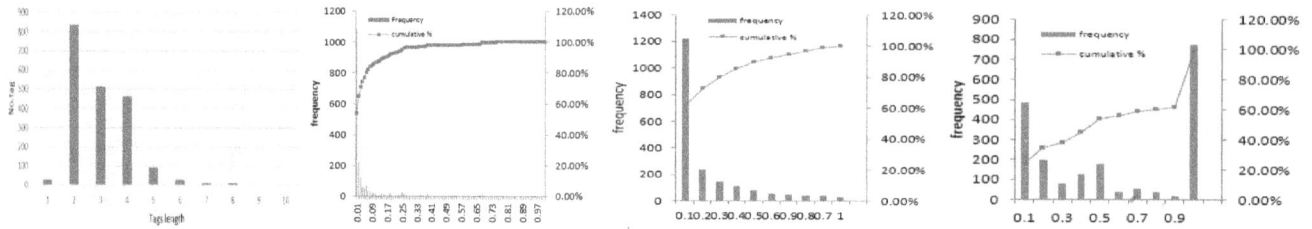

Figure 1: (1) The tags' length results; (2) the histogram of entropy results; (3) the histogram of Position of first occurrence; (4) the histogram of tags occurred frequency

$$P(x_i) = \frac{\text{Number of blog posts with the current tag contained in category } xi}{\text{Number of blog posts contained in category } xi}$$

Position of first occurrence: we calculated the first occurrence position of a tag in the blog post, divided the length of a blog post to normalize it. The higher values of the first position occurrence means the tag occur in the later of the blog post.

Whether the tag is contained in the blog post title: we judged whether the tag is contained in the title of the blog post.

Tag frequency: first, the stop words of the blog post were removed, and we counted the rest of words frequency to get the highest frequency of the word in one blog. Then we counted the occurrence frequency of tags in the blog post. Each tags' occurrence frequency was divided by the highest frequency word in the blog to normalize.

Inverse document frequency: The less documents a word contained, the bigger IDF is, and it means that the word has good separating capacity. The computed result is normalized using the following equation:

$$IDF(X) = 1 - \frac{\text{Number of documents contained the tag}}{\text{Total number of documents}}$$

Termhood: it was defined as the correlation degree between a candidate term and a specific domain concept [5]. The computed result is normalized using the following equation:

$$F(X) = \frac{\text{Frequency of the tag in foreground corpus}}{\text{Frequency of the tag in foreground corpus + Frequency of the tag in background corpus}}$$

We used blog posts crawled from the blog.sciencenet.cn as the foreground corpus and the corpus of "People's Daily" from January, 1998 to June, 1998 as the background corpus, which is one of the common used corpus for computing termhood. The higher occurrence frequency of the tag in the foreground corpus and the lower in the background corpus indicate that the termhood of the tag is high. Otherwise, the termhood is low.

3. RESULT ANALYSIS

First, the results of tags-based features were analyzed. Most tags were nouns (N=1620, 81.0%), then verbs (N=284, 14.2%) and adjectives (N=28, 1.4%). The lengths of most tags were 2 (N=839, 42.0%), 3 (N=514, 25.7%) or 4 (N=466, 23.3%), longer tags were rarely used to label academic blog posts, the results were shown in Fig.1 (1). 39% of tags were subject headings and 13% were named entities. Then, the results of content-based features were analyzed. 44% (N=880) of tags occurred in the title of blog posts, which indicated that the title's words are one of the important sources of tagging. Most tags had a low entropy, and 86% (N=1720) had an entropy within 0-0.1 as shown in Fig.1 (2). Fig.1 (3) showed that 89% (N= 1780) of tags occurred in the first half

part of the blog post, and only a few tags appeared in the latter half part of the blog. As shown in Fig.1 (4), 39% (N=774) of tags occurred frequently in blog posts, and tags which occurred rarely in blog posts were also used frequently. Moreover, the higher IDF of all tags (between 0.9 and 1) showed tags of academic blog posts had a good distinguishability, as shown in Fig.2 (left). Fig. 2 (right) showed the 88% (N= 1760) tags had higher termhood (between 0.9 and 1), which conformed to the academic blog post's tags characteristic.

4. DISCUSSION AND CONCLUSION

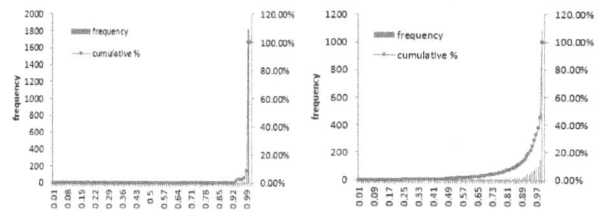

Figure 2: The histogram of IDF and termhood

Using tags of academic blog posts in the blog.sciencenet.cn as the research object, user's tagging behaviors were analyzed according to tags-based features and content-based features. The results showed that users intended to label academic blog posts with nouns, short words, a few named entities and some subject terms. The title was one of sources for users to annotate tags; most tags had a low entropy, which showed that most tags did not occur frequently; most tags occurred in the first half part of blog posts; users were inclined to label academic blog posts with frequently-occurred words and the less frequently words in the blog posts; tags of academic blog posts had a good distinguishability and the higher tag termhood. Based on the users' tagging behavior, the academic blog system can recommend high quality tags to satisfied user, which are beneficial for information organization and retrieval, and promote propagation of academic knowledge.

5. REFERENCES

[1] Sa, N. and Yuan, X., 2013. What motivates people use social tagging. In *Online Communities and Social Computing* (pp. 86-93). Springer Berlin Heidelberg. DOI=10.1007/978-3-642-39371-6_10

[2] Vander Wal, T., 2007. Folksonomy. *online posting, Feb, 7*.

[3] Farooq, U., Kannampallil, T.G., Song, Y., Ganoe, C.H., Carroll, J.M. and Giles, L., 2007, November. Evaluating tagging behavior in social bookmarking systems: metrics and design heuristics. In *Proceedings of the 2007 international ACM conference on Supporting group work* (pp. 351-360). ACM.

[4] Gupta, M., Li, R., Yin, Z. and Han, J., 2010. Survey on social tagging techniques. *ACM SIGKDD Explorations Newsletter*, 12(1), pp.58-72. DOI=10.1145/1882471.1882480

[5] Kageura, K. and Umino, B., 1996. Methods of automatic term recognition: A review. *Terminology*, 3(2), pp.259-289. DOI=http://dx.doi.org/10.1075/term.3.2.03kag

[6] Sood, S., Owsley, S., Hammond, K.J. and Birnbaum, L., 2007, March. TagAssist: Automatic Tag Suggestion for Blog Posts. In *ICWS*

Towards Identifying Potential Research Collaborations from Scientific Research Networks using Scholarly Data

Yanet Garay
Department of Computer Science
and Cyber-ShARE
University of Texas at El Paso, El
Paso, Texas, USA
ydgaray@miners.utep.edu

Monika Akbar
Department of Computer Science
and Cyber-ShARE
University of Texas at El Paso, El
Paso, Texas, USA
makbar@utep.edu

Ann Q. Gates
Department of Computer Science and
Cyber-ShARE
University of Texas at El Paso, El Paso,
Texas, USA
agates@utep.edu

ABSTRACT
Identifying research areas of researchers is a difficult task because of the various levels of abstraction in which information may be stored; however, such a task is essential for detecting potential research collaborations within an institution. This work describes an approach to create a scientific research network with topics identified from the researchers' scholarly data and relations between topics by analyzing data harvested from digital libraries and queries to domain ontologies. The relations are used to connect the researchers. Such networks have the potential for revealing the synergy between different topics and researchers within an institution. It will also show less explored research areas that can be targeted for further study. The poster will describe the approach and how it was applied to a biomedical domain at the university.

Keywords
Scholarly data; scientific research network; research collaborations.

1. INTRODUCTION
Gaining a better understanding of the current state of research within an institution is critical for its advancement towards its vision. In order to support collaborative and interdisciplinary work within and across academic institutions, it is vital to be able to curate and analyze scholarly data [5]. Institutional repositories have become a reliable medium for sharing scholarly work [2]. Study of scientific collaboration networks has been a field of intense interest in recent years because it not only depicts academic interactions and contributions, but also represents the knowledge structure in scientific communities [1][4].

The poster will describe the approach to construct a scientific research network (SRN) based on data harvested from metadata of scientific publications and academic activities by using domain-specific ontologies to identify and connect the researchers. The SRN can serve as the foundation for identifying possible research collaborations and new research directions. The construction of the SRN has three principal goals: 1) identify and represent individual researchers' research focus; 2) detect connections between researchers, and 3) discover potential research directions.

Permission to make digital or hard copies of part or all of this work for personal or classroom use is granted without fee provided that copies are not made or distributed for profit or commercial advantage and that copies bear this notice and the full citation on the first page. Copyrights for third-party components of this work must be honored. For all other uses, contact the Owner/Author.
Copyright is held by the owner/author(s).

JCDL '16, June 19-23, 2016, Newark, NJ, USA
ACM 978-1-4503-4229-2/16/06.
DOI: http://dx.doi.org/10.1145/2910896.2925439

The poster will describe and elucidate the approach by demonstrating how it was applied to a group of researchers at the University of Texas at El Paso (UTEP).

2. PROBLEM FORMULATION
Discovering potential research collaborations has traditionally been done by searching publications based on user-defined keywords. These keywords are defined by authors and aim at facilitating discovery by condensing research work into a few words. However, one of the challenges in this approach is that keywords are defined at different levels of granularity i.e., some keywords may be too abstract or too specific, making it difficult to 1) match keywords to identify related and potential research collaborations, 2) discover the main research area of a researcher and 3) trace how researcher's interests have changed over time, and 4) determine what the main areas of research of an organization are based on the publications of its researchers.

3. APPROACH
The approach constructs SRNs by analyzing data harvested from metadata of academic and research activities in a biomedical domain and by querying domain-specific ontologies to discover potential research collaborations.

The first step in the approach is to extract research publication and academic activity data. At UTEP, this was accomplished using Digital Measures (DM), a web-based data repository of faculty accomplishments. The effort targeted 92 faculty members from the biomedical research areas. For each of these faculties, a keyword list was constructed containing single-word keywords and two-word keywords. The next step is to calculate the keyword frequency by counting the number of times the keyword appears in the researcher's data from DM. To identify paths that link two or more keywords together, Ontobee [3] was used. Ontobee is a linked data server designed for ontologies that combines two basic features in the ontology-term search: 1) a web interface for displaying the search result details including hierarchy for a specific ontology term; and 2) a RDF/XML representation for ontology terms corresponding to the HTML web page results that can be accessed by Semantic Web applications. Ontobee provides access to ontologies covering domains such as: anatomy, health and experiments [3]. For this work, Ontobee is used to determine if the keywords included in the keyword list belong to a specific domain. This search allows us to discard words that were included in the keyword list, but should not be considered as keywords. On the other hand, there is a small possibility that a keyword would not be found in Ontobee, but should still be considered as a keyword. Once the keyword is determined to belong to the specific domain, the following is retrieved from Ontobee 1) the parent concept of the keyword, i.e., the immediate top level concept on the ontology hierarchy; 2) the asserted axioms of the keyword; and 3) the asserted axioms of the parent concept.

The semantic of the connection between a keyword and the parent concept can be read as an *is a* relationship. The asserted axioms are utilized to determine if the keyword is *part of* a more general concept. The concepts extracted from Ontobee will be included in the SRN of each faculty.

Using the approach described above, a method was created to generate the SRN representing the researcher's interests as a directed weighted graph. The directed edges in the graph are used to identify the source and target nodes. Similarly the weighted edges are used to classify the relationships between the nodes: *is a* = 1(strong), *is part of* = 5(less strong). The relation *is a* is considered to be more significant in the semantic of the SRN than relation *part of*. A keyword that *is a* concept X has a stronger relation with X than a keyword that is *part of* X. To determine how strong a relationship between two nodes is, the total weight of the path connecting the nodes is calculated. A smaller weight path signifies that the relationship is stronger. The method steps are described below:

1) For each faculty, compute their own keyword list consisting of nested pairs (keyword, frequency).

2) For each keyword k_i in the keyword list that is found in Ontobee, a node is created. The asserted axioms, the parent concept, and the asserted axioms of the parent concept are retrieved.

   2.1 The relationship k_i *is a Concept A (parent concept)* is obtained using the hierarchy of the ontology. *Concept A* is included as a node and an edge with the weight of 1 is created pointing to *Concept A*.

   2.2 The asserted axioms are used to look for the relationships a) *Concept A is part of Concept B; and* b) k_i *is part of Concept C*. *Concept B* and *C* are included as nodes and the respectively relationships with *Concept A* and k_i are created with a weight of 5.

3) If two nodes are connected by an edge with a weight of 1(A *is a* B), the direction of the edge (extracted from the concept hierarchy in Ontobee) will indicate which general concept will have its frequency incremented. The reasoning behind this is that the relationship A *is a* B implies that where A has been mentioned, B is also mentioned.

To illustrate, we apply the algorithm to the biomedical domain: Consider Faculty X whose keyword list is composed of nested pairs (keyword, weight) as follows: K= {(LH, 51), (hypothalamus, 42), (PVH, 69)}. After applying Step 2 of the algorithm the parent concept *Regional part of the brain* was obtained and the following relationships were extracted: 1) LH *is a* Regional part of the brain; 2) hypothalamus *is a* Regional part of the brain; and 3) PVH *is a* Regional part of the brain. After applying Step 3, the following is the updated keyword list: K = {(LH, 51), (hypothalamus, 110), (PVH, 69), (Regional part of the brain, 230)} Fig. 1 shows eight keywords (in color green) and six ontological concepts (in color gray) that were found by querying Ontobee. In addition, the semantics of the connections and paths between keywords and concepts is depicted. After applying the proposed algorithm, the keywords *Hypothalamic* and *Hindbrain* were extracted in the keyword list for Faculty X Ontobee was queried and a partial graph was built showing that the two keywords are related at a higher level by the concepts *Brain* and *Central Nervous System* if the next paths are followed:

Hypothalamic *is part of* Hypothalamus *is a* Regional part of the brain *is part of* Brain *is part of* Central Nervous System; Hindbrain *is part of* Brain *is part of* Central Nervous System.

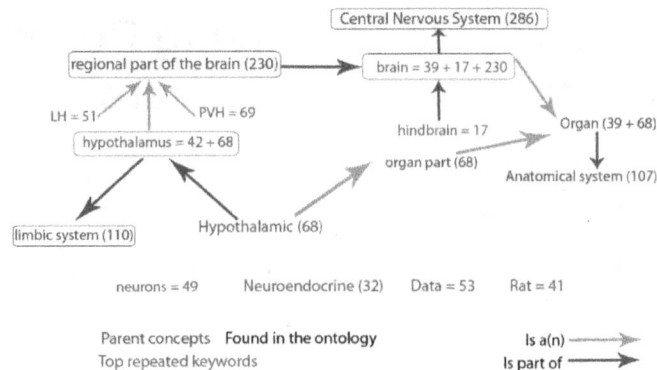

Figure 1. Partial graph for faculty X

The last step is to combine all the individual networks into one SRN. The overlapped nodes indicate a connection between scholars and nodes where the highest frequencies indicate the main research focus for the group of faculty.

4. CONCLUSION

This work proposes the preliminary work in defining an approach to construct SRNs. The approach is based on analyzing data harvested from metadata of scientific publications and querying ontologies to identify and connect the researchers. The work investigates detecting connections between researchers beyond the limitations depending on keywords selected by the research authors. Mapping researchers' scholarship using more general topics and more specifics allows detecting a wider range of connections. Future work includes completing the development of a tool that implements the described approach. Also the creation of a new method to detect the topics that are less explored in the SRN that could become new potential research directions is planned. This method will help in identify the expertise that could potentially be interested in focusing on these less explored topics. In addition, validation of the results with domain experts needs to be conducted to show the effectiveness of the approach.

5. ACKNOWLEDGMENTS

This work is supported in part by the National Science Foundation (NSF) grants HRD-1242122 and DUE-0963648. Any opinions, findings, and conclusions or recommendations expressed in this paper are those of the author(s) and do not necessarily reflect the views of the NSF.

6. REFERENCES

[1] Newman, M. E. 2004. Coauthorship networks and patterns of scientific collaboration. *Proceedings of the national academy of sciences*, *101*(suppl 1), 5200-5205.

[2] Schlangen, M. 2015. Content, Credibility, and Readership: Putting Your Institutional Repository on the Map. *Public Services Quarterly*, *11*(3), 217-224.

[3] Xiang, Z., Mungall, C., Ruttenberg, A., & He, Y. 2011. Ontobee: A Linked Data Server and Browser for Ontology Terms. In *ICBO*.

[4] Yang, Y., Man Au Yeung, C., Weal, M., & Davis, H. 2009. The researcher social network: A social network based on metadata of scientific publications. In: *Proceedings of the WebSci'09: Society On-Line, (*18-20 March 2009, Greece).

[5] Young, L., Denize, S., Simoff, S., Nankani, E., & Wilkinson, I. 2015. Researching The Structures and Processes of Collaborative Academic Networks. In *Proceedings of the 2010 Academy of Marketing Science (AMS) Annual Conference* (pp. 112-116). Springer International Publishing.

Personal Video Collection Management Behavior

Sally Jo Cunningham
University of Waikato
Hamilton, New Zealand
+64 7 838 4402
sallyjo@waikato.ac.nz

David M. Nichols
University of Waikato
Hamilton, New Zealand
+64 7 858 5130
dmn@cs.waikato.ac.nz

Judy Bowen
University of Waikato
Hamilton, New Zealand
+64 7 838 4547
jbowen@waikato.ac.nz

ABSTRACT
Video content typically consumes more storage space and bandwidth than other document types although users structure their content with the same organisational tools they use for smaller and simpler items. We analyze the 'native' video management behavior as expressed in 35 self-interviews and diary studies produced by New Zealand students, to create a 'rich picture' of personal video collections. We see that personal collections can have diffuse boundaries and many different intended uses—and that these information management needs are difficult to fulfill with their homegrown video collection management strategies.

CCS Concepts
• Information systems applications → Digital libraries and archives.

Keywords
Personal collection management, qualitative research, video information behavior.

1. INTRODUCTION
Personal information collections have expanded to include a diverse set of multimedia digital objects; in particular users now regularly create and download video files. Video content typically consumes more storage space and bandwidth than other document types although users structure their content with the same organisational tools they use for smaller and simpler items.

2. METHODOLOGY
We base this research on a set of self-interviews and diary studies conducted by 35 New Zealand tertiary students, in the context of a third-year university course in Human-Computer Interaction, offered in New Zealand in 2013. As a first step in a semester-long project to design and prototype a personal video management system, the students examined their own video collection behavior through a self-interview, and then through a diary study focusing on video document behavior.

Permission to make digital or hard copies of part or all of this work for personal or classroom use is granted without fee provided that copies are not made or distributed for profit or commercial advantage and that copies bear this notice and the full citation on the first page. Copyrights for third-party components of this work must be honored. For all other uses, contact the Owner/Author. ☐
Copyright is held by the owner/author(s).
JCDL '16, June 19-23, 2016, Newark, NJ, USA.
ACM 978-1-4503-4229-2/16/06.
http://dx.doi.org/10.1145/2910896.2925440

Self-interviews and diary study summaries (totaling 175 pages) are here analyzed for 35 students (21 (60%) male, 14 (40%) female; 32 (91%) aged 2 to 24, 3 (9%) aged 30 to 60). The analysis was based in grounded theory methods [1]; analysis proceeded through iterative reading, code development, and coding as the categories emerged inductively from the documents.

3. RESULTS
3.1 Size and Storage of Collections
The students typically estimated the size of their collections in number of videos and/or in memory usage. Collections ranged from the miniscule (three students had fewer than 20 videos in their collection) to the enormous (1.85 Terabytes on the student's personal media server, with an additional 2332 videos bookmarked, favorited, or otherwise linked to in online sources). On the other hand, the size of a collection can also be subjective; one of the moderately sized collections (approximately 150 Movies, TV episodes, and short clips) was described as "very large" by its owner, while another believed his 700 gigabyte collection to be "rather small for this day and age" [P20].

Table 1. Number of students utilizing each collection storage method or technique.

Physical storage		Virtual storage		Personal record	
Laptop / desktop	28	Facebook, social media	14	Bookmarks, favorites, 'likes'	23
External drive	18	YouTube subscription	6	Open browser tabs	2
Mobile	7	Cloud	5	Word document	1
USB memory stick	7	Personal YouTube channel	3	Email message with links	1
CD-ROM / DVD	4	iTunes	2	Links posted on blog	1
SD card	2	Netflix	1	Pinterest	1
Video camera	1			Memory	9
Gaming console	1				

To store or track these videos, the students used a wide variety of storage devices and techniques (Table 1). An initial, striking finding is that the students' personal collections are highly diverse and not limited to video files stored on physical devices under the students' control 'in the cloud' (e.g., in Dropbox or Google Drive); students also 'saved' videos virtually by posting them to

Facebook or uploading them to a personal YouTube channel. Students also considered videos that they had viewed through large online collections such as YouTube (through channel subscriptions), Netflix, etc. as being in some sense 'their' videos, in that the students could access the videos for re-viewing. Given this blurring of the division between private and public video collections,we note the obvious difficulties with maintaining a record of previously viewed videos, trusting that the video will not be removed from the collection, and maintaining a subscription to permit continued access.

Students also employed a variety of techniques to keep track of 'their' videos without necessarily storing them: the videos could be tagged by the student by bookmarking them in a browser, 'liking' or 'favoriting' it on a social media site; 'pinning' them on Pinterest; starting to stream the video and then simply leaving the browser tab open; keeping a collection catalog that might be simple (e.g., saving email messages that include links) or elaborate (e.g., posting links to a blog or maintaining a personal video catalog in a Word document); or simply relying on their memory to be able to re-find videos, rather than storing the file or a link. No student in the study used only a single mechanism from Table 1; instead, their collections were scattered across two to eight, with an average of five. This can necessarily make it difficult to access a particular video in the collection.

3.2 Reasons for adding a Video to a Collection

The primary reason for saving a video is, of course, 'to watch later'. This motivation can be teased apart to mean: to watch in the future, as watching now is inconvenient; to watch the video again, as it has been watched once and enjoyed; to watch at a more appropriate time, given that the video appears interesting but the student can't view it presently in its entirety; to have something to watch later when the internet can't be accessed or access is prohibitively expensive; to look more deeply into previously enjoyed videos; to intensively (re)view a video for its information content; to support the *possibility* of watching or re-watching the video, at some indeterminate future time. No student reported a useful technique or tool to differentiate between these intended future viewing purposes, and instead relied on memory of intent when adding a video to their collection.

Additional motivations for saving a video included: to share the video with others (where sharing included the gift of video copies to individuals and posting to social media sites); to retain a video as a memento or record of an event or experience (more common for self-created videos that are filmed in the moment, but other videos may be saved as reminders of the circumstances in which they were originally watched); as part of a themed sub-collection (television series, anime, etc.); and to improve a later viewing experience (by avoiding buffering in streamed video, to support a marathon viewing of a series, etc.). Again, the students had to invent their own techniques for supporting these intended uses in their collection (for example, dividing television shows / series into appropriately named files / folders on their storage devices). We also note that sharing and memento experiences are indeed sometimes 'recorded' in the email system or social media records for that student, but that these records are generally scattered across systems, media, and time—and so are not accessible or integrated into the collection.

3.3 "Keeping Track"

Another common task in managing a personal video collection is maintaining a record of one's interactions with it. Students reported a variety of interactions that they attempted to track, with varying degrees of success:

- marking their viewing progress through a sequence of videos (e.g., episodes in a season of a TV series);
- marking the place to begin watching again in a video whose viewing has been interrupted;
- keeping a list of of videos that have been added to the collection but that have not yet been viewed;
- differentiating between watched and unwatched videos in a stream (e.g., a subscription to a YouTube channel);
- tracking which videos have already been downloaded / added to the collection;
- marking one's viewing position in a partially watched video, to be able to pick up viewing again at that spot;
- selecting brief clips of interest embedded in longer videos

These tasks are not well-supported in the file systems used to store video files, so the students with collections on their own devices (hard drives, external drives, etc.) either had to rely on memory to track their viewing, or had to develop their own tracking system. Given that metadata for downloaded videos is not saved with the file and that filenames often vary between download sites, it can be difficult even to know which videos are already in the collection. A major difficulty lies in the absence of a detailed viewing / usage history supported directly by the file system (beyond the date of modification, which is often too crude a measure and further is visible only for a single file / folder rather than across an entire collection). The simple work-arounds could only handle one or two of the tracking tasks above. More complex schemes rely on the student's diligence in recording the relevant aspects of their viewing history—and these more onerous management techniques are often not rigorously applied

4. CONCLUSIONS

The results reinforce earlier findings that video content causes storage concerns for users in ways that are not present for other media types [3]. Although some participants did engage with metadata for collection organization, the familiar difficulties of maintaining order were common. Problems in naming objects were common for our participants; a file system survey using the approach of Henderson [2] would be a valuable complement to the reports in this paper. The provision of more meaningful default filenames by applications and devices would likely help users manage their collections more efficiently. Greater intelligence on the part of the operating system to use embedded metadata and heuristically use information in filenames are areas of future work for software developers.

5. REFERENCES

[1] Glaser, B., & Strauss, A. (1967) *The Discovery of Grounded Theory: Strategies for Qualitative Research*, Chicago.

[2] Henderson, S. 2011. Document duplication: How users (struggle to) manage file copies and versions. *Proceedings of ASIS&T'11*, 48(1). doi:10.1002/meet.2011.14504801013

[3] Odom, W., Zimmerman, J. & Forlizzi, J. 2011. Teenagers and their virtual possessions: design opportunities and issues. *Proceedings of SIGCHI '11*. ACM. 1491-1500.

Knowledge Extraction for Literature Review

Tatiana Erekhinskaya, Mithun Balakrishna, Marta Tatu, Steven Werner, Dan Moldovan
Lymba Corporation
901 Waterfall Way, Bldg 5
Richardson, Texas 75080
{tatiana, mithun, mtatu, swerner, moldovan}@lymba.com

ABSTRACT

Researchers in all domains need to keep abreast with recent scientific advances. Finding relevant publications and reviewing them is a labor-intensive task that lacks efficient automatic tools to support it. Current tools are limited to standard keyword-based search systems that return potentially relevant documents and then leave the user with a monumental task of sifting through them.

In this paper, we present a semantic-driven system to automatically extract the most important knowledge from a publication and reduces the effort required for the literature review. The system extracts key findings from biomedical papers in PubMed, populates a predefined template and displays it. This allows the user to get the key ideas of the content even before opening or downloading the publication.

Keywords

Literature review; knowledge extraction; semantic relation

1. INTRODUCTION

Researchers in many domains have the need to quickly grasp the big picture presented in current publications in various topic. Reviewing document repositories to find relevant publications and skim them for appropriateness is time consuming and labor-intensive process. There are recommendations [3] from experienced researchers to students on how to undertake the task in a more optimal way, based on heuristics on what sections of the paper should be scanned through first. In biomedical domain, the systematic review process goes from thousands of publications found by keyword-based search to tens that are reviewed in-depth, and the process of filtering remains manual.

There have been a few efforts targeted at providing the users with some overview information regarding the nature and content of the publication of interest. In general purpose information retrieval systems, the current approach is to provide snippets or citations to the user so that the relevance of the document can be assessed before reading the

Permission to make digital or hard copies of part or all of this work for personal or classroom use is granted without fee provided that copies are not made or distributed for profit or commercial advantage and that copies bear this notice and the full citation on the first page. Copyrights for third-party components of this work must be honored. For all other uses, contact the owner/author(s).

JCDL '16, June 19-23, 2016, Newark, NJ, USA.

© 2016 Copyright held by the owner/author(s).

ACM ISBN 978-1-4503-4229-2/16/06.

DOI: \doi{http://dx.doi.org/10.1145/2910896.2925441}

whole document. Another approach includes associating tags with the documents. However, these snippets and tags do not provide a coherent picture. MEDLINE, a large bibliographic database in biomedical domain, contains metadata associated with each citation, extracted in a partially automated way [2]. However, this metadata omits some important information such as dosage, explicit relations between intervention and outcome, etc.

Our approach combines the ideas of snippets and keyword annotations and populates predefined templates that are displayed with the publications. The predefined template is based on the PICO [4] model and represents the key findings presented in the paper along with its study settings. These hints about the content of the paper allow researchers to gain vital knowledge while saving time required to sift through large number of articles.

2. KNOWLEDGE EXTRACTION

The population of the template with key information is based on deep semantic parsing and knowledge extraction. Figure 1 shows the semantic representation of a sentence from a sample paper [6] and the populated template fragment. The system extracts concepts of interest and high-level relations. Such representation of all sentences with information of the document's structure is used to populate the template. The template slots include *problem* description (disease, condition, etc), *interventions* (medical procedures, diagnosis tests, medication), and *outcomes* (new values for vital sign measures, improvement, adverse effects, etc). An important part of the template is *study design* that includes the size of the trial group, and *patient* sociodemographic characteristics. Both concepts and relations are indexed in Apache Solr with concepts being indexed as tokens and relations being indexed as a separate Solr field.

2.1 Concept Extraction

The first step in the knowledge extraction process is concept extraction. This process is driven by ontologies and lexical patterns. In biomedical domain, the system benefits from existing medical ontologies: MeSH, SNOMED and UMLS Metathesaurus. Our hybrid approach to named entity recognition makes use of machine learning classifiers, cascade of finite-state automata, and lexicons to label more than 80 types of named entities. In addition to key medical categories like disease, vital sign, medication, procedure, etc, the module extracts their attributes: quantity, dosage, severity, time course, onset, alleviating and aggravating factors, as well as negative findings and family history.

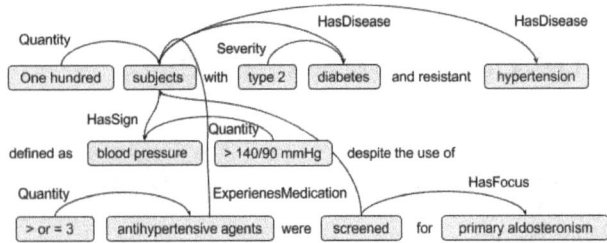

Category	Text Instantiation
Focus	Primary Aldosteronism
Study group:	
Group size	100
Condition	type 2 diabetes resistant hypertension
Current Medication	>3 antihypertensive agent
Outcome:	14% confirmed diagnosis of primary aldosteronism

Figure 1: Semantic representation of a sentence from a sample paper and the resulting template fragment for the paper [6].

2.2 Basic Semantic Parsing

The next stage in our automatic template population process is the extraction of basic semantic relations. The semantic parser extracts binary relations between concepts and content words in the sentence. We use 26 predefined relation types, following [5]. The relations are not limited by verb arguments, but include such relations as QUANTITY, PROPERTY, POSSESSION and others to represent semantic connectivity between all content words. These relations follow syntactic structures closely and can be automatically extracted in a robust manner.

We use a hybrid approach to semantic parsing: machine learning classifiers for argument pairs identified using syntactic patterns and filtered using ontology-based restrictions on candidate arguments. Finally, the overall semantic structure is analyzed to resolve the conflicts.

For example, in Figure 1, the following basic semantic relations are extracted: VALUE(resistant, hypertension), THEME (subjects, screened) and THEME(antihypertensive agents, use).

2.3 Semantic Calculus: Custom Relation Extraction

While basic semantic relations provide a robust representation of the semantic structure, they are of no interest to the end users and cannot be used for knowledge extraction directly. However, basic relations provide a foundation for extraction of domain-specific relations via Semantic Calculus [1]. The Semantic Calculus defines how and under what conditions a chain of relations can be combined into a high-level custom relation.

In a trivial case, Semantic Calculus rules relabel one basic relation into a more specific one. For example rule POSSESSION(c_1, c_2)&$ISA(c1, \ disease)$&$ISA(c_2, organism) \Rightarrow$ HASDISEASE(c_1, c_2) relabels POSSESSION(diabetes, subjects) into HASDISEASE. Another group of rules extracts the same 26 relation types via combination of two basic relations. This is used to propagate LOCATION and TIME relations and make the semantic structure more tight [1].

The most complex rules combine relation chains into high-level domain-specific relations. For example, relation HASSIGN in Figure 1 is not expressed directly, but can be extracted with axioms: *blood pressure* is a property of *hypertension*, and *hypertension* is related to *subjects*.

2.4 Template Population

The extracted relations are saved into an RDF store and then queried to populate the templates. Each template slot is filled via several SPARQL queries. For example to extract the group size, we are looking for x with the following query:

$$?x \text{ QUANTITY } ?y, \ ?y \text{ ISA } Patient,$$
$$?y \text{ THEME } ?z, \ ?z \text{ ISA } Intervention \quad (1)$$

The second line of this query is needed to make sure that the quantity is for the whole study group and not for a subset with a particular outcome. The output for the query is post-processed to avoid duplicates. Finally, the output is normalized: phrases head words are converted to lemmas and cardinals are replaced by their digit representation.

3. CONCLUSION

We tested our system on articles targeting treatment efficiency studies in the PubMed publication repository. We processed more than 8 million article abstracts in PubMed for the years from 2005 to 2015. The system can process around 100,000 articles per day per CPU core, and automatically extract knowledge to populate the predefined document template for each article. The automatically populated templates present key information from the paper which allows users to decide whether the paper is worth reading without reviewing it manually.

This approach can be applied to other domains to ease the burden of monitoring journals and conference proceedings.

4. REFERENCES

[1] E. Blanco and D. Moldovan. Composition of semantic relations: Theoretical framework and case study. *ACM Trans. Speech Lang. Process.*, 10(4):17:1–17:36, Jan. 2014.

[2] K. B. Cohen and D. Demner-Fushman. *Biomedical Natural Language Processing*. John Benjamin Publishing Company, 2014.

[3] J. Eisner. How to read a technical paper. https://www.cs.jhu.edu/~jason/advice/how-to-read-a-paper.html.

[4] X. Huang, J. Lin, and D. Demner-Fushman. Evaluation of PICO as a knowledge representation for clinical questions. In *AMIA Annu Symp Proc.*, pages 359–363, 2006.

[5] D. Moldovan and E. Blanco. Polaris: Lymba's semantic parser. In *Proceedings of LREC-2012*, pages 66–72, 2012.

[6] G. E. Umpierrez, P. Cantey, D. Smiley, A. Palacio, D. Temponi, K. Luster, and A. Chapman. Primary aldosteronism in diabetic subjects With resistant hypertension. *Diabetes Care*, 30(7):1699–1703, July 2007.

Question Identification and Classification on an Academic Question Answering Site

Bolanle Ojokoh
[1,3,4]Department of Computer Science,
Federal University of Technology,
Akure, Nigeria.
+234-703-0538346
bolanleojokoh@yahoo.com

Tobore Igbe
Rom-Flex Communication
Technology
Abuja,Nigeria.
+234-706-3376938
tobore2ng@gmail.com

Ayobami Araoye, Friday Ameh
+234-703-3102210,
+234-803-8024755
{araoyeayobami,
fridayameh85} @gmail.com

ABSTRACT
Online communities such as wikis, blogs, forums, scientific communities and other social networking services have enabled new levels of interactions and interconnections among individuals, documents and data and have become places for people to seek and share expertise. In this paper, we propose a systematic approach to identification and classification of questions. The questions were first identified using semantic occurrence of Part of Speech (POS) tag in English Language, after which they were classified based on maximum probability value of Naïve Bayes classification. The model was validated and evaluated with experiments on some crawled web pages from ResearchGate.

Keywords
Questions; Classification; Research Gate; Online Forums.

1. INTRODUCTION
Recent advances in Web 2.0 have enabled the proliferation of many online communities such as wikis, blogs, forums, scientific communities and other social networking services which are gaining popularity and are enhanced with dynamic information sharing among millions of people. These communities have enabled new levels of interactions and interconnections among individuals, documents and data and have become places for people to seek and share expertise. Search engines are not yet capable of addressing queries that require deep semantic understanding of the query or the document. Instead, it may be preferable to find and ask someone who has related expertise or experience on a topic. Web-based online communities are the places people often seek advice or help. An online forum is a web application for holding discussions and posting user generated content in a specific domain, such as sports, recreation, techniques and travel among others. Forums contain a huge amount of valuable user generated content on a variety of topics, and it is highly desirable if the human knowledge contained in user generated content in forums can be extracted and reused for the purpose of providing Question Answering (QA) services, including instant answers provided by search engines, QA search systems, and community-based Question Answering (CQA) services; improving forum management (including querying and archiving)[1]; augmenting the knowledge base of chatbot [2], among others.

A system capable of extracting and classifying questions becomes imperative to be able to find appropriate answers without reading all the content of a forum therefore building a QA system. This paper is

Permission to make digital or hard copies of part or all of this work for personal or classroom use is granted without fee provided that copies are not made or distributed for profit or commercial advantage and that copies bear this notice and the full citation on the first page. Copyrights for third-party components of this work must be honored. For all other uses, contact the Owner/Author.
Copyright is held by the owner/author(s).
JCDL '16, June 19-23, 2016, Newark, NJ, USA
ACM 978-1-4503-4229-2/16/06.
http://dx.doi.org/10.1145/2910896.2925442.

part of an ongoing research that explores the features for extracting quality answers from forums and blogs to provide a platform to encompass every category of question and enable QA systems to discover accurate answers to questions. There are some motives that compelled our view. Primarily, users of blogs could ask questions that do not flow with the conventional way of asking questions. Considering only specific type such as *Who, What, Where, Where, Which, Why and How*[3] are not sufficient to capture all possible questions. Rule based approaches, including text similarity measures [4] try to match the question with some manually handcrafted rules [5]. These approaches however, suffer from the need to define too many rules. Hence, there is the need for a Supervised Machine Learning Approach, adopted in this work.

2. METHODOLOGY
Extracting quality questions from online web logs (blogs) requires detailed processing and analyses of the blog. Fig. 1 is a three-section architecture that describes the processes involved. It consists of the pre-processing, question configuration and question classification sections. The question configuration module is a setup section for the system and is responsible for specifying the category of questions to be extracted from blogs. It is extensible, which makes it possible for the system to be adjusted to detect more categories of questions. Identification and classification of questions are carried out in the question classification section. This section iterates through the blogs extracted from the pre-processing section, disintegrates the blogs into sentences and annotates all sentences with Part of Speech (POS) tag in English Language. The tags in each of the sentences are extracted and analyzed with the tags obtained from the question configuration section. The analysis is performed using Naïve Bayes which is discussed later. The outputs of this section are questions with the corresponding category they belong. The question classification section applies Naïve Bayes classifier, a supervised machine learning probabilistic classifier that uses the label or attribute of a new instance to estimate the probability of its class or category.

Let B be the first post in a blog and B_t threads from the blog post B, all extracted text content in B and B_t are broken down into sentence units, using full stop as the delimiter

$$D = \text{Break}([.]B, [.]B_t) \qquad \text{Eq. 1}$$

where $D = \{BT_0 => (d[0], ..., d[m]), ..., BT_n => (d[0], ..., d[m])\}$ is an associative collection which represents the extracted sentence d, obtained from B and B_t, where m is the number of extracted sentences which are grouped together as BT and the relationship $(=>)$ between the group and the extracted sentences are treated as a group, and n is the size of the group.

$$D_a = \delta_a(A \rightarrow D) \qquad \text{Eq. 2}$$

$D_a = \{BT_0 => (d_a[0], ..., d_a[m]), ..., BT_n => (d_a[0], ..., d_a[m])\}$ is an array of labeled sentences with POS tag, A is a collection of part of speech tags in English Language (such as noun, verb, adjective, and so on). δ_a is a POS tagging function that assigns $(\rightarrow)$ tags in A to

D using Stanford parser that uses the principle of maximum entropy. Stanford parser is a java program that is capable of taking a sentence as input and producing a labeled output of each word in the sentence with its corresponding part of speech in English language.

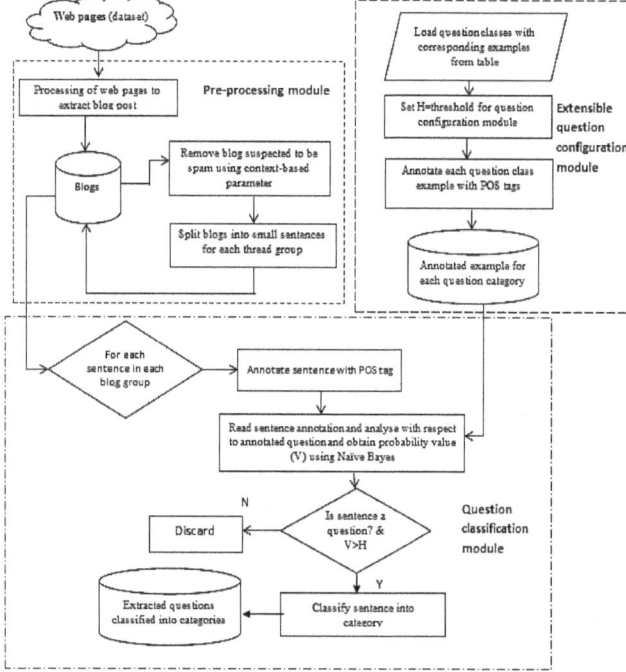

Fig 1: Question Identification and Classification architecture

Given categories of question classes C = {c_1, c_2,...,c_j }, each class having one or more question instance e, which forms a group g allotted to a class c_i, $g=\{e_1,e_2,...,e_k\}$. Therefore, C={$(g,c_1),(g,c_2)....,(g,c_j)$}.

Each question instance in g is marked with POS in English Language.

$$C_a = \delta_a(A \rightarrow C) \qquad \text{Eq. 3}$$

where $C_a = \{(g_a, c_1), (g_a, c_2) ...., (g_a, c_j)\}$ is the category of question with POS tag for each group in each question class, which is obtained from question configuration section and serves as the training record (dataset) for the classifier.

The learned Naïve Bayes classifier assigns tagged document d to its corresponding class c, and this is achieved by systematically searching for the structural occurrence of g_a tags in D_a, and assigning it to a class c in C_a.

$$W_c = \underset{c \in C_a\{1,,j\}}{\text{argmax}} \, p(C_k) \prod_{k=1}^{m} p(D_a|C_k) \qquad \text{Eq. 4}$$

$$p(d_a[i]|C_k) = \frac{count(a \rightarrow d_a[i],c) + 1}{(\sum_{i=1}^{R} count(a_i,c)) + |V|} \qquad \text{Eq. 5}$$

where W_c={$(Q[1],c)$, $(Q[2],c)$,..., $(Q[t],c)$} is the output of the Naïve Bayes classifier for sentences in D_a that contain questions $Q[1], Q[2], ... Q[t]$. Each question found in D_a is assigned a probability value based on the occurrence of tags found in d_a. Q is assigned a class in C based on the highest probability value of c, $p(C_k) = \frac{N_e}{N}$ where N_c is the number of question instance sentences e for a question group c, and N is the number of question instance sentences in all the question groups. Eq. 5 is laplace smoothing for Naïve Bayes to avoid the occurrence of 0 probability. $|V|$ refers to the total number of unique tags in C_a. $count(a \rightarrow d_a[i],c)$ refers to the total number of structural occurrence of tags a found in ($\rightarrow$) sentence $d_a[i]$ with respect to class c. $d_a[i]$ is said to be a question Q for class c if the maximum probability value exceeds the question threshold mark Q_{TM}, the value is adjustable to regulate the rate or

efficiency at which the system is able to detect question in documents[6].

3. RESULTS

Five hundred (500) web pages from ResearchGate website were crawled to retrieve pages containing user generated contents. Each of the downloaded pages is referred to as a group. 3487 sentences were obtained and 793 questions were identified and classified. We considered 23 question categories, with 171 instances distributed over the categories. The system was able to classify 782 questions correctly, 9 were wrongly classified due to the fact that it was not specified in the question configuration module and the remaining 2 wrongly classified questions was as a result of only one instance available for the question category which is not sufficient for the classification.

The results of evaluation of thirteen groups used to validate our model are shown in Table 1. The average result of 0.96 for identification indicates the high sensitivity of our system to detect question and a classification value 0.95 confirms the accuracy of the system in classifying extracted questions. These results make our model suitable to be applied in any domain for question extraction and classification.

Table 1. Evaluation Results for Question Identification and Classification

Groups	Question Identification		Question Classification
	Precision	Accuracy	Accuracy
Group 1	0.90	0.99	1.00
Group 2	0.93	0.98	0.90
Group 3	0.89	0.99	1.00
Group 4	0.79	0.95	0.92
Group 5	0.74	0.93	0.94
Group 6	0.77	0.94	0.92
Group 7	0.88	0.93	1.00
Group 8	0.85	0.96	1.00
Group 9	0.85	0.97	0.94
Group 10	0.88	0.96	0.94
Group 11	0.73	0.87	0.87
Group 12	0.83	0.95	1.00
Group 13	0.91	1.00	1.00
Overall	0.84	0.83	0.88
Average	0.91	0.96	0.95

4. ACKNOWLEDGEMENTS

This work was partially supported by the COMSTECH-TWAS Joint Research Grant (14-014 RG/ITC/AF/AC_C-UNESCO FR: 3240283404)

5. REFERENCES

[1] Shrestha, L. and McKeown, K. 2004. Detection of question-answer pairs in email conversations. In Proc. of COLING.

[2] Huang, J., Zhou, M., and Yang D. 2007. Extracting chatbot knowledge from online discussion forums. In Proc. of IJCAI.

[3] Mudgal, R., Madaan, R., Sharma, A. K., and Dixit, A. 2013. A Novel architecture for question classification based indexing scheme for efficient question answering. *arXiv preprint arXiv:1307.6937*.

[4] Ojokoh, B.A. and Ayokunle, P. 2013. Online Question Answering System, International Journal of Computer Science Research and Applications 3(3), 47-63.

[5] Prager, J., Radev, D., Brown, E., Coden, A. and Samn, V. 1999. The use of predictive annotation for question answering in TREC. In Proc. of the 8th Text Retrieval Conference (TREC-8).

[6] Jurafsky, D. 2013. Text Classification and Naïve Bayes. Gender, Genre, and Writing Style in Formal Written Texts, 23(3), 321–346.

Increasing Datasets Discoverability in an Engineering Data Platform using Keyword Extraction

Parthasarathy Gopavarapu
Purdue University
112 E Wood St
West Lafayette, IN 47906
+1 765 771 9122
pgopavar@purdue.edu

Line C. Pouchard
Purdue University
504 W State Street
West Lafayette, IN 47907
+1 765 494 3875
pouchard@purdue.edu

Santiago Pujol
Purdue University
550 W Stadium Ave
West Lafayette, IN 47907
+1 765 496 8368
spujol@purdue.edu

ABSTRACT

In this paper we describe the use of keyword extraction in a data management platform for the storage, publication, and sharing of scientific and engineering datasets primarily related to the stress of concrete structures under earthquake conditions. To improve discoverability of datasets and assist scientists who upload data, we designed an automated keyword extraction system that will propose keywords for uploaded datasets.

Keywords

Data discovery, data repository, keyword extraction.

1. INTRODUCTION

Datacenterhub (http://datacenterhub.org) is a platform for the storage, publication, and sharing of scientific and engineering datasets primarily related to the stress of concrete structures under earthquake conditions. Datacenterhub was created to provide a searchable and browsable platform to individual researchers who accumulate and analyze measurements and observation datasets of concrete structures that they have taken in the course of their research. Heterogeneous datasets include text descriptions, measurements, pictures, reports and drawings. Datasets are described with extensive metadata that includes experiment and case names, titles, contributor names, geo-coordinates, related publications, article citations, keywords, abstracts and other. Datacenterhub was developed as an extension to HUBzero®, a generic content management and collaboration platform developed and maintained at Purdue University.

One of the goals of Datacenterhub is to facilitate the discovery and exploration of datasets that have been uploaded in the platform, either by researchers who are interested in submitting datasets or by those who want to explore datasets underlying a publication. One obstacle to realize this goal is that researchers who submit their datasets often do not provide enough keywords for their datasets to enable powerful searches in Datacenterhub. This is compounded by the fact that datasets in the platform are self-published; thus the publication does not benefit from the assistance of a curator, for suggesting or adding new keywords.

Permission to make digital or hard copies of part or all of this work for personal or classroom use is granted without fee provided that copies are not made or distributed for profit or commercial advantage and that copies bear this notice and the full citation on the first page. Copyrights for third-party components of this work must be honored. For all other uses, contact the Owner/Author.
Copyright is held by the owner/author(s).
JCDL '16, June 19-23, 2016, Newark, NJ, USA
ACM978-1-4503-4229-2/16/06.
http://dx.doi.org/10.1145/2910896.2925443

We have designed a strategy to mitigate this situation and we are implementing a series of steps to increase the number of keywords for searching for datasets. Keywords obtained by keyword extraction are offered to researchers for annotating their data when they upload their experiment. The unique contributions of this poster include a method for increasing the searchability and access to datasets in the platform and the application of text mining methods to keyword extraction.

2. PROJECT DESCRIPTION

Figure 1 shows the flow of processes required for performing keyword extraction.

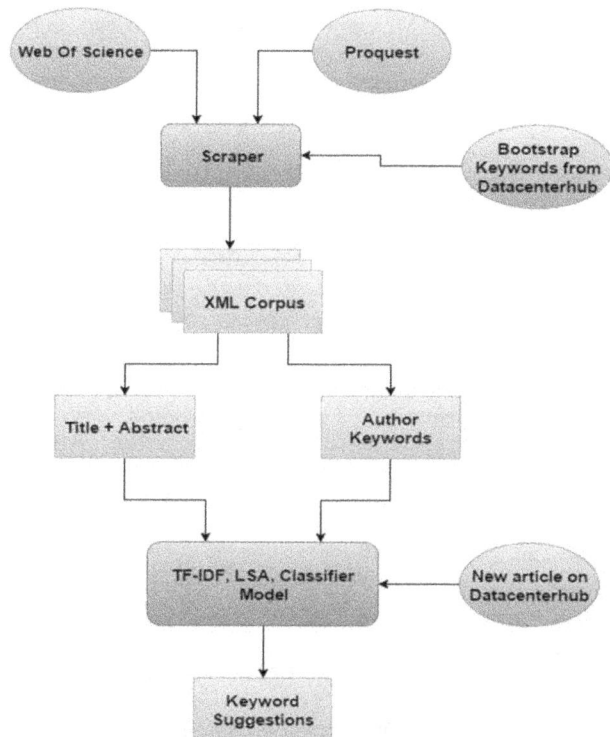

Figure 1: Workflow diagram for the Keyword Extraction Process. Ovals represent existing resources, rounded rectangles represent code/algorithms and rectangles represent created resources.

The keyword extraction process consists of **two major phases**. The **first phase** involves building a corpus of scientific articles in structural engineering, using title, abstract, and keywords from web based resources such as Web of Science (http://webofknowledge.com) and Proquest (http://search.proquest.com). The **second phase** consists of utilizing the corpus created in phase one, to train machine learning models that can extract keywords, given new documents such as abstracts. These abstracts are uploaded by users in the platform to document their experiments and datasets.

2.1 Phase 1

We use a bootstrap set of keywords obtained from Datacenterhub to initialize the process of corpus creation. Using these keywords, we build a corpus of scientific articles in the structural engineering domain. We use the title and abstract fields of these articles.

Bootstrap Keyword Set: This set is the list of keywords obtained from publicly available datasets on Datacenterhub. Some of the non-relevant keywords are eliminated and keyword normalization is performed.

Scraper: Once the normalized keyword list is created, each of these keywords is used as a search phrase on both Web of Science and Proquest. We use python scripts that utilize modules such as Mechanize (wwwsearch.sourceforge.net/mechanize) and BeautifulSoup (www.crummy.com/software/BeautifulSoup) to perform the search programmatically and process the results. Mechanize is used to fill and submit the search forms on these websites and BeautifulSoup is used to process the results obtained on submission. Once the search results are obtained, each of the result articles are processed to extract specific fields to create an XML document.

XML Corpus: The XML corpus contains one xml document per search result made of title and abstract. Duplicates are eliminated during the scraping process. Our corpus currently includes 36132 XML documents representing scientific articles amounting to 174 MB.

2.2 Phase 2

In Phase 2 we use the XML corpus of documents corresponding to the search results of the bootstrap keywords. We extract Title, Abstract and Keywords. The string obtained from concatenating Title and Abstract (Text) is used to represent the document and Keywords are considered labels for processing algorithms. We train a Multi-Label Binary Classifier using the Text and Keywords dataset created above. [1]

Dataset Representation: For each document the Text (Title+Abstract) is replaced using a feature representation learnt from the corpus. We use Latent Semantic Analysis (LSA) [2] along with TF-IDF [3] features so that the conceptual information of the document can be represented in addition to the importance of the terms in the document.

TF-IDF: Term Frequency - Inverse Document Frequency (TF-IDF) is a statistic used to measure the relevance of terms present in a set of documents to the content of the documents. The documents are represented using a TF-IDF matrix where each row represents one document from the corpus and each entry in the row represents the TF-IDF value for the corresponding document and word pair.

Latent Semantic Analysis: LSA is a document modeling technique which uses the occurrence matrix(M) of a corpus to find the topic distributions of the documents in the corpus. This matrix M is split into three matrices using Singular Value Decomposition(SVD). The matrix V_{mxk} represents the documents in a lower dimensional space and is considered as the topic distribution of the documents where k represents the number of

topics and m the number of documents. The TF-IDF and LSA features obtained are concatenated to form a new feature representation for the documents.

Keyword Suggestion: A list of words containing all the distinct keywords from the corpus is created. For each document a new binary vector of the same size as the keyword list is created which contains 1 if the corresponding word in the list is also a keyword for the document. This vector acts as the label for the document represented using TF-IDF and LSA.

Once the dataset is prepared with the feature representation of documents and the labels, we can use it to train classification tools [1]. We use K-Nearest Neighbor classifier in our implementation due to its ease of use and speed of training. Once the classifier is trained, the keywords for any new document can be predicted using the following process:

- Use the TF-IDF and LSA model to project the document into the new feature representation.

- Provide the feature representation obtained above as input to the classifier model trained using the corpus.

- This will output a binary vector of the same size as the list of keywords. All the words corresponding to entries containing 1 in the vector can be reported as the **keyword suggestions** for the new document.

2.3 Phase 3

In this phase, we integrate the results of the keyword extraction into the Datacenterhub interface. This phase is not represented in Figure 1, and is only in the planning stage at the time of this writing. We plan for the integration of a drop-down menu of keywords based on the suggestions extracted in Phase 2. This menu will reside on the upload interface of Datacenterhub.

3. CONCLUSION

We collected an XML corpus of scientific abstracts covering the domain of the datasets collected in Datacenterhub. We use it to create keyword extraction models so that researchers who submit their datasets to Datacenterhub are provided with additional keywords for their datasets. We offer these keyword suggestions to users to assist them in increasing the discoverability of their datasets.

4. ACKNOWLEDGMENTS

This material is based upon work supported by the National Science Foundation under Grant Numbers CIF21-DIBBS 1443027.

5. REFERENCES

[1] Hasan, KS. And Vincent Ng.2014. Automatic Keyphrase Extraction : A Survey of the State of the Art. In *Proceedings of the 52nd Annual Meeting of the Association for Computational Linguistics* (Volume 1: Long Papers), pages 1262–1273, 2014.

[2] Dumais, S.T. 2005. Latent Semantic Analysis. *Annual Review of Information Science and Technology*. 38,1(Sep. 2005) 188-230.

[3] Salton, G. and Buckley, C. 1988. Term Weighting Approaches in Automatic Text Retrieval. *Information Processing & Management*. (1988), 513-524.

Semantic Bookworm: Mining Literary Resources Revisited

Annika Hinze, Michael Coleman, Sally Jo Cunningham, David Bainbridge
Computer Science Department, University of Waikato
Hamilton New Zealand
hinze@waikato.ac.nz, mjc62@students.waikato.ac.nz, {sallyjo, davidb}@waikato.ac.nz

ABSTRACT
In this paper, we describe Semantic Bookworm—a tool that supports scholarly text analysis. In contrast to the text-based Bookworm tool, the Semantic Bookworm identifies semantic concepts.

Keywords
Semantic Analysis, Digital Humanities, Text Mining, Data Mining

1. INTRODUCTION & BACKGROUND
The large-scale digitization of print material makes it possible for scholars to expand the scope of their study to large—indeed, massive—collections of documents. Insights from traditional 'close reading' of small sets of texts now have the potential to be complemented by 'distant reading' [2] over these newly available digital resources, as data mining is brought to bear for the identification of unexpected patterns in corpora too large to be read.

This new style of humanistic research requires new tools to support analysis. One strand of tool development focuses on visual analysis, for example of the layout and structure of texts treated as images [5]; this approach obviously is particularly well-suited to documents that natively are primarily images. This present paper focused on a second, text-centered strand of research that treats a document as a sequence of *ngrams*, where decisions about the size of *n* and the choice of token as characters, syllables, or words are fundamental to this type of research. An ngram analysis tool is used to identify and quantify the occurrences of the specified token in the corpus (at a minimum providing a sum of the number of occurrences, and perhaps also offering statistical analysis of observed token frequencies as well), and then to visualize the occurrences (for example, by plotting frequency of token occurrence across time or against the structure of the underlying documents). Existing ngram analysis tools used in digital humanities research include the Ngram Statistics Package [1], Bookworm[1] [4], and the Google Ngram viewer[2] [5]. Recently a bookworm for the 4.6M public domain texts of the HathiTrust has become available.[3]

[1] https://github.com/Bookworm-project/BookwormDB

[2] https://books.google.com/ngrams

[3] http://bookworm.htrc.illinois.edu/

Permission to make digital or hard copies of all or part of this work for personal or classroom use is granted without fee provided that copies are not made or distributed for profit or commercial advantage and that copies bear this notice and the full citation on the first page. Copyrights for third-party components of this work must be honored. For all other uses, contact the Owner/Author. Copyright is held by the owner/author(s).

JCDL '16, June 19-23, 2016, Newark, NJ, USA
ACM 978-1-4503-4229-2/16/06.
http://dx.doi.org/10.1145/2910896.2925444

While these ngram analysis tools are demonstrably supporting new styles of humanities research that heretofore were not possible, the limitations of the tools are also becoming clear. Schmidt [7], for example, explores issues in using ngram analysis to tracking references to "the Enlightenment" as a historical period; the difficulties reported are caused to a large extent by the ngram analysis stripping away all cues (contextual, rhetorical, typographical) that allow a human reader to distinguish spurious uses of that phrase.

This paper introduces a *Semantic Bookworm* as a step towards combining the semantic, discriminative facilities of the human reader with the speed and coverage supported by automated mining tools. With Semantic Bookworm, not every occurrence of a word or phrase is counted, but rather the occurrence of a semantic concept. Section 2 introduces the architecture and implementation of the Semantic Bookworm, and Section 3 illustrates differences in results achievable with the Semantic Bookworm in comparison to the ngram-based (lexicographic) Bookworm.

2. SEMANTIC BOOKWORM
The original Bookworm software (Figure 1, blue and gray components) analyses a given document collection *lexically* using ngram analysis. The ngrams are then stored ready for search. The search function performs a look-up in the ngram index to identify the frequency of the ngram within the collection, and results are then visualized using, e.g., time graphs (examples in Sect. 3).

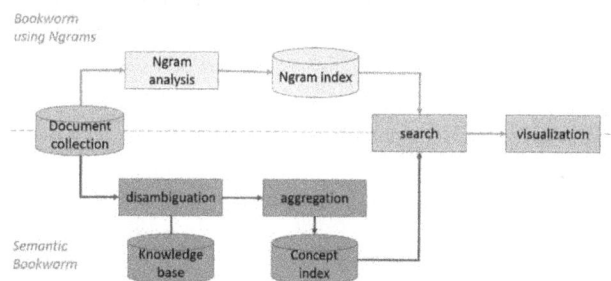

Figure 1: Combined architecture of Bookworm (original components blue and gray) and Semantic Bookworm (semantic components orange)

The Semantic Bookworm replaces those components that are shown in gray in Figure 1 by the components shown in orange. Here the document collection undergoes a disambiguation step using the knowledge base of semantic concepts we developed for Capisco [2]. In this process, all terms appearing in each document are mapped to their respective concept. This means that terms that are homonyms (same spelling, different meaning) may be linked to different concepts. Some terms may not be linked to any concept at all, as only those concepts are registered that are relevant to the document. The resulting concept information is then aggregated and stored in a concept index. For search and visualization, we use the original Bookworm components.

3. EXAMPLE VISUALISATIONS

We present two examples comparing the results of lexicographic analysis (using the original Bookworm) and concept analysis (using the Semantic Bookworm).

3.1 Analyzing books' structure

In the first example, we analyze two books by Charles Dickens, *David Copperfield* (orange line in Figures 2 and 3) and *Great Expectations* (blue line). The sequence of chapters is treated as a chronology in the Bookworm timeline, and the graphs plot the number of occurrences of terms (Figure 2) and concepts (Figure 3).

We here contrast the occurrences of the term "night" (counting each ngram) with the concept *Night* (counting each time the text deals with the concept rather than, for example, its occurrence in the farewell 'Good night'). Comparing these two sets of graphs, we note that the term "night" is overall mentioned more often throughout the books. This includes, for example, every mention of the word in phrases such as 'Good night'. We also note that even though in "Great expectations" the term "Night" is mentioned only somewhat less than in "David Copperfield", the concept of *Night* hardly ever appears in the former book and quite frequently in the latter.

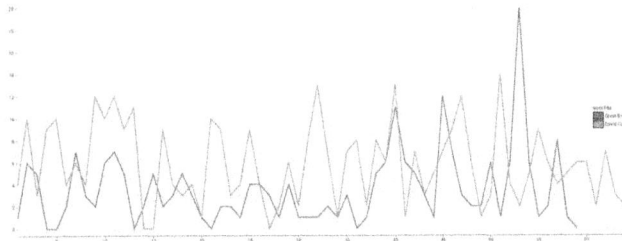

Figure 2: Term "night" across chapters of Dickens' books

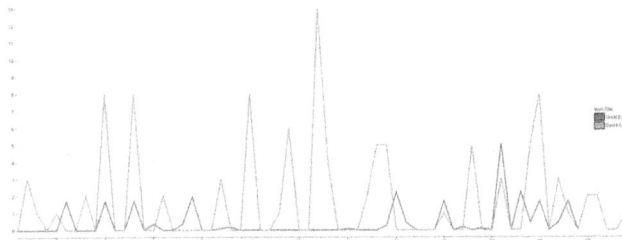

Figure 3: Concept *Night* across chapters of Dickens' books

Figures 4 and 5 show the distribution of the term and the concept of time, respectively. We note that overall the concept *time* occurs much more often than the term "time".

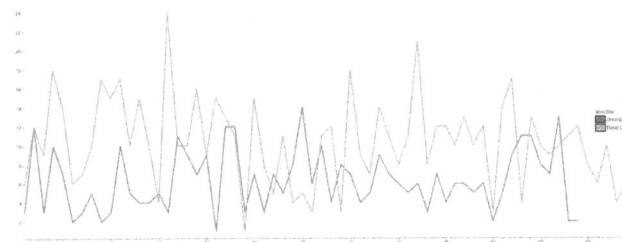

Figure 4: Term "time" across chapters of Dickens' books

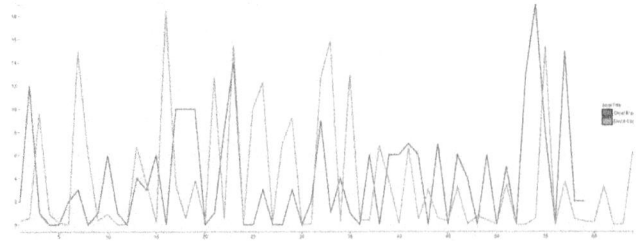

Figure 5: Concept *Time* across chapters of Dickens' books

3.2 Analyzing a collection structure

The second example analyses a collection of Charles Dicken's letters (here shown from 1835 to 53). We compare Dickens' use of the terms "god" (blue) and "philosophy" (orange) in Figure 6, left, with the occurrence of the concepts *God* and *Philosophy*, right. One can see that even though the term "Philosophy" is rarely used, topics of a philosophical nature appear quite often. On the other hand, the term "god" is used more often than the concept.

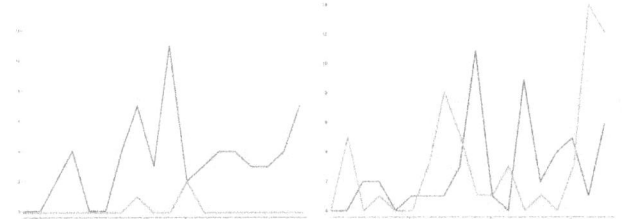

Figure 6: Bookworm (left) and Semantic Bookworm (right)

4. REFERENCES

[1] Banerjee, S., and Pedersen, T. 2003. The design, implementation, and use of the ngram statistics package. *Computational Linguistics and Intelligent Text Processing*, 370-381.

[2] Hinze, A., Taube-Schock, C., Bainbridge, D., Matamua, R., & Downie, J. S. 2015. Improving access to large-scale Digital libraries through Semantic-enhanced Search and Disambiguation. *JCDL '15*, 147-156.

[3] Kirschenbaum, M.G. 2007. The remaking of reading: Data mining and the digital humanities. *The NSF Symposium on Next Generation of Data Mining and Cyber-Enabled Discovery for Innovation.* 2007

[4] Leonard, P. 2014. Mining large datasets for the humanities. *IFLA WLIC 2014 Libraries, Citizens, Societies: Confluence for Knowledge*, http://library.ifla.org/930/

[5] Lin, Y., Michel, J.B., Aiden, E.L., Orwant, J., Brockman, W. and Petrov, S. 2012. Syntactic annotations for the Google Books ngram corpus. *ACL system demonstrations*, 169-174.

[6] Rushmeier, H., Pintus, R., Yang, Y., Wong, C. and Li, D. 2015. Examples of challenges and opportunities in visual analysis in the digital humanities. *IS&T/SPIE Electronic Imaging*, 939414-939414.

[7] Schmidt, James. 2013. Tracking 'the Enlightenment' Across the Nineteenth Century. *International. Conference on the History of Concepts*, 30-39.

Making Literature Review and Manuscript Writing Tasks Easier for Novice Researchers through Rec4LRW System

Aravind Sesagiri Raamkumar, Schubert Foo, and Natalie Pang
Wee Kim Wee School of Communication and Information
Nanyang Technological University, Singapore
{aravind002, sfoo, nlspang}@ntu.edu.sg

ABSTRACT

We demonstrate the recently built Rec4LRW system, meant for assisting researchers in three literature review and manuscript writing tasks. The system has been designed to be useful for all researchers, albeit the evaluation results show that it is more beneficial for research students and beginners. In this demonstration, we provide a walkthrough of the system by executing the tasks with sample research topics. The unique User-Interface (UI) and the task interconnectivity features are some of the highlighted aspects.

Keywords

literature review; manuscript writing; reading list; shortlisting feature; scientific paper information retrieval; scientific paper recommender systems

1. INTRODUCTION

The gap between novices and experts in research related activities is an apparent phenomenon, due to lack of experience in terms of task knowledge and execution skills [1, 2]. For mitigating this situation, both process-based human and technological interventions have been proposed. Most of the technological interventions are piecemeal approaches with researchers having to depend on multiple and disparate avenues for assistance. With our literature review and manuscript writing assistive system, we aim to address aspects such as task interconnectivity, information cues and serendipitous paper discovery along with the good quality recommendations.

2. REC4LRW SYSTEM

2.1 Brief Overview

The Rec4LRW system [3] has been built to help researchers in three main tasks of literature review and manuscript writing. The tasks are (1) Building an initial reading list of research papers, (2) Finding similar papers based on a set of papers, and (3) Shortlisting papers from the final reading list for inclusion in manuscript based on article-type preference of the researcher. The recommendation techniques of the tasks are based on seven criteria. These criteria represent the characteristics of the bibliography and its relationship with the parent scientific paper. The high level characteristics of the bibliography are captured using four criteria: References Count, Citations Count, Grey Literature Percentage and Coverage. The next set of criteria is

Permission to make digital or hard copies of part or all of this work for personal or classroom use is granted without fee provided that copies are not made or distributed for profit or commercial advantage and that copies bear this notice and the full citation on the first page. Copyrights for third-party components of this work must be honored. For all other uses, contact the Owner/Author.
Copyright is held by the owner/author(s).

JCDL '16, June 19–23, 2016, Newark, NJ, USA.
ACM 978-1-4503-4229-2/16/06.
DOI: http://dx.doi.org/10.1145/2910896.2925445

meant for capturing the relations between the scientific paper and each reference in the bibliography of the paper. They are Recency, Textual Similarity and Specificity. These criteria are used in the recommendation/retrieval techniques as per the individual task's requirement.

In task 1, coverage is used for ranking the final list of 30 papers from the output of a Content-based (CB) recommender that retrieves top 200 matching papers for the selected research topic. In task 2, the outputs of item-based collaborative filtering algorithm, title-based similarity matching and Textual Similarity & Specificity based document filtering techniques are merged. The seed basket is used as input for the aforementioned techniques. The final list of 30 papers is then ranked based on citation count. In task 3, a community detection algorithm is used to identify clusters of papers formed with the references and citations of the papers from the reading list. The number of papers to be shortlisted from these clusters is decided based on the article-type preference of the user. All the tasks in the system are interconnected using two collections called as *seed basket* and *reading list*. The seed basket serves as a collection of seed papers essential for running task 2 while reading list is a running collection of papers from both task 1 and 2. The reading list is one of the inputs for task 3. It is hypothesized that the system will be highly beneficial to research students and also for researchers who are venturing into new research topics.

2.2 Dataset and Technical Details

An extract of the ACM Digital Library (ACM DL) is used as the dataset. The dataset comprises of papers from proceedings and journals for the period 1951 to 2011. The sample set for the experiment was formed by filtering papers based on full text and metadata availability in the dataset. The final sample set contained a total of 103,739 articles. The back-end database is MySQL and JAVA is the main programming language used. The seven criteria values for all the papers in the sample set were measured as a pre-processing step. Apache Lucene and Apache Mahout libraries are used for the IR and RS mechanisms. The network analysis library JUNG is used exclusively in task 3 for creating the graphs and also for implementing community detection algorithms.

2.3 User-Interface of the System

The three tasks in the system are meant to be executed in a sequential manner. However, the tasks can be re-run as per user requirement if the intention is to mix different research topics in the same seed basket and reading list. This scenario potentially happens for multi-disciplinary research studies. Screenshot of one of these three tasks is provided in Figure 1. Certain novel UI features such as information cue labels (all tasks), shared co-relations with seed basket papers (task 2) and clustered papers option (task 3) have been included in the user interface to help researchers in relevance judgement and faster decision making.

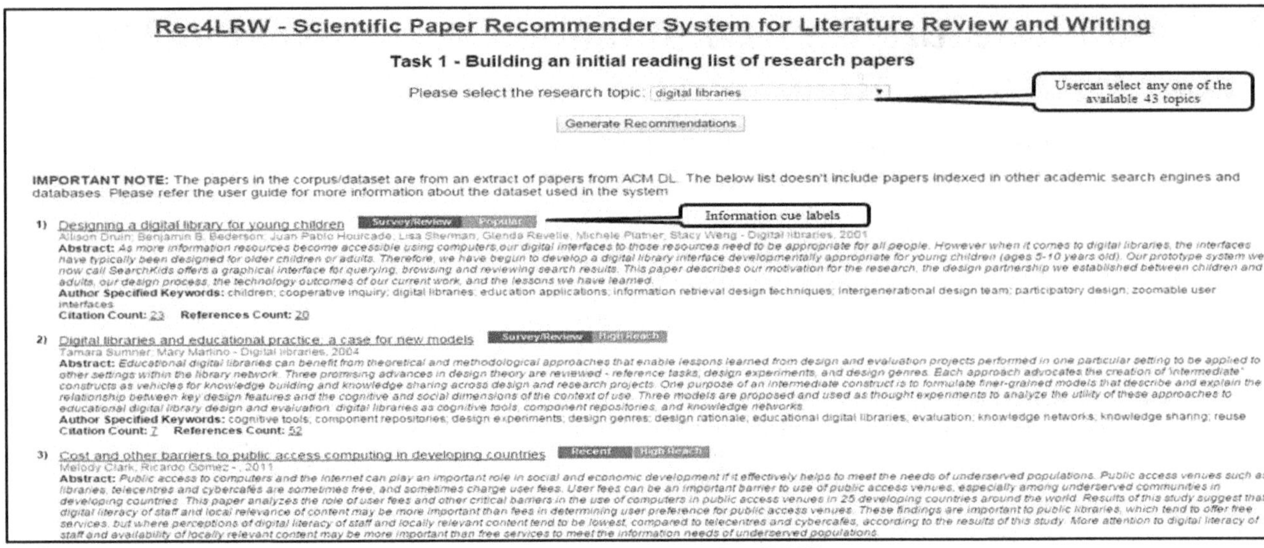

Figure 1. Screen of Task 1 from Rec4LRW system

3. USER EVALUATION STUDY

A user evaluation study was conducted to determine whether researchers using the tasks provided by Rec4LRW system can be efficient and effective in conducting the corresponding tasks in real-life settings. The participants had to select a research topic from a list of 43 provided topics. At the end of each task, participants had to answer mandatory survey questions and optional subjective feedback questions in evaluation questionnaires. System level evaluation questions were added to the questionnaire at end of task 3. Thee three system constructs chosen for the study are (i) Effort to use the System, (ii) Perceived System Effectiveness and (iii) Perceived Usefulness. As for the participants' demographics, 119 researchers participated in the whole study inclusive of the three tasks in the system. The reading list task (first task) was completed by 132 participants while 121 participants completed both the first and second task. 62 participants were PhD/MSc students while 70 participants were research staffs, academic staffs and librarians. The average research experience for PhD students was 2 years while for staffs, it was 5.6 years.

In Figure 2, the agreement percentages of the two study groups for the three system constructs are displayed. In the current study, an agreement percentage above 75% is considered as an indication of higher agreement from the participants. It is apparent from the percentages that students evaluated the system more favorably than staff. A significant difference of 14.18% was observed specifically for the Perceived Usefulness construct. This finding can be considered as an indication of the suitability of the system to students. The agreement is below 75% for the construct 'Effort to use the System' as participants found adding papers to the reading list as a rote activity performed solely for the study. The system's design rationale is to provide common recommendations for all users without taking user experience as a differentiating factor. However, students perceive the system to be more useful since it circumnavigates the apparent experience gap during execution of tasks.

4. FUTURE WORK

We plan to release a new version of the Rec4LRW system with more UI control features for enabling researchers to sieve through the results for better understanding the recommended papers. Additionally, we plan to set roles for the target users of the system so that personalization and customization features are made available. This feature is planned to be included in response to the qualitative feedback received from participants.

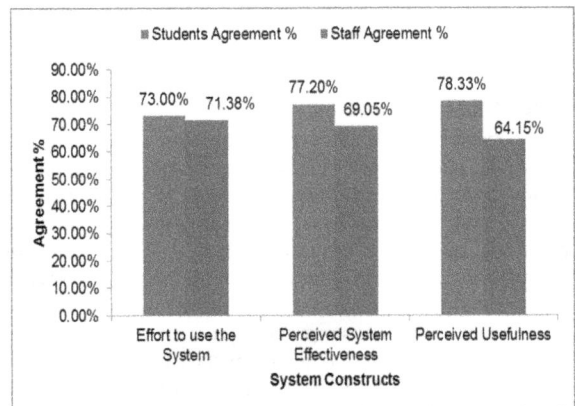

Figure 2. Agreement percentages of the system evaluation constructs

5. ACKNOWLEDGMENTS

This research was supported by the National Research Foundation, Prime Minister's Office, Singapore under its International Research Centres in Singapore Funding Initiative and administered by the Interactive Digital Media Programme Office.

6. REFERENCES

[1] Du, J.T. and Evans, N. 2011. Academic Users' Information Searching on Research Topics: Characteristics of Research Tasks and Search Strategies. *The Journal of Academic Librarianship*. 37, 4 (Jul. 2011), 299–306.

[2] Karlsson, L. et al. 2012. From Novice to Expert: Information Seeking Processes of University Students and Researchers. *Procedia - Social and Behavioral Sciences*. 45, (Jan. 2012), 577–587.

[3] Sesagiri Raamkumar, A. et al. 2015. Rec4LRW – Scientific Paper Recommender System for Literature Review and Writing. *Proceedings of the 6th International Conference on Applications of Digital Information and Web Technologies* (2015), 106–120.

Can Academic Conferences Promote Research Collaboration?

Xiaoyan Su, Wei Wang, Shuo Yu, Chenxin Zhang, Teshome Megersa Bekele, Feng Xia
School of Software, Dalian University of Technology
Dalian 116620, China
f.xia@acm.org

ABSTRACT

This work proposes to investigate the question of whether attending conference will breed new scientific collaboration based on the focal closure theory. Through the analysis of conference closure on individual and community level, we show that attending conference can promote new scientific collaborations, and conferences with more attendees and higher field ratings bring more new scientific collaborations.

Keywords

Academic social networks; Research collaboration; Focal closure

1. INTRODUCTION

Collaboration is playing an increasingly important role in scientific research because an individual scholar may not possess all the expertise and knowledge to address complex research issues. Consequently, tremendous efforts have been done to analyze the patterns and laws of coauthor behavior in order to enhance scientific collaboration. A scientific collaboration network extracted from coauthorships is usually static. However, it is of great importance in investigating how the network evolves over time, for example, the mechanisms of link formation and link extinction. One of the basic principles of dynamic network analysis is the triadic closure theory [2] which indicates that if two people have a common friend, they have a great chance to be friends in the future. However, in academia, new connection may happen between two unclose scholars who may not share common collaborators. Unfortunately, no previous work has been done on explaining this phenomenon.

In this work, we try to investigate this problem based on conference closure extended from focal closure [1]. Focal closure theory means that new connections may emerge between people who have joined in the same community. The basic idea of triadic closure and focal closure can be seen from Figure 1. To be specific, we calculate the probabilities of conference closure at individual and community

Permission to make digital or hard copies of part or all of this work for personal or classroom use is granted without fee provided that copies are not made or distributed for profit or commercial advantage and that copies bear this notice and the full citation on the first page. Copyrights for third-party components of this work must be honored. For all other uses, contact the owner/author(s).

JCDL '16 June 19-23, 2016, Newark, NJ, USA
© 2016 Copyright held by the owner/author(s).
ACM ISBN 978-1-4503-4229-2/16/06.
DOI: http://dx.doi.org/10.1145/2910896.2925446

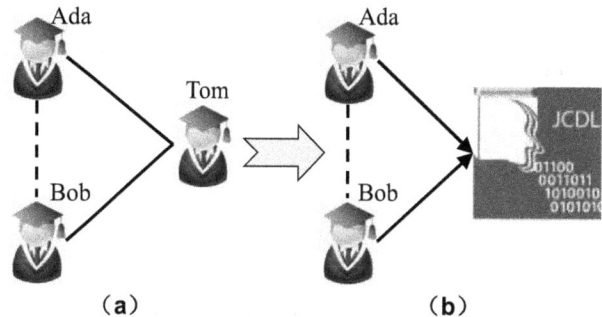

Figure 1: (a) Triadic closure; (b) Focal closure based on conference

level based on the cooperative behaviors of scholars who have published papers in the same conference in the field of Data Mining. Experimental results show that academic conference does bring new collaborations and conferences with more attendees and higher field rating are more able to promote scientific collaborations.

2. METHODS

2.1 Data Sets

Our study utilizes 12 influential conferences in Data Mining field from the computer science bibliography DBLP. We first extracted all the authors who have published papers in these conferences in 2010. The basic features of selected conferences are presented in Table 1. Then we gain their publications in the next five years to get their collaboration information.

2.2 Conference Closure

Conference closure means that two academic strangers who have not coauthored before are possibly to collaborate after attending a same conference. The conference closure can be studied at two different levels: (i) individual level and (ii) community level.

(i) Individual Level The ratio of conference closure at individual level can be calculated as:

$$CC_{indiv} = \sum_{i=1}^{n} \frac{N_i^c}{nN_i} \qquad (1)$$

where, N_i is the total number of new collaborators of scholar

Table 1: Statistics of selected conferences in 2010.

Conference	Founded time	Field rating[1]	No. of authors	No. of papers
FSKD	2002	11	1703	635
CIKM	1992	67	1103	374
ICDM	2001	56	960	353
ICDE	1984	104	660	217
KDD	1995	122	414	125
ICETET	2008	7	403	166
ADMA	2005	10	336	118
PAKDD	1998	33	292	100
SDM	2001	45	243	82
InCDM	2001	9	207	73
ICWSM	2007	19	197	72
DMIN	2005	7	165	62

[1] Field rating is got from Microsoft Academic Search.

Table 2: The ratios of conference closure at individual level in next 5 years.

Conference	2011	2012	2013	2014	2015
FSKD	**0.061**	0.052	0.039	0.041	0.032
CIKM	**0.077**	0.063	0.053	0.029	0.032
ICDM	**0.061**	**0.061**	0.045	0.023	0.023
ICDE	**0.059**	0.052	0.052	0.035	0.021
KDD	0.048	**0.055**	0.044	0.021	0.017
ICETET	**0.029**	0.006	0.010	0.013	0.000
ADMA	**0.038**	0.019	0.009	0.005	0.009
PAKDD	**0.032**	0.022	0.012	0.020	0.007
SDM	**0.035**	0.023	0.020	0.010	0.012
InCDM	**0.028**	0.019	0.023	0.021	0.009
ICWSM	**0.071**	0.049	0.025	0.031	0.013
DMIN	**0.018**	**0.018**	0.009	0.013	0.004

i after attending conference C, N_i^c is the number of scholar i's new collaborators who simultaneously attend C, and n is the total number of attendees of C. $\mathsf{CC_{indiv}}$ can reflect how attending a conference affects scholar's decision on choosing new collaborators.

(ii) Community Level The ratio of conference closure at community level can be calculated as:

$$\mathsf{CC_{com}} = \frac{N^c}{n} \qquad (2)$$

where N^c is the number of scholars who cooperate with other unfamiliar attendees of C. $\mathsf{CC_{com}}$ can better reflect how likely is it that the conference will promote new scientific collaborations.

3. RESULTS AND DISCUSSION

The ratios of conference closure at individual level in different years are shown in Table 2. We can see that there is an ascending trend for all conferences. This implies that most of the new cooperations happen in the first year after the conference, and the influence of conference closure gradually decreases over time. Meanwhile, the conferences with large scale also enjoy higher ratio of conference closure at individual level. Similar with conference scale, the ratio of

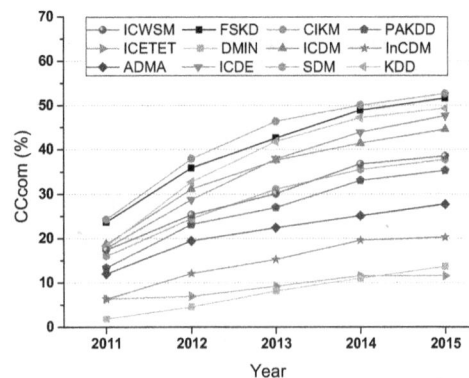

Figure 2: The ratios of conference closure at community level in next 5 years

conference closure at individual level is also positive related with field rating. In addition, the ratio of conference closure with low field rating (ICETET, ADMA, InCDM, DMIN) is very small (less than 0.010) in 2015.

Figure 2 shows the cumulative ratios of conference closure at community level in different years. We can find that there is a continuous growth for all conferences and the growth rate is relatively high from 2011 to 2013 and slightly goes down at the last two year. It indicates that attending a conference does promote new collaboration for many years. Meanwhile, the conferences with high field rating and more attendees enjoy higher ratio of conference closure at community level. Moreover, the probability reaches more than 50% for some large scale conferences (FSKD & CIKM).

Based on the analysis above, we can infer that the academic conference has a positive effect on promoting academic strangers to collaborate with each other, and conferences with more attendees and higher field ratings are more able to promote new scientific collaborations.

4. CONCLUSION

The theory behind our analysis is that new links may emerge between people who have joined in the same community. We verified this phenomenon based on the behavior of co-attending a conference. In future work, we will propose new mechanisms to promote scientific collaboration based on this verified theory.

5. REFERENCES

[1] G. Kossinets and D. J. Watts. Empirical Analysis of An Evolving Social Network. *Science*, 311(5757):88–90, 2006.
[2] A. Rapoport. Spread of Information Through A Population with Socio-structural Bias: I. Assumption of Transitivity. *The Bulletin of Mathematical Biophysics*, 15(4):523–533, 1953.

Coagmento 2.0: A System for Capturing Individual and Group Information Seeking Behavior

Matthew Mitsui
Department of Computer Science
Rutgers University
New Brunswick, NJ, USA, 08901
mmitsui@cs.rutgers.edu

Chirag Shah
School of Communication and Information
Rutgers University
New Brunswick, NJ, USA, 08901
chirags@rutgers.edu

ABSTRACT

In this demo, we present *Coagmento 2.0*, a Web-based, open-source platform that provides support for one working in individual or group projects spanning multiple sessions that involve looking for, collecting, and synthesizing information. The system also provides a highly customizable platform for researchers who want to investigate individual and group information seeking behaviors in a lab or a field setting. The demo not only shows back-end components and front-end interaction elements of the system, but also how one could easily configure *Coagmento* for user studies involving information seeking/retrieval with digital libraries (including the Web).

Keywords

Collaborative information seeking; information synthesis; sense-making; interactive search; exploratory search; CSCW

1. INTRODUCTION

Coagmento has been in development and use since 2007 and debuted to the public in 2009 as a platform for collaborative information seeking [5, 2]. This system has been inspired by and has been advancing the prior work of systems like Ariadne [6], Cerchiamo [3], CoSearch [1], and SearchTogether [4]. The fundamental change that *Coagmento* brought is its ability to support both individual as well as collaborative work in both synchronous and asynchronous contexts. Since its debut over 7 years ago, *Coagmento* has undergone several foundational shifts that will be presented here, as well as their implications towards future research in collaborative information seeking.

2. SYSTEM FOR END-USERS

Coagmento has always been a system for creating collaborative projects in which users can share information with each other. Users can bookmark, collect snippets, and annotate Web content in the scope of a project and share them with project collaborators. They can also live chat with collaborators and write on collaborative text editors. Users get started by making a free account and installing a free plug-in, available for Firefox, Chrome, Android, and iOS[1]. *Coagmento* users can also organize and interpret collected information in a browser view and can perform some basic text analysis. *Coagmento* allows individual users and collaborative groups to work in either single or multiple sessions, either synchronously or asynchronously. Figure 1 shows the Web layout and sidebar. Now, *Coagmento 2.0* also logs users' copy and paste behavior. We have found these behaviors to be much more common than snipping and bookmarking, and they can serve as implicit feedback of page usefulness. *Coagmento 2.0* also adds the ability to tag items, to filter them by tag, and to search them by text.

3. OPEN PLATFORM FOR RESEARCHERS

In the back-end, *Coagmento 2.0* is comprised of at least two major components. The first is Node.js[2], used to create a server-side notification framework that automatically reacts to users' updates and propagates them to collaborators. These "push notifications" are common in mobile applications like Twitter, where real-time reactivity is desirable but computational resources are scarce. Push notifications push live updates to project collaborators, such as new bookmarks.

Secondly, *Coagmento 2.0*'s server is coded in Laravel[3], a Model-View-Controller PHP framework that offers several constructs that make further Coagmento development very manageable. First, to extend Coagmento, an implementer will rarely need to manipulate databases directly. Implementers define database content in "models" - PHP scripts defining database structure. Examples in Coagmento are the query model that defines queries that users issued and the membership model that defines users' project membership. Updates can be made to the database structure with one-line "database migration" commands. These model code edits are immediately reflected in the database and are also reversible. Laravel also supports the use of several types of SQL databases, not exclusively MySQL. Second, database manipulation and retrieval can be defined through "service" PHP functions. New Web pages can be defined through PHP's "controllers" and "views". Views are created through templates so that minimal coding is required for new front-

Permission to make digital or hard copies of part or all of this work for personal or classroom use is granted without fee provided that copies are not made or distributed for profit or commercial advantage and that copies bear this notice and the full citation on the first page. Copyrights for third-party components of this work must be honored. For all other uses, contact the owner/author(s).

JCDL '16 June 19-23, 2016, Newark, NJ, USA

© 2016 Copyright held by the owner/author(s).

ACM ISBN 978-1-4503-4229-2/16/06.

DOI: http://dx.doi.org/10.1145/2910896.2925447

---

[1]http://coagmento.org/download.php
[2]https://nodejs.org/en/
[3]https://laravel.com/

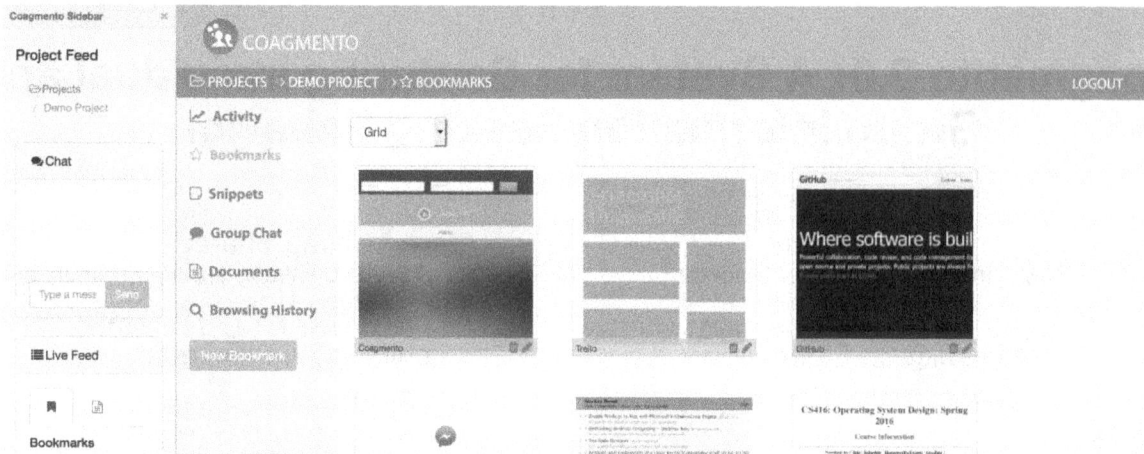

Figure 1: Coagmento 2.0 Web interface, including sidebar (left) and project page with thumbnails of collected bookmarks (center).

end interfaces. Any computer with PHP, Laravel, Node.js and a SQL database could be a *Coagmento 2.0* server.

Because of this convenience and extensibility, we have also recently launched *Coagmento 2.0* on GitHub as an open source tool[4]. Researchers can install PHP, Laravel, Node.js, and a SQL framework and download the GitHub repository to get started with their instance of Coagmento. Researchers can follow the Laravel framework to create new Web pages for user interaction and define new data types (e.g. more implicit user feedback signals). They can customize Node.js to create more live updates. We summarize the intended workflow in Figure 2; we maintain and host original *Coagmento* while any number of researchers can host their own custom instances. *Coagmento* has always allowed users to collaborate in real time, but researchers can now painlessly construct simple studies involving individual and collaborative information seeking/retrieval with digital libraries (including the Web), as well as actively contribute to *Coagmento* development.

4. DEMONSTRATION

In this demo, we will show some of the front-end functionality of *Coagmento* and help interested people set up their own instances of *Coagmento* and walk them through the customization process. We will show users how to install and get started with an installation of Coagmento. As an example of how to extend Coagmento, we will show how to create a new Web page view that displays copied and pasted Web content. We will also show examples of how to modify the database structure using Laravel.

5. ACKNOWLEDGMENTS

We would like to thank Kevin Albertson and Amanda Geng of Rutgers University for assisting with the development of this system. Work on Coagmento is supported through IMLS grant #RE-04-12-0105-12.

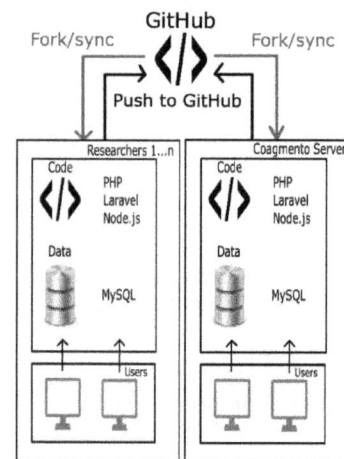

Figure 2: Overview of the intended use of the Coagmento infrastructure. Research fork the main code repository and locally store data.

6. REFERENCES

[1] S. Amershi and M. R. Morris. Cosearch: A system for co-located collaborative web search. In *Proceedings of CHI '08*, pages 1647–1656, New York, NY, USA, 2008. ACM.

[2] X. Fu, D. Kelly, and C. Shah. Using collaborative queries to improve retrieval for difficult topics. In *Proceedings of ACM SIGIR '07*, New York, NY, USA, 2007. ACM.

[3] G. Golovchinsky, J. Adcock, J. Pickens, P. Qvarfordt, and M. Back. Cerchiamo: a collaborative exploratory search tool. *Proceedings of CSCW*, pages 8–12, 2008.

[4] M. R. Morris and E. Horvitz. Searchtogether: An interface for collaborative web search. In *Proceedings of the 20th ACM UIST Symposium*, UIST '07, pages 3–12, New York, NY, USA, 2007. ACM.

[5] C. Shah, G. Marchionini, and D. Kelly. Learning design principles for a collaborative information seeking system. In *CHI '09 Extended Abstracts on Human Factors in Computing Systems*, CHI EA '09, pages 3419–3424, New York, NY, USA, 2009. ACM.

[6] M. B. Twidale, D. M. Nichols, and C. D. Paice. Browsing is a collaborative process. *Information Processing Management*, 33(6), 1997.

---

[4]https://github.com/InfoSeeking/Coagmento

Semantometrics

Towards Fulltext-based Research Evaluation

Drahomira Herrmannova
Milton Keynes, United Kingdom
d.herrmannova@gmail.com

Petr Knoth
Milton Keynes, United Kingdom
petrknoth@gmail.com

ABSTRACT

Over the recent years, there has been a growing interest in developing new research evaluation methods that could go beyond the traditional citation-based metrics. This interest is motivated on one side by the wider availability or even emergence of new information evidencing research performance, such as article downloads, views and Twitter mentions, and on the other side by the continued frustrations and problems surrounding the application of purely citation-based metrics to evaluate research performance in practice.

Semantometrics are a new class of research evaluation metrics which build on the premise that full-text is needed to assess the value of a publication. This paper reports on the analysis carried out with the aim to investigate the properties of the semantometric *contribution* measure [1], which uses semantic similarity of publications to estimate research contribution, and provides a comparative study of the contribution measure with traditional bibliometric measures based on citation counting.

Keywords

Research Evaluation, Citation Analysis, Text Mining

Acknowledgements

This work was supported by Jisc under contract no. 3790.

1. INTRODUCTION

We have introduced the idea of Semantometrics in [1] as a new class of metrics for evaluating research. As opposed to existing Bibliometrics, Webometrics, Altmetrics, etc., Semantometrics are not based on measuring the number of interactions in the scholarly communication network, but build on the premise that full-text is needed to assess the value of a publication.

In [1] we have attempted to create the first semantometric measure based on the idea of measuring the progress of scholarly discussion. Our hypothesis states that the added value of publication p can be estimated based on the seman-

tic distance from the publications cited by p to the publications citing p. This hypothesis is based on the process of how research builds on the existing knowledge in order to create new knowledge on which others can build. A publication, which in this way creates a "bridge" between what we already know and something new, which will people develop based on this knowledge, brings a contribution to science [1].

Until recently, it was still technically challenging for us to obtain an evaluation dataset on which properties of the contribution metric could be analysed. In this respect, we are now able to report on the first large-scale analysis of this metric. The goal of our study was to understand the properties and behaviour of the semantometric contribution measure in comparison with established research evaluation metrics. We chose to use citation counts obtained from the Microsoft Academic Graph (MAG) [4], as the representative of Bibliometrics, usage data (readership) obtained from Mendeley[1], as the representative of Altmetrics and research articles aggregated by the Open Access Connecting Repositories[2] (CORE) system as a representative sample for studying the characteristics of the contribution measure.

2. DATASET

Our experiments have been conducted on a dataset obtained by merging data from CORE, MAG and Mendeley. To assemble this dataset, we mapped DOIs of papers from CORE with MAG. Using MAG we then identified DOIs of papers citing and cited by the CORE papers. Finally, we used the DOIs to retrieve metadata, readership counts and primarily the titles and the abstracts using the Mendeley API. By merging these three datasets, we obtained a final dataset containing metadata, citation counts and reader counts of about 1.6 million Open Access papers. Additionally, we obtained metadata, including titles and abstracts of over 10 million papers which cite or are cited by the 1.6 million papers from CORE and are needed to calculate the contribution metric.

3. RESULTS

The main area of interest to us was the relation between the contribution measure and citation counts. The reason for this was the prevalence of use of citation counts in research evaluation. While using metrics based purely on citation counts has been subject to much criticism, these metrics still remain best known and most widely adopted. The aim was not to find a perfect correlation with citation counts,

Permission to make digital or hard copies of part or all of this work for personal or classroom use is granted without fee provided that copies are not made or distributed for profit or commercial advantage and that copies bear this notice and the full citation on the first page. Copyrights for third-party components of this work must be honored. For all other uses, contact the owner/author(s).

JCDL '16 June 19-23, 2016, Newark, NJ, USA

ⓒ 2016 Copyright held by the owner/author(s).

ACM ISBN 978-1-4503-4229-2/16/06.

DOI: http://dx.doi.org/10.1145/2910896.2925448

---

[1] http://dev.mendeley.com
[2] http://core.ac.uk

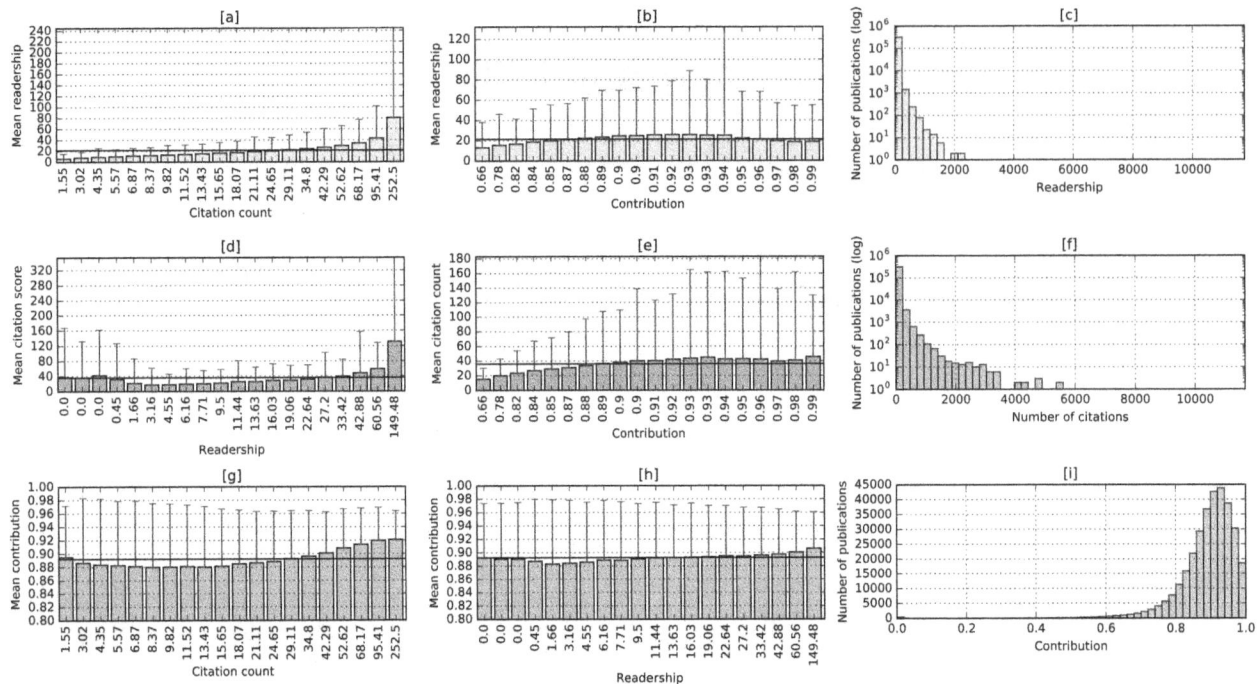

Figure 1: Results of the study. To produce figures [a], [b], [d], [e], [g] and [h], the data were split into 20 equally sized buckets by one of the studied metrics (x-axis). Mean (represented by height of the bars) and standard deviation (vertical lines on top of the bars) of a second metric (y-axis) was then calculated for each of the buckets. The solid horizontal lines represents the mean value across all buckets.

but rather demonstrate how does the contribution measure behave in relation to the well-known metric.

We have first investigated the distributions of the three metrics, these are shown in Figures 1 [c], 1 [f] and 1 [i]. As expected, the citation distribution (Figure 1 [f]) is a long tail (power law) distribution. This is consistent with existing studies [3]. The readership distribution (Figure 1 [c]) exhibits the same properties as the citation distribution. In contrast to the first two metrics, the contribution distribution (Figure 1 [i]) resembles a normal distribution.

To confirm our data are consistent with previous studies, we have investigated the relation between the citation and reader counts. We found that the two metrics are slightly correlated (Pearson $r = 0.3584$). A similarly strong correlation was reported by [2]. This correlation can also be seen when comparing the averaged values (Fig. 1 [a] and 1 [d]).

In contrast to the reader counts, we found no correlation between the citation counts and contribution (Pearson $r = 0.0871$). However, according to Figures 1 [g] and 1 [e] we can see that when comparing averaged values the behaviour of the contribution metric is not random, instead it is clearly correlated with citation counts. We can observe that publications with a citation score above a certain threshold achieve on average consistently higher contribution (Figure 1 [g]). Although the standard deviation shows it is not always the case, the results suggest that publications with more than 25 citations are more likely to have higher contribution. However, once a paper receives around 90 citations, higher citation counts do not lead on average to a higher contribution. We think this is an interesting observation that is consistent with our perception of research quality. One possible and highly simplified explanation could be that receiving around 90 citations is typically an indication of quality work. Higher citation counts then typically

reflect the size of the target audience community (impact) rather than higher quality of the underlying research work. This leads us to the conclusion that the contribution metric seems to capture different aspects of research performance than citation counts.

As in the previous case, there is no correlation between the contribution measure and reader counts, which is confirmed by Pearson $r = 0.0444$. Interestingly, while we observed a correlation between the averaged contribution and citation counts, there seems to be no such relation between averaged contribution and reader counts (Figures 1 [b] and 1 [h]).

4. CONCLUSION

We have demonstrated that new measures for assessing publication impact, which take into account the manuscript of the publication, can be developed and presented a comparative study of the semantometric contribution measure with citation and reader counts. The results of our study suggest that the contribution metric captures different aspects of research performance than citation counts. More specifically, we believe that Semantometrics have the potential to capture research quality and contribution rather than research impact.

5. REFERENCES

[1] P. Knoth and D. Herrmannova. Towards Semantometrics: A New Semantic Similarity Based Measure for Assessing a Research Publication's Contribution. *D-Lib Magazine*, 20(11/12), 2014.
[2] C. Schlögl, J. Gorraiz, C. Gumpenberger, K. Jack, and P. Kraker. Are downloads and readership data a substitute for citations? the case of a scholarly journal. *LIDA Proceedings*, 13, 2014.
[3] P. O. Seglen. The Skewness of Science. *JASIS*, 43(9):628–638, oct 1992.
[4] A. Sinha, Z. Shen, Y. Song, H. Ma, D. Eide, B.-j. P. Hsu, and K. Wang. An Overview of Microsoft Academic Service (MAS) and Applications. In *Proceedings of WWW 2015*, pages 243–246, Florence, Italy, 2015. ACM Press.

A Supervised Learning Algorithm for Binary Domain Classification of Web Queries using SERPs

Alexander C. Nwala and Michael L. Nelson
Old Dominion University, Department of Computer Science
Norfolk, Virginia, 23529
{anwala, mln}@cs.odu.edu

ABSTRACT

General purpose Search Engines (SEs) crawl all domains (e.g., Sports, News, Entertainment) of the Web, but sometimes the informational need of a query is restricted to a particular domain (e.g., Medical). We leverage the work of SEs as part of our effort to route domain specific queries to local Digital Libraries (DLs). SEs are often used even if they are not the "best" source for certain types of queries. Rather than tell users to "use this DL for this kind of query", we intend to automatically detect when a query could be better served by a local DL (such as a private, access-controlled DL that is not crawlable via SEs). This is not an easy task because Web queries are short, ambiguous, and there is lack of quality labeled training data (or it is expensive to create). To detect queries that should be routed to local, specialized DLs, we first send the queries to Google and then examine the features in the resulting Search Engine Result Pages. Using 400,000 AOL queries for the "non-scholar" domain and 400,000 queries from the NASA Technical Report Server for the "scholar" domain, our classifier achieved a precision of 0.809 and F-measure of 0.805.

CCS Concepts

•**Information systems** → *Clustering and classification;*

Keywords

Search Engines, Web queries, Query Understanding.

1. INTRODUCTION

In this paper we focus on domain classification of queries which targets two classes - the Scholar domain and the non-Scholar domain. The Scholar domain targets queries associated with academic or research content. For example, queries such as *"fluid dynamics"*, *"stem cell"*, *"parallel computing"* belong to the Scholar domain, while queries such as *"where to find good pizza"*, *"bicycle deals"*, and *"current weather"* belong to the non-Scholarly domain. In this work,

Permission to make digital or hard copies of part or all of this work for personal or classroom use is granted without fee provided that copies are not made or distributed for profit or commercial advantage and that copies bear this notice and the full citation on the first page. Copyrights for third-party components of this work must be honored. For all other uses, contact the owner/author(s).

JCDL '16 June 19-23, 2016, Newark, NJ, USA

© 2016 Copyright held by the owner/author(s).

ACM ISBN 978-1-4503-4229-2/16/06.

DOI: http://dx.doi.org/10.1145/2910896.2925449

we propose a novel method which does not rely on processing the actual query. Instead, we trained a classifier based on the features found in a Google SERP (Search Engine Result Page). The classifier was trained and evaluated (through 10-fold cross validation) with a dataset of 600,000 SERPs evenly split across both classes and the results were validated on 200,000 SERPs evenly split across both classes yielding a classification precision of 0.806 and F-measure of 0.805. We targeted a binary class, however our method could be scaled to accommodate other classes if the right features are found.

2. RELATED WORK

The problem of domain classification has been studied extensively. Jingbo et al. [4] built a domain knowledge base from web pages for query classification. Gravano, et al. [1] built a classifier targeting the geographical locality domain. Dou Shen et al. [3] built an ensemble-search based approach for query classification in which queries are enriched with information derived from Search Engines.

The query domain classification problem is not new and since queries are short, ambiguous, and in constant flux, maintaining a labeled training dataset is expensive. Therefore, we use Google SERPs instead of processing the query directly.

3. LEARNING ALGORITHM FOR DOMAIN CLASSIFICATION

Our solution can be summarized in two stages:

Stage 1. Building the classifier: First, identify the discriminative features. Second, build a dataset for the Scholar domain class and non-Scholar domain class. Third, train a classifier. Fourth, evaluate the classifier using 10-fold cross validation.

Stage 2. Classifying a query: First, issue the query to Google and download the SERP. Second, extract the features. Finally, use the classifier hypothesis function to make a prediction.

Feature Identification and Dataset Building: After extensive study, we identified 10 features to be extracted from the Google SERP:

The binary features **Knowledge Entity** - f_1 and **Images** - f_2 (Fig. 1b) represent the presence or absence of the Google knowledge entity and images respectively. The binary features **Google Scholar** - f_3 (Fig. 1b) and **Wikipedia** - f_7 (Fig. 1b) represent the presence or absence of a citation and a Wikipedia page respectively. The feature **Ad ratio** - $f_4 \in [0, 1]$ (Fig. 1a) represents the proportion of

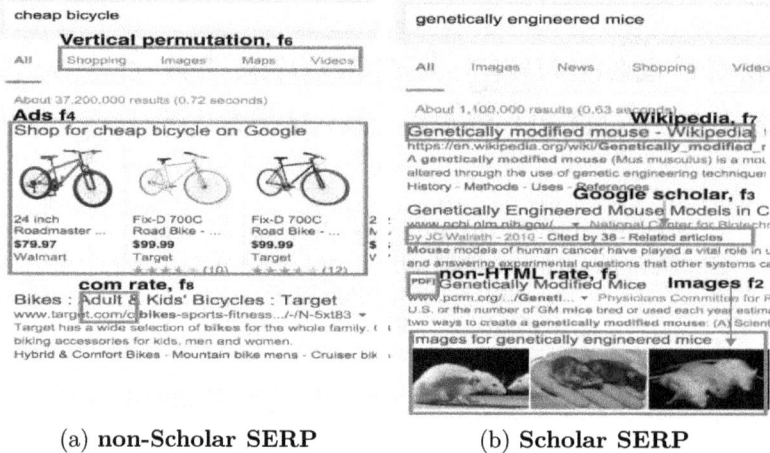

(a) non-Scholar SERP   (b) Scholar SERP

Figure 1: Example of features in the non-Scholar SERP (Left) and Scholar SERP (right). Non-Scholar queries typically feature "shopping" in the Vertical permutation (f_6), Ads (f_4), and are dominated by *com* TLDs (f_8). Scholar queries typically feature results from Wikipedia (f_7) and Google Scholar (f_3), as well as *non-HTML* types (f_5).

ads on the SERP. The feature ***com rate*** - $f_8 \in [0,1]$ (Fig. 1a) represents the proportion of *com* links on the SERP. The feature ***non-HTML rate*** - $f_5 \in [0,1]$ (Fig. 1b) represents proportion of non-*html* types on the SERP. The feature ***Vertical permutation*** - $f_6 \in [1, 336]$ (Fig. 1a) represents the ${}^8P_3$ possible page order of the SERP. The feature ***Maximum Title Dissimilarity*** - $f_9 \in [0,1]$, represents the maximum dissimilarity value between the query and all SERP titles: Given a query q, with SERP title t_i, and longest SERP title T, and Levinshtein Distance function LD, $f_9 = \max_{t_i} \frac{LD(q,t_i)}{|T|}$. Finally, the feature ***Maximum Title Overlap*** - $f_{10} \in \mathbb{Z} \in [0, \max_{t_i'} |q' \cap t_i'|]$, represents the cardinality of the maximum common value between the query and all SERP titles: Given a query set q with SERP title set t_i', $f_{10} = \max_{t_i'} |q' \cap t_i'|$

Figures 1a and 1b present a subset of the features for both classes. Note the ads present in the non-Scholar SERP and the absence of PDF documents. For the Scholar SERP, note the presence of a Wikipedia page, the PDF document and the Google Scholar article. Therefore, at scale, we could learn from not just the presence of a feature, but also its absence. After feature identification, we downloaded the Google SERPs for 400,000 AOL 2006 queries [2] and 400,000 NTRS (NASA Technical Report Server) 1995-1998 queries for the non-Scholar and Scholar datasets, respectively. Our method is not without limitations. For example, the datasets are presumed "pure." But this is not the case since Scholar queries exist in the non-Scholar dataset and vice versa, thus contribute to classification errors.

Classifier Training and Evaluation: Using Weka, we built a logistic regression model (Eqn. 1) on a 600,000 dataset evenly split across both classes. The model was evaluated using 10-fold cross validation yielding a classification precision of 0.809 and F-Measure of 0.805.

$$g_q = 2.7585 + \sum_{i=1}^{10} c_i f_i \qquad (1)$$

The coefficients matrix C^T contains the coeffients c_i for each feature f_i: $C^T = [c_1 \; ... \; c_{10}]$, $C^T = [0.8266, -1.1664, -2.7413,$

$-1.7444, 6.2504, -0.0017, -1.0145, -1.5367, 1.8977, -0.1737]$

Classifying a Query: To find the domain $d \in \{$Scholar, non-Scholar$\}$ of a query q,

First: issue the query to Google and download SERP.

Second: initialize all feature values $f_1 \; ... \; f_{10}$,

Third: use Eqn 1. to estimate g_q

Fourth: use logistic regression hypothesis (Eqn 2.) to estimate the class probability.

$$p(q) = \frac{e^{g_q}}{1 + e^{g_q}} \qquad (2)$$

Fifth: If $p(q) \geq 0.5$ predict $d = scholar$, else predict $d = non - scholar$

4. CONCLUSIONS

We define a set of features in SERPs that indicate if the domain of a query is scholarly or not. Our classifier which has a precision of 0.809 and F-measure of 0.805 can be further applied to other domains once discriminative and informative features are identified.

5. REFERENCES

[1] L. Gravano, V. Hatzivassiloglou, and R. Lichtenstein. Categorizing web queries according to geographical locality. In *Proceedings of the Twelfth International Conference on Information and Knowledge Management*, pages 325–333, 2003.

[2] G. Pass, A. Chowdhury, and C. Torgeson. A picture of search. In *Proceedings of the 1st International Conference on Scalable Information Systems*, 2006.

[3] D. Shen, R. Pan, J.-T. Sun, J. J. Pan, K. Wu, J. Yin, and Q. Yang. Q2C@UST: our winning solution to query classification in KDDCUP 2005. *ACM SIGKDD Explorations Newsletter*, 7(2):100–110, 2005.

[4] J. Yu and N. Ye. Automatic web query classification using large unlabeled web pages. In *Web-Age Information Management, 2008. WAIM'08. The Ninth International Conference on*, pages 211–215, 2008.

How to Identify Specialized Research Communities Related to a Researcher's Changing Interests

Hamed Alhoori
Department of Computer Science
Northern Illinois University
DeKalb, IL, USA
alhoori@niu.edu

ABSTRACT

Scholarly events and venues are increasing rapidly in number. This poses a challenge for researchers who seek to identify events and venues related to their work in order to draw more efficiently and comprehensively from published research and to share their own findings more effectively. Such efforts are hampered also by the fact that no rating system yet exists to assist researchers in culling the venues most relevant to their current readings and interests. This study describes a methodology we developed in response to this need, one that recommends scholarly venues related to researchers' specific interests according to personalized social web indicators. Our experiments applying our proposed rating and recommendation method show that it outperforms the baseline venue recommendations in terms of accuracy and ranking quality.

Keywords

Altmetrics; Personalized Recommendation; Scholarly Venues

1. INTRODUCTION

In addition to the challenges presented by the rising number of scholarly publications and venues, the task of identifying relevant research venues is further complicated because the research landscape is becoming less compartmentalized. There are, for example, increasingly complex academic sub-disciplines and emerging interdisciplinary research areas, events, and venues (e.g., journals, conferences, symposiums, workshops, and seminars). In this competitive and sophisticated research environment, researchers find it challenging to remain up to date on new findings, even within their own disciplines. Furthermore, "context-drift" in scholarly communities is becoming more prevalent as researchers expand, evolve, or adapt their interests in rapidly changing subject areas over time.

Generally, researchers learn of scholarly venues related to their research interests from limited sources: by word of mouth from lab members, departmental colleagues, and members of other scholarly communities; by conducting online searches and reviewing the research articles returned by these searches; from venue rankings; or from publishers' reputations. In the past, these approaches worked satisfactorily because relatively few related venues existed for any particular field. Today, however, given the more multifaceted scholarly environment, researchers become

acquainted with newly available and specialized venues only by spending considerable time browsing and evaluating.

In this study, we report on the effectiveness of a personal measure for evaluating venues we built based on user-centric altmetrics [1] and readings rather than conventional citation-based metrics. When applied, the measure recommends semantically related scholarly venues based on the researcher's specific interests and thus augments their awareness of relevant communities. In creating this measure, we drew on data from CiteULike,[1] a well-known social reference management system.

Prior to our work, few studies focused on methods for recommending scholarly events and venues. Among these, Klamma et al. [2] developed an approach that recommended academic events based on a researcher's event participation history. Boukhris and Ayachi [3] proposed a hybrid recommender for upcoming conferences in computer science based on venues from co-authors, co-citers, and co-affiliated researchers. Pham et al. [4] clustered users on social networks and used the number of papers published in a venue by a researcher to derive the researcher's rating for that venue. Other venue recommendation approaches based ratings on topic and writing style [5], title and/or abstract [6], and personal bibliographies and citations [7].

Most research to date has used citation analysis and researcher's publication or participation history to recommend venues. This approach is not useful for new researchers or graduate students who have yet to establish a record of scholarly activity. Furthermore, using only the venues in which researchers have previously published work undermines the "discovery" aspect of the recommendation process, as researchers might be interested in new areas in which they have not yet published. With these deficiencies in mind, our study explored a way to draw on a researcher's current personal article collections and readings to recommend tailored venues.

2. METHODOLOGY

Research articles can be associated with several metadata fields to produce recommendations. However, no direct metadata or ratings exist for venues. Nevertheless, references in a researcher's library can provide indirect information pertaining to a researcher's interests. We used such references and the years in which each was added to a researcher's library as factors in the measurement, which we refer to as personal venue rating (PVR). PVR takes into consideration how a researcher's interest in a given venue has changed over time. In Equation 1, we define PVR as a weighted sum for researcher u and venue v, and we refer to it as $r_{u,v}$:

Permission to make digital or hard copies of part or all of this work for personal or classroom use is granted without fee provided that copies are not made or distributed for profit or commercial advantage and that copies bear this notice and the full citation on the first page. Copyrights for third-party components of this work must be honored. For all other uses, contact the Owner/Author. Copyright is held by the owner/author(s).

JCDL '16, June 19-23, 2016, Newark, NJ, USA
ACM 978-1-4503-4229-2/16/06.
http://dx.doi.org/10.1145/2910896.2925450

---

[1] http://www.citeulike.org/

$$r_{u,v} = \sum_{i=y}^{1} w \log(v_{u,i} + 1) \qquad (1)$$

$v_{u,i}$ denotes the number of references in a researcher's u library from a specific venue v, which the researcher added during a certain year of the total number of y years, during which the researcher followed venue v. The weight w increases the importance of newly added references and is equal to i. PVR favors researchers who have followed a venue for several years over researchers who have added numerous references from a venue over fewer years. The log minimizes the effect of adding numerous references and helps to reduce shilling attempts. The addition of one allows for the case of one reference to be added to a library in a year. We used the year that a reference was added to the researcher's library, as it is more personalized than the published year.

We conducted an offline experiment using our CiteULike dataset, collected as described in [8]. We used user-based collaborative filtering (CF), item-based CF, SGD, and SVD++ algorithms. We compared researchers with similar interests in terms of their PVRs. To identify similarities among the researchers, we used the cosine similarity, the Pearson correlation similarity, and the Euclidean distance similarity.

We used a Boolean recommendation as a baseline and compared it with recommendations for scholarly venues based on PVR implicit ratings. Boolean ratings assume that all venues added by researchers are good venues and receive the highest rating.

3. RESULTS

We compared similarities that used PVR ratings and the user-based CF algorithm with the Boolean recommendation. The results demonstrate that PVR implicit ratings achieved higher precision (Figure 1), recall, and NCDG at lower neighborhood sizes. Additionally, using the PVR we were able to provide recommendations for up to 98% of users. We measured NMAE and NRMSE at different neighborhood sizes, and found that the Euclidean-weighting achieved the lowest NMAE and the lowest NRMSE. We compared the performance of four algorithms that used PVR ratings at different percentages of the training set, and we found that SVD++ achieved the lowest NMAE and the lowest NRMSE (Figure 2).

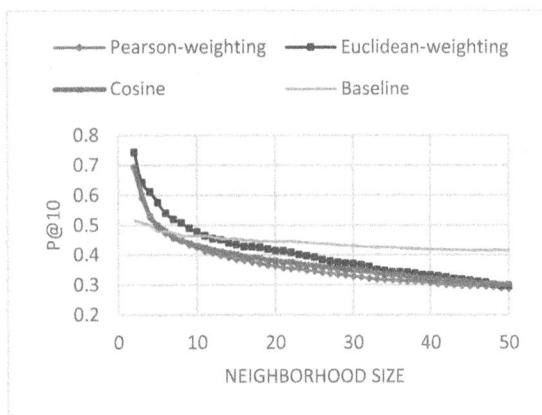

Figure 31. A comparison of user-based CF algorithm with similarities that use PVR ratings and the baseline at different neighborhood sizes

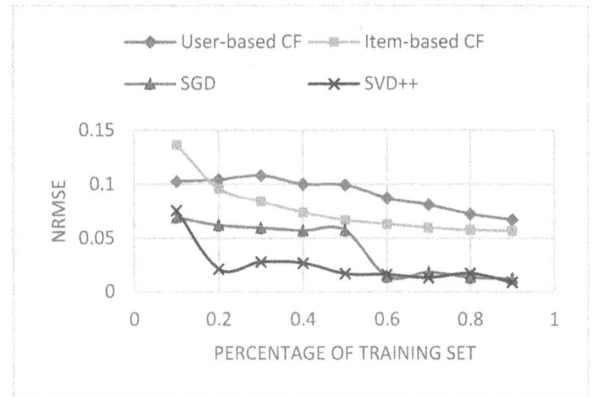

Figure 2. Comparison of algorithms at different training ratios

4. ACKNOWLEDGMENTS

This publication was made possible by NPRP grant # 4–029–1–007 from the Qatar National Research Fund (a member of Qatar Foundation). The statements made herein are solely the responsibility of the authors.

5. REFERENCES

[1] H. Alhoori, R. Furuta, M. Tabet, M. Samaka, and E. A. Fox, "Altmetrics for country-level research assessment," in *Proceedings of the 16th International Conference on Asia-Pacific Digital Libraries*, 2014, vol. 8839, pp. 59–64.

[2] R. Klamma, P. M. Cuong, and Y. Cao, "You never walk alone : Recommending academic events based on social network analysis," in *Proceedings of the First International Conference on Complex Science*, 2009, vol. 4, no. 1, pp. 657–670.

[3] I. Boukhris and R. Ayachi, "A novel personalized academic venue hybrid recommender," in *IEEE 15th International Symposium on Computational Intelligence and Informatics*, 2014, pp. 465–470.

[4] M. C. Pham, Y. Cao, R. Klamma, and M. Jarke, "A clustering approach for collaborative filtering recommendation using social network analysis," *J. Univers. Comput. Sci.*, vol. 17, no. 4, pp. 583–604, Feb. 2011.

[5] Z. Yang and B. D. Davison, "Venue recommendation: Submitting your paper with style," in *Proceedings of the 11th International Conference on Machine Learning and Applications*, 2012, vol. 1, pp. 681–686.

[6] N. Kang, M. A. Doornenbal, and R. J. A. Schijvenaars, "Elsevier Journal Finder: Recommending Journals for your Paper," in *Proceedings of the 9th ACM Conference on Recommender Systems - RecSys '15*, 2015, pp. 261–264.

[7] O. Kucuktunc, E. Saule, K. Kaya, and U. V Catalyurek, "TheAdvisor: A webservice for ac ademic recommendation," in *Proceedings of the ACM/IEEE Joint Conference on Digital Libraries*, 2013, pp. 433–434.

[8] H. Alhoori and R. Furuta, "Can social reference management systems predict a ranking of scholarly venues?," in *Proceedings of the 17th international conference on theory and practice of digital libraries*, 2013, vol. 8092, pp. 138–143.

Visualizing Published Metadata in Large Aggregations

Unmil P. Karadkar, Geoffrey A. Potter, and Shengwei Wang
The University of Texas at Austin, School of Information
1616 Guadalupe St. Ste. 5.202
Austin, TX 78701-1213 USA
+1-512-471-9292
unmil@ischool.utexas.edu

ABSTRACT

Large metadata aggregations provide access to documents held by multiple cultural heritage (CH) institutions. As CH institutions encode their metadata using different schemas and follow different data standards, aggregators must process the received data before making it available through a unified portal. Staff members at the contributing CH institutions don't receive feedback regarding the quality of the provided or the processed data. We are developing mechanisms that enable staff at the CH institutions to understand the effectiveness of their metadata with a goal of improving the visibility of their items in these large portals such as the Digital Public Library of America. This poster will present a classification of the DPLA metadata application profile highlighting compliance levels as well as a visualization framework for presenting the compliance of an institution's data with the DPLA data model.

Keywords
Digital Public Library of America; metadata visualization; metadata aggregation.

1. INTRODUCTION

Large metadata aggregations such as the The Digital Public Library of America (DPLA) and Europeana (http://www.europeana.eu) provide access to the holdings of multiple CH institutions, such as libraries, archives, and museums. The DPLA indexes metadata for over 11 million objects from more than 1,500 libraries, museums, and archives in the USA and it makes available through its Web portal (http://dp.la). The CH institutions, which the DPLA refers to as "data providers", continue to host the items that are indexed in the DPLA, using a variety of metadata schemas and standards to encode their data. The DPLA processes the received data to homogenize and map the data to a model called the metadata application profile (MAP) [2]. The accuracy of the data processing directly affects the visibility of an institution's items in the portal. However, staff at the contributing organizations often do not receive feedback regarding the efficacy of their data. While gauging the effectiveness of metadata by searching for their items is an option, this approach is neither systematic nor scalable. Further complicating such human-intensive efforts, the portal user interface does not display all the metadata associated with an item.

While the portal interface presents only a few elements, the DPLA makes all its harvested metadata publicly available via a RESTful application programming interface (API). Building on the openly available metadata in the context of the published MAP, we are

Permission to make digital or hard copies of part or all of this work for personal or classroom use is granted without fee provided that copies are not made or distributed for profit or commercial advantage and that copies bear this notice and the full citation on the first page. Copyrights for third-party components of this work must be honored. For all other uses, contact the Owner/Author.
Copyright is held by the owner/author(s).
JCDL '16, June 19-23, 2016, Newark, NJ, USA
ACM 978-1-4503-4229-2/16/06.
http://dx.doi.org/10.1145/2910896.2925451

developing tools to support data providers in assessing the fidelity between the source and the processed metadata. Our goal is to enable staff at the contributing institutions to view their published metadata well as to identify opportunities for enriching metadata.

2. PRIOR WORK

Metadata-based browsing and filtering—for example, faceted browsing—is now a common feature on popular web sites such as Amazon and eBay. In addition to browsing, significant research has explored the concept of metadata visualization for facilitating information access in domains such as videos [1] and scholarly search results [6]. Visualization has also been shown to be an effective technique for assessing and enhancing metadata quality. The VisMeB metadata browser provides a flexible framework for visualizing metadata and enables administrators to map elements to visualizations [7].

In the context of aggregated collections, the Aggregator's Workbench enables large collection managers in mitigating the effects of metadata heterogeneity by visualizing topical coverage of cultural heritage documents [3].Our past work in this domain has focused on semi-automatic enrichment of collection-level descriptions to augment the item-level metadata [5]. Building on the rich history of metadata visualization, the work described below complements the aggregators' view [3] by providing metadata assessment support to the contributors.

3. APPROACH

While our past work has viewed metadata aggregations through the lens of expressed collections, this research generalizes the notion of collections to include any grouping of items as specified by a contributor, much like the notion of dynamic collections that are generated in response to a query [4].

Thus, a collection manager may create a single profile for all items contributed by her institution or any subset as she sees fit. The DPLA MAP [2] includes core classes, which are required to be expressed in each item, and context classes, which may only be used when the relevant information is available. Within these classes, properties are further classified as required, strongly recommended, required when available, recommended, or optional. The complexity among these relationships is illustrated in figure 1. Thus, judging the impact of expressed metadata fields on improved discovery of items is not trivial. We have simplified this multi-level hierarchy to a three-level compliance: required, recommended, and optional in order to assist collection managers in prioritizing their efforts in metadata population.

4. VISUALIZATION

This framework is realized via the Web-based interface shown in figure 2. The visual interface, implemented using D3 (data-driven documents), highlights compliance of the institution's metadata at the three levels of compliance, each on its own tab. The interface favors functionality over form and adopts common color

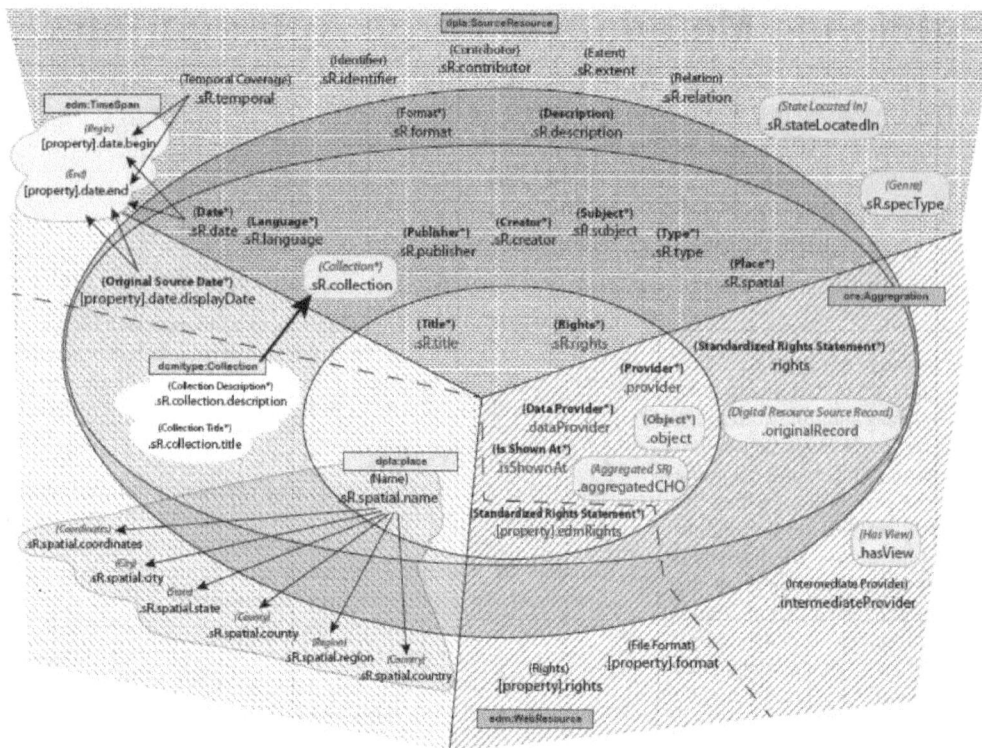

Figure 1. Compliance classification for DPLA fields.

provided by from small institutions from that made available through the DPLA portal. We are designing techniques to support collection managers in quickly assessing the high-need areas to enhance the discovery of their items. Our current efforts have focused on required fields and a subset of the recommended fields within the core classes. We are currently evaluating the developed visualizations using controlled experiments. The results of the evaluation will help us fine-tune the visualization in order to meet the needs of collection managers. Following the evaluation, we intend to broaden the repertoire to include optional fields as well as those in context (non-core) classes.

conventions to focus collection managers' attention on the task at hand. The compliance of the required field is shown using dual-distorted linear views. Enlarged Red blocks indicate missing values for required properties (the title field in figure 2). The interactive interface displays items with the missing values, enabling collection managers to identify errant items quickly. While the DPLA allocates unique identifiers to each ingested item, these ids are unsuitable for returning to the collection managers. Instead, the interface links to items via the institution's web page, which are meaningful to the staff. Beyond the mere presence of metadata, the interface also supports managers in separating rich descriptions from poor ones via visualization techniques, such as heat maps and scatterplots.

5. CONCLUSION AND FUTURE WORK

Staff at CH institutions have few resources and must optimize their efforts toward enhancing the discovery of items in the DPLA. Multiple layers of semi-automatic processing separate the metadata

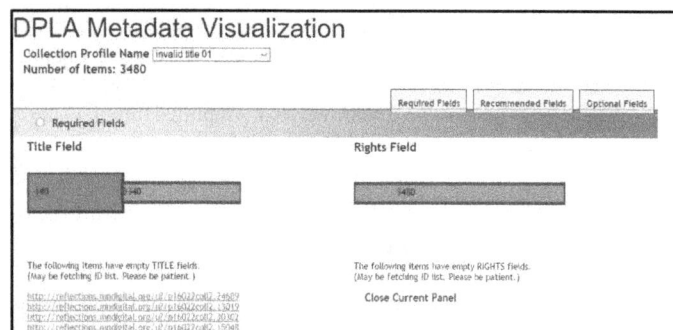

Figure 2. Visualization for compliance of required fields.

6. REFERENCES

[1]   Derthick, M. 2001. Interactive visualization of video metadata. *Proceedings of the 1st ACM/IEEE-CS joint conference on Digital libraries* (San Antonio TX, May 2001), 453.

[2]   DPLA 2015. Metadata Application Profile, version 4.0. Digital Public Library of America.

[3]   Fenlon, K., Efron, M. and Organisciak, P. 2012. Tooling the Aggregator's Workbench: Metadata visualization through statistical text analysis. *Proceedings of the American Society for Information Science and Technology* (Baltimore MD, Oct. 2012), 1–10.

[4]   Hill, L., Janee, G., Dolin, R., Frew, J. and Larsgaard, M. 1999. Collection metadata solutions for digital library applications. *Journal of the American Society of Information Science & Technology*. 50, 13 (Oct. 1999), 1169–1181.

[5]   Karadkar, U., Wickett, K., Parikh, M., Furuta, R., Sheehy, J., Junnutula, M. and Tzou, J. 2015. Computationally Supported Collection-level Descriptions in Large Heterogeneous Metadata Aggregations. *Proceedings of the 15th ACM/IEEE-CS Joint Conference on Digital Libraries* (Knoxville TN, Jun. 2015), 271–272.

[6]   Khazaei, T. and Hoeber, O. 2012. Metadata visualization of scholarly search results: supporting exploration and discovery. *Proceedings of the 12th International Conference on Knowledge Management and Knowledge Technologies* (Graz Austria, Sep. 2012), Article No. 21.

[7]   Klein, P., Reiterer, H., Mueller, F. and Limbach, T. 2003. Metadata visualization with VisMeB. *Proceedings. Seventh International Conference on Information Visualization* (London UK, Jul. 2003), 600–605.

MemGator - A Portable Concurrent Memento Aggregator

Cross-Platform CLI and Server Binaries in Go

Sawood Alam
Department of Computer Science
Old Dominion University
Norfolk, Virginia - 23529 (USA)
salam@cs.odu.edu

Michael L. Nelson
Department of Computer Science
Old Dominion University
Norfolk, Virginia - 23529 (USA)
mln@cs.odu.edu

ABSTRACT

The Memento protocol makes it easy to build a uniform lookup service to aggregate the holdings of web archives. However, there is a lack of tools to utilize this capability in archiving applications and research projects. We created MemGator, an open source, easy to use, portable, concurrent, cross-platform, and self-documented Memento aggregator CLI and server tool written in Go. MemGator implements all the basic features of a Memento aggregator (e.g., TimeMap and TimeGate) and gives the ability to customize various options including which archives are aggregated. It is being used heavily by tools and services such as Mink, WAIL, OldWeb.today, and archiving research projects and has proved to be reliable even in conditions of extreme load.

Keywords

MemGator; Memento; Aggregator; Web Archiving

1. INTRODUCTION

With the growth in the number of public web archives it is becoming important to provide a means to aggregate them for better coverage and completeness. The Memento protocol [3] provides a uniform API to lookup URIs in web archives. Due to the wide support of the Memento protocol in the archiving ecosystem, it is now easy to aggregate archives' holdings for any given query. However, current applications can either use an ad hoc aggregator implementation or rely on centralized services such as LANL's Time Travel portal[1] and ODU Memento Aggregator[2]. While centralized third party services are serving their purpose well, the convenience has the tradeoff of lack of customization and control such as the client application's inability to specify which archives are aggregated. Centralized services are usually good for general usage, but are not suitable for specialized purposes such as research or heavy traffic applications. For example, certain archives have IP-based traffic

[1]http://timetravel.mementoweb.org/guide/api/
[2]http://mementoproxy.cs.odu.edu/

Permission to make digital or hard copies of part or all of this work for personal or classroom use is granted without fee provided that copies are not made or distributed for profit or commercial advantage and that copies bear this notice and the full citation on the first page. Copyrights for third-party components of this work must be honored. For all other uses, contact the owner/author(s).

JCDL '16 June 19-23, 2016, Newark, NJ, USA

© 2016 Copyright held by the owner/author(s).

ACM ISBN 978-1-4503-4229-2/16/06.

DOI: http://dx.doi.org/10.1145/2910896.2925452

```
$ memgator --format=JSON --verbose http://example.com/
{
  "original_uri": "http://example.com/",
  "self": "http://localhost:1208/timemap/json/http:...",
  "mementos": {
    "list": [
      {
        "datetime": "2002-01-20T14:25:10Z",
        "uri": "https://archive.is/20020120142510/ht..."
      },
---TRUNCATED---
$ memgator --arcs=./archives.json --log=./memgator.log \
>          --agent="MemGator:1.0 Test Run <@WebSciDL>" \
>          --host=localhost --port=1208 \
>          --contimeout=20s --restimeout=45s server
MemGator Server is listening at:
http://localhost:1208/timemap/{FORMAT}/{URI-R}
http://localhost:1208/timegate/{URI-R} [Accept-Datetime]
---TRUNCATED---
```

Figure 1: CLI and Server Mode Examples

throttling policies that might limit the ability of centralized servers in case of heavy traffic. Similarly, the recent surge of OldWeb.today caused increased load on archives. As a result, one archive requested to be excluded from polling. This would have been an issue if they were using a centralized service.

There are a few open source aggregator implementations such as Memento Server[3] and Memento Java Client Library[4], but they are either outdated or require a server setup.

With these issues in mind, we created the MemGator tool that provides a standalone cross-platform binary without any external dependencies. It can be used as a one-off command to retrieve the response on the standard output or run as a web service to replicate necessary features of the centralized memento aggregator services (Figure 1). We tried to keep the service API as close to the LANL's Time Travel service as possible for greater interoperability. Both the modes (CLI and server) come with a handful of customization options that are documented in the binary itself and can be seen using standard help flag. One such configuration option is to supply a custom list of archives to be aggregated or use the archive profile [1] based archive ranking to query top-K archives only. We made the source code and binaries publicly available[5]. The tool is currently being used heavily in OldWeb.today and WAIL[6]. We are also running it as a web service[7] that is primarily being used by Mink [2].

[3]https://code.google.com/p/memento-server/
[4]https://github.com/ukwa/mementoweb-client-java
[5]https://github.com/oduwsdl/memgator
[6]http://machawk1.github.io/wail/
[7]http://memgator.cs.odu.edu/

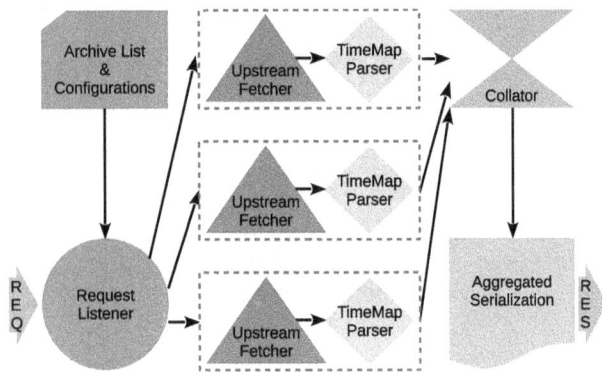

Figure 2: MemGator Workflow Diagram

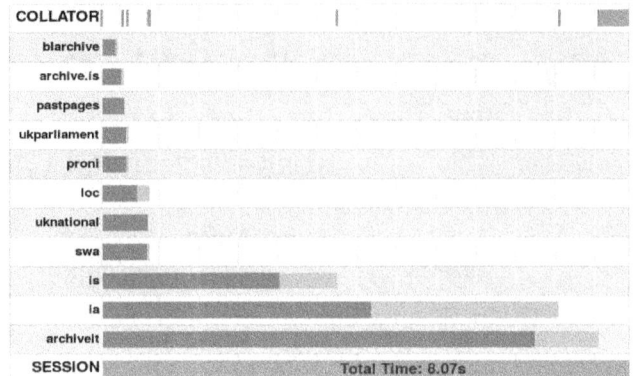

Figure 3: TimeMap Aggregation Request Timeline

2. IMPLEMENTATION

An aggregator is a good example of a concurrent application. It relies on various upstream archives which consumes the maximum amount of the overall time in network I/O while the process sits idle. Performing this operation sequentially will make it useless as the number of upstream services grows. We chose the Go language primarily because it is designed with concurrency in mind and has features that make development of concurrent web applications easy. Additionally, it provides the ability to create cross-compiled cross-platform static binaries.

Figure 2 illustrates the workflow of the MemGator implementation. The main thread (the request listener) loads the list of archives and other configuration options. When a lookup request is received, MemGator spins off goroutines (lightweight threads of Go) for each individual archive. These individual goroutines fetch the TimeMap from individual archives independently. If the response is successful the goroutine passes the data to a TimeMap parser via a channel (message passing mechanism of Go), which makes a linked list of the response in a chronological order. The parser sends the linked list data to the collator which accumulates responses from each individual goroutine and merges them while maintaining the sorting. Once all goroutines are completed or timeout occurs, the accumulator passes the aggregated linked list to the serializer. Depending on the format requested by the client (such as Link or JSON), the data is serialized and returned as the response to the user.

3. EVALUATION

We profiled individual functional blocks of a usual MemGator TimeMap request session with the microsecond precision and plotted them on a timeline to assess the gain of the concurrency. The top row of the Figure 3 shows activity in the main collator function when a response from an individual upstream goroutine is merged in the main linked list (while maintaining the canonical order). The far right activity in the first row is the time it took to serialize the response in the required format. The last row is the over all session time as observed by the MemGator. For a fairly large response (with 100,000+ Mementos) of `cnn.com` it took about 8 seconds. All the other middle rows show the time taken by the goroutines of individual archives for fetching the response (in red color) and parsing the fetched TimeMap (in yellow color) before passing the data to the main collator.

We then stress tested a server instance of MemGator using ApacheBench[8] for `cs.odu.edu` (with about 1,000 Me-

[8] https://httpd.apache.org/docs/2.2/programs/ab.html

Table 1: Stress Test Using ApacheBench

Concurrency	#Requests/sec (mean of 10 tests)
1	2.23
10	7.76
100	12.03
1000	64.70
>10000	ApacheBench I/O limit

mentos). Table 1 shows the number of requests MemGator was able to serve per second on various concurrency levels. Greater throughput on higher stress level is due to better utilization of the compute resources. For any individual request the processor is mostly sitting idle (and can be used for processing other requests), waiting for the network I/O to complete as illustrated in Figure 3 in red.

4. FUTURE WORK AND CONCLUSIONS

The project repository has various feature requests that we need to assess and implement in a clean way while maintaining the interoperability with the existing tools to the extent possible. So far the MemGator implements all the basic features of a Memento aggregator (such as TimeMap and TimeGate) and gives the ability to customize various options including which archives are aggregated. It is being used heavily by tools and services such as Mink, WAIL, OldWeb.today, and archiving research projects and has proved to be reliable even in conditions of extreme load.

5. ACKNOWLEDGMENTS

This work is supported in part by the IIPC. Mat Kelly, Ilya Kreymer, Herbert Van de Sompel, and Harihar Shankar provided helpful feedback for the MemGator development.

6. REFERENCES

[1] S. Alam, M. L. Nelson, H. V. de Sompel, L. Balakireva, H. Shankar, and D. S. H. Rosenthal. Web Archive Profiling Through CDX Summarization. In *Proceedings of 19th International Conference on Theory and Practice of Digital Libraries, TPDL 2015*, pages 3–14.

[2] M. Kelly, M. L. Nelson, and M. C. Weigle. Mink: Integrating the Live and Archived Web Viewing Experience Using Web Browsers and Memento. In *Proceedings of the 14th ACM/IEEE-CS Joint Conference on Digital Libraries*, pages 469–470, 2014.

[3] H. Van de Sompel, M. L. Nelson, and R. Sanderson. HTTP Framework for Time-Based Access to Resource States – Memento. RFC 7089, Dec. 2013.

Leveraging Tweet Ranking in an Optimization Framework for Tweet Timeline Generation

Lili Yao   Feifan Fan   Yansong Feng[*]   Dongyan Zhao
{yaolili,fanfeifan,fengyansong,zhaodongyan}@pku.edu.cn
ICST, Peking University, Beijing, China

ABSTRACT

When users search in Twitter, they are overloaded with a mass of microblog posts every time, which are not particularly informa- tive and lack of meaningful organization. Therefore, it is helpful to produce a summarized tweet timeline about the topic. The tweet timeline generation is such a task aiming at selecting a small set of representative tweets to generate meaningful timeline. In this paper, we introduce an optimization framework to jointly model the *relevance, novelty* and *coverage* of the tweet timeline, including effective tweet ranking algorithm. Extensive experiments on the public TREC 2014 dataset demonstrate our method can achieve very competitive results against the state-of-art TTG systems.

Keywords

Tweet timeline generation, optimization framework, tweet ranking

1. INTRODUCTION

When users search a query in Twitter, they are overloaded with a mass of microblog posts (or "tweets") every time. Therefore, it is helpful to produce a summarized tweet timeline about the topic. In TREC 2014 Microblog track, the organizer introduced the Tweet Timeline Generation (TTG) task[1], which can be summarized as "At time T, I have an information need expressed by query Q, and I would like a summary that captures relevant information".

In this paper, we introduce an optimization framework to jointly model the relevance, novelty and coverage of the tweet timeline, including effective tweet ranking algorithm. The main contributions of this work are: (1) We construct the semantic graph based on the relevance and novelty strategy, which can effectively filter out irrelevant tweets and decrease redundancy among the representative tweets. (2) Based on textRank algorithm[3], our tweet rank-

---

[*]Corresponding author

Permission to make digital or hard copies of part or all of this work for personal or classroom use is granted without fee provided that copies are not made or distributed for profit or commercial advantage and that copies bear this notice and the full citation on the first page. Copyrights for third-party components of this work must be honored. For all other uses, contact the owner/author(s).

JCDL '16 June 19-23, 2016, Newark, NJ, USA
© 2016 Copyright held by the owner/author(s).
ACM ISBN 978-1-4503-4229-2/16/06.
DOI: http://dx.doi.org/10.1145/2910896.2925453

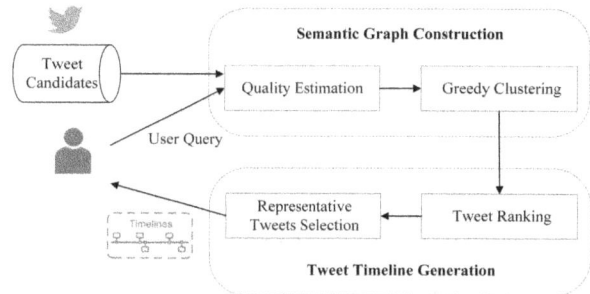

Figure 1: The architecture of our TTG system.

ing method which interpolates coverage characteristic can choose representative tweets effectively. (3) A set of experiments on public TREC twitter corpora demonstrate our method can achieve very competitive results against the state-of-art TTG systems.

2. PROPOSED APPROACH

2.1 Problem Formulation

Given a topic query Q, we obtain a tweet collection $C = \{T_1, T_2, ..., T_N\}$, and output a summarized tweet timeline which consists of relevant and non-redundant, chronologically ordered tweets. To address the issue, we characterize an effective timeline with following three key requirements.

Relevance. Given a query Q, we build an expansion language model $\theta_{Q'}$ based on the original word distribution θ_Q.

$$D_r(\theta_{T_i}) = D_{KL}(\theta_{T_i} \| \theta_{Q'}) \qquad (1)$$

Novelty. When dealing with a new tweet, we compare it with all other tweets before and determine whether the coming tweet is novel enough to form a new cluster.

Coverage. The coverage property of the summary, denoted as $Cov(T_i, S)$, reflects the proportion of the information contained in the cluster S covered by tweet T_i.

$$Cov(T_i, S) = \frac{\sum_{T' \in S} \mathcal{F}(IU(T_i) \cap IU(T'))}{\mathcal{F}(IU(S))} \qquad (2)$$

where function $IU(\cdot)$ gets all the information units in the corresponding tweets. $\mathcal{F}(\cdot)$ is the coverage calculating function.

2.2 Semantic Graph Construction

Fig.1 provides an overview of our system architecture. In the overall optimization framework, we firstly construct our semantic graph.

When a new tweet comes, we will add this tweet T to our semantic graph iff the relevance between query Q and tweet T satisfies the threshold α requirement. And then add T to the most similar cluster iff the novelty between T and the cluster is less than the threshold β. Furthermore, we will make an undirected edge between T and each tweet in the cluster with the weight of similarity. Otherwise, a new cluster will be established.

2.3 Tweet Ranking Method

After we construct the semantic graph, we can further utilize textRank algorithm to select important tweets.

$$W(T_i) = (1-d) + d * \sum_{T_j \in In(T_i)} \frac{W_{ji}}{\sum_{T_k \in Out(T_j)} W_{jk}} W(T_j) \quad (3)$$

However, the final values obtained after textRank runs to completion are not affected by the choice of the initial value of each tweet, which neglect the inherent attributes of coverage of each tweet. To overcome this limitation, we present our tweet ranking method based on textRank. And the main difference between them is that we jointly model relevance and novelty and interpolate coverage score in textRank. That is:

$$Score(T_i) = \gamma * W(T_i) + (1-\gamma) * Cov(T_i, S) \quad (4)$$

3. EXPERIMENTS

3.1 Experimental Setting

Data Preparation. We evaluate the proposed TTG systems over 55 official topics in TREC 2014 Microblog track[1].

Evaluation metrics. Following the TREC 2014 task on TTG, we mainly focus on the clustering performance as timeline quality. And the weighted F_1 score, denoted as $F_1{}^w$, is the main evaluation metric for TTG task in TREC 2014.

3.2 Methods to Compare

We note the following methods as comparisons in our experiments.

- **TTGPKUICST2:** Hierarchical clustering algorithm, which achieved the best performance in TREC 2014 Microblog Track.

- **EM50:** kNN clustering approach, which won the second place in TREC 2014 Microblog Track.

- **hltcoeTTG1:** The novel detection approach, which ranked third in TREC 2014 Microblog Track.

- **DivRank:** We implement the DivRank algorithm[2] that is also well known for jointly modeling only relevance and novelty without coverage.

- **StarClustering:** In star clustering[4], the final timeline is the representative tweets from each star-shaped clustering. This can also serve as a model that balances relevance and novelty.

Table 1: Performance of different methods.

Method	R	R^w	P	F_1	$F_1{}^w$
TTGPKUICST2	0.370	0.584	0.457	0.354	**0.458**
EM50	0.287	0.478	0.415	0.255	0.382
hltcoeTTG1	0.403	0.592	0.341	0.276	0.370
DivRank	0.506	0.680	0.338	0.351	0.403
StarClustering	**0.522**	**0.702**	0.268	0.269	0.328
RN	0.365	0.580	0.452	0.353	0.446
RN+tweetRank	0.369	0.585	0.459	0.358	0.454
RN+tweetRank*	0.371	0.585	**0.461**	**0.360**	0.456

- **RN:** This is the vanilla version of our proposed method modeling with relevance and novelty. And then directly select the tweet with the highest similarity score in the cluster as the representative one.

- **RN+tweetRank:** Based on the relevance and novelty score, we employ introduced tweet ranking method to select a tweet from each cluster.

- **RN+tweetRank*:** Furthermore, we interpolates coverage score in the tweet ranking method.

3.3 Results and Discussion

Table 1 shows the performance of different methods in TTG. Note that the abbreviations of R, R^w and P stand for *Recall*, weighted *Recall* and *Precision* respectively.

We can observe that DivRank and StarClustering modeling both relevance and novelty have achieved large recall along with unsatisfactory precision. With the proposed approach for balancing relevance and novelty, RN+tweetRank improves all the precision, recall and F_1 over RN, which demonstrates the effectiveness on tweetRank. By comparing RN+tweetRank with RN+tweetRank*, we can observe that the incorporation of the coverage also gives better performance. The strategy that combines relevance, novelty, coverage and tweetRank(i.e. RN+tweetRank*) together achieves the optimal performance for RN based methods. And our result is comparable with the state-of-art method TTGPKUICST2.

Acknowledgements

This work was supported by National Natural Science Foundation of China under Grant No. 61370116.

4. REFERENCES

[1] J. Lin and M. Efron. Overview of the trec-2014 microblog track. In *TREC'14*, pages 84–89, 2014.

[2] Q. Mei, J. Guo, and D. Radev. Divrank: the interplay of prestige and diversity in information networks. In *Proceedings of the 16th ACM SIGKDD international conference on Knowledge discovery and data mining*, pages 1009–1018. ACM, 2010.

[3] R. Mihalcea and P. Tarau. Textrank: Bringing order into texts. Association for Computational Linguistics, 2004.

[4] X. Wang and C. Zhai. Learn from web search logs to organize search results. In *Proceedings of the 30th annual international ACM SIGIR conference on Research and development in information retrieval*, pages 87–94. ACM, 2007.

Evaluating Cost of Cloud Execution
in a Data Repository

Zhiwu Xie, Yinlin Chen, Julie Speer, and Tyler Walters
University Libraries
Virginia Polytechnic Institute and State University
Blacksburg, VA, USA
{zhiwuxie, ylchen, jspeer, tyler.walters}@vt.edu

ABSTRACT

In this paper, we utilize a set of controlled experiments to benchmark the cost associated with the cloud execution of typical repository functions such as ingestion, fixity checking, and heavy data processing. We focus on the repository service pattern where content is explicitly stored away from where it is processed. We measured the processing speed and unit cost of each scenario using a large sensor dataset and Amazon Web Services (AWS). The initial results reveal three distinct cost patterns: 1) spend more to buy up to proportionally faster services; 2) more money does not necessarily buy better performance; and 3) spend less, but faster. Further investigations into these performance and cost patterns will help repositories to form a more effective operation strategy.

Keywords

Institutional repository; Big data; Cloud computing; Cost analysis.

1. EXPERIMENT DESIGN

We designed three controlled experiments to execute typical repository tasks in AWS: 1) data ingestion, where File Information Tool Set (FITS) was used to characterize the data files and create associated metadata to the Fedora Objects to be ingested, 2) fixity checking, where new file digests were calculated from the ingested data then compared with their current digest values; and 3) heavy data processing, where multiple Fast Fourier Transformation (FFT) operations were performed against the ingested sensor data. To run these experiments we first installed a Fedora 4 based data repository using a m4.xlarge Elastic Compute Cloud (EC2) instance. This repository instance had a large EBS storage volume attached to it and all data deposited to the repository would be considered locally stored. The cost of this instance was not counted towards the execution costs. The data used for experiments were vibration signals collected from 214 accelerometers mounted in Virginia Tech's Goodwin Hall [1-4], an engineering building and a highly

instrumented smart infrastructure laboratory facility. The data were written into one-minute interval zlib-compressed chunked HDF5 files. The experiments made use of three full days of data collected from the accelerometers totaling approximately 223GB. Data was stored at a temporary holding area in a Simple Storage Service (S3) bucket. We then allocated n EC2 instances, either in

Permission to make digital or hard copies of part or all of this work for personal or classroom use is granted without fee provided that copies are not made or distributed for profit or commercial advantage and that copies bear this notice and the full citation on the first page. Copyrights for third-party components of this work must be honored. For all other uses, contact the Owner/Author.
Copyright is held by the owner/author(s).

JCDL '16, June 19–23, 2016, Newark, NJ, USA.
ACM 978-1-4503-4229-2/16/06.
http://dx.doi.org/10.1145/2910896.2925454

type t2.medium or m4.large, where $n=1, 2, ...9$, to perform the processing. The S3, EBS storages and EC2 nodes were provisioned from the AWS US East Region, such that data movements among them were fast and free of charge.

2. RESULTS AND ANALYSIS

2.1 Speedup

Figure 1 shows the speedup results of the three experiments. For the ingestion experiment, a linear speedup was consistently observed when using faster m4.large instances. This may be attributed to the vastly parallelizable workload. Because each execution is largely independent from the others in terms of resources needed, doubling the resources cuts the time in half. Situations were markedly different when using smaller, cheaper virtual instances. A superlinear speedup was on display when $n < 5$, then drifted to the linear or slightly sublinear region with larger n. Typically, superlinearity may be achieved when multiple resources can be interleaved. The ingestion process requires chaining three different types of resources: 1) the temporary storage at S3; 2) the processing node using EC2 instances; and 3) the repository node using EC2. Their interleaving is indeed a plausible cause, with the superlinearity slowly disappearing due to the interleaving benefits been sufficiently exploited. However, it is not clear why slower processing nodes can in turn achieve faster ingestion rates, as clearly illustrated when $n > 6$.

For the fixity checking experiments, close to linear speedup was observed at lower n for both faster and slower processing nodes, then hit a roof. This indicated a bottleneck was reached, possibly at the repository read/write speed limit, at around 400GB/hour. Faster machines tend to reach this bottleneck faster.

In the heavy data processing case, the bottleneck observed at the previous case is far from being reached, with highest processing speed less than 1/10 previously observed. This allows the expected linear speedup pattern to sustain all experiments, and faster machines yield a slightly faster speedup.

2.2 Cost

We calculate the unit cost by dividing the hourly rate of the aggregated processing instances by the processing speed. This is slightly different from the actual cost, since the Amazon charge rounds up the last partial hour into a full hour.

As shown in Figure 2, the speedup characteristics of the three different workload result in three drastically different cost patterns. The heavy data processing use case illustrates the expected pattern associated with linearity, where using more processing nodes can process data faster, but at the same or slightly higher unit cost. This pattern is further supplemented by the fixity checking use case, where the predicted cost pattern takes a sharp turn up when a bottleneck is reached. Beyond this point, investing in more resources becomes wasteful. The rather surprising cost pattern is illustrated by the ingestion example, where throwing in more resources to some extent can save money and get the work done faster at the same time. When the data volume grows higher, searching for this optimal combination will be of particular interest to repositories.

In all three sets of experiments, using cheaper, slower instances tends to be more cost effective than using the faster ones if processing speed is not a concern. In some use cases, more expensive instances may be required in order to achieve higher processing speed to match the rate of data generation or collection. More money, however, cannot buy arbitrarily high speed.

3. SUMMARY

This paper describes a few interesting performance and cost patterns encountered in leveraging cloud computing for repository operations. Although the use cases under investigation are representative, we caution too literal a reading into the results. The speed and unit cost numbers are indicative, but are also specific to our cases. However, the trends and patterns illustrated in these cases may be useful in repository cost and service planning.

4. ACKNOWLEDGMENTS

This research is partially supported by Amazon AWS Research Grants.

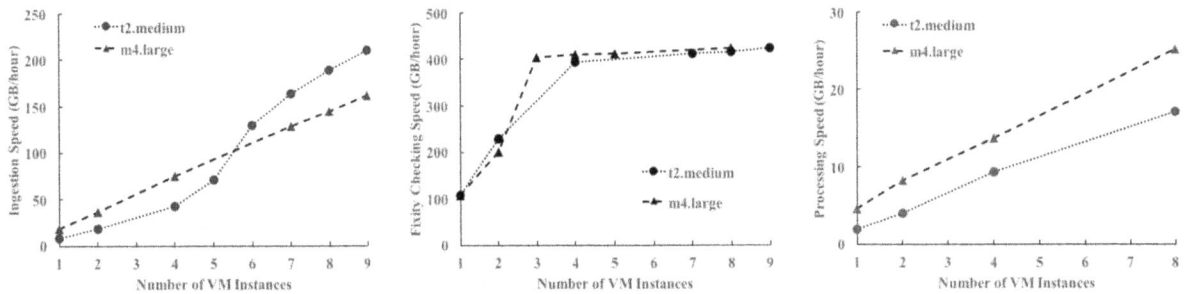

Figure 1. Speedup Using Multiple EC2 Instances.

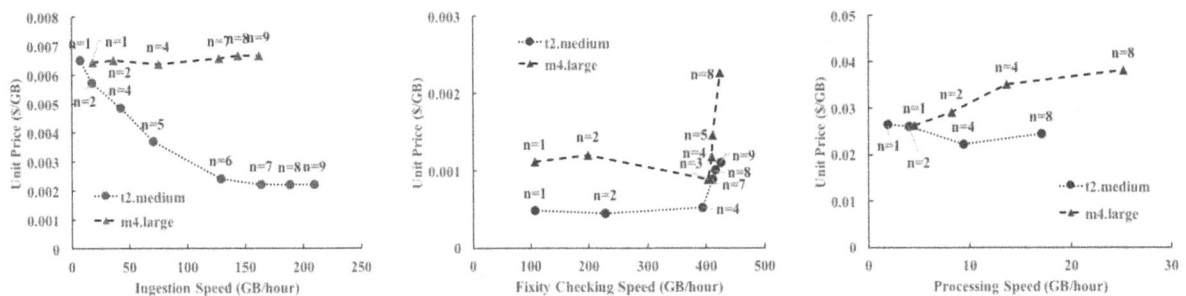

Figure 2. Unit Cost Using Multiple EC2 Instances.

5. REFERENCES

[1] Hamilton, J.M., Joyce, B.S., Kasarda, M.E. and Tarazaga, P.A. 2014. Characterization of Human Motion Through Floor Vibration. *Dynamics of Civil Structures, Volume 4*. F.N. Catbas, ed. Springer International Publishing. 163–170.

[2] Schloemann, J., Malladi, V.V.N.S., Woolard, A.G., Hamilton, J.M., Buehrer, R.M. and Tarazaga, P.A. 2015. Vibration Event Localization in an Instrumented Building. *Experimental Techniques, Rotating Machinery, and Acoustics, Volume 8*. J.D. Clerck, ed. Springer International Publishing. 265–271.

[3] Xie, Z., Chen, Y., Jiang, T., Speer, J., Walters, T., Tarazaga, P.A. and Kasarda, M. 2015. On-Demand Big Data Analysis in Digital Repositories: A Lightweight Approach. *Digital Libraries: Providing Quality Information*. R.B. Allen, J. Hunter, and M.L. Zeng, eds. Springer International Publishing. 274–277.

[4] Xie, Z., Chen, Y., Speer, J., Walters, T., Tarazaga, P.A. and Kasarda, M. 2015. Towards Use And Reuse Driven Big Data Management. *Proceedings of the 15th ACM/IEEE-CS Joint Conference on Digital Libraries* (New York, NY, USA, 2015), 65–74.

Games for Crowdsourcing Mobile Content:
An Analysis of Contribution Patterns

Dion Hoe-Lian Goh, Ei Pa Pa Pe-Than, Chei Sian Lee
Wee Kim Wee School of Communication and Information
Nanyang Technological University
{ashlgoh, ei1, leecs}@ntu.edu.sg

ABSTRACT

Crowdsourcing of mobile content through games is becoming a major way of populating information-rich online environments. A current research gap is that actual usage patterns of crowdsourcing games has been inadequately investigated. We address this gap by comparing content creation patterns in a game for crowdsourcing mobile content against a non-game version. Results show distinct differences in the types and distribution of content created.

Keywords

Crowdsourcing games; mobile content; content analysis.

1. INTRODUCTION

Crowdsourcing of mobile content has become a major way of populating information-rich online environments as well as an important source of big data. Typically, crowdsourcing systems employ volunteers or paid human experts. However, recruiting and retaining volunteers are challenging tasks since volunteerism is dependent on individuals' willingness to devote their time and effort to crowdsourcing projects. Paying for expertise is thus an alternative and has yielded positive outcomes, but this is potentially costly and is confined to those projects backed with adequate funding. Therefore, crowdsourcing projects need to consider alternative incentive mechanisms to widen their appeal.

Here, computer games are a possible means to attract participants for crowdsourcing projects due to the popularity of this entertainment medium. Consequently, games layered upon crowdsourcing tasks have emerged. Also known as human computation games or games with a purpose, players contribute their effort to a given endeavor through enjoyable gameplay [1]. As games for crowdsourcing mobile content gain traction, much research has emerged. Nevertheless, one gap present in prior work is that actual content creation patterns of crowdsourcing games have not been investigated adequately. We argue that understanding actual usage is essential in verifying the effectiveness of crowdsourcing games, as well as identifying the challenges that users face while using these applications.

We aim to address this research gap by fulfilling two objectives in the present study. First, we develop two crowdsourcing apps for mobile content creation: a game-based version that employs a virtual pet genre, and a non-game version.

Permission to make digital or hard copies of part or all of this work for personal or classroom use is granted without fee provided that copies are not made or distributed for profit or commercial advantage and that copies bear this notice and the full citation on the first page. Copyrights for third-party components of this work must be honored. For all other uses, contact the Owner/Author.
Copyright is held by the owner/author(s).

JCDL '16, June 19-23, 2016, Newark, NJ, USA
ACM 978-1-4503-4229-2/16/06.
http://dx.doi.org/10.1145/2910896.2925455

Second, we compare both apps to shed light on the types of content created by users.

2. APPLICATIONS DEVELOPED

The two mobile apps developed were: *Clash*, a competitive crowdsourcing game; and *Share*, a non-game version. We developed our own apps so that we had better control over the consistency of the interfaces and easy access to the contributed content. Both apps offer a map-based interface for creation of, and access to, content. Locations with content are indicated by map markers in the shape of houses (Figure 1a). Each house has a number of units, and each unit contains the crowdsourced content.

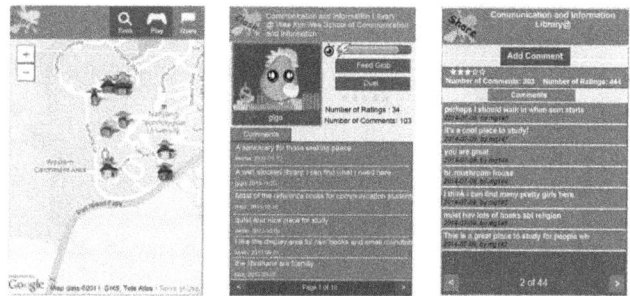

(a) Map-based interface.   (b) Pet's information in *Clash*.   (c) Comments in *Share*.

Figure 1. Screen shots of our mobile app.

Clash is a game in which players compete with others for pet ownership. Once a player has entered a house, a list of pets residing in each unit is presented. Selecting a pet will display information such as the name of the current owner (Figure 1b) and the crowdsourced comments associated with it. The player can challenge the current owner to a duel, and he/she will win the pet if the total sum of his/her strength and daily luck is greater than that of the challenged player The strength of each player is based on the quantity and recency of comments, and the number of ratings received from others. Thus, to win ownership of a pet in a duel, a player has to contribute location-based content.

Share is a non-game-based mobile app for crowdsourcing content that serves as a control. It does not have any game elements, and offers the basic features for contributing and accessing mobile content. A user accesses content by tapping on a mushroom house on the map, after which a list of units is presented. When a unit is selected, a list of comments associated with it is displayed (Figure 1c). From here, they can also create new comments.

3. METHODOLOGY

We recruited 160 participants (89 female) from two local universities. Their ages ranged from 21 to 46 years (M=23). Most were from computer science (47.8%), and engineering (38.8%). They used social network applications to share content via their mobile phones and the majority were game players. All participants used both apps in a counterbalanced design. They were required to use both on two different days, each spaced one day apart. Participants were told to use the application at any time where convenient to create and rate content, but the minimum usage was two half an hour sessions a day.

Content created was coded via an iterative procedure common in content analysis [3]. Content was classified based on categories derived from related earlier studies (e.g. [2]). Next, we inductively constructed new categories for those not-classifiable. Two coders were used, and the intercoder reliability using Cohen's kappa was found to be 0.841 for *Clash* and .927 for *Share*. The final set of 10 categories derived is shown in Table 1.

4. Results

In total, 3024 comments were contributed. Of these, 2059 were created using *Clash* and 964 were created using *Share*.

Table 1. Distribution of categories for contributed comments.

Category	Clash (N=2059)	Share (N=964)
Activities and events	187 (9.08%)	147 (15.25%)
App-related	462 (22.44%)	25 (2.59%)
Complaints and suggestions	81 (3.93%)	58 (6.02%)
Food	220 (10.68%)	101 (10.48%)
Humor	82 (3.98%)	53 (5.50%)
Places	449 (21.81%)	254 (26.35%)
Pleasantries	190 (9.23%)	84 (8.71%)
Queries	162 (7.87%)	97 (10.06%)
Spam	61 (2.96%)	17 (1.76%)
Status updates	165 (8.01%)	128 (13.28%)

The category showing the greatest difference between the two apps was "App-related", postings that were about the software or gameplay. In *Clash*, it formed the largest proportion of comments (22.44%). Examples include "*I just defeated the owner!*", and "*I have 2 fat pets now lol*". It appears that comments were used as a means to achieve *Clash's* objective of winning pets, and contained little informational value. For *Share*, the largest category of comments was "Places" (26.35%) and this was second for *Clash* (21.81%). Comments were descriptions of locations that participants found interesting or meaningful. Examples included recommending a park for taking photos ("*Yunnan Garden is a good place for a photoshoot*") and another suggesting a place to study in a university ("*Fantastic place to study or chill with friends during long breaks between lessons.*").

Categories which attracted 10% of comments or more, for at least one mobile app were: "Activities and events", "status updates", "food", and "queries". Next, categories that attracted less than 10% of contributions for either mobile app were "Pleasantries", "Complaints and suggestions", and "Humor". Finally, "Spam" was surprisingly the smallest category across both apps (2.96% for *Clash* and 1.76% for *Share*). This category refers to comments with meaningless words or irrelevant content. Such comments were used as a quick means to make contributions with little effort. Examples include terms such as "*fgfgfg*" or punctuation characters ("*?????*").

5. DISCUSSION AND CONCLUSION

Participants using *Clash* created more than double the amount of content than those using *Share*, suggesting that game-based approaches to crowdsourcing mobile content could better motivate contributions. Beyond quantity, there were also other notable differences in patterns of content created.

Although *Clash* produced more "App-related" content than *Share* which had little informational value, this may serve alternative purposes of entertainment through commentary or providing insights into other players. An outcome is that these contributions may draw and sustain interest in the game. In contrast, content creation was a solo activity in *Share*, and contributions did not garner any replies, signaling an absence of community.

Next, categories of crowdsourced contributions that conform more to the notion of location-based content being utilized as a means to learn about a specific place or for navigational purposes [4] include "Activities and events", "Complaints and suggestions", "Food", "Places", and "Queries". These categories constitute 53.35% of total content in *Clash* and 68.15% in *Share*. Contributions included what a particular location was about, what could be found there, what could be done, what was happening there, as well as an assessment or review of the location (e.g. "*... very crowded but offers a variety of food*").

A further comparison of the proportions of categories in Table 1 show that in most cases, *Share* had a larger percentage than *Clash*. This was due to the fact that for *Clash*, the "App-related" category was 18 times larger than *Share*. Further, the four location-based content categories (mentioned above) had a larger differential across apps than the other categories. Speculatively, we reason that to contribute meaningfully to these categories, participants had to be familiar with a particular location. Put differently, generating such content was more cognitively demanding, and because participants were tasked to win pets by competing against others, they turned to other content categories.

In conclusion, games can potentially attract participation in crowdsourcing tasks because of the enjoyment derived. However, the layering of a game changes users' behaviors as they respond to the excitement and challenge of accomplishing its objectives. Thus, developers of crowdsourcing games need to carefully strike a balance between entertaining game design and the production of useful contributions, since an over-emphasis in one may lead to a weakening of the other. However, our work has shortcomings that should be addressed. The first is that the profile of our participants were mostly from the engineering disciplines and were game players. Our study was also carried out within a short period of time in which all participants were new to the application. This may introduce novelty effects that could influence our findings.

Acknowledgments. This work was supported by MOE/Tier 1 grant RG64/14. The authors would also like to thank Wang Bin and Wang Chen for providing content analysis assistance.

6. REFERENCES

[1] Goh, D. H.-L. and Lee, C. S. 2011. Perceptions, quality and motivational needs in image tagging human computation games. *J. Inform. Sci.* 37, 5 (Oct. 2011), 515-531.

[2] Goh, D. H., Lee, C. S., and Low, G. H. 2012. I played games as there was nothing else to do: understanding motivations for using mobile content sharing games. *Online Inform Rev.* 36, 6 (Nov. 2012), 784-806.

[3] Neuendorf, K. A. 2002. *The content analysis guidebook*, Sage Publications, Thousand Oaks, CA.

[4] Yap, L.F., Bessho, M., and Sakamura, K. 2012. User-generated content for location-based services: a review. In *Virtual Communities, Social Networks and Collaboration*, A.A. Lazakidou, Ed. Annals of Information Systems. Springer, New York, NY, 163-179.

A Methodology to Evaluate Triple Confidence and Detect Incorrect Triples in Knowledge Bases

Haihua Xie

Institute of Computer Science & Technology, Peking University, Beijing, China
State Key Laboratory of Digital Publishing Technology (Peking University Founder Group Co. LTD.), Beijing, China
Postdoctoral Workstation of the Zhongguancun Haidian Science Park, Beijing, China
xiehh@founder.com.cn

Xiaoqing Lu and Zhi Tang
Institute of Computer Science & Technology
Peking University
Beijing, China, 100871
{lvxiaoqing, tangzhi}@pku.edu.cn

Mao Ye
Department of Knowledge Service Technology
Beijing Founder Apabi Technology Limited
Beijing, China, 100097
yemao.apb@founder.com.cn

ABSTRACT

The accuracy of the contents of a knowledge base determines the effectiveness of knowledge service applications, thus, it is necessary to evaluate the confidence of triples when a knowledge base is built. This study introduces a generic computational methodology to compute the confidence values of triples in knowledge bases and detect potentially incorrect ones for further verification. The major contributions of the proposed methodology are as follows: (1) A process to compute the confidence values of triples is designed; (2) New algorithms are proposed to adjust the term frequency and inverse document frequency values of each triple; (3) A method to build a support vector machine (SVM) classifier based on the selected triples used for incorrect triple detection is presented.

Keywords

Knowledge Base; Knowledge Service; Triple Confidence.

1. Introduction

Given the emergence of new technologies, digital libraries today are assuming the leadership in the new generation of knowledge management [1]. Among the many kinds of knowledge infrastructure, the knowledge base has received increasing attention. Triples are the key part of a knowledge base in many academic and industry applications. The accuracy of the contents of triples determines the effectiveness of knowledge service applications. In practice, information on building knowledge bases is extracted from various and miscellaneous data sources [2]. Errors in the source data or information extraction process may cause inaccurate contents in triples. Thus, the verification of triples is necessary once a knowledge base is built. However, the current verification methods are mostly based on manual checking of triples so they are often time-consuming and laborious.

Permission to make digital or hard copies of part or all of this work for personal or classroom use is granted without fee provided that copies are not made or distributed for profit or commercial advantage and that copies bear this notice and the full citation on the first page. Copyrights for third-party components of this work must be honored. For all other uses, contact the Owner/Author.
Copyright is held by the owner/author(s).

JCDL '16, June 19-23, 2016, Newark, NJ, USA
ACM 978-1-4503-4229-2/16/06.
http://dx.doi.org/10.1145/2910896.2925456

This study introduces a generic computational methodology to evaluate the confidence of triples in knowledge bases and detect potentially incorrect triples for further verification. We designed a process to compute the confidence values of triples and a way to build a support vector machine classifier for incorrect triple detection. Meanwhile, we conducted an experiment on data sets of industry applications to demonstrate how to apply our methodology in computation of triple confidence and detection of inaccurate triples.

2. Triple Confidence Computation

Triple confidence is the credibility of the relation between the Subject and Object in a triple. For example, the confidence of the triple <John, Supervisor, Michael> represents the dependability of the statement that John is the supervisor of Michael. The methodology introduced in this study tries to provide an appropriate value to assess the confidence of triples based on various data sources, and to detect potentially incorrect triples with low confidence for further verification.

The principle of our methodology is stated as follows: Based on a set of triples with relation R and a corpus with a large number of relevant sentences, appropriate statistical or machine learning techniques are used to extract feature words from sentences, which can characterize the relation R. Meanwhile, the weight of each feature word is calculated to evaluate the correlation of the word with the relation R. The confidence of each triple is then calculated based on the selected and weighted feature words. To achieve better detection results, cross-verification is applied in our methodology. That is, the dataset for feature words extraction and confidence evaluation is different from the data sources from which the triples are generated. Fig. 1 shows the process of triple confidence computation and incorrect triple detection in our methodology.

The critical steps in the process of calculating triple confidence are the selection of feature words and calculation of weight. Based on the idea of inverse document frequency (IDF) [3], the value of the weight for each word is calculated using the following formula:

$$\text{Weight}(w, R_i) = \text{TF}_{\text{Adj}}(w, R_i) * \prod_{k=1}^{m} \frac{1}{2^{\left(\frac{\text{TF}_{\text{Adj}}(w, R_k)}{\text{TF}_{\text{Adj,max}}(R_k)}\right)}} \quad (1)$$

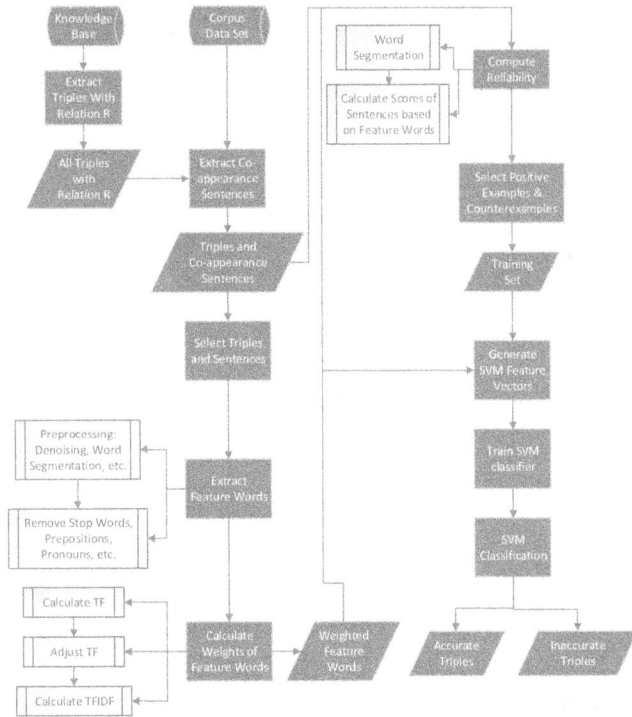

Fig 1. Process of Triple Confidence Computation

In Formula (1), $weight(w, R_i)$ is the weight of word w in relation R_i, and $TF_{Adj}(w, R_i)$ is the adjusted TF value of word w in relation R_i (see Equation (2)). $TF_{Adj,max}(R_k)$ is the maximum value of $TF_{Adj}(w_x, R_k)$ for all words w_x. m is the number of relations selected from the knowledge base to calculate the TFIDF value of word w in R_i. The adjusted TF value of each word is calculated using the following formula:

$$TF_{Adj}(w) = \frac{TF(w)}{\sqrt{Variance(w, T_0) + 1}} \qquad (2)$$

where $Variance(w, T_0)$ is the variance of the appearance frequency of word w in the triples in the triple set T_0.

After the weight value $Weight(w, R)$ is calculated for each word, the words with high weights are picked as the feature words for relation R. The number of feature words should be in the range of 100 to 200 based on our experience.

The set of selected feature words is denoted by W, and the number of feature words by num. The confidence of a triple Tr is calculated as follows:

$$Conf(Tr) = \frac{1}{SenNum(Tr)} \sum_{k=1}^{SenNum(Tr)} SenWeight(Sen_k, W) \quad (3)$$

where $Conf(Tr)$ is the confidence value of Tr, $SenNum(Tr)$ is the number of co-appearing sentences of Tr. A co-appearing sentence of Tr contains the subject and object of Tr. $SenWeight(Sen_k, W)$ is the accumulated weights of feature words contained in sentence Sen_k. A triple with higher confidence value is considered to be more reliable.

To build a SVM classifier for relation R, we choose the first n triples with highest confidence as the positive examples, and n triples with relation other than R as counterexamples. The SVM classifier is used to classify a triple set in the knowledge base O

and detect potentially incorrect triples by labeling them with "Incorrect".

Our experiment is conducted on two data sets of industrial applications, one of which is a knowledge base with 105,412 triples and 124 relations, and the other is an e-book library consists of 80,552 e-books of various types. A SVM classifier is developed based on the 400 triples and applied to classify 200 triples. Table 1 shows the experimental results of using different methods for calculating the weights of feature words.

Table 1. Results of Different Methods for Calculating the Weights of Feature Words

Weight of feature words	Accuracy%	Recall%	F Value
TF value	65%	64%	54%
Adjusted TF value	70%	74%	71%
IDF value of un-adjusted TF value	72%	73%	71%
IDF value of adjusted TF value	92.5%	93%	92.75%

3. Conclusion

This paper presents a methodology to computer triple confidence and detect incorrect triples in knowledge bases. The experiment conducted on data sets of industrial applications shows that the accuracy and recall rate of detecting incorrect triples are both high (> 90%) by using our methodology. The major limitation of our methodology is that the calculation of triple confidence values is only based on accumulated weights of feature words, and the attributes for building the SVM classifier are the scores of feature words contained in a triple.

We propose some future work to improve our methodology. First, our methodology should be applied in data sets of different languages to verify its validity in detecting incorrect triples. Second, more attributes should be considered to calculate the triple confidence value and build the SVM classifier, such as the syntax and semantics of sentences. Third, our methodology should be integrated into information extraction to improve both the accuracy rate and recall rates.

4. Acknowledgments

This work is supported by the projects of National Natural Science Foundation of China (No. 61472014 and No. 61573028), the Natural Science Foundation of Beijing (No. 4142023) and the Beijing Nova Program (XX2015B010). We also thank the anonymous reviewers for their valuable comments.

5. References

[1] Edward A. Fox. 2015. Introduction to Digital Libraries. In *Proceedings of the 15th ACM/IEEE-CS Joint Conference on Digital Libraries* (Knoxville, TN, June 21-24, 2015). JCDL '15. ACM New York, NY, USA, Pages 291-291. DOI = http://doi.acm.org/10.1145/2756406.2756927.

[2] Maximilian Nickel, Volker Tresp, Hans-Peter Kriegel. 2011. A Three-Way Model for Collective Learning on Multi-Relational Data. In *Proceedings of ICML*. DOI = 10.1.1.231.6909.

[3] H. C. Wu, R. W. P. Luk, K. F. Wong, K. L Kwok. 2008. Interpreting TF-IDF term weights as making relevance decisions. *ACM Transactions on Information Systems* 26 (3): 1. DOI = 10.1145/1361684.1361686.

Open Datasets for Evaluating the Interpretation of Bibliographic Records

Joffrey Decourselle
LIRIS, UMR5205
Université Lyon 1
Lyon, France
jdecours@liris.cnrs.fr

Fabien Duchateau
LIRIS, UMR5205
Université Lyon 1
Lyon, France
fduchate@liris.cnrs.fr

Trond Aalberg
NTNU
Trondheim, Norway
trondaal@idi.ntnu.no

Naimdjon Takhirov
Westerdals - Oslo School of Arts, Communication
and Technology - Faculty of Technology
Oslo, Norway
taknai@westerdals.no

Nicolas Lumineau
LIRIS, UMR5205
Université Lyon 1
Lyon, France
nluminea@liris.cnrs.fr

ABSTRACT

The transformation of legacy MARC catalogs to FRBR catalogs (FRBRization) is a complex and important challenge for libraries. Although many FRBRization tools have provided experimental validation, it is difficult to evaluate and compare these systems on a fair basis due to a lack of common datasets. This poster presents two public datasets (T42 and BIB-RCAT) intended to support the validation of the FRBRization process.

Categories and Subject Descriptors

H.3.7 [**Digital Libraries**]: Collection

Keywords

Migration, record interpretation, FRBRization, FRBR, dataset

1. INTRODUCTION

Libraries have traditionally relied on the MAchine Readable Cataloguing (MARC) format, available in different implementations such as MARC21 or UNIMARC, for the recording and exchange of bibliographic data. The semantics of MARC formats reflect the old-fashioned card catalogue which has obvious limitations and new models, such as the Functional Requirements for Bibliographic Records (FRBR) and its updated version Library Reference Model[1] (LRM), have been developed to provide library systems with a more sound and explicit information model for the next generation of library systems [2].

A major obstacle to the adoption of new models is the migration from the legacy MARC formats and the interpretation and transformation of existing data into the new models (e.g., FRBRization). In the last decade, many tools have been proposed to tackle this challenge [ ], but it is very complicated to compare tools: the experiments which are described in the papers are rarely reproducible, mainly because the datasets are not publicly available. A few catalog excerpts are provided, but they do not reflect the reality and the challenges of library catalogs because they are mainly used for illustrating specific cases [ ].

In this poster, we present two datasets (T42 and BIB-RCAT) for evaluating the FRBRization process. The goal of the first dataset is to identify the weak and strong points of a tool by testing all possible issues that libraries may face during FRBRization. The second dataset BIB-RCAT is extracted from catalogs of different cultural institutions and can be used for comparing or experimenting with the data quality that is typically found in real world catalogs. The datasets, released under a CC BY-NC licence[2], are available online at http://bib-r.github.io/.

2. DESCRIPTION OF THE DATASETS

In our context, a dataset is a set of collections. Each collection, which contains records, is available in two input formats (MARC21 and UNIMARC) and it is associated with an expert FRBR collection (gold standard). This expert collection has been manually created and verified by a librarian and three digital library researchers. The records have been extracted from real-world catalogs, and modified when needed to reflect bibliographic patterns and cataloging issues found in libraries.

2.1 Bibliographic patterns and issues

In bibliographic data there is a large diversity in the structure of entities and relationships needed to describe each item, but we can identify a set of patterns. Unfortunately, these patterns are often difficult to detect and FRBRize correctly [,]. The most frequent and thus **core pattern** includes a Work, an Expression, a Manifestation and (mostly) the Agent creator of the Work. Its FRBRization is relatively easy, unless the pattern is associated with cataloging

---

[1] http://library.ifla.org/1084/

Permission to make digital or hard copies of part or all of this work for personal or classroom use is granted without fee provided that copies are not made or distributed for profit or commercial advantage and that copies bear this notice and the full citation on the first page. Copyrights for third-party components of this work must be honored. For all other uses, contact the owner/author(s).

JCDL '16 June 19-23, 2016, Newark, NJ, USA

© 2016 Copyright held by the owner/author(s).

ACM ISBN 978-1-4503-4229-2/16/06.

DOI: http://dx.doi.org/10.1145/2910896.2925457

[2] https://creativecommons.org/licenses/

issues. The **augmentation pattern** is defined as an additional content to an existing Work, with the assumption that the new content does not alter the main Work (e.g., illustrations, forewords). Several scenarios occur to FRBRize this pattern, for instance the creation of a new Work or a note for the original Work. The **derivation pattern** means that one Work is the modification of another Work (e.g., translations, imitations), and it usually implies the creation of Expression(s) under the same Work or relationships between Works. The **aggregation pattern** is commonly described as a whole-parts relationship (e.g., ensemble, aggregative work). The FRBRization of aggregations mainly results in the creation of relationships between Works (and "super-Works") and optionally new Agents. The **complementary works pattern** aims at modelling a relationship with Works which have the same importance (e.g., sequels, accompanying works). Its FRBRization mainly results in the creation of relationships between Works.

In addition to bibliographic patterns, records may include cataloging errors. Authors of the TelPlus project have established six requirements for FRBRization [ ], that can be seen as errors in the initial records. They deal with **missing information**, namely record identifier, publication date, uniform title, original title, relator code and authoritative responsibility. These errors make it more difficult to FRBRize a record, for instance to discover the correct type of relationships between entities. We propose four new errors that can be found in catalogs. The **missing type and form of material** issue has an impact for correctly identifying Expressions (and sometimes Works). In UNIMARC, we can find **linkage error in title** and **linkage error in responsibility**, which means that the unavailable related record has a negative impact in terms of completeness when FRBRizing. Finally, libraries make use of standards such as the International Standard Bibliographic Description (ISBD), widespread normalization of values (e.g., country codes) or codes specific to individual libraries (e.g., for a book category, value "r" corresponds to a roman). These inconsistent **cataloging practices and norms** usually require human intervention to indicate how to process such fields.

2.2 Dataset T42

All records have an inherent bibliographic pattern (e.g., core, augmentation) and they may include any number of cataloging issues (e.g., missing relator code, title linkage error). The objective of the dataset T42 is to check whether a FRBRization tool is able to handle each possible case. We define a unit test as the combination of a pattern and an optional cataloging issue. Note that we do not include tests with more than one issue, since it would complicate the analysis of the results. We have ensured that the FRBRization is still possible when the issue deals with specific missing information. The dataset contains 42 meaningful unit tests which are crucial for testing specific aspects of FRBRization. For instance the *test 1.0* contains records with the core pattern and without issue, the *test 1.5* combines the core pattern with the missing uniform title issue and the *test 3.8* includes a derivation pattern and a missing relator code issue. The complete list of combinations is available online. Table 1 provides global statistics for the dataset T42 (second column). For example, this dataset includes records in three languages (English, French, German) and eight media types (e.g., books, movies, articles, audio).

Feature	T42	BIB-RCAT
Number of unit tests	42	-
Number of collections	126	3
Number of languages	3	1
Number of media types	8	4
Average (MARC) records	10/test	560
Average fields / record	18	17
Average (FRBR) entities	73/test	1922
Average (FRBR) properties	241/test	9517

Table 1: Statistics for datasets T42 and BIB-RCAT

2.3 Dataset BIB-RCAT

The BIB-RCAT dataset simulates real-world catalogs in which various bibliographic patterns and issues may be found. It contains three collections (MARC21 and UNIMARC formats, and the expert FRBR). It is mainly composed of records from various catalogs (e.g., a public French library). The size of this catalog (560 records) is smaller than the usual catalog in a library, since the expert FRBR collection requires a time-consuming effort to be manually produced and verified. Table 1 provides global statistics for the dataset BIB-RCAT (third column). For instance, the expert FRBR collection contains 1922 entities and 9517 properties.

3. CONCLUSION

In this poster, we present two datasets T42 and BIB-RCAT for evaluating the interpretation of bibliographic records. The first dataset enables to check how a tool performs when facing a specific bibliographic pattern or cataloging issue, while the second dataset reflects the data quality found in libraries. A perspective to this work deals with the definition of new metrics to evaluate the FRBRization process.

4. ACKNOWLEDGMENTS

This work has been partially supported by the French Agency ANRT (www.anrt.asso.fr), the company PROGILONE (www.progilone.com/), a PHC Aurora funding (#34047VH) and a CNRS PICS funding (#PICS06945).

5. REFERENCES

[1] T. Aalberg and M. Žumer. The Value of MARC Data, or, Challenges of FRBRisation. *Journal of Documentation*, 69:851–872, 2013.

[2] K. Coyle. FRBR, Twenty Years On. *Cataloging & Classification Quarterly*, pages 1–21, 2014.

[3] J. Decourselle, F. Duchateau, and N. Lumineau. A Survey of FRBRization Techniques. In *Theory and Practice of Digital Libraries*, pages 185–196, 2015.

[4] H. M. A. Manguinhas, N. M. A. Freire, and J. L. B. Borbinha. FRBRization of MARC Records in Multiple Catalogs. In *JCDL*, pages 225–234. ACM, 2010.

[5] P. Riva. Mapping MARC 21 Linking Entry Fields to FRBR and Tilletts Taxonomy of Bibliographic Relationships. *Library resources & technical services*, 48(2):130–143, 2013.

An Example of Automatic Authority Control

Anna Knyazeva
Institute of Computational
Technologies SB RAS,
Tomsk Polytechnic University
Tomsk, Russian Federation
aknjazeva@ict.nsc.ru

Oleg Kolobov
Institute of High Current
Electronics SB RAS
Tomsk, Russian Federation
okolobov@gmail.com

Igor Turchanovsky
Institute of Computational
Technologies SB RAS,
Tomsk Polytechnic University
Tomsk, Russian Federation
tur@hcei.tsc.ru

ABSTRACT

The automatic authority control problem is considered. One possible solution is to use the record linkage approach for authority and bibliographic records. The main aim of this paper is to figure out which concepts and methods are most useful for dealing with our data. An approach based on machine learning method (classification) is considered. A comparative study of different distances and feature sets is made. A study carried out on data of several Russian libraries. The data we deal with are in RUSMARC format which is a variant of UNIMARC popular in Russia.

CCS Concepts

•**Information systems** → **Entity resolution;** Deduplication; •**Computing methodologies** → *Classification and regression trees;* •**Applied computing** → *Digital libraries and archives; Document metadata;*

Keywords

Record Linkage; Name Disambiguation; Measuring Distances; Authority Records; Bibliographic Records

1. INTRODUCTION

The paper considers the implementation of record linkage methods to creating an automatic authority control technology for Russian libraries. Such technology allows to identify a real world object in bibliographic records by linking them with an authority records.

We have deal with data of several small Russian catalogs (bibliography and authority databases). In total we have about 300 000 bibliographic records and about 10 000 authority records. All records were translated to format RUSMARC. RUSMARC is a Russian bibliographic format based on UNIMARC. RUSMARC is a highly structured format of data. It contains strict instructions for every record field. But sometimes inaccurate or automatic creation of records leads to errors in filling the fields.

Permission to make digital or hard copies of part or all of this work for personal or classroom use is granted without fee provided that copies are not made or distributed for profit or commercial advantage and that copies bear this notice and the full citation on the first page. Copyrights for third-party components of this work must be honored. For all other uses, contact the owner/author(s).

JCDL '16 June 19-23, 2016, Newark, NJ, USA

© 2016 Copyright held by the owner/author(s).

ACM ISBN 978-1-4503-4229-2/16/06.

DOI: http://dx.doi.org/10.1145/2910896.2925458

2. RELATED WORK

The problem of automatic authority control has similarities with a more general class of problems known as record linkage [3], author name disambiguation [8], entity uncertainty [6], citation matching [5], duplicate detection [2] etc. Our approach combines a methods proposed in projects VIAF [1] and MARLIN [2].

The VIAF project (Virtual International Authority File) concerns of a duplicate detection problem. It aims to link two authority record if they describe the same person. Our approach has to deal with records of two types. The bibliographic records usually contain significantly less direct information of person, than the authority records. We use an Extended Authority Records for accounting indirect information about persons in the same way as VIAF. The only difference is that we had used dynamical Extended Authority Records existing only during the comparison process. The method proposed by VIAF developers is based on empirical analysis of authority records and choice of appropriate weight for every comparison feature. This requires a huge manual work.

Availability of labeled duplicates allows an approach that uses a binary classifier which computes a similarity function [2]. Given two databases containing records, that could be compared by k different fields, we can represent any pair of records by k-dimensional vector. Each component of the vector contains similarity between two field values computed using one of the similarity functions. A binary classifier is then trained on such supervision to discriminate between pairs of records corresponding to coreferent and non-coreferent pairs. There are a lot of different variants for the decision function creation: Bayesian classifiers [9], decision trees [3], Support Vector Machine [2] etc. In our work, we used the nearest centroid classifier with different distances in order to determine the most appropriate distance for our data.

3. OUR APPROACH DESCRIPTION

In this work we used the popular algorithm of record linkage consisting of four steps.

First step, *normalization* means for us a validation of records against requirements of format RUSMARC.

For a second step, *blocking* we use the popular method "the same initial of the first name and the same last name (iFfL)" [4] but add initial of other name because of its popularity in Russian.

For a *comparison on field-level* step we use three methods: strict matching of strings, fuzzy matching on base of Porter's stemming algorithm [7] for Russian and matching of dates. The Porter's stemming algorithm (Snowball) was chosen because it works well with different word endings so popular in Russian. During the comparison of dates we should parse a field values to determine birth date and (optionaly) death date. It is not a complicated task because the form of date is stabe enough in our records. We take into account only years, not full dates, in accordance with the VIAF's recommendation [1].

Sometimes field could contain more than one value (for example, subject terms). We use two methods to compare these fields. An indicator shows a presence or absence of the matching fields, and a ratio between the number of matchings and the number of field values in bibliographic record (not authority record).

We calculate Kendall rank correlation coefficient between every used feature and a resulting variable. So we can choose only statistically significant features.

The last step is a *decision* making on the base of the information from previous step. In this step we analyse a vectors of comparison feature values and make a decision about matching on the record-level. We use a learning set of record pairs in our work. We determine a centroids of two classes (coreferent and non-coreferent) and train a classifier to distinguish between these classes. In this work we consider five distances: Euclidean, Maximum, Manhattan, Canberra and Mahalanobis.

4. EXPERIMENTAL RESULTS

We evaluated the performance of our methods for field-level comparison and decision functions using three metrics: precision, recall and F1-measure. Firstly we created a dataset of pairs with known status (coreferent or non-coreferent). Then dataset was randomly splintered into learning and testing folds for cross-validation during each experimental run (we used 1000 runs).

The first aim of our experiments was to investigate the differences between an indicators and ratios for multivalued fields. The ratios showed better results on our data. So we are planning to use them in future work.

The second aim was to choose the best distance for classification. The best results for our data were shown by Mahalanobis distance. It is not surprising, Mahalanobis distance allows us to take into account the correlation between using features. As we try to involve more information, our features are significantly interdependent. At the same time, this distance requires using a set of not too interdependent features.

The concept of Extended Authority Records is only method to use an additional information about person (for instance, subject terms). But we detected that using of such records improves comparison results also for basic information which is in presence in authority records.

The best our result over different feature sets and distances is equal: *precision*=0.994, *recall*=0.99 and *F1*=0.992. We need to clarify a very high level of these measures. Our experiments were conducted on subset of our data which contains only records created under authority control. Such approach simplified our work because we did not need a manually review during a construction of learning and testing sets. Conversely it leads to work with data which is easy to disambiguate because of more high quality of them. We are planning to manually create more difficult testing sets on our data later.

5. CONCLUSIONS

The automatic authority control problem is considered. The problem is common in the situation of merging data from several libraries. In such case a great number of fuzzy duplicates among authority and bibliography records appear and many links between records are lost.

The approach used is based on machine learning method (nearest centroid classifier). Five distance measures are considered: Euclidean, Maximum, Manhattan, Canberra and Mahalanobis. The best results is reached with Mahalanobis distance. It allows us to take into account the correlations of the data set.

The concept of dynamical Enhanced Authority Records is used. This concept allows to increase the amount of bibliographic records which we can deal with from 20% to 77% of our bibliographic database. The reason is that indirect information about person is more often available in bibliographic records.

This paper describes work in progress. We wish to consider other blocking methods and classifiers in order to figure out which concepts and methods of the record linkage are most useful for our data. We need more learning and testing sets also. It is important to check out all conclusions on base records which were created without authority control.

6. ACKNOWLEDGMENTS

The reported study was funded by RFBR according to the research project No. 16-37-00070 мол_а.

7. REFERENCES

[1] R. Bennett, C. Hengel-Dittrich, E. T. O'Neill, and B. B. Tillett. Viaf (virtual international authority file): Linking die deutsche bibliothek and library of congress name authority files, 2006.

[2] M. Bilenko. *Learnable Similarity Functions and Their Application to Record Linkage and Clustering*. PhD thesis, Department of Computer Sciences, University of Texas at Austin, Austin, TX, August 2006.

[3] M. Elfeky, V. Verykios, and A. Elmagarmid. TAILOR: a record linkage toolbox. In *Proceedings 18th International Conference on Data Engineering*. IEEE Comput. Soc, 2002.

[4] B.-W. On, D. Lee, J. Kang, and P. Mitra. Comparative study of name disambiguation problem using a scalable blocking-based framework. In *Iternational Conference on Digital Libraries*, pages 344–353. ACM, 2005.

[5] H. Pasula, B. Marthi, B. Milch, S. Russell, and I. Shpitser. Identity uncertainty and citation matching. In *In NIPS*. MIT Press, 2003.

[6] D. A. Pereira, E. E. B. da Silva, and A. A. A. Esmin. Disambiguating publication venue titles using association rules. In *IEEE/ACM Joint Conference on Digital Libraries*. IEEE, sep 2014.

[7] M. Porter. An algorithm for suffix stripping. *Program*, 14(3):130–137, 1980.

[8] A. F. Santana, M. A. Goncalves, A. H. F. Laender, and A. Ferreira. Combining domain-specific heuristics for author name disambiguation. In *IEEE/ACM Joint Conference on Digital Libraries*. IEEE, sep 2014.

[9] W. E. Winkler. Overview of record linkage and current research directions. Technical report, Bureau of the census, 2006.

User Activity Characterization in a Cultural Heritage Digital Library System

Cyrille Suire
cyrille.suire@univ-lr.fr

Axel Jean-Caurant
ajeanc01@univ-lr.fr

Vincent Courboulay
vcourbou@univ-lr.fr

Jean-Christophe Burie
jcburie@univ-lr.fr

Pascal Estraillier
pestrail@univ-lr.fr

L3i laboratory, University of La Rochelle
La Rochelle, France

ABSTRACT

Digital access to large amount of heterogeneous data can create methodological biases regarding the discovery and exploitation of resources, particularly when it comes to Social Sciences. In order to provide relevant adaptivity for social scientists, it is important to fully consider their research practice diversity. To do so, we consider an activity-based approach for researchers' information search behavior. We have also conducted an experiment in a Cultural Heritage use case. The main result shows us that social scientists have the same research behaviors as those observed in exact Sciences.

Categories and Subject Descriptors

H.3.7 [**Information Storage and Retrieval**]: Digital libraries

Keywords

Information Seeking; User Modeling; User Behavior; Cultural Heritage; Task Models; Humanities

1. CONTEXT AND MOTIVATION

Social scientists and humanists have an increasing number of web platforms to access heterogeneous resources. The new challenge for researchers is the discovery and exploitation of these data. The tools commonly used to access this huge amount of data can create methodological problems [5]. Moreover, we know that the practices of social scientists are very diverse [3]. They need to be analyzed and understood to avoid most methodological issues. To investigate this, we present an activity-based approach. Following Marchionini's conceptual framework [4], users' research activities can be distinguished in two main groups: **lookup tasks** and **exploratory search tasks**. A recent paper by Athukorala

Permission to make digital or hard copies of part or all of this work for personal or classroom use is granted without fee provided that copies are not made or distributed for profit or commercial advantage and that copies bear this notice and the full citation on the first page. Copyrights for third-party components of this work must be honored. For all other uses, contact the owner/author(s).

JCDL '16 June 19-23, 2016, Newark, NJ, USA

© 2016 Copyright held by the owner/author(s).

ACM ISBN 978-1-4503-4229-2/16/06.

DOI: http://dx.doi.org/10.1145/2910896.2925459

et. al. [2] has shown that it is possible to distinguish the type of task the users are engaged in, when they are using a *scientific search engine*. The purpose of our work is to determine if this stands in another context — using a *digital library platform* and experimenting with a different type of public.

2. HYPOTHESE

As proposal, we want to prove that user behavior evaluation based on activity type is valid even if several points of our approach differ from [2]. Indeed, our system is significantly different and is built around the following considerations: its design and implementation is closer to a digital library web portal than a search engine like Google Scholar. Considering the work of [1] this kind of systems requires a specific evaluation. We implemented precise observers in our system to log users' behavior and compute features in two different ways. First, we focus on the first query iteration. A query is composed of every user events from the first input in the search field to the next one or to the end of the task. Then we focus on the overall task by averaging the values of each feature over all queries from the task.

- *Query Length (f_1):* this feature is defined as the number of terms in the query.
- *Duration (f_2):* duration in seconds.
- *Maximum scroll value (f_3):* This corresponds to the proportion of the page seen by the user. It reflects the number of items observable in the result list.
- *Number of clicked items (f_4):* how many resources were clicked on in the results page. That corresponds to an access to more precise metadata.
- *Position of those items in the result list (f_5):* this is a mean of the position of the items selected by the user inside the search engine results page.
- *Number of viewed documents (f_6):* how many original documents were actually opened by the user.
- *Duration dwelling (f_7):* time the user spent investigating documents outside the results page (in seconds).

3. EXPERIMENT

We conducted a first experiment with forty master students who are a the beginning of their specialization in the Cultural Heritage field of study. They have a medium level of topic knowledge and are able to adapt their behavior to the task type. Our experimental corpus must be precise enough to allow participants to perform realistic tasks. It contains 240 documents related to the Cultural Heritage field of study which the students are relatively familiar with. The resources of the corpus are heterogeneous: general works, scientific articles, iconographic documents, multimedia resources and even primary documents.

To carry out our experiment, we chose to make the students perform tasks in each Marchionini's overall category [4]. These tasks were designed by a specialist of the Cultural Heritage field of study. We defined the tasks such as follows.
Lookup category: Tasks T_1 and T_2 referred to the *fact retrieval* subcategory. For these two first tasks we suggested two straightforward questions. Participants had to find the date of a particular event and where an event took place. The search goal was simple and participants were able to decide when they had found the correct information. During the third task (T_3), students had to retrieve a precise document using given information. This task belongs to the *known item search* subcategory.
Exploratory category: We have identified one task for Marchionini's *learn and investigate* group referring in particular to the *knowledge acquisition* and *accretion* low level subcategories. The exploratory task (T_4) is an important and regular work for Humanities researchers and students. Participants had to identify and write a research problem on the Cultural Heritage topic in one of its aspect covered by our data set.

At the beginning of our experiment, all the participants received a fifteen minutes training on the use of our experimental platform. In order to control technical factors that could affect user behavior, all participants did the experiment under the same conditions. They used the same web browser connected to our experimental platform on a desktop computer and a 22-inch display. We gave participants the same instructions concerning the four required tasks. Users had to select the type of task inside a list and click on the start button to begin each task. At the end of the task, users had to click on the end button and provide the answers and results required by the current task.

4. RESULTS AND DISCUSSION

For the four tasks, features were computed regarding the first query iteration (f_n) and the entire task (f'_n). Because the raw data does not follow a normal distribution, we used non parametric methods. We performed a Friedman test on each feature, followed by a pairwise Wilcoxon signed rank test to evaluate the differences between two different tasks. Our results are consistent with the analysis made by [2]. Indeed, most of the features are fundamentally different when it comes to exploratory tasks. However, we find ourselves in a different context than the study led by Athukorala. Our system is a digital library storing not only scientific articles but more heterogeneous resources. Conducting the experiment with a different public — participants coming from social sciences and Humanities — leads us to the same results as Athukorala who took an interest in Computer Science researchers. Yet, these two types of researchers have very different habits in terms of information search.

Going further than the confirmation of previous results, we made the following additional observations. We can observe that some of the features presented in Table 1, computed on the first query and the overall task behave similarly. Identifying the type of task the user is engaged in as

		first query (f)			overall task (f')		
			T4			T4	
		T1	T2	T3	T1	T2	T3
			query length				
	p	***	***	***	*	***	***
	Z	-4.28	-3.33	-4.16	-2.56	-4.05	-4.08
			duration				
	p	0.1	***	***	***	***	***
	Z	1.61	-3.75	-3.78	-4.33	-4.55	-4.53
			max scroll value				
	p	0.06	**	**	**	0.18	*
	Z	-1.87	-2.97	-3.74	-2.64	-1.34	-2.09
			clicked items position				
	p	*	*	0.05	***	***	***
	Z	-2.25	-2.31	-1.96	-3.39	-3.92	-3.51

Table 1: **Statistical differences between an Exploratory task (T4) and three different Look-up tasks (T1, T2 and T3). The left-hand side of this table describe the results during the first query iteration, while the right-hand side concerns the overall task. We use a Wilcoxon signed rank test.** *p***-values with ***s are statistically significant, with * for** $p < 0.05$**, ** for** $p < 0.01$ **and *** for** $p < 0.001$**.**

early as possible is key to the system adaptation. To discriminate user's task as soon as possible, features f_1, f_2, f_3 and f_5 are significant. When looking at the results in Table 1, it seems that T_1 behave differently than T_2 and T_3 when compared to T_4. This is particularly true for f_2, f_3, f_6 and f_7, in the case of the first query iteration. We made another statistical test comparing T_1 and T_2 that confirmed this observation. It seems that when users discover the platform for the first time, some features are clearly impacted. This could be used to evaluate how difficult it is to get familiar with the platform and should be taken into account to efficiently contextualize user behavior traces.

5. REFERENCES

[1] M. Agosti, F. Crivellari, G. M. D. Nunzio, and S. Gabrielli. Understanding user requirements and preferences for a digital library Web portal. *Int J Digit Libr*, 11(4):225–238, Sept. 2011.

[2] K. Athukorala, D. Glowacka, G. Jacucci, A. Oulasvirta, and J. Vreeken. Is exploratory search different? A comparison of information search behavior for exploratory and lookup tasks. *J. Assoc. Inf. Sci. Technol.*, 2015.

[3] N. Audenaert and R. Furuta. What Humanists Want: How Scholars Use Source Materials. In *Proc. of the 10th JCDL*, pages 283–292, NY, USA, 2010. ACM.

[4] G. Marchionini. Exploratory Search: From Finding to Understanding. *Commun. ACM*, 49(4):41–46, 2006.

[5] I. Milligan. Illusionary Order: Online Databases, Optical Character Recognition, and Canadian History, 1997-2010. *The Canadian Historical Review*, 94(4):540–569, 2013.

A Mathematical Information Retrieval System Based on RankBoost

Ke Yuan, Liangcai Gao, Yuehan Wang, Xiaohan Yi, Zhi Tang
ICST, Peking University, Beijing, China
{yuanke,glc,wangyuehan,chlxyd,tangzhi}@pku.edu.cn

ABSTRACT

Mathematical Information Retrieval (MIR) systems are designed to help users to find related formulae and further understand the formulae in scientific documents. However, in existing MIR systems, nearly all the ranker models of MIR systems are based on tf-idf model, and few efforts have been made to discover the features besides the relevance between the query formula and related formulae. In this paper, we investigate a supervised ranking approach (RankBoost) in an MIR system, and we consider not only the relevance between a query formula and related formulae, but also the features of the query formula itself and plentiful features about the documents where the related formulae appear. Experimental results show that our system achieves better performance by comparing with state-of-the-art MIR systems.

Keywords

Mathematical Information Retrieval; Learning to rank; RankBoost

1. INTRODUCTION

As an important part of scientific documents, mathematical formulae are usually used to express the theoretical foundation of these scientific documents. It is not easy for researchers or students them to comprehend the unfamiliar formulae while reading scientific documents. Therefore, a formula based search engine is expected to help them to find some related formulae resources and further help to understand the formulae.

Mathematical Information Retrieval(MIR) systems are formula based search engine, and they are sprouting up since the definition of MIR first proposed. Nearly all ranking models of existing MIR systems are based on tf-idf model, however, tf-idf model cannot consider the structure features of formula. For example, in formula e^2 and e_2, the structure feature between e and 2 are different. Therefore, the designing of ranking models in MIR systems is still an open problem [1].

In this paper, we propose an upgraded MIR system based on WikiMirs3.0[3]. Compared with WikiMirs3.0, we employ a supervised learning to ranking model (RankBoost) as the ranker of the MIR system in order to integrate vast features of formulae and their corresponding documents. Most MIR systems just consider the relevance between query formula and related formulae, but consider few features about documents which contain the related formulae. In this paper, we consider not only the relevance, but also plentiful document features and the features of formulae themselves.

Permission to make digital or hard copies of part or all of this work for personal or classroom use is granted without fee provided that copies are not made or distributed for profit or commercial advantage and that copies bear this notice and the full citation on the first page. Copyrights for third-party components of this work must be honored. For all other uses, contact the Owner/Author.
Copyright is held by the owner/author(s).

JCDL '16, June 19-23, 2016, Newark, NJ, USA
ACM 978-1-4503-4229-2/16/06.
http://dx.doi.org/10.1145/2910896.2925460

2. Proposed System

2.1 Overview

The framework of the proposed system is illustrated in Figure 1. The dotted lines represent the offline workflows. Black dotted lines indicate the process of building the index file. Green dotted lines denote the learning to rank model training process. In the index building process, the relevance of formula and document together with features of documents are all extracted by feature extractor 0 (FE0), and then the formulae are parsed into terms by tokenizer. Afterwards, feature extractor 1 (FE1) extracts the structural features of formulae from the term candidate set. Lastly, the indexer stores the terms and features into an index file which will be used in the online workflow. In the training process, the training data is used to train a (local) ranking model. The learning system trains a ranking model which can assign a score to a given feature vector x.

The red solid line denotes the online workflow, namely the searching process. First users input the query by the interface, and then the query formula is parsed into terms by the tokenizer. Afterwards, documents which contain the terms of the query are collected from the index file which is built in the offline workflow. After that the features of the retrieved documents and query formula are extracted by feature extractor 2 (FE2), and then the retrieved documents are sorted via the ranking model. This paper mainly discusses how to build the ranker and the interface, tokenizer and indexer of proposed system are described in previous work [1,2].

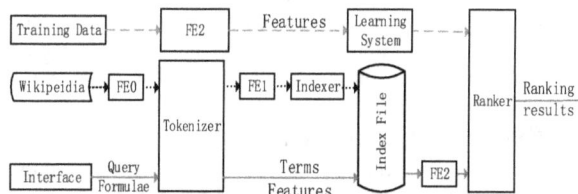

Figure 1. Framework of proposed system

2.2 Ranker of Proposed System

Ranker, as one of the most important module in an MIR system directly determines the ranking results. In this paper, we recall the related documents by the similarity between formula and related documents, and then use learning algorithms to rank the related documents. Although, listwise learning to rank algorithms perform better than pairwise learning to rank algorithms in many scenarios, listwise algorithms are ineffectively if the features of training data are sparseness. However, the features about formula are sparse. Due to the sparseness of formula features. This paper use RankBoost [3] as the ranking algorithm which is a representative pairwise learning to rank model.

In this section, we also explore the particular features of the MIR ranking task. All features we investigated, can be grouped into three categories, containing 255 dimension features as following. Each feature is normalized by the sum of all its values.

Formula-based Features: The semantic and structural information of query formulae are important features to help the final ranking. Moreover, we get the features of formulae in the corpus, because there may be higher probability for popular formulae to be searched.

Variable & constant: The number of variables and respective constant in the query formula.

Two-dimensional relation: The layer number of the semi-operator tree which is used to represent the structural information of formula. The semi-operator tree of formula is described in literature [1,2].

Frequency of the term: The frequency of the term in the inverted formula file.

Relevance-based Features: The relevance of query formula and the retrieved documents is the similarity between them. In order to evaluate it, we extract terms from the semi-operator tree which is used to represent formula, and then use several metrics to calculate the relevance. The computing methods below are detailed described in literature [1,2].

Frequency of the term occurring in a formula: The frequency of the query formula term occurring in a formula.

Formulae Level Distance: The distance of the matched terms on different levels between the query formulae and the related formulae in documents.

The match ratio between query and the formula: It is the matching score which is calculated by the total number of the terms in the query and a formula.

Independent score: The score which represents the similarity between the query and a single formula.

Comprehensive score: The score which is calculated by the similarity between a query and a document.

Document-based Features: Users who are searching formulae in MIR system may be interested in the articles which not only include the related formulae, but also the related formulae applied in the similar application scenarios. Therefore, features of document are useful to help ranker sort the retrieved documents.

Formula importance value: The importance of formula in a document.

Link number: Number of inlinks and outlinks in the document. We hypothesize that the stronger the association between a document and other documents, the more important of the document. The intensity of association can be reflected from link number.

3. Experiments and Evaluation

The proposed system uses the 2014-07-30 dump of Wikipedia as the corpus and in this paper we build a dataset for the training and testing process which includes 224 instances. Each instance is the query formula and top-50 retrieved documents. Half of the queries are randomly picked up from Wikipedia. Another half of the queries are randomly picked up from ArXiv. In addition, the relevance of documents with respect to the query is also given. The score will be higher when users think the retrieved document meets their need better. 0 denotes the retrieved document is irrelevant to the query, and 4 indicates the retrieved documents perfectly meet the user needs.

In order to evaluate the performance of RankBoost[3], we compare it with listwise model (ListNet)[4] and WikiMirs3.0[2] based on the metric of Normalized Discount Cumulative Gain (*NDCG*) WikiMirs3.0 is the representation of weighted tf-idf model, therefore this paper use WikiMirs3.0 as the baseline. In the model of ListNet, the learning rate is set to 0.0001, the iteration number is 1500.In the RankBoost model, the number of rounds to train is set to 250, and the threshold of candidates to search is 10.

3.1 Performance Comparison among Different MIR Systems

The ranking results of different systems in the test set are shown in Table 1. The results indicate that, our system achieves the best performance on the metrics. The ranking model of WikiMirs3.0 is based on weighted tf-idf model. While tf-idf model cannot integrate multiple useful features simultaneously. However, RankBoost can integrate multiple useful features effectively, which makes the proposed system outperform the baselines. The features about the formula are sparse which make the performance of ListNet worse than RankBoost. In addition, we take features of query and documents into consideration in the proposed system. All these make our system outperforms other systems.

Table 1. Results of *NDCG@k* of three systems

System	*NDCG@3*	*NDCG@5*
WikiMirs3.0	0.8295	0.8402
ListNet	0.8464	0.8652
Proposed system	**0.8712**	**0.8909**

3.2 Contribution of Different Features Categories

In order to validate the effectiveness of the three groups of features, we compare their effectiveness in RankBoost by removing one group of features at one time. The comparison results of different groups of features are listed in Table 2 as below.

Table 2. Effectiveness of *NDCG@k* different categories

System	*NDCG@3*	*NDCG@5*
Without Query-based features	0.8588	0.8784
Without Relevance-based features	0.8151	0.8493
Without Document-based features	0.8642	0.8838
All features	**0.8712**	**0.8909**

From the results above we can see that, the ranking results become worse when removing each one group of features, which proves that the three groups of features are all useful for the ranking of MIR system. Moreover, the relevance-based features affect the ranking results most significantly, as removing the features leads to the worst performances. Therefore, the relevance-based features are the most important basis to judge the relevance between query formula and the retrieved document.

4. Conclusion

In this paper we explore features of query formula and more document features in the MIR task. Then we apply learning to rank approach (RankBoost) to integrate those multiple features into the ranking model. The ranking performance of the proposed system has an improvement compared with the primary experiments.

5. Acknowledgments

This work is supported by the National Natural Science Foundation of China (No.61472014), the Natural Science Foundation of Beijing (No.4142023) and the Beijing Nova Program (2015).

6. References

1. Wang, Y., Gao, L., el at. WikiMirs 3.0: A Hybrid MIR System Based on the Context, Structure and Importance of Formulae in a Document. JCDL'15. 173-182. ACM. 2015

2. Lin, X., Gao, L., el at. A mathematics retrieval system for formulae in layout presentation. *SIGIR*. 697-706. ACM, 2014.

3. Freund, Y., Iyer, R., et al. An efficient boosting algorithm for combining preferences. *JMLR*. 4: 933-969. 2003.

4. Cao Z, Qin T, el at. Learning to rank: from pairwise approach to listwise approach. ICML'24. Pages:129–136. 2007.

Using Co-authorship Networks for Author Name Disambiguation

Fakhri Momeni
GESIS - Leibniz Institute for the Social Sciences
Cologne, Germany
fakhri.momeni@gesis.org

Philipp Mayr
GESIS - Leibniz Institute for the Social Sciences
Cologne, Germany
philipp.mayr@gesis.org

ABSTRACT

With the increasing size of digital libraries (DLs) it has become a challenge to identify author names correctly and assign publications to them. The situation becomes more critical when different persons share the same name (homonym problem) or when the names of authors are presented in several different ways (synonym problem). This paper focuses on homonym names in the computer science bibliography DBLP. The goal of this study is to implement and evaluate a method which uses co-authorship networks in order to disambiguate homonym names, especially common names. The results show that the implemented method has a good performance and can be used for author name disambiguation of sparse bibliographic records.

Keywords

Author name homonyms; Co-authorship network; Community detection; Louvain method; Gold standard

1 Introduction

In scholarly digital libraries authors are recognized via their publications. It is important for users to know about the author of a particular publication to access possible other publications by this author. For this purpose DLs provide search services by using the publication information in their databases. However, when several authors share the same name or authors provide their works under different versions of their name, DLs need more analysis on authors' oeuvres. Manual author identification in large DLs is very costly. Thus, as a consequence, automated solutions are to be found to analyze large sets of ambiguous author names. In addition, the demographic characteristics such as name origin and frequency of names used for authors influence the identification of authors. Therefore, all constraints of the underlying data should be considered to choose the appropriate method for author name disambiguation.

The author assignment and author grouping methods [3] are the two main types of method for author name disambiguation. The author assignment methods construct a

Permission to make digital or hard copies of part or all of this work for personal or classroom use is granted without fee provided that copies are not made or distributed for profit or commercial advantage and that copies bear this notice and the full citation on the first page. Copyrights for third-party components of this work must be honored. For all other uses, contact the owner/author(s).

JCDL '16 June 19-23, 2016, Newark, NJ, USA

© 2016 Copyright held by the owner/author(s).

ACM ISBN 978-1-4503-4229-2/16/06.

DOI: http://dx.doi.org/10.1145/2910896.2925461

model that represents the author and assigns proper publications to the model. It requires former knowledge about the authors. Nguyen and Cao [6] used these methods and proposed to link the author names to the matching entities in Wikipedia. The author grouping methods cluster the publications on the basis of their properties (co-authors, publication year, keywords, etc.) to assign a group of publications to a certain author. Following this framework, Caron and van Eck [2] applied rule-based scoring to clustered publications. In their approach they suppose that there is enough information about authors and their documents. Also, Gurney et al. [4] clustered publications with employing different data fields and integrated a community detection method.

In this paper we used an author grouping method (compare [3]) to cluster the publications of a set of random authors with the same name in the DBLP database. Considering the lack of rich bibliographic information in DBLP records, we applied co-authorship network analysis to detect similarities between publications. In addition, we investigated how the amount of homonym names affects the disambiguation results. In the end, we employed a community detection algorithm (Louvain method) to reduce the effect of common names in our evaluation.

2 Disambiguation Approach

We use an author grouping method in order to assign all publications of each person to a certain group. For this purpose all publications belonging to the same ambiguous author name are categorized into one block. In a next step we compare every pair of publications in each block with each other to find a similarity between them. If we have n blocks and m_i publications in a block i, the number of comparisons for all blocks is:

$$\sum_{i=1}^{n} \frac{m_i(m_i - 1)}{2} \qquad (1)$$

The result of each comparison is true or false. The *true* result means that two publications belong to one person and the same cluster. If one of them was compared with another one before and assigned to a cluster, the other one is added to that cluster too. If both of them were compared before and belong to different clusters, two clusters are rebuilt to one cluster. Otherwise a new cluster will be created and two publications are put in new cluster. In the next section we describe how to define the similarity indicator to build the clusters. The bibliographic information that we can obtain from publications in DBLP is limited mainly to author names (the names of all co-author names are listed), title and publication venue. We chose the co-author names as our similarity indicator. Therefore, we built a network of all authors and documents. Each pair of documents within every block has to be compared. To compare the publications the relations in the network are analyzed. If there is a path between two publications, their distance is defined as the length of the shortest path between them, otherwise it would be infinite. The length of the shortest path is equal to the number of nodes between two nodes. The less distance between two publications meansthat these publications were more likely to be written by one person. So, the distance between two publications is assumed as the similarity measure. Different thresholds can be considered for the distance.

3 Evaluation

In order to evaluate the output of the author disambiguation approach we need a gold standard of disambiguated author names. Many homonym author names in DBLP are disambiguated manually by the DBLP team and are identifiable with an id. For example, 'Hui Lin' belongs to four different persons: 'Hui Lin 0001', 'Hui Lin 0002', 'Hui Lin 0003' and 'Hui Lin 0004'. Thus, the set of publications for each person is recognizable. To build the gold standard[1] [5] we selected these identified author names and compiled all their publications into one set. In our gold standard we provide a list of publications that have at least one disambiguated author name. There are 5,408 authors who have an identification number (we mention them as disambiguated authors). These 5,408 authors and their publications form the gold standard.

To measure the performance of our method 1,000 disambiguated author names have been randomly selected from the gold standard. In total we have 2,844 different authors (with calculating their identifier) and 32,273 publications in our random sample. In the next section we evaluate the performance of our method against the gold standard. Some authors report that metrics like precision and recall have some constraints proving that are not suitable for evaluation of the effectiveness of clustering algorithms (see e.g. [1]). *BCubed* precision and recall [1] are metrics that satisfy these constraints and therefore we applied them to evaluate our method. For this purpose BCubed precision and recall were computed for each publication. The publication precision measures how many publications in its group belong to its author. The publication recall measures how many publications from its author appear in its group. BCubed precision, recall and F-measure were computed for every publication in every block. Then we considered their average as the BCubed precision, recall and F of the block.

4 Results and Discussion

For choosing the threshold we have checked the distances larger than 3, which results in a very low precision. Then we chose the threshold equal to 1 and 3. For the distance equal or less than threshold (1 or 3), we assign two publications

---

[1] Available at http://dx.doi.org/10.7802/1234

in the same cluster. The results of the evaluations for two thresholds are demonstrated in Table 1.

Table 1: Mean values of BCubed metrics for 1,000 blocks

	BCubed precision	BCubed recall	BCubed F
Threshold=1	0.99	0.77	0.81
Threshold=3	0.96	0.83	0.84

The results in Table 1 indicate that our co-author networks method performs well on the dataset and it can be utilized as author identification approach. Comparing the results for two thresholds (1 and 3) we can conclude that using threshold = 3 provides us with the better balance between precision and recall and a higher F (slightly better BCubed recall of 0.83 and F of 0.84). We observed that although using threshold=3 results the better performance generally, it is less efficient than using threshold=1 for common names. The reason is that common names enhance the probability of being authors with the same name in the same area of research activity and increase the likelihood of detecting the shared co-author for different researchers with the same name. Furthermore, it is more likely that these authors have co-authors with similar common names. This results in a higher probability of ambiguous co-authors and wrong connections between publications. Therefore, we should be more cautious when using the co-author of co-author as the similarity measure for these cases and verify the results more deeply. Hence, we applied a community detection algorithm to optimize the results (threshold=3) for the common names. We chose a subset of the names which have more than 200 publications (in total 28 names) in our DBLP dataset. To detect communities in the network we utilized the Louvain method with Pajek.

Because this method is based on co-author network, it is limited to multi-author papers. Therefore, a multi-aspect indicator is required for single-author papers. In this way, we can use the titles of publications to extract keywords and use this information to calculate similarity measures.

5 References

[1] E. Amigó, J. Gonzalo, J. Artiles, and F. Verdejo. A comparison of extrinsic clustering evaluation metrics based on formal constraints. *Inf. Retr.*, 12(4):461–486, 2009.

[2] E. Caron and N. J. van Eck. Large scale author name disambiguation using rule-based scoring and clustering. pages 79–86, 2014.

[3] A. A. Ferreira, M. A. Gonçalves, and A. H. F. Laender. A brief survey of automatic methods for author name disambiguation. *SIGMOD Record*, 41(2):15–26, 2012.

[4] T. Gurney, E. Horlings, and P. V. den Besselaar. Author disambiguation using multi-aspect similarity indicators. *Scientometrics*, 91(2):435–449, 2012.

[5] P. Mayr and F. Momeni. An open testbed for author name disambiguation evaluation.

[6] H. T. Nguyen and T. H. Cao. Named entity disambiguation: A hybrid statistical and rule-based incremental approach. In *The Semantic Web, 3rd Asian Semantic Web Conference, ASWC 2008, Bangkok, Thailand, December 8-11, 2008. Proceedings*, pages 420–433, 2008.

Real-time Filtering on Interest Profiles in Twitter Stream

Yue Fei   Chao Lv   Yansong Feng[*]   Dongyan Zhao
{feiyue,lvchao,fengyansong,zhaody}@pku.edu.cn
Institute of Computer Science and Technology, Peking University

ABSTRACT

The advent of Twitter has led to the ubiquitous information overload problem with a dramatic increase in the amount of tweets a user is exposed to. In this paper, we consider real-time tweet filtering with respect to users' interest profiles in public Twitter stream. While traditional filtering methods mainly focus on judging relevance of a document, we aim to retrieve relevant and novel documents to address the high redundancy of tweets. An unsupervised approach is proposed to model relevance between tweets and different profiles adaptively and a neural network language model is employed to learn semantic representation for tweets. Experiments on TREC 2015 dataset demonstrate the effectiveness of the proposed approach.

CCS Concepts

•**Information systems** → **Document filtering;** *Data stream mining;*

Keywords

Real-time Filtering, Neural Network Language Model, Adaptive Thresholding

1. INTRODUCTION

Social media sites such as Twitter are increasingly becoming better sources of information owing to the timeliness of news and users' interactions with friends. However, the dramatic increase in the amount of information a user is exposed to, greatly improves the chances of the user experiencing information overload.

Our main objective is retrieving tweets relevant to user's interest without redundancy. To find the accurate relevance boundry for different profile, we retrieve a list of candidate posts for each profile from the background corpus and set the score at top k relevant posts as relevance threshold. To

address the problem of vocabulary mismatch, we apply a neural network language mode to learn the semantics of texts and model the document representations. We evaluate our approach on the TREC 2015 microblog real-time filtering dataset. Experimental results show effectiveness of profile-biased adaptive thresholding method average pooling representation.

2. PROPOSED APPROACH

In this section we describe the proposed methodology for real-time filtering in tweet stream, which takes both relevance and redundancy into consideration. More specifically, given a real time tweet stream, where the tweet set $T = \langle t_1, t_2, t_3, ... \rangle$ arrives in a strictly chronological order, and users' interest profiles $P = \langle p_1, p_2, p_3, ... \rangle$, where each profile is denoted as a specific topic with a short phrase. our objective is to filter out relevant and novel tweet posts from the stream with respect to each interest profile.

2.1 Adaptive Thresholding

Traditional approaches filter tweets in a supervised manner [1, 2], which require labeled data and use fixed parameters across different profiles. Here we propose an unsupervised thresholding method to help identify interesting posts with regard to interest profiles in an adaptive manner. For each new coming document, our system will first decide whether it's relevant to the user's profile. The simplest way is to set a fixed threshold for every profile. However, a fixed threshold will result in two problems. On one hand, a fixed score threshold may not work well on different profile due to the variety of interest profiles. On the other hand, the content of relevant posts will change by time with a certain event involves or new subtopic emerges. Hence, the relevance threshold should be adaptive to both profile and time.

When initializing the relevance threshold for each profile, we run a Boolean Retrieval process to get candidate tweets relevant to the specific profile from the background corpus, i.e., the tweet collection of the last few days. The retrieved candidates are expected to be a reasonably accurate set since Boolean Retrieval is very strict. Then we compute the relevance scores between the candidates and the corresponding profile, rank the scores and cut out the top k scores as the initial threshold. Here k is an empirical parameter and can be set corresponding to the number of posts a user wish to read everyday. This threshold is timely updated with new coming posts in the same manner. In this way, we can get

---

[*]Corresponding author

Permission to make digital or hard copies of part or all of this work for personal or classroom use is granted without fee provided that copies are not made or distributed for profit or commercial advantage and that copies bear this notice and the full citation on the first page. Copyrights for third-party components of this work must be honored. For all other uses, contact the owner/author(s).

JCDL '16 June 19-23, 2016, Newark, NJ, USA

© 2016 Copyright held by the owner/author(s).

ACM ISBN 978-1-4503-4229-2/16/06.

DOI: http://dx.doi.org/10.1145/2910896.2925462

a reasonable initial thresholds and adapt the threshold with the evolution of topics.

This redundancy problem is very typical in microblog, since users often post messages with the same, or very similar content, especially when reporting or commenting on news and events. We employ a tweet pool retaining posts that have already been pushed to help get rid of redundancy. When a new relevant tweet is identified, we compare it with all the delivered tweets and justify whether it's novel according to a fixed redundancy threshold. We choose a fixed weak threshold since we assume that users view redundancy not as sensitive as relevance so that only very "redundant" documents are considered redundant.

2.2 Tweet Representation

We apply the average pooling of word embedding vector to tackle the vocabulary mismatch problem caused by the shortness of tweets [5] . The average pooling of word embedding vector utilizes word embeddings in a low-dimensional continuous space where relevant words are close to each other. The relationships among words are embedded in their word vectors, providing a simple way to compute aggregated semantics for word collections such as paragraphs and documents. In the previous study, a simple average pooling approach was proposed to derive document vectors from word embeddings. Letting $c_{i,j}$ denote the word embedding of the j-th word token of document i, the document vector v_i can be computed as Eq. 1, where J_i denotes the number of word tokens in the document i.

$$v_i = \frac{1}{J_i} \sum_{j=1}^{J_i} c_{i,j} \qquad (1)$$

3. EVALUATION

We evaluate our approach on the real-time filtering task of the TREC 2015 Microblog track [4]. The dataset is a sample from public tweet stream which begins from July 20, 2015 and lasts until July 29, 2015. We conduct preprocessing on the raw data including non-English elimination, stop words removal and stemming. There are 13,988,358 tweets left after preprocessing, while ignoring that some tweets are missed during sampling.

Totally 56 interest profiles are provided for evaluation. Each profile contains three parts: title, description and narrative. During the experiments, we find that both description and narrative introduce more noise than information for profiles. Hence, we will leverage the title information only for each profile. Two metrics are introduced for evaluating this task: the expected latency-discounted gain (ELG) and the normalized cumulative gain (nCG)[4]. ELG is a precision oriented metric while NCG values more recall.

We compare our tweet representation method with the BOW representation and paragraph vector representation [3]. Experimental results of the three representations with and without adaptive thresholding method are shown in table reftab:result. It's obvious that AP gains a statistically significant improvement in terms of ELG over BOW and PV, which implies the average pooling representation can better model semantic relations between tweet texts. Besides, the adaptive thresholding method significantly improves the filtering effectiveness using either filtering measures over those without. Moreover, our method is also comparable with the TREC 2015 best automatic run[4] in the last line. Figure

Table 1: Experimental results with different strategy. † denotes a statistically significant increase over BOW. Statistical significance is estimated with a paired t-test at ($p < 0.05$).

Run	ELG	nCG
BOW	0.2690	0.2415
BOW+Ada	0.2818 †	0.2722 †
PV	0.2709	0.2435
PV+Ada	0.3009 †	0.2745 †
AP	0.3037 †	0.2449
AP+Ada	**0.3067** †	**0.2806** †
TREC 2015 BEST	0.3150	0.2679

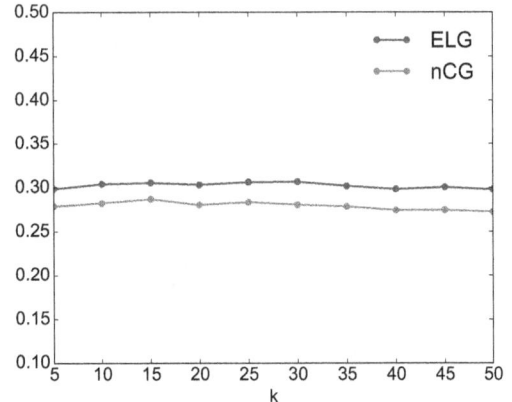

Figure 1: Sensitivity Analysis of k

1 shows the performance of adaptive thresholding strategy with k ranging from 5 to 50, which illustrates the robustness of our method. Overall, the results show the effectiveness of our average pooling and adaptive thresholding strategy.

4. ACKNOWLEDGMENTS

The work reported in this paper was supported by the National Natural Science Foundation of China Grant 61370116.

5. REFERENCES

[1] M. Albakour, C. Macdonald, I. Ounis, et al. On sparsity and drift for effective real-time filtering in microblogs. In *Proceedings of the 22nd ACM international conference on Conference on information & knowledge management*, pages 419–428. ACM, 2013.

[2] Y. Fei, Y. Hong, and J. Yang. Handling topic drift for topic tracking in microblogs. In *Advances in Information Retrieval*, pages 477–488. Springer, 2015.

[3] Q. V. Le and T. Mikolov. Distributed representations of sentences and documents. *arXiv preprint arXiv:1405.4053*, 2014.

[4] J. Lin, M. Efron, Y. Wang, G. Sherman, and E. Voorhees. Overview of the trec-2015 microblog track. In *Proceedings of TREC*, volume 2015, 2015.

[5] T. Mikolov, I. Sutskever, K. Chen, G. S. Corrado, and J. Dean. Distributed representations of words and phrases and their compositionality. In *Advances in neural information processing systems*, pages 3111–3119, 2013.

Preliminary Exploration of the Effect of Time Constraint on Search Interactions on Webpages

Chang Liu
Peking University
5 Yiheyuan Road
Haidian District, Beijing, P.R.China 100871
imliuc@pku.edu.cn

Tao Xu
State University of New York, University at Albany
1400 Washington Ave
Albany, NY 12222 USA
txu@albany.edu

ABSTRACT

This study explored the effect of time constraint on searchers' interactions during two kinds of tasks through conducting a user experiment. The results demonstrated users' did not tend to accelerate their reading or decision speed given time constraint, but to select fewer pages to read, i.e. visit fewer content pages and search result pages (SERPs); and they had more mouse clicks but fewer keystrokes per page when searching with time constraint. The results also showed the different effects of time constraint on search interactions on pages for two types of tasks. The results have implications for the design of digital library systems that take account users' time constraint or time pressure.

Keywords

Time constraint, task type, search interaction, search strategy

1. INTRODUCTION

Context is an important factor found to influence users' information seeking and search behavior. Several contextual factors including task type, users' domain knowledge, search skills, cognitive styles and etc., have been intensively examined. Time constraint is a contextual factor that is commonly existed in our daily life. Recently several studies began to focus on time constraint or time pressure and their effects upon search behaviors and search experience [2][4][5]. They have found that time constraint and time pressure affected searchers' assessments of search experience, i.e. pre-search confidence, search performance and satisfaction, and search difficulties.

In the literature of decision making, researchers have found that when consumers experience time pressure, there are three kinds of adaptation strategies to cope with time pressure: 1) acceleration, 2) selection of information, and 3) alteration of information search pattern (see [7] for the review). The empirical study by [7] found that participants did not adapt to time constraint through acceleration, but rather took more time on each item. In our study, we are also interested to see if users could accelerate or decelerate dwell time on each of the webpages when given time constraint. Crescenzi, Kelly and Azzopardi [3] investigated the impact of time pressure and system delays on search behavior from a user experiment. Results showed that participants in the time pressure condition issued queries significantly more frequently, viewed fewer documents per query and spent less time examining documents and SERPs. However, it is not clear whether searchers

would change their search strategies when given time constraint, and if so, how would they change search strategies; in addition, whether the effects of time constraint on users' search interactions are the same in two types of tasks.

2. User Experiment

A lab-based user experiment was conducted in this study. Forty undergraduate students (20 females and 20 males) from Peking University were recruited. Each participant first filled out a background questionnaire, and then searched for four assigned search tasks through a desktop computer. During search, participants were asked to respond to each task by typing or copying/pasting useful information for their tasks into a notebook file. We used Morae Recorder 3.3 (https://www.techsmith.com/) to record searchers' interactions on the computer and the computer screen unobtrusively. Several behavioral measures were calculated and examined from the Morae search log.

2.1 Time Constraint

The experiment assigned two conditions for participants to search tasks through the Internet: with time constraint (TC) and without time constraint (NTC). In TC conditions, participants were informed that they only had 5 minutes to accomplish the task before they started searching. Five-minute is a severe time constraint, which is less than 50% of the average time for the task in our pilot studies. This limit was determined for the purpose of according to prior studies in psychology (e.g. [6][7]). Each participant conducted searching under both conditions: two search tasks (one FF and one IU) in TC conditions and the other two search tasks (one FF and one IU) in NTC conditions. To eliminate the possible carryover effect given the within-subject design of time constraint, participants were given five-minute to take a break after they completed two search tasks in one time condition and before they switched to the other time condition. The order of search tasks and time conditions was systematically balanced using 2x2 Graeco-Latin Square design.

2.2 Search Tasks

In this study, we constructed two types of search tasks: Fact Finding (FF) and Information Understanding (IU). Each type of tasks consists of two tasks with different topics, and each task was constructed in a simulated work task situation following Borland's guidelines [1]. Task descriptions are shown below:

Fact Finding 1: *You heard that India has very interesting wedding traditions, and now you want to search for the following aspects of Indian Wedding: Wedding dresses, painted hands, and the type of food served.*

Fact Finding 2: *One of your friends said he was bitten by a rove Beetle, and felt very itching, and the wound festered after scratching. You were quite worried about this type of beetles. You want to search what is rove beetle? Is it poisonous? What should you do if you see a rove beetle? If bitten by a rove beetle, how should we treat?*

Permission to make digital or hard copies of part or all of this work for personal or classroom use is granted without fee provided that copies are not made or distributed for profit or commercial advantage and that copies bear this notice and the full citation on the first page. Copyrights for third-party components of this work must be honored. For all other uses, contact the Owner/Author.

Copyright is held by the owner/author(s).

JCDL '16, June 19-23, 2016, Newark, NJ, USA
ACM 978-1-4503-4229-2/16/06.
http://dx.doi.org/10.1145/2910896.2925463

Information Understanding 1: *Your nephew is considering trying out for a football team. Most of your relatives are supportive of the idea, but you think this sport is dangerous and are worried about the potential health risks. Specifically, what are long-term health risks faced by teen football players?*

Information Understanding 2: *Doric column is a distinctive architectural form in Ancient Greece architecture. Please search information about the general characteristics and representative works of Doric column, and whether Doric column has any influence on Chinese architecture? If so, what are the representatives?*

3. RESULTS

We compared the behavioral measures between NTC and TC when all tasks were considered, and then for FF and IU tasks respectively, using Mann-Whitney U tests. Results are shown in the Table 1. When all tasks were considered, the results showed that searchers visited more content pages and search result pages (SERPs) in NTC than in TC. This is also the case for IU tasks. But the pattern was different in FF tasks. For FF tasks, searchers visited more content pages in NTC than in TC, but there was no significant difference in the number of SERPs. For time-related measures, there is no significant difference on average dwell time on content page and SERPs between NTC and TC conditions for any types of tasks and when all tasks were considered.

4. DISCUSSION AND CONCLUSION

We examined the effect of time constraint on users' search interactions in this study. The results showed that when there was time constraint, participants did not accelerate or decelerate dwell time on each of webpages, but selected fewer content pages and SERPs to visit. Such result is different from [3], which found participants spent significantly less total time per document when there was time constraint. But they did not explain how the variable was calculated, so it is not clear whether the results from the two studies are comparable.

It is interesting to find time constraint had different impacts on the number of mouse clicks and keystrokes per page. Searchers tended to reduce unnecessary mouse clicks per page and often use keystrokes to locate specific pieces of information per page to cope with time constraint. Keystrokes and mouse clicks represented different types of interactions on pages. Searchers used mouse clicks to select, scroll, or click without any purpose; but they generally used keystrokes to express information need, either issuing queries on SERPs or locating specific text on content pages. Therefore, participants had much fewer mouse

clicks per page in TC for IU tasks might because they limited meaningless mouse clicks when there was strict time constraint. But for FF tasks, participants would often need to use keystrokes to locate specific pieces of information. We will examine users' keystrokes and mouse movements on pages in detail to explain such findings in future studies.

This is preliminary analysis of the effect of time constraint on uses' search interactions on pages, and our results showed users' did not tend to accelerate their reading or decision speed given time constraint, but to select fewer pieces of useful information to accomplish the task. Such results shed light on how to design search systems to help searchers accomplish search more efficiently when given time constraint. One possible way is to provide search result overview on SERPs for searchers to quickly understand the general results, and then make it easier to locate or select information on content pages.

5. ACKNOWLEDGEMENTS

This project is funded by National Nature Science Foundation of China (NSFC) #71303015. We thank participants in this experiments and student assistants for conducting the experiment and data cleaning.

6. REFERENCES

[1] Borlund, P. (2003). The IIR evaluation model: A framework for evaluation of interactive information retrieval systems. *Information Research, 8*(3): 1–34.

[2] Crescenzi, A., Capra, R., & Arguello, J. (2013). Time Pressure, User Satisfaction and Task Difficulty. *Proceedings of ASIS&T 13'.*

[3] Crescenzi, A., Kelly, D., and Azzopardi, L. (2015). Time Pressure and System Delays in Information Search. *SIGIR '15.*

[4] Liu, C., Yang, F., Zhao, Y., Jiang, Q., Zhang, L. (2014). What does time constraint mean to information searchers? *In the proceedings of IIiX 2014*, August, 26-31, Regensburg, Germany.

[5] Liu, C., Zhang, L., Jiang, Q., Yang, F., Zhao, Y. (2014). The influence of task type on search experience from the perspective of time constraint. *In the proceedings of ASIS&T 2014*, November 1-6, Seattle, US.

[6] Topi, H., Valacich, J. S., & Hoffer, J. A. (2005). The effects of task complexity and time availability limitations on human performance in database query tasks. *International Journal of Human-Computer Studies, 62*(3), 349-379

[7] Weenig, M. W., & Maarleveld, M. (2002). The impact of time constraint on information search strategies in complex choice tasks. *Journal of Economic Psychology, 23*(6), 689-702.

Table 1 The effects of time constraint and task type on searchers' behavior. Means (SD) and Mann-Whitney U test results.

	All tasks			FF			IU		
	NTC	TC	(*p*)	NTC	TC	(*p*)	NTC	TC	(*p*)
Number of content pages	**30.69 (22.58)**	**9.38 (5.21)**	**(<0.001)**	**27.50 (25.58)**	**9.06 (5.56)**	**(0.017)**	**33.67 (19.81)**	**9.77 (4.94)**	**(<0.001)**
Number of SERPs	**22.03 (14.58)**	**9.48 (5.64)**	**(<0.001)**	19.79 (16.07)	9.44 (5.59)	(0.07)	**24.13 (13.24)**	**9.54 (5.92)**	**(<0.001)**
Mean dwell time on content page (s)	13.85 (4.42)	14.99 (14.31)	(0.834)	12.80 (3.95)	16.01 (18.52)	(0.423)	14.84 (4.74)	13.74 (6.80)	(0.856)
Mean dwell time on SERP (s)	10.27 (4.38)	10.19 (3.82)	(0.016)	8.76 (3.51)	9.50 (2.91)	(0.101)	11.67 (4.75)	13.74 (6.80)	(0.088)
Number of mouse clicks in searching per page	**18.35 (7.24)**	**14.13 (6.50)**	**(0.013)**	14.64 (5.47)	12.26 (3.89)	(0.268)	**21.57 (7.18)**	**16.27 (8.21)**	**(0.016)**
Number of keystrokes in searching per page	**6.10 (8.97)**	**7.06 (5.57)**	**(0.128)**	**3.63 (2.61)**	**5.82 (4.06)**	**(0.012)**	8.24 (11.78)	8.48 (6.79)	(0.217)

Exploiting Network Analysis to Investigate Topic Dynamics in the Digital Library Evaluation Domain

Leonidas Papachristopoulos
Digital Curation Unit, IMIS,
'Athena' RC, Athens, Greece
l.papachristopoulos@dcu.gr

Michalis Sfakakis
Department of Archives, Library
Science and Museology,
Ionian University, Corfu, Greece
sfakakis@ionio.gr

Nikos Kleidis
Department of Informatics, Athens
University of Economics & Business,
Athens, Greece
klidisnik@aueb.gr

Giannis Tsakonas
Library and Information Center
University of Patras, Patras, Greece
gtsak@upatras.gr

Christos Papatheodorou
Department of Archives, Library
Science and Museology,
Ionian University, Corfu, Greece
papatheodor@ionio.gr

ABSTRACT

The multidimensional nature of digital libraries evaluation domain and the amount of scientific production published on the field hinders and disorientates the interested researchers who contemplate to focus on the specific domain. These communities need guidance in order to exploit the considerable amount of data and the diversity of methods effectively as well as to identify new research goals and develop their plans for future works. This poster investigates the core topics of the digital library evaluation field and their impact by applying topic modeling and network analysis on a corpus of the JCDL, ECDL/TDPL and ICADL conferences proceedings in the period 2001-2013.

Categories and Subject Descriptors

H.3 [**Information Storage and Retrieval**]: H.3.7 Digital Libraries

Keywords

Digital library evaluation; topic modeling; network analysis.

1. INTRODUCTION

Digital libraries (DL) evaluation domain focuses on diverse criteria, such as effectiveness, quality, and performance that can be viewed under different perspectives. Such heterogeneity poses significant challenges to individuals and communities who intend to study and contribute to the specific evolving domain. In this work we apply the Latent Dirichlet Allocation (LDA) method [1] to reveal the topics of the DL evaluation literature in the conferences JCDL, ECDL/TPDL and ICADL during the period 2001-2013. The outcome of this topic modeling process reveals not only the existence of key topics, but their interconnections too.

Permission to make digital or hard copies of part or all of this work for personal or classroom use is granted without fee provided that copies are not made or distributed for profit or commercial advantage and that copies bear this notice and the full citation on the first page. Copyrights for third-party components of this work must be honored. For all other uses, contact the Owner/Author(s). Copyright is held by the owner/author(s).
JCDL '16, June 19–23, 2016, Newark, NJ, USA.
ACM 978-1-4503-4229-2/16/06.
DOI: http://dx.doi.org/10.1145/2910896.2925464

Furthermore, through network analysis centrality measures, we determine the significance of each topic for the DL evaluation community. This work complements the results of a study over the identification and evolution of the topics emerged in the DL evaluation literature [2] and provides an insight into their interdependences. We specify the goals of this study to the following research questions:

1. Which are the most prominent topics emerged in the DL evaluation literature?

2. How these topics interact each other? Do they formulate larger semantic categories that effectively chart this domain?

2. PRELIMINARIES

The corpus of this study is composed by evaluation studies and was formed as follows: first, from the entire body of conference works (limited to full and short papers), a group of 395 papers formulated our corpus. The papers were classified as relevant to DL evaluation by applying a Naïve Bayes classifier. The DL evaluation identity of the composed corpus was validated, as well as the classifier was evaluated, by three domain experts who had previously achieved a high inter-rater agreement score [3]. Our next step was to discover key topic models from this corpus. Mimno's jsLDA web tool [4] was chosen for running the LDA algorithm and deriving the topic models. Mimno's jsLDA was chosen because of its advanced functionalities in the graphical presentation of interrelations among the extracted topics. The number of training iterations of the algorithm was set to 1,000 as the topic structure seemed to be more stable. In order to define the number of topics that describe adequately the corpus, several tests were executed (with 25, 20, 15, 14, 13, 11, 9 topics). Each extracted topic was arbitrary set to consist of ten words to achieve the necessary balance between the sufficiency of words and human ability for interpretation. Three domain experts, after examining the corpus and the number of topics from similar attempts in the field [5], concluded that the optimal interpretable number of topics is 13. The three experts labeled the topics taking into consideration the meaning of the words that the LDA algorithm suggested in the DL context.

Additionally, the jsLDA tool provided topic correlation functionalities, based on the Pointwise Mutual Information (PMI) measure. This compared the probability of two topics *a* and *b* occurring together in a document with the probabilities of occurring each one independently in the same document. The result of this computation was an adjacency matrix, which led to the generation of an undirected graph presenting the PMI of the topics, above a cutoff of 0.002. The graph (Figure 1) consisted of 13 nodes and 36 edges, where the thickness of an edge -derived from the corresponding value of the PMI between two topics- indicated the pair of topics, which are more likely to occur in the same document.

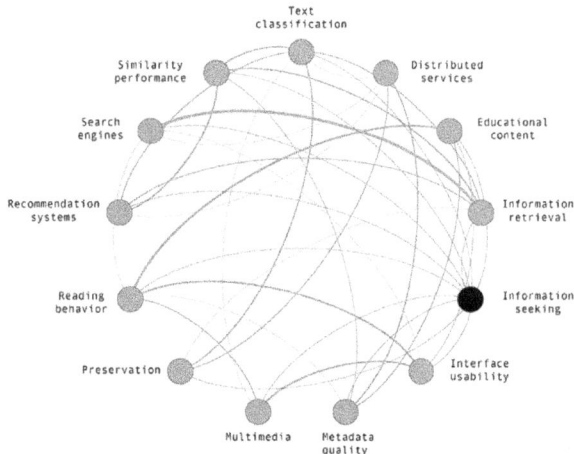

Figure 1. Topic correlation

A significant focal point of our network analysis was the revelation of nodes that play an important role. Three measures of centrality were applied: *degree centrality*, *betweenness centrality* and *closeness centrality*. Apart from the centrality measures, we also used in our analysis the *clustering coefficient* measure to localize neighborhoods of nodes that have strong relationships.

3. FINDINGS

Figure 2 presents the ranking of the topics according to their centrality values. All three centrality measures reveal that 'Information seeking' and 'Text classification' are the core topics of the domain. Indeed, as DLs are socio-technical information systems, the study of information seeking behavior is vital for their evaluation. On the other hand, 'Text classification' reflects the aim of the community for making system-wise organizational processes more efficient.

Degree		Closeness Centrality		Betweenness Centrality		Clustering Coefficient		Network analysis ranking				Legend	
								D	CC	BC	CL		
11	IS	1.083	IS	19.917	IS	0.833	EC	IS	IS	IS	EC	DS	Distributed services
7	TC	1.417	TC	4.367	TC	0.700	SP	TC	TC	TC	SP	EC	Educational content
6	RB	1.500	RB	3.033	MQ	0.700	RS	RB	RB	MQ	RS	IR	Information retrieval
6	IR	1.500	IR	2.950	SE	0.700	IU	IR	IR	SE	IU	IS	Information seeking
5	DS	1.583	DS	2.750	DS	0.667	P	DS	DS	DS	P	IU	Interface usability
5	SP	1.583	SP	2.167	RB	0.667	M	SP	SP	RB	M	MQ	Metadata quality
5	RS	1.583	RS	2.083	IR	0.600	RB	RS	RS	IR	RB	M	Multimedia
5	MQ	1.583	MQ	1.167	SP	0.600	IR	MQ	MQ	SP	IR	P	Preservation
5	SE	1.583	SE	1.000	IU	0.524	TC	SE	SE	IU	TC	RB	Reading behavior
5	IU	1.583	IU	1.000	M	0.400	MQ	IU	IU	M	MQ	RS	Recommendation systems
4	EC	1.667	M	0.783	RS	0.400	SE	EC	M	RS	SE	SE	Search engines
4	M	1.667	P	0.450	P	0.364	IS	M	P	P	IS	SP	Similarity performance
4	P	1.667	EC	0.333	EC	0.200	DS	P	EC	EC	DS	TC	Text classification

Figure 2. Topics ranking according to centrality values

All three centrality measures indicate that 'Information retrieval' belongs to the group of the core topics, proving the continuous interest for the advancement of the content discovery. 'Search engines' is also a topic that usually appears in the same papers with 'Information retrieval', a fact that reaffirms the obvious relation between these two topics. A thorough examination of the network analysis rankings indicates that, apart from 'Information seeking' and 'Text classification', the Top-5 topics were not the same in all centrality measures. For example, 'Metadata quality' has the third place in the *betweenness centrality* ranking, but it does not belong to the first five positions in the *degree* and *closeness centrality* list. This could mean that issues of metadata quality are pivotal in transiting the connections among various quality topics.

Another interesting point is the cohesive neighborhoods that exist in the DL environment. 'Educational content' has the largest *clustering coefficient* and therefore is the entry point to the semantically densest subgraph of topics, together with 'Reading behavior', 'Information seeking', 'Interface usability' and 'Metadata quality'.

4. CONCLUSIONS

Regarding our first research question, the examination of the centrality measures indicates that among the thirteen topics, 'Information seeking' and 'Text classification' have been in the center of the attention of DL community. The investigation of the second research question, which focused on the interaction of the topics, highlight the creation of a cohesive subgraph with 'Reading behavior', 'Information seeking', 'Interface usability', 'Metadata quality' and 'Educational content'. Another cohesive subgraph consists of 'Information retrieval', 'Search engines', 'Text classification' 'Similarity performance', 'Recommendation systems' and 'Information seeking'. This cohesion represents the formulation of large semantic spaces that can guide researchers in their exploration of the evaluation initiatives in the field of DLs.

5. REFERENCES

[1] Blei, D.M., Y Ng, A., and Jordan, M.I. 2003. Latent Dirichlet Allocation. *Journal of Machine Learning Research* 3, 993–1022.

[2] Papachristopoulos, L., Kleidis, N., Sfakakis, M., Tsakonas, G., and Papatheodorou, C. 2015. Discovering the topical evolution of the digital library evaluation community. In *Proceedings of the 9th International Conference on Metadata and Semantic Research*. CCIS No. 544, Springer, Berlin, 101–112.

[3] Afiontzi, E., Kazadeis, G., Papachristopoulos, L., Sfakakis, M., Tsakonas, G., and Papatheodorou, C. 2013. Charting the digital library evaluation domain with a semantically enhanced mining methodology. In *Proceedings of the 13th ACM/IEEE-CS Joint Conference on Digital Libraries*. ACM, New York, 125–134.

[4] Mimno, D. jsLDA: An implementation of latent Dirichlet allocation in javascript. https://github.com/mimno/jsLDA

[5] Pomerantz, J., Wildemuth, B.M., Yang, S., and Fox, E.A. 2006. Curriculum development for digital libraries. In *Proceedings of the 6th ACM/IEEE-CS Joint Conference on Digital Libraries*. ACM, New York, 175–184.

Inventor Name Disambiguation for a Patent Database Using a Random Forest and DBSCAN

Kunho Kim‡, Madian Khabsa*, C. Lee Giles†‡

‡Computer Science and Engineering
†Information Sciences and Technology
The Pennsylvania State University
University Park, PA 16802, USA

*Microsoft Research
One Microsoft Way
Redmond, WA 98005, USA

kunho@cse.psu.edu, madian.khabsa@microsoft.com, giles@ist.psu.edu

ABSTRACT

Inventor name disambiguation is the task that distinguishes each unique inventor from all other inventor records in a patent database. This task is essential for processing person name queries in order to get information related to a specific inventor, e.g. a list of all that inventor's patents. Using earlier work on author name disambiguation, we apply it to inventor name disambiguation. A random forest classifier is trained to classify whether each pair of inventor records is the same person. The DBSCAN algorithm is use for inventor record clustering, and its distance function is derived using the random forest classifier. For scalability, blocking functions are used to reduce the complexity of record matching and enable parallelization since each block can be run simultaneously. Tested on the USPTO patent database, 12 million inventor records were disambiguated in 6.5 hours. Evaluation on the labeled datasets from USPTO PatentsView competition shows our algorithm outperforms all algorithms submitted to the competition.

Keywords

Name Disambiguation; Random Forest; DBSCAN

1. INTRODUCTION

Querying by person name is frequent in digital library search. For example, users may want to find all patents invented by certain person in a patent search system. If there is no unique identifier for each person in the database, processing this query can be problematic. In order to do this, there are several factors to consider. First, a person's name can be found in different formats from record to record. For example, in one record has the full name, "John Doe" and in another the first name initial and last name, "J. Doe". Second, many inventors share a common name and that name will appear often in the database. This problem is particularly significant for names from Asian countries. Statistics

Permission to make digital or hard copies of part or all of this work for personal or classroom use is granted without fee provided that copies are not made or distributed for profit or commercial advantage and that copies bear this notice and the full citation on the first page. Copyrights for third-party components of this work must be honored. For all other uses, contact the owner/author(s).

JCDL '16 June 19-23, 2016, Newark, NJ, USA

© 2016 Copyright held by the owner/author(s).

ACM ISBN 978-1-4503-4229-2/16/06.

DOI: http://dx.doi.org/10.1145/2910896.2925465

shown that 84.8% of the population have one of the top 100 popular surnames in China, while only 16.4% for the United States. Third, there exist typographical errors in names.

Name disambiguation algorithms are often used to solve these problems. Name disambiguation is the task of distinguishing each unique name from all name records in the database. Here, we propose to use an author, name disambiguation algorithm for the patent database. Our algorithm follows the typical steps of author name disambiguation, with newly proposed set of features from patent metadata. We train a random forest pairwise linkage classifier [5],[7], and use DBSCAN for clustering records [3]. The publicly available USPTO database is used for evaluation.

2. DISAMBIGUATION PROCESS

Patent records and scholarly publications have similar metadata, e.g. both with data on persons who published(or invented) and their affiliations. Ventura et al. [8] showed promising results in adopting author name disambiguation algorithms for the patent database. Our algorithm follows similar steps.

2.1 Random Forest Classifier

As in [7] we train a random forest(RF) classifier to determine whether each pair of inventor records is same person or not. The RF classifier is a well-known and popular ensemble learning method that combines simple decision trees by aggregating the votes from the trees for classification [1]. We started with the feature set used in Ventura et al. [8], and tested additional features that are used in author disambiguation. We only kept features that had a meaningful decrease in Gini importance if they were removed. Table 1 shows all features used. Our RF classifier consisted of 100 trees, with 5 features tried for each split. Testing was on two different datasets, Common characteristics and Mixture(see Section 3). The out-of-bag(OOB) errors of the RF were 0.05% and 0.07% respectively.

2.2 Blocking

Patent databases have a fairly large number of records; the USPTO database contains more than 12 million inventor record mentions. Blocking functions for preprocessing are crucial for scaling, especially for millions of entities. Blocking splits whole records into several blocks, and the clustering is done within each block separately, assuming records from the same person rarely split into different blocks. We

Table 1: Features used in the random forest

Category	Subcategory	Features
Inventor	First name	Exact, Jaro-Winkler, Soundex
	Middle name	Exact, Jaro-Winkler, Soundex
	Last name	Exact, Jaro-Winkler, Soundex, IDF
	Suffix	Exact
	Order	Order comparision
Affiliation	City	Exact, Jaro-Winkler, Soundex
	State	Exact
	Country	Exact
Co-author	Last name	# of name shared, IDF, Jaccard
Assignee	Last name	Exact, Jaro-Winkler, Soundex
Group	Group	Exact
	Subgroup	Exact
Title	Title	# of term shared

Table 2: Disambiguation evaluation

Test Set	Training Set	Precision	Recall	F1 Score
ALS	Mixture	0.9963	0.9790	0.9786
	Common	0.9960	0.9848	0.9904
ALS common	Mixture	0.9841	0.9796	0.9818
	Common	0.9820	0.9916	0.9868
IS	Mixture	0.9989	0.9813	0.9900
	Common	0.9989	0.9813	0.9900
E&S	Mixture	0.9992	0.9805	0.9898
	Common	0.9995	0.9810	0.9902
Phase2	Mixture	0.9912	0.9760	0.9836
	Common	0.9916	0.9759	0.9837

Table 3: Comparison with the competition winner

Test Set	F1(Ours)	F1(Winner)
ALS	0.9904	0.9879
ALS common	0.9868	0.9815
IS	0.9900	0.9783
E&S	0.9902	0.9835
Phase2	0.9837	0.9826

use a simple blocking function with *full last name+initial of first name*, so that we can easily parallelize the algorithm.

2.3 Clustering Using DBSCAN

DBSCAN, a density-based clustering algorithm[2], clusters inventor records. It does not require a prior the number of clusters, and it resolves the transitivity problem [3]. We use the fraction of negative(0) votes of the trees in random forest as the distance function.

2.4 Parallelization

The parallelization proposed in [4] using GNU Parallel [6] was used to utilize all available processing units. We assign each blocks to each thread. Memory limitations limit complete utilization of all CPUs. In our algorithm, the amount of memory required is proportional to total number of records in the block. As such, we divided all blocks into 3 groups based on the total number of records, and set different maximum threads to run simultaneously.

3. RESULTS ON THE USPTO DATABASE

Recently there was an inventor name disambiguation competition for the USPTO database. We used the same evaluation datasets to compare with the results of the competition. The training dataset includes the Mixture and Common characteristics datasets, and the test dataset includes ALS, ALS common, IS, E&S, Phase2. Detailed explanation for each dataset can be found on the competition's web page[1]. We measured pairwise precision, recall, and F1 score for evaluation.

Table 2 shows the results for each training and test dataset. Results were slightly better with the Common characteristics dataset, as expected from OOB error of RF. We can also see that the recall is relatively lower compare to the precision. Blocking effects the recall, as it can remove some potential matches. Table 3 shows the comparison between our work and the best result from the competition. Note our algorithm has the best performance on all datasets.

4. CONCLUSIONS

Our Random Forest DBSCAN author name disambiguation algorithm works very well for inventor names and readily scaled to over 12 million inventor name mentions. For efficient memory usage for scalability, better blocking functions would be useful. It would be interesting to see if other

methods, such as graph or link data, could be incorporated as well.

5. ACKNOWLEDGMENTS

We gratefully acknowledge Evgeny Klochikhin and Ahmad Emad for helping us with evaluation and partial support from the National Science Foundation.

6. REFERENCES

[1] L. Breiman. Random forests. *Machine learning*, 45(1):5–32, 2001.

[2] M. Ester, H.-P. Kriegel, J. Sander, and X. Xu. A density-based algorithm for discovering clusters in large spatial databases with noise. In *Proceedings of the ACM SIGKDD International Conference on Knowledge Discovery and Data Mining(KDD'96)*, volume 96, pages 226–231, 1996.

[3] J. Huang, S. Ertekin, and C. L. Giles. Efficient name disambiguation for large-scale databases. In *Proceedings of the 10th European Conference on Principle and Practice of Knowledge Discovery in Databases(PKDD'06)*, pages 536–544, 2006.

[4] M. Khabsa, P. Treeratpituk, and C. L. Giles. Large scale author name disambiguation in digital libraries. In *IEEE International Conference on Big Data*, pages 41–42, 2014.

[5] M. Khabsa, P. Treeratpituk, and C. L. Giles. Online person name disambiguation with constraints. In *Proceedings of the ACM/IEEE Joint Conference on Digital Libraries(JCDL'15)*, pages 37–46, 2015.

[6] O. Tange et al. Gnu parallel-the command-line power tool. *The USENIX Magazine*, 36(1):42–47, 2011.

[7] P. Treeratpituk and C. L. Giles. Disambiguating authors in academic publications using random forests. In *Proceedings of the ACM/IEEE Joint Conference on Digital Libraries(JCDL'09)*, pages 39–48, 2009.

[8] S. L. Ventura, R. Nugent, and E. R. Fuchs. Seeing the non-stars:(some) sources of bias in past disambiguation approaches and a new public tool leveraging labeled records. *Research Policy*, 2015.

---

[1]http://www.dev.patentsview.org/workshop

Big Data Processing of School Shooting Archives

Mohamed Farag
Virginia Tech
Blacksburg, VA 24061
mmagdy@vt.edu

Pranav Nakate
Virginia Tech
Blacksburg, VA 24061
npranav@vt.edu

Edward A. Fox
Virginia Tech
Blacksburg, VA 24061
fox@vt.edu

ABSTRACT

Web archives about school shootings consist of webpages that may or may not be relevant to the events of interest. There are 3 main goals of this work; first is to clean the webpages, which involves getting rid of the stop words and non-relevant parts of a webpage. The second goal is to select just webpages relevant to the events of interest. The third goal is to upload the cleaned and relevant webpages to Apache Solr so that they are easily accessible. We show the details of all the steps required to achieve these goals. The results show that representative Web archives are noisy, with 2% - 40% relevant content. By cleaning the archives, we aid researchers to focus on relevant content for their analysis.

CCS Concepts

• **Information systems ~ Digital libraries and archives** • *Information systems ~ Clustering and classification*

Keywords

Web Archives; Big Data Processing; Classification; Digital Libraries.

1. INTRODUCTION

Many webpage archives are created by curators using the Internet Archive's service called Archive-It [2], which helps with harvesting, building, and preserving collections of digital content. The service takes URLs as input from a user. These URLs are used by Archive-It to crawl the web, guided by manual configuration details, and the resulting webpages are captured and stored in WARC files.

The captured webpages may not always be related to the event of interest; some are marketing pages linked to news pieces on the page with the given URL. The goal of our work was to take and clean a sample of webpage collections we curated, related to school shooting incidents: eliminate noise, remove non-relevant webpages, and organize the results. The output webpages would have to be accessible first for faceted searching and browsing, and later for analysis to add value for those in the social sciences as well as in diverse stakeholder communities.

There were three main tasks in this project. The first was to clean the webpages, which includes getting rid of HTML tags and stop words. The second task was to find the webpages relevant to the events of interest, which in the case of this project are shootings. The third task was to upload the cleaned and relevant webpages to

Permission to make digital or hard copies of part or all of this work for personal or classroom use is granted without fee provided that copies are not made or distributed for profit or commercial advantage and that copies bear this notice and the full citation on the first page. Copyrights for third-party components of this work must be honored. For all other uses, contact the Owner/Author.
Copyright is held by the owner/author(s).

JCDL '16, June 19-23, 2016, Newark, NJ, USA
ACM 978-1-4503-4229-2/16/06.
http://dx.doi.org/10.1145/2910896.2925466

Apache Solr, running on our big data cluster, so that they would be easily accessible, and amenable to further analysis.

2. SCHOOL SHOOTINGS

Table 1 lists the six school shooting collections along with the date, location, the number of HTML and non-HTML documents. The non-HTML documents include CSS, image, audio, video, and Javascript files.

Table 1. Shooting Collections

Collection	Date	Location	HTML	non-HTML
Alabama University Shooting	2/12/2010	Alabama, U.S.	73,307	33,175
Brazilian School Shooting	4/7/2011	Rio de Janeiro, Brazil	30,970	4,807
Connecticut School Shooting	12/14/2012	Connecticut, U.S.	11,697	13,609
Northern Illinois University Shooting	2/14/2008	Illinois, U.S.	3,995	12,298
Norway Shooting	7/22/2011	Norway	10,321	36,093
Youngstown Shooting	2/6/2011	Ohio, U.S.	11,710	32,315

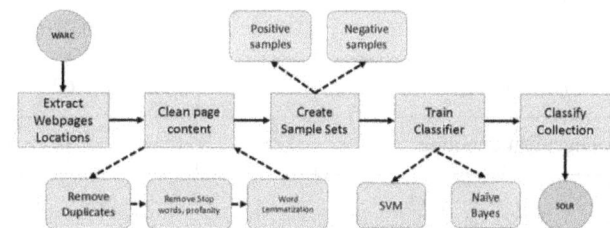

Figure 1. System Workflow

3. SYSTEM ARCHITECTURE

3.1 Cleaning and Preprocessing Collections

Figure 1 shows the design of the system developed to process the collections, showing the overall architecture. The system was implemented using Python [5] scripts. The cleaning process involves multiple subtasks, such as extracting the main text body of the page, word lemmatization, and removal of selected words and phrases.

In the first task, noise can be defined as stop words. In this step, we identified and removed all character sequences of stop words, which contribute little to the meaning of the page. We also extracted the main article of the webpage [6], getting rid of the non-relevant parts of the webpage (header, footer, and navigation). In the second task, the words of the text content of the webpage are lemmatized. This ensures that the content is standardized, to facilitate feature selection in the classification stage. We also removed duplicate webpages, which have the same title and same content. Table 2 shows the number of resulting documents after removing duplicates as well as invalid documents, i.e., those with HTML parsing errors that preclude easy text extraction.

Table 2. Number of unique and valid HTML documents in each collection

| Collection | Valid | | Invalid |
	Unique	Duplicate	
Alabama Univ. Shooting	6470	11659	12841
Brazilian School Shooting	1120	1813	1062
Connecticut School Shooting	3238	5657	2815
Northern Illinois Univ. Shooting	15385	31619	26303
Norway Shooting	7419	2002	900
Youngstown Shootings	3427	4549	3721

Table 3. Evaluation of SVM Classifier

Collection	Precision	Recall	F1
Alabama University Shooting	0.82	0.75	0.7
Brazilian School Shooting	0.53	0.73	0.61
Connecticut School Shooting	0.83	0.74	0.72
Northern Illinois University Shooting	0.83	0.74	0.72
Norway Shooting	0.73	0.65	0.62
Youngstown Shooting	0.26	0.51	0.34

3.2 Classifying Collections

The classification step involves multiple preprocessing steps such as creating training data, feature extraction, feature selection, and experimentation with machine learning classifier approaches. We used the 'scikit-learn' [4] machine learning library routines, written in Python [5], as part of the implementation.

We manually created a sample of positive webpages that are judged to be relevant to the content of the collection, and a sample of negative webpages that are not relevant. These sample sets are used to train a classifier for each collection. The labelled data is divided into 75%-25% split for training and testing, respectively.

We experimented with two types of classifiers: Naïve Bayes (NB) and Support Vector Machines (SVM). After converting the webpage text using the Vector Space Model (VSM), we applied the chi-square algorithm for finding the best K features. We have experimented with different values of K and will report results on the best value for each collection.

Table 3 shows the performance of the SVM classifier on the test data of all collections using precision, recall, and F1 score measures. We chose SVM classifiers as they showed better results than NB.

Results of classification (applying the trained classifier on the webpages in each collection) are shown in Table 4. The low precision, and the variability in precision values, are points of serious concern, and have led to much additional work in our research group, aimed to help curators of event archives more easily build collections of relevant documents.

Table 4. Classification Results

Collection	Rel. (%)	Non-rel. (%)	# HTML Pages
Alabama University Shooting	1.4	98.6	6470
Brazilian School Shooting	8.8	91.2	1120
Connecticut School Shooting	17.5	82.5	3238
Northern Illinois University Shooting	26.7	73.3	15385
Norway Shooting	13.5	86.5	7419
Youngstown Shooting	40.0	60.0	3427

Ongoing work includes: adding more shooting event collections, studying how the methodology developed can be applied to other types of collections (such as one on climate change), optimizing the process as it is applied on our 20-node Hadoop cluster, scaling up to support other types of events using the roughly 1.1 billion tweets we have collected, and connecting with focused crawling.

4. ACKNOWLEDGMENTS

This material is based upon work supported by the National Science Foundation under Grant No. NSF - IIS1319578: Small: Integrated Digital Event Archiving and Library (IDEAL).

5. REFERENCES

[1] Heritrix, http://www.crawler.archive.org/index.html accessed on 12/26/2015

[2] Archive-It, https://archive-it.org/, accessed on 12/26/2015

[3] E. A. Fox, D. Shoemaker, A. Kavanaugh, S. Sheetz, J. Bailey, M. Farag, S. Lee. Integrated Digital Events Archiving and Library (IDEAL), http://eventsarchive.org, accessed on 1/24/2016

[4] Sklearn, http://scikit-learn.org/stable/, accessed on 10/12/2015

[5] Python, https://www.python.org/, accessed on 10/12/2015.

[6] Readability, https://github.com/buriy/python-readability, accessed on 03/28/2016.

InterPlanetary Wayback: The Permanent Web Archive

Sawood Alam, Mat Kelly, and Michael L. Nelson
Old Dominion University, Department of Computer Science, Norfolk VA, 23529, USA
{salam,mkelly,mln}@cs.odu.edu

ABSTRACT

To facilitate permanence and collaboration in web archives, we built InterPlanetary Wayback to disseminate the contents of WARC files into the IPFS network. IPFS is a peer-to-peer content-addressable file system that inherently allows deduplication and facilitates opt-in replication. We split the header and payload of WARC response records before disseminating into IPFS to leverage the deduplication, build a CDXJ index, and combine them at the time of replay. From a 1.0 GB sample Archive-It collection of WARCs containing 21,994 mementos, we found that on an average, 570 files can be indexed and disseminated into IPFS per minute. We also found that in our naive prototype implementation, replay took on an average 370 milliseconds per request.

1. INTRODUCTION

The recently created InterPlanetary File System (IPFS) [2] is showing the potential to facilitate data persistence through a peer-to-peer network for dissemination and discovery. In this paper we introduce a scheme and software prototype[1], InterPlanetary Wayback (ipwb), that partitions, indexes, and deploys the payloads of archival data records into the IPFS peer-to-peer "permanent web" for sharing and offsite redundant preservation and replay.

The Web ARChive (WARC) format is an ISO standard[2] to store live web archive content in a concatenated record-based file. IA's web crawler, Heritrix [3], generates WARC files to be read and the content re-experienced in an archival replay system. OpenWayback[3] (written in Java) and pywb[4] (written in Python) are two such replay systems. We leverage and extend on the pywb codebase in this work.

To access the representations stored by an archival crawler, a replay system must refer to an index that maps the original URI (or, URI-R in Memento [4] terminology) and the time of capture (Memento-Datetime) to the record stored in a WARC file. CDX is one such indexing format along with the extended CDXJ format [1], with the latter allowing arbitrary JSON objects within each index record. In our initial prototype we take advantage of pywb's native support for CDXJ and use the arbitrary JSON data to store metadata

[1]https://github.com/oduwsdl/ipwb

[2]http://www.digitalpreservation.gov/formats/fdd/fdd000236.shtml

[3]https://github.com/iipc/openwayback

[4]https://github.com/ikreymer/pywb

Permission to make digital or hard copies of part or all of this work for personal or classroom use is granted without fee provided that copies are not made or distributed for profit or commercial advantage and that copies bear this notice and the full citation on the first page. Copyrights for third-party components of this work must be honored. For all other uses, contact the owner/author(s).

JCDL '16 June 19-23, 2016, Newark, NJ, USA

© 2016 Copyright held by the owner/author(s).

ACM ISBN 978-1-4503-4229-2/16/06. . . $15.00

DOI: http://dx.doi.org/10.1145/2910896.2925467

```
SURT_URI DATETIME {
  "id": "WARC-Record-ID",
  "url": "ORIGINAL_URI",
  "status": "3-DIGIT_HTTP_STATUS",
  "mime": "Content-Type",
  "locator": "urn:ipfs/HEADER_DIGEST/PAYLOAD_DIGEST"
}
```

Figure 1: A single-line CDXJ record template, shown on multiple lines for readability

about WARC records within IPFS (i.e., the content digest needed for lookup in IPFS).

IPFS is a content addressable peer-to-peer distributed file system [2]. By extracting the HTTP response body (henceforth "payload") from the records within a WARC file, IPFS allows our prototype to generate a signature uniquely representative of this content. This payload can then be pushed into the IPFS system and retrieved at a later date when the URI-M is queried. Content addressability allows for network-wide deduplication of the content. The digest of the content is used as the key to locate the content in the peer-to-peer network.

2. IMPLEMENTATION

CDXJ is a text-based file format that we utilize to store indexes of the archived content. Each line in the CDXJ file holds one index record. The line begins with a SURTed URI[5] and datetime followed by a single-line JSON block that stores reference to the content and other arbitrary metadata (Figure 1). We utilize the last field in a CDXJ record (a JSON object) to store the HTTP response headers and payload digests, original status code when the URI-R was crawled, the MIME-type of the content, and a UUID to identify a memento. The two digests that are used to locate the contents from the IPFS system and build the response are encoded into a single field called "locator" using a URN scheme[6].

In designing ipwb, it was critical to consider the HTTP header returned at crawl time separately from the HTTP response body. The HTTP response header's content will change with every capture, as the datetime returned from a server is temporally dependent. Compare this to the response body, which very often contains the same content on each access, more often for static resources. Were the HTTP header and response body combined then added to IPFS, every IPFS hash would be unique, nullifying the potential for de-duplication of identical content. Further, ipwb only retains response records. The rationale for this design decision is that the state of the art of web archive replay systems do not consider the WARC request record upon replay. While including request records may be useful in the future (for instance, to take into account the user-agent originally used to view the live website), WARC content is currently fully replayable without preserving the request records.

[5]http://crawler.archive.org/articles/user_manual/glossary.html#surt

[6]https://www.w3.org/TR/uri-clarification/

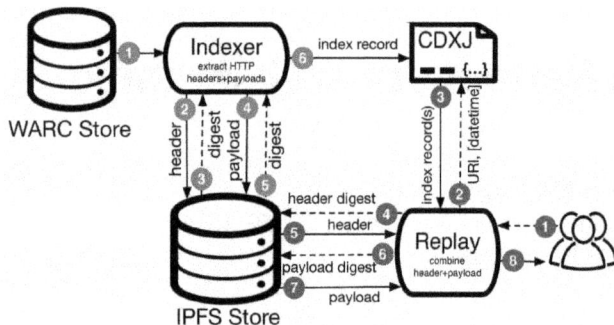

Figure 2: The ipwb indexer and replay workflow

Our prototype works in two phases, illustrated in Figure 2 with red (*Indexing*) and blue (*Replay*) annotations:

- *Indexing* – extracts records from the WARC store one record at a time, splits each record into HTTP header and payload, stores the two pieces into IPFS (compressing before storing, if necessary), and generates a CDXJ record using the returned references and some other metadata from the WARC record.

- *Replay* – receives request from users containing a lookup URI and optionally a datetime, queries for matching record in the CDXJ, fetches the corresponding header and payload from the IPFS Store (using references returned from the index record), combines them, and performs necessary transformation to build the response to the user.

3. EVALUATION

We tested our ipwb prototype on a data set from an Archive-It collection[7] about the 2011 Japan Earthquake consisting of 10 WARC files, each about 100 MB when compressed, totaling 1.0 GB on disk.

We indexed the WARCs using pywb's cdx-indexer and ipwb's indexer to generate a standard CDXJ file and one containing the IPFS-hashes (as described in Section 2), respectively. Generating ipwb's CDXJ file for 21,981 mementos in the data set took 66.6 minutes including the time required to push the data into the IPFS network and producing the IPFS hashes to be included in the CDXJ. The average indexing rate inclusive of the data dissemination to IPFS was 9.48 files per second. Because IPFS is in the early stages of development, performance when adding many small files to the IPFS network[8] consumes a large part of the time required for indexing.

To evaluate the replay time, we fetched 600 sample URI-Ms from each of pywb and ipwb independently, with both using the same WARC basis for CDXJ generation, performed prior to the replay procedure. The total time required for pywb to access the sample URI-Rs using local WARC files for lookup was 5.26 seconds. The same URI-Rs replayed in ipwb with the same WARC records disseminated into the IPFS system took 222 seconds. The increased latency is because of how IPFS works, however, it provides infinite cacheability and can benefit from CDNs. The latency is also because of our naive implementation where we fetch the header and payload sequentially rather than in parallel from the IPFS. Additionally, IPFS promises greater persistence (which is desired in archiving) with the cost of added latency. Figure 3a shows the amount of disk space required to convert and add compressed and uncompressed WARC content to IPFS. With the tested data set where there is very little duplication of HTTP response bodies because of URI-M uniqueness, the slope of the uncompressed additions was 1.10 while the slope of the compressed additions was 1.12. In practice,

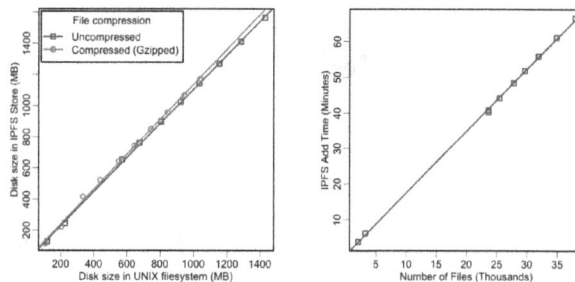

(a) Space cost   (b) Time cost

Figure 3: IPFS storage space and time cost analysis

where duplication of response body content is much more prevalent in a collection of WARCs, the file representative of the response body of the duplicated content will not need to be added to the IPFS, requiring only the file representative of the unique HTTP header (Section 2) to be added. This would result in a significantly smaller slope were the experiment extended to a larger collection. Figure 3b shows that as more files (extracted from the WARCs) are added to the IPFS system, the time required to do so correlates linearly with the number of files (not necessarily the size of the files for small files) with a slope of 1.74 (on average, 570 files per minute).

4. FUTURE WORK AND CONCLUSIONS

Because of the novelty of IPFS, particularly relative to web archiving, there are numerous applications to expand this work. Collection builders can share their collections by just exchanging the index while keeping the data in the IPFS network and others can optionally replicate the data in their storage for redundancy. Further considerations of access control can also be addressed to encrypt and restrict content based on privacy and security mechanisms. Another model of IPFS-based archiving system can be built entirely using IPFS and IPNS technologies without the need of external indexes.

In this work we developed a prototype to partition, disseminate, and replay WARC file records in the InterPlanetary File System (IPFS). Through experimentation on a 1.0 GB data set containing 21,994 URI-Ms, we found that extracting and indexing records from WARC files took 66.6 minutes inclusive of dissemination into the IPFS system. The average indexing rate inclusive of the data dissemination to IPFS was 570 files per minute on average.

5. ACKNOWLEDGEMENTS

We would like to thank Ilya Kreymer for his feedback during the development of the ipwb prototype and guidance in interfacing with the pywb replay system. This work was supported in part by NSF award 1624067 via the Archives Unleashed Hackathon[9], where we developed the prototype.

6. REFERENCES

[1] S. Alam, M. L. Nelson, H. Van de Sompel, L. Balakireva, H. Shankar, and D. S. H. Rosenthal. Web Archive Profiling Through CDX Summarization. In *Proceedings of TPDL '15*, pages 3–14.

[2] J. Benet. IPFS - Content Addressed, Version, P2P File System. Technical Report arXiv:1407.3561, 2014.

[3] G. Mohr, M. Kimpton, M. Stack, and I. Ranitovic. Introduction to Heritrix, an Archival Quality Web Crawler. In *Proceedings of IWAW '04*, September 2004.

[4] H. Van de Sompel, M. Nelson, and R. Sanderson. HTTP Framework for Time-Based Access to Resource States – Memento. IETF RFC 7089, December 2013.

---

[7] https://archive-it.org/collections/2438

[8] https://github.com/ipfs/go-ipfs/issues/1216

[9] http://archivesunleashed.ca

Improving Similar Document Retrieval Using a Recursive Pseudo Relevance Feedback Strategy

Kyle Williams[‡], C. Lee Giles[†‡]
[‡]Information Sciences and Technology, [†]Computer Science and Engineering
The Pennsylvania State University, University Park, PA 16802, USA
kwilliams@psu.edu, giles@ist.psu.edu

ABSTRACT

We present a recursive pseudo relevance feedback strategy for improving retrieval performance in similarity search. The strategy recursively searches on search results returned for a given query and produces a tree that is used for ranking. Experiments on the Reuters 21578 and WebKB datasets show how the strategy leads to a significant improvement in similarity search performance.

1. INTRODUCTION

Finding similar files is a common use case for search in digital libraries, as in research paper recommendation [1] or near duplicate detection. One of the requirements in similarity search is that the query documents have features in common with the authored documents, which may not always be the case even when documents are semantically similar [2]. This problem is commonly known as feature mismatch and relevance feedback methods based on user feedback or the top k results have been developed for query reformulation. We present a pseudo relevance feedback search strategy for similarity search. Unlike most work in relevance feedback where query reformulation is used based on a set of documents, we instead generate a set of new queries, where each new query is based on one of the top k returned search results. We perform this recursively on each search result and the output of our search is a tree, which we use for ranking.

2. RECURSIVE SEARCH AND RANKING

For an initial query Q that returns a set of results $\mathbb{R}$, the strategy involves recursively searching on the top $k \in \mathbb{R}$ for some recursive depth d and then combining and ranking the results of all searches. The output of the recursive search process is a tree as shown in Figure 1. In the tree, a directed edge from a node n_1 to a node n_2 represents the fact that n_1 was used as a query to retrieve n_2. For instance, the query Q was used to retrieve $r_{1,1}$ and $r_{1,2}$; $r_{1,1}$ was used to retrieve $r_{2,1}$ and $r_{2,2}$; $r_{2,1}$ to retrieve $r_{3,1}$, etc. We use this tree for ranking based on the intuition that if a document

Permission to make digital or hard copies of part or all of this work for personal or classroom use is granted without fee provided that copies are not made or distributed for profit or commercial advantage and that copies bear this notice and the full citation on the first page. Copyrights for third-party components of this work must be honored. For all other uses, contact the owner/author(s).

JCDL '16 June 19-23, 2016, Newark, NJ, USA

© 2016 Copyright held by the owner/author(s).

ACM ISBN 978-1-4503-4229-2/16/06.

DOI: http://dx.doi.org/10.1145/2910896.2925468

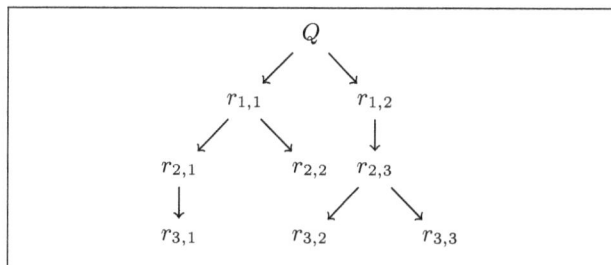

Figure 1: An example of a search result tree produced by the recursive search strategy.

was retrieved using the recursive feedback mechanism and not by the initial query, then it does not have features in common with the initial query and thus its score should be penalized. We propose to penalize search results based on their tree distance from the query document and, by doing this, we aim to account for the problem of performing blind relevance feedback on search results that are not relevant.

Assume a scoring function exists $\varphi(\cdot)$ exists that calculates the similarity between a query document q and a search result r. We then define a set of ranking formulas $\Psi(\varphi, T)$ that assign scores to documents based on both the similarity score φ and the search result tree T produced through the recursive search. Equations 1-5 represent a few simple formulas that are used in this study.

$$\psi_{Flat}(\varphi(q,r), T) = \varphi(q,r)^{\frac{T.depth(r)}{T.depth(r)}} \tag{1}$$

$$\psi_{Power}(\varphi(q,r), T) = \varphi(q,r)^{T.depth(r)} \tag{2}$$

$$\psi_{Decay}(\varphi(q,r), T) = \varphi(q,r)^{1+(1-\frac{1}{T.depth(r)})} \tag{3}$$

$$\psi_{Log}(\varphi(q,r), T) = \varphi(q,r)^{1+log_{10}T.depth(r)} \tag{4}$$

$$\psi_{Div}(\varphi(q,r), T) = \frac{\varphi(q,r)}{T.depth(r)} \tag{5}$$

The design of the ranking functions above is based on our intuition that the tree distance from the query document to a search result is correlated with relevance and that search results should be penalized for having higher tree distances. Thus, all of our ranking functions are designed to capture this in various ways by considering $T.depth(r)$, which is the depth in the tree T at which r occurs. The first ranking function, ψ_{Flat} (Equation 1), does not actually consider the

Table 1: Retrieval performance on Reuters and WebKB datasets. d is the recursive depth. $*$ and $\dagger$ represent statistically better performance than Baselines 1 and 2, respectively.

Ranking	Precision@10		MAP	
	d = 2	d = 3	d = 2	d = 3
Reuters				
Baseline 1	0.8591	0.8591	0.2664	0.2644
Baseline 2	0.8677	0.8677	0.4494*	0.4494*
Flat	0.8660	0.8653	0.4567*	0.4569*
Power	0.8703*,†	0.8698	0.4545*	0.4543*
Decay	0.8694	0.8689	0.4592*,†	0.4596*,†
Log	0.8698	0.8688	0.4573*,†	0.4576*,†
Div	**0.8706***	**0.8705***	**0.4610*,†**	**0.4611*,†**
WebKB				
Baseline 1	0.5127	0.5127	0.0812	0.0812
Baseline 2	0.5161	0.5161	0.1416*	0.1416*
Flat	0.5162	0.5153	0.1546*,†	0.1548*,†
Power	0.5174	0.5160	**0.1573*,†**	**0.1612*,†**
Decay	0.5154	0.5134	0.1568*,†	0.1589*,†
Log	0.5156	0.5128	0.1571*,†	0.1599*,†
Div	**0.5182***	**0.5167***	0.1543*,†	0.1579*,†

tree structure but instead has the effect of *flattening* the tree and each result is simply assigned its similarity score. The remaining functions all penalize the scores of results based on their tree distance from the query. The difference between them is in the severity of the penalization.

3. EXPERIMENTS

3.1 Method

We use the Reuters 21578 and WebKB datasets and, following other studies [3], we define two documents as being similar if they belong to the same category. The Reuters dataset contains news articles and we use the 10 most popular categories from the Reuters dataset [3]. The WebKB dataset contains categorized University webpages and we use data from Cornell University for testing. Queries are constructed from the documents based on the top 10 TF-IDF ranked terms and cosine similarity is used as the scoring function $\varphi(\cdot)$. We measure Precision@10 and Mean Average Precision (MAP). We consider two baselines. **Baseline 1 - regular search:** regular search is performed with no relevance feedback. **Baseline 2 - query reformulation:** the query is reformulated based on the top 10 TF-IDF ranked terms among the top 10 results for the initial query.

3.2 Results

Results are shown in Table 1. As can be seen from the table, Baseline 1 performs worst overall. All search strategies achieve a higher Precision@10 than Baseline 1 at a recursive depth of 2 and 3. Similarly, all search strategies also achieve better MAP. For the Reuters dataset, all of the recursive search strategies except the *Flat* ranking strategy achieve better Precision@10 than Baseline 2. The reason for this is that the Flat ranking strategy does not consider the tree structure but instead flattens the tree. This provides evidence to support our intuition that penalizing search results that appear lower in the search result tree can lead to better

ranking. The two ranking functions that achieve the highest Precision@10 are the Power and Div ranking functions. For the Power ranking function, the mean is significantly better than the mean for Baseline 2 at the 5% level based on a Wilcox signed-rank test. For this dataset, there is very little difference between the Precision@10 for a recursive depth of 2 or 3. We speculate that the reason is that too few results score highly enough to change the top 10 ranked documents.

For the WebKB dataset, the Power and Div ranking function have a higher Precision@10 compared to Baseline 2 and increasing to a depth of 3 leads to a decrease in Precision@10. In some instance, this decrease can be large as is the case for the Log ranking function where there is an over 2% decrease. As was the case with the Reuters dataset, the highest Precision@10 at depth 2 is achieved by the Div ranking method and was 0.52. It's interesting to note that, for both datasets, the Power and Div ranking functions achieve the highest Precision@10. This intuitively makes sense since these methods penalize results that appear lower in the tree more than the other methods. Therefore, the top k results are likely to be very similar to the case of when no recursive search is performed except still include additional documents that are highly similar to the original query document.

For the Reuters dataset, all recursive methods achieve higher MAP than Baseline 2. For the Div, Log and Decay ranking functions, the differences in MAP are significant at the 5% level. There is very little difference between the MAP achieved at a recursive depth of 2 and a recursive depth of 3, which was also observed for Precision@10. The highest MAP at depth 2 is achieved by the Div ranking function. For the WebKB dataset, all recursive methods also achieved higher MAP than Baseline 2. At a recursive depth of 2, all results are significant. For this dataset, increasing the recursive depth to 3 leads to a visible increase in MAP.

4. CONCLUSIONS

This paper presented a strategy for improving performance in similarity search and experiments showed how the recursive search strategies are effective in finding more relevant documents. Furthermore, for most of the experiments, the methods that take the tree structure into consideration perform best, indicating that the structure of the search result tree provides information that can be used to improve ranking. However, that being said, it is likely that the most appropriate ranking formula that takes the search tree into consideration is dependent on the dataset used. We leave investigating this for future work.

Acknowledgments

We gratefully acknowledge partial support by the National Science Foundation.

5. REFERENCES

[1] C. Nascimento, A. H. Laender, A. S. da Silva, and M. A. Gonçalves. A source independent framework for research paper recommendation. In *Proceeding of JCDL*, pages 297–306, 2011.

[2] J. Xu and B. Croft. Query Expansion Using Local and Global Document Analysis. In *Proceedings of SIGIR*, pages 4–11, 1996.

[3] D. Zhang, J. Wang, D. Cai, and J. Lu. Self-taught hashing for fast similarity search. *Proceeding of SIGIR*, pages 18–25, 2010.

Curve Separation for Line Graphs in Scholarly Documents

Sagnik Ray Choudhury
Information Sciences and
Technology
Pennsylvania State University
sagnik@psu.edu

Shuting Wang
EECS
Pennsylvania State University
sxw327@psu.edu

C. Lee. Giles
Information Sciences and
Technology
Pennsylvania State University
giles@ist.psu.edu

ABSTRACT

Line graphs are abundant in scholarly papers. They are usually generated from a data table and that data can not be accessed. One important step in an automated data extraction pipeline is the curve separation problem: segmenting the pixels into separate curves. Previous work in this domain has focused on raster graphics extracted from scholarly PDFs, whereas most scholarly plots are embedded as vector graphics. We report a system to extract these plots as SVG images and show how that can improve both the accuracy (90%) and the scalability (5-8 seconds) of the curve separation problem.

Keywords

Data Extraction; Line Graph; Vector Graphics

1. INTRODUCTION

Line graphs are 2D plots with single or multiple curves in the plotting region. They are heavily used in scholarly papers to compare multiple methods. A line graph is generated from a data table. It would be extremely beneficial to automatically regenerate that table[3]. An important step for that is curve separation: clustering each foreground pixel in separate curves.

Previous work in the curve separation problem has used figures extracted as raster graphics. Figures can be embedded in PDF documents in raster (PNG, JPEG) or vector formats (SVG, PS, EPS, PDF). It is hard to extract vector graphics from PDFs and recently some methods were proposed[2]. These methods extract the bounding box of a figure heuristically, then the PDF page containing the figure is rasterized (converted into a raster image) and the necessary region is cropped.

We examined a dataset of 40,000 figures extracted from 10,000 papers published in top 50 computer science conferences between 2004 and 2014. More than 70% figures were originally embedded in vector graphics formats. This motivated us to extract the figures as SVG (an XML based vector graphics format) images. When any image in a vector graphics format is embedded in a PDF, the commands are just transformed. When the same PDF is converted to an SVG, an inverse conversion happens. All paths or characters in the

Permission to make digital or hard copies of part or all of this work for personal or classroom use is granted without fee provided that copies are not made or distributed for profit or commercial advantage and that copies bear this notice and the full citation on the first page. Copyrights for third-party components of this work must be honored. For all other uses, contact the owner/author(s).

JCDL '16 June 19-23, 2016, Newark, NJ, USA

© 2016 Copyright held by the owner/author(s).

ACM ISBN 978-1-4503-4229-2/16/06.

DOI: http://dx.doi.org/10.1145/2910896.2925469

original image can be restored from the converted SVG. Whereas, if we extract the image by rasterizing a PDF page, all such information is lost. This simple and effective observation has gone largely unnoticed in previous work.

Our system converts any SVG into a flat (no grouping element) and "atomic" SVG where each path is separated into a set of painting commands each with exactly one argument and a bounding box. The paths and characters inside a figure bounding box are combined to produce an SVG image for a line graph. These SVG images are processed for curve separation.

2. RELATED WORK

Brouwer et al. [1] proposed methods to separate overlapping data points in scholarly scatter plots. A more comprehensive version of their architecture [3] reported curve extraction techniques for line graphs, but only for continuous curves. These works used raster graphics; our system uses a different paradigm and handle more generic cases.

3. EXTRACTION OF VECTOR IMAGES

An input PDF is split into pages and each page is converted into an SVG image using InkScape [1]. A "Path" command in an InkScape SVG can have multiple operations for drawing shapes such as lines, smooth and unsmooth Bézier curves and elliptical arcs. Each "operation" is of the form ("operator", "operand") and can be used in the absolute and the relative mode. Also, each operator can have a sequence of operands instead of a single one. Each path command is an XML node; the color and the stroke patterns are provided as the attributes. Multiple path commands can be grouped together with a grouping command ("g"). Each such group can be grouped further, leading to a hierarchical structure. Each path or group can have a "transform" attribute that changes the co-ordinate system by rotation, scaling or matrix multiplication.

An example path from an InkScape SVG is "*<path id="path170" d="m 2209.6, 3082.45 2114.25, 0 0, 1340.53 -2114.25, 0 0, -1340.53 z" />*". This path has a *moveto* command and a *relative lineto* command each with a sequence of arguments to draw two horizontal and the two vertical lines. This path can come from a marker or axis in a line graph. But unless we parse the path into smaller path commands (four separate line segments), they can not be combined to create such meaningful shapes.

SVG paths follow a context free grammar expressed through EBNF (Extended Backus-Naur Form). We wrote a parser combinator to parse an SVG path into a sequence of underlying operations. The parsers are regular expression based and capable of

---

[1] http://personal.psu.edu/szr163/svgconversionresults/converted.html

parsing a single operation. The combinator accepts a sequence of such parsers and returns a new parser as its output.

After retrieving such a sequence of operations (each with one or multiple operands) from a path command, we need to convert each operation into a sequence of *absolute* path commands each with a *single* argument. Any SVG path must start with an absolute move command, but all subsequent operations can be relative. Let us assume we have the absolute starting point for a relative lineto operation with three arguments (*m 2209.6, 3082.45 2114.25, 0 0, 1340.53 -2114.25, 0 0, -1340.53"*). Starting point for the first absolute lineto command will be the starting point for the whole path. End point for this command will be the argument itself. Starting point for the second absolute lineto command will be the end point for the lineto command created with the first argument. It is easy to see that a single operation can be transformed into a sequence of path commands using such a recursive formulation. A sequence of operations can again be treated in the same recursive manner to produce the final commands.

Next, the bounding box for each absolute path is calculated. While that is trivial for some operators (lines/ vertical lines), operations such as ellipse or Bézier curves need to converted into their parametric representations. More details are available in the code repository[2].

A path can have a transform attribute and it can belong to multiple groups. Transform operations from all these elements can change the bounding box coordinates. We first recursively traverse the tree structured SVG to create a "dictionary" data structure with the command ids as keys and a sequence of group ids as values. Each transform operation for a path is parsed (using a parser combinator) into a transform matrix and multiple such matrices (from the path and all the groups the path belongs to) are multiplied sequentially to generate a final transform matrix. This transform matrix is multiplied with the bounding box from the last step to produce the final bounding box for a path. Finally, all paths and characters within a figure bounding box are combined.

4. CURVE EXTRACTION

A curve in an SVG line graph is a collection of paths. But paths can draw axes or grid lines and tick marks as well. Horizontal and vertical paths painted in black or grey and spanning at least 70% of the image are probable axes or grid lines. Four such lines closest to the image boundary are classified as axes lines. Horizontal and vertical lines intersecting with the axes lines are classified as tic marks.

For color line graphs, all other paths are clustered based on the color and each cluster is output as a curve. Because we have "paths" instead of pixels, overlapping curves are extracted perfectly (figure 1, 2 out of 5 curves are shown).

A marker is a collection of paths that looks like a shape: a rectangle, star etc. For black and white (BW) graphs, we create groups of K paths such that any path in a group intersects with at least one other path in the same group. A rectangle is such a group with two horizontal and two vertical lines such that each horizontal line intersects both the vertical lines and vice versa. Similarly, we define rules for all other shapes. More details are available in the code repository[3]. Paths belonging neither to the marker groups nor to the axes and ticks are clustered based on their "style" attribute. If we can't find any marker, each cluster is output as a curve. Else, for each such cluster, we find out the marker group that intersects with the maximum number of elements in that cluster and all paths

---

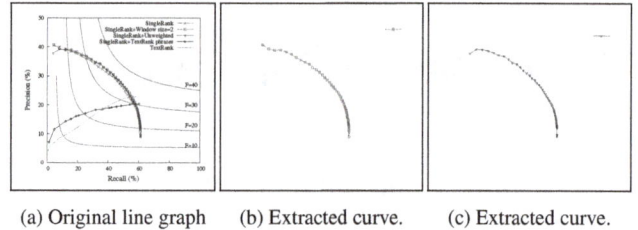

(a) Original line graph   (b) Extracted curve.   (c) Extracted curve.

Figure 1: Curve extraction from a color line graph.

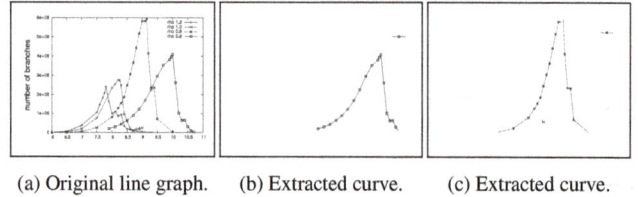

(a) Original line graph.   (b) Extracted curve.   (c) Extracted curve.

Figure 2: Curve extraction from a black and white line graph.

in that cluster are added to that marker group (figure 2, best viewed when zoomed in).

We experimented with 200 color and 200 BW line graphs extracted from 400 papers collected randomly from the CiteSeerX repository. Due to the lack of the gold standard data, we use visual evaluation: a curve is considered "correctly extracted" if a person can see at least 80% of the curve in the original plot and at most 10% of any other curve. Precision is defined as the number of correctly extracted curves/ total number of curves extracted and recall as defined as the number of correctly extracted curves/ total number of curves in the plot. The average precision and recall values for the color line graphs are 91% and 90%, respectively. For BW line graphs, these values are both close to 60%. While our approach works well for color graphs, BW graphs need improvement. In comparison, previous work[3] has considered only connected curves (no dashed line) with no markers on mostly synthetic datasets (the graphs were plotted, not extracted). Running time for the algorithm is 5-8 seconds per image on a quad core desktop with 16 GB memory, including the step for the SVG production.

5. CONCLUSION AND FUTURE WORK

We report a method to extract scholarly figures as vector graphics and show how that helps in an important problem: curve separation from line graphs. Compared to previous work, our methods are more robust. They are also scalable and accurate. Future work involves improving the accuracy of the problem for black and white line graphs.

6. REFERENCES

[1] W. Browuer, S. Kataria, S. Das, P. Mitra, and C. L. Giles. Segregating and extracting overlapping data points in two-dimensional plots. In *Proceedings of the 8th ACM/IEEE-CS joint conference on Digital libraries*, JCDL '08, pages 276–279, New York, NY, USA, 2008. ACM.

[2] C. Clark and S. Divvala. Looking beyond text: Extracting figures, tables, and captions from computer science paper. 2015.

[3] X. Lu, S. Kataria, W. J. Brouwer, J. Z. Wang, P. Mitra, and C. L. Giles. Automated analysis of images in documents for intelligent document search. *IJDAR*, 12(2):65–81, 2009.

---

[2]https://github.com/sagnik/svgimagesfromallenaipdffigures
[3]https://github.com/sagnik/linegraph-curve-separation

Issues of Dealing with Fluid Data in Digital Libraries

Soo-yeon Hwang (Organizer)
School of Communication and
Information, Rutgers University
sy.hwang@rutgers.edu

Melissa Cragin
National Center for Supercomputing
Applications, University of Illinois at
Urbana-Champaign
m_cragin@yahoo.com

Michael Lesk
School of Communication and
Information, Rutgers University
lesk@rci.rutgers.edu

Yu-Hung Lin
Rutgers University Libraries
liny4@rulmail.rutgers.edu

Daniel O'Connor
School of Communication and
Information, Rutgers University
dan.oconnor@rutgers.edu

ABSTRACT
This panel discusses the issues of dealing with fluid data and curating new data in digital libraries.

Keywords
Digital libraries; Big data; Curation; Fluid data; Velocity; Secondary analysis

1. INTRODUCTION
Digital libraries confront the issue of dealing with fluid data which changes over time and this is especially exacerbated with big data. One of the main characteristics of big data is its fluidity, in that it keeps expanding in volume and changing (also called the velocity characteristic of big data [1].) Many changes to big data sets might need to be curated, and the issue is how digital libraries cope with the fluid changes to the big data they are storing.

An additional issue involves secondary analysis. Transformations of data such as surface plot analyses and curvilinear model fitting can be done with standard data sets as well as big data sets. If someone uses the big data for secondary analysis, does the library need to store that data set as well? How would it curate new, derivative works' data? How is access provided to various iterations of a big data set? What would be the policy implications?

The expected audience for this panel includes those currently curating data sets and those complying with requirements to curate data and, if appropriate, make it publicly available. Also included here are those who work with and analyze data sets that change over time.

2. PANELISTS
- Melissa Cragin

  Executive Director, Midwest Big Data Hub, National Center for Supercomputing Applications, University of Illinois at Urbana-Champaign

  Melissa Cragin is the Executive Director for the Midwest Big Data Hub at the National Center for

Supercomputing Applications (NCSA), University of Illinois at Urbana-Champaign (UIUC). Prior to joining NCSA, Melissa was Staff Associate in the Office of the Assistant Director (OAD) of the Directorate of Biological Sciences (BIO) at the National Science Foundation (NSF), where she guided the development of data policy and accelerated community engagement on research data management and public access. Before joining the staff at NSF, Melissa served for two years in the BIO Directorate as an AAAS Science & Technology Policy Fellow. Prior to her work in the federal government, Melissa was on the faculty of the Graduate School of Library and Information Science at the University of Illinois, where she led the Data Curation Education Program and conducted research in the Center for Informatics Research in Science and Scholarship. She has a PhD from UIUC and an MLIS from Rutgers.

- Michael Lesk

  Professor, Dept. of Library and Information Science, School of Communication and Information, Rutgers University

  After receiving the PhD degree in Chemical Physics in 1969, Michael Lesk joined the computer science research group at Bell Laboratories, where he worked until 1984. From 1984 to 1995 he managed the computer science research group at Bellcore, and from 1998 to 2002 he was in charge of the Division of Information and Intelligent Systems at the National Science Foundation. Since 2003 he has been Professor of Library and Information Science at Rutgers University.

  He is best known for work in digital libraries, and his book "Understanding Digital Libraries" was published in 2004 by Morgan Kaufmann (second edition of a 1997 book). His research has included the CORE project for chemical information, early work on sense disambiguation, and he wrote Unix system utilities including those for tables, mail, and lexical analysis.

- Yu-Hung Lin

  Metadata Librarian for Continuing Resources, Scholarship and Data, Rutgers University Libraries

  Yu-Hung Lin is a Metadata Librarian for Continuing Resources, Scholarship and Data at Rutgers University. He works with faculty and researchers to plan and

Permission to make digital or hard copies of part or all of this work for personal or classroom use is granted without fee provided that copies are not made or distributed for profit or commercial advantage and that copies bear this notice and the full citation on the first page. Copyrights for third-party components of this work must be honored. For all other uses, contact the Owner/Author.
Copyright is held by the owner/author(s).

JCDL '16, June 19-23, 2016, Newark, NJ, USA
ACM 978-1-4503-4229-2/16/06.
DOI: http://dx.doi.org/10.1145/2910896.2926738

develop metadata application profiles to preserve digital scholarly publication and research data into RUcore (Rutgers Community Repository). In addition, he oversees and plans for access for users to print and electronic journals and databases in the library's catalog. Throughout his career, he has been working as cataloger, web application developer, systems librarian and digital services librarian at various types of libraries.

- Daniel O'Connor

Associate Professor, Dept. of Library and Information Science, School of Communication and Information, Rutgers University

Dan O'Connor has his MSLS and Ph.D. from Syracuse University and he is currently an Associate Professor in the Department of Library and Information Science at Rutgers where he teaches research methods in the undergraduate, masters and doctoral programs at the School of Communication & Information. Dan is currently Chair of the NJ Higher Education Leadership Council representing the interests of over 31,000 New Jersey faculty and staff. He is a nationally elected member the Executive Committee of the American Association of University Professors and a past-chair of the New Brunswick Faculty Council which includes over 60 academic departments. He has held consulting positions with the New York Public Library and the Metropolitan Museum of Art.

3. ORGANIZER

- Soo-yeon Hwang

PhD, Dept. of Library and Information Science, School of Communication and Information, Rutgers University

Soo-yeon Hwang recently earned a PhD from the School of Communication and Information, Rutgers University. Her research interests include time use with information, everyday use and social implications of information and communication technology, information system design, information ethics, and technology policy. She has a Master's degree in Information Economics, Management and Policy from the School of Information, University of Michigan, Ann Arbor, and a Bachelor's degree in Mass Communication from Yonsei University, Seoul, Korea. She has been writing computer programs since nine years old, has been an independent free and open source software developer, and has industry experience in all areas of software development on desktop, web, and mobile platforms.

4. REFERENCES

[1] Reinhalter, L., and Wittmann, R. J. 2014. The Library: Big Data's Boomtown. *The Serials Librarian*. 67, 4, 363-372. DOI= http://dx.doi.org/10.1080/0361526X.2014.915605.

Panel: Preserving Born-digital News

Edward McCain
University of Missouri, Columbia
mccaine@rjionline.org

Martin Klein
University of California, Los Angeles
martinklein0815@gmail.com

Matthew Weber
Rutgers, The State University
of New Jersey
matthew.weber@rutgers.edu

ABSTRACT

This panel examines the need for digital libraries to capture and preserve journalistic content in digital formats, especially online news.

CCS Concepts

• **Information Systems, Information systems applications, Digital Libraries and archives**

Keywords

Digital libraries; digital preservation; preservation repositories; preservation planning;

INTRODUCTION

News archives have proven value for a variety of researchers including historians, economists, sociologists, journalists, entrepreneurs, epidemiologists and many more. As journalistic content increasingly appears (and disappears) in digital formats, new paradigms are needed to capture and keep this valuable information.

This panel will explore some possible answers to the questions: How are we going to collect born-digital news content? What are the copyright issues involved? What are the possibilities for new kinds of algorithmic research? How can digital libraries help make this happen?

The expected audience for this panel includes those interested in the possibilities for working with digital collections of news content.

ORGANIZER

Edward McCain

Edward McCain serves as Digital Curator of Journalism at the Donald W. Reynolds Journalism Foundation and University of Missouri Libraries. He founded the Journalism Digital News Archive (JDNA) agenda and its related "Dodging the Memory Hole" outreach initiative. JDNA's purpose is to preserve and ensure access to born digital journalism. Using Theory of Change modeling, JDNA proposes to address the complexities of preserving born digital news by recognizing and engaging the stakeholders and the systems they employ in order to define a pathway toward long term, sustainable change. McCain's research has been supported by the Mizzou Advantage and the John S. and James L. Knight Foundation.

PANELISTS

Martin Klein

Martin Klein has a distinguished career in web preservation and digital libraries. His research is focused on the temporal aspect of the web, discovery and access of (archived) web resources, and scholarly communication. He has coauthored numerous articles in the web science and digital libraries domain and is the lead editor of the ResourceSync Specification (ANSI/NISO Z39.99). His research has been supported by the Library of Congress, NASA, Sloan Foundation, and the Andrew Mellon Foundation.

Mathew Weber

Matthew Weber is an Assistant Professor in the School of Communication and Information, and Co-Director of Rutgers' NetSCI Network Science research lab. Matthew's research examines organizational change and adaptation, both internal and external, in response to new information communication technology. His recent work focuses on the transformation of the news media industry in the United States in reaction to new forms of media production. This includes a large-scale longitudinal study examining strategies employed by media organizations for disseminating news and information in online networks. He is also leading an initiative to provide researchers with access to the Internet Archives (archive.org) in order to study digital traces of organizational networks. Matthew utilizes mixed methods in his work, including social network analysis, archival research and interviews. Matthew received his PhD in 2010 from the Annenberg School of Journalism and Communication at the University of Southern California.

Permission to make digital or hard copies of part or all of this work for personal or classroom use is granted without fee provided that copies are not made or distributed for profit or commercial advantage and that copies bear this notice and the full citation on the first page. Copyrights for third-party components of this work must be honored. For all other uses, contact the Owner/Author. Copyright is held by the owner/author(s).

JCDL '16, June 19-23, 2016, Newark, NJ, USA
ACM 978-1-4503-4229-2/16/06.
http://dx.doi.org/10.1145/2910896.2926739

Introduction to Digital Libraries

Edward A. Fox
Virginia Tech
Dept. of Computer Science
Blacksburg, VA 24061 USA
+1-540-231-5113
fox@vt.edu

ABSTRACT

This tutorial is a thorough and deep introduction to the Digital Libraries (DL) field, providing a firm foundation: covering key concepts and terminology, as well as services, systems, technologies, methods, standards, projects, issues, and practices. It introduces and builds upon a firm theoretical foundation (starting with the '5S' set of intuitive aspects: Streams, Structures, Spaces, Scenarios, Societies), giving careful definitions and explanations of all the key parts of a 'minimal digital library', and expanding from that basis to cover key DL issues. Illustrations come from a set of case studies. Attendees will be exposed to four Morgan and Claypool books that elaborate on 5S, published 2012-2014. Complementing the coverage of '5S' will be an overview of key aspects of the DELOS Reference Model and DL.org activities. Further, use of a Hadoop cluster supporting DLs will be described.

CCS Concepts

•Information systems → Digital libraries and archives;

Keywords

5S; Societies; Scenarios; Spaces; Structures; Streams

1. INTRODUCTION

Highlights of this tutorial include the applications of digital libraries [2] and the underlying technologies [3], which include: Exploration, Evaluation, Integration, Complex Objects, Annotation/Subdocuments, Ontologies, Classification, Text Extraction, Security, Content-based Image Retrieval, Education, Social Networks, Bioinformatics/eScience/ Simulation, and Geospatial Information.

Supporting all of those are integration methods, along with suitable schemes for evaluation [4]. By discussing all these topics we make clear that the 5S framework provides a comprehensive theoretical foundation for the field of digital libraries [1].

Permission to make digital or hard copies of part or all of this work for personal or classroom use is granted without fee provided that copies are not made or distributed for profit or commercial advantage and that copies bear this notice and the full citation on the first page. Copyrights for third-party components of this work must be honored. For all other uses, contact the owner/author(s).

JCDL '16 June 19-23, 2016, Newark, NJ, USA

© 2016 Copyright held by the owner/author(s).

ACM ISBN 978-1-4503-4229-2/16/06.

DOI: http://dx.doi.org/10.1145/2910896.2925429

2. DL TEACHING AND LEARNING

Educational resources from an US NSF funded grant to develop DL curriculum (see http://curric.dlib.vt.edu/) will be presented, including descriptions (aimed at teachers and learners) of the more than 30 major modules and sub-modules that cover the core DL topics and related topics (e.g., those used to teach in both undergraduate and graduate courses at Virginia Tech). Most of the modules have been reviewed, revised, field tested, and used at several locations. Further, NSF TUES support has aided integration of digital library coverage in each of 3 courses: Digital Libraries, Information Retrieval, and Computational Linguistics. Part of this involved problem-project based learning, with large collections and a Hadoop cluster. Based on the above, discussion of how to learn more about DLs, and how to teach others about DLs, will be tailored to the interests of the attendees.

3. TUTORIAL DESCRIPTION

3.1 Duration

Full day, on 19 June 2016.

3.2 Target Audience

Introductory or intermediate: Those new to the DL field, or coming to it from a different but related discipline, or just new to JCDL, should find this helpful, as they expand their involvement in the DL community.

This tutorial also should be of interest to those already involved in digital libraries, especially if they wish to organize/solidify their understanding and broaden their perspective, or to teach a DL course.

Expected number: 10-30

3.3 Tutorial History

Prior related tutorials have been given at: CIKM 95; DL 98-00; ECDL 00, 01, 05-07, 10; ICADL 00-05, 07; JCDL 01-06, 08-11, 13-15; MM 96, 98, 00; SIGIR 96, 01, 05; etc.

3.4 Learning Objectives

Attendees will be able to:

- Explain 5S; compare it with DELOS/DL.org works.

- Describe core DL content/services, informally and formally.

- Describe common DL application areas, from both a user and a system perspective.

- Describe common technologies that extend DL capabilities.

- Describe how to use a Hadoop cluster, with Solr, Mahout, Spark, etc., to handle large tweet and webpage collections, with clustering, classification, topic spotting, NER, etc.

- Identify modules of interest for study about DLs, or for use in DL courses, or in courses where DL content can be added.

- Learn/teach from the modules, and assess understanding.

- Add to the collection of modules, based on special expertise.

- Apply problem-project based learning in DL education.

3.5 Outline

This tutorial will cover many concepts and use multiple case studies. It will touch upon international activities, including DELOS/DL.org, but will focus on what is detailed in four recent books about DLs [2, 3, 4, 1], that build upon 5S, and cover

- Introduction; Exploration; Evaluation; Integration

- Complex Objects; Annotation/Subdocuments; Ontologies

- Classification; Text Extraction; Security

- Content-based Image Retrieval; Education; Social Networks

- Bioinformatics, eScience, and Simulation DLs

- Geospatial Information

Regarding DL Teaching and Learning, the following will be covered:

- Overview of the DL curriculum project and its methods

- Pedagogical and curricular recommendations

- Introduction to each of the 10 main curricular areas

- Discussion of particular modules of interest to attendees

- Discussion of problem-project based learning about DLs

- Discussion of how to meet attendee teaching/learning needs

4. BRIEF BIOGRAPHY

Edward Fox holds a Ph.D. and M.S. in Computer Science from Cornell, and a B.S. from M.I.T. Since 1983 he has been at Virginia Tech, where he serves as Professor. He directs VT's Digital Library Research Laboratory and the Networked Digital Library of Theses and Dissertations. He was a member of the Board of CRA (the Computer Research Association). He was chair of the IEEE Technical Committee on Digital Libraries, and earlier was chair of ACM SIGIR. He was chair of the steering committee for JCDL, and is on the international advisory committee for ICADL. He has been (co-)Principal Investigator on 122 research grants/contracts. He taught over 81 tutorials and has given 66 keynote/distinguished/ international invited talks. He has (co-)authored 18 books, 118 journal/magazine articles, 49 books chapters, 207 refereed conference/workshop papers, 71 posters, and about 160 other publications/reports, plus over 320 additional talks. Fox is editor for IR and DL for ACM Books. He was Co-Editor-in-Chief for ACM JERIC, and is on the boards of IJDL, JEMH, JIIS, J. UCS, Multimedia Tools and Applications, and PeerJ CS.

4.1 Contact information

- Dept. of Computer Science

- 114 McBryde Hall, M/C 0106

- Virginia Tech, Blacksburg, VA 24061 USA

- Tel: +1-540-231-5113 [direct], -6931[dept.]

- Mobile: +1-540-553-1856, Fax: +1-540-231-6075 [CS]

- Email: fox@vt.edu

- Website: http://fox.cs.vt.edu

5. ACKNOWLEDGMENTS

Thanks go to NSF for support through grants CCF-1032677; DUE-0121679, 0435059, 0840719, 1141209; and IIS-0325579, 0535057, 0535060, 0910183, 0910465, 0916733, 1319578. Thanks go to the National Inst. of Justice for NCJ 239049, to NIH for 1R01DA039456-01, and to QNRF for support through NPRP 4-029-1-007. The opinions expressed in this document are solely those of the author.

6. REFERENCES

[1] E. Fox, M. Goncalves, and R. Shen. *Theoretical Foundations for Digital Libraries: The 5S (Societies, Scenarios, Spaces, Structures, Streams) Approach.* Morgan and Claypool Publishers, San Francisco, 2012.

[2] E. Fox and J. Leidig. *Digital Library Applications: CBIR, Education, Social Networks, eScience/ Simulation, and GIS.* Morgan and Claypool Publishers, San Francisco, 2014.

[3] E. Fox and R. Torres. *Digital Library Technologies: Complex Objects, Annotation, Ontologies, Classification, Extraction, and Security.* Morgan and Claypool Publishers, San Francisco, 2014.

[4] R. Shen, M. Goncalves, and E. Fox. *Key Issues Regarding Digital Libraries: Evaluation and Integration.* Morgan and Claypool Publishers, San Francisco, 2013.

Introduction to the Digital Public Library
of America API

Unmil P. Karadkar
The University of Texas at Austin, School of Information
1616 Guadalupe St. Ste. 5.202
Austin, TX 78701-1213 USA
+1-512-471-9292
unmil@ischool.utexas.edu

Audrey Altman, Mark Breedlove, Mark Matienzo
Digital Public Library of America
c/o Boston Public Library, 700 Boylston St.
Boston, MA 02116 USA
+1-617-859-2116
{audrey,mb, mark}@dp.la

ABSTRACT
The Digital Public Library of America (DPLA) provides access to over 11 million objects from libraries, museums, and archives. In addition to serving as an open portal for cultural heritage, literature, art, and scientific materials, the DPLA provides access to extensive metadata related to these materials via an openly available, RESTful application programming interface (API). The open API enables third party developers to create targeted applications that enable new and transformative uses of the items indexed by the DPLA. This half day tutorial will introduce participants to the DPLA's data model, describe the API, explain how to retrieve data using the API, and how to work with the retrieved data using freely available software using both interactive and programmatic techniques.

Keywords
Digital Public Library of America; DPLA API; RESTful API

1. INTRODUCTION
 The Digital Public Library of America (DPLA) is a large metadata aggregation that provides access to over 11 million objects from over 1,500 libraries, museums, and archives in the USA through its Web portal (http://dp.la) [1]. Items available via the DPLA continue to be hosted by their home institution, which contribute only the metadata to the DPLA. These items cover a variety of topics including textual materials, works of art and culture, records of America's heritage, and scientific data sets. The DPLA is committed to making objects openly available for engaging citizens, students, and scholars, much as the American public libraries have done for the last two centuries.

In this spirit of openness, the DPLA makes all its metadata publicly available via a Web-based application programming interface (API) in order to enable "software developers, researchers, and others to create novel environments for learning, tools for discovery, and engaging apps". This tutorial will introduce attendees to the DPLA API. Participants will learn how to use the

API to access DPLA data via the Web-based interface, to store this data on their disks, view and explore the data using open, freely

Permission to make digital or hard copies of part or all of this work for personal or classroom use is granted without fee provided that copies are not made or distributed for profit or commercial advantage and that copies bear this notice and the full citation on the first page. Copyrights for third-party components of this work must be honored. For all other uses, contact the Owner/Author.
Copyright is held by the owner/author(s).
JCDL '16, June 19-23, 2016, Newark, NJ, USA
ACM 978-1-4503-4229-2/16/06.
http://dx.doi.org/10.1145/2910896.2925428

available software such as OpenRefine, and finally, to write programs for advanced data manipulation.

2. FORMAT AND SCOPE
This will be a half day tutorial.

Prior to the tutorial, we will send instructions to participants for pre-installing the necessary software on their computers as well as assist them in installing the software on the day of the tutorial.

During the tutorial will introduce the participants to the DPLA API and train them to use the API to retrieve and manipulate data without programming as well as using the Python and JavaScript wrappers that simplify programming tasks. Attendees will be given small programming tasks that require fetching and manipulating DPLA data.

2.1 Aims
This tutorial aims to introduce the DPLA conceptual data model, DPLA API, JSON data format, and command-line as well as programmatic interfaces for retrieving DPLA metadata.

2.2 Learning Objectives
This tutorial will enable the participants to:

- Understand and use RESTful APIs in general and the DPLA API in particular
- Locate relevant information on the DPLA developer pages
- Read the DPLA data model documentation
- Retrieve DPLA metadata via a Web browser and a command-line interface
- Manipulate saved DPLA data using OpenRefine
- Retrieve DPLA data using a modern programming language such as Python, PHP, JavaScript, or Java.
- Use Python wrappers such as dpla_utils and DPyLA – for Python programmers
- Use the JavaScript wrapper for JS programmers
- Retrieve and merge data from multiple pages
- Select, sort and count data values programmatically

3. TOPICAL OUTLINE
Here is a tentative list of topics that the tutorial will cover:

- Introduction to the DPLA and the Web portal
- Introduction to the developer pages
- Introduction to the data model (Metadata Application Profile- MAP)
- Introduction to the API and RESTful architecture
- Requests and responses
  - Sending a simple request
  - Receiving a simple response
  - Hands-on examples

- Introduction to JSON
- Viewing retrieved data with JSON browser plug-ins
- Selecting, sorting, and searching within fields
- Pagination
- Faceting
- Hands-on examples of advanced requests
- Saving the retrieved data to disk
- Viewing and manipulating data with OpenRefine
- Introduction to programmatic data retrieval
- Introduction to Python and JavaScript wrappers (DPyLA, dpla_utils)
- Introduction to JavaScript wrapper

4. TARGET AUDIENCE

As this is the first tutorial that we are proposing to be held during a major conference, we are unable to estimate the level of interest in the community. We expect that a large segment of the JCDL attendees will be interested in the topic. The location of the conference and its proximity to several universities in the Washinton, DC-Philadelphia-NJ-NYC metropolitan areas will help us attract students from these institutions.

The target demographic for this tutorial includes practitioners and scholars in Digital Libraries who are interested in working with DPLA data or those who want to learn about RESTful APIs in general.

4.1 Prior Knowledge

This is an introductory tutorial. No prior knowledge is expected of the audience.

5. EQUIPMENT NEEDS

The instructors will need access to the internet and a projector. We will bring our laptop computers to host the presentation. We will encourage participants to bring their laptop computers in order to follow along or complete tasks in the hands-on components of the tutorial.

6. INSTRUCTOR BIOGRAPHIES

Unmil P. Karadkar (unmil@ischool.utexas.edu) is an Assistant Professor in the School of Information at The University of Texas at Austin. He situates his work at the intersection of digital libraries, human-computer interaction, and visualization. He studies data practices of researchers with an eye toward identifying unmet information needs. Based on an understanding of these needs, he designs software to support their evolving practices and evaluates the impact of this software on their work. In the School of Information, Unmil teaches courses in Digital Libraries, Visualization, and Metadata Generation for Large Datasets and has used as well as trained his students to use the DPLA API.

Audrey Altman (audrey@dp.la) is a Developer for DPLA. She works with the DPLA Technology Team to design, develop, test, integrate, support, and document user-facing applications and back-end systems; support content management policies, process, and workflows, and contribute to the development of new ones; and collaborate with stakeholders to contribute to strategic and tactical planning and implementation of content stewardship applications and technologies. Audrey previously worked as a web developer for Digital Research and Publishing at the University of Iowa Libraries, and for the University of Iowa Digital Studio for Public Arts & Humanities. She holds a Masters of Library and Information Science from the University of Iowa, a M.A. in American Studies from the University of Alabama and a B.A. in Theater from Albion College. While Audrey doesn't have a single favorite DPLA item, she is partial to zoological drawings like those of the White Heron, Squat Lobster, Snail, and Collared Hedge Hog.

Mark Breedlove (mb@dp.la) is a Senior Developer for DPLA, who contributes to the design and implementation of the organization's ingestion, API, and front-end website. His work has been concentrated in the development of the ingestion system, which moves data from providers to the DPLA datastore, and the development of the organization's new DevOps systems. He works closely with the Director of Technology and the Content team. Before coming to DPLA, Mark was the Technical Director at See.me, a social discovery website for artists, and the American Museum of Natural History, building scientific web applications and content management systems for its Science Division. Mark's current favorite DPLA item is Gunn's Domestic Medicine, or Poor Man's Friend.

Mark Matienzo (mark@dp.la) is the Director of Technology for DPLA. As Director of Technology, Mark is responsible for the overall technology vision for the DPLA and overseeing its implementation. Mark also serves as the primary technical contact for outside organizations, partners, and developers. Prior to joining DPLA, Mark worked as an archivist and technologist specializing in born-digital materials and metadata management, at institutions including the Yale University Library, The New York Public Library, and the American Institute of Physics, and participated in projects such as the ArchivesSpace open source archival management system and AIMS – Born Digital Collections: An Inter-Institutional Model for Stewardship. Mark received a MSI from the University of Michigan School of Information and a BA in Philosophy from the College of Wooster, and was the first awardee (2012) of the Emerging Leader Award of the Society of American Archivists. Mark's current favorite item in DPLA is Children in Goat Cart.

7. REFERENCES

[1] Digital Public Library of America – About. 2016. Accessed Jan. 5, 2016, http://dp.la/info/.

Information Extraction for Scholarly Digital Libraries

Kyle Williams‡, Jian Wu‡, Zhaohui Wu†, C. Lee Giles†‡
‡Information Sciences and Technology, †Computer Science and Engineering
Pennsylvania State University, University Park, PA 16802, USA
kwilliams@psu.edu, jxw394@psu.edu, zzw109@psu.edu, giles@ist.psu.edu

ABSTRACT

Scholarly documents contain many data entities, such as titles, authors, affiliations, figures, and tables. These entities can be used to enhance digital library services through enhanced metadata and enable the development of new services and tools for interacting with and exploring scholarly data. However, in a world of *scholarly big data*, extracting these entities in a scalable, efficient and accurate manner can be challenging. In this tutorial, we introduce the broad field of information extraction for scholarly digital libraries. Drawing on our experience in running the Cite-SeerX digital library, which has performed information extraction on over 7 million academic documents, we argue for the need for automatic information extraction, describe different approaches for performing information extraction, present tools and datasets that are readily available, and describe best practices and areas of research interest.

CCS Concepts

•Information systems → **Extraction, transformation and loading; Information extraction;** •**Applied computing** → **Digital libraries and archives;**

Keywords

Information extraction, scholarly big data, digital libraries

1. SCHOLARLY INFORMATION EXTRACTION

In recent years, there has been an unprecedented increase in the number of scholarly documents produced. In 2014 it was estimated that at least 114 million English scholarly documents were accessible on the Web with 27% being freely available [1]. Given this ever increasing corpus of documents, it has become increasingly necessary to organize and manage the documents; allow for the exploration and discovery of new documents; explore the relationships between entities in documents; and to explore the *science of science* [2].

Permission to make digital or hard copies of part or all of this work for personal or classroom use is granted without fee provided that copies are not made or distributed for profit or commercial advantage and that copies bear this notice and the full citation on the first page. Copyrights for third-party components of this work must be honored. For all other uses, contact the owner/author(s).

JCDL '16 June 19-23, 2016, Newark, NJ, USA

© 2016 Copyright held by the owner/author(s).

ACM ISBN 978-1-4503-4229-2/16/06.

DOI: http://dx.doi.org/10.1145/2910896.2925430

Digital libraries facilitate this type of exploration and discovery through interfaces based on the metadata associated with scholarly documents and information extraction refers to the identification and labeling of this metadata. However, given the rate at which scholarly documents are produced and the heterogeneous nature of the data they contain, such as tables, figures and citations, it has become increasingly difficult to perform manual information extraction at scale, thus motivating the need for automatic methods.

Scholarly information extraction refers to the process by which metadata and entities are extracted from scholarly documents using automated algorithms and systems. These systems and algorithms need to be able to deal with the heterogeneity of the data, both in terms of the format of the documents and in terms of the data contained within the documents themselves. Furthermore, the approaches must be scalable in order to deal with the millions of documents that exist and that continue to be produced.

This half-day tutorial seeks to introduce the audience to the vast area of information extraction from scholarly documents. The tutorial will explore both the practical aspects of information extraction for scholarly digital libraries as well as the research opportunities that exist. The focus will be on information extraction in a world of *scholarly big data*.

2. ABOUT THE TUTORIAL

2.1 Scope

The tutorial will focus on digital libraries of scholarly documents, such as articles, slides, academic books, and technical reports. The benefit of focusing on the scholarly domain is that it is diverse and heterogeneous, while still being well defined and understood.

2.2 Learning Objectives

Attendees should leave the tutorial understanding:

- What is scholarly information extraction?

- What is the motivation for scholarly information extraction and what are the challenges?

- What approaches are there to scholarly information extraction and what readily available tools exist?

- How does information extraction fit into the larger digital library ingestion workflow?

- What research opportunities exist in information extraction and what are best practices?

2.3 Tutorial History

While this is the first time this tutorial is being presented, it is based on several conference presentations and publications [3, 4] as well as extensive experience in scholarly information extraction and digital libraries [5, 4].

2.4 Target Audience

The target audience is technical practitioners at a beginner or intermediate level who are interested in understanding how information extraction works, either for use in their own digital libraries or as an introduction to the research area.

2.5 Presenters

This tutorial will be prepared and presented by the following members of the CiteSeerX research group.

Kyle Williams A Ph.D. candidate in Information Sciences and Technology at Penn State University who has given several presentations on information extraction for scholarly digital libraries and integrated information extraction tools into document workflows.

Jian Wu A postdoctoral fellow in Information Sciences and Technology at Penn State University and the technical director of the CiteSeerX digital library. Dr Wu has experience in designing, implementing and maintaining information extraction workflows as part of the CiteSeerX digital library.

Zhaohui Wu A Ph.D. candidate in the Computer Science and Engineering at Penn State University with experience in extracting entities from heterogeneous data types and using them to build novel digital libraries.

C. Lee Giles The director of the CiteSeerX digital library project, with extensive experience in complex systems, digital libraries and the Web.

3. TOPICAL OUTLINE

The tutorial will cover the following topics:

Motivation and Challenges

The tutorial will begin by answering questions such as: *Why perform information extraction in scholarly digital libraries? What are the challenges? What does automatic information extraction enable?* The focus will be on the heterogeneous data entities that exist in scholarly data (or scholarly entities) and on the challenges and opportunities for their extraction in the big data setting. We will cover the definitions of various types of scholarly entities and the semantic relationships among them that could form a heterogeneous scholarly knowledge base. We will show how extracting these entities can enable enhanced digital library services and tools for exploring scholarly data. This will include a description of various specialized digital libraries that we have created based on specialized information extractors.

Approaches

Information extraction is an important task with increasing research attention not only in digital libraries, but also in NLP, IR, Web/Semantic Web, data mining, and knowledge engineering. Various approaches have be used for scholarly information extraction, by taking advantage of document templates, heuristics, crowdsourcing, knowledge bases, machine learning, and the Web [6]. We will describe various approaches that exist, identify their pros and cons, and describe situations in which each method is best suited.

Tools and Data

Various tools are readily available for extracting information from scholarly documents. We will cover a variety of existing open source tools, such as SVMHeaderParse, Grobid and ParsCit, as well as tools we have developed for CiteSeerX in order to give the audience a broad overview of tools available. These will include tools for well known extraction use cases, such as text, keyphrase and citation extraction, as well as tools for richer information, such as tables, figures and data. Where appropriate, we will provide empirical comparisons of different extractors [7]. We will also describe datasets and methods that exist for evaluating information extractors, including data from CiteSeerX repositories.

Information Integration

Drawing on our experience in running the CiteSeerX digital library, we will show how various tools for information extraction can be integrated into the digital library workflow as part of the document ingestion process. We will discuss issues related to pipelining, scalability, databases and indexing and describe APIs that can be integrated into existing document workflows.

Best Practices and Going Forward

We will describe best practices in information extraction for scholarly digital libraries and highlight ongoing challenges and research problems that may be of interest to the digital libraries, information retrieval, data mining, Web, and NLP research communities.

Acknowledgments

We gratefully acknowledge partial support by the National Science Foundation.

4. REFERENCES

[1] M. Khabsa and C. L. Giles. The number of scholarly documents on the public web. *PloS one*, 9(5):e93949, 2014.

[2] *The Science of Science Policy: A Federal Research Roadmap. Report on the Science of Science Policy.* National Science and Technology Council, 2008.

[3] C. L. Giles. Scholarly big data: information extraction and data mining. In *Proceedings of CIKM*, pages 1–2, 2013.

[4] K. Williams, J. Wu, S. R. Choudhury, M. Khabsa, and C. L. Giles. Scholarly Big Data Information Extraction and Integration in the CiteSeerX Digital Library. In *Proceedings of IIWeb*, pages 68–73, 2014.

[5] H. Li, I. Councill, W.-C. Lee, and C. L. Giles. CiteSeerX: An Architecture and Webservice Design for an Academic Document Search Engine. In *Proceedings of WWW*, pages 883–884, 2006.

[6] Z. Wu, J. Wu, M. Khabsa, K. Williams, H. H. Chen, W. Huang, S. Tuarob, S. R. Choudhury, A. Ororbia, P. Mitra, C. L. Giles. Towards building a scholarly big data platform: Challenges, lessons and opportunities. In *Proceedings of JCDL*, pages 117–126, 2014.

[7] M. Lipinski, K. Yao, C. Breitinger, J. Beel, and B. Gipp. Evaluation of header metadata extraction approaches and tools for scientific PDF documents. In *Proceedings of JCDL*, pages 385–386, 2013.

ACHS'16: First International Workshop on Accessing Cultural Heritage at Scale

Paul D. Clough
Paula Goodale
Information School
University of Sheffield, UK
Tel: +44 114 222 2664
p.d.clough@sheffield.ac.uk
p.goodale@sheffield.ac.uk

Maristella Agosti
Department of Information
Engineering
University of Padua, Italy
Tel: +39 049 827 7650
maristella.agosti@unipd.it

Séamus Lawless
ADAPT Centre, School of Computer
Science and Statistics
Trinity College Dublin, Ireland
Tel: +353 1 896 1000
seamus.lawless@scss.tcd.ie

ABSTRACT

The workshop aims to bring together researchers and practitioners to review and discuss ways of providing effective access to large-scale collections of cultural heritage content. The scale, variety and availability of cultural heritage content, combined with the variety of user groups with respect to background knowledge, specialist experience and needs is challenging in the context of existing access methods. In particular, we consider going beyond keyword search in large-scale cultural heritage digital libraries, in support of exploration and discovery. Our purpose for the workshop is to consider the opportunities and challenges presented by new and existing technologies, as well as the needs and experiences of diverse user communities. Our goal is to assess the current state-of the-art, to identify opportunities and establish future research priorities, informed by the combined knowledge and experience of academics and practitioners.

Keywords

Information retrieval, information access, exploration, discovery, digital libraries, cultural heritage, big data

1. INTRODUCTION

Large-scale digital libraries are becoming ubiquitous within and between cultural heritage (libraries, museums and archives) institutions, with increasing variety of content (media formats, metadata, and level of detail in text description), diverse user communities (from expert to novice) with differing, often poorly defined, and even unanticipated information needs, and widely varying interfaces to support more exploratory information seeking. In these 'big libraries' with challenges presented by both the volume and variety of content, we can also add the further challenges of needing to support a variety of users and uses.

Approaches to understanding and dealing with these challenges are many and varied, with complementary and competing alternatives in evidence, often using emerging and experimental techniques. Complexity arises in data processing for content preparation and presentation; interaction design to allow support for enhanced multimodal approaches to discovery and exploration, which go beyond the search box; and in evaluation of these digital libraries at multiple levels, including system, content and user-specific variables, as proposed for example, via the Interaction Triptych Model [1,2].

In this challenging, and constantly changing environment, it is important to review progress to date, and explore the future potential of emerging trends in information access functionality, interaction capabilities, and underlying techniques and technologies employed, in areas such as knowledge organization, content enrichment, visualization, personalization and adaptivity.

1.1 Workshop Description

We focus on challenges and opportunities, current and emerging, in exploration and discovery in large-scale digital libraries, with particular reference to cultural heritage. We consider the underlying enabling technologies, as well as interaction functionalities, and user evaluations. Our goal is to identify the needs of providers and their users, assess the current state-of-the-art, and to identify and prioritize areas of future research potential.

1.2 Objectives

The workshop is intended as a forum for knowledge sharing, discussion, and networking. Specific objectives are to:

- Identify outstanding information access challenges and understand their impacts on DL providers and users;
- Review latest developments for enhancing information access in CH digital libraries;
- Work towards a view of future research needs;
- Strengthen connections between academics and industry for potential collaborations.

1.3 Topics

The workshop is focused on all aspects of supporting information access, exploration and discovery within large-scale digital libraries, especially within the cultural heritage domain. Key topics include:

- Information discovery, exploration and serendipity
- User-centered information access and evaluation
- Multimedia and multilingual information retrieval
- Information needs and information behavior
- Information organization, ontologies
- Entity-centric information access
- Information extraction, content enrichment, text analytics, natural language processing
- Metadata and linked data
- Visualization of information spaces

Permission to make digital or hard copies of part or all of this work for personal or classroom use is granted without fee provided that copies are not made or distributed for profit or commercial advantage and that copies bear this notice and the full citation on the first page. Copyrights for third-party components of this work must be honored. For all other uses, contact the Owner/Author. Copyright is held by the owner/author(s).

JCDL '16, June 19-23, 2016, Newark, NJ, USA
ACM 978-1-4503-4229-2/16/06.
http://dx.doi.org/10.1145/2910896.2926733

- User modelling and adaptation
- Personalization and recommendation

2. FORMAT
The workshop will take place over a half day, and will include peer-reviewed papers, with authors allocated 15-20 minutes to present their research. In addition, there will be a panel discussion which will further explore matters arising during the course of the workshop. Workshop proceedings will be available online via CEUR.

2.1 Audience
The workshop will be of interest to researchers and practitioners working in the fields of digital libraries, cultural heritage, interactive information retrieval, content enrichment, evaluation and user studies, and other areas related to information access in large-scale digital libraries.

3. ORGANISERS
Paul Clough is Professor in Information Retrieval at the Information School, University of Sheffield. He received a B.Eng. (hons) degree in Computer Science from the University of York in 1998 and a Ph.D. from the University of Sheffield in 2002. His research interests mainly revolve around developing technologies to assist people with accessing and managing information. In particular Paul has published work in the areas of multilingual information retrieval, information access to digital cultural heritage, evaluation of information retrieval systems, geo-spatial search, text-based image retrieval, text re-use and search analytics. Paul is co-author of a book on multilingual information retrieval and over 100 peer-reviewed publications. He is head of the Information Retrieval group at Sheffield.

Paula Goodale is a researcher in the Information School, University of Sheffield. She holds Masters degrees in Information Management and in Librarianship, and is completing her PhD in Information Science, at the University of Sheffield. From 2004-2009, she was a Senior Lecturer in Information Management at the University of Huddersfield. Her current research focus is on information access in cultural heritage and digital libraries, with particular emphasis on user requirements and evaluation. Paula has worked on several research projects, including the EC-FP7 PATHS project, and the JISC Search25 project. She was co-chair of the 2nd SUEDL workshop.

Séamus Lawless is an Assistant Professor in the ADAPT Centre in the School of Computer Science and Statistics, Trinity College Dublin. Séamus' research has a strong user focus and all of his work aims to improve the experiences of users when interacting with content and information systems. His research interests are in the areas of information retrieval, information management and digital humanities with a particular focus on adaptivity and personalization. The common focus of this research is digital content management and the application of technology to support enhanced, personalized access to knowledge.

Maristella Agosti is full professor in computer science at the Department of Information Engineering, University of Padua, Italy. Group leader of the Information Management Systems (IMS) Research Group of the Department. Permanent Member of the Galilean Academy, Class of Mathematical and Natural Sciences. Her research interests are information access through search engines and digital libraries, user-oriented keyword-based search systems for structured data, annotation of digital contents, evaluation of digital libraries and archives,, and user interaction with digital cultural heritage collections. Principal investigator or senior researcher of several European Commission research projects including CULTURA, PROMISE, EuropeanaConnect, SAPIR, DELOS. Chair from 2009 to 2012 of the Steering Committee of TPDL.

4. PREVIOUS WORKSHOPS
The ACHS'16 workshop builds upon previous successful workshops on information access issues in digital cultural heritage, by the current organizers and colleagues:

4.1 SUEDL Workshops
The workshop on Supporting Users Exploration of Digital Libraries has been run on two previous occasions, collocated at TPDL 2012 and TPDL 2013 respectively. The first half-day workshop comprised four peer-reviewed papers, keynote, demonstration, and panel discussion. Proceedings are published on the workshop web site [3]. The program for the second full day workshop comprised eight peer-reviewed papers and demos, a keynote, and panel discussion. Proceedings are published in a combined volume with papers from other selected TPDL workshops [4].

4.2 ENRICH Workshop
The workshop on Exploration, Navigation and Retrieval of Information in Cultural Heritage was collocated at SIGIR 2013. The program comprised six peer reviewed papers, seven posters and demos, keynote and plenary session. Papers are available to download via the workshop web site [5].

5. REFERENCES
[1] Fuhr, N., Tsakonas, G., Aalberg, T., Agosti, M., Hansen, P., Kapidakis, S., and Papatheodorou, C. (2007). Evaluation of digital libraries. *Int. J. Digital Libraries*, 8(1), 21-38.

[2] Steiner, C.M., Agosti, M., Sweetnam, M.S., Hillemann, E.-C., Orio, N., Ponchia, C., Hampson, C., Munnelly, G., Nussbaumer, A., Dietrich, A., and Conlan, O. (2014). Evaluating a digital humanities research environment: the CULTURA approach. *Int. J. Digital Libraries*, 15(1), 53-70.

[3] Agirre, E., Fernie, F., Otegi, A. and Stevenson, M. (2012). *Proc. 1st International Workshop on Supporting Users Exploration of Digital Libraries*, (27 September, 2012, Valletta, Malta). SUEDL Workshop. http://ixa2.si.ehu.es/suedl/SUEDLproceedings.pdf.

[4] Bolikowski, Ł., Casarosa, V., Goodale, P., Houssos, N.,Manghi, P., and Schirrwagen, J. (Eds.). (2014). Theory and Practice of Digital Libraries - TPDL 2013 Selected Workshops: LCPD 2013, SUEDL 2013, DataCur 2013: Revised Selected Papers, (26 September, 2013, Valletta, Malta), Springer LNCS, Communications in Computer and Information Science, Vol 416. DOI=http://dx.doi.org/10.1007/978-3-319-08425-1.

[5] Workshop on Exploration, Navigation and Retrieval of Information in Cultural Heritage (ENRICH) *(1 August, 2013, Dublin, Ireland)*. http://www.cultura-strep.eu/events/enrich-2013/programme

Physical Samples and Digital Libraries

Unmil P. Karadkar
School of Information
The University of Texas at Austin
1616 Guadalupe St. Ste. 5.202
Austin, TX 78701-1213 USA
+1-512-471-9292
unmil@ischool.utexas.edu

Kerstin Lehnert
Lamont-Doherty Earth Observatory
Columbia University
61 Route 9W - PO Box 1000,
Palisades, NY 10964-8000 USA
+1-845-365-8506
lehnert@ldeo.columbia.edu

Chris Lenhardt
Renaissance Computing Institute
University of North Carolina
at Chapel Hill
100 Europa Drive Suite 540
Chapel Hill, NC 27517 USA
+1-919-445-0480
clenhardt@renci.org

ABSTRACT
Research in disciplines such as the earth and biological sciences depends on the availability of representative physical samples that have been collected at substantial cost and effort and some are irreplaceable. The EarthCube iSamples (Internet of Samples in the Earth Sciences) Research Coordination Network (RCN), funded by the National Science Foundation, aims to connect physical samples and sample collections across the Earth Sciences with digital data infrastructures to revolutionize their utility in the support of science. The goal of this workshop is to attract a broad audience comprising of earth scientists and other scientists working with physical samples, data curators, and computer and information scientists to learn from each other about the requirements of physical as well as digital sample and collection management.

Keywords
Internet of Samples in the Earth Sciences; iSamplES, Cyberinfrastructure; EarthCube

1. INTRODUCTION
Research in the many scientific disciplines depends on the availability of representative samples collected from our natural environment and even extraterrestrial bodies or those generated in experiments. In the earth sciences, these physical samples serve as fundamental references for generating new knowledge about the earth and the entire universe, contribute to a deeper understanding of the processes that created and shaped it, assess the availability of natural resources, and measure the risk of natural hazards. Many samples have been collected at great cost and with substantial difficulty, are rare or unique, and irreplaceable. The EarthCube Research Coordination Network (RCN) iSamples (Internet of Samples in the Earth Sciences) aims to advance the use of innovative cyberinfrastructure to connect physical samples and sample collections across the Earth Sciences with digital data infrastructures to revolutionize their utility in the support of science. The goal of this RCN is to dramatically improve the discovery, access, sharing, analysis, and curation of physical samples and the data generated by their study for the benefit of science and society as part of the EarthCube program. The RCN hosted its first workshop in Austin, TX, its second workshop in Chapel Hill, NC, and is coordinating its efforts with other EarthCube RCNs, such as the Earth-Centered Communication for Cyberinfrastructure (EC3), as well as national and international efforts to enhance access to scientific collections in general (e.g. CODATA Task Group, Scientific Collections International).

The proposed workshop will focus on designing a distributed data infrastructure required to make samples easily accessible, to ensure persistent access to relevant sample metadata, and to allow unambiguous linking of the physical objects to the digital data. This workshop is intended to attract a broad audience comprising of domain scientists, data curators, and computer and information scientists to learn from each other about the requirements of physical and digital sample and collection management. Attendees will address the issues and challenges in the creation, development and maintenance of collection management systems, citation of specimens, persistent identifiers, system architectures, administration, user interfaces, requirements engineering, evaluation models, and policy implications for digital collections.

2. OBJECTIVES
The goal of this workshop is to attract an inter-disciplinary community of researchers, curators, and practitioners who are interested in studying the issues involved in the management of samples, sample collections, and sample-based data in the field, in the lab, in repositories, in data systems and scientific publications. The intention is both to assemble the existing community as well as invite those with emerging interests in this area. A secondary goal is to focus the attention of the digital libraries community on the tremendous opportunities for research in this space and for collaborating with researchers in relevant science domains.

3. TOPICAL OUTLINE
The workshop will invite submissions on a broad range of topics at the intersection of physical samples in the sciences and digital libraries that facilitate the data collection, management, and use of samples. Topics include but are not limited to:

- physical sample collection curation
- information behavior and needs, user modeling
- evaluation of existing environments
- theoretical models
- system architectures
- social-technical perspectives on digital methods for sample management
- policies and workflows
- data analytics and visualization
- user interfaces
- cyberinfrastructure architectures, applications, and deployments
- distributed data management information systems
- impact of digital libraries on earth science sample collections

Permission to make digital or hard copies of part or all of this work for personal or classroom use is granted without fee provided that copies are not made or distributed for profit or commercial advantage and that copies bear this notice and the full citation on the first page. Copyrights for third-party components of this work must be honored. For all other uses, contact the Owner/Author.
Copyright is held by the owner/author(s).
JCDL '16, June 19-23, 2016, Newark, NJ, USA
ACM 978-1-4503-4229-2/16/06.
http://dx.doi.org/10.1145/2910896.2926736

- linked data and its applications
- personal information management of physical samples
- retrieval and browsing of samples
- scientific data curation, citation and scholarly publication
- social networks, virtual organizations and networked information
- sample collection archiving and preservation

4. FORMAT – FULL DAY WORKSHOP

We intend to host to a typical JCDL workshop, which includes position papers, presentations of ongoing work or results, and planning activities for building a community of scholars focusing on the creation, management, and use of scientific sample collections. The workshop will allow for plenty of discussion time between presentations as well as informally, during breaks. The workshop will invite posters and demonstrations (2 pages in the ACM proceedings format), position papers as well as works-in-progress papers (4 pages) and full papers, reporting on mature research (6 pages in the ACM proceedings format).

5. AUDIENCE

The expected audience is researchers and practitioners who are active in the management of scientific collection data as well as who have an interest in working at the intersection of earth science data and digital libraries. Thus, this workshop aims to bring together communities from multiple disciplines to develop a shared understanding of the needs to further scholarship and practice in this cross-disciplinary area.

Our intention is to engage 20-30 attendees approximately balanced between domain scientists and Computer/Information Scientists. A previous workshop accepted at JCDL did not attract a quorum of participants. With this experience, we have broadened the theme of the workshop to include all physical samples (not just earth samples, as we did last year), reached out to other communities and organizations, especially those geographically proximal to the conference location, and plan to advertise our workshop to cognate communities such as DataONE, and Research Data Alliance. We have also invited Chris Lenhardt, an Environmental Data Science Domain scientist at the Renaissance Computing Institute to serve as a workshop co-chair. Historically, the JCDL community has had a small but committed group of scholars working in the Earth Science domain, such as the DLESE project staff. We expect that the additional time afforded this year by the earlier JCDL notification will be beneficial for attracting participants.

6. IDENTIFICATION AND SELECTION

In order to attract attendees from a broad background, we will advertise this workshop to the geoscience and information science communities. Several SIG bulletin boards and mailing lists such as ACM SIGCHI, ASIS&T, TPDL, American Geophysical Union, EarthCube, Research Data Alliance, and DATAONE. We will also reach out to groups such as DLESE that have focused on the Earth Sciences within the digital libraries discipline. In addition, we invite the JCDL 2016 organizing committee to suggest other venues that will broaden dissemination of our workshop announcement.

A small program committee consisting of Computer Scientists and Earth Scientists will judge the merit and relevance of the papers as well as ensure that the presentations cover a breadth of topics in order to engage an audience with diverse interests.

Preliminary schedule:

May 15: Paper submissions due
May 22: Notify authors of acceptance
June 22, 23: Workshop at JCDL

The dates above may be tweaked to align with JCDL early registration deadline.

7. ORGANIZER INFORMATION

Unmil Karadkar (unmil@ischool.utexas.edu) is an Assistant Professor in the School of Information at The University of Texas at Austin. He situates his work at the intersection of digital libraries, human-computer interaction, and visualization. He studies data practices of researchers with an eye toward identifying unmet information needs. Based on an understanding of these needs, he designs software to support their evolving practices and evaluates the impact of this software on their work.

Kerstin Lehnert (lehnert@ldeo.columbia.edu) is a Senior Research Scientist at Columbia University's Lamont-Doherty Earth Observatory. She is the principal investigator of the NSF-funded EarthCube Research Coordination Network project: Earthcube RCN: iSAmplES: The Internet of Samples in the Earth Sciences, and has a long-term record designing data systems and digital infrastructure for samples and collections. She is Director of the Interdisciplinary Earth Data Alliance (IEDA), an NSF-funded data facility, chair of the EarthCube Leadership Council and president of the Earth & Space Science Informatics Focus Group of the American Geophysical Union

Chris Lenhardt (clenhardt@renci.org) is a Domain Scientist in Environmental Data Science and Systems at Renaissance Computing Institute, NC. He has worked on the management of digital scientific data throughout his career. Prior to coming to RENCI, he was the manager of NASA's Distributed Active Archive Center (DAAC) for Biogeochemical Data at Oak Ridge National Laboratory. His current research interests include the iSamples effort, agile data curation, and sustainable scientific software. He is part of the DataNet Federation Consortium (DFC) team at UNC. Mr. Lenhardt was part of the original SESAR (System for Earth Sample Registration) team. He also served as the president of the ESIP (Federation of Earth Science Information Partners) and is the Chair of NOAA's Data Access and Archiving Requirements Working Group (DAARWG).

8. ACKNOWLEDGEMENTS

The iSamplES Research Coordination Network is funded by the National Science Foundation through grant number: 1440351.

WADL 2016: Third International Workshop on Web Archiving and Digital Libraries

Edward A. Fox
Virginia Tech
Dept. of Computer Science
Blacksburg, VA 24061 USA
+1-540-231-5113
fox@vt.edu

Zhiwu Xie
Virginia Tech
University Libraries
Blacksburg, VA 24061 USA
+1-540-231-4453
zhiwuxie@vt.edu

Martin Klein
U. California Los Angeles
Research Library
Los Angeles, CA 90095 USA
+1-310-206-9781
martinklein@library.ucla.edu

ABSTRACT

This workshop will explore integration of Web archiving and digital libraries, so the complete life cycle involved is covered: creation/authoring, uploading/publishing in the Web (2.0), (focused) crawling, indexing, exploration (searching, browsing), archiving (of events), etc. It will include particular coverage of current topics of interest, like: big data, mobile web archiving, and systems (e.g., Memento, SiteStory, Hadoop processing).

CCS Concepts

•**Information systems → Digital libraries and archives; World Wide Web;**

Keywords

Web archiving; Internet Archive

1. INTRODUCTION

Our understanding of the past will, to a large extent, depend on our success with Web archiving. WADL 2016 (see http://fox.cs.vt.edu/wadl2016.html) will bring together international leaders from industry, government, and academia, who are tackling this important challenge. They will explore the integration of Web archiving and digital libraries, over the complete life cycle: creation/authoring, uploading, publishing in the Web, crawling/collecting, compressing, formatting, storing, preserving, analyzing, indexing, supporting access, etc. Table 1 gives a partial list of some of the topics discussed.

The objectives of this workshop are to:

- continue to build the community of people integrating Web archiving with digital libraries;

- help attendees learn about useful methods, systems, and software in this area;

Permission to make digital or hard copies of part or all of this work for personal or classroom use is granted without fee provided that copies are not made or distributed for profit or commercial advantage and that copies bear this notice and the full citation on the first page. Copyrights for third-party components of this work must be honored. For all other uses, contact the owner/author(s).

JCDL '16 June 19-23, 2016, Newark, NJ, USA

© 2016 Copyright held by the owner/author(s).

ACM ISBN 978-1-4503-4229-2/16/06.

DOI: http://dx.doi.org/10.1145/2910896.2926735

Table 1: Partial List of Topics

Archiving (events)	Big data	Classification
Community bldg	Crawling	Curation, Q/C
DBs / collections	Discovery	Extraction
Filling gaps	Globalization	Linking
Metadata	Mobile	Network science
Preservation	RDF	Social sciences
Standards,protocols	Systems,tools	Tweets

- help chart future research and practice in this area, so more and higher quality Web archiving occurs;

- produce an archival publication that will help advance technology and practice; and

- promote synergistic efforts including collaborative projects and proposals.

2. RELATED WORK

The most recent related workshop, WADL 2015, was held in conjunction with JCDL 2015. It led to a special issue of the IEEE TCDL Bulletin with 13 papers [4]. An earlier workshop, WIRE, focused on research leading to or making use of archives that preserve Internet content [8]. The first workshop on Web Archiving and Digital Libraries, WADL 2013, led to a summary [2] after a group responded to the call for meeting [3] as part of the JCDL 2013 workshop program. An earlier similar workshop at a prior JCDL took place in Ottawa in 2011 [6], partly as a result of the emergence of a cooperative to explore Web archiving [5]. Broader in scope but related are the annual General Assembly meetings of the International Internet Preservation Consortium (IIPC) [7].

3. LOGISTICS

3.1 Audience and Attendees

There is a growing community interested in this topic. Given that the prior WIRE workshop on a similar theme [8] had a significant number of participants from Rutgers University and that Columbia University played a lead role in a closely related Mellon funded initiative [1], we expect to have 15-30 attendees, including a solid representation of students. We will advertise, solicit submissions, have them reviewed by the program committee, and then organize an interesting program. Selections are guided by an international program committee of 13 people, in addition to the three co-chairs. We anticipate the program to include aspects from multiple disciplines such as Computer Science, Library and Information Science, Web Science, Social Sciences, etc.

3.2 Format and Duration

A full-day workshop is split it across two days, with invited speakers, selected papers, posters, demonstrations, and panels. A WebEx teleconference during the workshop can enable those unable to attend to be involved.

As in 2015, we expect to have a special issue of IEEE TCDL Bulletin; that led to a call for a special issue of IJDL, so if the timing is right, WADL 2016 contributions may go there too.

4. BIOGRAPHICAL AND CONTACT INFORMATION

4.1 Fox

Edward Fox holds a Ph.D. and M.S. in Computer Science from Cornell, and a B.S. from M.I.T. Since 1983 he has been at Virginia Tech, where he serves as Professor. He directs VT's Digital Library Research Laboratory and the Networked Digital Library of Theses and Dissertations. He was a member of the Board of CRA (the Computer Research Association). He was chair of the IEEE Technical Committee on Digital Libraries, and earlier was chair of ACM SIGIR. He was chair of the steering committee for JCDL, and is on the international advisory committee for ICADL. He has been (co-)Principal Investigator on 122 research grants/contracts. He taught over 81 tutorials and has given 66 keynote/distinguished/ international invited talks. He has (co-)authored 18 books, 118 journal/magazine articles, 49 books chapters, 207 refereed conference/workshop papers, 71 posters, and about 160 other publications/reports, plus over 320 additional talks. Fox is editor for IR and DL for ACM Books. He was Co-Editor-in-Chief for ACM JERIC, and is on the boards of IJDL, JEMH, JIIS, J. UCS, Multimedia Tools and Applications, and PeerJ CS.

Contact information
Dept. of Computer Science, 114 McBryde Hall, M/C 0106
Virginia Tech, Blacksburg, VA 24061 USA
Tel: +1-540-231-5113 [direct], -6931[dept.]
Mobile: +1-540-553-1856, Fax: +1-540-231-6075 [CS]
Email: fox@vt.edu, Website: http://fox.cs.vt.edu

4.2 Xie

Zhiwu Xie is an associate professor at Virginia Tech Libraries and leads its technology development team. He leads the development of transactional archiving based UWS, the Goodwin Hall Living Lab data management system, IMLS ETDplus, and VTechData, among others. He is deeply involved in Fedora/Hydra, APTrust, PREMIS, ResourceSync, and AltMetrics Data Quality. His research has received supported from Mellon, IBM, Amazon, and NSF XSEDE. He was a co-chair of WADL 2015. His website is at: http://scholar.lib.vt.edu/staff/zxie/.

4.3 Klein

Martin Klein holds a Ph.D. in Computer Science from Old Dominion University. He currently is a scientist in the Research Library at the University of California Los Angeles. He was program chair of DL 2014, poster chair of JCDL 2015, and is currently co-conference chair of iPres 2016. In addition, he is a board member of the Web Archiving Collaboration at Columbia University and guest editor of the International Journal on Digital Libraries as well as the Bulletin of IEEE Technical Committee on Digital Libraries. He also was co-chair of WADL 2015. Martin Klein is the lead editor of the ANSI/NISO Specification Z39.99 and has published numerous journal/magazine articles and conference/workshop papers. More information can be found at: http://www.library.ucla.edu/staff/martin-klein

5. ACKNOWLEDGMENTS

Our thanks go to NSF for support through IIS 0916733 and 1319578, to Columbia and the Mellon Foundation for supporting "Archiving Transactions Toward Uninterruptible Web Service," and to QNRF for support through NPRP 4-029-1-007. The opinions expressed in this document are solely our own.

6. REFERENCES

[1] Columbia U. Libraries. Web Resources Collection Program, 2015. https://library.columbia.edu/bts/web_resources_collection.html.

[2] E. Fox and M. Farag. Report on the Workshop on Web Archiving and Digital Libraries (WADL 2013), WADL Workshop Report. *ACM SIGIR Forum*, 47(2):128–133, 2013. http://sigir.org/files/forum/2013D/p128.pdf.

[3] E. A. Fox. Web Archiving and Digital Libraries (WADL 2013). Virginia Tech CTRnet announcement, 2013. http://www.ctrnet.net/sites/default/files/JCDL2013WorkshopWebArchiving20130603.pdf.

[4] E. A. Fox, Z. Xie, and M. Klein. Introduction to the Web Archiving and Digital Libraries 2015 Workshop issue: Web Archiving and Digital Libraries 2015 (WADL 2015) Overview. *Bulletin of IEEE Technical Committee on Digital Libraries*, 11(2), October 2015. http://www.ieee-tcdl.org/Bulletin/v11n2/papers/intro.pdf.

[5] H. Garcia-Molina, F. McCown, M. Nelson, and A. Paepcke. Web Archive Cooperative making web archives useful today, supported by the NSF (1009916), Stanford University, 2011. http://infolab.stanford.edu/wac/.

[6] H. Garcia-Molina, F. McCown, M. Nelson, and A. Paepcke. Web Archive Globalization Workshop. In conjunction with JCDL 2011, Ottawa, Canada, June 16-17, 2011. http://cs.harding.edu/wag2011/.

[7] IIPC. International Internet Preservation Consortium homepage, 2015. http://netpreserve.org/.

[8] M. Weber, D. Lazer, K. Carpenter-Negulescu, and A. Kosterich. Working with Internet Archives for Research (WIRE 2014 Workshop, Cambridge, MA, June 17-18), 2014. http://wp.comminfo.rutgers.edu/nsfia/.

5th International Workshop on Mining Scientific Publications (WOSP 2016)

Petr Knoth
Mendeley Ltd.
London, UK
petr.knoth@mendeley.com

Lucas Anastasiou
Knowledge Media institute
The Open University
Milton Keynes, UK
lucas.anastasiou@open.ac.uk

Drahomira Herrmannova
Knowledge Media institute
The Open University
Milton Keynes, UK
drahomira.herrmannova@open.ac.uk

Nancy Pontika
Knowledge Media institute
The Open University
Milton Keynes, UK
nancy.pontika@open.ac.uk

1. INTRODUCTION

Digital libraries that store scientific publications are becoming increasingly central to the research process. They are not only used for traditional tasks, such as finding and storing research outputs, but also as a source for discovering new research trends or evaluating research excellence. With the current growth of scientific publications deposited in digital libraries, it is no longer sufficient to provide only access to content. To aid research, it is especially important to leverage the potential of text and data mining technologies to improve the process of how research is being done.

This workshop aims to bring together people from different backgrounds who: (a) are interested in analysing and mining databases of scientific publications, (b) develop systems that enable such analysis and mining of scientific databases (especially those who run databases of publications) or (c) who develop novel technologies that improve the way research is being done.

2. TOPICS

The topics of the workshop will be organised around the following themes:

1. The whole ecosystem of infrastructures including repositories, aggregators, text-and data-mining facilities, impact monitoring tools, datasets, services and APIs that enable analysis of large volumes of scientific publications.

2. Semantic enrichment of scientific publications by means of text and data mining, crowdsourcing or other methods.

3. Analysis of large databases of scientific publications to identify research trends, high impact, cross-fertilisation between disciplines, research excellence etc.

Topics of interest relevant to theme 1 include but are not limited to:

- *Infrastructures including repositories, aggregators, text-and data-mining facilities, impact monitoring tools, datasets,, services and APIs for accessing scientific publications and/or research data.* The existence of datasets, services, systems and APIs (in particular those that are open) providing access to large volumes of scientific publications and research data, is an essential prerequisite for being able to research and develop new technologies that can transform the way people do research. We invite papers presenting innovative approaches to the development of these systems that enable people to access databases and carry out their analysis. Papers

Permission to make digital or hard copies of part or all of this work for personal or classroom use is granted without fee provided that copies are not made or distributed for profit or commercial advantage and that copies bear this notice and the full citation on the first page. Copyrights for third-party components of this work must be honored. For all other uses, contact the Owner/Author.
Copyright is held by the owner/author(s).

JCDL '16, June 19-23, 2016, Newark, NJ, USA
ACM 978-1-4503-4229-2/16/06.
http://dx.doi.org/10.1145/2910896.2926737

addressing Open Access are of special interest. We also welcome submissions discussing the technical aspects of supporting Open Science, in particular reproducibility of research, sharing of scientific workflows and linking research data with publications. Finally, we also invite papers discussing issues and current challenges in the design of these systems.

Topics of interest relevant to theme 2 include but are not limited to:

- *Novel information extraction and text-mining approaches to semantic enrichment of publications.* This might range from mining publication structure, such as title, abstract, authors, citation information etc. to more challenging tasks, such as extracting names of applied methods, research questions (or scientific gaps), identifying parts of the scholarly discourse structure etc.

- *Automatic categorization and clustering of scientific publications.* Methods that can automatically categorize publications according to an established subject-based classification/taxonomy (such as Library of Congress classification, UNESCO thesaurus, DOAJ subject classification, Library of Congress Subject Headings) are of particular interest. Other approaches might involve automatic clustering or classification of research publications according to various criteria.

- *New methods and models for connecting and interlinking scientific publications.* Scientific publications in digital libraries are not isolated islands. Connecting publications using explicitly defined citations is very restrictive and has many disadvantages. We are interested in innovative technologies that can automatically connect and interlink publications or parts of publications according to various criteria, such as semantic similarity, contradiction, argument support or other relationship types.

- *Models for semantically representing and annotating publications.* This topic is related to the aspect of semantically modeling publications and scholarly discourse. Models that are practical with respect to the state-of-the-art in Natural Language Processing (NLP) technologies are of a special interest.

- *Semantically enriching/annotating publications by crowdsourcing.* Crowdsourcing can be used in innovative ways to annotate publications with richer metadata or to approve/disapprove annotations created using text-mining or other approaches. We welcome papers that address the following questions: (a) what incentives should be provided to motivate users in contributing, (b) how to apply crowdsourcing in the specialized domains of scientific publications, (c) what tasks in the domain of organising scientific publications is crowdsourcing suitable for and where it might fail, other relevant crowdsourcing topics relevant to the domain of scientific publications.

Topics of interest relevant to theme 3 include but are not limited to:

- *New methods, models and innovative approaches for measuring impact of publications.* The most widely used metrics for measuring impact are based on citations. However, counting citations not taking into account the publication content and the qualitative nature of the citation. In addition, there is a delay between the publication and the measurable impact in citations. We in particular encourage papers addressing new ways of evaluating publications' impact beyond standard citation measures.

- *New methods for measuring performance of researchers.* Methods for assessing impact of a publication can be often extended to methods that can assess the impact of individual researchers. However, there are also other criteria for measuring impact in addition to publications, such as the development and publication of research data, economical and market impact that should also be taken into account. We welcome papers addressing these aspects.

- *Evaluating impact of research groups.* The same as for impact of individuals holds for research communities.

- *Methods for identifying research trends and cross-fertilization between research disciplines.* Identifying research trends should allow discovering newly emerging disciplines or it should help to explain why certain fields are attracting the attention of a wider research community. Such monitoring is important for research funders and governments in order to be able to quickly respond to new developments. We invite papers discussing new methods for identifying trends and cross-fertilization between research disciplines using methods ranging from social network analysis and text- and data-mining to innovative visualization approaches.

- *Application and case studies of mining from scientific databases and publications.* New methods and models developed for mining from scientific publications can be applied in many different scenarios, such as improving access to scientific publications, providing exploratory search in digital collections, identifying experts. We encourage papers describing innovative approaches that use scientific publications and data to solve real-world problems.

- *Improving the infrastructure of repositories to support the development and integration of new impact and performance metrics.* New ways of improving the repository infrastructure can include, for example, tracking accesses and downloads, researcher profiling and the interlinking of repository data with external services.. These can be in turn used for developing new impact metrics. We welcome papers addressing these issues.

3. SPECIAL OPEN PUBLICATIONS DATASET TRACK

This year we would like to invite the workshop participants to makes use of the CORE publications dataset containing large volume of research publications from a wide variety of research areas. The dataset contains not only full-texts, but also an enriched version of publications' metadata. This dataset provides a framework for developing and testing methods and tools addressing the workshop topics. The use of this dataset is not mandatory, however it is encouraged.

4. EXPECTED AUDIENCE

The workshop on Mining Scientific Publications aims to bring together researchers, digital library developers and practitioners from government and industry to address the current challenges in the domain of mining scientific publications.

5. PREVIOUS ORGANISATION

The 1st International Workshop on Mining Scientific Publications (http://core-project.kmi.open.ac.uk/jcdl2012/) was previously held in conjunction with JCDL 2012. The 2nd run of this workshop was held in conjunction with JCDL 2013 (http://core-project.kmi.open.ac.uk/jcdl2013/). The third run was especially popular and was associated with DL2014 in London (http://core-project.kmi.open.ac.uk/dl2014/). Finally, the 4th run was associated with JCDL 2015 (http://core-project.kmi.open.ac.uk/jcdl2015/) All runs of the workshop have been extremely successful in terms of attracting submissions and participants from leading institutions in the area including Cambridge University, Microsoft, British Library, Elsevier, National Library of Medicine, Library of Congress, University of Pennsylvania (CiteSeerX), Know-Center Graz, University of Athens (OpenAIRE project) and Mendeley.

6. FORMAT

We plan this workshop as a one whole-day event. The workshop is organized this year for the fifth time (the four previous workshops were also in association with JCDL) and is planned to take place yearly. The workshop will consist of two invited talks, a series of presentations followed by a short discussion, a short work in groups session dedicated to addressing specific issues in the field and a final round table discussion at the end of the day. The workshop participants will be also encouraged to visit and experience demonstrations that will be presented during coffee breaks. In the evening, the workshop participants will have the possibility to attend an informal dinner.

7. SUBMISSION FORMAT

We invite submissions related to the workshop's topics. Long papers should not exceed 8 pages and short papers should not exceed 4 pages of the ACM style. Furthermore, we welcome demo presentations of systems or methods. A demonstration submission should consist of a maximum two-page description of the system, method or tool to be demonstrated. All submissions will be uploaded to EasyChair for a peer-review.

8. PEER REVIEW

All submissions will be peer-reviewed and meta-reviewed by members of the Programme Committee. Each publication will be assigned a score and the best publications will be selected. In this sense, the process will be the same as in the last years.

9. PUBLICATION

We will closely work with D-Lib to publish accepted short and full papers as a special issue. The proceedings of the special issues from the last years are available at:

http://www.dlib.org/dlib/july12/07contents.html

http://www.dlib.org/dlib/september13/09contents.html

http://www.dlib.org/dlib/november14/11contents.html

http://www.dlib.org/dlib/november14/11contents.html

10. ORGANIZING COMMITTEE

Petr Knoth, Mendeley Ltd., UK

Drahomira Herrmannova, Knowledge Media institute, The Open Univ., UK

Lucas Anastasiou, Knowledge Media institute, The Open Univ., UK

Nancy Pontika, Knowledge Media institute, The Open Univ., UK

11. PROGRAMME COMMITTEE (TENTATIVE)

The Programme Committee will be officially established shortly after the acceptance of the workshop. The Programmme Committee will likely consist of its members from the last years and additional new members. The following people are expected to form the Programme Committee:

Bruno Martins, Technical University of Lisbon(IST), Portugal

Eloy Rodrigues, University of Minho, Portugal

Francesco Osborne, Knowledge Media institute, The Open Univ., UK

Iryna Gurevych, Darmstadt University of Technology, Germany

Martin Klein, Los Alamos National Laboratory, USA

Natalia Manola, University of Athens, Greece

Paolo Manghi, ISTI-CNR (DRIVER, OpenAIRE), Italy

Pável Calado, Technical University of Lisbon(IST), Portugal

Robert M. Patton, Oak Ridge National Laboratory, USA

Robert Sanderson, Digital Library Systems & Services, Stanford, USA

Roman Kern, Know Center Graz, Austria

Zdenek Zdrahal, Knowledge Media institute, The Open Univ., UK

Tanja Urbancic, Jožef Stefan Institute, Slovenia

Wojtek Sylwestrzak, University of Warsaw, Poland

Stelio Piperidis, Institute for Language and Speech processing (META-SHARE), Athena Research Center, Greece

Ziqi Zhang, Department of Computer Science, Univ. of Sheffield, UK

12. WORKSHOP WEBPAGE & DISSEMINATION

The workshop web page will be deployed maximum one week after the workshop acceptance. The workshop will be then disseminated through a number of channels including WikiCFP, Twitter, Facebook and the mailing lists of The European Library/Europeana, Jisc, OpenAIRE, UKCoRR, META-SHARE, OpenMinTeD, Mendeley and others.

We expect the keynote presentations to address the issues of developing a) e-Infratsructures for text and data mining of research papers and b) large open citation databases to help bibliometrics researchers.

Joint Workshop on Bibliometric-enhanced Information Retrieval and Natural Language Processing for Digital Libraries (BIRNDL 2016)

Guillaume Cabanac[1], Muthu Kumar Chandrasekaran[2], Ingo Frommholz[3],
Kokil Jaidka[4], Min-Yen Kan[2], Philipp Mayr[5], Dietmar Wolfram[6]
[1]University of Toulouse, France; [2]NUS School of Computing, Singapore;
[3]University of Bedfordshire, UK; [4]Adobe Systems Inc., India;
[5]GESIS - Leibniz Institute for the Social Sciences, Germany; [6]Univ. of Wisconsin-Milwaukee, USA
[1]guillaume.cabanac@univ-tlse3.fr; [2]{muthu.chandra,kanmy}@comp.nus.edu.sg;
[3]ingo.frommholz@beds.ac.uk; [4]jaidka@adobe.com; [5]philipp.mayr@gesis.org; [6]dwolfram@uwn.edu

ABSTRACT

The large scale of scholarly publications poses a challenge for scholars in information-seeking and sensemaking. Bibliometric, information retrieval (IR), text mining and NLP techniques could help in these activities, but are not yet widely used in digital libraries. This workshop is intended to stimulate IR researchers and digital library professionals to elaborate on new approaches in natural language processing, information retrieval, scientometric and recommendation techniques which can advance the state-of-the-art in scholarly document understanding, analysis and retrieval at scale.

CCS Concepts

•**Information systems** → **Information retrieval;** *Link and co-citation analysis;* •**Applied computing** → **Digital libraries and archives;**

Keywords

Bibliometrics; Information Retrieval; Digital Libraries; Natural Language Processing; Text Mining

1. INTRODUCTION

Current digital libraries collect and allow access to digital papers and their metadata – inclusive of citations – but mostly do not analyze the items they index. The scale of scholarly publications poses a challenge for scholars in their search for relevant literature.

After the success of two parent workshops series – the 1st NLPIR4DL workshop in 2009, and the series of three Bibliometric-enhanced Information Retrieval (BIR) workshops in 2014, 2015 and 2016 – BIRNDL[1] will focus on scholarly pub-

---

[1]http://wing.comp.nus.edu.sg/birndl-jcdl2016/

Permission to make digital or hard copies of part or all of this work for personal or classroom use is granted without fee provided that copies are not made or distributed for profit or commercial advantage and that copies bear this notice and the full citation on the first page. Copyrights for third-party components of this work must be honored. For all other uses, contact the owner/author(s).

JCDL '16 June 19-23, 2016, Newark, NJ, USA

ⓒ 2016 Copyright held by the owner/author(s).

ACM ISBN 978-1-4503-4229-2/16/06.

DOI: http://dx.doi.org/10.1145/2910896.2926734

lications and data. The workshop will investigate how natural language processing, information retrieval, scientometric and recommendation techniques can advance the state-of-the-art in scholarly document understanding, analysis and retrieval at scale. Researchers are in need of assistive technologies to track developments in an area, identify the approaches used to solve a research problem over time and summarize research trends. Digital libraries require semantic search, question-answering as well as automated recommendation and reviewing systems to manage and retrieve answers from scholarly databases. Full document text analysis can help to design semantic search, translation and summarization systems; citation and social network analyses can help digital libraries to visualize scientific trends, bibliometrics and relationships and influences of works and authors. These approaches can be supplemented with the metadata supplied by digital libraries, such as usage data.

This workshop will be relevant to scholars in several fields of computer science and computational linguistics; it will also be of importance for all stakeholders in the publication pipeline: implementers, publishers and policymakers – with this workshop we hope to bring a number of these contributors together. Today's publishers continue to seek new ways to be relevant to their consumers, in disseminating the right published works to their audience. Formal citation metrics are increasingly a factor in decision-making by universities and funding bodies worldwide, making the need for research in such topics more pressing.

The event is split into two parts: the paper presentations and the CL-SciSumm Shared Task.

2. WORKSHOP TOPICS AND FORMAT

Our goal is to encourage insights from bibliometrics, scientometrics and informetrics to applications in digital libraries. We invite stimulating submissions on topics including – but not limited to – full-text analysis, multimedia and multilingual analysis and alignment as well as citation-based NLP, information retrieval, information seeking and digital libraries (DL). Specific examples of fields of interests include (but are not limited to):

- Summarization of scientific articles; automatic creation of reviews and automatic qualitative assessment of submissions; question-answering for scholarly DLs

- Recommendation for scholarly papers, reviewers, citations and publication venues
- Navigation, searching and browsing in scholarly DLs; niche search in scholarly DLs; new information access methods for scientific papers
- Network analysis and citation analysis in scholarly DLs; citation function/motivation analysis; novel bibliometric metrics; topical modeling analysis; information retrieval for scholarly text, e.g. citation-based IR
- Knowledge discovery and analysis of the ancestry of ideas
- Translation, multilingual and multimedia analysis and alignment of scholarly works; analyses of writing style in scholarly publications
- Metadata and controlled vocabularies for resource description and discovery; automatic metadata discovery, such as language identification
- Disambiguation issues in scholarly DLs using NLP or IR techniques; data cleaning and data quality

The workshop will start with an inspirational keynote by Dietmar Wolfram (University of Wisconsin–Milwaukee) followed by paper presentations. There will be a special session with presentations of the participating groups in the CL-SciSumm Shared Task as well as a planned fishbowl-style panel.

3. THE CL-SCISUMM SHARED TASK

To highlight and bring together the scholars working on above topics, BIRNDL will also host a shared task on scientific document summarization on open access literature in the computational linguistics (CL) domain. The output summaries will be of two types: faceted summaries of the traditional self-summary (the abstract) and the community summary (the collection of citation sentences or *citances*) [4]. This task follows up on the successful CL Pilot Task conducted as a part of the BiomedSumm Track at the Text Analysis Conference 2014 (TAC 2014), and re-uses the SciSumm14 manually-annotated dataset [2], to enhance impact and visibility. In this shared task, we will extend the SciSumm14 dataset of ten, by releasing pairs of training and test datasets: each pair comprising the annotated citing sentences for a research paper, and summaries of the research paper. The resulting CLSciSumm16 corpus is expected to be of interest to a broad community including those working in computational linguistics and natural language processing, especially in the sub-disciplines of text summarization, discourse structure in scholarly discourse, paraphrase, textual entailment and text simplification. Microsoft Research Asia is generously supporting the development, annotation and dissemination of the dataset as well as the organization of this shared task.

4. PREVIOUS RELATED WORKSHOPS

Our workshop is a continuation of several previous ones on similar topics. We present a summary of some relevant recent events, which underpin our claim of the workshop topic being spot-on and relevant.

- The 1st Workshop on text and citation analysis for scholarly digital libraries (NLPIR4DL) was held in conjunction with ACL-IJCNLP 2009, Singapore.

- Scholarly Big Data: AI Perspectives, Challenges, and Ideas at AAAI 2016 - This workshop is related to our topics but appears earlier in 2016. It indicates a high degree of interest for our topic, and will be synergistic due to its complementary date.
- 3rd Workshop on Argumentation Mining at ACL 2016 - This related workshop is synergistic and complementary. We overlap to a small extent in being interested in argumentation (their workshop) in scientific documents (our workshop).
- 3rd Workshop on Bibliometric-enhanced Information Retrieval (BIR2016) at ECIR 2016 [3]. The scope of the BIR workshops (2014, 2015 and 2016) were on information retrieval, information seeking, science modelling, network analysis, and digital libraries, applying insights from bibliometrics, scientometrics, and informetrics.
- 1st Workshop on Mining Scientific Papers: Computational Linguistics and Bibliometrics at ISSI 2015 [1] brought together researchers to study the ways Bibliometrics can benefit from large-scale text analytics and sense mining of scientific papers, thus exploring the interdisciplinarity of Bibliometrics and NLP.

5. OUTLOOK

This workshop is the first step to foster the reflection on the interdisciplinarity and the benefits that the disciplines Bibliometrics, IR and NLP can drive from it in a digital libraries context. In the future we plan follow-up workshops at IR, NLP and Digital Libraries venues. Furthermore we are working with the *International Journal on Digital Libraries* to offer a special issue on topics discussed at BIRNDL, for extended versions of BIRNDL workshop papers, shared task descriptions, as well as a general call for submissions. Dates for first submission of camera-ready papers will likely be around September 2016, with a target of producing an issue by mid 2017.

6. REFERENCES

[1] Iana Atanassova, Marc Bertin, and Philipp Mayr. Proceedings of the First Workshop on Mining Scientific Papers: Computational Linguistics and Bibliometrics. Istanbul, Turkey, 2015.

[2] Kokil Jaidka, Muthu Kumar Chandrasekaran, Beatriz Fisas Elizalde, Rahul Jha, Christopher Jones, Min-Yen Kan, Ankur Khanna, Diego Molla-Aliod, Dragomir R Radev, Francesco Ronzano, et al. The computational linguistics summarization pilot task. In *Proceedings of Text Ananlysis Conference*, Gaithersburg, USA, 2014.

[3] Philipp Mayr, Ingo Frommholz, and Guillaume Cabanac. Proceedings of the Third Workshop on Bibliometric-enhanced Information Retrieval. Padova, Italy, 2016.

[4] Preslav I Nakov, Ariel S Schwartz, and Marti Hearst. Citances: Citation sentences for semantic analysis of bioscience text. In *Proceedings of the SIGIR'04 workshop on Search and Discovery in Bioinformatics*, pages 81–88, 2004.

Author Index

www.ingramcontent.com/pod-product-compliance
Lightning Source LLC
Chambersburg PA
CBHW080931220326
41598CB00034B/5749